EDUCATIONAL MEDIA AND TECHNOLOGY YEARBOOK

BRENDA BRANYAN-BROADBENT and R. KENT WOOD,
Editors

EDUCATIONAL MEDIA AND TECHNOLOGY YEARBOOK

1990

VOLUME 16

Published in Cooperation with the
Association for Educational Communications
and Technology

1990

Libraries Unlimited, Inc. • Englewood, Colorado

LIBRARIES UNLIMITED, INC.
P.O. Box 3988
Englewood, Colorado 80155-3988

ISBN 0-87287-851-1

ISSN 8755-2094

To
Harvey Raymond Frye
and
Marie McMahan

Contents

Part One
EDUCATIONAL MEDIA AND TECHNOLOGY
The Year in Review

Part Two
TECHNOLOGY UPDATE

Part Three
LEADERSHIP PROFILES IN EDUCATIONAL
MEDIA AND TECHNOLOGY

Part Four
ORGANIZATIONS AND ASSOCIATIONS
IN NORTH AMERICA

Part Five
GRADUATE PROGRAMS

Part Six
MEDIAGRAPHY
Print and Nonprint Resources

Preface

The year 1989 has been one of landmark events for AECT and the educational media and technology professions. A number of state legislatures are considering technology initiatives in education, and we hope to report the successful passage of those initiatives in *EMTY 1991*.

In assuming the editorship of the *Educational Media and Technology Yearbook* by invitation of the publisher, we have assumed the burden that comes at the end of each year. We note with enthusiasm the closing of a decade of economic stagnation that slowed the diffusion and impact of our field. Although there were some pockets of advancement in theory and practice, it was a discouraging decade for many who faced cutbacks in library media programs in public education and the elimination of the fledgling instructional design and development divisions in higher education. There were bright spots within business and industrial settings. Corporations such as IBM discovered the power of effective instructional design and development. Some, such as Jack Bowsher, began making influential speeches, noting that instructional designers are the "educational architects" of the future:

> In almost every organization, hundreds of people make or influence key decisions about education. In a few organizations, the total number is several thousand, including people in operations overseas. Where there is a need for massive change, which is the case in education, people need to see a vision. Where are we going? Why are we doing this? These questions will be asked over and over again.
>
> The majority of people who do not immediately "buy in" to the vision are not people who automatically resist change. They are simply people who do not understand what the leaders of the new programs have in mind. Massive change involves a massive communication task. The leaders of change must be willing to devote a large part of their time to explaining the value of new education systems....
>
> Today, we are applying the lessons we learned from computers and the experience derived from the application of the systems approach to sell and implement major changes in education. In our environment, we are defining a systems approach to education as a process for developing instruction that is based on defined business requirements and that produces gains in knowledge and skill to improve job performances.*

Educating America: Lessons Learned in the Nation's Corporations by Jack E. Bowsher. New York: Wiley, 1989, pp. 107-8.

It is our desire that *EMTY* will continue to be a "mind tool" to improve both knowledge and skill performance in education, business and industry, government, and the defense communities. As we leave the decade of the 1980s we note the enthusiasm returning to our colleagues. One could say, as will be the theme for AECT 1991, THE MAGIC IS BACK!

Abbreviations Used

The following abbreviations are used in this yearbook:

Act. Dir..................Acting Director
admin.................... administrator
ALA......American Library Association
approx.................. approximately
Assn....................... Association
Assoc....................... Associate
Asst........................ Assistant
bi-mo......................bimonthly
bi-wk...................... biweekly
Chair.................... Chairperson
Co-Dir(s)................Co-Director(s)
comp(s)....................compiler(s)
Coord.................... Coordinator
d. .... daily
Dept. Dir..........Department Director
Dir. .... Director
dist.........................distributed
Div. .... Division
ed(s). .... editor(s)
exec........................ executive
indiv..................... individual(s)
info.......................information
inst. .... institution(s)
irreg........................irregularly
Lib. Coord..........Library Coordinator
libr........................... librarian
libs...........................libraries
Mgr........................ Manager

Mng. Dir.............Managing Director
mo............................monthly
nat............................national
n.d...........no date or date not known
no............................number
n.p.....no pagination or pages not known
Off. .... Officer
organ....................organization(s)
pa......................... paperbound
pna..................price not available
pp............................pages
Pres........................President
prog........................ program
Prof........................ Professor
pub......................... publisher
q............................quarterly
rep......................representative
rev........................... revised
Secy.........................Secretary
semi-ann.................. semi-annual
semi-mo.................. semi-monthly
sr............................ senior
Treas....................... Treasurer
Univ. .... University
V.P.....................Vice-President
vol(s). .... volume(s)
wk............................ weekly
yr............................ year

Part One

Educational Media and Technology
The Year in Review

Introduction

The trends and issues section of *EMTY* this year is particularly rich, with meaty analyses of the field. Following up on his excellent overview of the field in volume 15, Don Ely presents a second major overview of educational technology. This summary is must reading for all professionals in the field.

Pea and Soloway's report to the federal government proposes methods and programs to enhance technology in American education. Apart from the success or failure of the proposals, the paper provides an excellent summary about what is known about the impact of technology on learners and the learning/teaching process.

Bork's fine article summarizes the various approaches schools have used in adopting computer technology. He then proposes a number of advanced ideas for the utilization of this technology in ways that will maximize its impact.

Caffarella and Sachs review ten years of doctoral work in the country, demonstrating that the production of doctoral students and the number of studies being added to the field's research pool are growing.

Finally, Holloway provides an overview of the activities of AECT for 1989.

Trends and Issues in Educational Technology, 1989

Donald P. Ely
ERIC Clearinghouse on Information Resources
Syracuse University
Syracuse, New York

Since trends are difficult to determine from year to year, the analysis that began in 1988 continued in 1989. A trends report is now planned for every other year, so the next one will be published in 1991. Last year was the starting point for analyzing trends and issues in the field of educational technology (Ely, 1988). This year's report builds on that initial effort in an attempt to create a database for longitudinal analysis of trends in the field over the years. The only previous attempt to discern trends in the field for ERIC was reported by Allen (1970).

As we might expect, many of the 1989 trends are the same as those in 1988. Year-to-year trends are not as variable as decade-to-decade trends. The fact that certain trends are repeated is, in a sense, a confirmation of their importance. Confidence is increased as a trend appears over several years.

The trends as reflected in the literature are more a reflection of the status quo than a prediction of the future. Content analysis usually reveals the topics of current interest, perhaps with a lag time between the events reported and their appearance in the publication. The trends should be viewed from this perspective.

INTRODUCTION

(The reader who is interested only in educational technology trends may omit this section and resume reading on page 10.)

The way in which trends are determined may be as valuable as the trends themselves. This section describes the procedures used in reading the conclusions that are the focus of this study. A rationale for content analysis as the vehicle for determining trends is given first. Then the specific procedure used by the author is described. Trends in 1988 and 1989 are compared, and the literature sources are named. Finally, the rank order of topics for 1988 and 1989 is given.

Why Content Analysis?

To ensure consistency, the same procedures, with minor revisions, were followed in 1989. A modified content analysis was used for determining the trends. A careful look at *what* professionals in the field are saying in their own professional writings seems to be one of the best ways to identify trends. Even though the focus on content of publications, convention programs, doctoral dissertations, and ERIC input means looking backward, it was this retrospective look that provided specific, measurable content units upon which to base extrapolations of future movements. One alternative for eliciting trends is to use the informed specialist (as Allen did in 1970) to name trends from that person's vantage point. It would seem that one person's viewpoint, as unbiased as that person may try to be, is open to criticism for its subjectivity. As with individuals, the best predictors of future performance in professional fields would seem to be past behaviors.

Beyond Content Analysis

Frequency counts of content units serve as the basis for the trends in 1989. These quantitative results have been complemented and supported by position papers, policy statements, and ongoing state-of-the-art studies issued by opinion leaders and organizations they represent: professional associations, state and federal governmental offices, and quasi-governmental nonprofit bodies. Statistics gathered and reported by organizations who specialize in such data collection have been used to provide quantitative profiles of growth and direction and to confirm the content analysis. Using these sources, the author generated the trends. The categories created for the content analysis sometimes directly influenced the determination of a trend and sometimes indirectly influenced it. The complementary literature was used to enhance, explain, and provide examples related to the trends. The reader should note that there is no *direct* relationship between the quantitative categories and the trends. They are used as *indicators* of trends and are interpreted by the author to tease out trends.

Top Topics

The trends for 1989 are more qualitative than those of 1988. This publication points out the subtle shifts and probes some of the reasons for the directions in which the field of educational technology appears to be heading. For example, in reviewing the trends, "Instructional Processes" (which includes instructional design) leads the coverage many times over its nearest competitor, "Technical Developments," which moved from third place last year to second place this year (see table 1).

Table 1.

Rank Order of Content Analysis Categories

	1988	**1989**
Instructional Processes	1	1
Personnel	2	6
Technical Developments	3	2
Management	4	3
The Field	5	4
Services	6	5
Society and Culture	7	7
Research/Theory	8	8

In an attempt to be more specific about "Instructional Processes," our team created new subcategories so that specific elements of each category could be broken out for further analysis. The "Personnel" category fell from second position in 1988 to sixth position (out of eight) for 1989. When categories showed consistency in retaining their position (all except "Personnel"), further exploration was made to determine *why*. Then supplementary documents, not included in the formal content analysis, were used for getting behind the data to determine the political, social, and economic reasons for the findings.

External Pressures

Educational technology seems to be on the tongues of more educators every year. Lay people are more involved and newspaper reporters actively seek information about technological innovations in education and training settings. The general feeling seems to be that many new technologies, primarily those using computers and telecommunications, are going to be an integral part of our culture, and that the schools ought to be preparing young people to be intelligent producers and users of the information technology hardware and software. Newspapers, magazines, and broadcasting are making people aware of the potentials of technology, and many adults often ask, "Why not in the schools?" This question is beginning to haunt educators and appears more often in the literature than ever before. There is an accounting for such attitudes in the trends.

Limitations

One limitation of this study that must be recognized is that the trends identified in it were created largely by people who are in the field of educational technology. If the journals, conventions, and dissertations are used as the basis for analysis, it stands to reason that these sources attract contributions from people *within* the field. It is only when the general literature created by opinion leaders and visible organizations is factored into the equation that the strong influence of professionals in the field is tempered by the broader perspectives and opinions of other educators and policymakers. Even with this observation, it seems reasonable to say that the literature mainly reflects the trends as seen by those who spend their daily lives working within the field.

Rationale for Identifying Trends

The rank order of each trend was determined by using its frequency in the literature; i.e., the topic that is the subject of the most articles, papers, and documents is listed as trend number one. This ranking was further substantiated by examples from the literature, statistics from reliable sources, and policy statements from opinion leaders and organizations. Each trend grew out of the topics and subtopics as classified in table 2, page 8. This procedure permits both quantitative and qualitative data to be interpreted for determination of trends. Ultimately, the author's responsibility is to identify the trends and to write the supporting rationale.

Table 2.

Rank Order of Top 13 Recording Units

	1988 n = 1,443	1989 n = 1,514
Design and Development	448	259
Evaluation	97	99
Status (of the field)	61	95
Computer Related	82	90
Interactive Video	29	83
Distance Education	61	81
Curriculum Support	25	79
Professional Education	145	72
Society and Culture	72	71
Telecommunications	14	71
Research/Theory	45	57
Roles and Responsibilities	51	38
Logistics	43	32
Others (36 recording units)	270	387

Issues

In the process of analyzing data to identify trends, there are likely to be varied points of view on topics of importance to professionals in the field. In this report, an *issue* is a problem or question for which there are two or more points of view. An attempt is made to state each point of view without resolution.

Future Trends

This study is not an exploration of "futures." As trends are identified they should be monitored to determine their future potential force and direction. Predictions about the future can be valid only by using trends over a period of years. The ERIC effort to identify trends has just begun, and it is difficult to make predictions based on data from only two years. However, in the absence of soothsayers or crystal balls, these trends can serve as points of departure for extrapolations leading to future movements within the field.

Methodology

Sources for the content analysis used in this study were four leading professional journals in educational technology, papers given at annual conventions of three professional associations, dissertations from five universities that have a high level of doctoral productivity, and the educational technology documents that have been placed into the ERIC database (figure 1). The 1989 report covers the period from October 1, 1988, through September 30, 1989.

Journals

British Journal of Educational Technology
Educational Technology
Educational Technology Research and Development (a merger of the *Journal
    of Instructional Development* and *Educational Communications and
    Technology Journal,* both of which were analyzed separately in 1988)
TechTrends

Dissertation Sources

Arizona State University
Florida State University
Indiana University
Syracuse University
University of Southern California

Conferences

Association for Educational Communications and Technology
Educational Technology International Conference (United Kingdom)
National Society for Performance and Instruction

Figure 1. Content sources.

ERIC Input

Examined were all documents in the area of educational technology put into the ERIC system from October 1, 1988, to September 30, 1989.

Independent reviews of each item from each source were made by at least two reviewers, who then compared their analyses, usually in the presence of the author of this report, and collectively made decisions about classification using a form with forty-nine recording units. (A recording unit is a designated label for subject matter content; e.g., for the category "Evaluation," there are four recording units, one of which is "Product Evaluation.") The classification scheme duplicated the 1988 procedure with minor modification of recording units (see appendix A). Several topics were assigned additional recording units to permit finer distinctions of subject matter. Several recording units used in 1988 were eliminated because of infrequent use. The rank order of the top thirteen recording units is given in table 2. The complete compilation of frequencies by topic and source is in the appendix.

Additional sources used to confirm the quantitative data were policy papers and reports published in 1989 by organizations with high public visibility that are in a position to influence public and professional opinion. Used for example, were *Linking for Learning: A New Course for Education*, issued by the Office of Technology Assessment of the U.S. Congress; *Results in Education 1989: The Governors' 1991 Report on Education*, released by the National Governors' Association; and statements of the National Education Association.

Glenn LeBlanc and Crystal Yancey served as data analysts.

TRENDS IN EDUCATIONAL TECHNOLOGY, 1989

Caution

Trends can be described in the same way that the five blind men described the elephant — each perceived the animal differently depending on the place of contact. Likewise, it is difficult to determine trends for an entire field like educational technology since the field is often interpreted differently by persons with varied perspectives. Part of the problem is the broad definition of the field and part is in its multiple manifestations at various levels and in many locations. Thus, a trend applicable to elementary and secondary schools may not be visible in postsecondary institutions. A professional working with artificial intelligence and expert systems sees the field quite differently than the specialist working in the creation of video products. When educational technology principles and practices are applied in medical and business training sectors, the trends look considerably different than when applied in training for adult literacy or learning English as a second language, even though basic premises and procedures may be the same. The purpose of this disclaimer is to point out the potential misinterpretations that could emerge from wholesale acceptance of all the following trends. Each statement should be screened with a contextual filter to be sure that it applies in the setting where it is to be used.

Trend #1

Concern for design and development of instructional products and procedures dominates the professional literature.

Design and development are concerned with several subtopics: needs assessment, task analysis, learner characteristics, message design, product development, and motivational strategies. The dominance of these topics in the literature of 1989 is brought about by an increasing recognition of the importance of instructional material design and the strategies used to deliver information. It is a swing away from a preoccupation with hardware that dominated the field in its early days toward a concern for the systematic development of software. Much of the literature in this area emphasizes the design of products using new tools such as HyperCard. HyperCard has emerged as one of the most frequently discussed topics at professional conferences and has become the subject of articles in every journal reviewed for this study. One journal initiated a regular HyperCard column in 1989. This specific interest in the use of an authoring program to create instructional materials is indicative of the heightened interest in the process of instructional design and development.

There is usually a distinction between instructional *design* and instructional *development*. Instructional design focuses on the product itself and the lesson is the unit of analysis; instructional development is broader and usually deals with the course as the unit of analysis. The terms are often used interchangeably, but the distinction is important to practitioners and theoreticians alike. Instructional designers are likely to look at the "micro" level of instruction and use knowledge and skills of task analysis, interpretation of learner characteristics, message design, and motivational strategies. Professionals who practice instructional development work at the "macro" level and are more concerned with needs assessment, goal definition, systematic arrangement of components, delivery systems, evaluation, and management of the enterprise. In practice, some of the specific areas of interest for instructional designers are artificial intelligence and expert systems, interactive video, and problem solving. All three of these areas are frequently found in the literature and conference programs of 1989. Instructional developers, on the other hand, are involved in distance education and course development, which also frequently appear in the 1989 literature.

When discussing instructional design and development, the medium is usually secondary. To be sure, the medium *is* important and is sometimes the starting point for instructional designers and developers. The ideal case would determine the most appropriate medium *after* decisions about goals, objectives, and context of use have been made. Analysis of learners and task analysis should also precede the selection of a medium. Many practitioners tend to focus on the medium because it is a visible delivery system; the hardware has more public appeal and is more observable than the software. For example, the literature speaks of "the computer" or "interactive video," which then produces a mindset of the devices that deliver the information rather than the information itself. (In this content analysis, the items that emphasize *equipment* are placed in the "Technical Developments" category; those that describe *materials* or *software* are placed in the "Design and Development" category.)

There continues to be a concern for the proper balance of hardware and software in teaching and learning. The Center for Technology in Education at the Bank Street College of Education has a mission "to conduct research and development leading to an understanding and demonstration of how technology can improve student achievement, and consequently school productivity" (Fox & Saunders, 1989). In this instance, technology is interpreted as hardware and software in a school setting.

Results in Education 1989 (National Governors' Association, 1989) reports a growing concern among educators that "regardless of the current emphasis placed on computer use instruction, schools do not appear to be taking advantage of the unique uses of technology in teaching subject matter and in helping students develop higher-order thinking skills.... The predominant focus seems to be on expanding access to technology with little or no attention given to using technology to restructure schools or to teach higher-order thinking." Even with extensive coverage of the design and development function in the educational technology literature, there remains a public perception that it has not yet reached a creative and sophisticated level.

Issues

- Under what conditions should the medium of instruction be selected *before* versus *after* the design process?

- How can the distinction between instructional *design* and instructional *development* be made clearer?

- Is there a direct relationship between software quality and the use of specific design models and/or procedures?

- How can instructional materials be designed to help learners use high-order thinking skills?

- How can technology be applied to assist learners in problem solving?

Trend #2

Evaluation is becoming an integral part of the instructional design and development process.

Evaluation has always been an integral part of the instructional design and development process, but it is currently enjoying an increased recognition in the professional literature of educational technology. Like the many faces of instructional design and development, evaluation can be subdivided into at least four areas: product evaluation, process evaluation, cost-effectiveness (productivity) evaluation, and formative evaluation. Product evaluation (summative evaluation of instructional materials or software) and formative (or en route) evaluation during the design and development process are often included in the literature of instructional design and development.

During 1989 there were many articles and conference papers that highlighted evaluation. The dominant theme for most of these papers was product evaluation, most frequently discussing the effectiveness of computer programs used in schools and colleges. Many of the papers were case studies of the outputs of design and development efforts. The process evaluation area also included program evaluation, that is, the summative conclusions reached after a program or project has concluded. Evaluation of teaching and impact of technology fall into this category.

Evaluation seems to be emerging as a distinct area within the larger category of instructional design and development and has established itself within the field of educational technology. Seventy-four percent of the professional academic programs now include courses in evaluation as part of the curriculum (Johnson, 1989a).

Issues

- Should evaluation of instructional products be medium-specific or generic? (For example, should there be one evaluation procedure for computer-assisted instruction and another for audiotapes, or could one evaluation protocol serve all instructional resources?)

- Should evaluation competencies be developed independently of design and development competencies? (That is, is evaluation separate from or integral to the process of instructional design and development?)

- When should evaluation be used? When should research be used?

Trend #3

There is increasing use of research and development knowledge to solve current problems of teaching and learning.

Much of the literature of 1989 seemed to draw upon earlier works. Summaries of research and development findings, meta-analyses of research in specific areas, and reports of case studies reflected recognition of existing work as useful for current efforts. Educators have often complained that information that is already known is not used, and the wag says, "There's nothing new under the sun." However, when existing knowledge is synthesized it often becomes more useful than separate and isolated facts. When successful programs are publicized, they are more likely to be adopted.

Most of the existing knowledge derived from the literature and case studies focuses on the use of educational technology principles and practices in teaching and learning. For example, forty of the programs out of the 250 listed in the 1989 National Diffusion Network (NDN) catalog, *Programs That Work*, are technology-oriented. After these programs have gone through a rigorous review process, they are listed in the NDN catalog with a "seal of approval." A national review panel looks at the programs and carefully judges them according to set criteria. Schools across the nation adopt and implement these programs.

More specific to the subject of this report on trends is *Tapping the Potential of Educational Technology*, published by the Southeastern Educational Improvement Laboratory. This catalog of 105 educational technology projects was created with information gathered from state education agencies. The introduction says that

> some projects appear to be disarmingly simple, while others are at the forefront of new ways to incorporate technology in the classroom to meet a critical need. But all add to our understanding of how technological capacities can be harnessed to address the instructional needs of all students. (Southeastern Educational Improvement Laboratory, 1989)

The 49 entries for computers are proportionate to the general literature of the field. Other categories reflect less emphasis but are nonetheless indicative of current activities in many of the nation's schools: CD-ROM (7 entries); Distance Learning Technologies (9 entries); Robotics (5 entries); Telecommunications (14 entries); Videodisc (10 entries); Video Production (6 entries), and Videotape (5 entries).

Issues

- To what extent are existing research findings and case study results applicable in new settings?

- How can research findings be made more generalizable?

- What research questions appear to be paramount today in the field of educational technology?

Trend #4

Computers can be found in almost every public school in the United States.

Quality Education Data (1989) reports that 76,395 of the 79,693 public schools in the United States have two or more microcomputers. When the total number of microcomputers is calculated, there are 1,596,715 units, or an average of 19.8 units per school. A more revealing figure is the average microdensity of 25.4 students per microcomputer. (Microdensity is the term that indicates the number of students in a school or school system divided by the number of microcomputers available for instructional purposes.) Schools with a microdensity of one to nine students per computer number 5,228. Despite improvements in these figures every year, the fact remains that "the average student spends only about one hour per week on the computer" (National Governors' Association, 1989).

Nonpublic schools do not fare as well. Of the 23,026 Roman Catholic and other private schools, 8,440 report that microcomputers are available. Microdensity has not been calculated.

The Apple II series dominates the market with 84 percent of the schools having access to this brand; 21 percent of the schools have access to Radio Shack, 25 percent to Commodore, and 15 percent to IBM. The 1989 figures show that IBM-compatible and Macintosh have less than 2 percent availability in the schools. All of the above figures show double counts when more than one brand is available in a school (Quality Education Data, 1989).

There is no doubt that use of the computer in schools at all levels continued to dominate the literature in 1989 as it did in 1988. Journals specifically dedicated to computers in schools were not included in the content analysis since they would skew the findings. There are at least thirteen journals that specifically address the use of computers in education. If those sources were used, computer literature would be far above any other category in this study. It seems appropriate, therefore, to review some of that literature separately to augment the general review of educational technology literature.

Electronic Learning has surveyed state education agencies annually since 1980. The ninth annual survey of all fifty state education agencies (plus the District of Columbia and Puerto Rico) revealed that 77 percent of the states are planning new, technology-related programs, and 93 percent of the states provide in-service computer education for certified teachers. Computer courses in teacher education programs are required for certification in twenty-three states and the District of Columbia. This survey also indicated that factors likely to hinder the development of educational technology (defined here as use of computers and video technologies) are funding and teacher education. Funding was named by 64 percent of the states as a major impediment to continued growth, and teacher training was reported to be a limiting factor by 21 percent of the states. With regard to special problems for which technology provided some solutions, thirty-five states named special education as receiving the most support, and twenty-seven reported the use of technology with gifted and talented programs. Twenty-one states use technology to address equity issues (ninth annual survey of the states *Electronic Learning*, 1989).

More professional educators and associations appear to be endorsing technology in the schools. The National Education Association's Special Committee on Educational Technology reported to the Representative Assembly in 1989. "Today every teacher needs a computer," the report stresses, "because teaching now also means handling administrative tasks, spurring the technological revolution in learning, reforming the curriculum, and restructuring the schools." One NEA officer said, "The focus must be on technology as a means to restructure the school environment—not as a piecemeal appendage grafted onto the current school structure and curriculum, and not as a way to further routinize learning" (Weiss, 1989b).

The momentum for computer use in education is accelerating. Administrative and clerical applications have become routine in most schools. Universities have varied mixes of computer access—mainframes, microcomputer clusters, and individual personal units; but most of the use appears to be for management of the institution, research, and writing. The computer does not constitute a major movement in the process of teaching and learning. The most common use of microcomputers in elementary and secondary schools is to teach computer "literacy." Other primary uses are for word processing and "drill and practice" exercises. There is some indication that schools are not buying as much microcomputer software. Hope Reports (1989) calculated a sharp increase in microcomputer software sales from 1982 until 1985 and then a significant decline each year through 1988. There may be several explanations. First, school budgets are tighter and purchasing may have been reduced. Second, those who purchase software may not know what is available. Third, if people know what is available, they may feel that it is not appropriate to the needs of a school or that it is insufficient in quality.

The potential for computers in teaching and learning has not been advancing. The lack of progress can be attributed to the lack of teacher knowledge and skills, the lack of time to create and adapt materials, and the lack of support for introducing ideas. Mary Futrell, immediate past president of the National Education Association (NEA) said, "In the future we also need to do a better job of training teachers to use instructional technologies. Whether the technology is a calculator, computer, VCR, or laser, we need to help teachers integrate technology into the curriculum" (Futrell, 1989). The NEA's Special Committee on Educational Technology says only half of the nation's teachers report that they have used a computer, and only a third indicate that they have had up to twenty hours of computer training.

One finding coming out of a five-year research program at the Educational Technology Center (ETC) at Harvard University's Graduate School of Education underscores the need for greater teacher involvement in the use of technology in schools.

Involving experienced teachers as partners in collaborative research requires time and explicit efforts to link the work of the schools with the work of universities. ETC established laboratory sites in several schools to learn what implementation of the Center's innovations entails. This research revealed that incorporating technology-enhanced guided inquiry approaches into regular classrooms requires changes not only in technology but also in curriculum and teaching approaches (Fox & Saunders, 1989).

Schools are not the only educational institutions lacking in computer applications to teaching and learning. Frank Newman, president of the Education Commission of the States, said in a keynote address to CAUSE 89: "In the teaching and learning function of the university, we are still in the category [of computer use] that we in the academic world euphemistically call 'potential.' That is to say we have made practically no progress. To put it in perspective, the average university in this country, in terms of its use of information technology in teaching, is substantially behind the typical elementary and secondary school" (Newman, 1989).

Concerns about computers in the schools led in 1989 to an international conference sponsored by UNESCO. Entitled "Education and Informatics: Strengthening International Co-operation," the ten-day conference produced a series of conclusions, recommendations, and suggestions for action. The 500 delegates also issued a "declaration" that calls for a

> new impetus to the consultations that are so urgently needed in this field and to take steps to ensure that the international community gives sufficiently high priority to international plans and programmes aimed at co-operation on new information technologies in education to ensure that they cater for all countries expressing needs for assistance. (UNESCO, 1989)

ISSUES

- How can more attention be directed to the teaching and learning functions of computers in education settings?

- How can schools provide access, training, and time for teachers to gain computer skills?

- What constitutes "good" computer software?

- How can computer-assisted instruction be integrated into the curriculum?

- How can access to computers be enhanced for *all* learners?

Trend #5

Interactive video is widely accepted as a research and development product but not in schools and higher education.

In 1989 there were three times as many articles in the interactive video category as in 1988. The increasing activity in this area reflects growth in the production and use of laser discs. The more common laser discs for computer use, CD (compact disc, audio) and CD-ROM (compact disc-read only memory), have increased interest in the larger format videodisc, which stores more visual information. The videodisc has been around for almost ten years, with applications limited largely to commercial motion pictures for home use. Using a digitized format, and combining it with microcomputer control, the videodisc has become an interactive system with potential for individualized teaching and learning. A frequent combination reported in the literature is the use of HyperCard software with a videodisc. This combination permits exploration of concepts in depth and use of an inquiry approach to learning through the hierarchical structure of HyperCard, supported by computer graphics with still and moving images stored on the videodisc. In some cases the computer is coordinated with a videotape recorder as a less expensive, and slower, inter-active video system.

For education, it is clear that interactive video is still in its infancy and is more a research and development product than one that is ready for wholesale adoption. Quality Education Data (1989) reports only 1,177 schools with videodisc players. Of that number, only 805 have an interactive capability. In actual numbers, Hope Reports (1989) estimates that there are 3,500 videodisc players in the schools and 3,900 in the colleges. Other estimates are much more optimistic. Pollak (1990) says, "There are 125,000 to 150,000 videodisc systems currently in use in the nonconsumer arena. Of these, it is estimated that 30,000 are in use in education." Clearly, there are major discrepancies between the data and the estimates. Regardless of the number of units, it is highly likely that relatively few are being used interactively in education, even though the medium is frequently used in military and industrial training.

In the *Electronic Learning* ninth annual survey (1989), all of the thirty-one states reporting on the use of technologies (other than the computer) said that television was available in 80-100 percent of their K-12 schools and that videotape recorders were almost as ubiquitous. Videodisc players and CD-ROM were found in the smallest percentage of schools.

The potential contributions of interactive video were reported in the research findings of the Educational Technology Center (ETC) (Fox & Saunders, 1989). In science, "computer simulations that visually represent normally unobservable aspects of scientific phenomena can help students to change their deeply rooted everyday ideas ... and to more readily grasp important accepted scientific theories and concepts." In mathematics, "results so far suggest that the external visual representations presented by the software help students to construct more sophisticated mental representations of the target mathematical ideas."

There are schools where interactive video is being used. Ten existing projects in ten states are described in *Tapping the Potential of Educational Technology* (Southeastern Educational Improvement Laboratory, 1989). These projects would have to be called "pilot" since they are using products that are custom-made or not widely available. The interactive video developments build on the interactive characteristic of computers. It is a marriage of two basic hardware systems, with specialized software to provide increased access to resources in a minimum time.

The *potential* of interactive video is recognized by educational technologists and educational leaders alike. Seymour Papert, of the M.I.T. Media Lab, says: "We will stop making distinctions between computers and video. We will probably have computer-controlled systems that use video and databases and involve interaction" (Papert, 1989). Ruth Randall, former chief state school officer of Minnesota, shares Papert's perspective: "Video, along with live interactive television, will also play a larger role in distance learning. Instructional video can bring many experiences to schools that are isolated, or that don't have teachers with expertise in every area" (Randall, 1989).

It is important to distinguish between *interactive video* and videodiscs. It appears that more videodiscs are available than ever before. The 1989-1990 *Videodisc Compendium for Education and Training* contains over 700 videodisc titles from ninety-three producers, an increase of sixty-one from the previous edition. Most of the titles are in the science and computer areas. The strongest areas of growth are in art, language arts, and the social studies (Pollak, 1990).

Issues

- Can interactive video be justified as a cost-effective teaching tool?

- How can more than one learner use an interactive video workstation at the same time?

- What is the role of CD-I (compact disc, interactive)?

- Who will prepare the sophisticated interactive video software for schools?

Trend #6

Distance education has become established as a major vehicle for instruction at all levels of education and training.

Distance education is prominent in the educational technology literature. The organization and management of distance education encompasses much more than the delivery systems that are so visible. Yet, it is delivery systems that establish the relationship between distance education and educational technology. There is virtually no distance education program that does not involve some aspect of hardware and software as well as the design and development of courseware. The emphasis on design of course materials is critical for learners who are working independent of face-to-face contact with a teacher. Much of the literature falls into the field of educational technology.

There are journals devoted specifically to distance education (*The American Journal of Distance Education*, *The Canadian Journal of Distance Education*, and several published outside of North America). None of these journals were part of the content analysis. A cursory review of these specialized journals reveals that many of the articles are devoted to organization, management, retention, evaluation, and other topics that tend not to emphasize communication technology. There appeared to be no one technology that exceeded others in frequency. Broadcasting and telecommunications media were used as frequently as microcomputer discs and multimedia packages. Broadcasting involves open channel stations, point-to-point satellite, cable, and low-power transmission (Instructional Television Fixed Service — ITFS). Telephone lines are used for computer networking, two-way audio, and graphic display (electronic chalkboard). Some programs are self-contained on microcomputer discs for individual learning, and still others offer a combination of textbook, workbook, audiocassette, and various video materials (videocassette, slides, illustrations). Some distance education programs have created various media configurations using some of each of the technologies. No one technology or system works for every situation. Trend #9 provides further information about telecommunication delivery systems.

The 1989 publication of *Linking for Learning: A New Course for Education* by the Office of Technology Assessment (OTA) of the U.S. Congress, signified a current and growing interest in distance education. The OTA report includes the results of a survey describing distance education activities of almost every state at the elementary/secondary and postsecondary levels. The dominant theme is technology delivery systems, with dozens of case studies described in detail and comprehensive cost-effectiveness results. This level of interest confirms an earlier estimate that distance education may be a viable response to many problems facing American education, e.g., shortage of teachers especially in rural areas, lack of specialized instruction in many schools, and limited opportunities to learn without the timebound and placebound restrictions of formal educational institutions. The OTA report points out that "the Star Schools Program, begun in 1988 to develop multi-state, multi-institutional K-12 distance education, has helped to focus attention on distance learning." It also credits the National Telecommunications Information Administration and the Rural Electrification Administration with support for distance education through their funding mechanisms. Like other OTA reports, this report makes a series of recommendations. They focus on *telecommunications policy*; *research, evaluation, and dissemination*; *support for teachers*; and *expansion of the infrastructure*.

Other countries have discovered the potential of distance education, especially at the postsecondary level. The Open University in Great Britain has been well established for more than twenty years. Many developing nations of the world have embraced distance education as one solution for providing increased access to education. A briefing paper for a UNESCO-International Council on Distance Education roundtable (Timmers, 1989) summarized the trends in developing nations and spelled out the needs for the future. The United States has become a recent adopter of this innovation. To be sure, there had been correspondence courses and self-study programs before, but not in such an organized and comprehensive fashion as the current programs demonstrate. State governors have been tracking this development and, in their 1989 report (National Governors' Association, 1989), they confirm increasing activities in distance education.

> Continuing the trend of the past two years, distance learning, which brings educational instruction via television, satellite, cable, or microwave, is the most prominent area of state involvement in technology. Distance learning initiatives and expansions were reported by thirty-seven states. States are either implementing, expanding, studying, or funding distance learning programs to provide special courses to schools with at-risk students, to enhance teacher education, and/or to offer instruction in locations where there are insufficient teachers or very low enrollments. (p. 31)

It is possible that educational technology and distance education may be closely related. Distance education starts with the individual learner and designs learning materials for one person at a time — one premise of design and development in educational technology. Distance education uses a full spectrum of media resources to deliver content — another dimension of educational technology. Distance education requires a management system that tracks each student — and educational technology uses the concept of system in most of its work. Distance education has a major evaluation component with feedback mechanisms — and educational technology considers evaluation an integral part of its definition. Many educational technologists have found their way into distance education and it is likely that more will be needed.

The most common unit for distance education appears to be the course. Some courses are packaged to create a complete degree (or certificate) program at a distance. Open universities in Europe, Asia, and the Far East are already offering the entire degree program at a distance. Whether or not university-level distance education in the United States will reach the numbers involved in other parts of the world remains to be seen. The fact is, in most parts of the United States there is adequate access to postsecondary education institutions, which is not the case in Europe or in many developing nations of the world. It may be that *access* determines the need for education at a distance.

Issues

- Which face-to-face instructional functions can effectively be replaced by distance education materials?

- For what type of subjects and what type of learner is distance education most appropriate?

- What is the lowest educational level for which distance education can be effectively used?

- How does the instructor's role change when distance education is used?

Trend #7

The definition, conduct, and status of professional education in the field continues to preoccupy practitioners.

Professionals in any field are usually concerned about the status of their field. They ask questions about their changing roles and responsibilities. They worry about the education of future professionals and the upgrading of current practitioners. They look for recognition, especially from external colleagues, and they try to identify leadership from among their ranks. Certification or licensing are means to preserve standards of professional competence. The field of educational technology is no exception. The literature in 1989 included items on all of these topics, but especially *professional education* and *roles and responsibilities* of professionals in the field.

Most of the concerns were expressed at professional meetings. Such meetings are probably the place to "sound off" about professional matters because attendees come from many parts of the country, and if actions are eventually called for, it would be the professional association that would likely initiate and implement actions related to status, roles, certification, and professional education. Conferences serve as a forum for such expressions of concern. Again, the field of educational technology is no exception. One such conference, of Professors of Instructional Design and Technology (PIDT), focused on four major themes: (1) redefining the field; (2) improving graduate studies; (3) conducting research; and (4) identifying the role of educational technologists outside academic programs (Klein, 1989). These themes are consistent with much of the current literature.

Academic programs in higher education are often the genesis of professional concerns. This fact occurs because professors are questioning the content of their courses and are concerned about placement of their graduates. Professors also tend to write more for the professional journals and are more likely to attend national conventions than practitioners. Annual surveys are conducted each year by Logan. In 1989 he queried the chairs of academic programs about trends that they saw in their programs. One major trend has to do with increased placement in business and industry settings, with fewer graduates going to academic settings. Another trend refers to curricular emphasis. There is much more activity (courses, interest, product development) with computers in education and in the area of instructional design and development. These emphases seem to be at the expense of more traditional activity in media production and management. The complete listing of master's and doctoral programs in the field is found in the *Educational Media and Technology Yearbook 1989*. Also appearing in 1989 was the third edition of *Master's Curricula in Educational Communications and Technology: A Descriptive Directory* (Johnson, 1989a). An analysis of the publication (Johnson, 1989b) compares academic programs and the information given in the second and third editions. For example, 44 of the 213 master's programs listed in 1985 are no longer being offered; but 23 new doctoral programs have begun since 1985. She also notes that terminology describing the programs has changed.

Hutchinson and Rankin (1989) published a salary survey of Association for Educational Communications and Technology (AECT) members. Similar studies, published in 1984 and 1987 by the same authors, provided some basis for comparison. Such studies provide one measure of professionals in the field. They reported that "the average AECT member is 45.5 years of age, has been employed in the field for 15.5 years, has held his or her position for 8.9 years, and is paid $40,316." Since the last study, salaries have increased more than 16 percent, but the 12.5 percent inflation rate wiped out much of the gain. Other findings report on level of education, number of months worked each year, types of positions held, and salary comparisons between men and women.

Issues

- What changes are necessary in the programs to prepare professionals for service in the field of educational technology in light of the many technological changes that have occurred recently?

- Is there a role for the educational technologist in the K-12 schools? If so, what is it?

- Should educational technology practitioners be certified? If so, by whom?

- Where are the future educational technologists coming from?

Trend #8

The impact of technology on individuals in the society at large continues to be considered by educational technology professionals.

One sign of professional growth is that people within the field of educational technology are asking questions about the consequences of their efforts on individuals who use the products and systems created by educational technology procedures. For example, one of the perennial concerns raised by people inside and outside the profession is the effect of commercial television on young children. The issue continues to be explored, debated, and perpetuated because of conflicting data and opinions. The most recent analysis is *The Impact on Children's Education: Television's Influence on Cognitive Development* (Anderson & Collins, 1988), sponsored by the Office of Educational Research and Improvement of the U.S. Department of Education. The authors examined nine common assertions about the effects of television on children and report their findings on each assertion. They conclude that the research literature is sparse but they offer the following responses to the common assertions:

- There is no evidence that television has a mesmerizing effect on children's attention caused by color, movement, and visual changes.

- While preschool and early elementary school-age children's comprehension of television can be fragmented, this holds primarily for relatively complex adult-level dramatic presentations.

- Even preschool children demonstrate frequent inferential activities while television viewing.

- There is no evidence that children generally get overstimulated by television.

- There is little evidence that television viewing displaces valuable cognitive activities.

- The assertion that television viewing shortens attention span is difficult to test since the term *attention span*, as commonly used, has no certain technical meaning.

- There is no clear evidence that television influences imaginativeness, but one study indicates that television may negatively affect verbal "ideational fluency," i.e., ability to think of alternative uses for an object.

- There is some weak evidence that television availability reduces reading achievement.

- There is no evidence that television asymmetrically influences brain development.

Helping students (and others) to interpret what they see and hear via mass media continues to be the subject of some of the literature in this category. *Visual literacy* is the term attached to this movement and, though interest in it peaked during the late 1970s, there is still a residue of writing about how it is taught in schools and colleges (Wood, 1989b).

After more than 500 people from 93 countries and 29 international organizations met in Paris for the International Congress on Education and Informatics, they issued a *Declaration* (UNESCO, 1989) that highlights some of the societal concerns raised in other quarters. Several statements from that document are illustrative of the concerns held by participants in that Congress:

- We strongly feel that with the introduction of new information technologies in education, educational disparities may further grow within and between countries unless immediate and determined steps are taken to avoid such development by adopting corrective measures both nationally and internationally.

- We declare that, by virtue of its important role in every society, new information technologies should form part of the culture available to the entire population.

- We recognize the multiplicity of the roles new information technologies play not only as a tool in education but as a new approach and culture for effective transaction in teaching and learning, management of information, and accelerated development of society.

These are healthy concerns of reflective practitioners who view "ends" as being as important as "means." In both 1988 and 1989 there were many such items in the literature, most of them coming from documents entered into the ERIC database.

Issues

- How can learners of all ages be taught critical viewing and listening skills?

- What are the consequences on learners of using technology in the school?

- How can home use and school use of technology be brought together for productive results?

- What special roles can technology fulfill that teachers cannot do as well?

Trend #9

The applications of telecommunications used in the society at large are reflected in the schools and in postsecondary institutions.

Telecommunications is defined here as the electronic connection between a receiver and a sender. Either receiver or sender could be a person or an electronic device. At the simplest level, there is the telephone, which has permitted telelectures (an individual speaking from a remote location to a group or groups using an amplified speaker at the receiving end) and teleconferences (groups meeting simultaneously at two or more locations with audio or audio/video communication). Telephonic connections also permit computer conferencing, searching remote databases with a personal computer, using computer-based bulletin boards, and communicating with electronic mail. More recent technologies include video connections with regular and low-power broadcasting, cable distribution, and satellite. Very often, combinations of several telecommunications systems are used to deliver information.

Previous trends reported in this paper have referred to telecommunications in relation to computer utilization. Mainframe and microcomputers often use telecommunications for connection to other people and information resources. The distinction is blurring as these two technologies become mutually dependent. However, in educational settings, video is still a distinct medium.

There are 377,700 video cassette recorders (VCRs) in the 102,719 public and nonpublic schools in the United States. Colleges and universities own 50,200 units (Hope Reports, 1989). There are 1.5 million videotapes in 79,693 videotape collections and television receivers in practically every school. Eighty-six percent of all the schools indicate that they will purchase the same or more hardware in 1989-1990, and 96 percent say they will purchase the same or more software during the same period (Quality Education Data, 1989). These data confirm the penetration of television in the schools.

There are no data on the number of cable connections, but the current literature reports that some school districts have arrangements with local cable companies to use one public channel for educational programming.

Perhaps the most visible and controversial use of television in the schools occurred in 1989 when Whittle Communications announced free availability of a fifteen-minute daily television newscast *with commercials*. For schools that are willing to cooperate, Whittle Communications' "Channel One" provides television monitors for every classroom, two videotape recorders, and an installed satellite dish. "Channel One" is designed to present a teenage perspective on news and current affairs to students in grades 6 through 12. The program was piloted for five weeks during the spring of 1989 in five secondary schools and one middle school, and a comprehensive evaluation was completed (*Whittle Communications*, 1989). The results were generally favorable and the commercials did not appear to distract from the educational value of the newscasts. Despite continuing controversy, 500 schools in twenty-four states have subscribed to the service, which is scheduled to begin in March 1990. The Whittle organization predicts that about 8,000 schools with a potential audience of about 6 million pupils will be using the service by December 1990.

The Turner Broadcasting System began "CNN Newsroom" on August 14, 1989. This daily fifteen-minute commercial-free program, geared to middle and high schools, is broadcast at 3:45 a.m., EST, each weekday. Participating schools are permitted to tape record the programs free of charge. CNN and major cable operators will absorb the costs for connecting schools to the cable. The Discovery Channel began "Assignment: Discovery" on September 18, 1989, with a one-hour daily program geared to middle and high schools. Each hour is made up of two segments, each twenty to twenty-five minutes, that can be videotaped for later use. Each day follows a specific theme: Monday, *Science and Technology*; Tuesday, *Social Studies*; Wednesday, *Natural Science*; Thursday, *Arts and Humanities*; and Friday, *World Events and Contemporary Issues*. There are no commercials.

Each of the broadcasting services provides teacher guides and other support material to augment the programs. Each of these three new services will be watched and studied during 1990. Results will be reported in future trends papers.

Another important component of the telecommunications picture is satellite delivery of instruction to schools, colleges, and training settings. By 1989, 10,476 schools had installed satellite dishes (Quality Education Data, 1989). The Star Schools projects, funded by the U.S. Department of Education, used satellite communication to deliver courses. A number of states and consortia are now operating distance education programs and courses by satellite in Oklahoma, Washington, Missouri, Texas, and Kentucky (Jordahl, 1989). Some satellite-based programs have grown to multistate operations. The Texas Interactive Instructional Network (TI-IN) serves twenty states and broadcasts over 100 hours of live secondary level courses every week. In Kentucky, 250 secondary schools receive televised instruction via satellite, much of it interactive. The Oklahoma Arts and Sciences

Teleconferencing Service offers courses to 102 schools in eight states. Other states have satellite delivery of instruction in various stages of development. Coupled with distance education developments, satellite-based communication is clearly one of the growth areas of educational technology.

In higher education, the National Technological University (NTU) continued to offer courses to students in remote locations via satellite. NTU is a consortium of more than twenty engineering schools that broadcasts about 5,500 hours of credit and noncredit courses to about forty corporate sites across the United States. Growth to this level has occurred in the five years since its beginning (Mays & Lumsden, 1989).

Issues

- What types of connections should schools be able to make (e.g., cable satellite, low-power broadcasting)?

- What are the appropriate uses of networks among schools and colleges?

- Should schools use programs during the school day that contain commercial messages?

- What is the appropriate role of the school in producing instructional programs for transmission to other schools and colleges?

- What are the cost/benefits of connecting schools to other schools and communication sources?

Trend #10

The results of research do not appear to have much effect on applications and operations of educational technology.

Translating research and theory into practice is a problem that has always been expressed by educators. In part, the problem is perceived differently by researchers and practitioners and its resolution is still waiting. Researchers wonder why practitioners do not use the results of their scholarly efforts, and practitioners wonder why researchers do not provide useful principles, expressed in understandable terms, that can be used directly in day-to-day classroom activities. These positions, which are now new, are nevertheless incorporated into the 1989 trends report because there seems to be a preponderance of reports on *practice* in the current literature and very little on research and theory. Where research and theory are the subjects of articles and papers, they tend to emphasize *models*. Models, in these cases, are usually diagrammatic representations of instructional design and development procedures. Some models are based on research, but most seem to use empirical observations as the rationale to support the generalizations represented by each model.

One of the conclusions of the Harvard Educational Technology Center research program focuses on the need to link teacher knowledge with research findings. "Teachers [should] collaboratively rethink educational goals, strategies, and roles and invent ways to connect their own wisdom with the products of educational research" (Fox & Saunders, 1989). This position places the responsibility directly on the doorstep of teachers. While teachers wait for "the products of educational research," researchers are calling for more research in order to be able to provide the results that will be directly useful. For example, Anderson and Collins (1988), in their comprehensive study on the influence of television on learner's cognitive development, say:

> The research literature provides little support for most of the common beliefs about the influence of television. For a number of reasons, however, it is difficult to conclude that television has no major effects. First, there has been almost no research on a number of major issues, including the influence of entertainment television on children's academically relevant knowledge. Second, considerations of what is known about television viewing suggest possible negative effects (for example, on listening skills) that have not been explored in research. Third, some of the existing research can be challenged on methodological grounds. (p. 5)

Many of the forty papers submitted to the 1989 annual convention of the Association for Educational Communications and Technology, Division of Research and Theory, were based on doctoral dissertations and make little attempt to derive principles for practice. In contrast, the major conference in the United Kingdom, Educational Technology International Conference 1989, presents mostly case studies of educational technology applications with almost no mention of research or theoretical bases. It appears that the translation process is lacking and that the dichotomous positions are being maintained by both researchers and practitioners. Educational technology is not unique in this matter.

There is another potential for confusion in the matter of research and practice, and that is the interpretation of *evaluation* as research. Misunderstanding of the purpose and procedures of evaluation may lead to erroneous conclusions. Usually, the purpose of evaluation is to gather data to help make decisions, e.g., to continue a program, to market a product, to hire a new staff member. The purpose of research is to explore new areas or test hypotheses in order to discover new facts or to revise existing knowledge. It may or may not have direct practical applications. Evaluation and research often use the same or similar procedures in gathering data. Both report findings and come to conclusions. It is understandable that they are confused. Such confusion is not clarified in the literature so that evaluation often passes for research and vice versa.

Issues

- Where do teachers go to get information about teaching and the design of learning materials?

- In what form would research findings be both responsible and useful?

- How can teachers be built into research and evaluation activities?

- Who facilitates the translation of research into practice?

Trend #11

The curriculum support function is an important element of educational technology programs.

In the 1950s and 1960s, when the educational media movement was in place, practitioners emphasized the organization and management of programs in schools and colleges. One important maxim was the "3 Rs": the *R*ight material and equipment, in the *R*ight place, at the *R*ight time!

As the field evolved and there was a gradual shift toward instructional design and development, the emphasis and urgency of administrative matters seemed to wane. However, the literature of educational technology in 1989 still displays the residue of this earlier function. The terminology has changed to *curriculum support* and the locus of activity has shifted to the school library *media* center, but the management and logistics concept remains. Authors in 1989 reported on ways in which they facilitated the use of educational media and technology activities in their settings. They describe the nature of the services and special procedures that they have introduced to make programs operate more effectively and efficiently. Some of the papers describe ways in which teachers and learners have been taught skills to use the resources that are available in schools and colleges today. Some specify new information services that are intended to help teachers and learners become more responsible for their own learning. These are the functions that help educators and students implement and use the hardware and software being introduced under the umbrella of educational technology.

The importance of curriculum support services is noted in the research report of the Harvard Educational Technology Center: "Implementation assistance must therefore include ... logistical help with issues such as schedules, equipment, and curriculum materials" (Fox & Saunders, 1989, p. 4). The Center for Technology in Education at the Bank Street College of Education stresses the same concern in its research program funded by the U.S. Department of Education: "A program of 'design experiments' will be carried out collaboratively with schools to design and study the optimal conditions for the integration of technology into schools under varying constraints" (Fox & Saunders, 1989, p. 177).

Recognition of the need for curriculum support is evident in the joint publication of *Information Power* by the American Association of School Librarians and the Association for Educational Communications and Technology. This publication presents the "standards" for media and technology in schools. It is beginning to be discussed in the educational technology literature, mostly in publications related to school library media programs. Its focus is on curriculum support.

Issues

- Which management functions formerly performed by educational technologists in the school can be handled by school library media specialists?

- What incentives have to be offered to involve professional educators in the process of curricular integration of media and technology resources?

- What hardware and software ought to be available in every classroom and which from a central location?

- How can the profession monitor effectiveness in the use of media and technology in formal education environments?

APPENDIX A: TRENDS BY
TOPIC AND SOURCE

	Journals	Disser-tations	Confer-ences	ERIC	Total
TRENDS					
The Field					
History	4	0	0	1	5
Status	10	0	38	47	95
Future	4	0	2	8	14
Ethics	1	0	3	10	14
Legal Aspects	1	0	2	3	6
The Standards	1	0	8	0	9
Personnel					
Roles/Responsibilities	7	0	24	7	38
Recognition	0	0	1	1	2
Certification	0	0	0	2	2
Leadership	0	0	2	0	2
Professional Education	21	0	33	18	72
Management					
Organization	1	0	4	0	5
Logistics/Operations	3	0	20	9	32
Procedures/Policies	2	0	13	13	28
Facilities	1	0	3	3	7
Finance/Budget	1	0	6	1	8
Planning Processes	4	0	6	11	21
Diffusion	6	2	12	18	38
Implementation	7	1	22	18	48
Technical Developments					
Computer-related	19	0	20	51	90
Telecommunications	2	0	10	59	71
Video	3	0	7	19	29
Audio	0	0	3	4	7
Photography/Holography	0	0	0	0	0
Instructional Processes/Services					
Distance Education	5	0	48	28	81
Simulations/Games	4	1	9	4	18
Problem Solving	3	0	9	13	25
Interactive Video	11	0	53	19	83
AI/Expert Systems	7	1	16	22	46
Design and Development					
Needs assessment	0	0	20	3	23
Task analysis	1	0	5	3	9
Individual differences/ learner characteristics	3	6	12	17	38
Message design	7	1	22	6	36
Course development	4	0	11	9	24
Product development	5	0	34	10	49
Courseware design	9	0	8	5	22
Hypermedia	11	0	20	5	36
Motivational Strategies	3	2	17	0	22

(Appendix A continues on page 28.)

Appendix A (*continued*)

	Journals	Disser- tations	Confer- ences	ERIC	Total
Evaluation					
Product Evaluation	11	0	24	28	63
Process Evaluation	2	0	11	7	20
Cost-effectiveness Evaluation	2	0	3	5	10
Formative Evaluation	2	0	3	5	10
Services					
Literature and Reading Guidance	0	0	0	1	1
Curriculum Support	12	1	23	43	79
Skills Instruction	3	0	9	6	18
Information Services	2	0	12	9	23
Research and Theory					
Research Methodologies	1	0	4	6	11
Theory and Model Con- struction/Application	8	1	25	12	46
Society and Culture	5	0	6	60	71

Grand Total 1,507

REFERENCES

Allen, William H. (1970). *Trends in instructional technology*. Stanford, CA: ERIC Clearinghouse on Educational Media and Technology. ED 043 242.

Anderson, D. R., & Collins, P. A. (1988). *The impact on children's education: Television's influence on cognitive development*. Washington, DC: Office of Educational Research and Improvement, U.S. Department of Education.

Ely, Donald P. (1989). *Trends and issues in educational technology 1988*. Syracuse, NY: ERIC Clearinghouse on Information Resources. ED 308 859.

Fox, J., & Saunders, C. (1989). *Major research findings, selected accomplishments, and publications 1985-1988*. Washington, DC: Office of Research and Improvement, U.S. Department of Education. ED number to be assigned.

Futrell, Mary H. (1989, Winter). Future classrooms need technology. *AIT News-Letter, 20* (1), 7-8.

Hope Reports. (1989). *Educational media trends through the 1990s: A sequel*. Rochester, NY: Hope Reports.

Hutchinson, J. A., & Rankin, P. M. (1989, September). 1989 AECT member salary survey. *TechTrends, 34* (4), 10-15.

Johnson, Jenny K. (1989a). *Master's curricula in educational communications and technology: A descriptive directory* (3d ed.). Washington, DC: Association for Educational Communications and Technology.

Johnson, Jenny K. (1989b, September). The degrees to which.... *TechTrends, 34* (4), 16-19.

Jordahl, G. (1989, February). Communication satellites: A rural response to the tyranny of distance. *Educational Technology, 29* (2), 34-38.

Klein, J. (1989). Enhancing instructional design and technology academic programs: A summary of the fifth meeting of the professors of instructional design and technology. *Educational Technology Research and Development, 37* (3), 103-106.

Logan, Edwin. (1989). Highlights of the status and trends of instructional technology/media related programs at the doctoral and master's level. In D. P. Ely (Ed.), *Educational media and technology yearbook 1988* (pp. 153-215). Englewood, CO: Libraries Unlimited.

Mays, M., & Lumsden, D. B. (1989, May/June). NTU—A technological university for a technology-based society. *TechTrends, 34* (3), 18-23.

National Diffusion Network. (1988). *Programs that work* (14th ed.). Longmont, CA: Sopris West, Inc.

National Education Association. (1989). *Educational technology: NEA special committee report*. Washington, DC: NEA. ED number to be assigned.

National Governors' Association. (1989). *Results in education: 1989. The governors' 1991 report on education*. Washington, DC: National Governors' Association. ED number to be assigned.

Newman, Frank. (1989, November 28). *Uneven marriage: The university and the management of information technology*. Keynote address presented at the CAUSE National Conference on Managing Information Technologies: Facing Issues, San Diego, California.

Ninth annual survey of the states. (1989, October). *Electronic Learning, 9* (2), 22-28.

Papert, S. (1989, Winter). Future classrooms need technology. *AIT Newsletter, 20* (1), 8-9.

Pollak, R. A. (1990, January/February). The state of videodiscs in education and training. *Instruction Delivery Systems, 4* (1), 12-14.

Quality Education Data. (1989). *1989-90 Catalog of educational mailing lists and marketing services*. Denver, CO: Quality Education Data.

Randall, R. (1989, Winter). Future classrooms need technology, *AIT Newsletter, 20* (1), 9-10.

Southeastern Educational Improvement Laboratory. (1989, March). *Tapping the potential of educational technology*. Research Triangle Park, NC: SEIL.

Timmers, Shannon. (1989). *Higher level distance education and the needs of developing countries*. Vancouver, BC: Open Learning Agency.

UNESCO. (1989, April). *Education and informatics: Strengthening international cooperation*. Paris: UNESCO.

U.S. Congress, Office of Technology Assessment. (1989). *Linking for learning: A new course for education*. Washington, DC: U.S. Government Printing Office. ED 310 765.

Weiss, Stefanie. (1989a, September). Cable networks compete for classroom market. *NEA Today*, p. 3.

Weiss, Stefanie. (1989b, September). For the '90s: A Computer on each teacher's desk. *NEA Today*, p. 32.

Whittle Communications. (1989). *Overview of Whittle Communications Educational Network*. Knoxville, TN: Whittle Communications.

Wood, D. B. (1989a, September 29). Schoolroom newscasts – minus ads. *Christian Science Monitor*, p. 11.

Wood, D. B. (1989b, October 4). College students learn "visual literacy." *Christian Science Monitor*, p. 10-11.

Mechanisms for Facilitating a
Vital and Dynamic Education System
Fundamental Roles for Education Science and Technology

Roy D. Pea
and
Elliot Soloway
Cognitive Systems, Inc.
234 Church Street
New Haven, Connecticut 06510

Final Report
for the
Office of Technology Assessment*
U.S. Congress

October 31, 1987

EXECUTIVE SUMMARY

This report was prepared as one component of an OTA project entitled "Educational Technology: An Assessment of Practice and Potential," requested by the U.S. House Committee on Education and Labor. The objectives of our particular project were: (1) synthesize current activities and directions of research in education science (the cognitive, social and instructional sciences), and (2) characterize how opportunities brought about by theoretical advances in education science and developments in multimedia, interactive, information processing technologies can be brought profitably and effectively to bear on American education.

There is an ever widening gap between the school and rest of society: what students do in school makes less and less contact with what is required of them to function as productive citizens in a participatory democracy. The key to bridging that gap lies in revitalizing the educational process. A cornerstone in that effort can be education science. In particular, research in the cognitive, social, instructional, and computational sciences has brought about a fundamental change in our thinking about learning and teaching. In particular,

*This report appears in summary form as part of a larger OTA project report. The full report, *Power On! New Tools for Teaching and Learning*, is available from the Government Printing Office, Washington, DC 20402-9325. Order GPO number 052-003-01125-5, $11.00. Call 202-783-3238 to verify price.

there has been a paradigm shift from viewing education from a curriculum/subject matter perspective to viewing education from a learner and teacher perspective. Rather than students having to adapt to a given curriculum, we can now draw on our fine-grained theories of how students actually go about learning to adapt the curriculum to the student. Moreover, advances in information processing technologies enable these new insights into learning and teaching to be embodied in qualitatively different sorts of educational products: computer-based microworlds, where, through the medium of high-quality, color graphic simulations, students can explore the inner workings of the living cell, or design and test mini mechanical robots; intelligent tutoring systems, capable of providing true one-on-one instruction in subjects such as geometry and algebra.

We present a framework, consisting of the following categories, for organizing the R&D directions considered most promising by experts in the field: (1) changing what students do; (2) changing how we track learning; (3) changing what's taught; (4) changing what teachers do; and (5) changing the schooling environment. In each category, we first discuss the theoretical justification that supports the changed view. Then, we identify specific technological innovations embodying the theoretical principles that create promising new learning and teaching environments.

Our analyses suggest that there are many reasons why it has been difficult to transfer advances in the scientific understanding about educational processes and the prototype technologies influenced by them to educational practice. Several major reasons for these difficulties have been: funding primarily from military or business contracts that has focused efforts on relatively narrow, training issues; unstable and insufficient funding resources in fundamental education science at the precollege level; inadequate coordination of R&D efforts with the teaching profession and other educational organizations, as well as commercial technology developers and professional publishers.

A range of mechanisms are needed in order to bring about the major changes that are envisioned for education through education science and the innovative use of technology. We outline three options for a Federal role in supporting the development and nurturing of such mechanisms: from a significant increase in support, to a modest increase, to no increase. Moreover, we assess these three options with respect to their potential for developing mechanisms that can achieve goals such as: providing a base for the development and exploration of new ideas and technologies in education science, developing a community infrastructure, providing for the integration of classroom teachers into all phrases of the research and development process, and providing links to the commercial sector in order to effectively produce and disseminate quality technological products.

A cornerstone of the first two options is our call for Centers of Interactive Technology and Education (CITEs). A CITE is an interdisciplinary, educational science and technology research and development center, that will also serve to coordinate significant activities in graduate, professional, and educator training, and educational technology product development. CITEs would operate with core federal support, with significant contributions from corporate, foundations, state and local institutional sponsors. The cost of 1 CITE for a year will be about $10 million. Fully a third of this will go for "in practice" activities: supporting an associated school, supporting teacher education, etc. The types of CITE activities proposed, as well as staff levels and composition, reflect theory-practice integration by design, as well as the belief that education science and technology is fundamentally an engineering and not a pure science.

The magnitude of the problems facing us in education is large. In order to make an effective dent, we need to commit ourselves to a substantial program of research and development. Education science coupled with innovative uses of technology has an unparalleled potential for meeting the challenges. With sufficient Federal support, that potential can be actualized.

INTRODUCTION:
BRIDGING THE GAPS

There are ever-widening gaps between schools and society. Our report highlights three such gaps. These gaps are detrimental not only for the economy of our nation, but for future prospects of enlightened citizens as the foundation and beneficiaries of a participatory democracy. In particular, there are substantial gaps between the knowledge students are capable of using after formal schooling and the knowledge they need to participate effectively as productive citizens in a democracy; and between the tools for learning and problem-solving utilized in society and those involved in the nation's educational activities. The final gap—whose narrowing with technologies holds promise for narrowing the other gaps—is between research knowledge of learning as a cognitive, socially situated process, and educational practices primarily dependent on "transmitting" information or procedural skills for manipulating symbols.

Widespread attention has been devoted to documenting the ills of present American education. This state is described in several dozen reports from book-length reports and special commissions appointed by governmental, business, and research agencies (6, 17, 34, 50, 77, 79, 93, 100a, 115, 129a, 148c, 153, 173, 174). We know that illiteracy is widespread, that education in mathematics, science, and technology is not sufficient, that understanding of culture, humanities, social affairs, and history is impoverished. Participation in science and mathematics education is decreasing, yet it is key to the nation's technological vitality in an increasingly competitive world economy (57, 64, 86, 116, 120, 131, 131a, 180, 187), and particularly underrepresented by women and minorities (1a, 43, 50, 120, 178). Employers find too few high-school and even college graduates prepared in the basic educational competencies needed to function effectively in organizations (127a, 144a, 185b). These are not just vocational concerns, but issues of deep educational significance and effective development of human resources.

The knowledge gap. The problem of students' knowledge utilization, also described as "transfer," is a serious underachievement of much present education. Research and findings from the National Assessment of Educational Progress and other sources indicate that students have difficulties in reasoning and problem-solving where they must put what has been learned in school to use in writing, scientific and mathematical reasoning, critical thinking about complex issues facing society, and other real activities (36, 77, 130, 153). Proposals to orient teaching and learning so that it is "situated" in contexts of application rather than as isolated general skill-training or fact-memorization may help ameliorate this condition (95, 127a, 147, 185a). And schools as yet have placed far too little emphasis on the inquiry skills required to make effective use of vast information databases, much less the knowledge integration and communication skills needed to make use of the information acquired through such search (15, 49, 86, 145).

The technology gap. As this report will document, very rapid changes are taking place in the mass market computer-based technologies used to support learning, problem-solving, and entertainment activities in society, both in the workplace and in homes. Market trends and projections, as well as research, suggest that the gap has widened and will, given today's directions, continue to widen between societal and school-based educational uses of technologies (11, 64, 65, 116a, 186). This is not important strictly because of the prevalence of technologies in society, but because the ones that are in use are commonly empowering humans in helping them to better reason, learn, communicate, and collaborate (136, 138). And students are largely not getting access to these advantages. Optimistic popular reports citing statistics on the growing numbers of computers in schools are deceptive, since they include substantial quantities of primitive equipment with only marginal educational uses—typically for "computer literacy" or low-level computer programming with no future application.

The research-application gap. Although a broad consensus has emerged about needed changes in educational practices from the cognitive, social, and instructional sciences—what we henceforth call in shorthand "the education sciences"—there have been few changes that have taken place in the state of the nation's education as a result. While the research-practice link has always been problematic, these research communities have begun to engage in a new paradigm of work, involving educational practitioners and real educational settings in research and development activities, that holds great promise for narrowing this traditional gap (26, 50, 58, 65a, 82, 116, 116a, 128, 162).

Possible relations between the knowledge and technology gaps. As we will show, concerted federal efforts are required to "yoke" societal uses of technology that are human-centered to educational uses of technology. This process, designed so as to narrow both the knowledge and the technology gaps, should be guided by the best research the cognitive, social, and instructional sciences has to offer for how processes of learning for understanding take place, and for how people are better enabled to realize their creative and productive potentials, and to lead fulfilling lives.

Roles for Research and Development for Bettering Education through Technologies

Research in the cognitive, social, and instructional sciences, and the accompanying use of theory-guided educational technologies, could do much to narrow these gaps.

The strategy to be pursued should whenever possible involve the application of such sciences to the design, development, and use of technologies in education that are *human-centered*, not technology-centered (136). The reason for these provisions is that there is no reason to believe that the uses of technology per se will improve education. As artifacts, computers neither teach nor intrinsically carry good, but serve as implements of imagination (or its absence). Indeed, technology as often as not can cause as many problems as it solves (5). And although we believe there are important reasons for keeping pace with technology developments in society, it would be foolhardy to make education technology "driven," rather than critically responsive to educational potentials of new technologies. As in the case of computers in complex organizations (101), many planful, purposive, and effortful acts beyond the technology—how it is designed, thought about, used, supported, how it is integrated with other activities and tools of teaching and learning—are integral to its effectiveness as catalyst of human development and educational attainments (26, 42, 50, 70, 148). Where research-guidance from these human sciences can be expected to make a positive difference in the educational tools provided and used, it should be exploited. And as we shall see, various incentive structures could improve the utilization of research and development results for technologies in educational settings.

It is essential to keep examining whether computer technologies can, as many theorists and researchers conjecture, dramatically improve the processes of teaching and learning (16, 19, 20, 24, 26, 28, 42, 51, 52, 110, 144, 145, 166). Several indications support this belief, even though the features and uses of many educational technologies fall seriously short of what will be required for such changes to occur. Many of the advances in understanding the nature of thinking and learning in the cognitive sciences have been dependent upon the use of the computer as a device for explicitly modelling or revealing mental processes (25, 66, 73, 81, 84). The methods and tools emerging from this research, now exploited commercially in artificial intelligence and in cognitive tools, can be brought to serve the processes of education. The symbol storage and manipulation capabilities of computers used in this research have also served society in allowing for the creation of powerful cognitive tools, such as writing systems, graphics and animation programs, relational databases, project planning and management tools, and expert systems (13, 95a, 136). Many of these tools act as imagination and intelligence "extenders," serving to make new kinds of reasoning, prediction, understanding, cooperation, and creative expression possible (119, 136, 138, 139, 146, 148, 181, 190, 202). The ability to provide mind-like artifacts in educational processes such as intelligent tutors, intelligent help for learning to use tools, and "interactive" books may also prove important.

The Complexities of Education Require Scientific Understanding to Guide Practice

We are in a new era of sciences on processes of education. Those who examine the science of learning and the detailed practices of effective instruction have come to appreciate the much, much greater *complexity of education* than heretofore recognized (e.g., 116, 120). The society at large must come to appreciate the extraordinary complexity of what we ask people to master in education. Otherwise, patchwork solutions like "longer school days," without more fundamental analyses of cognitive, social, and instructional aspects of learning, will continue to be proposed and implemented with marginal effects.

To effectively guide the practices of education, the development of educational technologies including curricula and computer tools, and the education of teachers for promoting student learning, we need a deep scientific understanding of how minds in society learn.

The research community commonly compares our scientific understanding of mind in education today to our understanding of body and medicine in the early 1800's. Folk theories of medicine predominated then, and folk practices in education largely predominate today. Just as the everyday citizen feels expert in judging what is wrong with education, and how to do it better, so the everyday citizen felt expert in the 1800's in diagnosing and treating the body's ills. Everyone had elixirs and cures. The everyday citizen was wrong then, and except for some areas of learning that can be informally acquired outside formal schooling, that citizen is largely wrong about education today. What transformed medical practice was medical science, requiring the best minds in highly-focused empirical attacks on the nature of disease and biological systems, and use of the most advanced technologies available, tuned specifically to the problems' dimensions.

Understanding the workings of mind in learning in society is one of the major frontiers of science. Until the complexities of education are better appreciated, we cannot expect popular enthusiasm about research and development for educational technologies. We cannot expect substantive funding at the high levels required to achieve a sufficient scientific understanding of how the mind works in education, or to attract the best minds to improving education (120). Instead, we may see continuation of past funding efforts, perceived by the education science community as largely sporadic, short-term, and isolated in nature. This problem is further borne out by the astonishing fact that federal support for research in education has expenditures of one-tenth of one percent of the education budget, in contrast to 20 times that figure for the health budget, and 150 times that figure for the defense budget (116). Education will go on suffering with such inattention. Yet we cannot continue to practice folk medicine with student's minds.

Computers Are Different Than Any Previous Educational Invention

We all know about the information revolution, and the computer's role as a "once in a century" innovation (172a). It has served to kindle fundamental rethinking of the nature of education, for three major reasons. First and foremost it has provided the microscope for new conceptions of mind — how it works in reasoning and learning. Secondly, since it is a "metamedium" for information creation, storage, transformation, and communication, it has become a universal multimedia instrument for education. And thirdly, in the prosthetic powers it provides for scaffolding mental activities and managing information complexity, it has opened doors on human potential and possibilities that have fired the imaginations of educators around the world.

These are great reasons for hope. But they come with great costs of realization, since they make clear that we are no longer in a period of education "business as usual," but a new technological era. What have we come to see about education, in part through the arrival of information technologies? What kinds of insights and new levers might the humane use of computers offer?

Computers have within a short decade of use in mass society placed in great relief the plights of education. Of course there have been other contributions to these recognitions. But through their use as simulation tools for constructing cognitive science theories of mind, we have begun to see, in a manner not at all apparent in the neo-behaviorist theories of learning in decades past, how poorly education achieves the aims of sound reasoning in its rich varieties, of adequate comprehension and communication of ideas and images, of invention and creativity, of lifelong learning and a fulfilling existence.

COGNITIVE, SOCIAL, AND INSTRUCTIONAL ASPECTS OF THE EDUCATION SCIENCES

We will focus here on the changes that have taken shape in the scientific understanding of education, and the repercussion they have for every facet of its conception and practices. While frontier studies in this field debate the particular details of how knowledge is mentally represented, and the processes and mechanisms involved in conceptual change and acquisition of problem-solving strategies, it is nonetheless generally agreed that the consensus directions highlight the necessity of substantial reforms in educational practices and in the very idea of "education." We will characterize changes in consensus views on:

- The nature of the learner
- The nature of "understanding"
- What materials are needed for learning
- What pedagogical tasks and strategies are effective and why
- Roles of the social context in learning with technologies

View of the Nature of the Learner

A new consensus view of the learner, incongruent with most present-day practices, characterizes present research in the education sciences. Research concludes that the dominant *transmission* view of knowledge is deeply misguided (reviewed in 23, 80, 102).

According to this view, the major pedagogical activity is to provide well-structured presentations of material to be learned, primarily through lecture, demonstration, and recitation (124). Instead, we now see that new learning is *constructed* in terms of prior knowledge by an active learner in a social context, that knowledge is best acquired in functional contexts with similarities to situations for future knowledge transfer, and that learners need to learn strategies and methods for autonomous "repair" of understanding when applications of prior knowledge ot a novel situation fails.

The new view of the learner, influenced by the work of Piaget (148b), Ausubel (7), Bruner (26a) and others in the 1960's and 1970's (38, 80, 184), sees the development of intelligence generally, and of subject-matter understanding in education in particular, as actively constructed by the individual (e.g., 152). New knowledge is acquired in relation to previous knowledge, building upon intuitive, informal experiences. Such "experiential knowledge" must be reckoned with in education. Much recent research involves "diagnosing" the understandings, preconceptions, and interests that learners bring to formal instruction, so that instruction may bridge experiential and formal, school-based learning. Such bridging is important because severe limits arise in the kinds of problems these informal reasoning methods can solve. Analyses of preconceptions have been particularly revealing for topics in science (32, 33, 39, 40, 48, 58, 60, 61, 88, 106, 122, 123, 140, 142, 193, 194, 201), mathematics (21, 29, 35, 75, 100, 154, 155, 168), and programming (14a, 95b, 101a, 148a, 177, 177a). Research work in the development of reading (6, 10, 133, 143) and writing skills (12, 26, 58a) also reveals the importance of helping students build upon a rich set of communicative strategies, techniques, and experiential topics derived from oral language use that makes sense to them.

An understanding of subject matter so that problems can be solved or creatively posed requires a richly interconnected network of concepts, principles, and skills (41, 76, 81, 84, 107). The necessity of subject matter knowledge in expertise has been recognized for centuries. What is new is the research-based recognition that it is *not* a knowledge base of facts per se that should be an instructional goal. Instead, students need to acquire facts, principles, or theories as *conceptual tools* for reasoning and problem solving that they can see makes sense because they have consequences in meaningful contexts (18, 26, 50, 185a). The knowledge base acquired through education should not be inert, memorized for recall on tests, but active, conditionalized for application to appropriate contexts of use (77). The new educational awareness of the pedagogical priority of facts-in-use has led to an increasing emphasis on what have been described as "guided microworlds," "apprenticeship learning," or "learning by doing" (52, 65a, 95, 153). In such methods, students acquire knowledge-in-use, experiencing and employing new ideas in contexts of application with many similarities to their desired contexts of transfer.

Learners, even expert learners, routinely face novel situations for knowledge application. Experts will self-consciously exploit analogies, reasoning by related cases, and use other heuristics in order to make connections between previous knowledge and the present case (84). The domain expert is distinguished from the novice not only by having more knowledge for automatic application to situations (through processes of recognition), but by having more strategies (and better control over their use) for "repairing" prior knowledge, recovering when it fails (165). Research with novice learners (e.g., for multidigit subtraction [25a, 193a], and for algebra equation-solving [84]) suggests that systematic patterns of procedural repair are used when prior knowledge fails. These findings imply that repair processes are basic to learning, and may be exploited by instruction so that learners exert autonomous control over learning repair activities (84). The instructional result would be more flexible understanding, ready to meet the novel situations an uncertain future world presents.

View of the Nature of "Understanding"

Detailed comparative studies of the processes and outcomes of reasoning about problems by experts and novices in different knowledge domains have led to major reconceptualizations of what it means to "understand" a topic (134a). While this issue is one of the most complex of all topics in the cognitive sciences, there are nonetheless several major points of agreement arising from research on psychological understanding. The importance of this topic for education is momentous, since much present school-based "learning" does not result in understanding (6, 33, 153).

The first major point is that understanding is an active process, guided by prior knowledge and expectations. Whether the domain is reading narratives, solving physics problems, or creating an algebraic model of a situation, people expect regularities. These regularities constitute basic categories of experience, "frames" or "schemas," that are associated in memory with prototypic features (163). Schemas bring order into a world that would otherwise consist of entirely novel experiences. Expert learners have highly elaborated and differentiated knowledge schemas that often lead to "automatic" recognition of a problem type and deployment of the appropriate actions to solve the problem (2, 3, 84). Those with high levels of domain understanding also can reason analogically from prior cases, evaluating the utility of discoveries made through such analogies, and reason counterfactually, in order to determine "what-if-not?" (e.g., in mathematics [168], social science [193a], electronic troubleshooting [24a], and medical diagnosis [46]).

A second and related point is that domain experts have well-developed "mental models" of how complex systems function, such as electrical circuits, steam plants, economic systems, computer programs, ecosystems, or aircraft navigation systems. These mental representations are functionally important because they can be used to "run" mental simulations of such a system in order to qualitatively reason about its hypothetical future states and determine "what if?" (14, 69). The utility of such virtual machines in memory is apparent in reasoning about malfunctioning systems, or about the predicted consequences of changes in the properties of a particular system component upon system behaviors. Technical training in military and industrial settings has benefited from these scientific insights (85a, 91a, 185).

A third key aspect of understanding is the rich interconnectivity of knowledge schemas. Research indicates that the knowledge of a novice may be represented in isolated "packets" in memory (62a, 165), so that contradictions may arise between beliefs which have never been brought together before in explaining events. Consistent and coherent belief systems are not easily achieved, but require special educational attention. This is a particularly deep problem in science education (33, 38a, 58, 89). Teachers may need to go to elaborate ends to elicit students' conceptions so that such cognitive conflicts are made manifest, in the hopes of subsequent instructional progress if they can guide students to integrate such formerly-isolated belief "packets." On the positive side of this problem, great power resides in the multiple representations of knowledge in a connected memory system. For then much more flexibility is enabled in paths of thinking about a problem. One perspective or representation may serve much better than another in coming to a problem solution. Knowledge "participates" in various knowledge structures, so that a deadend in reasoning about a problem in one way may be overcome by trying another path of inquiry. Such relational matrices among concepts and skills seem to be "compiled" in memory through experience in working with variegated examples (75a).

A fourth important aspect of understanding is the use of both domain-specific and general strategies in problem-posing and problem-solving (76, 84, 183). Part of the facility of the domain expert resides in the use of powerful strategies for reasoning that are finely-tuned to the characteristics of problems that arise in that space (e.g., strategies for solving algebraic problems, or reasoning in social science).

Finally, great importance has been attributed to the use of "metacognition" for learning (23, 51, 168, 182). This term refers either to *reflective cognition*, one's awareness of particular characteristics of one's mental states or processes (e.g., that list is too long for me to remember; I will make mistakes in multiplying such large numbers in my head), or to *regulative cognition*, one's use of executive or monitoring strategies for guiding mental activities in problem-solving (e.g., time allocation in studying; strategy selection for overcoming lack of understanding in reading). Among the major pedagogical goals arising from this research to date is the fostering of autonomous learners through direct instruction in learning-to-learn strategies, and comprehension-monitoring strategies in reading (44, 170).

View of Materials Needed for Learning

Massive curriculum reforms in precollege mathematics and science were funded by the federal government in the 1960's and early 1970's, including those of the Physical Science Study Committee, the Biological Science Study Committee, Chemical Bond Approach, Project Physics, and the School Mathematics Study Group (121). Although these projects were designed to produce materials so that students could acquire subject "understanding" of the kind we have been discussing, these materials made their major breakthroughs by providing deep, structural analyses of the subject matter, which were then reflected in the curricular structures that were developed (116, 121). For the past several decades, education has been correspondingly *curriculum-centered*.

The major change wrought through recent learning research in the education sciences is a *learner-centered* view, or what we will call the **"cognitive shift."** Even though educational topics, examples, and subject matter structure and sequence still need analysis and careful design, there is a broad consensus that they must begin with the knowledge states of the learner, and build from there. We know practice with variegated problems is important, but much more basic research is needed to match problems with student knowledge and needs.

Substantial evidence indicates that most present curricula as used poorly promote subject matter understanding (e.g., 57, 58, 68, 88, 92, 116, 123, 131, 149, 154). We also know that the lack of specified relationships between traditionally-distinct curricula leads for most students to isolated knowledge structures that correspond but too well to the curriculum boundaries (18, 20, 147), Concerns emerge in the common lack of transfer of school learning to experiential situations outside school in society and work, and in the nonutilization of experiential knowledge (such as invented algorithms for addition and subtraction) in school settings (37, 50, 61, 102, 108, 153, 155, 156, 169). The calls for reform are founded, for example, on cognitive research indicating the conceptual isolation of knowledge acquired in mathematics, science, and language arts, whereas concepts and skills involved in these disciplines are needed in an integrated manner for reasoning and communicating in order to solve real-world problems. Calls for reform also highlight the "inert" nature of much knowledge acquired through formal education, whose conditions of application are left unspecified. And even the most well-structured curricula from a subject-matter perspective may not be learned because of conflicting preconceptions learners have that are derived from experiential knowledge, or because of the limited nature of knowledge representations that are offered (e.g., text only, when pictures or diagrams would help).

Present learning materials have several other major problems besides lack of integration. They are often comprised primarily of referentially-isolated activities, without regard to their meaningfulness in relation to real tasks (153, 164). Prominent examples include syntactic drills in arithmetic and algebra, memorization of vocabulary definitions, rote enactment of cookbook lab experiments, and part-of-speech sentence diagramming. Perhaps not surprisingly, many studies of classroom instruction have shown how little actual instruction takes place of the whole activities of reading, writing, mathematical modelling of situations, or scientific inquiry (10, 12, 168, 173, 179). Documentation of such experiential deficits cries for curricular reform.

In new "functional learning environments," what have typically been characterized as "basic skills" are not taught as ends in themselves, but as component tasks whose fluency is required for success in real activities (26, 50, 53, 143, 168, 185a). Real applications of knowledge to be acquired are at the core of instruction, and students are "scaffolded" as they become increasingly more proficient in taking on parts of the whole, meaningful task, with instructional support "fading" as competencies are achieved (52, 148ab, 153, 154a). The aim of autonomous or collaborative real task performance is explicit from the start, not promised at the end of isolated drill activities with unspecified conditions of applicability. Instructional studies utilizing such methods for reading comprehension (143), composition instruction (12), and mathematical problem solving (168) have been highly successful in improving student capabilities with this approach.

Even such functional learning environments carry with them the newly-documented need for teachers to understand, at an individual student level, the *preconceptions* a student has about the subject of instruction. Substantial cognitive research in science learning shows how proto-theories students hold about light, gravity, motion, heat and temperature, weight and density, biological organisms, and other physical phenomena are unlikely to be integrated with the knowledge conveyed by formal instruction (32, 33, 38a, 39, 40, 58, 60, 61, 74, 106, 116, 122, 123, 142, 193, 194, 201). Science education research suggests that using sensitively-designed curricula where recurrent preconceptions are explicitly recognized, diagnosing and discussing preconceptions and the strengths of formal alternatives, may help students build upon their preconceptions (116). Similar findings appear for the social sciences (193a), writing (12, 26, 58a, 148), reading (6, 96), and technology (148a), although less work with this orientation has been carried out for such subjects. Work with expert teachers has shown part of their success arising from recognizing *types* of preconceptions and developing specific strategies to deal with them (12a, 109a).

A related point, also concerned about individualization, emerges from research on individual differences in experience with and capacity to learn from different modalities, such as text, pictures and diagrams, graphs, equations (38, 89a, 176a, 176b). A principle distinction between text-based and graphically-based modes of learning finds some research support (68a, 119a, 144b), and has critical implications for basic research and development activities in creating and testing new applications of computer technologies that offer unique opportunities for enhancing the visual learning environments of education.

Beyond considerations of individual differences, a core insight of cognitive science has been the utility of *multiple representations of knowledge* for supporting learning, reasoning, and problem-solving activities. Each representational system — natural language, symbolic equations, logical formalisms, pictures, functional diagrams (e.g., of circuits, or processes), graphs, etc. — has specific strengths and weaknesses in the features it provides to support or guide problem-posing and problem-solution processes (13a, 97, 107a). Expert reasoners in a subject area tend to be highly flexible in the representations they choose to exploit for posing and solving problems (84), so a desirable goal of curricular design should be to facilitate fluency in the various representations of knowledge that a student will need to use.

A last and deeply significant way in which curricula must change is tied directly to information technologies. What one "needs to learn" has for millennia been *conditional* on the technologies available for thinking and reasoning. In an oral culture, rhetoric held sway. The ingredients of literacy were dramatically changed with the advent of a written language medium, and later a print-based one (141, 150a). The widespread availability of word processors and other writing tools such as outliners and an on-line thesaurus and spelling checker, as a recent OECD report (26, cf. 70, 148) indicates, are radically redefining what students are doing in language arts. Requisite mathematical knowledge and skills have been similarly contingent on technologies (68, 97, 131, 190). Graphing programs allow students to develop intuitive understanding of relations between graph shapes and equation specifications that formerly required laborious hand-plotting of point. Symbolic manipulation programs available for $100 can "get A's" in college mathematics courses, and suggest redefinitions in what one needs to do and learn from precollege mathematics courses. Databases in science and history are being used in secondary schools throughout the country to foster original inquiry by students, previously possible only with great labor. The professional subject-matter teaching organizations such as CBMS (55), NCTE (160), NCTM (131), NSTA, and more broadly, NSF (131a) have been hard at work redefining curricular priorities and topics. The reasons are that one may now treat topics with information technologies that were not possible at all before at the precollege level (e.g., systems dynamics modelling; robotics; graphics animation), and that some topics should now be omitted from curricula (e.g., long division) because low-level algorithmic activities formerly taught may now be automatically carried out by the computer (68, 131). Many of these computer uses have been designed to overcome cognitive or instructional "bottlenecks," and thus emancipate the learner.

View of What Pedagogical Tasks and Strategies Are Effective and Why

With new conceptualizations of the learner, and of appropriate curricula, comes a new understanding of what the pedagogical activities of a classroom should be in order to promote effective learning and understanding. Many of these insights are implicit in what has already been said, and many of the techniques have been used by expert teachers for many years. But there is a new specificity to why such techniques work that supercedes previous understanding. Clearly much more attention to the preconceptions of individual learners is needed for formal knowledge to be acquired by more students through teaching and learning activities. This requires "knowledge diagnosis" of a kind that is more labor-intensive and teaching-relevant than traditional classroom assessment measures (71, 116). "Linking" activities have teachers solicit from students, as well as provide, connections between what is being learned and previous learning. Linking is seen to aid knowledge transfer processes, even among traditionally poor learners (23, 67, 142, 143).

A central lesson from education science investigations of classroom learning is *sociological* individuals create, revise, and contribute not only to their own knowledge but that of the culture. But education tacitly espouses counterproductive belief systems for what knowledge is, and what a learner's role is in the knowledge acquisition process (50, 124, 133, 168). To facilitate this awareness of the purposive and constructed nature of knowing—rare among students but common in the disciplines—the teacher needs to create a *community*, in which thinking and problem-solving of the kinds required for the discipline(s) under study is contributed by all members of the group (12, 22, 52, 89, 147, 153). Several kinds of activities appear necessary for this community to be established: (1) the teacher thinks-aloud about problems, including ones that are novel to her and for which answers are not immediately apparent, describing reasons for making certain strategic decisions and not others, working through reasoning steps; (2) the teacher solicits contributions to this process from classroom members so that they come to collaborate in the problem-solving process, even when they would be unable to carry out the whole task alone; (3) students come to take on "roles" or subtasks in complex collaborative problem-solving, and rotate in these roles; and (4) group discussions take place on such processes, reflecting on and consolidating what has been learned. Small group learning, peer tutoring, and apprenticeship learning have also been demonstrated as effective techniques with implications for educational technology development and use (50, 52, 78).

The role of reflection in these processes deserves special mention. Expert problem-solvers routinely pause on completing the solution of difficult problems and reflect on what has been learned—whether there were reasoning dead-ends, inept analogies, or productive generalizations that could be useful to remember for the future (168). New information technologies make possible the recording and abstracted playback of problem-solving sessions for such reflective analyses (51).

View of the Role of the Social Context in Learning with Technologies

There is also a broader recognition than in the past of the potent roles of social context in the learning process. Research on teacher cognition and classroom activity planning, peer collaborative problem-solving, homework and parents, and on motivational and attributional aspects of learning activities has contributed to this new understanding (50, 102, 120).

Curricula and tools for learning in the classroom rarely have direct effects on learners. The lessons and empowerments that they offer are typically mediated through the activities, expectations, and shaping influences of the teacher, the students' peers, and parents. Correlatively, the learning a specific individual is capable of is not solely a characteristic of that person, but of the social contexts in which such performances are carried out. The shaping characteristics of learning environments are thus complex and multifaceted, and we have only recently begun to chart the dimensions of their influence (50).

For example, teachers can make a difference in whether they create and maintain an open environment in which making mistakes is an accepted part of the learning process, and in which different approaches to problems are welcomed as opportunities for group learning. Such an environment appears to have shaping influences in whether a student treats work on a problem as an opportunity for learning or as an occasion for failure and diminished self-worth. A student's concept of self-as-learner thus has important causal influences on both achievement motivation and reactions to learning feedback (63a). And negative teacher expectations for a student's performance often become self-fulfilling.

Social relations with peers in the classroom can also be harnessed to contribute to cognitive growth. Numerous studies in a Piagetian tradition indicate that peer discussions of strategies for solving a problem may serve as important facilitators of cognitive growth, by making explicit different beliefs and arguments for their warrants (148aa).

WHAT SPECIFIC RESEARCH AND TECHNOLOGY DIRECTIONS COULD BRIDGE THE GAPS?

Given these new understandings in the education sciences, how should educational practices be influenced? How might specific research and technology directions in education bridge the gaps we have described? What *changes* would need to occur? Cognitive, social, and instructional science studies have documented an incredible number of specific learning problems that arise in education. Examples of "basic competencies" often served up to illustrate what is lacking or deficient are insufficient vocabulary, grammar, procedural skill in algebra, or calculational talents. These are but symptoms of deeper problems. Training or longer school days aiming for better performance on the achievement tests crafted for these diagnostic purposes misses the point. Education must help students learn to put their minds intentionally to work in categorizing, analogizing, critiquing, designing, inventing, modelling, and like activities. How can we better help students learn to comprehend and imagine as they read, to compose text for expression as well as for learning, to think mathematically, to reason scientifically, to reason critically, to take control of their own education within and beyond formal settings? The grassroots and research community calls for focus on "complex" or "higher order" thinking skills express these aims (44, 170).

We have seen how the cognitive, social, and instructional sciences have transformed views of the learner, of understanding, of curriculum, of pedagogy, of social context. How might these works find application and continual renewal through research and development activities with computers and related computational media? As an organizational strategy, we have grouped the emergent trends and themes from our consultations with experts in the field into five categories of goals. These goal categories, overlapping to some extent because of the *system*-based nature of what makes learning work (120), correspond to those of our analysis of what has been learned. These goals present a framework within which we can place the various research and development directions and themes considered central to plans for improving the quality of education.

For each category of research and development activities described as goals, we provide a brief rationale linking it back to the research, and remarks concerning issues of overall priorities. It is important to observe that many uses of technology now common in educational practice (11, 186) were *not* considered high priority for federal support by our respondents. These paradigms include standard drill and practice software (especially in arithmetic and language), some rigid branching CAI programs, and in general, "computer-based management" approaches to computer use to mechanize existing testing procedures, scoring, and reporting.

We also note that a tension exists within the field of education science as applied to educational technology and evaluation issues. The tension is between making technologies that can be evaluated as "working," given present achievement-test metrics of effectiveness (not measuring understanding), and making technologies that enable students to engage in qualitatively different and superior learning experiences, better geared to providing "learning as understanding," but for which new measurement techniques need to be developed (116, 120). New work in cognitive psychometrics at the Educational Testing Service and other laboratories is moving in this latter direction (28, 77, 117b). Strategies for providing measures of accountability in the educational technology field are in flux because of this basic issue. For example, the classic benchmark is Benjamin Bloom's findings of a "2-sigma" advantage for individual human tutoring over conventional classroom-based instruction (12b). This means that the tutoring method puts the *average* student who is tutored in the *top five percent* of a student population conventionally taught. This dramatic result can serve as a goal for any of the technology-enhanced methods of education, once measures of conceptual change are determined for the cognitive-shift paradigms we will be outlining.

In addition, while it is highly unlikely that technology is appropriate for every activity in education, our analyses are technology-focused since that is our charge in this report. Given this constraint, we need to be sure to focus where indications are that research and development work in this field will have significant payoffs for investments of effort, talent, and costs. We also highlight opportunities for educational benefits arising from technical developments that many believe can be fruitfully exploited by the research and educator communities.

It is necessary to distinguish education from training. Many technologies, from the business tools of office automation to the interactive videodiscs for subject-matter learning in military training have quite a restricted focus. They are designed for very special environments, with deeply-engrained assumptions about the social environment, the age and goals of its users, and with narrowly-defined performance objectives. While we hope to learn from such technologies and to exploit such inventions whenever possible, they are not easily or even desirably adaptable for classroom uses for education. It is certainly important to recognize that research and development in business, industry, and military training does not translate into educational technologies for precollege education (28).

Before characterizing high-priority categories of R&D activities in educational technologies, it is important to briefly sketch the dimensions of technological development trends, and to set out where educational technologies are now in schools. While unpredictable factors may alter these considerations (e.g., the pace with which emerging superconducting materials will find their way into everyday powerful computers), they serve as influential constraints to heed in the directions of R&D the Federal government decides to pursue.

Advancing the Educational Technology
Available to Schools

There are important constraints to recognize in the pace of change with which new technologies for education are coming into schools, and in how new programs are created and marketed. Recognition of these constraints is important, for they have not figured in much R&D planning for educational technologies. Given projected continuation of the organizational behaviors to be described, the Federal government can either work to confront and overcome the constraints with novel programs of support and incentives, work within them, or implement some mixed strategy. In any regard, closer attention to present organizational constraints in the design and implementation of research and technology development in education promises to improve the impact of R&D on educational practices.

Constraint 1: The installed base of technology defines present markets in educational computing. During the past decade, schools and parent-teacher organizations moved quickly and often at a grass roots level to buy computers for classroom use (11). While this has been important in familiarizing teachers and students with fundamental operating concepts of computing, and basic paradigms for software use, it is becoming apparent that there are side-effects of these early moves to computerize the classroom. Schools buy new machines to match their old so as to capitalize on teacher training, student familiarity with programs, and the installed base of hardware and software (186). As many analyses of computing in organizations have shown, there are large "buried costs" of new technologies (5, 101). In this case, they include the costs of teacher education, student familiarization, time for practitioners to develop skill in making a specific technology work in the classroom, seeking out and evaluating alternative options for updating technologies, hardware and software technology maintenance and upgrading, renovation costs to retrofit existing spaces for the electrical, space, and furniture needs of computer technologies, etc. The schools' attention to such costs revealed with the installed base strategy is parallel to concerns in business when they consider upgrading technology, as IBM found with their 360 series of computers.

With respect to hardware, the Apple II family computers are the dominant precollege machines (with over 1 million in schools, mostly Apple-IIes, amidst computers from IBM, Commodore, Tandy, etc.). Schools also rarely get rid of equipment, but instead find a lower "niche" for its use, so that older computers such as Texas Instrument-99s, Commodore-PET computers are used for barebones programming instruction in the early grades. 128K (kilobyte) machines are not yet the majority of microcomputers in school use. Since the dominant Apple-II family computers are rugged machines, professional educational software developers and publishers we interviewed consider it likely that they will remain in school use over at least the next 5 years. Apple IIgs computers, which have more powerful graphics, audio, and processor capabilities, are coming into use slowly, and are the most advanced computers such developers have begun to create software for commercially. Market surveys indicate that schools are acquiring this level of machine primarily because the Apple IIgs run their installed software base (largely for Apple-II family computers). By 1992, IIgs's are expected to be standard 4 megabyte (4000K) machines, and widely available in schools.

An emphasis on the higher-end hardware recommended in previous policy reports misses the point of what schools can or want to do in their purchasing within at least the next 5-10 years, given current trends in financing educational computing. This point applies to IBM-PC/ATs or Apple Macintosh computers, much less university-level advanced function workstations such as Suns, Microvaxes, Macintosh-IIs, or IBM-Personal System computers. Yet it is true that systems of this level are needed to run graphics-intensive and multitasking software applications typical of integrated tool environments (129). They unfortunately do not allow schools to use their installed base. For example, none of the Apple Macintosh computers can run Apple-II family software. The more successful educational software developers also will not take the financial risk of working with "niche" machines (in particular, those with only a school but not a home market, as in the case of the now defunct IBM-PC Jr.).

Finally, a key figure to note is the 10-15 year time period from when a new chip is developed in sampling quantities in laboratories to when there is likely to be an installed educational software base in schools that use the chip. From lab chips to shipped computers using those chips has typically taken 3 years, developing an operating system for the chip takes 3-4 years (e.g., IBM OS-2) and may take longer as chips increase in complexity, 1-2 years more for software developers to use the operating system to create applications, and several more years at minimum for the installed base of the new level of computer to reach the critical mass required to attract a broad range of developers to create applications specifically for schools.

Constraint 2: Since little educational software is purchased by schools, educational software development is financially risky for commercial developers. Needed research to make programs effective cannot be afforded. Software purchasing behavior of schools is also very conservative. In Fortune 1000 companies, the budget for software typically exceeds the hardware budget, whereas schools only spend 17% of their hardware budgets on software. The success of software sales in education, even for tools such as word processors, is often explicitly linked to textbooks, and expected gains in achievement test scores. And schools on average purchase only 14 software programs per year of the thousands produced (186). Parents spent six times more last year (over $200 million) on educational software than did schools (Future Computing).

Over 11,000 educational software titles have been produced, and 150 new ones appear each month, with a bare minimum of testing, primarily to overcome functional flaws in program operation. Very rarely do companies have the money available to engage in formative testing in classroom situations to see if the product can be used effectively by teachers, or whether students learn from it. Evaluations of educational software consider only 5% of present products outstanding, and even these evaluations are not based on observations of classroom use but professional evaluator assessments based on first-hand inspection of the program. The evaluation principles used fall seriously short of the cognitive evaluations we have described as central to closing the gaps between learning theory and educational practices.

Emerging Computing Standards for Undergraduate Educational Technology

It is critical to heed the hardware and software technology that is in our schools today, and to compare it with what is being used as the development and testing environments for new educational technologies in research universities, centers, and laboratories. Perhaps the most instructive comparison will be with undergraduate education.

The minimum hardware requirements defined at the undergraduate educational computing level are known as the "3M" machine—a million-instruction-a-second processor, a bit-map screen display with a million dots (pixels), a million bytes (megabyte) of main memory, virtual memory, and a LAN connection (9, 129, 202). For example, such specifications provide the capacities to display and transform interactively images used for learning in mathematics (e.g., graphs), science (e.g., interactive simulations), and with text (e.g., relational databases, idea organizer programs, hypertext). Berkeley UNIX is the operating system being used in these machines to allow for multi-tasking and some software transportability, and windowing systems like CMU's Andrew or X-Windows are being used so that the programmer-side of UNIX is not visible to the student user. This approach has been called "interpersonal computing," since it links together a student's advanced function workstation and a mainframe fileserver so that it appears to the student as if one has all one's data and programs locally (electronic mail, remote access to large databases, statistics). Such workstations with educational discounts meeting these specifications from Apple, DEC, IBM, and SUN Microsystems are now available in the $5000-$8000 range and are expected to reach the desired $3000-$4000 level within two years (10% of a student's four-year tuition).

Theory-based Educational Technology Research and Development Strategy

It is important to recognize that the relationship between theory, research, and technology development in education is (to some measure) different than many other fields, which have sharp distinctions between basic and applied research. Many leaders in the field now recognize that the theory-practice link for educational technologies is not a one-way application of knowledge to action (e.g., 65a, 82). For when a theory of learning and pedagogy is embodied in an educational tool, and then tested in real contexts of use, feedback is provided on the soundness of the theories, not only the tool. And the very nature of the settings in which the technology will be used and in which the learning will occur should be used to shape the design and features of the technology. The theory itself will develop responsively through such applications to learning in real settings. Many hope that technologies can better enable a "cybernetic education system," in which feedback loops between outcomes and practices can provide a more adaptive, dynamic educational system of learning and teaching activities than previously possible (28). This aim will require new kinds of assessment measures that characterize conceptual change and cognitive growth through levels of proficiency for valued education outcomes.

These observations recommend a mode of work that incorporates the insights and activities of teacher/practitioners, education science researchers, technology developers, subject matter specialists, and, to insure real-world market penetration of research-based materials, professional publishers (25, 112, 113, 120, 121). Our policy discussions in the final section of this report elaborate on technical and cost requirements of work models incorporating these groups and their activities. Related discussions of interdisciplinary integration of the kind required to advance the practical impacts of this field are available (45, 87).

Changing What Students Do

Research on the nature of the learner in the cognitive, social, and instructional sciences (earlier described) has profound implications for what students should do in order to learn, whether in schools or other settings for learning such as community centers, clubs, or libraries. We also must emphasize the importance of *universal* access to quality uses of educational technologies. Research has indicated that in addition to the knowledge and technology gaps we have highlighted between schools and society, there is a highly divisive gap that puts at a disadvantage students in rural schools, the largely minority students in poor urban schools, and female students (11, 43, 50, 65, 120, 178). Federal attention is needed to insure that the changes outlined here for what the research says students should be doing in education involved these groups and settings, so that these education environments may take the fullest advantage of the fruits of educational technology research and development.

There are a variety of paradigms that have become established in the research and development communities during the past decade for building and using educational technologies. What we describe in the sections that follow are the key areas that were highlighted by experts in the field as important priorities for Federal support.

An important observation is that *very few of the priorities experts recommended are now in use in schools*. Although survey data indicate that tools such as word processors and microbased science laboratories are entering the classroom, most present uses are for drill and practice and tutorial CAI (11, 64, 65), which previous survey reports have concluded offer little to improving student understanding (25, 112, 113, 120). Unfortunately, in only a few cases are paradigms recommended by our experts being used to *commercially* implement educational technologies that schools could hope to exploit within the next five years. For these reasons, federal efforts should closely examine the ways in which research and development activities could be more intimately related to technology transfer activities of the kind that software developers and commercial publishers are technically able to implement with appropriate incentives. Further analyses of the nature of possible Federal R&D/commercial relationships are provided in the concluding policy section of our report.

The major categories for our discussion of "changing what students do" will be intelligence extenders, microworlds, "intelligent" tutors and coaches, networking, and hypermedia and multimedia learning environments. It will become apparent as we examine other topics in subsequent sections—changing how we track learning, changing what's taught, changing what teachers do, changing the schooling environment—that there are intimate relations between these different facets of the student/teacher/materials/environment system. But we believe these categories offer helpful distinctions for thinking about the ways in which experts recommended how research and development activities in the cognitive, social, and instructional sciences should change education, and what technologies it should employ to support its work.

Since the cognitive view of education is student-centered, it is no surprise that the bulk of priorities we will discuss involve changing what students do. It is also important to note that these categories have been reasonably distinct in modern research and development efforts. Although there have sometimes been ideological grounds for these separations, we believe they are primarily due to hardware and software limitations and the early stage of work in the field, whose scientists have tended to direct their efforts to one or another paradigm. There are many reasons to believe that integrating these paradigms of information technology use in education to create hybrid systems will be important to do. For example, knowledge representation methods for inferring a students' conceptual model of a domain now used in "intelligent" tutoring systems and coaches could complement the microworld approach, or a student's strategies for using tools in some learning activity could be inferred and result in hints from an "intelligent" help system. We see comparable trends in the "functional eclecticisms" of today's interior design directions, and in combinations of rule-based, object-oriented, and logic-based paradigms for new high-level programming languages (13).

Intelligence Extenders

There is a major class of tools for learning and problem-solving, also found to be very useful in teaching, which have been described as "cognitive technologies," "intelligence extenders," "cognitive workbenches," or "mental prostheses." These tools make qualitatively easier the specific mental activities involved in complex tasks such as collecting information and crafting idea structures in writing, comprehending intricate mathematical relationships through dynamic graphs, and designing and running experiments. What they have in common is making more accessible, with less mental effort, the achievement of what are considered to be "complex" acts of mind. Development efforts of this type often create qualitatively different learning and teaching experiences. Many of our experts suggested that for education "machines that think" may be less essential than new tool systems that enable students to better express and build on their own intelligence and creativity (53, 65a, 70, 98, 132, 154a, 166).

What computational media commonly afford in such applications is great speed and accuracy in the transformations of symbols, including pictures, text, diagrams, numbers and sound, that allow for extensions of human intelligence. Many different tools may be integrated in such cognitive workbenches, facilitating multitasking and the construction of single documents comprised of multiple media. The rapid interactivity of these tools enables the thinker to engage in the incremental refinement and revision processes— whether the task is algebraic modelling, persuasive writing, or planning a scientific experiment—that have been associated with expert performance in a host of disciplines (84). These rapid interactive properties, developed at Xerox PARC for business and programming environments (13, 176), are now standard features of the Apple Macintosh environment, and in "windowing" packages for IBM and other computers. As we have seen, they are also central to university-level educational computing, as a key component of the standard arising from planned synthesis activities of the InterUniversity Consortium for Educational Computing (based at Carnegie-Mellon University).

Such tools are important for they help close the gap between the worlds of school and the workplace. Content delivery is comparatively inefficient from the perspective of nearly all the educational technology developers we spoke with, since a new program is needed for every new piece of curriculum. It is also inefficient for schools, because teachers and students must often re-learn how to use the different software programs because of inconsistent design and functioning. And as designed today, there is too much emphasis on the technology's surface features, which are created to appeal to and hold student attention through extrinsic motivation. Various experts considered that tools will probably have the most payoff, especially those used in reading and writing. For under $100, a word-processing program designed for students 8 years old and up can be purchased—with 60,000 word spelling corrector, and combined thesaurus and 50,000 word dictionary. Micro-based laboratories available today provide compelling examples of how we can help students learn science by doing it. The Lego-Logo Project at MIT, in which elementary students write Logo programs to control Lego machines, reveals how one can connect programming and real-world objects such as gears, levers, and sensors, so as to introduce key concepts in physics, engineering, and robotics through an experiential approach (132).

Developments are now approaching second-generation, or "integrated" tool levels. Present systems being commercially developed, unfortunately with minimal research support, are for early reading and writing, K-6 mathematics, and micro-based lab science. They will be customizable by teachers and publishers for different curriculum areas and topics. The analog in the business world is *dBase III*, which is a powerfully general database system complete with a programming language for creating database applications. While it is acknowledged that there are better database programs available, this one has spawned several hundred companies that all make applications (e.g., accounting or inventory overlays to *dBase III*). The same has happened with Lotus 1-2-3 in the world of spreadsheets and financial modelling. Various experts consider the development of comparably powerful "engines" for education to be a high priority, expecting that similar branch-off developments would occur, leveraging the impact of Federal investments (112, 118). Creating tool "engines" is just the approach taken in the past five years at the university level, lead by Project Andrew at Carnegie-Mellon (129), Project Athena at MIT (9), and Brown University's IRIS Project (202).

This approach thus builds on substantial prior investments in software and hardware engineering by industry, business, and university education, and would represent an important continuity between the precollege and college computing experiences.

Present precollege efforts underway with federal foundation support along these lines include a tool environment for scientific inquiry (*Inquire:* Bank Street College: 89), graphical tools for science and mathematics (e.g., *Sketch:* Carnegie-Mellon; *Functions*, U. California, Berkeley), for systems modelling and theory building (TERC/Lesley College: 190), for network-supported collaborative research in earth science (*Earth Lab:* Bank Street College: 133a) and environmental science (TERC/National Geographic: 189), a set of tools for learning and doing statistics (Bolt, Beranek & Newman: 158), a decision-analysis support tool environment for social studies (*IDEA*, New York University: 147a), and a powerful environment for students and teachers to create such tools, called *Boxer* (U. California, Berkeley: 62, 63). For example, the *Modeling Project* (TERC/Lesley: 190) allows high-school students to learn about systems dynamics and system modelling by using icons to build models. In building models of population growth or toxic waste impact, icons would represent levels (e.g., population; pollution) and rates (births/deaths; accumulation/absorption), and interaction is used as the calculation mode to "run" the model. Thus students can work intuitively with the basic ideas of differentiation and integration which formerly required formal instruction in calculus.

What these and other efforts begin to make apparent is that learning general purpose programming languages is an anachronism unless one plans to become a computer scientist or programmer. While programmable functions will be available for many of the tools above, the clear trend is toward creating application-specific, special-purpose programming languages for tool use and control, and these are often not even being called "programming" any longer because of the technical image that conveys.

Many experts whose advice we sought placed high priority on creating many more tool environments for precollege education, that should be designed to simultaneously provide powerful new learning environments for education, and "mini-research laboratories" for studying the acquisition of complex cognitive skills (82). They suggested that schools should be involved in having students use cognitive workbenches, such as outlining tools and text-editors, database access and information organization systems, drafting and animation programs, theorem-proving assistants, algebra assistants (such as those under development at Bolt Beranek & Newman; Harvard Educational Technology Center; Rand Corporation), spreadsheets, graph plotters, and multimedia design tools. A key educational goal in these efforts is to provide means for students to make conjectures and hypotheses, just as in the worlds of science and society, that can be tested and discussed with a teacher's guidance (50, 135). Numerous experts also stressed the need for enhancing students' capacities to design communications, to be able to manipulate the language with ease and grace, through written and oral expression, and graphical means (26, 70). Communicative expression permeates virtually everything a person does, and cross-cuts the entire curriculum. Research examining effects of using word processors in education has barely scratched the surface of this important, broader problem (26, 148).

The most liberating of the uses of technology in this category which we know about are those invented for exceptional students (127, 154a, 159, 191). Reports have begun to appear of how educational technologies may remarkably enhance opportunities for the physically handicapped (e.g., cerebral palsied, at Francis Orthopedic School, Riverside, CA), for blind (e.g., Tennessee School for the Blind), deaf (Clark School for the Deaf/ Smith College), learning disabled, and hyperkinetic students so that they can be mainstreamed into regular classes from special educational settings. Some of the innovative projects include braille word processors for the blind, specially-designed materials for teaching English syntactic structure to improve the reading and writing skills of the deaf, and the use of speech synthesis output and graphics-tablet generated speech to initiate and then support communicative expression for students with either no or very limited oral language (e.g., autism, cerebral palsy, Down's syndrome: City of Hope National Medical Center & George Washington University). Many of the projects foster a new independence on the part of such students. While these are some of the most moving cases of how technology may enable the expression and fulfillment of human potential, more planned synthesis of research and documentation of projects in this area is called for, so that these effects can be widely replicated.

Microworlds: Context-Based Learning

Microworlds (113, 144) are uses of the computer for providing dynamic models of systems, or small parts of systems, that students can explore and study, either without instructor support, or with instructional guidance built into the program ("guided microworlds": 198). Such paradigms for learning have also been described as "discovery worlds" or "simulations" (although many earlier simulations did not allow students to change the properties of the systems, much less construct their own).

Such microworld systems have been created for early physics learning (*Dynaturtle*: MIT: 60, 199; *ThinkerTools*: Bolt Beranek & Newman: 198), for exploring electrical circuit behavior (*Sophie* [24a], *Quest* [196, 197]: Bolt Beranek & Newman), for economic systems (*Smithtown*: University of Pittsburgh: 118), and for physical systems such as a steam plant (*Steamer*: Bolt Beranek & Newman [185], UCSD [91a]). Simpler versions of simulations developed commercially for microcomputers (with little learning research input) include *Geography Search* (Tom Snyder Productions), *Island Survivors* (Holt, Rinehart & Winston)—part of Bank Street College's Voyage of the Mimi multimedia series for mathematics and science education, and the microworld *Rocky's Boots* (Learning Company), for creating logic gates.

Microworlds are seminal learning tools because they highlight cognitive objectives demonstrated to be central to "understanding"—i.e., how things work. For example, those proficient in scientific reasoning have mental models of the physical system in which phenomena of interest occur, and are thereby better able to predict what will happen given certain changes of system design or system variables (14, 59, 69, 84). Insofar as using microworlds or simulations encourages the formulation in memory of knowledge structures and mental processes that allow such science understanding, they serve key educational goals, often overlooked in a textually-based science education (116, 120). Recent studies of precollege science textbooks show that often more new vocabulary is introduced in science than in a foreign language text, with insufficient attention paid to prior conceptions, visual and interactive experiences of the world, or of world models (116). Research needs to determine effective designs for learning and teaching activities with microworlds, and their place in relation to experience with the added complexities of real world systems. New microworld topics for R&D from experts we interviewed included ecological simulations so students can examine science-technology-society issues such as acid rain, toxic wastes and underground hydraulics, sewage and water supplies, and depletion of natural resources such as rain forests. The *Vivarium Project* (Apple Computer, MIT: 132) aims to provide future microworlds where students will be able to craft worlds of realistic animal agents, and then "play them," watching how the animals interact in an ecosystem.

The strength of microworlds from the perspective of research on the nature of student learning and understanding is potentially great. Students can learn by doing, by acting on microworlds rather than merely observing phenomena take place in demonstration mode. They may acquire understanding of the properties of systems and relationships among changes in their properties through their actions upon the systems. Some microworld systems let students build or program their own worlds, and they can then explore how they work, examining the consequences of changes in their properties. An example is the microeconomic simulation *Smithtown* (118), in which students can vary price and population and observe effects on demand, and use tools such as electronic spreadsheets and graphing programs to support laboratory investigations. Microworlds can be constructed for close resemblance to real-world activities, so that transfer of learning from working with the microworld and the world of concrete action are closely coupled. New actions that are possible with these microworlds—due to the ability to make changes of scale in space, time, size, and relationships—allow for other powerful teaching and learning opportunities (112). Imaginary microworlds can also be constructed—non-Newtonian universes and the like—which offer new capabilities to bring to life and render apparent for students things that they could never see or imagine without the technologies (109). Generally, multiple learning paths are made possible that have much in common with "hands-on learning" with physical objects advocated in the science curriculum reforms of the 1960's and 1970's, but which introduce the novel opportunities just described (as well as limits—since a model is never complete).

Support is needed for R&D at a much higher level than currently available for creating microworlds for student use in schools and other learning settings. Few laboratories have had projects of sufficient duration or with the right organizational partners to allow for commercial development and widescale implementation of this learning tool paradigm. Stable programs of scientific research to provide basic knowledge of microworld learning for different subject areas, innovative tools for creating microworlds more broadly, and microworlds to be co-developed for key curriculum areas in cooperation with software developers and publishers, are all required for this paradigm to find its appropriate place in education.

"Intelligent" Tutors and Coaches

The "Intelligent" Tutor paradigm, which has been developed over the past 10-15 years in research laboratories, relies heavily on artificial intelligence and cognitive theory, methods, and programming languages. Some of the most elaborated scientific theories of learning and memory have been incorporated in their development (4, 109, 175, 192a). The term "intelligent" is used because such tutors can by themselves, once programmed, generatively solve new problems of the type they are designed to teach, even though answers for those problems have not been programmed. This paradigm has students work on problem-solving tasks, and then from their responses, builds a model of the student's level of understanding in terms of specific rules and knowledge representations. A theory of instruction for the tutor's knowledge domain is also part of the program. It is then used by the program to offer individualized instruction, reactive to the specific understandings a student is inferred to have. Some experts we consulted find this paradigm appealing, since it "automates" the delivery of instruction and may come to approximate the dramatic improvement in level of student learning found in human tutoring research (although obviously not providing social-affective support, help with unpredictable problems students may have, etc.). They argue that the problem of growing teacher unavailability, particularly in the areas of mathematics, science, and technology education, can be in part met through such technologies. Several existence proofs are offered in the *Lisp Tutor* (Carnegie-Mellon: 4a), in which undergraduates take a semester-long course in introductory LISP programming with the Lisp Tutor, and the *Geometry Tutor* (Carnegie-Mellon: 4), at the classroom-testing stage, which teaches geometry proof skills in junior high school.

Intelligent Coaches offer more free rein to the student, but at the expense of requiring considerable sophistication in a pedagogical theory of coaching and hints (30, 175). We presently have little scientific understanding of how to build coaching systems such as *West* (developed for informal learning of basic arithmetic in a game environment at Xerox PARC: 30) that promote effective learning (25). Coaches allow the student a great deal of control over the situation, and do not inflexibly correct errors in student responses that deviate from optimal performance as in Neo-CAI. The communication problems inherent in coaching systems seem to be solvable only under very special circumstances, such as in the especially constrained task domain of WEST. Solving this communication problem, given the intricacies of natural language understanding, would entail putting almost as much structure on the curriculum as older CAI programs (e.g., PLATO, TICCIT).

The key problem in the near-term with the intelligent tutor and coach paradigms is that they are very capital-intensive and require very advanced computing power, technical knowledge, and art (25). Only a few laboratories in the country are presently equipped with the advanced programming environments and hardware, and the research and development talent in computer science, cognitive psychology, artificial intelligence, and psychometrics that is required for quality work with this orientation. This basic science community in artificial intelligence and cognitive theory is hard at work on the problems of knowledge representation, expertise modelling, and student model-building. Less work has focused on providing an empirical basis for the theory of instruction/coaching built into such systems, or at the "microsystems" design level, in which the classroom conditions for their effective implementation is examined (50, 120). Such research, investigating the knowledge, strategies, and practices of expert teachers and coaches in real educational settings, is considered a high priority for informing these efforts (117a). Several experts suggested that this approach would benefit from having new designs in which students help resolve the ambiguities of the student model being dynamically created during instruction. Presently, it is a difficult technical problem to infer the student's knowledge states from responses to problem-solving tasks, as efforts in understanding the development of subtraction skills (Xerox PARC: DEBUGGY, 29, 192a) and simple Pascal programming indicate (Yale: PROUST, 95b). Students could select one of a set of states of knowledge the program presently has insufficient data for distinguishing, in effect making the knowledge diagnosis task a collaborative one between student and computer.

In the sciences, *Quest* (Bolt Beranek and Newman: 196, 197) has been used as an intelligent tutor to teach electronic circuit troubleshooting to high-school students, and *Guidon* (Stanford: 47) is used to teach medical diagnosis. There are also numerous specialized tutors for very small learning tasks that have been developed for commercial or military training, with little application to precollege education unless it is vocational. Other experimental ITSs are now only partially implemented, but begin to show the magnitude of cost and scale for a broadly-used approach of this type: *Proust* (Yale: 164a, 117b, 177b) and *Debuggy* (Xerox PARC, CMU: 29, 192a). Our experts consider that because of their costs, it is now most likely that intelligent tutors and coaches will enter educational practice eventually through programs of work initiated by business and/or military research and development. But since these systems are unlikely to match the needs of precollege education, funding needs of new efforts directly working on problems at this level should be better capitalized than at present. The intelligent tutor approach seems likely to be most effective in mathematics and some topics in the sciences. It was generally noted by experts we consulted that even with the technical complexities of knowledge diagnosis and student modelling this paradigm requires, such uses of technology in education will be possible on a broad scale by the end of the century. Advances in the basic science required for success along these lines are considered important to inform next-generation learning technologies and theories (25, 112, 113, 120).

Present estimations of development time and costs of such circumscribed intelligent tutors range between 500-1000 hours development time per hour of successful lesson, with minimal use of graphics and no video. For more open-ended tutors, where natural-language like dialogs are offered, we can expect much higher development costs. For comparison, we note that a single university course (non-computer, but using video extensively) at the highly-regarded Open University in England takes a team two years and over $1 million to develop. One expert expects that it would cost $1-2 million to create each tutor of this type for procedural skills in select areas in mathematics, English grammar, phonological decoding, and some aspects of chemistry and biology. These methods are unlikely to work wherever understanding and declarative knowledge, and not only procedural skill, are required for success, as in word problems, reading comprehension, and those areas of learning requiring huge fact bases (e.g., spelling, science). These areas where such tutors do not work are thus high priority research areas. Such work would be advanced by much more basic research on expert teachers' knowledge used to teach such non-procedural areas. More research is also needed on conditions under which such systems are useful in learning, or serve as a crutch, providing answers as hints if students are having special difficulties.

It is important to distinguish the diverse scientific groups working on variants of the student-centered cognitive approach to education science and technology development, and further developments of computer-assisted instruction in the 1960's traditions. Advanced systems for instruction in calculus (Stanford) or set theory and logic (New York University), build on technical/theoretical developments in neo-behaviorist learning theory during the 20 years of development of over 10,000 curriculum hours of computer-based instructional materials behind the approach of PLATO and TICCIT. A major difference is that these systems are not concerned with changes in the nature of knowledge representations of students taking place with learning, but mathematical models of performance variation with practice. Among the experts we consulted, the cognitive shift in research studies during the past decade in the education sciences poses fundamental problems for this previous perspective. They argued that since it is people who are learning, it should be constraints in their knowledge (such as preconceptions) that should determine how learning and teaching transpire, not the structure of curricular materials. They ask, why should the structure of the problem types of the curricular domain be highlighted to the exclusion of the cognitive and social contexts in which prior understandings arose and in which new education is made possible?

Networking

The advent of communication satellites, local area network technologies for linking together computers, and the use of modems for remote telecommunications has changed the kinds of work that can be done in education, and has potential for positively changing the nature of communication within educational settings (99a, 24, 26, 135, 136) as well as in the scientific community (189, 192). As we now know from the case of the telephone (but never predicted at the time of its invention), changes in communicative structure have dramatic social consequences. How could these be positively exploited for education? Many experts noted how networking in effect "breaks down the walls" of the school classroom, allowing two-way flow of documents, messages, and interactive dialogues that extend the material and intellectual goods that a class has available as learning and teaching resources. More remarks on these "environmental" aspects of networking are provided in subsequent discussions of changing the school environment.

Clearly the kinds of activities students participate in for learning may also change with networking. But how should they? Several prototype projects, *Earth Lab* (Bank Street College: 133a) and *Kids Network* (TERC and National Geographic: 189), offer some direction. In each case, students will be involved in doing collaborative science, collecting original data either remotely, throughout the country (on acid rain, as in *Kids Network*) or in coordinated efforts locally (in New York City for the Earth Lab Project). In these cases, networks allow for the coordination of learning and teaching activities across classrooms throughout the country, or across individual workstations within a classroom. In other efforts originating from UCSD and University of Illinois, cross-cultural communication networks established between the US, Japan, Israel, England, and other nations are being used to coordinate joint science inquiry by students on astronomy and ecological issues, and to compare and contrast cultural differences on these topics (26, 114).

University-level research and development work in this area has focused on defining standards for what is described as "interpersonal computing," in which a student's computer workstation has high-level local computing power but also provides an invisible gateway to university mainframes for loading tools, obtaining access to very large databases, or for computation-intensive calculations. How might such an approach be made feasible at the precollege level?

Research and development issues in this area are complex and deserve much more attention. Some of these problems are technical and engineering issues — such as establishing communication standards that would allow for compatibility of network systems and protocols, making cheaper communication software and hardware, and lowering service costs for greater accessibility to school systems. Other projects are directed toward technical and conceptual problems involved in effectively *coordinating* information exchange across individuals and groups (90, 119).

Many of the fundamental problems of learning-through-networking have yet to be addressed by the cognitive, social, and instructional science communities. Under what conditions and for what topics would cooperative study, or other cooperative learning activities (such as project-based work), be beneficial? In the past two years, a major new area of advanced research and technology development has appeared that is described as "computer-supported cooperative work" (138, 181). The aim of such investigations is to establish the functional needs of collaborative work groups in business and science laboratory settings, and to create prototypes of the technical infrastructure of tools and operating systems necessary to sustain such activities. Since a substantial body of instructional research has begun to define conditions under which collaborative small group learning is an effective paradigm for education, one direction of research could center on coordinating findings and methods from the business/laboratory communities and the precollege studies. The link to education is that even workgroups in business are involved in learning.

Multimedia Learning Environments

Apart from the microworlds described above, which have yet to be distributed broadly in education, most of the paradigms for educational technologies described are print-based. This may be because print characterizes information environments in schools today. For most instructional activities, minimal use is made of voice, music, and other sounds, or visuals such as pictures and diagrams in books, and filmstrips, slides, or uses of video in cassette, videotape, or videodisc formats — even though these media may be highly effective for learning. The "text-reading eye" has been the primary sensory channel for most education, and yet this is a radical impoverishment, given the senses available from which learning takes place in the world.

This state of affairs will very soon change. Picture the elementary school teacher discussing earth science and plate tectonics with her students, pulling up for computer projection on-line dramatic video clips of volcanoes, student activities centering on an interactive microworld for examining how continental drift operates, and slides of fossil remains from different continents showing the former connectedness of now-dispersed land masses. One student has the idea of photographing local geological strata, another brings in a home video of television footage on volcanoes he thinks might be relevant, and when they return the next day these images are scanned into the classroom archives for other students to use, too. Electronic messages flow between students and from teachers to students on difficulties or new ways of thinking about what is being learned. The students work at their own multimedia composition workstations, revealing what they have learned by constructing and revising their own reports about plate tectonics from these and other materials they can draw on.

While today this scenario might seem fantastic, it may not be by the end of this century. Dramatic developments in the consumer electronics, telecommunications, and electronic publishing industries are rapidly making available low-cost, high quality, and high volume editing and storage technologies for high-speed computer access to high-quality audio and still and full-motion imagery (1, 31, 104, 105, 167a). While we cannot begin to review the momentous changes in sound and image processing, storage, and transmission underway, several highlights must be mentioned. Numerous experts mentioned the importance of carrying out the necessary research in the education sciences to exploit the potency of these multimedia environments for education. And as some ongoing research studies at Vanderbilt using a commercially-available multimedia system (*Handy*, IBM: 18-20) indicate, students need to be "producers" of multimedia documents and knowledge, not only "consumers," for effective learning to take place. What might the new "multimedia literacy" become, and how might tools and patterns of communication change, in society and in education? And how might such media — already including the use of techniques such as audio-supported, computer-aided reading tools that speak an unknown word when it is selected (122a, 134, 191), and multi-leveled games directed to fostering component reading skills development (70a, 70b) and vocabulary acquisition (127b) — help learners acquire text-based literacy?

The recent technical developments in this field center around CDs, or compact optical disks for mass storage and retrieval of images, text, and sound (104). Each thin, 150-gram iridescent CD can store 550 megabytes of multimedia memory, equivalent to 150,000 printed pages. While CD-ROM is now useful primarily for archival, read-only purposes, read-write media with similar properties are expected to become commercially available in 1990. Related developments in CD-Interactive (9, 27), the new GE/RCA Digital-Video Interactive (DVI: 200), and other technologies should make possible dynamic, interactive multimedia learning environments that can tap vast archives of text, image, and sound for the uses of education. The *Palenque Optical Disc Prototype* (Bank Street College: 200) shows some of the pontentials of the DVI medium in its dynamic mix of talking book, audio-video encyclopedia, and educational movie activities for 8 to 14-year-olds home learning about Mayan archaeology, culture, and ecology.

Over 100 CDs are commercially available, including Grolier's 20-volume Academic American Encyclopedia, Books in Print, and replications of various vast databases previously available on-line. Lancaster and other scholars have documented how the paperless society is on the way. How far behind will a paperless education be? The Library of Congress has established *The Center for the Book*, to explore how changes in information technologies will change the way in which the information in books and other documents will be composed, stored, accessed, and perceived (49). The Library of Congress is putting its vast visual reference materials on CDs, and the Smithsonian Institute has similar efforts underway. MIT is placing its 300,000 graphic works on CD, and art museums throughout the country are investigating opportunities to disseminate compact editions of their collections on CDs. Apple Computer, Lucasfilm, and National Geographic recently announced a joint project to create multimedia educational materials with CD technologies. And in related developments, the entertainment industry, including such movie makers as Warner Brothers, Columbia, Paramount, Lucasfilm, are supporting research and development activities to create low-cost (digital) optical disc movies (132), and interactive television (6a). Even today, (analog) interactive videodiscs of movies are broadly purchased, and the potential interest in home video is revealed by the 40 million videocassette recorders in American homes. Since each CD can store vast numbers of images, local home or school access to image archives will be possible. Network access (167) and copying of imagery onto local storage and replay/editing devices will be a parallel developing activity, depending on how the economics of central storage and access charges is settled.

Particular excitement among educators has been generated by the recent availability of "hypertext" and "hypermedia" systems. Hypertext is an information structuring paradigm designed to match the nonlinear, associative nature of human thinking, which is poorly supported with present linear, text-based technologies (56, 85, 192). In effect, it is the generalized footnote. These complex interdependencies among ideas are particularly evident in documents such as dictionaries, encyclopedias, and training manuals, but they formerly required lots of fingers and thumbs for flipping back and forth between books and book sections (195). Hypertext technologies provide ways of pointing from one place in a text-space to another, and labelling the type of pointers for computer search capabilities. Labelled links forming conceptual maps or "webs" among ideas may be created—in what are called "hypermedia" systems (146, 202)—by students, teachers, and researchers in between text fragments, graphics, timelines, and video clips, to be "travelled" by readers of these hypermedia compositions. These webs of relations can be saved, revised, shared, just as a text or musical piece might be in previous media, creating dramatic new opportunities for providing multiple contexts for learning concepts.

Optical disc storage of text will also be commonplace, with the important exception that information retrieval techniques developed in computer science will provide for full indexing and concordance capabilities, so that entirely new kinds of reading and research activities will be possible with these interactive, multimedia books. Relations among reading, writing, editing, publishing, are likely to change as readers annotate and engage in debates in the electonic "margins" of documents and create communities of interpretation (1, 56). The Brown University experience with their prototype *Intermedia* software environment in teaching cell biology and nineteenth-century English literature this year has captured much popular attention (202). Faculty consider the rhetoric of hypertext particularly well-suited to promoting the "understanding" involved in multiple interpretations of ideas and their relationships, whether in humanities or in the sciences.

Similar hypermedia R&D efforts at the precollege level in the next decade would provide on-line access to the vast archives of images and sound for education being converted to electronic form throughout the country, including maps, speeches, radio broadcasts, music, drawings, paintings, photographs, and full-motion video and film. The first hypertext product appeared commercially for Apple Macintosh computers this year (*Guide*), and several others will be appearing in 1987-1988. And there are at least ten different hypertext systems under development in major software, hardware, and research laboratories (56).

Beyond local storage of large media archives on optical disc, network access to images will become commonplace once broadband, fiber optics transmission provides the information gateway served by phonelines today (167). There is a trend to local mass storage, but costs of many CDs are high now because of low volume sales. Industry researchers predict this will change late in this century with fast transmission rates of broadband transmission and the availability of cheap color bit-map advanced function workstations. Electronically delivered magazines and movies, personalized television news and radio (MIT Media Laboratory: 182), multimedia home shopping for consumer goods and real estate, will all provide market forces contributing to the availability of these multimedia information services and technologies. A prototype of such a vast multimedia information service is in development for the *Telesophy Project* at Bell Communications Research (167: "telesophy" means "knowledge at a distance"—the modern extension of "telephony").

Though it may be several decades before standards are defined for image indexing and retrieval schemes, and until large volumes of graphics and texts become available through these media, research is needed on creating tools so that students and teachers can make effective use of these materials for learning. It is a broad consensus of the information sciences and telecommunications communities that these technologies will become commonplace. But unlike what happened with network television, the educational community should be ready with research that speaks to issues of specific needs for teaching and learning, and which builds on the best analyses of education from the cognitive, social, and instructional sciences. What this will require is prototype development and research activities using these new developments with precollege students and teachers, throughout the different areas of learning. New creative challenges are being faced by writers, artists, musicians, and filmmakers, using these new integrated media, and the expressive dimensions of their union will be under exploration for a very long time. Education science should help lead the way in creative work with these media. Research is also needed on what multimedia manipulation and composition tools are needed for education; including design issues concerning notational languages, text-audio-image editors, and characteristics of integrated tool systems for multimedia composing for communication (*Multimedia Literacy Project*, New York University). It is unlikely that needed developments for educationally-appropriate, electronic multimedia education environments will emerge from the commercial marketplace alone. But federally-funded research could make a significant difference in the decades ahead.

As one example, we note that all obtainable NSF-funded elementary science curriculum materials created with tens of millions of federal dollars during the 1960's and 1970's (approximately 15,000 pages) have just been made commercially available with indexing software for only $150 (a CD player costs $900-$1000). This disk should provide an important source for research and development activities in science learning to build upon.

There will also need to be technology transfer efforts specifically designated for education, such as the provision of inexpensive digital scanners of text and images, easy-to-use, low-cost videorecorders/editors for student and teacher use, and low-cost color printers for computer-accessed imagery.

Networking technologies are already making radically different information access possible for the classroom, although such access is largely text-based thus far. One barrier to student access to on-line databases has been that the language for formulating queries varies for almost every database. Now in *Einstein* (Addison-Wesley), one query language is available for students that enables access to the materials in about 900 databases. Einstein serves as a translating "front-end" to these databases, converting the students' queries in its language to the required format for any of the other databases. But information access does not make education. Students need to know how to formulate inquiries that information search may play a role in, and then to know how to filter and organize the information they obtain through searches in order to address the questions that led them to their initial search. Students will need special browsing tools for examining large information databases designed to take account of features of their understanding and of learning environments (146). Cognitive and instructional research on reading comprehension and writing has focused primarily on single texts (23), and needs to be extended so that we know more how students can learn to synthesize information from diverse sources collected for a variety of purposes. How should searches and inquiries be formulated? What are the information age equivalents to what used to be taught as library skills?

We unfortunately know very little about student learning from even presently available video, film, and interactive videodisc materials (20). Research is needed to guide educational practices for when such media are helpful, under what conditions, and for what topics. Good education does not always require broadcast studio quality, and some research indicates that for some learning objectives, line drawings may be superior to pictures (which include many instructionally-irrelevant details. We also need to investigate how to utilize the interactive potentials of computers to design interactive or "smart" pictures, graphs, and diagrams, that can explain themselves to students, depending on answers students give to questions posed by such visuals (93a). More intelligent and consistent methods will need to be developed for indexing, retrieving, manipulating, and editing images, sounds, text, and other data from mass storage media, particularly if they are to be accessible to students and not only teachers. Previous work on standards that has led to acceptance of user-interface protocols, such as the Apple Macintosh's "cut and paste" editing methods, needs to be extended for integrated multimedia environments and for educational users.

Changing How We Track Learning

The research in the cognitive and instructional sciences on the nature of "understanding" we earlier described has profound implications for how the educational establishment tracks learning and measures developmental progress in achieving educational goals. At present, very little school assessment is directed toward diagnosing students' conceptual understanding (71, 77). These issues are not only critical for improving education. They are also important from an economic perspective, since determining the quality of the content or the design of an educational technology cannot be determined solely from inspecting it. From a policy perspective, we need measures of the impact on learning outcomes of an educational technology (under specific use conditions). These measures should match what cognitive research on "understanding" indicates to be the objectives of education (25, 28, 113, 177b).

But to achieve this goal, major changes are needed in prevailing methods for learning assessment. A National Research Council committee report states that: "Tests also play a role in the learning process itself. They tell students what in the curriculum is important and shape the teaching and learning process.... If, for example, testing is confined to memorizable end results, students will concentrate on these end results, ignoring the more sophisticated levels of understanding and reasoning to which teachers and test makers may be rendering lip service" (120, p. 25).

On one extreme, theorists argue that we need to devise assessment strategies that check for the attainment of nontrivial skills (153, 166). They suggest that particular attention should be paid to "complex thinking skills," such as the ability to generalize appropriately, to invent analogies and use them critically, to decompose problems into interacting parts, to effectively manage and deal with complexity, to lay out a procedure as a sequence of approximations which converge to solution, to analyze a situation from a viewpoint other than one's own.

On the other extreme, theorists argue that we cannot expect to be able to measure such general capacities, since they may be developed distinctly in each substantive domain of learning (44, 76). They suggest that we may make assessments of one's level of progress in conceptual development for each subject domain of interest, based on empirical data studying the course of individual learning in that area. Assessment in this case is tied to theories of conceptual development, and stages of task proficiency. Both orientations consider today's item assessment tests inadequate as measures of understanding or skills. Finally, many empirical analyses imply that learning to engage in *self*-evaluation as one is learning, for example, testing one's comprehension in reading or in acquiring new ideas in science, and strategically working to overcome learning difficulties, should be educational priorities (23, 51, 125, 153, 170).

A substantial body of research findings on students' experiential learning outside school indicates that students often have alternative conceptual frameworks that constitute "preconceptions" from the perspective of formal learning, and that run into conflict with traditional instruction that does not recognize the potency of their previous beliefs. There is substantial evidence, for example, of the superficiality of student understanding of force and motion after instruction: they demonstrate misapprehensions in qualitative reasoning about the same situations that they can set up and solve formal equations for! Such curricula do not prevent everyone from understanding science, but it is widely conjectured in the cognitive research community that a much greater proportion of students would learn science with understanding if we tracked learning and taught with awareness of these alternative frameworks (25, 33, 58, 120, 142). Since the cognitive and instructional science research studies indicate that we need to teach to the student's present level of conceptual understanding, teachers need better diagnostic instruments for ascertaining what students believe about what is being taught. They also need more refined developmental theory of subject matter understanding than presently available to guide instructional interventions, and uses of technologies, once one has an accurate knowledge diagnosis.

For these reasons, a substantial federal investment should contribute to the creation of new research-guided precollege curricula, coupled to new assessment instruments for measuring deep conceptual understanding and diagnosing prior understandings.

Changing What's Taught

The cognitive shift in education provides the foundation for calls of curricular reform from the research community. Thus, we now know that our central goals in education are to have particular knowledge structures represented in students' memories that ensue in appropriate action, and that capturing subject matter knowledge structure in the curriculum to be taught is insufficient. *The reason is that knowledge is not "transmitted" by education, but constructed by learners from educational activities in relation to what they already know.* Key attention is paid to analysing students' alternative conceptual frameworks for reasoning about the topics they are being taught, and whether they are making progress toward the formal understanding of subject matter knowledge represented by the mature field. A rigid following of curriculum guidelines can ignore what students might want to know to help them in learning.

This cognitive shift has major implications for what should be the nature of curriculum, and more broadly what is taught in education. Under "what is taught," we include not only the textbooks, teacher lectures and demonstrations, and activities such as reading, working problems, and class discussions which constitute the bulk of instructional interactions used in schools, but also the enrichment activities, such as movies, videos, field trips, and laboratory experiments, that are adjuncts to the main content of a course.

Below we note the major observations that have arisen as consensus points in the cognitive and instructional research scientific communities, so that students learn for deep understanding rather than surface proficiency in recalling facts and formulas and symbol manipulations. We then present research and development activities suggested by the experts we consulted as means for closing the knowledge and technology gaps.

Too much is being taught to be learned for understanding. One of the most important lessons of cognitive studies of subject-matter learning is that teaching for understanding is much more demanding of classroom time than present instruction, which teachers literally need to race through to "cover everything" (116, 120). And the breadth of this "coverage" continues to accelerate as otherwise well-meaning subject matter organizations, such as the American Chemical Society (187), or the American Physics Society, recommend including yet more topics in the precollege curriculum. But "less is more" when conceptual understanding is the aim of educational activities. This conclusion was reached in a 1986 research agenda planning workshop at University of California, Berkeley and Lawrence Hall of Science (116: funded by NSF) in which forty-five mathematicians, scientists, cognitive scientists, mathematics and science teachers, and curriculum and technology experts participated. *But deciding what central topics need to be taught for understanding will depend on what we consider to be the tasks at which students need to do well.*

To take but one example, an interdisciplinary group at Harvard's Educational Technology Center has after three years of research devised a one-month unit, using educational software and novel teaching methods, that is highly effective in leading ninth graders to understand the heat-temperature distinction (201a). This is a conceptual hurdle for precollege science, and since it is the first time energy is treated, it is intimately related to understanding the molecular model of matter, and thus a focal part of any science curriculum. But only 5-6 days typically is allowed to cover this topic.

New curricula must recognize the existence of students' alternative conceptual frameworks and be responsive to them. Curricula need to be developed that not only present appropriately structured subject knowledge, but materials that address known preconceptions students have for the subject matter to be learned. There is a great deal of research identifying alternative conceptual frameworks students have in science (32, 33, 38a, 39, 40, 58, 60, 61, 74, 106, 116, 177b, 122, 123, 142, 193, 194, 201). But we know far less about how to provide instruction that would enable students to construct new understandings reflecting the structure of modern knowledge. Large-scale research and development projects should address these concerns systematically for major chunks of central curricular topics. Once students' alternative conceptual frameworks for each curricular area are reasonably well-specified, the use of knowledge representation languages and artificial intelligence methodologies might be used to help automate the process of diagnosing a student's current conceptual framework. We also know too little about how experiential activities prior to schooling contribute to the formation of students' alternative conceptual frameworks; yet such understanding could help guide the design of new learning environments for promoting conceptual change toward the formal standards of subject understanding conveyed in school (89, 116).

Functional learning environments can be designed to narrow gaps between knowledge acquisition and application settings in society and in education. As earlier discussed, the acquisition of new learning in performing whole tasks (such as newspaper writing/editing, research in social studies or science, or applied mathematics) under the guidance of more able peers or a teacher can connect school learning to real societal contexts. Technologies can play key roles in this process, and the feasibility of widescale implementation of existing prototype efforts with this orientation should be examined.

We must systematically examine how technologies can make higher learning and complex thinking more accessible to more learners. Curricula need to change to reflect what it is possible for students to do and understand with new technologies. We have heard frequent references to the "complexity barriers" involved in learning formal topics, particularly in mathematics, sciences, and technology (62, 94, 98, 116, 171, 190). It is the belief of many researchers and developers of educational technologies that many of the features of such complexities are media-specific, and that new learning tools can overcome them. More extensive research and development collaborations with this theme need to take place between professional educator organizations in the subject disciplines and the education science community. Innovations are slowly appearing in which calculators and computers play integral parts of student activities in existing curricula (116, 120), but much more comprehensive and innovative efforts will be required. Three major directions of curricular tools, building on research earlier described, were commonly mentioned as bearing great promise in this regard.

The first is crafting learning environments with multiple representations of knowledge whenever possible, since multiple ways of knowing may make a topic more accessible to certain learners. If possible, such representations should be linked so that the learner may establish intuitive understanding of how changes across the representational media are related (97, 154a). Software environments with these properties are under development for reasoning about intensive quantities (ratio, proportion) and algebraic modelling at Harvard's Educational Technology Center (65a, 97), and for modelling systems dynamics (TERC/Lesley College: 190). The *Boxer* programming environment (U. California, Berkeley: 63) will provide students with linked program outcome and control program representations that are now finding their way into professional programming environments. Many more topic areas could utilize this approach, and research examining the conditions of its effectiveness for learning is an important need.

The second need is deeper understanding of the role of visual representations, of pictures, diagrams, graphs, flowcharts, and other non-text media in learning processes. Random access videodisc and compact optical offer much more provocative but little understood educational possibilities than linear videotape. The need for research understanding of how such representations function in the learning and reasoning processes of students is particularly critical because new information technologies provide opportunities for much greater exploitation of non-text media. Object-oriented graphics editors, digital scanners for photos and video frames, and animation tools, are available at reasonably low cost for computers in the $2000 range, and are being used for these purposes in learning technology development work (1).

The third need is for programmatic R&D efforts to provide new materials that allow the linking and co-articulation of subject matter understanding across now-isolated curriculum areas, so that students will remember and use task-appropriate collections of understandings to solve real problems—which researchers find rarely respect the curriculum boundaries established in school. Project work at Vanderbilt University with this emphasis, using existing interactive videodisc technologies under microcomputer control for promoting integrated learning of mathematics, science, and reading, has resulted in promising learning outcomes for at-risk middleschool and elementary students (18-20). A particular priority and opportunity with this emphasis would be creating learning environments for discrete mathematics and statistics—for which there are essentially no texts and no teachers at the precollege level—even though these have become critical topics for students to understand as they enter college.

In contrast, we found that experts consider curriculum reforms designed primarily to "keep pace with the information explosion" to be unrealistic. While some have argued that the main need for curriculum reforms is the pace of knowledge change, which requires new and up-to-date texts and curricula, it is clear that such an emphasis, relying as it does on a "knowledge transmission" metaphor for the role of education, is fighting a losing battle. There is no way to keep pace, so a growing recognition is for the need to teach generative learning skills, exercised against the best available substantive materials, with clear recognition and communication to students that knowledge will continue to change. Educators should also stress the acquisition of productive inquiry skills so that students can find and reconfigure needed knowledge for their own purposes, rather than having information stuffed into their minds at a faster and faster pace.

Changing What Teachers Do

Research in the cognitive and instructional sciences earlier described on the nature of teaching and learning has major implications for what the activities of teachers should be. (Since another OTA subreport will deal centrally with such issues of teacher education and educational technologies, we will not focus on them here.) But several points deserve special mention. The statistics available paint a bleak picture for the teaching profession. We have heard expressed particular concerns about the low levels of teacher certification in mathematics, science, and English; the lack of subject matter understanding even among many of those certified; the drop in numbers of new teachers being educated; the lowering SAT scores of teachers entering the profession; the high rate of forthcoming teacher retirements; and the poor image of career opportunities many teachers profess (93).

Technology has a curious but intriguing role in this picture, and unfortunately, little research is available that will help guide decision-making about it. Many different roles were described for the teacher-technology relation (116a). Only a few of the experts we consulted described the preferred role of the technology to be directed at *replacing* the teacher. Some believe that this is what "intelligent" tutors are being designed to do, but the general belief was that relatively little of formal education can be mechanized in that fashion.

Most experts instead highlighted the ways in which the computer can be used to *revitalize* the teaching profession in many ways (93, 116a, 203), including: (1) providing better education to teachers about the incremental change (rather than all/none) nature of the development of subject matter understanding, and teaching pedagogical methods for diagnosing students' preconceptions so that they will better be able to know where students are in the learning process; (2) changing teachers' roles and making their work more interesting—in particular making their role more one of "coach" than delivery agent of learning (the assumption being that small groups or individual students can focus on thinking and problem-solving through the use of such tools as micro-based labs, micro-worlds, word processors, and database programs); (3) promoting more effective learning of subject matter, reasoning skills, and pedagogical methods through uses of the technology itself, through in-service, pre-service, and networking activities. Perhaps the greatest satisfaction of all for teachers, if present research understanding finds its way into practice, will reside in providing students with better understanding than they have before. And while few now believe that computers will necessarily make teachers' lives easier, they may make their work much more interesting and challenging intellectually.

Our experts consider a focus on teachers to be essential. As one research scientist assessed the present state: "The problem with education now is not what *students* are capable of, but what *teachers* are capable of, given their previous education. There is a general consensus, at least in science learning, that teachers need to teach to students' conceptual understanding. Students interpret curriculum in terms of their preformal conceptual frameworks. The major problem of educational research and development is to educate teachers about this consensus view, and in how to diagnose students' alternative frameworks for thinking about what is being taught" (Dr. Susan Carey, MIT).

Changing the Schooling Environment

Research from the education sciences revealing the influence on learning of the social context and schooling environment has major implications for designs of school learning environments. Some directions considered promising for change are those in which teachers teach partly by modelling thinking processes (e.g., in reading comprehension) and engaging students in "cognitive apprenticeships," in which an environment is created for promoting students' positive self-images as learners, and in which peer collaboration and tutoring, and small-group learning are encouraged (51, 52, 153, 154a). But these opportunities are poorly understood at the present time in relation to technologies, even though they are integral to effecting school change that builds on research knowledge. For this reason, new empirical studies are required. Research and technology development activities at this level of analysis, which has been described as "microsystems," simultaneously studies the social organization of instruction and curriculum content (120).

Technologies may have a special role to play in the future of microsystems research. Networking technologies would fundamentally change the communication systems of classrooms, connecting teachers and students to other learning and teaching resources, both human and information databases. Telecommunication technologies such as major networks and local-area networks (LANs) are currently cumbersome and costly for schools to implement. The importance of the planned NSF support for developing high-speed, high-bandwidth compatible national networks to replace the present Arpanet system has been aptly described as providing the information equivalent to the interstate highway system. Smaller-scale but parallel federally-initiated efforts should work at the school-level, and could solicit complementary local and state education funds for this purpose. Research and development efforts are needed that aim for cheap, compatible networking hardware and software to support collaborative project work and cooperative learning activities within and across schools, and access to information databases on-line. Such work would require basic studies of human-computer interaction for student-appropriate interface designs (71a). Satellite transmission of educational materials also requires careful study, but it is important that the cognitive shift in education outlined throughout this report be reflected in experiments involving this technology.

While these telecommunications may dramatically expand the learning and teaching resources available for students and teachers, some concern has been expressed that the communication infrastructure of schools is vastly underdeveloped to support these changes: since so few classrooms have telephones, how likely is it that they will support costs of modems, local-area network cabling, networking, and satellite transmissions?

Other Needed Research and Development Activities

Several priorities were described which do not fit well in the categories outlined above, because in an important sense they involve all of the categories.

Comparative research evaluations are needed of different approaches to the same instructional task to test the strengths and weaknesses of different learning theories. Several experts suggested that present development environments for the programming of prototypes of education technology such as *InterLisp-D/LOOPs* (Xerox PARC: 13) or *Boxer* (U. California, Berkeley: 63) would allow graduate students to do this in a semester. Implementations would be tested formatively (for interest, comprehension), summatively (for learning outcomes), and in terms of the quality of the revised learning theory generated. More graduate students, hardware, and laboratory schools would be required to do this any more broadly than at two or three research-oriented laboratories (e.g., U. Pittsburgh, Carnegie-Mellon).

A cluster of other important issues centers on establishment of standards, compatibility, and R&D that would contribute to improving production economy for educational technologies.

Standards in interface design are needed to reduce for teachers and students learning time and to ensure compatibility for cognitive workbenches such as text editors, drafting programs, theorem proving assistants, algebra assistants, outlining tools, spreadsheets, graph plotters. Additional work on interface conventions for accessing/storing data that would be readily accessible to, for example, elementary school children will be important. (Much like what has occurred in the acceptance even by IBM, in their new Personal System series of computers, of Apple Macintosh interface conventions such as files-as-icons, multiple windows, and pull-down menus). These developments are not likely to take place in the commercial arena because of the low-profitability of educational technology materials, but will be critical for education.

Helping reduce costs of producing technological media is another goal mentioned by experts as an appropriate federal role (28, 126, 159a). For example, "courseware" development, as defined by sharp domain boundaries and clear sequential strategies for instruction, is often provided, particularly in commercial and military training applications, by instruction-controlled videodisc, videocassettes, intelligent tutors, which are highly expensive. It has been observed that typical expensive production methods, coupled with keen commercial competition, has resulted and will continue to result in poor quality instructional goods. This problem also exists, but to a lesser extent, for the costs of course-ware production involving more flexible browsing/resource systems (CD-ROM, data-bases), where many activities are locally adapted and not specified at great levels of detail since they are under greater user control.

Two strategic approaches may meet this problem of costs (159a). One involves lower-ing development costs, the other improves the analysis/evaluation of instructional products. These approaches are in contradistinction to the present trends of increasing the effectiveness and variety of such educational media.

Lower development costs and more efficient production would be likely to arise from better theories of learning, since empirically-grounded principles would lead to better first prototypes, and instructional development costs are dramatically reduced by how good a version of a product one begins with in testing. Such an objective calls for basic learning research aimed at facilitating effective instructional design and intervention, and increasing our capacities to assess competencies in knowledge domains. Without goals for educational products, drives for more-economic development are aimless. As discussed elsewhere in this report, present testing measures are inadequate to these purposes, since they do not provide the needed instructionally relevant observations about a learner's level of under-standing and skills, and qualitative observations of student performance are insufficiently rigorous. We are in particular need of such methods for determining competence in the broadly taught school subjects, and their availability could have critical impact on the quality of teaching and learning, and the design and production of instructional technologies.

The other strategy aims at reducing costs of both the synthesis of educational tech-nology materials. As for synthesis, there are high costs associated with gathering and extracting information — textual and graphical — required for design of instruction. This activity is often underemphasized since reference materials are considered to be widely available for presently taught school subjects. Requisite tools include those for automated indexing, and AI-supported information retrieval methods. Substantial basic research on techniques for effectively indexing and retrieving graphics are needed. Instructional designers would often like information menus for choosing content, and readily-reconfigurable databases devised for these purposes could also be used by teachers for preparing lessons, and for students in research activities and report preparation. A related goal is to develop highly-automated camera and videorecording/editing equipment, so that urgent educational problems may be met creatively by teachers without the over-emphasized (from a pedagogical perspective) broadcast production aesthetics of present educational video.

POLICY SUGGESTIONS: PLANS FOR REVITALIZING AMERICAN EDUCATION

In the foregoing, our primary intent has been to describe in the somber tones of academic prose the advancements in education science and technology that presage funda-mental changes in education. However, our intent is also to generate genuine excitement for a vision of the future where education is a vehicle for empowerment; where learning is exciting, stimulating, fun; where kids are active participants in a profoundly important individual and social ritual — that of idea creation and idea interchange. For example, consider the following technological products that are literally just around the corner:

Doing history, not just reading about history: Developing interpretations for events is a key activity of historians. Imagine, then, that you are trying to understand the influence of various paintings on the writings of Robert Browning. You can select a piece of Browning's text, and call up — on your computer screen — the paintings that Browning was thought to have known about. You then piece together an argument on "influences": the golden color of the wheat in this painting appears to be reflected in this poem, and so forth. However, given the uncertain travel arrangements — which you get by looking at travel documents, also on your computer screen — it seems unlikely that Browning could have seen the painting before he wrote the line. And so on. Without the computer, this historical investigation would either have been impossible or highly problematic — especially for a student in a rural school nowhere near the primary sources.

Doing science, not just reading about science: Acid rain is a hot research topic in science today. A rich corpus of data is going to be crucial to pin down exactly how this phenomena works: there are surely multiple lines of causation and interacting factors by which acid rain occurs. What if 25,000 students collected data on this topic in different regions of the country, and collected data on various environment factors, e.g., the amount and type of industry in the area, numbers of smokestacks, and so on. And, what if these students were able to put these data on-line, so that all 24,999 other students might have access to it for analysis, for on-line discussions of the trends, and to spur further research. And, what if data analysis tools were available, and simulation programs to model acid rain's effects. It is not implausible that some students may develop fine conjectures and scientific explanations for aspects of the acid rain problem: the data and the analysis tools accessible by the 25,000 students are comparable to that accessible by a "true" bench scientist. Who is the real scientist now?

Doing art, not just reading about art: Everyone at one point or other dreams about being a movie producer. Talent aside, the logistics prevent all but the most motivated to get a chance. However, through the use of "video design programming languages" and electronic networks tied to databases of video-images, students can create their own personalized videos — while sitting at their desk.

The above vignettes are not blue-sky, wishful thinking: education science and technology has developed the theory and the technological base for creating these sorts of dynamic educational products. In fact, each of the above are in the prototype stage now.

What are called for, then, are mechanisms through which a systematic multitude of vignettes of the above sort can be realized. More generally, mechanisms are needed by which the broad, but focused changes described earlier, in what students do, how they are taught, etc., can be brought about. What should be the federal role in developing and nurturing such mechanisms?

In this section, then, we present three alternative courses of action for the Federal government.

Option 1: Significant increase in Federal spending. In this plan, we call for the creation, over a 10 year period, of 6 major Centers for Interactive Technologies in Education, plus the need for a substantial increase in funding of individual researchers.

Option 2: Modest increase in Federal spending. In this plan, we call for the creation of only 1-2 centers, with only a minimal increase in funding of individual researchers.

Option 3: No increase in Federal spending. Under this option, the Federal role would be as it is now. The burden of furthering education, then, would fall to the private sector.

We go on to assess the effectiveness of the mechanisms in each of these options with respect to the following four goals for educational vitality emphasized by many of the experts we interviewed. The achievement of these goals will provide the basis for the wide-ranging, deep changes we indicated earlier were beginning to take shape:

Goal 1: Producing and exploring new ideas in education science and technology. Our storehouse of ideas in education science needs considerable expansion. We need more deep theories of learning, teaching, understanding, expertise, etc. Moreover, we need to explore these ideas in a systematic fashion. Under the current environment, researchers must often drop a line of inquiry due to the vagaries of funding without an adequate assessment of its potential. Still further, we need to develop ways to quickly, and cost effectively, prototype and evaluate technological innovations.

Goal 2: Developing an extensive community infrastructure. Work in education science is inherently multi-disciplinary, and labor-intensive. Simply put, we need a major influx of talented individuals who are committed to doing something significant in the field. We need to provide clear avenues for the development of first-class researchers and developers.

Goal 3: Providing professional development opportunities. High on the list of priorities must be ways to involve the classroom teacher more actively in all phases of innovation: from idea conception to research, product development and evaluation, teachers need to be involved as first-class citizens. A plan of action that does not allocate a substantial portion of its budget to "in practice" issues will not result in the changes we described earlier.

Goal 4: Producing and disseminating technological products. The cost of developing high-quality, educationally-principled technological artifacts is high—and the return on investment may well not be there. This is a plain fact that educational software houses and publishers, for example, know only too well. Creative strategies need to be developed to support commercial concerns, while not unduly constraining researchers' imaginations. Current modes of marketing and distributing technological products are both costly and oftentimes ineffective. Again, strategies need to be explored that bring products to the public in a timely and affordable manner.

In what follows we examine the potential of each of the three options for achieving the above four goals.

Option 1: Significant Increase in Federal Spending

This first option has a 10 year duration, with three overlapping phrases:

> *Phase 1: Establish Infrastructure* — create Centers for Interactive Technology and Education (CITE) where research, development, dissemination, and evaluation take place in a realistic learning and teaching situation.

> *Phase 2: Begin Dissemination to Public Schools* — facilitate active commercial distribution of the CITE products, and develop the baseline technologies that will enable teachers and students in the schools to have nationwide access to products, information bases, etc.

> *Phase 3: Accelerate to Nation-wide Dissemination* — provide access for every school to a Resource Center that can assist teachers in integrating the ideas and technology from education science into their classrooms.

This option is based on: (1) our analyses of effective organizational structures in comparable fields (e.g., biomedical engineering) and (2) on recommendations from the experts we interviewed. For example, almost universally, our experts stressed the need for nationally sponsored centers that would bring together a critical mass of people, with ideas, talents, and skills, to work on the complex, important problems in education. Moreover, essentially all the previous reports on policy recommendations have suggested comparable mechanisms (25, 112, 113, 116, 120, 121, 131).

Phase 1: Establish Infrastructure. There are two major thrusts to be accomplished during Phase 1:

- Develop Centers for Interactive Technologies in Education

- Increase support for individual investigators as well as provide supports for commercial enterprises that are involved with educational technology.

Centers for Interactive Technologies in Education

A major innovation proposed is the establishment of 6 Centers for Interactive Technologies in Education (CITEs) across the US, over the next five years. Two centers would be established in Year 1, while one center would be established in each of the 4 succeeding years (of Phase 1). Each CITE would be intimately tied to both a K-12 school system and a major research institution. There would be two major functions of each CITE: (1) conduct both basic research in education science (the cognitive, social and instructional sciences), and (2) carry out development and dissemination of technological products. In addition, each CITE would have the following sorts of functions:

- holding workshops for teachers in the CITE-associated school and for other teachers and educators in the area,

- hosting visiting faculty and post-doctoral fellowships,

- providing research/development facilities for graduate students,

- disseminating the CITE developed products on a large-scale, e.g., interact with commercial enterprises for the marketing and support of technological products.

As detailed in Table 1, the cost of one center, when equipment and support personnel are added in, is estimated to be approximately $10 million per year. This figure is higher than that typically associated with centers (e.g., Learning Research and Development Center at the University of Pittsburgh, or the Educational Technology Center at Harvard).

Table 1.

Staffing Levels and Cost for a CITE Per Year

[1]Senior Staff	5	$200,000	$1,000,000
[2]Support Staff	35	100,000	3,500,000
Post-doctoral Fellowships	10	100,000	1,000,000
Visiting Faculty	10	100,000	1,000,000
Graduate Fellowships	10	40,000	400,000
[3]Staff to work with school teachers	13	100,000	1,300,000
[4]Equipment/School/Hardware per student	390	3,000	1,170,000
Equipment/School/Software per student	390	500	195,000
[5]Equipment/School/Hardware per teacher	13	4,000	52,000
Equipment/School/Software per teacher	13	2,000	26,000
TOTAL			$9,643,000

Cost of Phase 1

Year 1 (2 CITEs)	19,286,000
Year 2 (1 new CITE, total 3 CITEs)	28,929,000
Year 3 (1 new CITE, total 4 CITEs)	38,572,000
Year 4 (1 new CITE, total 5 CITEs)	48,215,000
Year 5 (1 new CITE, total 6 CITEs)	57,858,000
Year 6 (6 CITEs)	57,858,000
Year 7 (6 CITEs)	57,858,000
Year 8 (6 CITEs)	57,858,000
Year 9 (6 CITEs)	57,858,000
Year 10 (6 CITEs)	57,858,000
Total for all CITEs	$482,150,000

[1]Of the $200K per senior researcher, approximately $80K goes for salary, while the remaining $120K goes for "indirect costs" and equipment. This level of "burden" is typical of active research and development environments.

[2]Of the $100K per researcher/developer, approximately $40K goes for salary while the rest goes for indirect costs and equipment.

[3]There will be one resource person assigned to each grade (class) in the CITE school whose explicit role will be to facilitate the back and forth transfer issues associated with using the technology in the classroom.

[4]We estimate 30 students per class for each of 13 grades (classes).

[5]Each classroom teacher needs to have a modest hardware (and software) budget.

However, as we briefly outlined above, a CITE would be a much larger enterprise than are the current centers. However, as Table 1 clearly shows, close to 30% of a CITE's support goes for "in practice" support: providing the children and teachers in the attached school with hardware and software, providing staff to work with teachers and schools in the region, and providing support staff for the dissemination of the CITE-developed technological products. These functions are not a major part of any current center; by and large these functions just aren't being carried out.

Each CITE should be located at a major center of research. This model is one that is currently being employed (e.g., the Educational Technology Center is located at Harvard). Moreover, to foster both synergy and diversity—and to create a critical mass—we propose that a CITE be composed of 5 senior researchers and a staff of approximately 50 associate researchers and developers. (In addition to full-time staff personnel, research and development groups will draw on visiting faculty and CITE-sponsored graduate students.) The 1:10 ratio is one that is common in productive research laboratories. Thus, a CITE is a major institutional structure.

We propose that the CITEs not be chartered to focus on particular curricular topics, particular grade levels, or particular technologies. Rather, we propose that CITEs be encouraged to explore the full spectrum of topics, grade levels and technologies. The multimedia, interactive technologies actively facilitate the crossing of subject boundaries. In the "acid rain project" cited earlier, writing, communicating, and mathematical skills arise naturally in the context of the scientific research that the students are carrying out. And numerous experts consider grade-level accessibility of complex concepts and skills quite malleable with computer technology supports.

Following the guidelines for the new NSF centers, and for other comparable institutions (e.g., MCC in Austin, TX), the cost of a CITE would be borne in part by the federal government, and in part by private industry. A commercial concern would buy in for a share, and have access to various center resources. Similarly, DOD would be encouraged to participate in the CITE program. While the details need to be carefully worked out, the point is that such joint federal-commercial funding relationships have recently been found to be effective, and thus we have reason to believe that such an arrangement would work in this area also.

With that brief description of the functional architecture of a CITE, let us now assess the utility of a CITE with respect to the four goals identified earlier as being critically important for revitalizing American education:

Goal 1: Producing and exploring new ideas in education science and technology.

Support the integration of research and development. Over and over again, our experts made strong recommendations that theory must not be divorced from practice. That is, the most common model of research and development is that research constructs a theory, hands it off to the developers, who then make it into a product. However, this model of the relationship between research and development has not been an effective one in education. Rather, education must be viewed more as an engineering discipline than as a pure science: in education, theory must lead to products, feedback from which helps to reshape theory. In what follows, we sketch four reasons why the CITE model in Option 1 puts significant emphasis on facilitating the integration of theory and practice.

First, theorists need to study real phenomena: the phenomena under study in the cognitive, social, and instructional sciences do not lend themselves to "laboratory study," where small, isolated components are studied and for which circumscribed theories are constructed. Theories of nonsense syllable memory, while permitting controlled experimentation, simply do not scale up to realistic learning situations. Rather, laboratories for developing viable theories of learning and teaching are just the naturally occurring learning, teaching situations themselves.

Second, developers need a direct channel to researchers, since realizing complex theories in an educational product requires considerable interaction between theorists and developers. The costs of producing technological products can be dramatically cut as a result of the close collaboration between researchers and developers. In particular, armed with better theories, the developer has a better chance of developing a more effective prototype the first time around. Without such a theory to use as a guidelines, one is surely less confident that what one initially produces will be at all useful.

Third, there must be a direct link between the researchers/developers and the school teachers, who ultimately have the responsibility for employing the developed technology in the classrooms. There are a number of reasons for the need of this direct link. For one, teachers need to be integrated into the process of educational technology research and development, from conception to final product delivery. Second, education is like the fields of medicine and engineering: new ideas and products are constantly being produced, and thus medical professionals and engineers need to be life-long learners about their fields. Similarly, teachers need to contribute to and be kept abreast of new developments. If such inservice interchanges are integrated into the research and development laboratories, then the lag time between an idea and its dissemination is considerably shortened. Moreover, the critical feedback by the teachers can provide key insight for the researchers and developers.

Fourth, since, as we argued earlier, education is exceedingly complex, education science researchers are often quite surprised by the interaction that results when students meet theory-motivated, technological products. Researchers may need to substantially change their theories, while developers may need to substantially change the design of their products. In sum, then, we feel that the organizational structure employed in bio-medical and bio-engineering research is an appropriate one for educational technology research: there theory and practice are integrated in an effective synergy.

Support for the sustained interaction of colleagues from many disciplines. Research in education science is inherently multi-disciplinary; the production of insightful theories and effective technological products requires the active participation of psychologists, educators, computer scientists, anthropologists, sociologists, graphics designers, subject matter experts, video producers, human-factors specialists, etc.

Provide a rich source of technology for experimentation. Technology creates new possibilities; what can be done with technology often outstrips what people believe it is possible to do. Researchers and developers in educational technology need to have access to a wide range of technologies; they need channels into the manufacturers for experimenting with the latest equipment. While it may take time for the latest technological innovation to percolate down to the schools, nonetheless, researchers and developers who have access to the latest in technology can plan an orderly, effective transition between what is now available and what will be available. In addition, the technology often permits the researcher and developer to do things that couldn't be done before: the technology opens up whole new avenues. For example, CD-ROM permits an individual to literally have at his/her fingertips as much information as was available before in a small library. Given that this enormous amount of information is now available on immediate demand, we need to rethink how information needs to be organized, so as to facilitate the cognitive processes of information search and utilization.

Goal 2: Developing an extensive community infrastructure. In order to insure a sufficient number of researchers and developers to reach a critical mass in education science, adequate training environments and career paths must be provided. While there are schools of education, the majority of research in the cognitive, social and instructional sciences is taking place outside schools of education, by isolated investigators working in the traditional departments of psychology, anthropology, sociology, mathematics, computer science, or small to medium sized laboratories of research and development. Those disciplines have their own well-established methodologies, evaluation criteria, career paths, etc. Oftentimes there is conflict between the traditions of a discipline and the goal of producing theory and product in education. For example, if one is a graduate student in computer science, working on a Ph.D. in artificial intelligence, the objective must be to produce something acceptable to computer scientists, not to educators. Thus, concern for education must remain secondary in these traditionally-structured departments.

In contrast, CITEs can provide a "home" for researchers and developers to contribute to education science. A CITE offers the setting in which training of individuals can be effectively carried out. Moreover, given the proposed extended life span of the CITEs, it would be a reasonable place for career satisfaction and advancement.

Goal 3: Providing professional development opportunities. It is critical that classroom teachers become involved in ideas and developments of education science and technological innovations. In line with our emphasis on integrating theory with practice, CITEs can provide an excellent environment for teacher professional development. CITEs, as part of their basic charter, should run a wide range of workshops and courses expressly designed for classroom teachers. CITE researchers and developers will be encouraged to involve classroom teachers during even the earliest phases of their projects. Thus, teachers will be linked into the new ideas at all levels: from basic research to dissemination and use.

Goal 4: Producing and disseminating technological products. All too often researchers and developers ignore the significant costs and talents involved in successfully marketing and distributing a product. One-of-a-kind deals between publishers/software houses and researchers/developers just don't offer any economies of scale. CITEs can expressly be designed to provide a continuous stream of products for the commercial sector. This continuity of product availability makes it worthwhile to establish high-bandwidth, long-term relationships with commercial enterprises. In turn, these serious relationships will cut down on the unconscionable delay that now exists between conception and realization: there will be a clear, well-defined, well-oiled path from idea to utilized products.

In sum, then, the CITE model seems like a good candidate mechanism for achieving these critically important goals.

In the above discussion, we have highlighted the "pros" of the CITE strategy. We now turn to addressing specific "cons" that can, if not dealt with explicitly, detract from the effectiveness of the center concept:

> There is a danger that centers will lose their innovativeness. Key to lessening the chances of such a loss will be mechanisms that provide for renewal and for interaction with other CITEs, individual researchers, and organizations. For example, CITEs should explicitly rotate their staff through other CITEs: this mechanism will help to spread good ideas, and to provide infusions of new ideas. Also, we suggested that CITEs not necessarily be mission-oriented; the senior staff, as well as the associates and teachers themselves should provide a drive for innovation and diversity.

There is a danger that there will be conflict between a CITE and its host institution or other institutions in the field. For example, there is a concern that CITEs will swallow up research personnel; non-CITE universities may not be able to provide an attractive enough environment. Staffing is a problem: there are presently not enough qualified individuals to populate CITEs and universities. However, there is good reason to believe that staffing problems will lessen: CITEs will be major training grounds, and increased recognition of the importance and support of education science will result in its ability to draw high-quality individuals into the field.

There is a danger that support for CITEs will become unduly influenced by political, regional, administrative, etc., considerations. Channeling significant resources to CITEs (and individual investigators) will naturally attract attention. One of the functions of a CITE is dissemination: such an activity will provide the basis for informed decision-making.

In sum, the center concept is not without its risks. Nonetheless, the demand for centers was almost unanimous among the experts we interviewed. Thus, the risks were deemed well-worth the undertaking: the benefits of centers outweighed the risks. Given the importance of centers, it is definitely worth the effort to find ways to minimize their drawbacks.

Our suggestion for six CITEs is based on a number of factors. First, our experts repeatedly spoke of the need for a diversity of ideas: a few CITEs might well not provide enough material in the gene pool, so to speak. Also, our experts spoke of the power of synergy arising from a critical mass of top-flight workers interacting. While CITEs may each have different theoretical stances, interaction among CITEs will expressly be fostered. Second, the commitment of significant resources, in terms of a substantial number of CITEs, will have its own impact on various fields and individuals. It is our sense that once world-class scientists and scholars see that America is serious about dealing with education, they will come and join, even if just temporarily, in the work of a CITE. The contribution of these individuals will be significant. Students will then be able to experience the excitement of dealing with the frontiers of knowledge first hand; they won't need to wait years until their textbooks are updated.

As detailed in Table 1, the cost of developing and maintaining 6 CITEs over the 10 year period is roughly $500 million. While on the surface this figure might seem high, we hasten to point out: (1) that this amount would be spent over a 10 year period, and (2) if we can use the F-14 fighter plane as a unit of measure, the CITE portion of Option 1 can be viewed as costing less than one F-14 per year for 10 years. It is important to note that what we are proposing would not "naturally" happen: current levels of funding for research and development in education do not come close to what is needed, nor would the commercial or DOD sectors naturally put forward this level of support. Thus a major "delta" is needed by the Federal government in order to make this plan happen.

Support for Individual Investigators and Commercial Concerns

While Centers for Interactive Technologies in Education will be the major cost of Phase 1, there is a second mechanism that needs to be in place to insure progress in this area. Namely, support will still be needed for individual investigators working at their home institutions. Centers by their nature will encourage a focusing of attention on specific problems from specific paradigms. However, the independence of the individual investigator allows him/her to be less tied to a reigning paradigm. Note too that graduate students are often supported by such research grants. Moreover, given the variety of directions within education science and technology, we need many projects that explore the myriad of potential avenues. While current funding levels appear to be only marginally adequate for even today's researchers, as the field grows more and more individuals will be competing for funds. Thus, this pot needs a significant infusion of funds in order to keep abreast with the increasing numbers of researchers competing for support.

In addition, we need to set up a mechanism by which developers of technology-based products can gain support for their efforts. For example, currently software houses are frankly loathe to undertake development for the education market: development costs are high, and the market is perceived as limited and fickle. Upfront risk money and planned subcontracts through CITEs could be provided to ease the burden of developers; a return of the percentage of profits would be an acceptable cost for this type of assistance.

Phase 2: Begin Dissemination of Ideas and Technology. The objective of Phase 2 is to begin to get the ideas and technology developed by the CITEs (and by individual investigators) out into the schools. We see two major mechanisms for this transition: (1) the active participation of the commercial sector, and (2) the use of technology itself—high-bandwidth, nationwide computer networks, and machine readable information bases—to provide for the dissemination of product and information. We propose that Phase 2 begin in Year 2 of Phase 1. There is no reason to wait for the completion of Phase 1: the development of both mechanisms will take time, and thus they should be started early, and products should already be coming out of the pipelines at the CITEs by the end of year 2 of Phase 1. Since the technological developments of this phase will interact with the commercial sector's activities, we will address this issue first.

Computer networks promise to fundamentally change how information is distributed. Right now, there are elaborate schemes for moving physical objects—that contain graphics, text, music, etc.—from one place to another. However, it doesn't take a crystal ball to see that, if the information in those physical objects is placed on a "machine readable medium" (e.g., CD-ROM), and if each school desk is wired to a computer network which enables the student at the desk to tie into a computer thousands of miles away—instantly—then access to information no longer is a problem. Any (and each) student can have all the letters written by George Washington to Benjamin Franklin "on his desk"—in micro-seconds.

We need to set in motion a systematic plan for creating just such computer networks and machine-readable databases. The DOD will continue to upgrade their telecommunications network (the ARP Anet). Education needs its champion to put up the resources for building the analogue of the national highway system for the nation's schools. Commercial concerns will contribute to this effort, since, as we argue below, it is in their best interest to have high-bandwidth conduits to and from schools. Similarly, while the Library of Congress will no doubt be converting portions of its collection to machine-readable form, this process also needs an extra jolt of support, focusing on high-use educational materials, in order to accelerate the process.

The agreements between CITEs and commercial enterprises ("book" publishers, software development houses, etc.) will be especially economically viable if CITEs can readily transmit products to these enterprises in a format that requires little subsequent transformation on the part of the enterprises themselves. For example, if a CITE personnel wants to publish a book, the cost of producing a hardcopy version of that book would certainly be reduced if the author can simply transmit machine-readable text directly to the typesetters. Similarly, if "book" publishers can transmit to customers essentially what the author sends in, then the cost will again be reduced. The mechanism for both transmissions is computer networks. Clearly issues of copyright, cost, etc., need to be thought through and equitably worked out (e.g., a charge for use scheme may well be viable). Note that publishers and software houses need not wait for the existence of the computer networks to begin the process of finalizing, marketing and distributing products developed at a CITE.

State and local institutions need to enter the picture in Year 2, at the beginning of Phase 2. Clearly, they will play a key role in (1) shaping the partciular products coming out of the centers, as well as (2) in planning and facilitating the dissemination paths from the CITEs to the schools. Some formula will need to be developed whereby state and local governments contribute funds to support these activities.

In effect, Phase 2 simply takes the "integration of theory with practice" one step further: ideas and products need to move from the schools associated with the CITEs to schools nationwide.

Phase 3: Accelerate to Nationwide Dissemination of Ideas and Products. During this final phase of the ramp-up effort, the objective is to make the fruits of the research and development available on a national scale. The key factors during this phase are: (1) teacher education, and (2) commercial involvement.

Not unreasonably, teachers will not have had much exposure to the ideas of education science, as we have described them here, nor to the diverse types of interactive, multi-media technology, and the educational products that employ those technologies, that are coming to be available. A significant effort needs to be made to provide teachers with professional development opportunities that will aid them in understanding and using these ideas and technology products. Summer workshops, in-service seminars, sabbatical leaves to work at a CITE, etc., will need to be supported. We can't stress this need too highly: considerable funds need to be made available for this effort.

Similarly, the ideas and technologies developed through Option 1 support need to move into schools of education, and traditional academic departments at universities and colleges. We propose that CITE staff rotate out into the academic community in order to carry the ideas and technology first hand. Similarly, we see visiting faculty playing a critically important role in facilitating the transition to non-CITE locations.

Just as teachers are the ultimate implementors, commercial concerns are the ultimate distributors. We have argued previously that incentives, supports, grants, etc., need to be developed in order to provide commercial concerns with that critically important assistance in the volatile educational market.

A National Advisory Board should be set up to oversee and assess the progress made at the various CITEs and by the other participants (individual researchers, commercial concerns). This body would not have a regulatory role. Rather, there is great need in this sort of endeavor for providing alternative perspectives: we all need help seeing the forest for the trees. The Advisory Board will provide valuable feedback to CITEs, to funding agencies, etc., on these institutions' directions and themes.

Option 1 will work only if its funding is continuous. The experts we interviewed repeatedly stressed that the infrastructure of the education science and technology field must be stable in order to attract and keep the key players, and it must be stable in order to provide for orderly transition of graduate students into career paths. While particular CITEs (or individual investigators, commercial concerns, etc.) may go "out of business" the overall level of support for the plan must be stable. While we recognize that minor glitches may arise, significant reduction in funding would be disastrous. During the last decade, support for research in science education virtually disappeared for a few years. Not unreasonably, many of the best people left the field. It is the consensus of the field that we are only now beginning to recover from that instability of funding.

Note that the CITEs will continue to operate at full capacity during Phases 2 and 3. It is not the case that they will solve the problems of education during Phase 1. Education is a dynamic process, and we need to respond to changes in principled ways. Ongoing efforts at the various CITEs (and continued support for individual investigators) will provide American education with the capacity to be both reactive and proactive to our constantly changing world.

Lest this point has gotten lost in the detail: Option 1 is one that was developed on the basis of analyzing comparable work models in other fields, and on the basis of recommendations from a broad range of leading experts in education science and technology. While there will surely be disagreement about particular points of Option 1 from our experts, we feel confident that we have represented their expert opinion fairly.

Finally, what kinds of outcomes can we predict will flow from Option 1? There are essentially two: (1) the field of education science coming into its own as a significant field of study, with rich, powerful theories that deal with real learning and teaching phenomena, and (2) a wide range of principled, technological products that should provide the critically important leverage that is needed to enable American education to meet the challenges of the 21st century.

Option 2: Modest Increase in Federal Spending

While Option 1 called for a 10-year effort, with six Centers for Technology and Education (CITE), plus substantial increase in funding for individual investigators, Option 2 calls for the following: (1) 1-2 CITEs, plus (2) only an increment increase in support of individual investigator research. This level of funding is still substantial by comparison to the current situation. Since the community is currently productive even with limited resources, we see the increment in funding, while modest, will nonetheless result in enhanced productivity. In particular, this increased level of support should definitely result in many more spotlighted projects.

However, the main weakness of this level of support lies precisely in its producing spotlights, and not a coherent, systematic exploration of ideas and technology. The experts we interviewed by and large stated that what is needed are major demonstration projects of significant scope and duration; piecemeal demonstrations — spotlights — are where we are now. One or two CITEs would not be able to undertake many large-scale projects. Moreover, our experts often voiced a concern that support for only a very limited number of such large-scale projects might well be risky: only a limited number of ideas would be explorable, thereby potentially directing the field (and considerable resources) down less productive paths.

Each CITE in this option would still be a robust center: the staffing levels would be at least as high as a CITE proposed in Option 1. In fact, a CITE in this option might well have additional staffing needs. The increase is due to the enhanced role that a CITE would need to play on the national level. Essentially, a CITE would need more resources to engage in dissemination and training.

Option 2 can be viewed as the "go slow" strategy. For example, experts voiced some concern that a significant input of resources, as in Option 1, to education science at this time would raise expectations too high. Delivery on those expectations might not be forthcoming in the short term, and thus a backlash might well result. In turn, funding might be cut off precipitously. Such a boom and bust funding cycle is, as experience has taught us, particularly detrimental to a growing field.

Ultimately, the question that must be answered is this: is Option 2 commensurate with the problem? Will this level of funding make a dent in the serious problems facing American education today — and tomorrow? While Option 2 will most definitely facilitate a growth in education science, that level of development may well be out-paced by the ever changing nature of society and the educational problems that such change engenders.

Option 3: No Increase in Federal Spending

In effect, this option is saying that the current efforts by the Federal government are sufficient to deal with the problems of education. The mechanisms currently in place will provide the ideas and products that will help America cope with its education problem. While the education science community has clearly made progress under the current mechanisms and funding arrangements, the rate of progress does not approach that of the present and arising problems in American education.

Interestingly, the commercial sector is showing increased interest in using education science ideas and technology in developing more effective training programs. Such programs, while costly, may well give companies the competitive edge that is needed. However, the focus will be clearly on training that is relevant to the concerns of the commercial enterprise. Moreover, the concepts and techniques developed in the commercial sector will, not unreasonably, be proprietary; these ideas and technological innovations will not be made widely available. In effect, the gap between learning in the workplace and learning in the school will continue to grow—adding yet more tear to the fabric of our society.

Moreover, as the commercial sector does become more active in this area, invariably there will be a drain of skilled personnel from the educational sector into the commercial sector. With limited numbers of key investigators in the field currently, this would only exacerbate the problem.

Possibly the greatest impact of this option will be felt on the classroom teachers themselves: we have ineffective mechanisms currently for involving teachers in development, exploration, and effective use of new ideas and technology. The CITE model, with 30% of its resources going directly for "in practice" efforts, quite clearly is a mechanism that attempts to remedy a current weakness. Option 3 provides precious few options for teachers.

We desperately need new mechanisms for the production and distribution of effective educationally-oriented technological products. Our current ones simply do not encourage individuals to engage in the resource intense process needed to develop effective technological products. Again, Option 3 does not address this critical need.

In sum, we do not feel that Option 3 is a viable one—if America is serious about its commitment to making positive changes in education.

REFERENCES

1. Ambron, S., & Hooper, K. (1987). *Multimedia in education.* Cupertino, CA: Apple Computer, Inc.

1a. American Association for the Advancement of Science (1984). *Equity and excellence: Compatible goals: An assessment of programs that facilitate increased access and achievement of females and minorities in K-12 mathematics and science education.* AAAS publication 84-14. Office of Opportunities and science. Washington, DC: American Association for the Advancement of Science.

2. Anderson, J. R. (1982). Acquisition of cognitive skill. *Psychological Review, 89,* 396-406.

3. Anderson, J. R. (1985). *Cognitive psychology and its implications.* (2nd ed.). San Francisco: W. H. Freeman.

4. Anderson, J. R., Boyle, C. F., & Reiser, B. J. (1985). Intelligent tutoring systems. *Science, 228,* 456-467.

4a. Anderson, J. R., & Reiser, B. J. (1985). The LISP tutor. *Byte, 10,* 159-178.

5.   Anderson, K. T., & Beeman, W. O. (1986). *An annotated bibliography of research on computers and society*. Providence, RI: Office of Program Analysis, Institute for Research in Information and Scholarship, Brown University.

6.   Anderson, R. C., Osborn, J., & Tierney, R. (Eds.) (1983). *Learning to read in American schools*. Hillsdale, NJ: Erlbaum.

6a.   Anderson, T. (1987). Beyond Einstein: A case study in interactive television. In S. Ambron & K. Hooper (Eds.), *Multimedia in Education* (pp. 209-233). Cupertino, CA: Apple Computer Inc.

7.   Ausubel, D. P. (1968). *Educational psychology: A cognitive view*. New York: Holt, Rinehart and Winston.

8.   Bairstow, J. (1986, October). CD-ROM: Mass storage for the mass market. *High Technology*, 44-51, 69.

9.   Balkovich, E., Lerman, S., & Parmelee, R. P. (1985, November). Computing in higher education: The Athena experience. *Communications of the ACM, 28*, 1214-1224.

10.   Beck, I. L., & Carpenter, P. A. (1986). Cognitive approaches to understanding reading. *American Psychologist, 41*, 1098-1105.

11.   Becker, H. J. (1987, June). *Instructional uses of school computers: Reports from the 1985 National Survey*. Issue No. 4. Center for Social Organization of Schools. Baltimore, MD: John Hopkins University.

12.   Bereiter, C., & Scardamalia, M. (1986). *The psychology of written composition*. Hillsdale, NJ: Erlbaum.

12a.   Berliner, D. (1987). In search of the expert pedagogue. *Educational Researcher*.

12b.   Bloom, B. S. (1984). The 2 sigma problem: The search for methods of group instruction as effective as one-to-one tutoring. *Educational Researcher*, June/July 1984, 4-16.

13.   Bloomberg, D. (Ed.). (1986, May). *Digests of recent research: Intelligent systems laboratory: Mid 1983-mid 1986*. Palo Alto, CA: XEROX Palo Alto Research Centers.

13a.   Bobrow, D. G. (1975). Dimensions of representation. In D. G. Bobrow & A. Collins (ED.), *Representation and understanding: Studies in cognitive science* (pp. 1-34). New York: Academic Press.

14.   Bobrow, D. G. (Ed.). (1985). *Qualitative reasoning about physical systems*. Cambridge, MA: MIT Press.

14a.   Bonar, J., & Soloway, E. (1985). Preprogramming knowledge: A major source of misconceptions in novice programmers. *Human-Computer Interaction, 1*, 133-161.

15.   Boorstin, D. J. (1980). *Greshman's Law: Knowledge or information?* Washington, DC: Library of Congress.

16.   Bork, A., & Weinstock, H. (1987). *Designing computer-based learning material*. New York: Springer-Verlag.

17.   Boyer, E. L. (1983). *High school: A report on secondary education in America*. New York: Harper and Row.

18.   Bransford, J., Hasselbring, T., Barron, B., Kulewicz, S., Littlefield, J., & Goin, L. (1987). Uses of macro-contexts to facilitate mathematical thinking. In R. Charles & E. Silver (Eds.), *Teaching and evaluating mathematical problem solving*. Reston, VA: National Council of Teachers of Mathematics, in press.

19.   Bransford, J., & Hasselbring, T. (1987, June). *Technology can help children who are at risk of school failure*. Paper presented at The Conference on Technology and Students at Risk of School Failure, St. Charles, Illinois, June 28-30, 1987.

20.   Bransford, J., Sherwood, R., & Hasselbring, T. (1987). Effects of the video revolution on development: Some initial thoughts. In G. Forman & P. Pufall (Eds.), *Constructivism in the computer age.* Hillsdale, NJ: Erlbaum, in press.

21.   Briars, D. J., & Larkin, J. H. (1984). An integrated model of skill in solving elementary word problems. *Cognition and Instruction, 1*, 245-296.

22.   Brophy, J. E., & Good, T. L. (1986). Teacher behavior and student achievement. In M. C. Wittrock (Ed.), *Handbook of Research on Teaching*, (3rd Ed.). New York: Macmillan.

23.   Brown, A. L., Bransford, J. D., Ferrara, R. A., & Campione, J. C. (1983). Learning, remembering, and understanding. In J. H. Flavell & E. M. Markman (Eds.). *Handbook of child psychology: vol. 3. Cognitive development* (4th ed., pp. 77-166). New York: Wiley.

24.   Brown, J. S. (1983). Process versus product: A perspective on tools for communal and informal electronic learning. In S. Newman & E. Poor (Eds.), *Education in the electronic age.* New York: Learning Lab, WNET/Thirteen Educational Division.

24a.   Brown, J. S., Burton, R. R., & de Kleer, J. (1982). Pedagogical, natural language and knowledge engineering techniques in SOPHIE I, II, and III. In D. Sleeman & J. S. Brown (Ed.), *Intelligent tutoring systems* (pp. 227-282). New York: Academic Press.

25.   Brown, J. S., & Greeno, J. (1985). (Chairmen). Research briefing panel on information technology in precollege education. In *New pathways in science and technology: Collected research briefings: 1982-1984* (pp. 298-317). New York: Vintage Books.

25a.   Brown, J. S., & VanLehn, K. (1980). Repair theory: A generative theory of bugs in procedural skills. *Cognitive Science, 2.*

26.   Bruce, B. (1986). *Information technologies and written expression.* Centre for Educational Research and Innovation, Technical Report. CERI/NT/86.02. Prepared for the International Conference of National Representatives and Experts, Organization for Economic Co-operation and Development, Paris, October 13-15, 1986.

26a.   Bruner, J. S. (1966). *Toward a theory of instruction.* Cambridge, MA: Harvard University Press.

27.   Bruno, R., & Mizushima, M. (1986, July-August). New developments in optical media: An outline of CD-I. *Optical Information Systems*, 318-323.

28.   Bunderson, C. V. (1987). *Suggested goals and priorities for federal support of research in educational technology.* Unpublished manuscript, Educational Testing Service.

29.   Burton, R. R. (1982). Diagnosing bugs in a simple procedural skill. In D. Sleeman & J. S. Brown (Eds.). *Intelligent tutoring systems* (pp. 157-184). New York: Academic Press.

30.   Burton, R. R., & Brown, J. S. (1982). An investigation of computer coaching for informal learning activities. In D. Sleeman & J. S. Brown (Eds.). *Intelligent tutoring systems* (pp. 79-98). New York: Academic Press.

31.   Canter, M. (1986). The new workstation: CD-ROM authoring systems. In S. Lambert & S. Ropiequer (Eds.). *CD Rom: The new papyrus* (pp. 359-375). Redmond, WA: Microsoft Press.

32.   Carey, S. (1985). *Conceptual change in childhood.* Boston, MA: Bradford Books/The MIT Press.

33.   Carey, S. (1986). Cognitive science and science education. *American Psychologist, 41*, 1123-1130.

34.   Carnegie Forum on Education and the Economy. (1986). *A nation prepared: Teachers for the 21st century.* The Report of the Task Force on Teaching as a Profession. Washington, DC.

35.   Carpenter, T. P. (1985). Learning to add: An exercise in problem solving. In E. Silver (Ed.). *Teaching and learning mathematical problem solving: Multiple research perspectives.* Hillsdale, NJ: Lawrence Erlbaum Associates.

36.   Carpenter, T. P., Linquist, M. M., Matthews, W., & Silver, E. A. (1984). Achievement in mathematics: Results from the national assessment. *Elementary School Journal, 84*, 485-495.

37.   Carraher, T. N., Carraher, D. W., & Schliemann, A. D. (1985). Mathematics in the streets and in schools. *British Journal of Development Psychology, 3*, 21-29.

38.   Case, R. (1985). *Intellectual development: Birth to adulthood.* New York: Academic Press.

38a.   Chaiklin, S., & Roth, C. (Eds.) (in preparation). *Physics knowledge and instruction.* (Papers presented at the 1986 NSF Bank Street College Conference on Novice Physics Problem Solving and Education).

39.   Champagne, A. B., Klopfer, L. E., & Gunstone, R. F. (1982). Cognitive research and the design of science instruction. *Educational Psychologist, 17*, 31-53.

40.   Champagne, A. B., Klopfer, L. E., & Gunstone, R. F. (1985). Instructional consequences of students' knowledge about physical phenomena. In A. L. Pines and L. H. T. West (Eds.), *Cognitive structure and conceptual change.* New York: Academic Press.

41.   Chi, M. T. H., Feltovich, P. J., & Glaser, R. (1981). Categorization and representation of physics problems by experts and novices. *Cognitive Science, 5*, 87-119.

42.   Chipman, S., & Butler, P. A. (1985, July 5). *Gazing into the silicon chip: The impact of microcomputers on teaching and learning.* Learning Technology Center Technical Report #85.2.3, Peabody College of Vanderbilt University, Nashville, TN.

43.   Chipman, S. F., and Thomas, V. G. (1984). *The Participation of women and minorities in mathematical, scientific, and technical fields.* Paper prepared for the Committee on Research in Mathematics, Science, and Technology Education, Commission on Behavioral and Social Sciences and Education, National Research Council, Washington, DC.

44.   Chipman, S. F., Segal, J. W., & Glaser, R. (Eds.). (1985). *Thinking and learning skills: Current research and open questions. (Vol. 2).* Hillsdale, NJ: Erlbaum.

45.   Chubin, D. E. (1986). Interdisciplinary integration within technology assessments. In Daryl E. Chubin, Alan L. Porter, Frederick A. Rossini, & Terry Connelly (Eds.), *Interdisciplinary analysis and research: Theory and practice of problem-focused research and development: Selected readings.* Mt. Airy, MD: Lomond Publications, Inc.

46.   Clancey, W. J. (1983). The epistemology of a rule-based expert system: A framework for explanation. *Artificial Intelligence, 20*, 215-252.

47.   Clancey, W. J. (in press). *Qualitative student models. Annual review of computer science.* Palo Alto: Annual Reviews, Inc.

48.   Clement, J. (1982). Students' preconceptions in introductory mechanics. *American Journal of Physics, 50*, 66-71.

49.   Cole, J. Y. (Ed.). (1987). *Books in our future: Perspectives and proposals.* Washington, DC: Library of Congress.

50.   Cole, M., & Griffin, P. (1987). Contextual factors in education: Improving science and mathematics education for minorities and women. Prepared for the Committee on Research in Mathematics, Science, and Technology Education, Commission on Behavioral and Social Sciences and Education, National Research Council. Madison, WI: Wisconsin Center for Education Research.

51.   Collins, A. M., & Brown, J. S. (in press, a). The computer as a tool for learning through reflection. In H. Mandl & A. Lesgold (Eds.), *Learning issues for intelligent tutoring systems.* New York: Springer.

52.   Collins, A. M., & Brown, J. S. (in press, b). The new apprenticeship: Teaching students the craft of reading, writing, and mathematics. In L. B. Resnick (Ed.), *Cognition and instruction: Issues and agendas.* Hillsdale, NJ: Erlbaum.

53.   Collins, A. M. (1985). Teaching, reading, and writing with personal computers. In J. Orasanu, (Ed.), *A decade of reading research: Implications for practice.* Hillsdale, NJ: Erlbaum.

54.   Committee on Basic Research in the Behavioral and Social Sciences. (1987). *Ten-year outlook on research opportunities in the behavioral and social sciences.* Final report of the committee, Commission on Behavioral and Social Sciences and Education. Washington, DC: National Academy Press.

55.   Conference Board of the Mathematical Sciences. (1983). *The mathematical sciences curriculum K-12: What is still fundamental and what is not.* In The National Science Board Commission on Precollege Education in Mathematics, Science and Technology, *Educating Americans for the 21st century* (Source Materials: pp. 1-23). Washington, DC: National Science Foundation.

56.   Conklin, J. (1987). A survey of hypertext. *IEEE Computer*, in press.

57.   Crosswhite, F. J., Dossey, J. A., Swafford, J. O., McKnight, C. C., & Cooney, T. J. (1985). *Second international mathematics study summary report for the United States.* Champaign, Ill.: Stripes Publishing Company.

58.   Driver, R., Guesne, E., & Tiberghien, A. (Eds.). (1985). *Children's ideas in science.* Philadelphia: Open University Press.

58a. de Beaugrande, R. (1984). *Text production: Toward a science of composition.* Norwood, NJ: Ablex.

59.   deKleer, J. (1985). How circuits work. In D. G. Bobrow (Ed.), *Qualitative reasoning about physical systems.* Cambridge, MA: MIT Press.

60.   diSessa, A. A. (1982). Unlearning Aristotelian physics: A study of knowledge-based learning. *Cognitive Science, 6*, 37-75.

61.   diSessa, A. A. (1983). Phenomenology and the evolution of intuition. In D. Gentner & A. Stevens (Eds.), *Mental models* (pp. 15-33). Hillsdale, NJ: Erlbaum.

62.   diSessa, A. A. (1984, September). *The third revolution in computers and education.* Prepared for the Committee on Research in Mathematics, Science, and Technology Education, Commission on Behavioral and Social Sciences and Education, National Research Council.

62a. diSessa, A. A. (1985). *Knowledge in pieces.* Address presented to the Piaget Society Symposium on "Constructivism in the Computer Age," Philadelphia, PA.

63.   diSessa, A. A., & Abelson, H. (1986). BOXER: A reconstructable computational medium. *Communications of the ACM, 29* (9), 859-868.

63a. Dweck, C. (1986). Motivational processes affecting learning. *American Psychologist, 41*, 1040-1048.

64.   Education Commission of the States (1983). *A 50-state survey of initiatives in science, mathematics and computer education.* No. sm-83-1. Denver, CO: Education Commission of the States.

65.   Education Turnkey Systems, Inc. (1985). *Uses of Computers in Education.* Washington, DC: National Commission for Employment Policy.

65a. Educational Technology Center. (1987). *Teaching for understanding in the age of technology: A position paper from the Educational Technology Center, Harvard Graduate School of Education.* Cambridge, MA: Harvard University.

66.   Estes, W. K., Shiffrin, R. M., Simon, H. A., & Smith, E. E. (1982). The science of cognition. In National Research Council, *Outlook for science and technology: The next five years.* San Francisco: W. H. Freeman.

67.   Feuerstein, R., Rand, Y., Hoffman, M. B., & Miller, R. (1980). *Instrumental enrichment.* Baltimore, MD: University Park Press.

68.   Fey, J. T. (1982). Mathematics education. In H. E. Mitzel (Ed.), *Encyclopedia of educational research.* (5th ed.), Vol. 3, pp. 1166-1182. New York: Free Press.

68a. Fleming, M. L. (1979). On pictures in educational research. *Instructional Science, 8*, 235-251.

69.   Forbus, K. D. (1985). Qualitative process theory. In D. G. Bobrow (Ed.), *Qualitative reasoning about physical systems*. Cambridge, MA: MIT Press.

70.   Frase, L. T. (1987). Technology, reading, and writing. In J. R. Squire (Ed.), *The dynamics of language learning* (pp. 294-308). Urbana, IL: National Conference on Research in English, ERIC Clearinghouse on Reading and Communication Skills.

70a.   Frederiksen, J. R., Warren, B. M., & Rosebery, A. S. (1985a). A componential approach to training reading skills: Part 1. Perceptual units training. *Cognition and Instruction, 2*, 91-130.

70b.   Frederiksen, J. R., Warren, B. M., & Rosebery, A. S. (1985b). A componential approach to training reading skills: Part 2. Decoding and use of context. *Cognition and Instruction, 3/4*, 271-338.

71.   Frederiksen, N. (1984). The real test bias: influences of testing on teaching and learning. *American Psychologist, 39* (3), 193-202.

71a.   Frye, D., & Soloway, E. (1987). Interfaces to educational software: A neglected topic. *Proceedings of the Computer-Human Interaction Conference '87*. Toronto, Canada.

72.   Gagne, R. M. (1985). *The conditions of learning and the theory of instruction* (4th ed.). New York: Holt, Rinehart & Winston.

73.   Gardner, H. (1985). *The mind's new science: A history of the cognitive revolution*. New York: Basic Books, Inc.

74.   Gelman, R., & Brown, A. L. (1986). Changing views of cognitive competence in the young. In N. J. Smelser & D. R. Gerstein (Eds.), *Behavioral and social science: Fifty years of discovery* (pp. 175-207). Washington, DC: National Academy Press.

75.   Gelman, R., & Gallistel, C. R. (1978). *The child's understanding of number*. Cambridge, MA: Harvard University Press.

75a.   Gick, M. L., & Holyoak, K. J. (in press). The cognitive basis of knowledge transfer. In S. M. Cormier & J. D. Hagman (Eds.), *Transfer of learning: Contemporary research and applications*. Orlando, FL: Academic Press.

76.   Glaser, R. (1984). Education and thinking: The role of knowledge. *American Psychologist, 39* (2), 93-104.

77.   Glaser, R. (1987). *The nation's report card: Improving the assessment of student achievement*. Cambridge, MA: National Academy of Education, Harvard Graduate School of Education, 1987.

78.   Good, T. L., & Marshall, S. (1984). Do students learn more in heterogeneous or homogeneous groups? In P. L. Peterson, L. C. Wilkinson, and M. Hallinan (Eds.), *The social context of instruction* (pp. 15-38). London: Academic Press.

79.   Goodlad, John I. (1984). *A place called school*. New York: McGraw-Hill.

80.   Greeno, J. G. (1980). Psychology of learning, 1960-1980: One participant's observations. *American Psychologist, 35* (8), 713-728.

81.   Greeno, J. G. (1983). Research on cognition and behavior relevant to education in mathematics, science, and technology. In *Educating Americans for the 21st century, volume 2*. Washington, DC: The National Science Board Commission on Precollege Education in Mathematics, Science, and Technology.

82.   Greeno, J. (1985, April). *Advancing cognitive science through development of advanced instructional systems*. Paper presented at the American Educational Research Association Meetings, Chicago, Illinois.

83.   Greeno, J. G., Brown, J. S., Foss, C., Shalin, V., Bee, N. V., Lewis, M. W., & Vitolo, T. M. (1987, in press). Cognitive principles of problem solving and instruction. *Machine Mediated Learning*.

84.   Greeno, J. G., & Simon, H. A. (1986). Problem solving and reasoning. In R. C. Atkinson, R. Herrnstein, G. Lindzey, and R. D. Luce (Eds.), *Stevens' handbook of experimental psychology* (revised ed.). New York: John Wiley & Sons.

85.   Halacz, F. G., Moran, T. P., & Trigg, R. H. (1987, April). Notecards in a nutshell. *Proceedings of the ACM CHI & GI '87 Conference*, Toronto, Canada.

86.   Hamburg, D. A. (1984, June). Science and technology in a world transformed. *Science*, 943-946.

86a.   Halff, H. M., Hollan, J. D., & Hutchins, E. L. (1986). Cognitive science and military training. *American Psychologist, 41*, 1131-1139.

87.   Handscombe, R. D. (1983). University-based technology transfer. In S. R. Epton, R. L. Payne, and A. W. Pearson, (Eds.), *Managing interdisciplinary research*. Chichester, Great Britain: John Wiley & Sons.

88.   Harms, N. C., & Yager, R. E., (Eds.). (1981). *What research says to the science teacher*. Washington, DC: National Science Teachers Association.

89.   Hawkins, J., & Pea, R. D. (1987). Tools for bridging the cultures of everyday and scientific thinking. *Journal for Research in Science Teaching, 24*, 291-307.

89a.   Hegarty, M., & Just, M. A. (in press). Understanding machines from text and diagrams. In H. Mandl & J. R. Levin (Eds.), *Knowledge acquisition from text and pictures*. Elsevier Science Publisher B.V.: North Holland.

90.   Hiltz, S. R., & Turoff, M. (1985). Structuring computer-mediated communication systems to avoid information overload. *Communications of the ACM, 28*, 680-689.

91.   Hirsch, E. D., Jr. (1987). *Cultural literacy*. New York: Houghton-Mifflin.

92.   Holdzom, D., Lutz, P. B. (1984). *Research within reach: Science education*. Washington, DC: National Institute of Education.

93.   Holmes Group. (1986). *Tomorrow's teachers*. East Lansing, MI: Michigan State University.

93a.   Hooper, K. (1979). *Intelligent pictures*. Paper presented at the Wellesley College, Luce Foundation Series on Language and Cognition.

94.   Hutchins, E., Hollan, E., & Norman, D. A. (1986). Direct manipulation interfaces. In D. A. Norman & S. Draper (Eds.), *User-centered system design*. Hillsdale, NJ: Erlbaum.

95.   Institute for Research on Learning. (1987, March). *A view of the Institute for Research on Learning*. Palo Alto, CA.

95a.   Jackson, P. (1986). *Introduction to expert systems*. Reading, MA: Addison-Wesley.

95b.   Johnson, W. L., & Soloway, E. (1985). Automatic bug detection. *Byte Magazine*, April.

96.   Just, M. (1987). *Psychology of reading and language comprehension*. Boston: Allyn & Bacon.

97.   Kaput, J., Luke, C., Poholsky, J., & Sayer, A. (1986, September). *The role of representations in reasoning with intensive quantities*. Technical Report 86-9, Harvard University, Educational Technology Center.

98.   Kay, A. C. (1983). New directions for novice programming in the 1980's. In P. J. L. Wallis (Ed.), *Programming technology* (Vol. 2, pp. 209-247). Elmsford, NY: Pergamon Infotech.

99.   Kiesler, S. B., & Turner, C. F., (Eds.). (1977). *Fundamental research and the process of education*. Committee on Fundamental Research Relevant to Education, National Research Council. Washington, DC: National Academy of Sciences.

99a.   Kiesler, S. B., & Sproull, L. (1987). *The computer and change on the campus*. Cambridge: Cambridge University Press.

100.   Kintsch, W., & Greeno, J. G. (1985). Understanding and solving word arithmetic problems. *Psychological Review, 92*, 109-129.

100a.   Kirsch, I., & Jungeblut, A. (1986). *Literacy: Profiles of America's young adults: Final report*. Report No. 16-PL-02. Princeton, NJ: Educational Testing Service.

101. Kling, R. (1987, in press). Defining the boundaries of computing across complex organizations. To appear in R. Boland & R. Hirschheim (Eds.), *Critical issues and information systems research.* John Wiley and Sons.

101a. Kurland, D. M., & Pea, R. D. (1985). Children's mental models of recursive Logo programs. *Journal of Educational Computing Research, 1* (2), 235-243.

102. Laboratory of Comparative Human Cognition. (1983). Culture and cognitive development. In W. Kessen (Ed.), *Mussen's handbook of child psychology* (4th ed.), (Vol. 1, pp. 295-356). New York: Wiley.

103. Laird, J. E., Newell, A., & Rosenbloom, P. S. (1987, January). *Soar: An architecture for general intelligence.* Cognitive Science and Machine Intelligence Laboratory, Technical Report No. 2. Ann Arbor, MI: University of Michigan. (To appear in *Artificial Intelligence.*)

104. Lambert, S., & Ropiequet, S. (1986). *CD-ROM: The new papyrus.* Richmond, WA: Microsoft Press.

105. Landauer, T. K. (1987). Education in a world of omnipotent and omniscient technology. To appear in R. Nickerson & P. Zodhiates (Eds.), *Education in 2020: Roles for technology.* Hillsdale, NJ: Erlbaum.

106. Larkin, J. H. (1982). The cognition of learning physics. *American Journal of Physics, 49,* 534-541.

107. Larkin, J. H., McDermott, J., Simon, D. P., & Simon, H. A. (1980). Expert and novice performance in solving physics problems. *Science, 208,* 1335-1342.

107a. Larkin, J. H., & Simon, H. A. (1987). Why a diagram is (sometimes) worth ten thousand words. *Cognitive Science, 11,* 65-99.

108. Lave, J. (1987). *Cognition in practice.* New York: Cambridge University Press.

109. Lawler, R., & Yazdani, M. (Eds.). (1987). *Artificial intelligence and education.* Norwood, NJ: Ablex.

109a. Leinhardt, G. (1983). Novice and expert knowledge of individual students' achievements. *Educational Psychologist, 18* (3), 165-179.

110. Lepper, M. R. (1985). Microcomputers in education: Motivational and social issues. *American Psychologist, 40,* 1-18.

111. Lepper, M. R., & Malone, T. W. (1985). Intrinsic motivation and instructional effectiveness in computer-based education. In R. E. Snow & M. C. Farr (Eds.), *Aptitude, learning and instruction: III. Cognitive and affective process analyses.* Hillsdale, NJ: Erlbaum.

112. Lesgold, A. M. (1986). *Chairman's report.* Prepared for the International Conference of National Representatives and Experts, Organization for Economic Co-operation and Development, Centre for Educational Research and Innovation, Paris, October 13-15, 1986.

113. Lesgold, A. M., & Reif, F. (1983, June). *Computers in education: Realizing the potential (Chairmen's report of a research conference, Pittsburgh, PA, November 20-24, 1982).* Washington, DC: U.S. Department of Education Office of Educational Research and Improvement.

114. Levin, J. A., Riel, M. M., Rowe, R. D., & Boruta, M. J. (1985). Muktuk meets jacuzzi: Computer networks and elementary school writers. In S. W. Freedman (Ed.), *The acquisition of written language: Revision and response.* Hillsdale, NJ: Erlbaum.

115. Lightfoot, S. L. (1983). *The good high school.* New York: Basic Books.

116. Linn, M. (1986, August). *Teaching in the information age—education and the challenge of technology: Proceedings of a conference on technology and teacher education, August 5-8, 1986, Monterey, California.* Cupertino, CA: Apple Computer, Inc.

116a. Linn, M. C. (1986, May). *Establishing a research base for science education: Challenges, trends, and recommendations (Report of a national conference, funded by the National Science Foundation, held January 16-19, 1986).* Lawrence Hall of Science and the Graduate School of Education, University of California, Berkeley.

117.   Lippman, A. (1981). *Movie manuals: Personalized cinema as an instructional partner.* Media Technology Group, Massachusetts Institute of Technology.

117a.   Littman, D., Pinto, J., & Soloway, E. (1986). An analysis of tutorial reasoning about programming bugs. *Proceedings of National Conference on Artificial Intelligence.* Philadelphia.

117b.   Littman, D., & Soloway, E. (1987). Evaluating intelligent tutoring systems: The cognitive science perspective. In J. Jeff Richardson & M. Polson (Eds.), *Intelligent tutoring systems.* Hillsdale, NJ: Erlbaum.

118.   Learning Research and Development Center. (1987, May). *Research in intelligent CAI at the Learning Research and Development Center of the University of Pittsburgh.* Pittsburgh, PA.

119.   Malone, T. W., Grant, K. R., Turbak, F. A., Brobst, S. A., & Cohen, M. D. (1987). Intelligent information sharing systems. *Communications of the ACM*, in press.

119a.   Mandl, H., & Levin, J. R. (Eds.). (in press). *Knowledge acquisition from text and pictures.* Elsevier Science Publisher B.V.: North Holland.

120.   March, J. G. (Chair). (1985). *Mathematics, science, and technology education: A research agenda.* Committee on Research in Mathematics, Science, and Technology Education, Commission on Behavioral and Social Sciences and Education, National Research Council. Washington, DC: National Academy Press.

121.   March, J. G. (Chair). (1987). *Interdisciplinary research in mathematics, science, and technology education.* Committee on Research in Mathematics, Science, and Technology Education, Commission on Behavioral and Social Sciences and Education, National Research Council. Washington, DC: National Academy Press.

122.   McCloskey, M., Caramazza, A., & Green, B. (1980). Curvilinear motion in the absence of external forces: Naive beliefs about the motion of objects. *Science, 210*, 1139-1141.

122a.   McConkie, G. W., Zola, D., & Winograd, P. (in press). Computer aided reading for adult illiterates. In M. Pennington (Ed.), *Teaching English with computers: First and second language perspectives.*

123.   McDermott, L. C. (1984). Research on conceptual understanding in mechanics. *Physics Today, 37*, 24-32.

124.   Mehan, H. (1979). *Learning lessons.* Cambridge, MA: Harvard University Press.

125.   Meichenbaum, D. (1977). *Cognitive behavior modification: An integrated approach.* New York: Plenum.

126.   Melmed, A. (1987, May). *A new educational technology: Need and opportunity.* Paper presented at Lugano, Switzerland Conference on Computer-Assisted Approaches to Training, sponsored by the Gottlieb-Duttweiler Institute, Zurich, Switzerland in collaboration with New York University. Proceedings to be published by North-Holland Press.

127.   Meyers, L. F. (1984). Unique contributions of microcomputers to language intervention with handicapped children. *Seminars in Speech and Language, 5.*

127a.   Mikulecky, L. (1982). Job literacy: The relationship between school preparation and workplace actuality. *Reading Research Quarterly, 17*, 400-419.

127b.   Miller, G. A., & Gildea, P. M. (1987, September). How children learn words. *Scientific American, 257* (3), 94-99.

128.   Minstrell, J. (1982). Conceptual Development Research in the Natural Setting of the Classroom. In M. B. Rowe (Ed.), *Education in the 80's — science.* Washington, DC: National Education Association.

129.   Morris, J. H., et al. (1986, March). Andrew: A distributed personal computing environment. *Communications of the ACM, 29* (3), 184-201.

129b.   National Assessment of Educational Progress. (1986). *The reading report card: Trends in reading over four national assessments 1971-1984.* Princeton, NJ: Educational Testing Service.

130.   National Commission on Excellence in Education. (1983). *A nation at risk: The imperative for educational reform.* Washington, DC: U.S. Government Printing Office.

131.   National Council of Teachers of Mathematics. (1980). *An agenda for action: Recommendations for school mathematics in the 1980's.* Reston, VA: National Council of Teachers of Mathematics.

131a.   National Science Board Commission on Precollege Education in Mathematics, Science and Technology. (1983). *Educating Americans for the 21st century: A plan of action for improving mathematics, science, and technology education for all American elementary and secondary students so that their achievement is the best in the world by 1995.* Washington, DC: National Science Foundation.

132.   Negroponte, N. (1987). *MIT Media Laboratory.* Annual Report of Activities (Videodisc).

133.   Neisser, U. (Ed.). (1987). *School achievement of minority children: New perspectives.* Hillsdale, NJ: Lawrence Erlbaum Associates.

133a.   Newman, D., Goldman, S., Brienne, D., & Jackson, I. (1987). *Earth lab: Progress report, May 1, 1986 to December 31, 1986.* Technical Report. Center for Children and Technology. New York: Bank Street College of Education.

134.   Nickerson, R. S. (1985, Summer). Adult literacy and technology. *Visible Language, 19* (3), 311-355.

134a.   Nickerson, R. S. (1985). Understanding understanding. *American Journal of Education*, vol. 93, pp. 201-239.

135.   Nickerson, R. S. (1986b, October). *Technology in education in 2020: Thinking about the not-distant future.* Background paper for Harvard Educational Technology Center Panel on Technology in Education in 2020, Vermont.

136.   Nickerson, R. S. (1986c). *Using computers: The human factors of information systems.* Cambridge, MA: MIT Press.

137.   Nickerson, R. S. (1986a, May 2). *Preliminary notes re: Psychological research priorities.* Prepared for American Psychological Association Ad Hoc Planning Group on Scientific Developments, chaired by Lew Lipsitt.

138.   Nielsen, J. (1987). Computer-supported cooperative work: Trip report from the conference in Austin, December 3-5, 1986. *SIGCHI Bulletin, 19* (1), 54-61.

139.   Norcio, A. F., & O'Hare, J. J. (Eds.). (1987, April 24). *Report on the Workshop on Research and Development in Naval Human-Computer Interactive Systems.* NRL Memorandum Report 5971. Washington, DC: Naval Research Laboratory.

140.   Novak, J. D., & Gowen, D. B. (1984). *Learning how to learn.* Cambridge: Cambridge University Press.

141.   Ong, W. J. (1982). *Orality and literacy: Technologizing the word.* New York: Methuen.

142.   Osborne, R., & Freyberg, P. (1985). *Learning in science.* Auckland, Australia: Heineman Publishers.

143.   Palincsar, A., & Brown, A. L. (1984). Reciprocal teaching of comprehension-fostering and comprehension-monitoring activities. *Cognition and Instruction, 1*, 117-176.

144.   Papert, S. (1980). *Mindstorms: Computers, children, and powerful ideas.* New York: Basic Books.

144a.   Park, R. (1984). Improving basic skills in the workplace. *Training and Development Journal*, 76-80.

144b.   Paivio, A. (1971). *Imagery and verbal processes.* New York: Holt, Rinehart & Winston.

145.   Pea, R. D. (1985). Beyond amplification: Using the computer to reorganize human mental functioning. *Educational Psychologist, 20*, 167-182.

146.   Pea, R. D. (1987, April). *Human-machine symbiosis: Cognitive and cultural implications of hypermedia.* Paper presented at an international conference on Computers, Cognition, and Epistemology, University of Aarhus, Denmark (to appear).

147.   Pea, R. D. (1987, in press). Socializing the knowledge transfer problem. *International Journal of Education Research.*

147a.   Pea, R. D., Cohen, J., Brunner, C., Mellen, N., & Webster, K. (1987). *IDEA: Tools for learning systematic decision analysis.* Paper presented at the Annual Meeting of the American Educational Research Association, Washington, DC.

148.   Pea, R. D., & Kurland, D. M. (1987). Cognitive technologies for writing. *Review of Research in Education, 14.*

148a.   Pea, R. D., Soloway, E., & Spohrer, J. C. (1987). The buggy path to the development of programming expertise. *Focus on Learning Problems in Mathematics, 9* (1), 5-30.

148aa.   Peterson, P. L., Wilkinson, L. C., & Hallinan, M. (Eds.). (1984). *The social context of instruction.* Orlando, FL: Academic Press.

148ab.   Pettito, A. L. (1985). Division of labor: Procedural learning in teacher-led small groups. *Cognition and Instruction, 2,* 233-270.

148b.   Piaget, J., & Inhelder, B. (1969). *The psychology of the child.* London: Routledge & Kegan Paul.

148c.   Ravitch, D., & Finn, C. E., Jr. (1987). *What do our 17-year-olds know? A report on the first national assessment of history and literature.* New York: Harper & Row.

149.   Reif, F. (1985). Acquiring an effective understanding of scientific concepts. In L. H. T. West & A. L. Pines (Eds.), *Cognitive structure and conceptual change.* New York: Academic Press.

150.   Reif, F. (1987). Interpretation of scientific or mathematical concepts: Cognitive issues and instructional implications. *Cognitive Science,* to appear.

150a.   Resnick, D. P., & Resnick, L. B. (1977). The nature of literacy: An historical exploration. *Harvard Educational Review, 47* (3), 370-385.

151.   Resnick, L. B. (1983). Mathematics and science learning: A new conception. *Science, 220,* 477-478.

152.   Resnick, L. B. (1984). Toward a cognitive theory of instruction. In S. G. Paris, G. M. Olson, & H. W. Stevenson (Eds.), *Learning and motivation in the classroom.* Hillsdale, NJ: Lawrence Erlbaum Associates.

153.   Resnick, L. B. (1987). *Education and learning to think: Subcommittee report.* Paper prepared for the Committee on Research in Mathematics, Science, and Technology Education, Commission on Behavioral and Social Sciences and Education, National Research Council, Washington, DC.

154.   Resnick, L. B. (in press). Understanding algebra. In J. Sloboda & D. Rogers (Eds.), *Cognitive processes in mathematics.* University of Keele, England: Oxford University Press.

154a.   Resnick, L. B., & Johnson, A. (1987, July). *Intelligent machines for intelligent people: Cognitive theory and the future of computer assisted learning.* Unpublished manuscript. Learning Research and Development Center, University of Pittsburgh.

155.   Resnick, L. B., & Omanson, S. F. (1987). Learning to understanding arithmetic. In R. Glaser (Ed.), *Advances in instructional psychology* (Vol. 3, pp. 41-95). Hillsdale, NJ: Erlbaum.

156.   Rogoff, B., & Lave, J. (Eds.). (1984). *Everyday cognition: Its development in social context.* Cambridge, MA: Harvard University Press.

157.   Romberg, T. A., & Carpenter, T. P. (1985). Research on teaching and learning mathematics: Two disciplines of scientific inquiry. In M. C. Wittrock (Ed.), *Handbook of research on teaching* (3rd Ed.). New York: Macmillan.

158. Rosebery, A. S. (Ed.). (1986). *Research digest: Cognitive and instructional sciences.* Cambridge, MA: Bolt Beranek and Newman Laboratories.

159. Rosegrant, T. J. (1984). Fostering progress in literacy development: Technology and social interaction. *Seminars in Speech and Language, 5*, 47-57.

159a. Rothkopf, E. Z. (1987, July). *Putting educational technology to work: Solutions for unglamorous problems.* Unpublished manuscript. New York: Teachers College, Columbia University.

160. Rothman, R. (1987, August 7). "Summit meeting" of leading English teachers calls for reforms in instruction at all levels. *Education Week, 6* (39), Extra Edition, 1, 29.

161. Rowe, M. B. (1983). Science education: A framework for decision-makers. *Journal of the American Academy of Arts and Sciences, 112.*

162. Rubin, A. D., & Bruce, B. C. (1986). Learning with Quill: Lessons for students, teachers and software designers. In T. E. Raphael (Ed.). *Contexts of school basic literacy* (pp. 217-230). New York: Random House.

163. Rumelhart, D. E., & Norman, D. A. (1981). Analogical processes in learning. In J. R. Anderson (Ed.), *Cognitive skills and their acquisition.* Hillsdale, NJ: Erlbaum.

164. Russell, S. J. (1987, Winter). Math in the real world: Used Numbers project explores practical skills. *Hands On! 10* (1), 8, 21.

164a. Sack, W., Littman, D., Spohrer, J., Soloway, E. (1986). Evaluating the performance of PROUST in the classroom. Yale University, Department of Computer Science, Technical Report. New Haven, CT.

165. Schank, R. C. (1986). *Explanation patterns: Understanding mechanically and creatively.* Hillsdale, NJ: Erlbaum.

166. Schank, R. C., & Slade, S. (1985, October). *Education and computers: An AI perspective.* Yale University, Department of Computer Science, YALEU/CSD/RR #431. New Haven, CT.

167. Schatz, B. R. (1986, September). *Telesophy: A system for browsing and sharing inside a large information space.* TM-ARH-006-094. Morristown, NJ: Bell Communications Research.

167a. Schwartz, J. (1987). Dreamworlds. *Daedulus.*

168. Schoenfeld, A. (1985). *Mathematical problem solving.* New York: Academic Press.

169. Scribner, S. (1985). Knowledge at work. *Anthropology and Education Quarterly, 16*, 199-206.

170. Segal, J., Chipman, S., & Glaser, R. (Eds.). (1985). *Thinking and learning skills: Relating instruction to basic research: Vol. 1.* Hillsdale, NJ: Erlbaum.

171. Sheil, B. A. (1981). *Coping with complexity.* (CIS-15). Palo Alto, CA: Xerox PARC.

172. Shymansky, J. A., Kyle, W. C., Jr., & Alport, J. M. (1983). The effects of new science curricula on student performance. *Journal of Research in Science Teaching, 20* (5), 387-404.

172a. Simon, H. A. (1981). *The sciences of the artificial,* 2nd ed. Cambridge, MA: MIT Press.

173. Sirotnik, K. A. (1981). *What you see is what you get: A Summary of observations in over 1000 Elementary and secondary classrooms.* A Study of Schooling. Technical Report No. 29. University of California, Graduate School of Education, Laboratory in School and Community Education, Los Angeles.

174. Sizer, T. (1984). *Horace's compromise: The dilemma of the American high school.* New York: Houghton Mifflin.

175. Sleeman, D., & Brown, J. S. (Eds.). (1982). *Intelligent tutoring systems.* New York: Academic Press.

176. Smith, D. C., Irby, C., Kimball, R., & Verplank, B. (1982, April). Designing the Star user interface. *Byte.*

176a.   Snow, R. E. (1986). Individual differences and the design of educational programs. *American Psychologist, 41*, 1029-1039.

176b.   Snow, R. E., Frederico, P., & Montague, W. E. (Eds.). (1980). *Cognitive process analysis of aptitude.* Hillsdale, NJ: Erlbaum.

177.   Soloway, E. (1985). From problems to programs via plans: The content and structure of knowledge for introductory LISP programming. *Journal of Educational Computing Research, 1*, 157-172.

177a.   Soloway, E. (1986). Learning to program = Learning to construct mechanisms and explanations. *Communications of the ACM, 29* (9), 850-858.

177b.   Spohrer, J. C., & Soloway, E. (1986). Novice mistakes: Are the folk wisdoms correct? *Communications of the ACM, 29* (7), 624-632.

178.   Stage, E., Kreinberg, N., Eccles (Parsons), J., & Becker, J. (1985). Increasing the participation and achievement of girls and women in mathematics, science and engineering. In S. S. Klein (Ed.), *Handbook for achieving sex equality through education.* Baltimore, MD: John Hopkins University Press.

179.   Stake, R. E., & Easley, J. A., Jr. (1978). *Case studies in science education.* NSF Se-78-74. Available from the U.S. Government Printing Office, Washington, DC, National Science Foundation.

180.   Steen, L. A. (1987). Mathematics education: A predictor of scientific ompetitiveness. *Science, 237*, 251-252, 302.

181.   Stefik, M., Foster, G., Bobrow, D. G., Kahn, K. M., Lanning, S., & Suchman, L. A. (1987). Beyond the chalkboard: Using computers to support collaboration and problem solving in meetings. *Communications of the ACM, 30* (1).

182.   Sternberg, R. S. (1983). Criteria for intellectual skills training. *Educational Researcher, 12*, 6-12, 26.

183.   Sternberg, R. J. (Ed.). (1984). *Mechanisms of cognitive development.* New York: W. H. Freeman & Co.

184.   Sternberg, R. S. (1984). Toward a triarchic theory of human intelligence. *The Behavioral and Brain Sciences, 7*, 269-315.

185.   Stevens, A., and Roberts, B. (1983). Quantitative and qualitative simulation in computer-based training. *Journal of Computer-Based Instruction, 10*, 16-19.

185a.   Sticht, T. G. (1987). *Functional context education: Workshop resource handbook.* San Diego, CA: The Applied Behavioral and Cognitive Sciences, Inc.

185b.   Sticht, T., & Mikulecky, L. (1984). *Job-related skills: Cases and conclusions.* Information Series No. 285. Columbus, OH: The Ohio State University, ERIC Clearinghouse on Adult, Career, and Vocational Education.

186.   Talmis. (1986, May). *The future of computers in education: A district-level view.* Talmis #1956. New York: Talmis (215 Park Avenue South, NY, NY 10003).

187.   Task Force for the Study of Chemistry Education in the United States. (1984). *Tomorrow.* Washington, DC: American Chemical Society.

188.   Thurow, L. C. (1987, May). A surge in inequality. *Scientific American, 256* (5), 30-37.

189.   Tinker, R. (1987, Winter). Network science arrives: National Geographic-coordinated school experiment generates student-scientists. *Hands On!, 10* (1), 1, 10-11.

190.   Tinker, R. (1987, Winter). Turning math curricula upside down: Applying math models in tenth grade. *Hands On!, 10* (1), 9.

191.   Trachtman, P. (1984, February). Putting computers into the hands of children without language. *Smithsonian*, 42-51.

192. Trigg, R. H., & Weiser, M. (1986). TEXTNET: A network-based approach to text handling. *ACM Transactions on Office Information Systems, 4* (1), 1-23.

192a. VanLehn, K. (1983). On the representation of procedures in repair theory. In H. P. Ginsburg (Ed.), *The development of mathematical thinking*. New York: Academic Press.

193. Viennot L. (1979). Spontaneous reasoning in elementary dynamics. *European Journal of Science Education, 1*, 205-221.

193a. Voss, J. F., Greene, T. R., Post, T. A., & Penner, B. C. (1983). Problem-solving skill in the social sciences. In G. H. Bower (Ed.), *The psychology of learning and motivation: Advances in research and theory*. (Vol. 17, pp. 165-213). New York: Academic Press.

194. West, L., & Pines, A. L. (Eds.). (1985). *Cognitive structure and conceptual change*. Orlando, FL: Academic Press.

195. Weyer, S. A., & Borning, A. H. (1985). A prototype electronic encyclopedia. *ACM Transactions on Office Information Systems, 3* (1), 63-88.

196. White, B. Y., & Frederiksen, J. R. (1985, July). QUEST: Qualitative understanding of electrical system trouble-shooting. *Sigart, 93*.

197. White, B., & Frederiksen, J. (1986). *Progressions of qualitative models as a foundation for intelligent learning environments*. Bolt Beranek and Newman Report No. 6277. Cambridge, MA (*Artificial Intelligence*, to appear).

198. White, B. Y., & Horwitz, P. (1987). ThinkerTools: Enabling children to understand physical laws. In *Proceedings of the Ninth Annual Conference of the Cognitive Science Society* (pp. 336-347). Hillsdale, NJ: Erlbaum.

199. White, B. Y. (1984). Designing computer games to help physics students understand Newtons laws of motion. *Cognition and Instruction, 1*, 69-108.

200. Wilson, K. S. (1987). *Palenque: An interactive multimedia optical disk prototype for children*. Technical Report No. 44, Center for Children and Technology. New York: Bank Street College of Education.

201. Wiser, M., & Carey, S. (1983). When heat and temperature were one. In D. Gentner & A. Stevens (Eds.), *Mental models*. Hillsdale, NJ: Lawrence Erlbaum & Associates.

201a. Wiser, M. (1985). *Designing a microcomputer-based laboratory to induce differentiation between heat and temperature in ninth graders*. Technical Report 85-17. Cambridge, MA: Harvard University, Educational Technology Center.

202. Yankelovich, N., Meyrowitz, N., & van Dam, A. (1985, October). Reading and writing the electronic book. *IEEE Computer, 18* (10), 15-30.

203. Yff, J. (Ed.). (1985). *Education in the information age: The impact on teacher education and training, International Yearbook on Teacher Education 1985*. Washington, DC: International Council on Education for Teaching.

A Historical Survey of Computer Technology in Education

Alfred Bork
Educational Technology Center
Information and Computer Science
University of California, Irvine

INTRODUCTION

There is effectively a standard history of how computers and related interactive technologies are used in educational environments. This history can be the history of an entire country, or it can be the history of a particular group within a country. While there are variants from country to country, and from group to group, it is standard enough that it bears considering. The history, in many ways, is not encouraging. Many of the earlier stages can be considered regrettable. Both schools and training show similarities in computer patterns, but schools receive more attention.

The history of technology in education, worldwide, is still an incomplete history. In the last section of this paper I discuss a desirable final stage of this history, if we are to move toward a use of technology that improves education. We have serious problems all over the world in our educational systems. Technology offers us the promise, but not the certainty, of being able to cope with those problems. Technology can enhance learning. The last stage in my history reflects what needs to be done to improve educational systems in the world.

Interactive information technologies have been widely discussed and used in learning environments of all types. But the results are often disappointing or poor. A technology with great potential is often poorly used. So far, there seems to be only a little learning from previous mistakes. The tendency is for a new group or a new country to start with patterns previously used that are now recognized by sophisticated users as incorrect. But perhaps early stages and mistakes are necessary for later developments. And some aspects of early stages are useful for later development. By bringing these ideas and this developmental pattern into the open, it may be possible to avoid constant repetition of mistakes. There is some sign that this can happen.

I do not mean to imply that development involving technology in education is a strictly linear process, although it does seem that some stages precede other stages. As with any complex human activity there is some oversimplification in viewing this complex process linearly. Perhaps a history of this kind might better be written in hypertext! But in much of the description that follows I will talk about the history in a linear fashion, since I am dealing with a linear medium, text. The variation from group to group also confuses the patterns. And statistical data about the progression of steps is not available, and perhaps not really useful. Many of the features of this history are like those seen with other innovations, but I will not review the more general situation. My attempt is to represent honestly

91

the advantages and disadvantages of interactive technology in all types of learning activities.

The situation is, for convenience, grouped in three stages. First I will discuss beginning stages in the history. Then I will discuss intermediate stages — stages that usually follow the beginning stages. Finally, I will talk about the desirable future of this history. Again the reader is warned that the outline presented should not be taken in too linear a sense. There are many variations in this history in individual situations. But the patterns are common. The reader might want to compare these stages with a similar history of the use of books in education.

BEGINNING STAGES

The stages discussed in this section represent the most common beginning activities in the use of computers and related technology in education. These stages can occur together, although the drive toward computer literacy, in its simpler forms, may be later than the others examined. We can see this pattern both at the individual school level, and often at the level of a whole country.

"Let's Get Lots of Hardware"

The drive to acquire computers, to move as many computers as possible into schools or universities, is typically the first strong movement we see for technology in education. The acquisition of hardware is the major consideration in this stage. Training activities sometime reflect this early stage also. Teachers given a video projector, but no education in video, would not find the equipment useful.

Teachers and administrators are involved in this strong push toward as much equipment as possible, as quickly as possible. For some, this is perceived as a way to gain visibility. But the main forces involved are probably the commercial world, and the parents. The commercial world is involved for an obvious reason — the desire to market their machines. The parents are driven by another consideration, the vague notion that there is something wrong with a school or university that does not "have" computers. Usually no one involved — the school officials, the teachers, the sellers, or the parents — have a clear idea of what the computers are to be used for; only equipment counts. The pattern is different if the school or country cannot afford the hardware; in a sense, the cases of this kind are fortunate, because they can avoid the purchase of large amounts of useless, and soon obsolete, hardware.

Sometimes there is *a* use for the computers, a single use that is promoted heavily. This is a slightly more advanced stage, but it is still primarily a hardware-oriented stage. The philosophy is "let's get many computers all running X, and train the teachers so that marvelous things will happen in our school." The life of the typical student is hardly affected by the new hardware, and this software thrust is often short-lived.

Like many stages, this stage does not die, but continues to repeat on and on. We can still see today either the pure hardware acquisitions, or the hardware acquisition driven by one piece of software. This stage is lacking curriculum and learning consideration, an essential component of educational environments that I will frequently return to in this discussion. We can think of possible historical analogies to this situation. We might speculate that in the early days of printing, schools acquired printing presses, with the notion that they would make considerable difference in how things were done. Schools today may acquire video players for all rooms, with little consideration of what educational tapes are available, how they can be obtained, and the role they play in student learning. Unfortunately, educational issues take second place to technological issues in these considerations. That also happens with computers when the emphasis is primarily on acquiring computers — getting hardware.

Within the United States public primary and secondary schools we now have about 2 million computers. One could question whether it was wise to buy that many computers, given the limited effective use of those computers within classes. It is not necessary for everyone to proceed this way. In Japan, where both software and hardware technology exist, we see a conscious effort to avoid putting computers into classes, at least at an early stage. In other countries computers have been avoided too, but primarily because they were too expensive, or difficult to produce, for the countries involved. This last group may be the luckiest!

"Let's Teach Languages"

Once the hardware has been acquired in many of these schools there is distinct embarrassment. What is it to be used for? What do students do? The situation is desperate. One type of software is almost always available, the simple programming languages. They come with the computer in many situations, so one common use of these initial machines is to use them for teaching programming. Learning a computer language is usually not what the parents, the teachers, and the administrators have in mind; but it is possible, and like many things in technology, if something is possible, it often happens without consideration of whether it is desirable. So students learn a computer language, or a fragment of a language.

Given that programming is to be taught, and given that teacher and administrators are good at finding reasons for doing something, we begin to see rationales developed for students learning to program. We hear statements like "almost everyone will need to program in the future," "one can understand computers only if one writes programs," or "programming increases problem-solving capabilities." These are all dubious, vague assertions with little experimental backing, although the third may eventually prove, with good curriculum units, to be true.

Undoubtedly, programming is useful for some people, and perhaps even for everyone, although that is yet to be demonstrated. Many of the advocates of teaching programming relate it to learning general problem-solving strategies. But the research on problem solving have not demonstrated transfer of problem-solving capabilities. Problem solving in one area is often unrelated to problem solving in another area, it would appear. Nevertheless, there may still be some interesting possibilities in that direction, to be discovered in the future, as suggested. My view is that far more interesting learning environments, and material, for programming are needed. We can begin to see some possibilities with the development of the Martino the Robot material in Italy, and the Informatics material developed by the USSR Academy of Sciences and Moscow State University. Both of these projects are curriculum-based, not language-based. More work is needed.

The question of whether programming should or should not be taught is at least an open question, and a question that has many associated subquestions: *how* it should be taught, *to whom* it should be taught, *when* it should be taught, and *what* it should replace. When programming is taught in schools, there are three major problems. First there is inadequate curriculum material typically for the teaching of programming. Second, the teachers in schools typically know little about modern programming or software engineering. Third, the languages most likely to be used in teaching programming in schools are poor, low-level languages.

I will not comment on the lack of curriculum material for learning to program, except to say that most of the textbooks in this area are written by people with little previous programming experience. The situation with regard to teachers is more obvious. Modern programming is not a simple activity. The software engineering principles involved are not something that can be learned by beginners in a few weeks of a summer program. We would not dream of certifying people to teach mathematics based on a sole mathematical experience of a few weeks in a summer institute, yet we do a similar thing in programming. A competent teacher of programming needs just as much training as a competent teacher of mathematics. (We are fast approaching the point in the United States where we do not have competent teachers of high school mathematics, either. Recent figures show that only a little more than half of our mathematics teachers are certified to teach mathematics; that is a separate issue.)

The issue of languages requires more attention. Here, too, there is a "history," repeated in many situations. Almost inevitably the initial language is BASIC, although this may be slowly changing. Few computer scientists believe that there is any value in anyone learning BASIC. BASIC was an early language, which did not meet many of the demands of later software engineering. It develops bad habits in the students, almost inevitably in practice — habits extremely difficult to overcome at a later time. The original language has diverged in many directions. There is adequate commentary already, but BASIC continues to be widely taught.

I do not think that the situation is much better with Logo in classes today. Logo does have the possibility of program structure, through its use of procedures, so it is superior in that sense to many variants of BASIC. But Logo is an old language at this point, with a strange syntax, compared to more recent languages. Logo in classes turns out to be about 99 percent turtle graphics, with little to do fundamentally with Logo, since this graphic facility was a later addition after the language was developed. Turtle geometry can be and has been added to almost any language. Most teachers do not understand Logo, and teach accordingly. So results in most schools are poor.

In the United States, the Advanced Placement exam in computer sciences, leading to college credit, has had a beneficial effect on what language is used, but still the fundamental issues raised above are not touched. The Advanced Placement exam requires a structured language, Pascal. Since over 95 percent of introductory university computer science courses are based on Pascal, it is not surprising that the Advanced Placement exam in computer science uses Pascal. But the problems mentioned above, with teachers, are still often present. More curriculum material is available.

I remind the reader that I still regard the teaching of computer languages as an open issue. More research is needed, and more experimentation with different ways of learning about programming and problem solving. But even if one ignores all these problems associated with "let's teach languages," this use of computers has little effect within the school environment. Students are studying algebra, physics, English, history, and many other topics. If the computer plays no role in those courses, it is unlikely to have much total effect on the educational system. Hence, the thrust to teach languages, even if it were carried out in an extremely successful fashion, would still represent a limited use of the computer in education, and one using student time that might better be devoted to other purposes. There is general agreement about this in the technical community, but nevertheless languages continue to be taught, often poorly.

"Let's Teach Computer Literacy"

This historical development is often a stage beyond the two just discussed. It starts, often, as another name for the teaching of programming languages, one that seems more acceptable to many people. The argument is similar to that for language teaching: that everyone will need to be computer literate in the society of the future, because computers will be widely used in all activities. Parents, teachers, and administrators tend to agree on these issues. But agreement is lost when one needs to consider what the content of a computer literacy course should be. Computer literacy is like motherhood in that most people are in favor of it. But unlike motherhood, it does not have a clear and precise definition. People agree that they like computer literacy only because they do not explore carefully what it is that they have in mind by the term *computer literacy*.

Computer literacy is something of a bridging mechanism from the beginning stages of the history of computers in education to the intermediate stages I discuss next. At one stage computer literacy is indistinguishable from the teaching of programming languages perhaps at a simple level. Indeed, some textbooks for computer literacy are fundamentally programming texts. All the considerations in the last section apply. But, as suggested, computer literacy can have a wide variety of meanings. At the lowest level, it can be simply, "Can I turn the computer on, and insert a disk, and run a program." It may include the use of business-related tools, such as spreadsheets and word processors. The meaning of computer literacy continues to evolve, in all countries.

One aspect of computer literacy does seem important, but difficult to get across to students. People need to consider the ethical and moral problems associated with the use of computers. Computers exert a powerful effect on our society. They can exacerbate major social, personal, and economic problems, or they can contribute to the solution of these problems. But the discussion of these issues is handled, if at all, superficially in most computer literacy courses.

Another frequently stated goal of computer literacy courses is to motivate students. Student motivation, in all areas, is important, as it can increase quality time on task, an important factor in how much students learn. My experience in looking at schools that claim to have a computer literacy program is that a fair amount of this turns into game playing with computers. We get various rationales, primarily the notion that somehow the game is overcoming barriers that the student may have in using computers. I do not see these barriers, particularly with children. Good user-friendly computer material runs with students with no attempt at trying to convince them that computers are good for them. Or the issues of student excitement are often raised, in using game-like programs. One could equally argue that pinball machines, free candy, or open sex are valuable within classrooms because they excite the students.

Computer literacy courses have also come to emphasize the learning of common business tools, such as spreadsheets. This is discussed in a later section of this paper.

Toward the end of this historical phase the term *computer literacy* begins to fall into ill repute. Sometimes it is replaced by other names. In Europe and in many other countries the name *Informatics* is popular, although it often denotes a higher-level course than one associated with the term *computer literacy*.

"Let's Train the Teachers"

Almost no teachers now in schools have had any acquaintance with computers. Indeed, the teachers now coming out of schools of education have almost zero acquaintance with computers, because very few schools of education anywhere in the world are in a position to deal with this question adequately. So a movement begins to arise that emphasizes teacher training. As with many of the other stages considered, this is seen as a panacea. We continue to spend large sums of money in this direction, with little in the way of positive results.

This movement is different in different stages of the history. When it comes first in this early stage, it is often concerned with languages and computer literacy. It also follows some of the stages to be discussed later, such as acquaintance with tools. The major difficulty with all this is what the teacher should be trained to do. Typically, the content of teacher training in technology reflects the stage of the history, as suggested. The fact that there is no coherent use of the computer in education, as will be consistently pointed out here, raises great difficulties in the issues of preparing teachers to use computer effectively.

To some extent what happens with training teachers about computers now might be thought of in the following fashion. We decide that the overhead projector is to be extensively used in education. We run courses on how to use the overhead projector, but we don't supply teachers with much in the way of adequate material, so these courses are content-free. We would not expect under these circumstances that courses of this kind would be too valuable. This suggests that teacher training will not be successful until we have adequate curriculum material using the technology. At that point we will also need something else that is lacking at present: good materials for training the teachers to use these technology-based courses.

NEXT STAGES

At this point the history becomes somewhat more confused, in that not all of these stages are pursued by all groups. Furthermore, the order becomes more variable than that just suggested. Often "national policies" of a country, after the initial failures represented in the first stages, begin to come into play, determining these new directions. But the net effects may be similar to grassroots approaches coming from teachers. This middle stage in our "history," has a variety of possibilities. There is no clear-cut order in these possibilities and arguments erupt about the "correct" order. Various philosophical positions favor one or the other stage, often almost at the level of fads. So, the order in which the following sections are presented should not be taken as strict historical order.

"Let's Use Advanced Hardware"

The first stage in this history was the drive to acquire computers. Middle history reflects a similar hardware intensity but the grounds have shifted. Now more powerful equipment is considered. A variant of this hardware drive occurs in prestigious universities. There it is simply not the equipment that is wanted, but the most advanced (and expensive) equipment that the university feels they can own. Often large amounts of money go into purchasing this equipment and developing system software associated with it. I won't mention names, but examples will be well known to many readers. Education takes second place; most of the students are unaffected by this advanced hardware, and most classes continue as they were, without the new computers. It is often argued that these "experiments" help determine future directions, but the experiments seldom are done carefully enough, and are too individualistic, to provide such data.

Another aspect of this rush to use the latest equipment concerns the use of new technology related to the computer, such as the videodisc and the many variants of the compact disc. Some groups rush from one piece of equipment to another, looking for the pot at the end of the rainbow. This is not to say that these devices won't eventually prove to be useful in learning. I believe they will. But if we always proceed by jumping on the bandwagon of the latest device, the computer will never have any major effect on education! We never seem to use the technology that we have, but rather many individuals are eager to proceed to a newer technology. We *already* have the technology to make major improvements in education in all countries and at all levels. This will be further considered in the final stage of this history.

Again, we see a mistaken emphasis on the hardware, and a lack of attention of what can be done in courses. The computer, with all the new peripherals, still should be considered the major device, because it alone brings interactivity and individualization. But the question of what technology should be used should not be driven by the latest piece of equipment around. Rather, it should be driven by pedagogical considerations. Decisions made without taking into account the full learning context are likely to be inadequate decisions. Thus, if we examine interactive video, the combination of the computer and the videodisc, there are some areas where visual information will be extremely important, either for direct content or for motivational reasons, and there are other areas where it may be of little consequence. Deciding in advance that I am going to use equipment X is often a poor decision.

"Let's Develop Small Programs for Use in Standard Courses"

The reaction in this case is to a comment already made in the earlier section. The computer, used in the vein suggested in the early history, has no effect on most of the curriculum, and little effect on most students. Most of the courses taught are in subject matter areas. If the computer is to affect education significantly, it must be used in these subject matter areas. Educators slowly begin to realize this.

Hence, we see the beginning development of computer-based learning material. Normally this early development is at a cottage-industry level. A teacher, knowing a little bit about programming, writes a program for his or her students. Large numbers of teachers proceed in this way. The programs are all small, because the teachers have limited time and capability in this area. Then organizations are founded to take the teachers' programs, modify them, improve them, and make them available, perhaps commercially. Thus, organizations may begin to develop their own small programs. Many, but not all, of the companies distributing computer-based material have histories such as this.

The hallmark of these materials is that they are *small*, not taking students much time. That is, they do not represent any extensive amount of material, but are bits and pieces, minute programs, perhaps occupying an hour or so of student time. Because of this, it is not too surprising that these sequents typically have little effect on the courses in which they are used. A traditional course, based primarily on lectures and textbooks, has a few pieces of computer-based material introduced at certain points. Not too surprisingly, the overall course is little altered. The student time spent with the computer is likely to be small compared to the time spent listening to lectures or reading books. So the courses are only slightly altered. Only a small percentage of student time goes to using computer material. The courses that use such small programs already exist, and are typically based on print material developed many years ago. So their form and content reflect precomputer strategies and hence they cannot make full use of the new technologies.

Another problem with many of these small programs is that of quality control. Since they are often developed on an individual scale, without adequate resources, and often by individuals with little experience in developing learning materials, it is not too surprising that the quality is often poor. Yet, many of these programs do get used, for the reason already suggested: the computers are in the schools, and there is some drive to show that the computers are useful in some way to justify the cost of the hardware. Many become commercially available. Some good programs do exist, but too few to improve education for most students, and the programs themselves occupy too little student time to have much effect.

Another interesting, but educationally unfortunate, phenomenon arises in connection with these small programs. Programs that have almost nothing to do with educational content, as it is understood in the traditional fashion, or by those who look toward future systems, become widely used, because they exist, and are perhaps entertaining to children. Thus, the enthusiasm for creating computer-based posters, greeting cards, and banners, having little to do with the learning process, reflects the existence of software for doing this. In a sense the software situation is very similar to that with regard to languages, as previously discussed. We have it, so we use it! Since the software exists, it is used, sometimes heavily. Hence, the computer has an unfortunate effect on education; it takes away valuable student time from important components of learning and invests it in material that has little intrinsic learning value.

Several types of small programs have been developed, and again large philosophical discussions break forth about which type is "correct." These philosophical discussions are seldom based on pedagogical or empirical considerations about the learning needs of students in a course. They are simply widely held sets of beliefs. Nevertheless they are often argued vigorously. What is lacking is much empirical information to support the arguments, in any direction. Some of the types of small programs are described in the following paragraphs.

Tutorials. One common type of material is tutorials, units that try to help the student in the learning process. Higher-level tutorial material attempts to work somewhat the way an individual tutor might work. At its best, seldom realized, this material can individualize the learning experience for each student, and can make learning an active experience. It also plays a major role in maintaining student interest. Groups of excellent teachers can be effective in designing such units. This is the approach we follow at Irvine. But little tutorial material of this kind exists at present, and it suffers from the same problems as any small amount of material. So although this stage in history holds greater potential, it is yet to be realized. This topic will receive further discussion in the next major section.

At the lower end of tutorial is drill and practice, giving students practice in using the material. Drill and practice is often derided, yet in many courses, as they are taught today, drill in learning the materials is almost essential. For example, almost any calculus course taught anywhere in the world today requires a large amount of practice and drill in the arts of differentiation and integration. Whether this is a reasonable procedure or not deserves further consideration, but it is unfair to criticize drill and practice on the computer when it is heavily used in noncomputer components of the curriculum. Drill and practice with the computer has distinct advantages over the usual drill and practice, such as the possibility of immediate feedback and assistance to students.

Simulations. Another type of small program that has its strong philosophical adherents is the simulation. Simulations go under various names. At Irvine we call them "controllable worlds." If they are done in Logo they tend to be called "microworlds." Sometimes they are called "free environments." The notion of a simulation is straightforward. The computer simulates some part of a real or imaginary world, creating conditions that allow the user to "play" with that world, change it, and observe what happens.

There is a strong pedagogical purpose for simulation, although that purpose is not often understood. Simulations are most useful in the important task of helping students build their intuition about particular areas, to develop insight. This experiential phase is an important component of learning, often neglected by our traditional processes. Insight can be stimulated by a rich collection of student experiences provided by simulations. But the typical small simulations suffer frequently from a fatal flaw. They are not interactive, so they cannot react to what the student is doing or not doing, and so cannot determine whether the student is building intuition or gaining any other form of knowledge in the process. Student difficulties are ignored in many simulations. A few students may be learning with the simulation, but the many who are not tend to be bored by the material, since they do not see what is happening or why they are involved in it. The designers of simulations often assume that student help will come from teachers, but given typical class size this expectation is not at all reasonable in most situations. Student motivation is often a serious problem. Simulations are often far more interesting to the developers than to the students! Students do not understand why they are using the simulation.

I call a simulation that completely ignores what the user is doing, a naked simulation, because it does not have the "clothes" that it needs to be a full pedagogical unit. An effective simulation needs to watch carefully what the student knows and does not know, offering help and assistance. But few of these programs do. Naked simulations are seldom useful with typical students, although they may work for very good students with very good teachers. They need to be clothed in pedagogy. A friend tells me that the term *naked video* has a similar meaning.

Microcomputer-based laboratory. There is a recent alternative to simulations that also is connected with building student intuition, through providing a wide range of experience. This alternative is the microcomputer-based laboratory. The notion is to attach a probe directly to the computer, a probe that measures some aspect of the outside world, such as temperature, distance of an object, etc. As with other types of material, little empirical information is now available on how this approach compares with the approach of the "pure" simulation. Many scientists favor actual laboratory equipment, even though it is, as in the case of a microcomputer-based laboratory, removed from direct manipulation by the student. Typically these programs produce graphs of whatever the probe measures, or whatever can be calculated from this, versus time.

As with the simulations, most of the microcomputer-based laboratory programs do not pay attention to what the student is doing. So the problems mentioned for simulations also occur. The assumption once more is that the teachers will provide this additional information, without regard for the fact that in the large typical classroom it is usually impossible for the teacher to do this for everyone.

* * *

Some tutorials and simulations get the word *intelligent* attached to them, but these programs seldom actually use the methods of artificial intelligence. We do find a few experimental programs that use these methods, and we find other programs without artificial intelligence methods that clothe the simulation. But these are rare at this current stage of the history. The potential, however, is again large.

A serious problem with many tutorials and simulations is that they are elitist and work only with a few very good students. The typical student is quickly in trouble. Learning material of this kind deserves to be called *elitist software.* Given privileged students, or extremely competent teachers, elitist software can provide the things that are missing in the naked simulations and simple tutorials, at least to a few students. Even here however, the chance of being able to supply the missing details to everyone in the class is likely to be small. Too many students are present. Hence, software of this kind often is glowingly reported based on its use with a few bright students and teachers, but it fails in typical courses.

"Let's Use Authoring Systems"

The drive toward producing small pieces of learning material quickly becomes frustrated, because the teachers involved know little or nothing about programming. Hence, entrepreneurs see a new direction: authoring languages and systems. Teachers are told that they do not need to know anything about programming. "We have this easy way of allowing you to write learning material, through the magic of computers, where no programming is needed." Anyone can do it, the promoters claim. Languages may start within a professional organization (IBM and Coursewriter, for example).

Authoring languages and systems are heavily promoted and advertsied products. At the 1988 ADCIS meeting in Philadelphia, for example, about half of the exhibitors were promoting authoring systems. Many of these are fifteeen or so years old. Some reappear under different names. It seems that profits are to be made in this area, given the considerable commercial interests that market authoring systems and languages.

Little quality material is written in these systems. If the systems are easy to use, as advertised, then they produce only simplistic material. As they get more complicated they become less easy to use, but provide a general range of material. When this happens, the systems typically are removed from the hands of the authors, and a new level of professional uses the system. The original advertising promises are then forgotten. But these authoring facilities are seldom designed by competent computer scientists who know what a complex programming language or developmental environment should be like, and so they are typically not adequate to the task. Further, they often have a restricted built-in view of the nature of the learning process, or they can produce only certain types of materials. They do, however, absorb great quantities of resources, money and time, and so their net effect on the promotion of computers in education has been negative; they use up money that could be better spent elsewhere. The net result of most authoring systems is to make money for the promoters.

But almost every novice getting into the field believes, unfortunately, that the first choice is to pick an authoring system or language! New systems keep appearing, suggesting that some systems make a profit. But little effective material is produced with these systems. It is often not realized that authoring systems, as opposed to sets of tools, are not needed to create high-quality interactive learning material. The problem is primarily a specialized problem in software engineering.

"Let's Catalog Existing Software"

Since many of these small, low-quality programs are developed, the numbers suggest that we need lists of them. So we find organizations that prepare these lists and distribute them. Sometimes these organizations are called clearinghouses; they also may make available some of the material on these lists. Not too surprising, clearinghouses list material of variable quality. If anything has potential, it may be picked up commercially, and so will not be a candidate for the clearinghouse. So these lists, even relegated to particular fields, seldom turn out to be of much use. A few exceptions exist.

"Let's Evaluate the Small Programs"

A step beyond cataloging is some attempt to evaluate the material. This is certainly desirable, because it begins to give some ideas about which small programs might conceivably be useful in which classes. This could be related, in schools, to the state and local frameworks that guide the curriculum.

But evaluation can have many meanings. What evaluation usually implies at this stage of the history is peer evaluation, the program being examined by another teacher who did not write it, but who is familiar with the students in the area. The critical issue, however, is how effective the programs are in helping students to learn. Peer evaluations emphasize teaching, not learning. Many of the materials glowingly described in peer evaluations turn out to have severe problems when ordinary students are involved in a summative evaluation. Materials liked by teachers, as already suggested, may not work with students; this is not unique to computers. While some useful things can come from peer evaluation, these evaluations miss the major direction for evaluation: testing with typical target audiences. Summative evaluation, well done, is expensive and time-consuming in most situations.

The net result of these evaluations, even though the quality of the effort is poor, is to confirm what has already been pointed out — that there is little effective learning material available in the small program category. The nature of the programs, their smallness, almost ensures that this will be the case. The material is not extensive enough to make a real difference.

"Let's Teach Students about Tools"

An entirely different approach is often seen toward the end of this middle stage of our history. The argument resembles what we have already seen in computer literacy, at least in its earlier stages. It goes something like this. Powerful computer tools are now generally available in our society. Students may almost certainly use these tools after they graduate from school or university. Hence, let's be sure to teach them all about the tools that are currently available. As with learning languages, this philosophy can be questioned. The first thing to note is that the tools usually being referred to — word processors, spreadsheets, database manipulators, graphics programs — have almost all come from the business community. That is, *none of them* were developed for use in the learning process. I sometimes refer to this stage in the survey as "picking up the crumbs of the business tables."

How have these business tools impacted education? Because they were developed for business considerations to meet business needs, it would seem almost obvious that these tools are not ideal for educational purposes. But this seems to have escaped most of the people who pursue this direction. Often the tools used are not exactly those that were developed for business. The reason for this is that the computers they are running on are computers that businesses refuse to buy! Thus, weaker forms of the business programs, imitations for the weaker computers, are often developed for the school or university environment. Schools often do not use the "best" business tools, even when they have the appropriate computers.

Where should the tools be taught? Often the computer literacy course is revived in this context, and it becomes a course for learning about word processors and other tools. But we also see use of tools within subject matter classes, and some of these approaches are useful, at least slightly. Thus, a spreadsheet may get used in a mathematics or science class. The published literature contains many examples of this kind, and we find enthusiasts for this use.

Perhaps the most important use of such tools within a class is the use of word processing in a writing class. Word processors will soon be almost universally used in almost any type of writing activity, so the presence of word processors in writing courses, and in other courses that involve substantial writing, is not surprising. The ability to make corrections easily, without the laborious processes involved in rewriting and retyping entire papers, shows the potential for improving writing. Spelling checkers also play an important role. It may be the student's responsibility to learn how to use the word processor well enough to meet course requirements. This is often the case, for example, in junior- and senior-level English courses in universities, where it becomes almost impossible to survive in the course, given the amount of writing needed, without a word processor. Learning to use the tools is not simple, and often little help is provided.

The word processor is only one of many computer-based tools that can be useful in the writing environment. Furthermore, learning to write involves a whole methodology of which word processing is only a small segment. Learning to write has undergone a revolution recently, with emphasis on viewing the entire process of writing, not just the actual writing activity. The notion that there are tools that can assist with the prewriting process, and tools that can help with the postwriting or revision process, is central to using computers effectively in a process approach to improve writing. Yet, these tools are often fragmentary, and are seldom put together in a full-scale curriculum designed for learning writing and later developing productive writing skills. There are, however, some new, less commonly used tools developed for writing and other specific areas of the curriculum. To some extent these tools overlap types of software considered previously, particularly simulations. As with the business tools, problems arise from the issues of curriculum.

The emphasis on a curriculum context, as discussed in the use of word processing in the teaching of writing, is an important and neglected consideration for most of these tools. Having the tools alone, whether they are word processors, spreadsheets or other things, is seldom sufficient. What is needed is a whole collection of software to use with the tools. This software needs to address the following questions.

- How is the student to learn to use the tools? How many hours of valuable class time in a writing course are going to be devoted to teaching people the mechanism of various tools? Or is there some more effective way of doing this?

- How do the tools integrate with each other, and how do the students understand that the important thing is not the tools themselves, but the curriculum material that one is trying to get across?

- How do the tools fit with other aspects of the curriculum?

- Does the tool make any attempt to determine if the student is learning anything?

- Does the tool offer any individualized assistance to the student who is in difficulty? Or does it assume that the already overworked teacher will work individually with each student in a large class?

All these questions are seldom answered, because the tools are plucked from business applications, with little pedagogical context surrounding them. The problem is not too different from the problem of the naked simulation, mentioned above. The focus is not on learning, and on helping students to learn, but on the technology. A friend likes to say that any piece of learning without a curriculum context is like a "one night stand." The analogy seems to me a good one; no full, rich relationship is developed.

But even if we can answer all these questions carefully, and develop a full curriculum context for the use of tools, the question remains as to computer use in many other areas of the curriculum where the tools may not be as vital, but where other kinds of technology-based learning material may play a more important role. The notion that somehow education needs to use only the tools that have been developed for business is a very peculiar notion, reflecting the poverty of education today.

"Let's Use Networks"

One stage that is eventually reached in many countries and in many individual projects is the stage that focuses on the use of networks — first local, then long-distance. That is, the standard personal computer is no longer seen as adequate, but the student also needs connections between computers and the resources that networks can provide. It is not necessary that every user be networked all the time; many long distance networks assume that only occasionally will there be a connection made by phone, sometimes without knowledge of the student.

Initially, the use of networks becomes almost purely a matter of convenience and bookkeeping. The convenience comes because it is no longer necessary to deal with all the floppy disks. The bookkeeping comes because now it is possible to keep better records of what the student has or has not done. The next stage is the use of electronic mail and bulletin boards, often poorly coupled with the curriculum; these activities can be valuable if integrated with the curriculum.

But seldom has any learning material been developed that *demands* the network, other than the use of electronic mail and bulletin boards. A few exceptions exist, such as the National Geographic/TERC science units. Although there would seem to be some interesting possibilities for pedagogical developments that could take place in network environments, and could not take place in other environments, these possibilities have scarcely been touched. So networks become an expensive addition, not contributing much to the learning situation. But like many of the early stages in the history, they reflect a potential that might be realized if the final stage of history is ever attained.

"Let's Develop Management Systems"

At some time, usually early in the second stage, the notion of using the technology to provide course management, with or without any of the rest of the material in the course involving the computer, is broached. The argument for management systems is reasonable. Teachers spend much time with paperwork, time they do not consider interesting. If the management system can indeed cut down this time, then it has considerable appeal for the teachers.

At the simplest level the management systems become simply the replacement for the teacher's record book, a way of recording the grades and progress of the course by the teacher directly. Thus, the teacher gives tests, and instead of entering grades in a written form in a record book, they are entered online, hopefully with a friendly query-type program. Perhaps the computer does some mathematics, such as averaging the grades. Such use is of minimal interest. More advanced forms of management systems may tie in directly with other material on the computer, so that the information is recorded automatically. Systems of this kind do exist. Probably we can expect more of them in the final stage of the history. The integrated system available from such companies as Computer

Curriculum Corporation and WICAT combines management systems with extensive curriculum material.

The purpose of management systems is not given much consideration. Often they are regarded as an aid only to the teacher, who uses them to record information and supply various reports. But equally, and perhaps of greater importance eventually, is a management system that supplies help directly to the student. Such a system is necessary if the student is to understand what he or she needs to work on further. Management systems can thus offer a variety of interfaces, for different users.

FINAL STAGE

Up to this point there has been, I believe, historical accuracy in telling what has happened. However, like any archetypical history that tries to encompass an entire movement, the individual details may be different than those described. The account we have so far brings us roughly up to the present. The computer, the videodisc, and the compact disc are still having little impact on improving education. Some of the reasons for this were discussed in earlier sections. But this historical survey is incomplete; we have not reached the desirable final stage: effective use of computers within the classroom environment. The next stage of the history has not yet taken place in any country or in any organization, although some are closer to it than others. In this section, I provide a quick view of what I regard as the next stage of the history. Many of my papers and books expand this in more detail.

We might describe the last stage in this historical survey as the "let's develop full curriculum using computers" stage which I believe includes at least five elements.

1. *Future learning systems.* I find surprisingly little discussion of the desirable forms of future learning systems, of any type. This discussion is much needed; it is difficult to know how to improve schools if we do not have a target for the future. Most of the use of technology in education has ignored this issue.

2. *New courses and curricula.* The only way interactive information technologies can be used effectively in education, just as the only way the book could be used effectively, is to develop entirely new courses and curricula. These new courses need to assume from the beginning of the development process that *all* educational media, including those from modern interactive technology, are available. Such material would lead to new curricula. It would go far beyond the bits and pieces of technology-based material now available. These courses could well differ greatly in form, content, and teacher role from existing courses, because they were developed later. Content needs change because of our changing society. New forms for course structure are suggested by new learning technologies. Exciting possibilities exist that would have been impossible with the older learning media.

But little in the way of resources have been devoted to full curriculum development based on interactive technology. Indeed, most of the money associated with computers in education, in the United States, is still invested in the earlier stages already mentioned in the first two parts of this discussion, even today. Some full courses have been developed: the logic and set theory courses at Stanford University, the physics course at the University of California, Irvine, and the Writing to Read course for young children. But these courses are a drop in a very large bucket, if we consider all the systems of education in existence. This lack of full-scale interactive courses is curious. Hundreds of full video-based courses have been developed, some slightly interactive, but only a very small number of computer-based courses. We cannot realize the full potential of interactive learning technology without newly designed courses. I find it hard to understand why video has had so much more support, given that most video-based courses are not interactive.

3. *Teacher training.* The fact that we are considering courses that are quite different from previous courses, including different teacher roles, indicates the great importance of educating the teacher. Current efforts at educating the teacher in something called "technology" are typically unsuccessful, because the technology is not tied down to pedagogical situations. We do not train teachers to use books! The training of teachers must be associated with each of the new courses developed, and the development of this material for teachers must be considered an integral part of the development of the courses. One of my friends, Jacques Hebenstreit, has emphasized this recently in private correspondence. He comments, "The constructive use of computers is not a problem in hardware and not even a problem in software. It is a problem of making teachers confident."

4. *Evaluation.* The focus of the final stage will be on full course development and evaluation, so that we can rebuild schools and universities with technology-based courses that were not possible with the older technologies. One can see glimmerings beginning in a few countries, but still it is a stage that we are perhaps not yet ready for. These full courses also need to be accompanied by full summative evaluations. The importance of testing learning material with students has already been stressed in discussing evaluation in the previous stage. It is desirable that several such courses will be available in each area, so that these courses can be compared for student effectiveness not only with the conventional courses, but with each other. Writing to Read has been evaluated in this sense, but such evaluations are seldom done.

5. *Implementation.* The implementation of these new courses in all areas of learning is a complex task. Educational institutions of all types are conservative and do not change easily. But we know, from industry experiences, something about implementation of major changes in education. That experience will be useful here.

CONCLUSION

The potential for this last stage in our history of computer technology in education is exciting. We have great problems in education, and it is only with the redevelopment of our courses and schools that we can begin to face those issues that are certain to challenge future generations.

An Analysis of Doctoral Dissertation Productivity in Instructional Design and Technology from 1977 to 1988

Edward P. Caffarella
College of Education
University of Northern Colorado, Greeley

Steven G. Sachs
Instructional Technologies and Extended Learning
Northern Virginia Community College

This study is an analysis of doctoral dissertation research completed by students in instructional design and technology (ID&T) programs from 1977 through 1988. This dissertation research was completed at forty-six institutions throughout the United States. The first section is an analysis of the number of dissertations completed during each of the twelve years. The second section deals with the forty-six institutions and the number of doctoral degrees in ID&T awarded by each. The third section identifies the individuals who chaired the dissertations. The fourth section is a historical analysis of dissertation research in ID&T. The fifth section is a comparison of the research during the present period with dissertation research completed since 1921. The last section is a comparison of the ten most productive ID&T programs over the last seven decades.

METHODOLOGY

The analysis is based largely upon the data presented in two recent Association for Educational Communications and Technology publications—*Doctoral Research in Instructional Design and Technology: A Directory of Dissertations, 1977-1986* (Caffarella and Sachs, 1988) and *Doctoral Research in Instructional Design and Technology: A Directory of Dissertations, 1987-1988* (Caffarella, in press). These two publications contain listings of dissertations completed by doctoral students at ID&T programs in the United States.

These publications and this article provide an opportunity to better define the doctoral research in the field of instructional design and technology, thereby helping the profession to identify valuable studies and research trends. By building upon the research of others, future researchers can advance the field more collectively than one individual working in isolation could do.

The data in the two directories (Caffarella and Sachs, 1988; Caffarella, in press) were supplied directly by the universities in the United States that offer graduate programs in instructional design and technology. These various programs are offered under a wide variety of titles, including instructional development, educational media, instructional technology, and instructional systems. The initial list of institutions was taken from the list of doctoral and masters programs in the *Educational Media and Technology Yearbook 1986* (Miller & Mosley, 1986). These lists were checked against the membership list for the Professors of Instructional Design and Technology organization to ensure that the list included as many institutions as possible.

Each participating institution supplied the following information for each doctoral student who graduated between 1977 and 1988:

- Student's name

- Year of the degree

- Dissertation title

- Institution name

- Dissertation chairperson(s)

The intent was to make the listing inclusive rather than exclusive. The decision to partici- pate and which dissertations to submit were left to the individual institution. Since most of the institutions elected to participate, the directories include the majority of doctoral graduates from programs in instructional design and technology.

The list for dissertations completed from 1977 through 1986 was collected during the fall of 1987 and the winter of 1988. The data for 1987 and 1988 were collected from the institutions during the winter and spring of 1989.

DISSERTATIONS COMPLETED

During the period 1977 through 1988, 1,518 dissertations were completed at forty-six institutions (see figure 1, page 108). The original directory (Caffarella and Sachs, 1988) has 1,220 entries, covering 1977-1986, from forty-two institutions. The 1987-1988 directory has 298 dissertation titles completed at thirty-nine institutions. From 1977 through 1988 the number of dissertations completed each year ranged from a low of 106 in 1980 to a high of 149 in 1983 and 1985. During this twelve-year period there was a relatively steady output of dissertations, with an average of 127 completed each year.

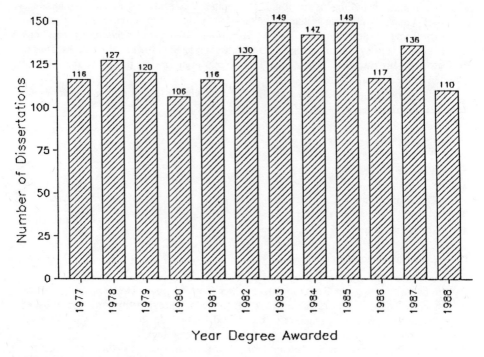

Figure 1. ID&T doctoral dissertations for each year, 1977-1988.

INSTITUTIONAL PRODUCTIVITY

The analysis of institutional productivity as displayed in table 1 shows that most of the dissertations were completed at a relatively small number of institutions. The table is arranged in order by the total number of dissertations completed at each institution. In addition to the total number for the institution, table 1 also displays the number of dissertations completed during each year. The last three columns show the cumulative total, the percentage of dissertations completed at each institution, and the cumulative percentage.

Table 1.
Number of Dissertations for Each Institution for Each Year in Order by Total for Institution

	1977	1978	1979	1980	1981	1982	1983	1984	1985	1986	1987	1988	Tot	Cum Tot	%	Cum %
Indiana University	27	24	24	22	12	25	13	14	18	12	16	9	216	216	14.23	14.23
Univ. of S. California	9	12	7	9	6	7	17	18	5	3	9	6	108	324	7.11	21.34
Boston University	5	6	9	4	16	10	9	11	12	12	6	7	107	431	7.05	28.39
Syracuse University	16	10	6	6	9	6	5	10	5	8	4	3	88	519	5.80	34.19
University of Pittsburgh	5	5	7	1	5	9	13	7	9	6	8	5	80	599	5.27	39.46
Florida State University	4	6	8	6	0	13	16	10	4	3	5	4	79	678	5.20	44.66
Brigham Young University	6	8	5	3	2	7	4	7	10	7	3	9	71	749	4.68	49.34
East Texas State Univ.	3	12	9	3	7	4	4	4	2	3	4	7	62	811	4.08	53.43
Michigan State University	5	8	3	5	4	4	4	3	10	4	3	2	55	866	3.62	57.05
Pennsylvania State Univ.	0	2	7	7	1	0	2	7	5	5	8	4	48	914	3.16	60.21
University of Illinois	0	1	0	4	0	1	1	1	2	6	21	10	47	961	3.10	63.31
Wayne State University	2	0	2	3	8	2	8	5	8	5	2	2	47	1008	3.10	66.40
University of Iowa	0	2	1	2	8	4	7	3	6	6	2	2	43	1051	2.83	69.24
Northern Illinois Univ.	9	3	4	5	4	5	3	2	4	1	0	2	42	1093	2.77	72.00
University of Wisconsin	0	2	3	4	4	1	5	4	6	3	3	7	42	1135	2.77	74.77
Rutgers University	6	3	6	5	3	5	3	5	4	1	0	0	41	1176	2.70	77.47
Ohio State University	1	3	2	3	1	1	3	1	4	3	4	2	28	1204	1.84	79.31
Louisiana State Univ.	5	2	5	1	2	4	4	1	0	1	1	0	26	1230	1.71	81.03
Arizona State University	1	1	0	1	3	4	3	4	4	1	0	2	24	1254	1.58	82.61
University of Oklahoma	2	1	1	3	2	0	2	2	3	3	4	1	24	1278	1.58	84.19
New York University	1	7	1	0	3	0	0	1	3	0	2	2	20	1298	1.32	85.51
State Univ. of NY at Buffalo	0	1	0	0	2	2	1	3	0	4	3	2	18	1316	1.19	86.69
Columbia University	0	0	0	0	2	6	6	3	0	0	0	0	17	1333	1.12	87.81
University of Minnesota	1	2	3	1	3	0	2	1	1	0	3	0	17	1350	1.12	88.93

(Table 1 continues on page 110.)

Table 1 – *Continued*

	1977	1978	1979	1980	1981	1982	1983	1984	1985	1986	1987	1988	Tot	Cum Tot	%	Cum %
Univ. of Northern Colorado	1	0	0	0	2	1	1	2	1	2	3	2	15	1365	.99	89.92
University of Virginia	1	0	0	1	1	1	2	0	2	3	1	3	15	1380	.99	90.91
University of Washington	1	2	2	0	0	0	1	2	3	1	1	1	14	1394	.92	91.83
Virginia Polytechnic Inst.	2	1	0	0	1	3	0	0	0	2	3	1	13	1407	.86	92.69
Univ. of Texas at Austin	0	0	0	0	0	0	1	2	2	2	3	2	12	1419	.79	93.48
University of Connecticut	0	1	1	1	2	0	3	1	1	0	1	0	11	1430	.72	94.20
University of Georgia	0	0	0	0	0	0	1	0	2	0	1	7	11	1441	.72	94.93
Kansas State University	0	0	0	0	0	1	0	2	3	2	2	0	10	1451	.66	95.59
Georgia State University	0	0	1	0	0	2	1	1	1	3	0	0	9	1460	.59	96.18
Kent State University	1	0	1	3	1	0	1	0	1	0	0	1	9	1469	.59	96.77
Utah State University	0	0	0	0	0	0	2	1	0	2	2	1	8	1477	.53	97.30
Iowa State University	1	0	1	0	1	0	0	1	1	0	1	1	7	1484	.46	97.76
Oklahoma State University	0	0	1	1	0	0	0	1	1	1	1	0	6	1490	.40	98.16
University of Toledo	0	1	0	0	1	1	0	0	0	0	1	3	6	1496	.40	98.55
S. Ill. Univ. at Edwardsville	0	0	0	1	0	0	0	0	1	1	2	0	5	1501	.33	98.88
University of Colorado	0	0	0	0	0	0	1	0	3	0	1	0	5	1506	.33	99.21
Temple University	1	1	0	1	0	0	0	1	0	0	0	0	4	1510	.26	99.47
University of Oregon	0	0	0	0	0	0	0	1	1	1	0	0	3	1513	.20	99.67
Univ. of Tenn. at Knoxville	0	0	0	1	0	1	0	0	0	0	0	0	2	1515	.13	99.80
Oregon State University	0	0	0	0	0	0	0	0	0	0	1	0	1	1516	.07	99.87
University of Nebraska	0	0	0	0	0	0	0	0	1	0	0	0	1	1517	.07	99.93
University of New Mexico	0	0	0	0	0	0	0	0	0	0	1	0	1	1518	.07	100
TOTAL	116	127	120	106	116	130	149	142	149	117	136	110	1518			

An analysis of the data in this table yields some interesting conclusions about the productivity of each institution and the distribution of graduates among the institutions. During the twelve-year period, 49 percent of the graduates did their studies at only seven institutions. The graph (see figure 2) clearly shows the distribution of graduates among these seven institutions.

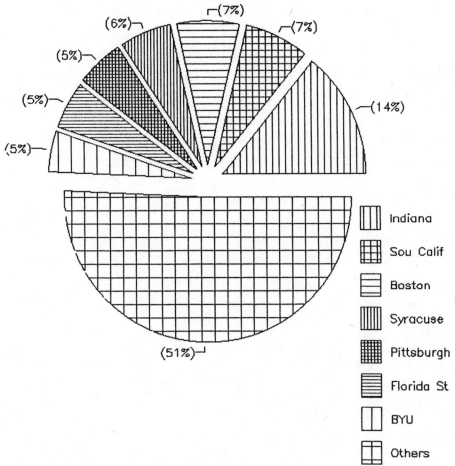

Figure 2. Seven most productive ID&T institutions, 1977-1988.

The largest number of ID&T students graduated from Indiana University with 216 dissertations. The other institutions among the seven most productive included Boston University, University of Southern California, Syracuse University, Florida State University, University of Pittsburgh, and Brigham Young University. The remaining thirty-nine institutions produced 51 percent of the dissertations.

The list of institutions producing larger numbers of doctoral graduates was relatively consistent from 1977 through 1988. Table 2, page 112, shows the three most productive institutions for each year from 1977 through 1988.

Table 2.

Most Productive Institutions for Each Year

1977 Indiana (27)	Syracuse (16)	S. Calif. (9)
1978 Indiana (24)	S. Calif. (12)	East Texas (12)
1979 Indiana (24)	East Texas (9)	Boston (9)
1980 Indiana (22)	S. Calif. (9)	Penn. State (7)
1981 Boston (16)	Indiana (12)	Syracuse (9)
1982 Indiana (25)	Florida St. (13)	Boston (10)
1983 Florida St. (17)	S. Calif. (16)	Indiana & Pittsburgh (13)
1984 S. Calif. (18)	Indiana (14)	Boston (11)
1985 Indiana (18)	Boston (12)	Brigham Young & Michigan St. (10)
1986 Indiana & Boston (12)	Syracuse (8)	
1987 Illinois (21)	Indiana (16)	S. Calif. (9)
1988 Illinois (10)	Indiana & Brigham Young (9)	

The number in parentheses next to the institution name is the number of dissertations for that year. Over the twelve-year period, Indiana University was one of the top three producers during every year and first for seven years. The University of Southern California and Boston University were in the top three producing institutions for six years. Syracuse University was in this group three times during the twelve years from 1977 through 1988.

Within the institutions the numbers of graduates varied widely from year to year (see table 1). For example, Indiana University had 27 graduates in 1977 but only 9 during 1988. The number of graduates at the University of Southern California ranged from 18 graduates in 1984 to 2 graduates in 1986, while the graduates at Boston University ranged from 16 in 1981 to 5 in 1977.

In each year from 1977 until 1982, only 25 to 27 of the 46 institutions produced graduates. In each year from 1983 until 1987, that number increased to 32 to 36 institutions producing graduates. In 1988 only 30 institutions of the 46 produced graduates.

DISSERTATION CHAIRS

There were 286 professors who chaired dissertations in instructional design and technology. Each chairperson directed an average of 5.44 dissertations, with a range from 89 to 1.

Approximately 25 percent of the dissertations were completed under the direction of eleven professors (see table 3).

Table 3.
Dissertations for Each Chairperson for Each Year, 1977-1988.

	Tot	Cum Tot	%	Cum %
Kelley, Gaylen B. Boston University	89	89	5.72	5.72
Casey, Robert. Univ. of S. California	40	129	2.57	8.30
Knirk, Fred. Univ. of S. California	37	166	2.38	10.68
Schwen, Thomas. Indiana University	32	198	2.06	12.73
Pett, Dennis. Indiana University	31	229	1.99	14.73
Childs, John. Wayne State University	27	256	1.74	16.46
Hughes, Lawson. Indiana University	26	282	1.67	18.14
Titus, Robert L. East Texas State Univ.	26	308	1.67	19.81
De Vaney, Ann. University of Wisconsin	23	331	1.48	21.29
Merrill, M. David. Brigham Young & Univ. of S. Calif.	23	354	1.48	22.77
McConeghy, Gary. Northern Illinois Univ.	22	376	1.41	24.18
Belland, John. Ohio State University	21	397	1.35	25.53
Welliver, Paul W. Pennsylvania State Univ.	21	418	1.35	26.88
Dwyer, Francis. Pennsylvania State Univ.	20	438	1.29	28.17
Seels, Barbara. University of Pittsburgh	20	458	1.29	29.45
Berry, Louis H. University of Pittsburgh	19	477	1.22	30.68
Gentry, Castelle G. Michigan State University	19	496	1.22	31.90
Razik, Taher A. State Univ. of NY at Buffalo	18	514	1.16	33.95
Cox, Robert A. University of Pittsburgh	17	531	1.09	34.15
Keller, John. Syracuse U. & Florida State U.	17	548	1.09	35.24
Smith, Jay C. University of Oklahoma	17	565	1.09	36.33
Sullivan, Howard. Arizona State University	17	582	1.09	37.43
Bhola, Harbans S. Indiana University	16	598	1.03	38.46
Levie, W. Howard. Indiana University	16	614	1.03	39.49
Molenda, Michael. Indiana University	16	630	1.03	40.51
Holloway, Robert. Columbia University	15	645	.965	41.48
Ely, Donald. Syracuse University	14	659	.900	42.38
Morgan, Robert M. Florida State University	14	673	.900	43.28
Stahl, Albert. Wayne State University	14	687	.900	44.18
Allen, William. Univ. of S. California	13	700	.836	45.02
Davies, Ivor. Indiana University	13	713	.836	45.85
Heinich, Robert. Indiana University	13	726	.836	46.69
Roberts, Charlie W. Louisiana State University	13	739	.836	47.52
Spiro, Mary. University of Pittsburgh	13	752	.836	48.36
Blasingame, Ralph. Rutgers University	12	764	.772	49.13
Bratton, Barry. University of Iowa	12	776	.772	49.90
Others	742	1518	50.1	100

Half of the dissertations were directed by thirty-six chairs. There were 147 faculty members who chaired only one or two dissertations. Thus, a relatively small number of professors directed most of the dissertations in instructional design and technology. As might be expected, most of the professors with larger numbers of students were faculty members at the seven institutions producing the largest number of dissertations.

EARLIER COMPILATIONS

Several earlier studies compiled lists of dissertations in what is now known as instructional design and technology. The first compilation (Moldstad, 1956) includes the earliest dissertation in the field, completed at the George Peabody College for Teachers in 1921. Between then and 1988 approximately 3,200 dissertations were completed in instructional design and technology. There has been a continual growth in the number of dissertations completed each year.

Moldstad compiled three supplements (1958, 1959, 1961) to the original list; these were also published in *Audio-Visual Communication Review*. Each of the lists includes the dissertations completed during the intervening years and also includes any dissertations overlooked in earlier lists. The Moldstad compilations showed that approximately 50 percent of the studies were completed at eight institutions. This is consistent with the finding in the current study that the majority of the studies were completed at a small number of institutions.

Huang (1979) compiled a list of dissertations completed during the years 1960 to 1970. His list includes 468 dissertations and overlaps by one year the last Moldstad list. A summary report on the dissertations from 1960 to 1970 was published by Huang (1980). Huang reports that 69 percent of the dissertations were completed at five institutions. This concentration is slightly higher than was reported by Moldstad or the current study. The difference can be explained by the much tighter definition of the field used by Huang. Kirschner, Mapes, and Anderton (1975) developed a listing of dissertations completed in educational media from 1969 through 1972.

The Caffarella and Sachs (1988) compilation covers the years 1977 through 1986. The second compilation (Caffarella, in press) covers 1987 and 1988. There are 1,518 dissertations in these two volumes.

As shown in figure 3, there has been a relatively constant growth in the number of dissertations since the first dissertations in the 1920s. Although there were a few dissertations completed before 1950, the real growth in doctoral study in instructional design and technology started in the early 1950s. The slightly lower figures during 1961-1970 are due to a much tighter definition used by Huang (1979). Therefore, the 1961-1970 lists contain fewer references than would have been included if the same definitions had been used for all lists. An averaging of the numbers of dissertations during the periods 1966-1970 and 1977-1980 yields a probable estimate of 450 dissertations during 1971-1976.

The total number of dissertations on all lists is 2,695 actual entries. Including the estimate for the years 1971-1976, approximately 3,200 doctorates have been awarded in instructional design and technology by institutions in the United States. Of this total approximately 47 percent were awarded during the twelve-year period from 1977 through 1988.

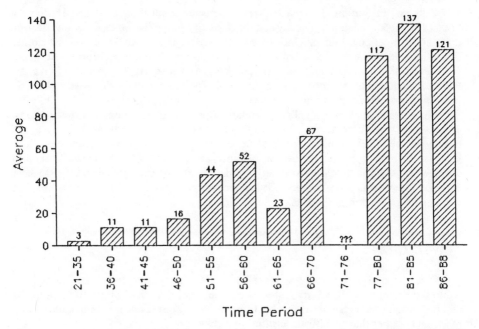

Figure 3. Average number of ID&T dissertations for each year during each period from 1921-1988

CHANGE OVER TIME

Since 1921 the predominant institutions in instructional technology have changed several times. Table 4 shows the ten most productive institutions for each of three periods: 1921-1956, 1960-1970, and 1977-1988. Within each column the institutions are ordered by the number of dissertations completed during each period.

Table 4.
Ten Most Productive Institutions for Each Period.

1921-1956	1960-1970	1977-1988
Columbia	Indiana	Indiana
New York	Syracuse	S. Calif.
Indiana	New York	Boston
Iowa	S. Calif.	Syracuse
Penn. St.	Michigan St.	Pittsburgh
Wisconsin	Ohio St.	Florida St.
Ohio St.	Columbia	Brigham Young
Chicago	Nebraska	East Texas
Stanford	Florida St.	Michigan St.
U. Michigan	Boston	Penn. St.

Only one institution, Indiana University, appears in all three columns. During the period 1921-1956, Indiana University had the third highest number of dissertations. During the other two periods, Indiana University was the most productive institution. Five other institutions, including Syracuse University, University of Southern California, Michigan State University, Florida State University, and Boston University, are included in the last two time periods but do not appear in the first. The current study shows that these six institutions continued the dominance they established during the 1960s.

The current study also highlighted some major differences among the time periods. The most striking differences are between the first and last columns of table 4. Two of the most productive institutions in the two earlier periods, Columbia University and New York University, do not appear in the list for the most recent period. Ohio State University also appeared on the lists for the two earlier periods, but was seventeenth for the most recent period. Pennsylvania State University is included in the 1921-1956 and 1977-1988 lists, but was less dominate during the 1960s.

CONCLUSION

Over the past seven decades, some institutions have expanded while others have reduced the number of ID&T graduates. Given the concentration of dissertations among a relatively small percentage of the faculty, these shifts may be the result of individual faculty retirements rather than significant institutional change of focus.

During the last seven decades there has been a steady increase in the number of doctoral dissertations completed at institutions in the United States. Approximately 127 dissertations in the field are now being completed each year at forty-six institutions of higher education. These dissertations are the latest in a long line of dissertations dating from 1921. The field of instructional development and technology is a growing and viable field with a substantial body of doctoral dissertation research.

REFERENCES

Caffarella, E. (in press). *Doctoral research in instructional design and technology: A directory of dissertations, 1987-1988.* Washington, DC: Association for Educational Communications and Technology.

Caffarella, E. P., & Sachs, S. G. (1988). *Doctoral research in instructional design and technology: A directory of dissertations, 1977-1986.* Washington, DC: Association for Educational Communications and Technology.

Huang, C. (1979). *Monograph of doctoral studies in educational technology: 1960-1970.* New York: City University of New York, York College, Center for Educational Technology. ED 184 555.

Huang, C. (1980). Analysis of doctoral production in educational technology: 1960-1970. *Educational Communications and Technology Journal, 28* (1), 3-9.

Kirschner, C. D., Mapes, J. L., & Anderton, R. L. (1975). *Doctoral research in educational media 1969-1972.* Stanford, CA: ERIC Clearinghouse in Information Resources.

Miller, E., & Mosley, M. L. (1986). *Educational media and technology yearbook 1986* (vol. 12). Littleton, CO: Libraries Unlimited.

Moldstad, J. (1956). Doctoral dissertations in audio-visual education [1921-1956]. *Audio-Visual Communication Review, 4* (2), 291-333.

Moldstad, J. (1958). Doctoral dissertations in audio-visual education: Supplement I [1956-1957]. *Audio-Visual Communication Review, 6* (1), 33-48.

Moldstad, J. (1959). Doctoral dissertations in audio-visual education: Supplement II [1957-1958]. *Audio-Visual Communication Review, 7* (2), 142-153.

Moldstad, J. (1961). Doctoral dissertations in audio-visual education: Supplement III [1958-1960]. *Audio-Visual Communication Review, 9* (4), 220-229.

AECT
The Year in Review

Robert E. Holloway
Instructional Technology
Center for Excellence in Education
Northern Arizona University, Flagstaff

The Association for Educational Communications and Technology (AECT) is the largest and oldest educational media and technology organization in the United States. With a core membership of approximately 5,000 and affiliates representing another 9,000, AECT continues to serve as the primary national association which addresses a wide range of educational technology policy issues.

The most significant events for AECT this year were (1) increasing the focus on national policy; (2) revising governance procedures; (3) establishing a funded cash reserve policy; and (4) approving new national offices. Each of these represents a milestone in the development of the association.

OPERATIONS

Stan Zenor, executive director, was offered and accepted a two-year contract renewable annually. This was a vote of confidence for the quality of the work of the executive director. At the same time, discussions of new priorities were initiated and, working with the strategic planning task force, the Executive Committee suggested increasing the time spent on membership growth, strengthening the national office, and developing a work plan for each year. A new marketing plan, developed by Karen Gourlay of the national office staff, was presented to the AECT Board and approved. The change from an antiquated computing system was completed and a new membership directory was published. A new coordinator of conventions, Donna Hoffman, ably took over planning national meetings.

The most significant symbolic change was approval to seek new offices in Washington, D.C. For the first time, AECT has a national office with a conference room large enough for the AECT Board to meet. The new address is:

1025 Vermont Avenue, N.W.
Washington, DC 20005
(202) 347-7834
FAX (202) 347-7839

Also for the first time, the Executive Committee and most of the AECT Board are functionally connected by electronic mail. For the most current list of addresses, contact

Ed Caffarella on BITNET at CAFFAREL@VCUVAX. (If you have BITNET access, you may also want to subscribe to the EDTECH bulletin board at EDTECH@OHSTVMA.)

GOVERNANCE

The AECT Assembly, made up of councils representing the major constituency groups—divisions, state affiliates, and national affiliates—meets at each national convention. The attempt to involve constituent groups has had mixed success, primarily because delegates have had little advance preparation and an unclear mission. Over the last three years changes have been made and tested to improve the quality and efficiency of the Assembly operation. The Assembly will now have copies of the strategic plan for the Association before the national convention. Rules for self-governance of the Assembly have proven successful. Credit for the success is given to the steering committee chairs.

An increase in the number of regional chapters, a concept implemented by Don Smellie, past president, suggests this form of local membership has met needs in many locations.

The Renaissance and Reformation theme of the 1989 summer leadership conference (held in Roanoke, Virginia) expresses the current evolutionary state of AECT. This culminated with a complete revision of the bylaws, chaired by David Graf, and proposed revisions to the constitution (Articles of Incorporation) for 1991. In addition to passing an operating budget of over a million dollars, the AECT Board approved the major move of the national office to a new leased facility (see above).

ACTIVITIES

One of the major functions of an association is to provide the membership with continuing education opportunities. The major professional development conference was hosted by Mike Molenda at Indiana University. The focus was distance education in both education and business and industry training. One outcome was a *TechTrends* interview with Jason Ohler, one of the principal speakers.

Workshops and regional meetings help those who are able to attend, but the major contribution of AECT has been the refurbishing of both periodical and nonperiodical publications. The major periodicals, *Educational Technology Research and Development*, and *TechTrends*, are timely harbingers. Other recent nonperiodic publications are *Standards for College and University Learning Resources Programs*, *Copyright and Instructional Technologies*, and *Guidelines for the Accreditation of Programs in Educational Communications and Information Technologies*. These and more are available from the AECT Bookstore.

A major teleconference on Star Schools started the national convention in Dallas, Texas. Jim Picquet and Lee Crowley arranged for on-site production of a panel discussion by all recipients of Star Schools grants and, representing the sponsor of the Star Schools legislation, Amanda Broun, education counsel for Senator Kennedy's office. The videotape of this conference was added to the materials available from the AECT Bookstore.

As part of a long-term commitment, AECT participated in a major project on "information literacy" brainstorming by the National Commission on Libraries and Information Science and AASL. The result is an umbrella organization, the National Forum for Information Literacy, chaired by Patricia Breivik, ALA; Bob Holloway is vice chair.

THE PROFESSION

A number of policy issues will be exceptionally important in the near future. Federal funding has again proved to be a stimulus. Although funding levels are far below those of the early NDEA projects, the requests for proposals have focused and shaped thinking in the field. The invested effort and increased discussion help other funding sources, private and state, assign priorities. This is especially true of distance education, but is also observable with regard to interactive technologies. AECT serves on the consulting boards formulating guidelines when invited and testifies on legislation.

Accreditation and certification are inseparable issues. Accredited programs usually offer the experiences for certification and so are a control point for any profession where certification is recognized. The processes are at a crossroads. These generally dull issues, except to those being evaluated, are increasingly under siege by those who prefer no regulations, other interest groups with overlapping constituencies, and changes in the field itself. To respond to this growth and change, the AECT Board has formed a task force, chaired by Edward Caffarella, to coordinate the separate activities in the Association and develop strategy. This is an important function of the national association and one which cuts across the interest groups in the profession. It is likely the most significant activity of the decade and one to which AECT will devote its most valuable resource, the energy of the membership.

Part Two

Technology Update

Introduction

The purpose of this section is to continue the tradition of keeping readers current on the technical developments of the year.

The current interest in expert systems is explored by Jones, Li, and Merrill, who explore essential components of instructional design if an expert system is to be of value.

David Moursund, one of the pioneers of educational computing, is interviewed by Carolyn Knox-Quinn. In the interview he gives a short history of his early efforts to establish educational computer associations and educational computing journals. He brings those efforts up to date here.

Because of the current interest in interactive media, Brockenbrough S. Allen provides a descriptive essay on how professionals are being educated to produce and develop this technology. Jonassen and Wang continue that discussion with an exploration of hypertext and its implications for designers.

Francine Fukui provides a fascinating look at Japanese education for those who want to make comparisons with their own systems.

Thomas Russell summarizes a conference at Indiana University dealing with distance education and the section is completed with a summary of significant events in 1989 by Rockley Miller and John Sayers.

Expert Systems in Instructional Design

Mark K. Jones
Zhongmin Li
and
M. David Merrill
Department of Instructional Technology
Utah State University, Logan

INTRODUCTION

There has been considerable interest in recent years in the application of artificial intelligence methods to a variety of enterprises. This renewal of interest has principally been motivated by the practical and commercial success of computer programs called expert systems, which attempt to capture the knowledge and experience of a human expert and apply this to decisionmaking in some discipline. While computer programs have served for years as tools to practitioners, the interest in expert systems relates to the programs' abilities to reach conclusions despite incomplete or missing data.

Not surprisingly, instructional design researchers have looked at expert systems to see if these would be valuable tools for our field (Jones & Massey-Hicks, 1987; Gustafson, 1990; Ranker, 1990). Our own research at Utah State University, the Second Generation Instructional Design Research Program, began in this way. ID EXPERT v1.0 was implemented on a VAX computer using the expert system shell *S.1*. This prototype was primarily rule-based with a linear interface. It did, however, demonstrate the feasibility of an instructional design expert. This v1.0 prototype is able to guide a limited content analysis, make reasonable recommendations for course organization, and make reasonable recommendations about possible transactions within this course organization for a limited domain of subject matter. This prototype explored various rule structures, including the accumulation of evidence using certainty factors for decisions involving a large number of attributes (Merrill & Li, 1988). This prototype was funded by the Army Research Institute for the Behavioral and Social Sciences, in cooperation with the U.S. Office of Personnel Management and Human Technology, Inc.

Our experience with this first system had an interesting effect. We found that our principal problems in building the system came not from the technology but from the limitations of theory in instructional design. The methodology for constructing an expert system begins with a knowledge acquisition process in which the facts and rules of a domain are elicited from an expert, or group of experts, in the domain, and then translated into code for the expert system program. This procedure works best with well-structured domains. Unfortunately for instructional design, we often found ourselves unable to express the knowledge of our field in specific, consistent, and useful rules.

This will not come as news to the practitioner of instructional design. While current ID theory provides some useful guidelines, frequently the designer is left to his or her own intuition and experience. For example, much has been written on how to write an instructional objective. But where are the prescriptions for organizing an instructional module consisting of a given set of objectives? We know how to perform an audience analysis, but what rules exist for the customization of instructional strategies based on learner characteristics? Most importantly, in our view, the content analysis methods of conventional ID delineate the components of knowledge to be instructed, but provide no guidance for generating instruction that integrates these knowledge components into the cohesive "mental models" which students must acquire if they are to comprehend dynamic and complex phenomena.

Our conclusion is that while it is possible to construct an expert system to aid instructional designers to use existing methodology, the usefulness of such systems will be limited. What is required is a new generation of instructional design theory that will provide a richer and more complete knowledge base about instruction and its design and delivery from which a more effective expert system can be constructed. The goal of our research is to help develop such theory.

LIMITATIONS OF ID_1

We identify a number of specific shortcomings to the current generation of instructional design theories, which we term ID_1. These have been discussed in detail elsewhere (Merrill, Li, & Jones, 1990); in summary they are:

Limitation 1. Content analysis does not use integrated wholes, which are essential for understanding complex and dynamic phenomena. First generation instructional design methods attempt to identify the components of subject matter. These constituent components are then used to prescribe course organization and sequence. The elements of this analysis are individual content components such as facts, concepts, principles (rules), or procedures. The resulting instruction may be effective in teaching these pieces of the content, but is often not effective in helping students to integrate these components into meaningful wholes. Hence, students are able to pass exams but cannot apply the knowledge in a wider context.

Limitation 2. Limited prescriptions for knowledge acquisition. While ID_1 methods prescribe content structure as a result of the content analysis, none prescribe the subject matter components necessary to build a complete knowledge base for this structure. Hence, the resulting structures are little more than content outlines for which the designer must still gather considerable additional material in order to build the course.

Limitation 3. Limited prescriptions for course organization. For most ID_1 methods there is a gap between content analysis and course organization strategies. The prescription for course organization strategies is either not present or superficial. Prescriptions range from a one-to-one correspondence between content structure elements and instructional modules, to the bottom-up sequences suggested by Gagné hierarchies. But none of these ID_1 methods adequately accounts for different levels of instructional outcomes, such as familiarity versus basic instruction versus remediation. And none of the ID_1 methods considers the highly interactive nature of the new technologies and how to prescribe highly interactive sequences.

Limitation 4. Existing theories are essentially closed systems. There is no means of incorporating fine-grained expertise about teaching and learning, gained from research, and applying this in the design process. While there remains much to understand about how people learn, we in fact know a great deal already. The designer of instruction must, however, apply this knowledge separately from the application of ID_1 theory, as no hooks are built into the theory to incorporate and apply new and better knowledge as it is discovered.

Limitation 5. ID_1 fails to integrate the phases of instructional development. Methodology based on ID_1 defines five phases of instructional development: analysis, design, development, implementation, and evaluation. While the outcomes of each phase are inputs to the next, and the development cycle is iterative, that is the extent of the integration of the phases. Separate tools are used, and separate knowledge representations are maintained in each phase. Theory provides no prescriptions for how changes made in one phase should lead directly to changes in another.

Limitation 6. ID_1 teaches pieces but not integrated wholes. Each of these ID_1 methods attempts to prescribe the characteristics of the stimulus presentation to the student. These presentation components consist of elements such as definitions, examples, nonexamples, practice problems, attention-focusing help, and prerequisite information. In every case the instructional designer must compose an instructional strategy from such elements to make a complete whole. Often these strategies take on a disjointed character in which one content element is taught after another but little is done to integrate a series of elements into a whole.

Limitation 7. Instruction is often passive rather than interactive. Most of the ID_1 theories were formulated before interactive media (computer-based instruction, interactive video, intelligent tutoring systems) were readily available. As a consequence, most of these models concentrate on the stimulus elements of the presentation rather than on input elements. Instruction based on ID_1 is frequently passive rather than interactive, requiring little mental effort on the part of the student. ID_1 theories are display-orientated (our own work is called *Component* Display *Theory*) rather than transaction- or interaction-oriented. They prescribe examples and nonexamples but have little to say about the use of experiential interactions, simulated environments, or controllable worlds. (See Merrill, 1988.)

Limitation 8. Every presentation must be constructed from small components. With ID_1 methods the designer must always compose every instructional strategy from basic display elements, e.g., definitions, rules, examples, and helps. This means that for each lesson the designer must analyze and select every display element for presentation to the student. If one were to consider a larger content element, a mental model, then it is conceivable that there is a corresponding instructional transaction for promoting the acquisition of this mental model. Composing instruction from larger transaction units would mean considerable savings in development time and resources. By analogy, first generation instructional design is a little like limiting a chemist to the basic elements. Chemists can make anything, but to get water they must start with hydrogen and oxygen and make the compound first. We need some instructional compounds that can be used as wholes. However, none of the ID_1 methods identify such transaction wholes.

Limitation 9. Current ID is labor-intensive. Current instructional design and development practices are extremely labor-intensive. Even though the hardware is affordable, the courseware frequently is not. A development/delivery ratio of more than 200:1 is too high. The current ratio for designing and developing instruction for the new interactive technologies exceeds 200 hours of design/development for each one hour of delivered instruction (Lippert, 1989). Some estimates suggest ratios exceeding 500:1 just for programming.

PROPOSED SOLUTION

The Second Generation Instructional Design (ID$_2$) Research Program addresses these problems directly, by creating a new generation of instructional design and development procedures and tools for use with technology-based, interactive instructional delivery systems. Current research is supported in part by a grant from International Business Machines Corporation.

ID$_2$ builds on existing theories of instructional design, but addresses the shortcomings noted above. Specifically, ID$_2$ will be capable of: aiding the development of instruction to teach integrated knowledge; prescribing instructional strategies; incorporating new knowledge about teaching and learning and applying this in the design process; and integrating the phases of instructional development.

ID$_2$ will comprise the following components:

- A model for representing domain knowledge

- A library of instructional transactions

- A means of prescribing pedagogic decisions

- An online intelligent advisor program that dynamically customizes the instruction during delivery

Knowledge Representation for ID$_2$

An important aspect of human cognition is representation. The same information may be represented in different ways, such as textual, graphical, or verbal. Research has indicated that even inside human memory, different forms of representations may be used to represent the same information. To avoid the details of various forms of representation in the human brain, the term *mental model* is used to mean the internal representation of knowledge. It is assumed that when learning occurs, a student either forms a new mental model, or modifies an existing mental model of the learned subject. However, from the instructional knowledge analysis perspective, the form in which the mental model exists is less critical. Which form of mental model a piece of instruction should promote is a question to be addressed during the course organization phase of the instructional design rather than the knowledge analysis phase.

An advantage to tying knowledge analysis to mental models is that the analysis is based on wholes and relationships of wholes rather than on components only, which is typical of the first generation of instructional design theories.

As the mental model is the internal representation of knowledge, a knowledge structure is defined as a computational (external) representation of the same knowledge. Mental model is used here as a generic term for an internal (cognitive) representation of knowledge. In the same manner, knowledge structure is used as a term for any computational knowledge representation mechanism. There is a correspondence between a mental model and a knowledge structure in that they both represent the same knowledge but in two different media. For instructional purposes, a knowledge structure is all the knowledge required to promote the acquisition of a given mental model, including its components, its organization, and its elaboration. It is hypothesized that if a student is taught the computational knowledge representation, this will promote the development of an internal representation of the knowledge that corresponds to but may not necessarily have the same form as the knowledge structure.

Key to ID_2 is the acquisition and representation of course content. We propose to represent knowledge in terms of objects we call frames; each frame has an internal structure (slots, which contain values for the structure), and links to other frames. These (both internal and external) are termed elaborations of the frame. The set of all elaborated frames together, which contains all the knowledge to be instructed by a course, is called an elaborated frame network.

It is hypothesized that there are three fundamental frame types:

- Entities, which correspond to some thing, for example, a device, object, person, creature, place, or symbol

- Activities, sets of related actions to be performed by the learner

- Processes, sets of related actions that are entirely external to the learner

There are also three types of elaborations:

- Components, which correspond to the internal structure of a frame (for an entity, the components would be parts of the entity; for an activity, steps; and for a process, events and causes)

- Abstractions, which correspond to a "kinds-of" class/subclass hierarchy into which the frame may be classified

- Associations, meaningful links to other frames in the network

The network structure of the knowledge representation allows information to move through the structure, so that data contained in one part of the net affects the data stored elsewhere. Two principal means by which this occurs are:

- Inheritance, in which attributes of a class or superclass in an abstraction hierarchy are passed to a subclass or instance

- Propagation, in which the contents of a frame influence the contents of another frame connected to it via an association link

Knowledge analysis and acquisition is the process of gathering and organizing all of the information required for the student to acquire a given mental model or set of mental models. The product resulting from the knowledge analysis and acquisition process is an elaborated frame network. For a more detailed account of the knowledge analysis and representation, see Jones, Li, & Merrill (1990).

Transactions

A transaction is defined as a mutual, dynamic, real-time give and take between the instructional system and the student in which there is an exchange of information. The purpose of a transaction is to promote the acquisition of one or more mental models. Instruction designed using ID_2 is in terms of a sequence of these transactions.

The adequacy of a transaction is determined by a number of factors, including the degree of active mental processing involved, the completeness with which the transaction promotes acquisition of the target mental model, the degree to which the transaction elaborates a prerequisite mental model, and the degree to which the transaction can be customized to the special needs of individual students or groups of students. Transactions are categorized by the content elements instructed (for example, the component — parts — elaboration of an entity frame), and by the instructional strategy implemented for that content.

Frequently the effective implementation of a particular instructional strategy will require more than a single transaction. The set of transactions that implements a given instructional strategy to teach a particular elaborated frame in a particular domain, in order to promote the acquisition of a given mental model by a given student, is referred to as a *transaction frame set*. Similarly, the set of transactions necessary to achieve a given instructional goal is referred to as a *transaction goal set*. Note that these terms refer to the effects of the transactions, not to collections of code segments. A transaction is not a piece of code or an instructional artifact but the effect of executing a piece of code or an instructional artifact. It is a logical construction, not a physical one.

The code segment which when executed causes a transaction to take place is called a *transaction instance*. This is created by the transaction configuration system (TCS) as a result of an object-oriented design process. A class "transaction" is defined, with a subclass structure beneath it corresponding to the different types of possible transactions that can be generated by the system. A given transaction is instantiated by the TCS from this class hierarchy, and the capabilities of the transaction instance are inherited through the class structure. The instructional artifact thus created may be stored in a library of such artifacts for reuse. For efficiency, the TCS may access the library and recommend instantiated transactions in place of generating new transactions. The ability to assemble courses from such previously prepared standard components will be a major source of economy in the instructional design process using ID_2.

It is important to recognize that the delivery method for a transaction is not constrained by ID_2. In addition, existing instruction, not created with ID_2, may be categorized, placed in the library, and recommended by the system. To be included in the library, it is necessary only that a transaction be describable in terms of its intended instructional outcomes and the type of domain knowledge instructed. Examples of possible transactions range from a teacher-given lecture, through CAI and interactive video presentations, to intelligent tutoring systems.

Pedagogic Prescriptions

Instructional strategy specifies a pedagogy for selecting, sequencing, customizing, and integrating instructional units. Strategy exists at several levels. There is strategy embedded into a transaction that controls the presentation of the transaction. This may be termed *Microstrategy*. Above this level, there is the strategy which directs the assembling of a set of transactions into a transaction frame set, to instruct a particular elaborated frame. There is the higher-level strategy which integrates the instruction for a set of elaborated frames, each with its own transaction frame set, into a larger instructional unit which corresponds to an instructional goal. At the highest level there is strategy to integrate all goals into a course. These levels may be termed *macrostrategies*. In this section we are concerned only with macrostrategies.

The identification of instructional goals is critical to the design of instruction for ID_2. A goal corresponds to some learned capability or performance which the student will attain as a result of the instruction. The achieving of a goal may require the acquisition of one, or a set of, mental models by the learner.

An instructional (macro) strategy is implemented with one or more transaction frame sets. A transaction frame set, as discussed above, is constructed to include all the transactions necessary to promote the acquisition of a given mental model. The pedagogic strategy determines which of the possible transaction instances should be generated to achieve the instructional goal. Any given frame set will include only a few of the transaction instances which could be generated for that type of knowledge structure. Hence the pedagogic strategy serves to direct and constrain the application of the transactions. In addition, because each transaction requires only certain elements of the knowledge structure, the strategy also directs and constrains the knowledge acquisition to just the portions of the knowledge structure required for the goal. Without such constraint, the knowledge acquisition process would be completely open-ended.

A limitation of ID_1 is the lack of pedagogic prescriptions. ID_2 will contain rules for prescribing instructional strategies, which in turn will prescribe transactions. The prescription of instructional strategies will result from an analysis of the requirements and constraints of a particular instructional situation, and will lead to the identification of instructional goals.

Information gathering is the first requirement of strategy analysis. Relevant information includes an analysis of the application to which the learning will be put, the characteristics of the learner population, and the environmental conditions under which the instruction will be administered. Using this information about a particular instructional situation, strategy analysis provides both *prescriptions* and *filters* for the knowledge acquisition process. The knowledge acquisition process is general, that is, a Knowledge Acquisition System knows about frame components, organization, and elaboration but not which of these elements may be appropriate for a given situation. A *prescription* indicates that a particular goal requires a given level of abstraction (organization) and certain links between *frames* (elaboration). A *filter* indicates that a particular goal does not require certain frame components, certain organizational structures and certain elaborative links. ID_2 would provide rules for selecting prescriptions and filters that correspond to particular kinds of goals. A Strategy Analysis System would guide the user to select a goal type consistent with the course to be developed and would then provide prescriptions and filters which would direct the knowledge acquisition process.

An Intelligent Advisor

This integration continues through to the delivery of instruction by means of an online advisor program. The prescriptions made at design time are based on the designer's best estimate of the learner population. During the delivery of instruction, information about the learner, his or her aptitude, specific goals, motivation, familiarity, and other factors, as well as the learner's expressed preferences, may be taken into account to modify those prescriptions.

The advisor would have access to the knowledge base, both for the domain and the pedagogic prescriptions. In addition, it would maintain a student model that contained information about the learner. Using the information gathered about the student, the advisor would adjust design decisions to customize the instruction to more adequately meet the characteristics of the student. The advisor could also engage in a mixed-initiative dialog with the student which would allow the student to participate in this decisionmaking.

Similarly to the domain knowledge representation, we propose to implement in the advisor what would be characterized as a "weak" student model: one that is not capable of simulating the actual state of the student's knowledge, or identifying as a result of such simulation the faulty conceptions, or bugs, in that knowledge. Rather, information about the student would be gathered, categorized, and entered as data for the miniexperts responsible for pedagogic strategy decisions, in particular the selection and sequencing of transactions.

CONCLUSION

The development of intelligent tools to perform the functions described above, and their integration into a complete ID$_2$ system, is the goal of the research currently being performed. Considerable progress has been made towards a knowledge acquisition and analysis system, with the knowledge representation methodology having been developed in detail. A small number of prototype transactions exist, with a major project on the transaction library about to get under way. Research is in the early stages on the pedagogic prescriptions and the intelligent advisor.

This work will be useful to many with interests in the field of instructional technology. The novice instructional designer will be aided by a set of intelligent tools which guide him or her in the development of quality instruction; the experienced designer can use the same tools to rapidly prototype different approaches to design before selecting a particular design for development; and the managers and customers of instructional development will benefit from more cost-effective development processes. Researchers and theoreticians in instructional design should view ID$_2$ as a framework that structures knowledge about instructional development, and highlights areas where additional empirical and theoretical knowledge is needed. Finally, learners will benefit from instruction delivered on interactive devices that fully exploits the potential of these technologies.

REFERENCES

Gagné, R. M. (1965). *The conditions of learning* (1st ed.). New York: Holt, Rinehart, & Winston.

Gagné, R. M. (1985). *The conditions of learning* (4th ed.). New York: Holt, Rinehart, & Winston.

Gustafson, K. L., & Reeves, T. C. (1990). IDiOM: A platform for a course development expert system. *Educational Technology.*

Jones, M. K., Li, Z., & Merrill, M. D. (1990). Knowledge acquisition and analysis. *Educational Technology.*

Jones, Marlene, & Massey-Hicks, M. (1987). *Expert CML: The next generation.* Paper presented at the Computer-assisted Learning in Tertiary Education Conference, Sydney, Australia (November 30-December 2).

Lippert, R. C. (1989). Expert systems: Tutors, tools, and tutees. *Journal of Computer Based Instruction, 16* (1), 11-19.

Merrill, M. D. (1988). Applying component display theory to the design of courseware. In D. H. Jonassen (Ed.). *Instructional designs for microcomputer courseware.* Hillsdale, NJ: Lawrence Erlbaum.

Merrill, M. D., & Li, Z. (1988). *Implementation of an expert system for instructional design* (phase 2). Army Research Institute technical report.

Merrill, M. D., Li, Z., & Jones, M. K. (1990). Second generation instructional design. *Educational Technology.*

Ranker, R. A. (1990). A computer based lesson development advisor. *Educational Technology.*

Dave Moursund on ISTE
The ICCE and IACE Merger*

Carolyn Knox-Quinn
Editor
UPDATE Newsletter
International Society for Technology in Education
University of Oregon, Eugene

People see you as the founder of ICCE. Can you tell me how it was that ICCE started?

During 1970, the National Science Foundation was beginning to fund statewide systems grants for education. In Oregon a group of people got together and decided to apply for a statewide math education grant. This occurred at essentially the same time that a number of people were getting together to think about forming a computer in education group for the state of Oregon. I was one of the people who was involved in the meetings that led to the start of the Oregon Council for Computer Education, but I was in no sense responsible for starting that organization.

The Oregon Council for Computer Education had its first organizational meeting in the fall of 1971. Relatively soon it became clear that the National Science Foundation wasn't about to fund two very large statewide grants in one state. So, that computer group piggybacked on the math grant. I became the computer person on the math grant and received part-time support for about five years, from 1971 through 1976, from the math grant.

The Oregon Council for Computer Education got a certain amount of money through that math grant each year to support its activities. Our periodical publication during those early years usually consisted of minutes of the board meetings, but eventually, in 1974, I said that I would start a periodical for the Oregon Council for Computer Education. In May 1974, I put out the first issue of *Oregon Computing Teacher*. Remember, during that time, I was partly supported by the National Science Foundation grant, so that in esscence you can trace this publication to financial support of the National Science Foundation grant if you like.

I put out *Oregon Computing Teacher* pretty much single-handedly for about five years. *Oregon Computing Teacher* came out kind of randomly, depending on when materials became available or when I had time to do it. By 1979, we were reaching only about 500 people in terms of circulation. It was a pretty widely distributed circulation, scattered throughout the country, but there was one heck of a lot of work going into putting out a periodical that reached such a modest number of people. I was relatively tired of working on it, and I remember talking to the board, saying that something's got to change, somebody else has got to take this over, or we have to do something differently.

That's when Bob Albrecht called up. Bob Albrecht was founder and editor of *Calculators and Computers* magazine. *Calculators and Computers* magazine was on the verge of

---

*Explanation of acronyms used in the article is on p. 138.

closing down because its paid circulation had not reached a viable number. I worked out an agreement with Bob whereby *Calculators and Computers* magazine ceased publication, their subscribers received a copy of *Oregon Computing Teacher*, and their advertisements were carried in *Oregon Computing Teacher*.

Oregon Computing Teacher had been a modest-sized publication with very little money involved. The money used to publish it came from the paid circulation, and most of the labor was done free. This arrangement with Bob Albrecht meant my needing to contract with advertisers for $1,500 or $1,800 worth of advertising and fulfilling a subscription obligation of 1,500 copies or so. These financial obligations led me to incorporate; I incorporated as the International Council for Computers in Education, which, indeed, was ICCE. That was August 1979, about five years after the first issue of *Oregon Computing Teacher* came out.

The original ICCE board of directors overlapped heavily with the board of directors we had for the Oregon Council for Computer Education. I was president of the new organization. I think I remained president five years before we finally got our act together well enough to have appropriate types of elections and ways of getting officers and new board members.

During the first three or four years of the International Council for Computers in Education we gradually moved toward finding reasonable ways to develop an elected board; not having a board consisting entirely of people from the Pacific Northwest; building membership; building circulation; and making various decisions about who would be ICCE members. By four or five years into the development of the organization, we got a mechanism in place so that the board became a pretty broad-based group. After five years we elected another president and moved into a relatively politically stable, very rapid-growth state of affairs.

Who was your initial audience and what was your initial objective?

The national association for Educational Data Systems started in the early 1960s and developed a number of geographical affiliates. The Oregon Council for Computer Education came into existence at a time when an Oregon AEDS organization existed. The orientation of the AEDS organization tended to be administrative data processing. When the Oregon Council was starting, their focus was toward teachers, a grassroots approach to meet the needs of individual teachers. These teachers felt that there was a substantial difference between their needs and the needs of the educational data processing people. One of the strawmen in terms of these needs was the date of the annual meeting. Would annual meetings be held during weekdays, or would they be held during weekends? There was some tendency for AEDS organizations to hold their meetings during weekdays, when teachers felt they couldn't attend. The Oregon Council held its meetings on weekends, when teachers could more easily attend.

Relatively early on, the Oregon AEDS group and the Oregon Council began to cooperate, holding some joint meetings, and they eventually considered merger. There wasn't great animosity between the two groups. The Oregon Council for Computer Education had gotten to be a number of times bigger than the Oregon AEDS group, and when the vote for merger actually came, my recollection is that the Oregon AEDS group voted for merger, but the Oregon Council members did not. The level of suspicion from the teachers, or the grassroots approach versus the educational administrators, was still quite high, so the merger did not occur. The two groups, after that, sort of went their own way.

The structure of the International Council for Computers in Education was patterned after the National Council of Teachers of Mathematics. The idea was that there would be regional affiliates. We developed a structure in which the affiliates put people on the board in sort of a rotating fashion. That lasted until we started to get lots of affiliates. Then it became clear that this wasn't a good approach. More direct democracy in terms of some better way of holding elections gradually won out. Our current ISTE method of having a national election by direct ballot was sort of a logical outcome of the problem of representing the constituencies.

Historically, about 1984, Dennis Spuck from AEDS and I began to talk seriously about how to improve cooperation between the two organizations. We attempted several different things; for example, occasionally we arranged for people in one organization to join the other's board meetings at a discounted price. We looked for other methods of cooperation, and began to look seriously at a merger.

However, 1984 was a long time ago and the AEDS organization and the ICCE organization boards were tremendously suspicious of each other in terms of their orientation. At that time, ICCE was still very much a teacher-oriented, grassroots, precollege computer in education organization. The board of the AEDS organization, then, was still dominated by educational administration and data processing people. During the next few years, tremendous changes occurred in both organizations. The AEDS organization struggled with a name change to IACE, and it struggled with not knowing which group of members to serve. It identified three constituent audiences: the education data processing audience, teachers at the precollege level, and the higher education computer in education market. It saw itself as being a computer in education group, serving all three markets. As a relatively small organization it didn't have the resources nor the membership to adequately serve all three of those markets.

AEDS, from relatively early on, was one of the sponsors of the American Federation of Information Processing Societies (AFIPS). AFIPS, as it became financially successful, decided to share the profits it made from its conferences with its members. AEDS, as a partial owner of AFIPS, received a substantial amount of money. One year it amounted to about $80,000. The AEDs organization, with somewhat over 1,000 members, received in that one year the equivalent of $60 or $70 per member from AFIPS. The AEDS conferences were also quite successful financially at that time, so the combination of the membership fees and the profits from the conferences and the substantial income from AFIPS allowed them to run an organization that spent $200 per member per year. Even though their dues were reasonably high, their costs for running the organization were maybe three times their annual dues rate. Financially, this left them very vulnerable to any change in either the success of their conferences or the success of the AFIPS conference, and both of those ran into trouble at approximately the same time. The AEDS organization then ran into some financial trouble due to lack of this income, and they sort of went into a holding pattern while they regrouped and raised some money. They were able to start up their newsletter and research journal again. During the same period of time as it regrouped, the structure of the AEDS board began to change. The AEDS (or IACE) board became less administrative data processing-oriented and more teacher-oriented—more grassroots-oriented if you like. It was at that time that serious discussion about an IACE and ICCE merger began to occur. I think that captures the essence of what was going on there.

Did merger discussions proceed smoothly?

The initial merger discussions as a whole were fraught with considerable difficulties from the boards of both organizations. But the merger discussion committees in each organization consisted of people who really wanted the merger to occur. In essence, we had presidents of each organization at that time who were supportive of a merger. These presidents managed to put together a merger committee from each organization that were supportive, or at least entered the discussion with a positive attitude. In terms of the structure of the board and those particular presidents, a unique opportunity had occured. I think we had two things going on simultaneously: the merger discussion committees were convinced that a merger should occur, but the boards of the two organizations themselves were still being pretty darn suspicious of each other and not at all sure that they wanted a merger to occur.

What was the purpose of the merger?

As IACE began to get back on its feet, there was relatively serious competition between the two groups. We had two groups whose names were relatively similar, each aiming at all of the fields of computers in education. The IACE group was still attempting to meet the needs of the full range of computers in education. The ICCE group still continued to focus its energy at the precollege level. There was growing awareness that the similarity of names and purposes was confusing members. There were quite a large number of people in each organization that belonged to the other. I think roughly a quarter of the IACE members were ICCE members, for example. From the ICCE point of view, ICCE had to decide either to start its own refereed research journal or pursue a merger vigorously, because a research journal was a missing component of its set of publications. I think from the IACE point of view, they were financially viable through very good fund-raising efforts, but they were still spending money more rapidly than they took it in through membership.

IACE was putting out a research journal that tended not to meet the needs of their largest constituency, the precollege educators. So, it became clear that in terms of meeting the total needs of all the stakeholders and addressing the total group of stakeholders, a merger would be highly desirable. A merged organization would have the resources to address the precollege people and the Information Processing Administrators of School Systems (IPASS) or the Information Resource Manager (IRM) audience, and it would have the combination of the publications, special interest groups, and so on, and could create additional ones that would serve a pretty broad audience.

The merger brought together a group of people with two still relatively different points of view. ICCE board meetings had always been relatively informal; for example, no policy manual was developed. The IACE organization had a large policies and procedures manual, and its meetings tended to be run quite formally. The politics of teachers versus administration tended to enter into meetings, making it difficult to reach consensus on major decisions. So, in structuring the merger, a whole lot of thought went into what constituencies would be represented by the merged group, and how many votes on the board should be devoted to each constituency. The decision to have a certain number of directly elected members at the elementary level, the college/university level, the international level, or the IRM level was based upon very careful thought about what the membership profile would look like after the two organizations merged.

This hasn't been done perfectly. For example, about 4 percent of the total membership was from outside of the United States and Canada at the time the merger occurred, and we decided to make sure that we always had one board member from outside the United States and Canada. On a twelve-person board, one out of twelve is much more than 4 percent, but we decided we wanted to be an international organization and have at least one truly international representative there. The IPASS or the IRM, in terms of total numbers of members in the merged organization, was hard to tally, but our estimate was that about one-third of IACE fell into that category, which would make it only a modest percent,

3 percent or so, of the total merged organization. The decision to have an IRM person on the board was a forward-looking decision. It is one of the constituencies that we want to definitely serve. So, at the time of the merger it was clear that there was a variety of constituencies that we wanted to serve.

At the time of the merger we also gave a lot of thought to the private sector. We realized that there were groups of people we wanted to interface with. The decision to have a Private Sector Council required a lot of thought and a lot of discussion on the part of the merger group. It was another very forward-looking idea. The sense of direction of the field of computers in education or of education as a whole includes more interface with the private sector, but the private sector people and the education people are pretty suspicious of each other. The education people on the merger discussion committees were somewhat suspicious that we were selling out to business/industry. We haven't yet got fully into place our private sector organization, but it's clear that that's a very forward-looking and right sense of direction.

You describe two groups with some historical animosity: teachers and the private sector, teachers and the Information Resource Managers. Is there some overriding reason that is making the merger successful?

ISTE is working on a mission statement and we are doing work on strategic planning. The merger discussion committees agreed that the mission of the organization was to improve education at all levels, throughout the world, and for all types of education. So they're talking about private and public education, in business and industry, and so on. As the merged organization has begun to settle down and has had a chance to think more carefully about what it's doing, the mission statement to improve education through appropriate use of technology at all levels and throughout the world has come forth as the guiding light, as our sense of direction. That sense of direction, I think, overcomes, indeed overwhelms, animosity. When you have a higher purpose and it's a purpose that all people can agree is a right purpose, then it helps formulate decisions. It helps the group to eyeball each other and say, "Well, we're coming at this from different points of view and in some sense we're still suspicious of each other, but it's clear that we're attempting to make decisions that will contribute to the world of computers in education as a whole.

Could you briefly describe how the field would benefit as a whole by the IRMS and teachers getting together?

Part of the process of doing strategic planning or long-range planning is to have a vision of where you're headed. The field of computers in education is just barely getting off the ground. You can trace the history of computers in education back thirty years or forty years or more and you can say, "My gosh, we've had computers in the public schools since 1958 or earlier. We've had computer science departments in universities now for more than thirty years. What do you mean the field is just getting off the ground?" But in terms of computers having a significant impact upon the nature of our educational system, having a significant impact on individual students, we're just barely getting started.

If you look a reasonable distance into the future, you can see such things as all students having quite good computer facilities and telecommunications that link all students to each other, and telecommunications to link all students to massive data banks like the Library of Congress. Such a total system would give students access to a wide range of aids to learning at all levels. You can see that students at all levels may some day have access to the research databases like the Human Genome project.

We get just little tiny hints of these things happening as we see special project schools in which a very large amount of equipment is made available. The teaching load for teachers in such projects has been reduced to four periods a day instead of five or six; teachers interact with each other more; the curriculum is a cross-discipline curriculum; teachers plan projects that their students in a number of classes work together on; and so on. As one begins to see this type of vision emerging, one sees that it requires a massive telecommunications system, a massive sharing of purpose among administrators, students, and teachers. You have a narrowing of the number of levels of bureaucracy. You come closer to the quality circles of participatory management. The goal is higher than preserving one's turf or saying, "I'm a teacher and I do only certain things," or "I'm an administrator and I do certain things," or "I'm a math teacher and I only teach math," and so on. The interdisciplinary, interlevel, and interorientational nature of the job gradually gives way to a goal, which is to help students get the best possible education that they can get in a world that is massively different because of the information age technologies and the types of problems that people have to deal with in these information age technologies.

This analysis suggests that the IRM stands in a unique position between a top-down and a bottom-up approach to instructional use of computers. Both the teachers/students and the school administrators need access to large parts of the same parts of information. The IRM is in a unique position to facilitate the development of the information system that would serve the students and the teachers as well as the school administrators and the state administrators. ISTE is committed to developing lines of communication between these groups.

I think the key idea is that the field of computers in education is still in its infancy, and the future is very bright. ISTE will make a major contribution to that future.

* * *

Acronyms Used in This Article

AEDS — Association for Educational Data Systems

AFIPS — American Federation of Information Processing Societies

IACE — International Association for Computing in Education

ICCE — International Council for Computers in Education

IPASS — Information Processing Administrators of School Systems

IRM — Information Resource Manager

ISTE — International Society for Technology in Education

Graduate Training for
Interactive Multimedia Designers*

Brockenbrough S. Allen
Professor of Educational Technology
San Diego State University
President
Division for Instructional Development
Association for Educational Communications
and Technology

In the early 1980s, the Department of Educational Technology at San Diego State University (SDSU) began offering a one-semester course on interactive video instruction as part of its master's degree program. During the last seven years, graduate students in EDTEC 653 have used a range of delivery systems and collaborated with a variety of organizations to produce six interactive videodiscs. Some of these have served as useful prototypes; others have come to fruition as usable products. In the final analysis, however, the most important yield of the course has been in the skills of graduates who now contribute to the ongoing development of interactive multimedia technology.

WHITHER INTERACTIVE MULTIMEDIA?

A description of EDTEC 653 (and a forecast of its future) is best framed by a review of the technology on which the course is based. After a decade of slow maturation, interactive video is now merely one of several technologies that rely on optical-laser technology for storage of information in general, and storage of "natural video" imagery in particular. The broader advance of technologies that is increasingly referred to (by both Apple and IBM) as interactive multimedia employs a variety of software standards and storage systems in different combinations. The result is an alphabet soup of emerging technologies, including CD-ROM (Compact Disc — Read Only Memory), CDV (Compact Disc Video), CD-I (Compact Disc — Interactive), and DVI (Digital Video Interactive).

As with earlier communications technologies, serious debate about the viability and usefulness of interactive multimedia hardware and software is obscured by the glib predictions of marketeers. However, interest in multimedia technology is growing. The

---

*Dr. David M. Sharpe, Coordinator of Instructional Development team taught EDTEC 653 with Brockenbrough Allen from 1983 to 1989.

Dee Emery assisted in the preparation of this article, portions of which appeared in *DET/CHE News*, a copyrighted publication of the Directors of Educational Technology, California Higher Education (used with permission).

optical storage industry has established a firm footing on the success of the compact disc, first introduced in 1983, and on the much more modest success of the older videodisc format. Interactive video seems poised to emerge into the public consciousness as interactive kiosks appear in shopping malls, hardware stores, and hotels. The installed base for interactive videodisc systems now exceeds 125,000. One interactive videodisc company is reportedly selling 300 units a month to schools in the Los Angeles basin.

In 1989, the interactive videodisc industry produced about 700 titles, up from about 100 titles in 1986. It is tempting to speculate that the technology is therefore entering the early phases of an exponential growth curve. But observers who remember the marketing failures of videodisc companies in the early 1980s will be skeptical about such prognostications.

The business of designing and producing interactive video has not produced great wealth on the scale of a Bill Gates or a Steven Jobs. But after many years of asking, "If we're having so much fun, why aren't we making any money?" some developers are now able to turn a modest profit.

THE STATE OF THE ART

Conventional interactive video instruction relies on computers to select and display video and audio segments (stored on optical laserdiscs) in response to viewer input. The random-access capabilities of laserdiscs allow "natural" video images to be retrieved by computer — based on input from the viewer. The effect of this "editing" capability has been likened to a "personal film" — a nearly seamless assemblage of video segments adjusted to the needs and responses of the individual learner. The design of conventional interactive video instruction has coupled techniques based on computer-assisted instruction with the traditions of instructional television.

The term *multimedia* was applied by educational technologists in the 1960s to describe the integration or coordinated delivery of print and nonprint materials in media centers and libraries (Hicks & Tillin, 1970). The audiovisual industry also used this term to refer to complex computer-controlled, multiple-projector slide presentations that blended photography, graphics, narration, and music in rapidly changing mosaics that (paradoxically) often assumed panoramic dimensions. (Eventually, *multi-image* became the standard term for these extravaganzas.) The modifer *interactive* was added in the late 1980s to describe computer-based systems that combine "two or more media such as text, graphics, writing and video and audio signals" (Wright, 1990, p. 84).

The value of interactive multimedia as a paradigm for informing and instructing (and as a means for creating and synthesizing new knowledge) will become clearer as the 1990s unfold. In any case, courses on interactive multimedia can now claim generic value as a vehicle for training instructional design students. Development of interactive multimedia software fosters acquaintance with diverse production technologies, ranging from television cameras and flatbed scanners to MIDI keyboards and audio digitizers. Instructional design takes place at a nexus of convergent communication modalities where crucial issues often involve new (and sometimes untried) methods for combining text, graphics, photographs, video motion, speech, and music. Experience with design problems that involve integrated delivery systems and multimodal messages provides a broad foundation for diverse careers in educational product development.

TRAINING PROFESSIONAL MULTIMEDIA DESIGNERS

We may be facing a shortage of trained interactive multimedia designers. Until recently, industry experience was limited to a small cadre of experts who "paid their dues" during the pioneering phase of interactive video. During this innovative period, designers acquired their knowledge primarily by participating in various research and development efforts and small-scale commercial projects. Training was informal, dominated by collegial exchanges and mentorships. Interactive multimedia design is still an expensive trial-and-error process in most organizations. Exploiting the technology in an orderly and efficient manner now requires a more systematic and formal approach.

A COURSE ON INTERACTIVE MULTIMEDIA

Competent development of interactive multimedia instruction requires a new synthesis of diverse skills and efficient coordination of numerous specialists. The designer is only one member of a team that may include project managers, subject matter experts, writers, actors, directors, video production specialists, video editors, computer programmers, and representatives of disc mastering facilities.

Purpose and Organization

EDTEC 653 is closely articulated with other courses in the SDSU master's degree program. Students are typically in their late twenties or thirties and highly motivated. Many are actively pursuing new careers and have completed the bulk of their coursework, which usually includes two or three courses on instructional design, courses on educational computing and HyperCard authoring, and a course in basic video production. Most will have completed required courses in statistics and evaluation, and some will have completed a course in project management.

EDTEC 653 accommodates a limited number of advanced students from the University's Department of Telecommunications and Film and one or two working professionals who are interested in learning about interactive technologies. They are invited to participate not only for the video expertise they can lend, but because of their access to production resources that can supplement the Department of Educational Technology's spartan video facilities.

EDTEC 653 attempts to integrate and extend previously acquired experience through seven skill strands:

1. Instructional design

2. Interpersonal skills

3. Project management

4. Development of control structures (using, for example, flowcharts)

5. Interactive technologies

6. Authoring software

7. Video production

Activities in these seven areas become increasingly complex as students progress through the two course projects. In the first project, students "interactivate" (repurpose) an existing videodisc. In the second project, they work in teams to develop a Level 3 videodisc* from scratch, or they develop a detailed prospectus for a novel application of interactive technologies.

The course is not designed to train production specialists or computer programmers. Rather, it aims to train instructional designers who will work on a development team. It affords students with opportunities to learn the problems faced by other team members, even as they master skills specifically associated with design.

Project One: Interactivating Existing Video

The first project extends knowledge acquired by students in previous instructional design courses. The goal is to interactivate a short segment of linear video using the capabilities of a Level 3 videodisc system. Allen (1986) defines interactivation as "a process in which linear, fixed-pace media (including audiotapes, videotapes, and films) are transformed so as to allow the selection, pacing and sequencing of messages to be based on the responses of the learner" (p. 107). Project One helps students to extend their instructional design skills to interactive multimedia delivery platforms without requiring that they develop original video footage. Interactivation is not presented as a means for developing interactive multimedia products (although it has some utility for this purpose), but rather as an exercise that helps students to transition their thinking from the familiar paradigms of linear video to the new paradigms of interaction.

Students work in teams of two. The original video material consists of excerpts from a commercially produced videodisc about 35mm photography. *The Creative Camera* (Holzmann, 1981) uses the constant angular velocity (CAV) format. In theory, the random-access capabilities of CAV discs support true interactive designs. However, the organization of *The Creative Camera* is linear, differing little from a videotape. The information is also extremely dense, which makes it especially well-suited to an exercise where the central problem is how to transform a short "information dump" into instruction that promotes specific learning outcomes.

Project One is based on a three-stage, fifteen-step model described by Allen (1986). In Stage One, students determine the instructional goals and objectives of the existing video and specify additional objectives if necessary. In Stage Two, they subject the continuous structure of the linear video to a detailed four-phase analysis. Four separate phases or structures are logged against an absolute time scale, measured in seconds and in videodisc frame numbers. Video cinematic structure is analyzed as a set of components: scenes, shots, camera angles, etc. Audio cinematic structure is analyzed in terms of music, narration, dialog, field sounds, and so on.

The other two phases of the analysis are concerned with the *instructional* function of audiovisual representations. Video and audio channels are each assumed to carry a sequence of more or less discrete instructional messages. Each message is seen as a component in an overall instructional strategy. Merrill's (1983) Component Display Theory (CDT) provides a set of descriptors for identifying these components and for describing their relationship. As modified for use in the four-phase analysis, CDT provides about

---

*Level 1 systems allow viewers to determine the pace of information delivery. The user can freeze the action, step frame by frame in forward or reverse, scan the disc, or proceed in slow motion. Level 2 players possess an on-board, programmable microcomputer. This permits a videodisc to be programmed to respond to a user's input. Level 3 systems link a videodisc player with an external computer, allowing complex branching patterns and computer text and graphics overlays.

thirty descriptors ranging from "motivator" and "expository generality" to "directions" and "learning strategy."

The four-phase analysis helps students to catalog existing pictorial and aural representations, to determine the structure and function of the existing instructional strategies, and to locate points where the continuous structure of the linear video can be interrupted without damaging cinematic "continuity." The analysis also provides students with a basis for deciding how additional components (to be delivered via computer text and graphics) might enhance the existing instruction or adapt it to new purposes.

Once the four-phase analysis is complete, students develop a flowchart that incorporates existing video as part of an instructional algorithm. Most flowchart symbols include a brief content description and a CDT descriptor that explains the function of the component within the instructional algorithm/strategy. Flowcharts serve as instruments for communication among team members. They permit preliminary validation of instructional strategies and verification of program logic during informal reviews with team members and instructors.

The next step is to develop the instructional messages in more complete detail. A storyboard frame is developed for each message specified in the algorithm. A standardized form includes space for describing video, audio, and computer displays; for indicating programming branches; and for specifying subroutines. Storyboard frames are cross-referenced to corresponding flowchart symbols. Since Project One relies on existing video, original video segments and audio content are transferred to storyboards unmodified.

In the final phases of Project One, students use VideoHype (Berlfein & Allen, 1989), a HyperCard-based authoring system, to control the disc player and to drive text and graphic displays. VideoHype only hints at the complexity (and in some cases the power) of expensive commercial programs for interactive multimedia. However, the system is easy to use and is accompanied by an online tutorial.

Project Two: Designing and Producing Original Software

Development of interactive multimedia software is a team effort. No one student is expected to have the expertise or the time to accomplish this task alone. Just as all seven skill strands overlap and intertwine in Project One, so do the responsibilities of the team members overlap and intertwine in Project Two.

The project is typically developed for a "client" organization recruited by the instructors. In the past, clients have ranged from corporations and government agencies to schools and museums. Clients are coached by the instructors so as to have reasonable expectations of a graduate student undertaking.

Project Two involves a team of over twenty people and requires development of a complete Level 3 videodisc from scratch in eight weeks. The class is divided into four or five independent development teams. Team members assume roles as instructional designers, HyperCard authors, or video producers. A student manager is designated for each team and several students are asked to serve as coordinating designers or producers for the entire class.

MacProject II (Willrett & Young, 1987), a computer-based project planning tool, is used to coordinate about thirty separate tasks related to design and production. Each student spends about fifty hours on the project. Workloads during the eight-week period vary with individual roles and responsibilities. Certain tasks on the critical path, such as video editing, may generate peak workloads of twenty hours in one week for some students. Total person-hours devoted to Project Two usually exceeds 1,500. See table 1, page 144, for a listing of typical project tasks.

Table 1.

Task List for 1988 Multimedia Prototypes.
Boldface indicates milestones. Prototypes typically require several
hundred hours of additional work before they are suitable for field
testing. Not included here are tasks related to specification and integration of hardware and software or tasks related to preparation of
project documentation for student portfolios.

TASK DESCRIPTION	DUE	LEADER
Start	**March 3**	**Instructor**
Integrate hardware and software	24	Technician
Establish learning outcomes	24	Lead ID
Develop preliminary treatment	24	Lead ID
Develop treatment and prospectus	24	Lead ID
Critique prospectus	**24**	**Team**
Review flowcharts	31	Lead ID
Develop flowcharts	April 7	Manager
Draft storyboards; time segments	14	Lead ID
Review storyboards	14	Lead ID
Plan logistics of shoot and editing	21	Instructor
Translate storyboards	21	Translator
Obtain talent, props, scenery	28	Producer
Obtain and organize production resources	28	Instructor
Write scripts	28	IDS
Finalize storyboards, flowcharts	28	Lead ID
Develop shot sheets	28	Assoc Producer
Conduct rehearsals and audio recording	28	Talent
Conduct video shoot	**May 5**	**Producer**
Draft HyperCard program files	8	Lead ID
Specify sequence of tape segments	9	Assoc Producer
Revise and debug HyperCard program files	9	Lead ID

TASK DESCRIPTION	DUE	LEADER
Edit video (rough)	9	Producer
Develop graphics displays	12	Lead ID
Develop digitized sound files	12	Assoc Producer
Develop text displays	12	Lead ID
Test programs on dummy disc	12	Lead ID
Complete master videotape	**12**	**Producer**
Integrate and smooth flow between displays	19	IDs
Debug program files	19	Manager
Edit graphics files	19	IDs
Edit text files	19	Lead ID
Obtain videodisc	**19**	**Instructor**
Debug program with actual disc	19	Lead ID
Demonstrate completed program	**26**	**Team**
End	26	Instructor

The initial phases of Project Two focus on analysis of the instructional problem. Working with a subject matter expert supplied by the "client," the coordinating instructional designers use task-analysis methodology, semantic networks, and other techniques to capture and analyze subject matter. They also analyze the target population's age, educational background, prior knowledge, attitudes, and motivation. Instructional goals and objectives are based on this information. When possible, a preliminary analysis is done during the preceding semester by interested students under the auspices of an independent study course.

Following the analysis phase, students develop instructional strategies and represent these strategies as narrative treatments accompanied by "block diagrams" that depict the large-scale control structures of the proposed software. These plans are usually evaluated by the entire class—an important activity in terms of student experience, as well as software development. Rigorous critiques at this stage ensure that all "specialists" have a chance to express reservations and doubts about the soundness and feasibility of the designs. Following the review, the instructional designers develop detailed flowcharts and storyboards, incorporating suggested changes. Coordinating instructional designers, producers, and HyperCard authors then meet with team designers and instructors to review the storyboards and freeze the design.

The coordinating producers—in consultation with the instructors—then plan the logistics of video production. They organize talent, scenery, and props and schedule rehearsal time, drawing on resources provided through the "client," the SDSU Telecommunications and Film Department, and companies associated with any working professionals who are taking the course.

Meanwhile, HyperCard authors begin developing software "stacks," using VideoHype to generate buttons and "scripts." Since flowcharts and storyboards provide detailed specifications, HyperCard authoring is relatively independent of other production activity. Stacks are tested and debugged using a "dummy disc." Any standard laserdisc can serve this function; the primary concern is to ensure that the scripts in the stack control the disc player as specified in the design documentation.

Coordinating producers are responsible for videotaping, editing, and postproduction. The tape is edited in conformity with storyboards and specifications provided by the coordinating programmers. Music and narration are dubbed and the final tape is sent to a mastering facility for conversion to disc. When the disc is received from the mastering facility, frame numbers for all critical segments are logged on to flowcharts and storyboard forms. Frame numbers are then inserted into the HyperTalk scripts, replacing the frame numbers used with the dummy disc.

One incentive for the high level of student involvement and commitment required by Project Two is the value that project materials can add to a student's portfolio. Students are encouraged to make videotape copies of a sample run-through of the final interactive multimedia program. Project documentation is equally important. Students use this documentation to provide prospective employers with concrete examples of their design experience. Documentation is also used by students as a reference aid for future projects.

Project Two deliverables include an executive summary of the project, an analysis of the subject matter and the target audience, instructional objectives, narrative descriptions of proposed instructional strategies and lessons, flowcharts and storyboards, videodisc, and HyperCard stacks. Evaluation is based on the quality of instructional strategies, flowchart and storyboard accuracy, clarity and layout of text and graphics, and use of interactive multimedia capabilities. Evaluation of individual student performance is based on the quality of the product as evaluated by the instructors and peer evaluations of individual contributions.

PROTOTYPES AND PRODUCTS

The prototypes (and products) described below serve several functions. First and most important, they provide opportunities for student designers to see how plans and design documents relate to the prototype development process. Second, the prototypes provide interested parties (who in some cases contribute modest funding) with working examples that help them to envision how multimedia is related to current or future needs. Finally, the prototype development process serves as a context in which to test models and theories and as a source of serendipitous discoveries of new approaches to multimedia design.

Preparing Subcutaneous Injections, 1985

The first videodisc-based prototype to emerge from EDTEC 653 was produced with limited resources and equipment. The delivery platform consisted of an NTSC monitor and an Apple II + computer controlling a Pioneer 1000 player through a VMI interface. The program was written in BASIC.

Footage of simple tabletop demonstrations was shot and edited in VHS and mastered as a DRAW (Direct Read After Write) videodisc recorded by Spectraimage, Inc. of Burbank, California. DRAW discs are widely used by "sitcom" producers for automated editing and are designed for temporary use only. Image quality is poor and information on the discs often begins to deteriorate after a few months. The principal advantage of DRAW technology is price (about $300 for a single standard-size disc) and turnaround time (one day).

Preparing Subcutaneous Injections was developed as a prototype for use by Commander Anne M. Devney in training Navy medical corpsmen (Allen, Devney, & Sharpe, 1986). Devney was interested in promoting care and vigilance required in proper aseptic technique and dose preparation. The program demonstrated several procedures and included tutorials and practices. It also employed a novel strategy in which learners are shown segments of the procedure with and without errors. Learners were instructed to press the space bar when they detected a violation of aseptic technique. A subroutine determined whether the space bar was activitated within a "time window" and provided appropriate feedback such as "no error occurred," and "You correctly detected an error. Which of these statements best describes the error?" Repeated failure to detect an error resulted in a repeat showing of the video segment in which the action is frozen at the point of the violation. The "error detection strategy" developed for *Preparing Subcutaneous Injections* was later elaborated into a general model for using interactive video to teach procedures (Allen, Lipson, & Fisher, in press).

Taming Tomatoes, 1986

This project was shot on 3/4-inch tape using borrowed industrial cameras and studio space. Editing was completed at the University's public broadcast station and the Department of Telecommunications and Film. A single "glass" disc was mastered by Laservideo, Inc. in Anaheim, California. The delivery platform consisted of an Apple II + with a VMI interface, a Pioneer 1000 player, and a Microkeyer video overlay card. (Overlays were used primarily for text labels and simple graphics.)

Taming Tomatoes was developed as a pilot project for Foodmaker, Inc., the parent company for Jack-in-the-Box restaurants. The program won a Silver Cindy Award from the Association of Visual Communicators. It was designed to demonstrate how a Level 3 interactive video system can be used to train restaurant employees to operate standard food preparation equipment safely and in accordance with company guidelines.

The program is divided into three sections. The first section, "Parts, Functions and Procedures," illustrates and describes two tools used to slice and chop tomatoes – the tamer and wedger. This section demonstrates correct procedures for tool use, shows consequences of incorrect use, and provides details on the tools' parts and functions.

The second section, "Error Detection," uses an adapted version of the strategy described for *Subcutaneous Injections*. Section three, "Review, Practice, and Testing," provides learners with an opportunity to review their knowledge of parts, functions, and procedures.

DISCourse: Finding Your Way to a Negotiated Agreement, 1987

DISCourse was developed on a beta-test version of Mentor/MacVideo, the first system for authoring interactive video programs on the Macintosh computer (Edudisc, 1989). The delivery platform coupled a Macintosh with any one of several models of video-disc player. Video was shot on 3/4-inch tape with high-quality cameras in studio sets prepared by students from the SDSU Department of Telecommunications and Film. Students from the Drama Department assumed most major roles. The 3/4-inch tape was first mastered as an 8-inch glass disc by Laservideo and later transferred to 1-inch tape for a run of plastic discs mastered by the Pioneer Communications of America. The completed interactive program is distributed under the Edudisc label as an example of how to use Mentor/MacVideo software.

DISCourse is designed to demonstrate how to use interactive video tutorials and simulations to teach the art of principled negotiation. The program made extensive use of audio, high-resolution graphics, and computer-generated text in a manner now associated with interactive multimedia.

The program is divided into two tutorials (active listening and options for mutual gain) and two simulations. The simulations involve a disagreement between an imaginary training corporation and a training department in a hypothetical city government. The learner plays the role of a project manager who must work with the city's stubborn training director to resolve the dispute amidst growing political controversy over city resources.

DISCourse uses a hierarchy of menus to represent situations resulting from user choices. The Macintosh also presents contracts, memos, newspaper articles, and telephone and radio messages. The user actively communicates with the program by reading or sending information and by requesting interactions with other characters in the dispute. *DISCourse* makes extensive use of simulated dialogs in which the learner responds to comments by actors through multiple-choice formats.

Prototypes for SDSU's Language Acquisition Resource Center, 1988

The three major prototypes that emerged during this year were partially funded by a State Lottery Funds Grant, which paid for disc mastering and some equipment. Foreign language faculty were granted release time to serve as subject matter consultants. Additional work on the prototypes was carried out by graduate students (paid and unpaid) when the course was over.

The two-screen delivery platform consisted of a Macintosh SE driving a Pioneer LD-V4200 through a phone port. HyperCard was used as the authoring environment for all prototypes except *Voyage en France*, which used the Mentor/MacVideo authoring system. Two discs were produced from 3/4-inch master tapes: a single 8-inch glass disc mastered by Laservideo, and a set of 75 plastic discs produced by Pioneer. Sources of found footage included a documentary on Baja California originally produced by KPBS, a commercial videotape on language instruction. Original footage was shot by students and edited in the facilities of the SDSU Department of Telecommunications and Film.

Un Voyage en France **(a trip to France)** was designed to increase students' French vocabulary and improve comprehension of spoken French while heightening interest in French language and culture. Developed as a prototype for SDSU's Language Acquisition Resource Center, the program combines footage of a native French speaker (shot by the students in local surroundings) with footage from a commercially available videotape (used with permission). The tape, *France from Within* was developed by Bernard Petit, a professor of French at the State University of New York at Brockport. Petit specializes in shooting documentary footage of daily life in France. Three vignettes were laid down on the disc: "Life in a Student Apartment," "How to Make a Normandy Tart," and "The 2CV."

Only "The 2CV" was developed as a working interactive prototype; remaining footage was left for future development. The 2CV is an inexpensive subcompact auto—a French alternative to the VW Beetle beloved for its ruggedness, reliability, and "character." All interaction and dialog for this segment is conducted in French. The program begins with an audio sequence representing an airport departure in the United States. Upon arrival in Paris, the learner is greeted at the airport by Natalie who serves as hostess, guide, and coach for each of the segments. In the "walk-around" of the 2CV, the learner is treated as an active participant in the dialog. Natalie makes queries about vocabulary or events involved in the owner's explanation of the car. Typical questions are: "Why should I buy a 2CV?" and "How fast can the 2CV go?" Brief video segments featuring Natalie provide generic feedback: "No, I don't think that's correct." (These are also intended for use with the other, undeveloped vignettes on the student apartment and the Normandy tart.) Specific feedback is provided as text and audio only.

Aventura en Baja was developed as a prototype interactive video adventure game designed for second-year Spanish students. A companion tutorial stack introduces vocabulary and frequently used phrases. The adventure game format was selected for *Aventura* to provide a framework where language would be used as a tool for solving problems and implementing choices. It is rarely finished in one sitting. Preliminary field testing suggests that students will spend six to seven hours before completing the game.

Using spoken and textual scenarios conveyed by audio, video, and computer graphic/text stimuli, the player travels through Baja California in search of the missing half of an ancient amulet. The actual path taken through the game structure depends upon items held in an inventory (flashlight, water, first-aid kit, money, passport, gasoline, etc.), and on decisions made by the student about how to deal with obstacles and opportunities. Decisionmaking takes the form of directional movement and choosing responses based on the interpretation of audio or textual content. The player may add or drop inventory items at any point in the game.

Several features of the game promote active language processing. All choices and options are presented in Spanish. An online, searchable dictionary contains over 200 frequently used vocabulary items. The program also includes an online *cuaderno* or notebook which automatically stores for future reference captions that describe game events. Students may add their own comments to the notebook as well. The notebook can also capture other text information such as brief passages from famous Hispanic authors. Notebook comments can be saved to a standard ASCII text file at the end of a game session and edited by the student or reviewed by a teacher.

A unique feature of the notebook allows teachers or instructors to adapt the game to specific educational goals by designating an unlimited number of "writing prompts" which will then appear in the notebook automatically at a designated point in the game.

Following the class work on *Aventura*, graduate assistant Ellen Berlfein spent several hundred hours refining the software, focusing on a low-cost compact version which would fit on two standard 800K Macintosh disks and which eliminated the interactive video content.

IMPART (Interactive Multimedia Paired Associate Rehearsal and Training) is a HyperCard-based prototype authoring system for developing interactive multimedia drill and practice lessons (Allen & Eckols, 1989). Designed to support vocabulary drills in any foreign language that can be represented by Macintosh keyboard characters, IMPART allows authors to specify the items presented in a lesson as well as underlying assumptions about drill operations. The system is intended primarily for teaching associations between pairs of objects (symbol-word, picture-word, word-word, etc.) when these require a degree of rote memorization.

IMPART helps lesson designers to select and manage: (1) the representational modality (text, speech, picture) of the stimulus (responses are always represented as text); (2) the context or meaning of the link between the paired elements; and (3) the events involved in rehearsal of stimulus-response pairs.

Four Prototype Museum Exhibits, 1989

These programs were developed for the Scripps Institution of Oceanography Aquarium-Museum as a means of informing museum staff and prospective donors about potential application of interactive multimedia to Scripps' new museum (due to open in 1992). The prototypes were all designed to run on the Macintosh-HyperCard-Pioneer LD-V4200 platform described previously. Three of the prototypes were shot and edited on 3/4-inch tape using a variety of equipment (the fourth utilized an existing disc). The original master edit was transferred to 1-inch tape and used to create two identical full-size videodiscs. A fourth prototype used an existing commercial videodisc.

As a result of the students' work, the Aquarium-Museum has expanded its range of exhibit formats, planning more complex and more sophisticated exhibits that build upon the lessons learned from the prototypes. Scripps produced a promotional videotape for potential exhibit sponsors narrated by former astronaut Wally Schirra which illustrates how the interactive exhibits work. The viewer sees actual footage of aquarium visitors interacting with the exhibits as well as additional examples of the types of video footage that will be incorporated into the final product.

Exploring an Oceanographic Research Vessel takes the visitors on tours of research ships in the Scripps fleet. By selecting locations on a schematic of a ship, the viewer can "visit" locations and observe crew activities, which are briefly explained through combined use of text, graphics, and audio. Scripps operates three basic types of research vessel. The prototype also includes introductions to RV FLIP (FLoating Instrument Platform) and the RV ORB (Oceanographic Research Buoy); these are meant to serve as starting points for additional program design and development. Most of the footage for the prototype was shot documentary style by students. Additional footage was obtained from existing Scripps documentaries and film records.

El Niño examines climatic phenomenon associated with the reversal of important ocean currents in the Pacific. Viewers navigate through a "story line" to learn about El Niño and then test themselves by predicting its effects. How widespread is it? How does it look from space? How does it affect ocean life?

Remote sensing satellite images are used to represent sea surface temperatures. Corresponding locations of phytoplankton populations illustrate some of the techniques fisherman use to determine locations of large tuna populations. Visitors use a simple simulation that allows them to select values for ocean water temperature and observe effects on tuna fish population.

Live video images include preexisting footage of storms caused by the 1983 El Niño. These were obtained from KFMB, a commercial television station. The exhibit also includes a motion sequence obtained from the California Space Institute that is an actually a time-series of satellite images taken of the 1983 El Niño.

Sharkey's Believe It Or Not was designed for sustained interactions as part of the museum's classroom and docent-guided activities. The exhibit explores shark physiology and anatomy while defusing the sensationalism and myths surrounding sharks. *Sharkey's* uses "gee-whiz" statements to capture the attention of young children and adults alike. Don Wilkie, director of the Aquarium-Museum, dissects a shark and reveals the inside workings of the shark's gut and other internal organs.

The exhibit uses an attract loop consisting of sharks with "believe it or not" statements superimposed on the video screen. Concurrently, a menu of these "believe it or not" statements is displayed on the computer screen. This menu is also available to viewers at many key points in the program, enabling them to explore the information according to their interests. The viewer who chooses to discover more about sharks' diets and feeding habits is exposed to the concept of sharks as "opportunistic" eaters. A submenu lists choices such as "Jaws and Teeth," "Senses," "What Sharks Eat," and "Digestion." For this prototype, the branches on "What Sharks Eat" and "Senses" were fully developed. The portion on digestion was partially implemented.

The Fist Encyclopedia prototype uses an existing videodisc by the same title as a source of motion video imagery. Tom Dwyer developed PioneerScripter, an authoring system for generating Level 2 videodisc control programs and downloading them into a Pioneer LD-V6000 player. PioneerScripter eliminated the need to program the LD-V6000 with a remote control device. Control sequences can be developed on the Macintosh and downloaded on demand. Twelve examples of underwater animal life were selected from forty-five species on the videodisc.

Former EDTEC 653 Students:
What Are They Doing Now?

Steven Rodriguez (1984) is now Assistant Professor of Educational Technology at San Jose State University (California), where he teaches courses on instructional design and interactive video. After completing his coursework at SDSU, Rodriguez earned a doctorate at Florida State University, Tallahassee, where he also developed interactive video software for employment training.

Cheryl Dean (1985) is Senior Instructional Designer at Darox Interactive, a company specializing in interactive video training and education. Darox is internationally known for its *Dexter* medical training simulations. Dean manages a team of fifteen designers and is currently designing an interactive video program on literacy.

Mark Better (1986) is an instructional designer at IVID Communications, a company that develops interactive video training for Fortune 500 companies. Better is past president of the San Diego chapter of the International Interactive Communications Society and recently served as a judge for the Association of Visual Communicator's Cindy Awards. He is currently working on interactive video programs to teach service technicians who will work on Nissan's new Infinity automobile.

(Continued on page 152.)

Patrick E. Walker (1987) is a Senior Scientist at Horizons Technology, Inc., which develops custom software and integrated systems for desktop computer applications. He is currently planning the company's new Multimedia Resources Division. Walker is also co-owner and chief engineer at WalkerVision Interarts, an audiovision production company specializing in interactive video and affective/artistic resources for multimedia design and development.

Kathleen Lindstrum (1988) is a Lead Instructional Designer for Courseware/ Andersen Consulting, a division of Arthur Anderson, Inc., which specializes in development of multimedia training software. Lindstrum has used IBM authoring software to create interactive videos for IBM market representatives and consumer product buyers. She recently worked on a design team that developed interactive courseware for Apple Computer Company's new multimedia system.

Steven Wagner-Davis (1989) is a freelance multimedia consultant whose design experience following EDTEC 653 included a stint at WICAT Systems, where he designed interactive video programs for training flight attendants and an interactive adventure game for the San Diego Zoo. Wagner-Davis has also designed interactive video programs for Science Applications International Corporation and Perceptronics, Inc.

CHANGES IN THE OUTLOOK FOR EDTEC 653

In recent years it has become increasingly difficult to organize EDTEC 653 coursework so as to strike an appropriate balance between theory and practice. The arduous process of designing and producing relatively "bulletproof" software has traditionally set the tone for the last ten weeks of ECTEC 653 and has helped to establish its reputation in the San Diego training community. But these activities also took time that might have been used to visit local firms, to critique exemplary commercial projects, and to examine broad trends in the technology. In the future, more time will be allocated to emerging technologies (e.g., CD-I and DVI), and more exotic developments such as virtual reality (see Brand, 1987 for a discussion of virtual reality).

In 1990, the design and production of an actual videodisc will be dropped to make room for a broader perspective on rapidly changing developments. The first project will remain intact as an introduction to techniques for designing and authoring interactive multimedia software. In lieu of producing an actual disc, the second project will require development of an original proposal for applying interactive multimedia technology to a real or hypothetical educational problem. Some or all of these proposals will be developed for interested "clients," thus maintaining the real-world, project-based orientation of the course. The proposal will consist of (1) a technical report detailing the technologies, methods, and strategies for using a particular variant of interactive multimedia technology (accompanied by a literature review) and (2) a short videotape (to be designed and produced by the students) that will help interested parties to "envision" the look and feel of the proposed application. These changes in the course outlook are consistent with the Department of Educational Technology's emerging philosophy about training instructional designers as specialists in prototype development.

HyperCard as a Tool for Rapid Prototyping of Interactive Multimedia

Much has been written about the flexibility and convenience of HyperCard. It has become the lingua franca of the SDSU Educational Technology program because it is easy to learn, because it runs on the Macintosh (the most common machine in our labs), and because it can be used to develop diverse software ranging from databases and hypertext programs to tutorials and expert systems.

From the standpoint of graduate training of interactive multimedia designers, HyperCard's most important advantages appear to revolve around the concept of *rapid prototyping*. In this approach, designers use computer-based development tools and delivery systems to create prototypes that are sufficiently functional to (1) communicate the "look and feel" of a proposed product to reviewers and decisionmakers, (2) permit formative evaluation with representative learners, and (3) serve as a detailed guide for completion of a final version which may be developed and delivered through systems other than HyperCard and by specialists other than designers. HyperCard can be used, for example, to create scripts and storyboards for video and tape/slide productions. HyperCard prototyping for high-technology delivery systems is also becoming more widespread. It is the tool of choice for the early prototyping of CD-I products, according to Richard Currier, president of Vortex, Inc., a CD-I design firm.

A special advantage of HyperCard for rapid prototyping is that screen displays and user controls can be quickly and easily modified by designers who have little programming expertise. It may take several minutes for a skilled programmer to relocate or resize a "hotspot" (area sensitive to mouse or touchscreen activation) using a conventional programming language, whereas the same modification can be implemented on HyperCard in seconds by a designer with no programming experience. This kind of "editing" power makes detailed paper-and-pencil designs less important, perhaps changing the need for rigid approaches to paper-based design documentation. More importantly, "editing power" supports more direct involvement by designers, perhaps reducing the need for artists, programmers, and other "go-betweens" during prototype development.

Rapid prototyping may eventually become the norm in the development of educational products. If so, then graduate programs that train instructional designers may find it advantageous to focus on the kind of tools, theory, and practice that support development and testing of computer-generated prototypes rather than emphasizing completion of finished products for any specific delivery system.

Advantages of HyperCard as a Training Tool

For two decades, the rule of thumb for evaluating the effectiveness of computer authoring systems and languages was: expect to trade power and flexibility for ease of use. Historically, easy-to-use authoring systems were limited in capability and burdened with restrictive assumptions about the nature of instructional interactions.

A new generation of authoring tools exemplified by systems such as CDI/Genesis, IBM's LS-1, and SuperCard attempt to overcome this trade-off by providing multiple levels of access and by integrating authoring activities at these various levels. Higher levels (more removed from direct access to the machine's architecture and operating systems) support design work with graphics, audio, video, and text editors. These high-level authoring environments also support development of links between displays without requiring programming expertise.

Multilevel authoring systems include built-in programming languages (HyperTalk, in the case of HyperCard that can be used to: (1) create more sophisticated displays, (2) build and maintain complex data structures, and (3) generate complex algorithms for governing interactions with learners. Multilevel authoring systems can call subroutines developed in general-purpose high-level languages such as "C" or Pascal. They can also "launch and return" the user to and from applications programs such as word processors, spreadsheets, or graphics programs. Access to high-level languages such as "C" and Pascal affords a means for developers and producers to create their own custom authoring tools.

Many conventional authoring systems treat learning as a preplanned algorithmic process; while they favor the development of "branch-on-performance" tutorials, they are not well-suited for the development of programs that combine information access with instructional support. Nor are they compatible with emerging notions of hypertext and hypermedia as environments in which users navigate through "knowledge networks" according to their own interests and predilections.

HyperCard is well adapted for creating programs that help learners to explore, link, and structure information, but it is also supports development of the kind of mastery-oriented designs that characterize conventional computer-based instruction. It therefore appears well-suited as a means for training designers about how to develop computer-based learning environments that have varying ratios of informational and instructional content. There is, in addition, HyperCard's potential for developing instruments (a third "I"). These are tools for creating new knowledge through simulation, exploration, and synthesis. For example *Aventura en Baja*, a multimedia adventure game developed by EDTEC 653 students in 1988, provides students of Spanish with an online notebook for keeping track of clues, making comments, and responding to writing "prompts" embedded in the game by their teacher.

HyperCard can also be used to *create* authoring systems, another class of "tool," perhaps more relevant to the training of instructional designers. VideoHype, previously mentioned as an easy-to-use general-purpose multimedia authoring system, was created in about 250 person-hours. IMPART (previously described) is an example of a special-purpose HyperCard-based authoring system developed in EDTEC 653. Authors can use IMPART to generate ASCII text files that store information about text items, videodisc clips, and digitized "sound bites." In theory, these files could then be accessed by programs running on other multimedia delivery platforms such as IBM Infowindow.

Potential Limitations of HyperCard

One of the concerns expressed about HyperCard as a tool for training designers is that skills may not be transferable to other delivery platforms, for example MS-DOS-based systems. One response to this concern is that HyperCard can be used as a tool for proto-typing designs that will be implemented on more difficult, or less powerful, authoring systems. A second response is that several HyperCard-like authoring systems are now under development for MS-DOS environments, although the notion that they will compete effectively is arguable. A third response — one that directly reflects the philosophy of most of the faculty in the SDSU Department of Educational Technology — is that the primary mission of the department's master's program is to train educational product designers rather than computer users per se. Most of the faculty feel that HyperCard is a more efficient means for exposing students to design methods and techniques than are MS-DOS-based authoring programs.

Another concern, given somewhat more weight by the SDSU Educational Technology faculty, is that the flexibility of HyperCard may result in undisciplined approaches to software development—leading to "spaghetti" programs that are unfathomable to developers other than the original authors. This concern can be addressed through careful attention to design documentation, structured programming techniques, use of shell programs and templates, and, most importantly, through consideration of recent theories on the design of hypertext, hypermedia, and interactive multimedia programs.

Finally, there are concerns relating to HyperCard's current lack of color graphics, its propensity for generating large files, the lack of efficient compilers, and an absence of any Apple-supported hardware for superimposing HyperCard displays over videodisc images. The faculty expects that these problems will be addressed as successors to HyperCard, such as Silicon Beach's SuperCard, reach the market.

REFERENCES

Allen, B. S. (1986). Interactivating linear video. *Journal of Computer Based Instruction, 13* (4), 107-112. EJ 344 302.

Allen, B. S., & Eckols, S. E. (1989). IMPART: A prototype authoring system for inter-active multimedia tutorials and drills. *Canadian Journal of Educational Communication, 18* (3), 207-220.

Allen, B. S., & Erickson, D. M. (1986). Training interactive videodisc designers. *Journal of Instructional Development, 9* (2), 19-28. EJ 345 884.

Allen, B. S., Lipson, J. I., & Fisher, K. M. (in press). EPOSODE: Enhanced procedural orchestration through student observation and detection of errors. *Machine-Mediated Instruction*.

Berlfein, E., & Allen, B. S. (1989). VideoHype 1.2 (HyperCard-based authoring system for interactive multimedia). Available from Brockenbrough S. Allen, 6964 Caminito Entrada, San Diego, CA 92119.

Brand, S. (1987). *The Media Lab*. New York: Viking Press.

Edudisc, Inc. (1989). Mentor/MacVideo (interactive video authoring software). Nashville, TN.

Hicks, W., & Tillin, A. (1970). *Developing multi-media libraries*. New York: R. R. Bowker.

Holzmann, J. (producer), & Benz, F. (director). (1981). *The Creative Camera* (Level 1, interactive videodisc). Montvale, NJ: Pioneer Electronic Corporation & Valley Isle Productions. (No longer commercially available.)

Merrill, M. D. (1983). Component display theory. In C. M. Reigeluth (Ed.), *Instructional design theories and models*. Hillsdale, NJ: Lawrence Erlbaum Associates.

Willrett, D., & Young, S. D. (1987). MacProject II (computer program). Cupertino, CA: Claris Corporation.

Wright, K. (1990, March). The road to the global village. *Scientific American*, 83-94.

Hypertext, Learning, and Instructional Design

David Jonassen
and
Sherwood Wang
University of Colorado, Denver

INTRODUCTION

Interest in hypertext and hypermedia (hereafter referred to by the more generic term *hypermedia*) in recent years has been growing rapidly and steadily. Hypermedia is a soft technology for organizing and storing information in a knowledge base to be accessed and generated nonsequentially by authors and users. Hypermedia systems are being used extensively in software engineering and collaborative problem-solving applications, for online documentation and information retrieval and help systems, as writing aids, and, more recently, as authoring tools for instruction and learning. Such diverse applications show both the flexibility of hypermedia and the difficulty of creating a discrete definition of hypermedia. Although hypermedia did not evolve as an instructional medium, its characteristics mimic the associative properties of the mind, making it a potentially powerful new learning technology.

In the first section of this paper, we will outline the characteristics of hypermedia systems and some of the problems that may be encountered. Next, we will examine some of the learning applications of hypermedia systems, emphasizing the different types of learning they can facilitate. Finally, we will explore the relationship between hypermedia and instructional design and make some concluding remarks.

CHARACTERISTICS OF HYPERMEDIA

We begin by defining generalized characteristics of hypermedia. Of course, not every hypermedia knowledge base or system possesses every characteristic. In fact, one of the distinguishing features of hypermedia systems is their flexibility in adapting to the needs of different applications. These definitions include inherent features, (nodes, links, networks of ideas, and paths) and ways that users and authors interact with them (interactivity, annotation, and authoring).

Nodes

Probably the most pervasive characteristic of hypermedia is the node, which consists of chunks or fragments of text, graphics, video, or other information. The size of a node varies from a single picture or a few words to the size of a document. Nodes, also referred to as frames, are the basic unit of information storage. Rather than encountering a continuous flow of information, such as a book or a motion picture film, hypermedia places information into nodes that are interrelated to each other in some way. Modularizing information enables the user of the information system to determine what node of information to access next. It may be a node that consists of an elaboration, an opposing point of view, or an example or illustration of the information in the original node.

The most popular metaphor for nodes is notecards, which typically limits the amount of information in a node to a single screen. Perhaps the most important characteristic of nodes is that they may be amended or modified by the user. The user may add to or change the information in a node or crate his or her own node of information for the hypermedia system. Many "browsing" systems, however, provide a set of predetermined nodes that may not be amended. Nodes may be unalterable because they reflect the information-processing requirements of a task as defined by the goal of the system.

Links

The interrelationships between nodes of information are defined by links, the interconnections between the nodes. Links in hypermedia systems are typically associative, that is, they define an associative relationship between the node pairs that they connect. The links transport the user through the information space to the nodes that he or she selects. Links enable the user to navigate through the hypermedia knowledge base. Links also provide organizational information, typically stating explicitly the nature of the relationship between the interconnected nodes. Linked transfers are activated by a pointing device (e.g., mouse, keystroke, light pen, finger on a touchscreen) being directed at a "hot button" on the screen. Many hypermedia systems permit the user to either amend the existing links or create new ones.

Links may be embedded in the text or picture, so that simply pointing at a word or part of a picture will transport the user to another node. Links may be placed in a dedicated screen area outside the information space. Links may be referential or organizational (Conklin, 1987). Referential links refer to information in another node and then permit the user to return via the same link. Organizational links are typically organized in a network of related nodes. Links may also be value, text, or lexical links (Collier, 1987). Value links point from one node to another. Text links connect text to nodes. Lexical links connect regions of text to nodes.

Network of Ideas: Organizational Structure

Nodes are linked together in meaningful ways. The node structure and the link structure form a network of ideas. A network is an interrelated and interconnected group or system of ideas. The ideas in a hypermedia network are the nodes interconnected by the links. Nodes may be linked together based upon semantic relationships in the subject matter or the information processing required by a task. The network may also emanate from the user, who imposes his or her own structure on the information.

The organizational structure of any hypermedia system determines the information model of the hypermedia knowledge base. The information model describes the organization of ideas and their interrelationships which, if explicitly signaled, may help the user to comprehend better the information or problem that is embedded in the system. The information model also facilitates locating and retrieving information in the system. Once again, the information model may be amended by the user, in which case it reflects (to some extent) the semantic network of the user.

Graphical organizers are often used to give an overview of the links and nodes in a hypermedia system. Strategic placement of organizers help to orient the user in the hypermedia system. The use of distance as a metaphor for semantic "closeness" is questioned by some authors. Landow (1990) makes the point that all nodes one link away from a starting node are the same "distance" away, irrespective of their relatedness to the central node. Nevertheless, graphical browsers appear to be popular with users (Leggett et al., 1990) and are included in many hypermedia systems.

Paths

Paths may be determined by the author, the user/learner, or by shared responsibility. Author-generated paths refer to predetermined links within the information space, known as "guided tours" through the knowledge base. Users who do not wish to determine the sequence of access to information frequently traverse systems in this linear manner. Users or learners may also create their own paths. These paths are typically individualized reflections of the logic that a learner uses to traverse the knowledge base. Most systems enable the user to save these paths for later review and annotation. These trail histories can reveal assumptions that the user makes while navigating through the knowledge base. Users or learners also may share these paths in collaborative systems or add their paths to the knowledge base.

Interactivity and Learner Control

Hypermedia permits users to determine the sequence in which to access information (browsing), to add or amend the information to make it more personally meaningful (collaboration), or to build and structure their own knowledge base. The level of user control varies with the system and its purpose. What is important is that users are meaningfully interacting with, and dynamically controlling, the information. They can accelerate/decelerate, change directions, expand their information horizons, argue/fight back, or even switch intellectual vehicles. Unlike most information systems, hypermedia users *must* be mentally active while interacting with the information. Interaction is a hallmark of most information systems. Hypermedia permits a higher level of dynamic user control.

Constructive Environment

Hypermedia systems are typically flexible browsing tools. Some hypermedia systems have become popular and commonly used authoring environments for creating computer-based instruction, for personal note taking or information management, and for communicating with peers; they are also used as cognitive learning tools for organizing and storing users' own knowledge. Many of these applications do not exhibit other characteristics of hypermedia. However, they are important and useful information applications. Therefore, the broadest conception of hypermedia is a software environment for building or conveying knowledge, collaborating, or solving problems.

Hypermedia Structures

The most signficant problem in creating hypermedia is deciding how and how much to structure the information in the knowledge base. The answer to this question depends, in part, upon how the hypermedia will be used. The various applications of hypermedia require different access and information structures.

Unstructured Hypermedia

Unstructured hypermedia is random, node-link hypermedia in which only referential links are used. This type of hypermedia provides random access directly from any node to any other node that is linked to it. Two nodes are linked because one node contains a reference to the information in the other. The user jumps immediately to any topics within the hypermedia by pointing at the item.

The major task in designing an unstructured hypermedia system is to identify the concepts or information fragments to point to and comprise each node. Text analysis systems that can analyze textbooks (contents list, index, and key words) for important terms or ideas. Whenever ideas co-occur, associative links connect the ideas. No overall conceptual structure is implied necessary for unstructured hypermedia.

Structured Hypermedia

Structured hypermedia implies an explicit organization or arrangement of nodes and associative links. In designing structured hypermedia, the designer is saying that there is a subject matter structure or a knowledge structure that ought to be conveyed in the link structures and node structures. Structured hypermedia consists of sets of nodes, each set accessible from any other set. Each set is explicitly arranged to depict the structure of the information. Hypermedia structures assume various conceptual models.

Several possible structures for organizing hypermedia emerge:

- *Semantic structures* reflect the knowledge structure of the author or an expert.

- *Conceptual structures* include predetermined content relationships such as taxonomies.

- *Task-related structures* are those that resemble or facilitate the completion of a task. Primary tasks include retrieving information, such as in information retrieval systems, and learning from instructional systems.

- *Knowledge-related structures* are those that are based upon the knowledge structures of the expert or the learner.

- *Problem-related structures* simulate problems or decisionmaking.

Hypermedia Variables

Along with these general characteristics, hypermedia systems vary along several continua. First, hypermedia systems can be created and described in terms of the content format. This ranges from text-only nodes to full integrated sound, graphics, and animation. Similarly, the type of delivery systems can range from printed hyperbooks with page number links, to computer knowledge bases utilizing interactive videodisc players and distance communication networks.

Size issues relate to different aspects of hypermedia systems. Size or granularity (McAleese, 1990) of nodes is an author-defined characteristic of all hypermedia systems. Systems with small-grained nodes divide the content into a greater number of smaller chunks, while large-grained systems have larger chunks of information and a smaller number of nodes. Related to granularity is the number of links a hypermedia system contains. As the number of links increases, the need for organizing links into understandable patterns also increases. The size of the entire hypermedia knowledge base is also an important variable. Brown University's Intermedia project (Yankelovich et al., 1987) is a knowledge base consisting of thousands of nodes and links. Systems like Intermedia create more potential problems for navigation and also require a mainframe computer to manage the large memory requirements.

Interactivity is another variable that greatly affects the nature of any hypermedia system. The level of interactivity determines the nature of a hypermedia system in at least three ways, as shown in figure 1.

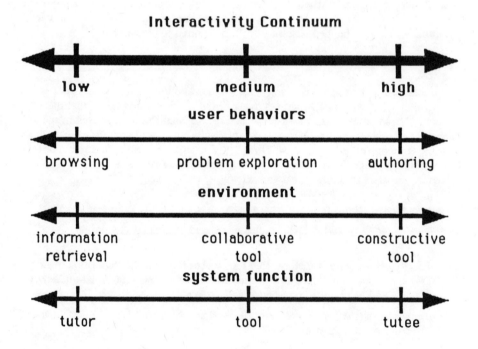

Figure 1.

When users spend the majority of their time browsing, the environment is used predominantly for information retrieval, and the system functions as a tutor for the user. When system interactivity is moderate, users can engage in problem exploration, which can include collaborative efforts. Here users manipulate and modify parts of the system. Authoring requires a system that facilitates reorganization and construction of knowledge through a high degree of interactivity. In this case, the user is actually adding new knowledge and "teaching" to the system.

POTENTIAL PROBLEMS USING HYPERMEDIA

Navigating through Hypermedia

The most commonly identified user problem is *navigating through hypermedia*. Many hypermedia systems consist of hundreds and even thousands of nodes with a potentially confusing array of links connecting them. It is well documented that in such systems, users can easily become lost, not knowing where they came from, where they should go, or even how to exit the part of the program they are in. Users are frustrated by this experience, frequently losing sight of their original purpose in using the hypermedia. They often give up without acquiring any information from the hypermedia.

Integrating Information

A problem related to navigation and equally important to learning applications is integration of new knowledge by the learners into their own cognitive structures. Learning (which will be discussed in more detail in the next section) is the creation or reorganization of the learners' knowledge structures and entails the acquisition of information and the reorganization or restructuring of that information to make it more meaningful. The less structured the hypermedia, the greater the processing load placed on the learner to organize and integrate the information acquired.

If hypermedia can be structured to replicate content or knowledge structures, then it should provide the necessary anchors for restructuring the learner's knowledge. What is not known is how likely users are to assimilate these structures or to use them to integrate what they have learned. The attempt to replicate effective stimuli (users' knowledge structures) with the nominal stimulus (e.g., written word, page, or screen) has met with little success. This is primarily due to the fact that no picture of the effective stimulus is available to replicate. The effective stimulus is also in a constant state of change both within an individual and among individuals.

Synthesizing Information

Learning requires another process in addition to the processes of acquisition and integration — *synthesis* of the information into smooth and automated behavior. Synthesis is similar to the cognitive process of *tuning* in Norman's model of learning (accretion, restructuring, and tuning). Once a learner has acquired information and integrated it into his or her knowledge structure, a new structure evolves. The learner fine-tunes the new knowledge structure by practicing with it and generalizing it to novel situations. As with integration, unstructured, node-link hypermedia is less likely to facilitate the process of synthesis.

Cognitive Overhead

The number of learning options available places on learners increased cognitive demands that they are often unable to fulfill. Hypermedia browsers must be able to monitor their own comprehension of the information presented in the hypermedia, select appropriate strategies for correcting any misconceptions, and develop information-seeking strategies that facilitate integrating information and synthesizing information from the hypermedia. These are known as meta-cognitive strategies, and they require additional effort on the part of the browser. We know that good learners use them and that poor learners do not. Browsing hypermedia places significant demands upon the user, demands that may take energy from the more important process of learning.

Learner Control

Learner control is an instructional strategy that permits learners to direct the sequence of instruction, that is, to make decisions about the type and amount of instructional support they think is necessary. Rather than the instruction directing the learner, the learner is allowed to adapt the instruction to personal preferences or abilities. Learner control is justified by the beliefs that learners know what is best for them and that if learners are in control of instruction, they will invest more mental effort in their learning. Hypermedia use is premised on learner control.

Unfortunately, the research on learner control has not generally supported any learning benefits. This is especially true with average and below-average learners. Research has shown consistently that learners, when given control over instructional variables, do not make the best decisions. Those who need the most instructional support (under-achievers) frequently select the least, and those who need the least (overachievers) frequently select the most. Learners in learner control treatments have regularly learned less than those in treatments controlled by the instructor or by an adaptive instructional design. When compared with teacher-directed or computer-programmed decisionmaking, learner control has generally yielded less learning. These results call into question the fundamental premise of hypermedia—interactivity.

HYPERMEDIA AND LEARNING

There are many conceptions of learning, far too many to review in this chapter. Descriptive theories of learning include cognitive/information processing, behavioral, cybernetic, and others. For the purpose of designing instructional systems, learning is thought of in terms of tasks or learning outcomes, such as Gagne (Gagne, R. M., 1985), Bloom and his colleagues (Bloom et al., 1956), and Merrill (Merrill, 1983). When relating hypermedia to learning, three learning processes seem to be best supported: information retrieval, knowledge acquisition, and problem solving.

Information Retrieval

An important step in any learning process is satisfying information needs—seeking information that answers a question, makes a decision, solves a problem, or aids comprehension. Information about any domain of knowledge is stored in a variety of forms in many places and is organized in different ways. When seeking information, what most people are concerned about is accuracy, understandability, and access time (Chen, 1982). Interactivity can vary from low to high, although there are no specific requirements for high levels of interactivity. Information retrieval is a fundamental learning activity, precursive to many others.

A distinct advantage of hypermedia for information seeking is its ability to integrate large corpi of information in alternative representations. Access to the information is facilitated by the associative organization of the information in hypermedia, which resembles the associative structure of human memory. Hypermedia is capable of providing different organizational structures for libraries of information, thereby providing access to information in ways that more closely resemble the information-seeking behaviors and needs of users.

Knowledge Acquisition

Conceptually, learning is the reorganization of knowledge structures. Knowledge structures refer to the organization of ideas in semantic memory. Ideas are referred to as *schemas*. A schema for an object, event, or idea is composed of a set of attributes. Attributes are the associations that an individual forms around an idea. The schemas are arranged in a network of interrelated concepts known as our semantic network.

Schemas in our semantic network are linked together by attributes or associations. These interconnections enable learners to combine ideas, infer, extrapolate, or otherwise reason from them. Properly structured hypermedia networks describe what a learner knows, which provides the foundations for learning new ideas, that is, expanding the learner's semantic network. This is the richest conceptual model of learning from hypermedia. Learning, then, results from the interactive processes of accretion, restructuring, and tuning (Rummelhart et al., 1978).

Accretion

Accretion describes the accumulation of information in order to fill existing schemata. The learner adds information (arguments or attributes) to the knowledge structure that exists. Accretion can also result in the addition of new schemas that use existing schemas as their model (Norman, 1976). No reorganization of knowledge occurs in the learner's cognitive structure during accretion. Accretion is prerequisite to restructuring.

Restructuring

As knowledge is acquired, learners' schemas expand to a point where the schemas are unable to adequately accommodate or interrelate all of the information. Learners begin to restructure their knowledge by adding schemas or developing new conceptualizations for existing ones. While restructuring of knowledge is the least common learning activity, it is the most important. Restructuring is facilitated instructionally by the use of metaphors, analogies, and inferences, all of which are cognitively difficult. The results of restructuring are new knowledge structures, which enable learners to interpret or access their knowledge in new ways.

Tuning

After all of the schemas have been developed and reorganized by the learner into a coherent knowledge base, minor adaptations are made to make performance more efficient. Through practice or consistent use of new knowledge structures, they are tuned or finely adjusted. Schemas are modified to meet specific task demands or adapted to particular knowledge domains or contexts. Tuning might entail refining a procedure, filling in inferences, or adapting the schemas to new situations.

Sequence

The sequencing of these processes is not invariant. Typically, the learner begins with accretion or the building up of information until it forces restructuring, which occurs for some time. Over time and with practice, the learner tunes his or her knowledge structures, so that it is the dominant mode during the latter stages of learning. However, these processes are carried out simultaneously. While restructuring some schemas, the learner may also be adding new information to other information while fine-tuning other topics. The goal of the accretion-restructuring-tuning sequence is to reach a state of intellectual equilibrium. After developing finely tuned schemas, the learner may enter the accretion mode later when new information becomes available. If that new information is substantial enough, it may elicit some additional restructuring.

Learning from hypermedia includes accretion, restructuring, and tuning. Hypermedia is the ultimate accretion medium, a knowledge base of interrelated ideas that can be readily accessed and assimilated. On the interactivity continuum, accretion is located toward the low end. Accretion implies more than acquisition. It also implies adherence or attachment to a knowledge structure. Providing a basic hypermedia structure, as discussed above, and making the relationship of the nodes to the structure obvious through the link structure will facilitate accretion.

The problem of integration of information into the learners' knowledge structure (discussed above) is a learning process of restructuring. Learners must be able to explicitly reorganize their own ideas in order to better accommodate new information. Restructuring is permitted by the dynamic control capabilities of creating and reorganizing links in the system. This requires a moderate level of interactivity to be effective.

Tuning is the most difficult of the learning processes to simulate in any system because it requires application of the content to make the fine adjustments in the user's knowledge structures. Tuning is facilitated by hypermedia environments that enable authoring and collaboration.

Problem Solving

From an information-processing perspective, problem solving starts with a problem, which includes a goal state, a starting state, and solution paths to reaching the goal, all of which constitute the problem space (Newell and Simon, 1972). Problem solving assumes an unsatisfied goal state. When the starting state and goal state are consonant, no problem exists. Problem solving entails three processes—problem representation, knowledge transfer, and evaluation (Gagne, 1985).

Problem Representation

Regardless of the nature of the problem space, the problem solver first must represent the problem in a meaningful way. This requires accessing enough relevant schemas to make sense out of the problem. The problem must be stated in terms that the solver understands. This stage is the most important to the problem-solving process, because it determines what knowledge will be activated by the solver. One of the strengths of hypermedia is its ability to alternatively represent the problem. Problem-solving applications such as IBIS represent information in the system in constrained nodes, such as issue, position, and argument nodes (Conklin and Begeman, 1987).

Transfer

The problem representation, be it a formal statement, such as a formula, or an informal description of the problem, activates relevant knowledge. This knowledge is then applied to the problem as possible solutions. Problem solvers typically apply some strategy for solving a problem, such as means-ends analysis, brainstorming, or analogical reasoning. Hypermedia may facilitate the transfer process by providing alternative representations of information, such as analogical links. The collaborative nature of many hypermedia environments facilitate brainstorming and means-ends activities.

Evaluation

The problem solver evaluates a solution by whether it produces the goal state with a reasonable amount of effort in a reasonable amount of time. Solutions that do not meet minimal criteria reactivate the knowledge retrieval process in search of alternative solutions. Collaborative environments can facilitate this process.

The information-processing model is also partially dependent on the level of interactivity. Problem representation, like accretion, needs only a low level of interactivity. Transfer, like restructuring, requires a moderate level of interactivity. Many times, evaluation is facilitated by high levels of interactivity. Figure 2 shows the parallels between interactivity, knowledge acquisition, and problem solving.

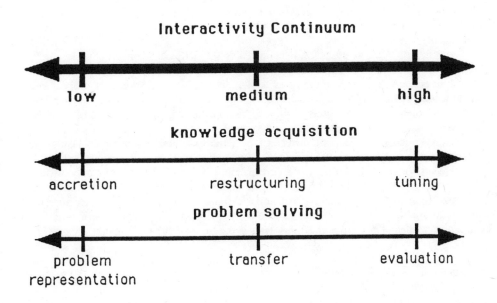

Figure 2.

HYPERMEDIA AND
INSTRUCTIONAL DESIGN

Because hypermedia systems can be comparatively unstructured and because there are problems in using them (such as navigation, integration, synthesis, and cognitive overload), many regard hypermedia as inconsistent with principles of instructional design and development (IDD). Instructional design models are typically linear and procedural operations (e.g., task analysis, producing instructional materials). They are more likely to be closed systems. Hypermedia systems, on the other hand, are less deterministic than traditional instructional designs, not based upon convergent, objective-referenced purposes. They are minimally intervening and are predicated upon cognitive activity instead of behavioral outcomes. A learner's interactions with hypermedia are not predictable, while most instructional designs focus on predictability of responses.

Commonalties in Theoretical Approach

Instructional design is becoming more influenced by cognitive learning theories, which incorporate principles based upon information processing theory, memory and retention theory, and schema theory (Di Vesta and Riebner, 1987). Hypermedia design principles also incorporate principles from cognitive psychology (note that not all hypermedia systems, like IDD systems, uniformly exemplify cognitive principles). The network of ideas that make up a hypermedia can mimic semantic networks of associated ideas in memory that provide meaning for each of the ideas in human memory. Hypermedia may be schema-based, with each node comprising a schema that is associated with other nodes in an associative structure. Hypermedia are able to map the expert's schemas or to accommodate to the user's.

Another theoretical basis for hypermedia is the active structural network. Active structural networks are structures that are composed of nodes and ordered, labeled relationships connecting them (Norman et al., 1976). The nodes are instances of propositions and the links describe their relationships. Since active structural networks are used to represent what a learner knows, hypermedia may be used to map the knowledge of both the expert and the user (Jonassen, 1990).

If hypermedia and IDD still differ, it is a matter of function. Hypermedia can serve many functions (e.g., information retrieval, instruction, collaborative problem solving), whereas instructional design defines a circumscribed process for producing only instruction. Structured hypermedia systems direct the learner's processing but do not control it as is typically prescribed by many instructional designs. If function follows structure, as argued above, then hypermedia multifunctionality results from its malleable structure. The structural malleability of hypermedia systems is the topic of the next section.

Mapping Instructional Designs
on to Hypermedia

The hypermedia model is a generic collection of nodes, links, and structures. Its authoring software "is just a tool for creating, manipulating, and displaying nodes of information embedded into a network structure" (Halasz, 1988, p. 850). The computer system treats all nodes and links the same—as objects to be stored, connected, retrieved, and displayed (Halasz et al., 1987). No meaning accrues to nodes and links until they are authored. Structure depends upon content, not the hypermedia authoring system. Many hypermedia systems are tailorable and extensible to a variety of applications. Designers in flexible hypermedia authoring systems may tailor the hypermedia interface and structure to their own application or extend and adapt the system to meet the needs of an instructional design. These characteristics enable hypermedia to reflect many types of information structures. Since instructional designs seek to structure information in meaningful ways, hypermedia systems may also be used to directly reflect different instructional designs. For instance, hypermedia may map content according to elaboration theory (Reigeluth & Stein, 1983). The content may be elaborated, with nodes and links emanating from an epitome node. Hypermedia reflecting an elaboration structure might contain nodes that depict the organizing structure (procedural, conceptual, or theoretical) in a graphical browser. Links displayed at any time would constrain the options available to the user. For instance, the epitome node(s) would permit access to only the first level elaboration nodes. Those nodes in turn would permit access to strategy, analogy, or summarizer nodes. Users would have to access synthesizer nodes prior to returning to nodes on any higher elaboration level.

Most instructional design models can be mapped explicitly with hypermedia authoring because of its structural malleability. Learning prerequisite designs, such as Gagne's, can be modeled directly by hypermedia by sequencing nodes in a prerequisite sequence. That is, learners would have to complete prerequisite information prior to moving onto the next step. Note that not all hypermedia authoring software is capable of mapping all designs. Like all software, it varies in capabilities and features.

Hypermedia as an IDD Environment

Hypermedia systems may also function as instructional development tools for creating instructional sequences. The Instructional Design Environment (IDE) is an interactive hypermedia system that helps designers create courses by structuring the content and creating instructional sequences (Jordan et al., 1987; Russell et al., 1987). It is built on NoteCards, an idea-processing hypermedia system (Halasz et al., 1987). IDE creates node/link structures that contain information such as class size, preferred delivery vehicle, prior knowledge, course objectives, and learning principles. It leads the designer through a series of decisions about domain knowledge, how the student will learn the skill, and the presentation strategies. These decisions result in a series of outputs, including a knowledge (content) structure, student model (comprehension, bugs, learning styles, etc.), course control (sequencing and inclusion prescriptions based upon strategy and tactics cards), and the instructional units or actual course delivery materials. Each of these elements is defined by types of cards which contain information or rules that may control or inherit information from other cards. Two major analysis tools are provided by the system—a rationale tracer which displays the rationale that designers have given for each decision and a checker which maps elements from one area onto those in another area based upon defined relationships. Decisions are based upon information that the designer supplies and rules that IDE supplies (e.g., after presenting three concepts in a row, test for understanding of one of the concepts). IDE is a sophisticated design environment that is built on a highly-structured hypermedia system.

CONCLUSION

Hypermedia is a flexible information technology that provides a powerful environment for designing, developing, and displaying instruction. The most common applications of hypermedia to date have not been in the instructional area. However, a number of potentially powerful instructional applications are being investigated (Jonassen & Mandl, 1990). Hypermedia is not without some potentially serious drawbacks. Navigation, learner control, and cognitive overload have the potential for mitigating many of the benefits of hypermedia for learners and instructional designers, if these factors are not taken into account. The theoretical foundations of hypermedia are consistent with contemporary instructional design and development models, albeit with a more consistent cognitive and systemic emphasis than many. Hypermedia systems provide sophisticated tools that may advance the integration of cognitive learning principles into practice in the instructional design and development field.

REFERENCES

Bloom, B. S., Englebart, M. D., Furst, E. J., Hill, W. H., & Krathwohl, D. R. (1956). *Taxonomy of educational objectives: Handbook I. The cognitive domain.* New York: Longman.

Chen, C. (1982). *Information seeking: Assessing and anticipating user needs.* New York: Neal-Schuman.

Collier, C. H. (1987). Thoth-II: Hypertext with explicit semantics. In *Proceedings of Hypertext '87 conference.* Chapel Hill: University of North Carolina, Computer Science Department.

Conklin, J. (1987). Hypertext: An introduction and survey. *Computer, 20* (9), 17-41.

Conklin, J., & Begeman, M. (1987). IBIS: A hypertext tool for team design deliberation. In *Proceedings of Hypertext '87 conference.* Chapel Hill: University of North Carolina, Computer Science Department.

Di Vesta, F. J., & Riebner, L. J. (1987). Characteristics of cognitive engineering: The next generation of instructional systems. *Educational Communications and Technology Journal, 35,* 213-230.

Gagne, E. D. (1985). *The cognitive psychology of school learning.* Boston: Little, Brown.

Gagne, R. M. (1985). *The conditions of learning,* 4th ed. New York: Holt, Rinehart, & Winston.

Halasz, F. G. (1988). Reflections of notecards: Seven issues for the next generation of hypermedia systems. *Communications of the ACM, 31* (7), 836.

Halasz, F. G., Moran, T. P., & Trigg, R. H. (1987). NoteCards in a nutshell. In *Proceedings of the 1987 ACM conference on human factors in computer systems* (pp. 45-52). Toronto, Ontario, April 5-9, 1987.

Jonassen, D. H. (in press). Semantic network elicitation tools for structuring hypertext. In C. W. Green & R. McAleese (Eds.), *Hypertext: Theory into practice, II*. London: Blackwell.

Jonassen, D., & Mandl, H., Eds. (in press). *Designing hypertext/hypermedia for learning*. Heidelberg, FRG: Springer-Verlag.

Jordan, D. S., Burton, R. R., Jensen, A. S., & Russell, D. M. (1987). A hypertext environment to support the task of instructional design. In *Proceedings of Hypertext '87 conference*. Chapel Hill: University of North Carolina, Computer Science Department.

Landow, G. P. (in press). Popular fallacies about hypertext. In Jonassen & Mandl, p. 3.12.

Leggett, J., Schnase, J. L., & Kacmar, C. J. (in press). Hypertext for learning. In Jonassen & Mandl, pp. 2.7-2.8.

McAleese, R. (in press). Concepts and hypertext nodes: The ability to learn while navigating through hypertext nets. In Jonassen & Mandl, p. 6.3.

Merrill, M. D. (1983). Component display theory. In C. M. Reigeluth (Ed.), *Instructional design theories and models: An overview of their current status*. Hillsdale, NJ: Lawrence Erlbaum Associates.

Newell, A., & Simon, H. A. (1972). *Human problem solving*. Englewood Cliffs, NJ: Prentice Hall.

Norman, D. A. (1976). *Studies in learning and self-contained education systems, 1973-1976*. Tech Report No. 7601. Washington, DC: Office of Naval Research, Advanced Research Projects Agency. ED 121 786.

Norman, D. A., Gentner, S., & Stevens, A. L. (1976). Comments on learning schemata and memory representation. In D. Klahr (Ed.), *Cognition and instruction*. Hillsdale, NJ: Lawrence Erlbaum Associates.

Reigeluth, C. M., & Stein, F. (1983). The elaboration theory of instruction. In C. M. Reigeluth (Ed.), *Instructional design theories and models: A current view of the state of the art*. Hillsdale, NJ: Lawrence Erlbaum Associates.

Rummelhart, D. E., & Norman, D. A. (1978). Accretion, tuning and restructuring: Three modes of learning. In J. W. Cotton & R. Klatzky (Eds.), *Semantic factors in cognition*. Hillsdale, NJ: Lawrence Erlbaum Associates.

Russell, D. M., Moran, T. P., & Jordan, D. S. (1987). The instructional design environment. Palo Alto, CA: Xerox Palo Alto Research Center, Intelligent Systems Laboratory.

Yankelovich, N., Landow, G., & Heywood, P. (1987). *Designing hypermedia "idea-bases"—The Intermedia project*. Brown University IRIS Technical Report 87-4, Providence, RI.

Japan ... High-Tech Country ... High-Tech Education? What Can America Learn?

Francine Fukui
Assistant Professor
Department of Elementary Education
Utah State University, Logan

Few will disagree that Japan has risen to be one of the most competitive countries in the world. Economically it is internationally prominent, and its products, particularly high-tech items, are valued everywhere. In recent years, American presidents, legislators, journalists, and even educators have been claiming that the astonishing economic success of Japan must be linked to their superior school system. So today, just as it occurred in 1958 when Russia launched Sputnik, an impetus for rethinking our American education system has emerged. Are there lessons our education system can learn? As a result of a year-long experience working within Japan's education system, I believe there are.

JAPAN, "THE LAND OF THE RISING SUN, ECONOMY, AND TEST SCORES"

Most think of Japan as a small country — even the Japanese do. Japan may seem small on a world map because its size is dwarfed by its nearby neighbors, China and the Soviet Union. For Americans, the best comparison in terms of both landform and population would be considering the combined areas of New York, New Jersey, Pennsylvania, and all of New England, except Maine. However, square mileage alone as a measure of national size can be very misleading. A more meaningful measure of a nation's size is population, and Japan ranks seventh in the world, behind China, India, the Soviet Union, the United States, Indonesia, and Brazil. Another important measure of a country's size is its productive power or gross national product (GNP) — the multiple of its resources, its population, and the skills of its people. In this category Japan ranks third, behind the United States and the Soviet Union.

Despite its largeness by some measurements, Japan is much smaller than its square mileage would suggest. The entire country is so mountainous that less than a fifth of it is level enough to permit agriculture or other economic production. Because of this, Japan has by far the highest density of both population and production per square mile of any country in the world. Japan's population is approximately 125 million people; this would mean that one-third of the United States' population would be crammed into the land size of Montana.

In just a few decades, the phrase "made in Japan" has gone from being a sign of shoddy workmanship to a sign of top quality and highly reliable products, especially for high-tech items such as cars, audiovisual equipment, and computers. In fact, "made in

Japan" has grown to mean higher quality than "made in USA." Americans are now hearing about the so-called "Japanese threat" to American business. Burstein (1988) revealed some of the ways the Japanese yen has become so visible.

1. The United States has come to depend on Japanese investors to directly finance as much as 30 percent of the American government's budget deficit. Throughout 1985-87, the leading Japanese securities firms were almost always among the largest buyers of long-term U.S. Treasury bonds at auction.

2. All ten of the world's ten largest banks (ranked by deposits) are today Japanese. Only one American bank—Citicorp—even makes the somewhat more broadly defined list of the world's top ten bank holding companies. Thirty years ago not a single Japanese bank was counted in the world's top fifty; as recently as 1980 only one Japanese bank ranked in the American-led top ten.

3. If U.S. subsidiaries of Japanese-owned companies (Nissan, Honda, Sony) were ranked in the *Fortune 500*, they would already account for thirty of the biggest U.S. industrial corporations. The Japanese-owned sector is growing 400 percent faster than the rest of the U.S. economy on the strength of direct investments approaching $10 billion for 1987.

4. A quarter-million Americans already work for Japanese employers in the United States. Economists expect that number to rise to a million in the 1990s.

5. The total value of all stocks listed on the Tokyo Stock Exchange surpassed the total value of all stocks listed on the New York Stock Exchange early in 1987. Tokyo's lead has continued to widen since. A single Japanese company—Nippon Telegraph and Telephone (NTT)—is worth more than IBM, AT&T, General Motors, General Electric, and Exxon combined.

6. Japanese investors bought about $18 billion worth of prime U.S. real estate between 1985 and 1988. Among the notables in New York: the Tiffany, Mobil, Exxon, and ABC buildings, 666 Fifth Avenue, and a chunk of the Citicorp tower; in southern California, Arco Plaza, La Costa Spa Resort, and one-third of all downtown L.A. office buildings; in Washington, D.C., the U.S. News & World Report Building; in Las Vegas, the Dunes Hotel. Continuing to buy such high-visibility flagships, Japanese investors are now moving into office and commercial real estate in cities such as Atlanta, Boston, Indianapolis, Cleveland, and Charlotte.

7. In Hawaii, Japanese investors own more than 75 percent of the equity in the twenty hotels along the Waikiki beachfront—just a small part of their $6.5 billion Hawaiian realty portfolio.

In 1953 the Japanese per capita income was $188—less than that of Brazil and Malaysia. But today, Japan's per capita income exceeds that of the United States and most other countries. Japan's low rates of infant mortality, youth delinquency, and adult crime also indicate how well the Japanese are doing. They have extremely high standards of health and high life expectancy. The prosperity of the Japanese and their achievements in world leadership have put a spotlight on their education system.

Japan's current education system is credited for diminishing the many class divisions created by Japan's feudal system. Prior to World War II, the place of birth alone determined the career and status for which an individual qualified. But today compulsory education and scores from strict examinations determine the future for every Japanese child. Japan has been transformed from a class-bound society to one controlled by meritocracy.

This new education system also must be acknowledged for the continual top ranking of Japanese students when various nations' students are compared in knowledge, skills, and even IQ (Ravitch, 1986). The Japanese have repeatedly excelled in hypothesis testing, problem formulation, and factual mastery. Japanese high school students have been found to be two years ahead of their Western counterparts in mathematics and physics. Most Japanese young people can read music, know calculus, and have a fair grasp of basic statistical analysis. Tasker (1987) reported that the average Japanese IQ is 111, compared to the average American IQ of 100. This finding also means that 10 percent of the Japanese population has an IQ above 130, compared to 2 percent of the American population.

In addition to producing students who obtain very high scores on objective tests, the Japanese graduation record is very impressive. About 96 percent graduate from Japanese high schools compared to the 76 percent who graduate from U.S. high schools. Over 50 percent of Japanese high school graduates go on to some form of further education, with approximately 37 percent graduating from a university.

The Japanese school system is also extremely effective in producing a highly literate and productive society. Despite the complexity of their written language, 99 percent of the Japanese population is functionally literate, compared with under 80 percent in the United States. It seems that the excellent educational standards have made it possible for the Japanese to meet the challenge of the technologically more advanced methods of the West and to achieve world leadership in many fields today.

HIGH-TECH COUNTRY ...
HIGH-TECH EDUCATION?

Given these impressive findings and sweeping claims, a closer examination of the Japanese school system is in order. Because Japan has become one of the world leaders in technology, one would expect these technological advances to be readily present in all walks of Japanese life, particularly the public education system. One would assume that Japanese schools would be filled with a wide variety of high-tech equipment—computers, videodisc players, electronic equipment, etc. But this high-tech image that Westerners have of the Japanese education system would be surprisingly shattered if visits were made to Japanese public schools. From the outside, the typical Japanese school doesn't look all that different from the typical American public school. But unlike American schools, where computer labs are not "an exception to the rule," the discovery of a computer lab in a Japanese public school classroom would be "an exception to the rule."

In 1984, Japan's Ministry of Education completed a national survey on school use of microcomputers. This survey revealed how very few computers could be found in Japanese public schools. The results indicated that 27 (0.1 percent) out of 21,802 elementary schools owned computers; 94 (0.9 percent) out of 10,802 junior high schools owned computers; and 1,970 (49.8 percent) out of 3,954 high schools owned computers. A second problem highlighted by this survey was the lack of actual computer training and even the lack of interest in being trained among Japanese teachers. Table 1 summarizes these findings.

Table 1.

Computer Training of Japanese Teachers

School Level	% Trained	% Desiring Training
Elementary	0.9	3.2
Junior High	1.4	3.5
High School	6.1	4.8

This same survey also revealed that 63 percent of all the schools owning computers used their computers primarily for "managing instruction" – data processing of student records; only 32 percent of the school actually used their computers in some form of computer-assisted instruction.

A second survey on school computer ownership was completed in 1985 and published by the Asian Seminar on Educational Technology. This survey found that computer ownership had increased slightly in Japanese schools: kindergartens, 0.35 percent; elementary schools, 0.58 percent; junior high schools, 3.09 percent; and high schools, 56 percent. A more specific breakdown of computer ownership is shown in table 2.

Table 2.

Number of Computers Owned

Number of Computers	Percentage of Schools
1	36.3
2	16.3
3	11.3
4	7.3
5	5.4
6	3.5
7	3.3
8	2.1
9	2.8
10	2.6
11-15	5.2
16-20	2.1
over 20	1.7

The breakdown above reveals some very interesting information. This study revealed that 52.6 percent of those schools that do own computers have only one or two computers and that 76.6 percent own five or fewer computers. With so few computers within one school setting, student exposure to computers would be minimal.

The preceding statistics are the most recent Japanese accountings of computer usage within their school system currently available in English. Although these surveys may seem dated, personal observations made during the 1988-1989 academic year within various Japanese elementary and junior high schools revealed that very little had changed from these 1984 and 1985 findings.

If high tech is difficult to find in the Japanese school system, what can be found? What is the Japanese school system doing to produce what seems to be student marvels of the modern world? What can we learn from Japanese education?

JAPANESE EDUCATION: AN INSIDE LOOK

Global surveys and national comparisons of test scores have provided a surface picture of the Japanese education system. However, a phenomenological view would also provide another perspective. By allowing the data collection tools to examine the day-to-day happenings within the Japanese school system and within the Japanese culture, new insights and understandings may emerge. The power of daily observation allows a deeper and more intimate understanding of the subject. The following narrative, which shadows Taro, a Japanese junior high student, is derived from a year of observation within Japan's education system.

Taro, a typical thirteen-year-old, lives in the city of Gotemba, a small resort town resting at the foot of Mount Fuji. According to the Japanese, Gotemba is considered to be a small country town because its population is only 76,000. Taro lives with his parents, one sister, and his paternal grandparents.

At 6:30 a.m., Taro, a seventh grader, is awakened by his mother. Unlike his American counterpart, there is no question as to what he will wear to school. Taro must wear his school uniform—a black serge jacket with brass buttons, black slacks, black socks, and black shoes. He also knows that his sister, Junko, will be wearing her white and blue sailor suit. Their schools carefully regulate not only student clothing, but also hair styles, book bags, and even pencil cases. Girls are forbidden to wear any type of jewelry, makeup, or long hair styles. Both Taro and Junko know that any deviation from the norm would be severely reprimanded and the dress code would be carefully reiterated.

Taro has long since learned the close link between academic achievement and success in life. His parents, grandparents, and teachers have instilled within him the firm belief that his success in school will lead to his success in later life. Taro knows that he can secure a job with a top company in Japan only if he is successful throughout his school career.

His mother continually prods him and Junko to ensure that they perform their scholastic tasks. Taro's mother, along with all other Japanese mothers, have become known by the common term *kyoiku mama* or "education mom." This title highlights the very special role of Japanese mothers—to ensure the educational success of their children. All educational decisions are the responsibility of the mother. Taro's mother does not work because she has totally devoted herself to her children's education and character development. She warmly encourages both Taro and Junko to do their best and to *gambare*—never give up. She also gives them practical help. Despite household crowding, they have both been given their own separate study areas to complete their school homework. She ensures that their study areas are quiet and comfortable. They each have a desk surrounded by partitions, which their mother claims increases their concentration. Taro's mother has also provided

Junko and him with a bell to request her assistance or a snack. She often studies along with Taro from a duplicate set of textbooks and visits his classes regularly so that she will understand his teacher's methods of teaching. She periodically invites his teachers to her home for meals because she wants to establish a close alliance with his teachers to ensure that Taro will fully realize his potential.

Taro's school day begins at 8:25 and concludes at 3:30, Monday through Friday. Unlike his American counterpart, Taro has yet another four hours of school on Saturday. In total, Taro's school year consists of 240 days. Figure 1 shows Taro's weekly schedule.

PERIOD		M	T	W	T	F	S
8:25-8:40	HR	SHORT HOMEROOM					
8:40-9:30	1	MORNING ASSEMBLY HOMEROOM	INDUSTRIAL ARTS	P.E.	P.E.	ENGLISH	ENGLISH
9:40-10:30	2	SOCIAL STUDIES	↓	MATH	JAPANESE	SCIENCE	MATH
10:40-11:30	3	FINE ARTS	JAPANESE	ENGLISH	MUSIC	JAPANESE	SOCIAL STUDIES
11:40-12:30	4	↓	SOCIAL STUDIES	SCIENCE	PRACTICAL ARTS	SOCIAL STUDIES	HOMEROOM & CLEAN UP
12:40-1:00		LUNCH					
1:10-2:00	5	HOMEROOM CLASS ACTIVITY	MATH	JAPANESE	SCIENCE	MUSIC	
2:10-3:00	6		P.E.	MORAL ED.	CLUBS	MATH	
3:00-3:30	HR	SHORT HOMEROOM PERIOD AND SCHOOL CLEAN-UP					

Figure 1. Taro's weekly schedule.

Taro's daily morning homeroom time, or what he and his friends call "short homeroom," lasts fifteen minutes. This time is generally used for a daily morning assembly for all the students in Taro's school. Because winter is nearing, today's "short homeroom" will be held in the gymnasium rather than outside on the playing field. During this assembly, Taro and all his classmates must stand at attention for the fifteen-minute lecture that Mr. Takahashi, his principal, delivers on some aspect of behavior and the values connected with that behavior. Today's lecture was on group loyalty and how important this is to build a strong Japan. Mr. Takahashi used the well-known Japanese saying to emphasize his point: "If a nail sticks up, it must be hammered down." He explained how useless a nail is if it sticks up. The nail that sticks up does not "belong"—it isn't doing what it was meant to do. This nail doesn't contribute to the cause—it serves no purpose.

After "short homeroom," Taro will experience a day of six fifty-minute periods, separated by ten minutes between each class. Because most of Taro's classes are held in his homeroom class, he will enjoy these ten minutes as an unsupervised time used for stretching and social interaction while his teachers move from homeroom group to homeroom group. This is unlike American junior high schools' transition periods, where the ten minutes are used by students to get to their next classroom.

This year Taro's homeroom class consists of forty-five students. Mr. Suzuki is Taro's homeroom teacher. Taro knows that this is the most important group he will encounter throughout his junior high career. It is to this group that he must learn to "belong," because this single class will stay together all day, all year, throughout Taro's entire junior high career. All activities of Taro's school revolve around homeroom classes. Mr. Takahashi and Mr. Suzuki have been repeatedly explained that the major intent of the homeroom group is to provide students the opportunity to get along within this group, instead of constantly searching for new friends in a larger and larger circle.

Taro will spend approximately ten hours a week in special nonacademic homeroom activities designed to develop a sense of belonging, a spirit of unity, and a feeling of community among the members of the class. He is looking forward to this year's homeroom activities — athletic activities, musical events, and the extended overnight field trips. Taro and his classmates are fully aware that these special homeroom activities are all carefully scheduled and spaced throughout the year to instill more and more group loyalty. For example, last week Taro's junior high school's homeroom groups engaged in an annual choral competition in which each homeroom selected a class song, practiced it diligently for several months, and finally presented it as a part of an almost daylong choral contest. The students sensed the seriousness of this contest when they saw the many outside judges who had been called upon to render the decision. For five hours, the entire student body of Taro's school sat on the floor in the unheated gymnasium while one homeroom after another presented its song. Each homeroom was accompanied on the piano by a member of that homeroom.

During the months of practice for this choral competition, Mr. Suzuki explained how competitions in their junior high were always aimed at achieving mastery of whatever skill, knowledge, or attitude is involved. So this choral competition meant that their homeroom would need to master to perfection their musical selection. Mr. Suzuki also explained that most homeroom activities would usually involve group competitions rather than having individuals compete against each other. According to Mr. Suzuki, this would teach each homeroom group identification and loyalty without involving the criticism of others. Group cohesiveness is also strengthened by students' sense of national purpose. In his short homeroom, Mr. Takahashi has explained how important the youth of Japan are to the national effort to come from behind as a nation. The Japanese have been committed to a mentality that they are "number two," and therefore have to constantly try harder. They see themselves as always having to catch up to the more modern Western society.

Taro's homeroom also engages in more academically related activities. A great deal of time is devoted to providing Taro and his classmates with feedback on examinations taken during the year. Daily and weekly class schedules are presented. Taro must keep a daily journal of his progress, to which Mr. Suzuki regularly responds in writing. Mr. Suzuki acts as Taro's academic adviser since the Japanese junior high has no school counselor. If Taro were to have any academic or social problems, Mr. Suzuki would deal with the situation. He is also responsible for all academic assignments that Taro will be given over vacation breaks. Mr. Suzuki is also the crucial link between home and school during junior high. He frequently writes to Taro's parents and attends the many parent meetings that occur at the school. Taro's report cards are completed by Mr. Suzuki.

Taro enjoys a great variety in his school curriculum. A glance at figure 1 reveals that no two days are the same. Taro will rarely have more than three classes per week in any subject, including mathematics and language. Mr. Takahashi has explained that social studies, science, mathematics, Japanese language, and English all make up the basics and that mastery in each is critical for success in Japan today. Throughout the week, Taro is also required to have classes in physical education, music (usually choral music), fine arts, industrial arts, and practical arts (similar to American home economics).

Once each week one of Taro's class periods is devoted to a club activity of his choice. He has chosen to join the tennis club, while his other friends have joined either the English, basketball, baseball, gardening, swimming, or Japanese calligraphy club. Taro, as does every Japanese student, knows how important participation in a club really is. He knows that if he doesn't join a club, he would be *nakama hazure* or outside the group. This is absolutely unthinkable to any Japanese. Taro's tennis club membership often requires that he meet in the mornings and afternoons, before and after school, on Saturdays, and sometimes even on Sundays. Miss Serizawa, the home economics teacher, is the faculty sponsor of the tennis club and accompanies them on outings on Saturdays and Sundays.

Taro also has a weekly class in moral education, usually involving what Americans would term "character development." These weekly class sessions emphasize an attitude of "wholeheartedness," a spirit of "power of positive thinking," and the "ability to choose to do the hard thing."

In addition to specific instruction on moral education, much of Taro's school curriculum and the entirety of his life at school are permeated with moral education. Two examples illustrating the importance of moral education in Japan's education system are the required student involvement for lunch preparation and school cleanup. These two activities are common events in Taro's school life and are intended to strengthen the same important moral precept—"do your share and take responsibility for your group." As a regular part of the school day, Taro, along with every Japanese junior high student, may serve as both a lunch worker and a custodian. For the next two weeks, Taro will serve with his *han* or small group on lunch duty. This lunch duty includes changing into special lunch-duty clothing and preparing, serving, and cleaning up the lunch for his homeroom. Taro constantly reminds himself to not forget his lunch-duty uniform, since doing so would extend his time on this duty.

Every student participates in school cleanup the last half hour every afternoon and on Saturday mornings. Taro's subgroup, along with every other *han*, is assigned a part of the duties involved in cleaning the school. Classrooms, hallways, teachers' offices, and even bathrooms are cleaned carefully by every student in the school. This daily cleanup will be the last duty of the day before school dismisses. Taro, along with the other students in his *han* enjoy the informality of this time and actually look forward to this peer insteraction time. They all hope that they are displaying the "wholeheartedness" that their teacher discussed in their moral education class.

During each class session, instruction is usually constant. Taro rarely spends class time doing seatwork. Taro's teachers are models of direct instruction. In Taro's homeroom, students sit in traditional rows—a double row of girls next to a double row of boys, all facing forward with their eyes on the teacher and their backs to the rest of the class. Mr. Suzuki, as does each of Taro's teachers, usually stands at the front, often behind a lectern, since teachers' desks are not allowed in the classrooms. Because the teachers rotate from class to class during the day, the teachers' desks and materials are in the faculty room. Taro's teachers spend long hours before, during, and after school in the faculty room, which adjoins the principal's office. Each of Taro's teachers is proud to be a *sensei* or a teacher. Teachers are viewed as highly educated and highly paid members of a highly honored profession. The title of *sensei* is one of special honor in Japan and is applied equally to kindergarten teachers and university presidents. Japanese teachers will usually devote their lives to their profession. Few will leave the classroom for more attractive offers elsewhere.

Taro's past seven years of schooling has taught him not to ask questions. His mother has explained repeatedly that curiosity, clarification, or the expression of personal opinion is not part of the Japanese junior high. Taro knows that it is his teachers' responsibility to teach the required curriculum and, likewise, it is his responsibility to master it. Thus, he must listen intently to his teachers.

Taro will spend many hours each week during junior high developing citizenship, loyalty, duty, and obligation. The design of his homeroom class, homeroom activities, club activities, and school ceremonies and rituals are all focused on developing and maintaining group citizenship. When Taro leaves junior high, he will be ready to become a loyal worker for life in whatever situation he may find himself — family, corporation, or military. He will understand, accept, and enthusiastically embrace being Japanese. Taro will know that successful membership in the groups in his life is a prerequisite to advancement in life at all stages.

The spirit of *gambare*, endurance, and commitment pervades every activity in which Taro will be involved in junior high. Taro learns from every teacher and every assignment that quitting or slacking off are not options. Commitments, once made, are final. Changing plans, altering agreements, or giving up on a chosen objective are not options in junior high. The cold classrooms, lengthy assignments, and incredibly high standards are all intended to teach students to persevere and to never give up.

Although it is thirty-five degrees Fahrenheit, Taro knows that his school will not be heated. Taro's school, like every other public Japanese school, has no central heating system. The lack of heat exists because of an apparent concensus among Japanese educators, supported by parents, that the lack of heat contributes to learning to endure hardships, a central goal of the Japanese school. It is for this reason, and not because of the lack of money, that frequently the heat is not turned on until late in the autumn, long after the temperature outside has reached close to freezing. Even late into winter, the hallways, the auditorium, the gymnasium, and other large areas are never heated. Only classrooms and offices are heated, and then often only by a single kerosene stove in the middle of the room. Taro's endurance is also tested during the warmest times of the year, when temperatures can be in the nineties. Just as there is no heating system, air conditioning is nonexistent.

Closely related to the spirit of endurance is the Japanese concept of mastery. The ever-present expectation in the classrooms of Taro's junior high is that students should work for mastery of whatever task they undertake. Creativity, uniqueness, and individuality are foreign in Taro's education. Taro knows that he will be required to learn 2,000 *kanji* or language characters prior to graduation from junior high. Taro will endeavor to be able to reproduce these characters exactly as they are taught by his teacher. He knows that he must give no thought to personal perspective here, or in mathematics, social studies, or any other area of the curriculum. Even in industrial arts, where he works on the design and construction of individual projects, the emphasis is on reproducing the model presented by his teacher. For Taro, the epitome of mastery is exemplified by the most famous and highly regarded Kabuki dancers. The most prominent of these are those who are able to exquisitely reproduce the movements of the masters, not those who are creative or have their own personal style.

In junior high, Taro has been told that it is effort, not ability, that counts. His teachers, and consequently all the students, believe that everyone arrives at the door of the junior high with a clean slate and with the ability to succeed. Taro firmly believes that success is totally dependent upon the amount of effort he extends. Mr. Takahashi, along with all of Taro's teachers, have repeatedly stressed that there are no gifted students, only those who work especially hard.

Effort relates to the amount of time one expends in learning, and Taro will spend considerably more time engaged in learning than does the typical American junior high student. Not only is the school day, school week, and school year longer for Taro, he also attends three different *jukus*, or after-school schools, five days a week. Taro usually completes his club activities around 5:00 p.m. and then returns home for dinner. After dinner on Mondays, Wednesdays, and Fridays, he attends a private *juku* from 6:30 to 9:00 p.m., where he studies mathematics and English in more depth. Taro also attends a second *juku* on Saturday afternoons and a third *juku* all day Sunday. These two weekend *jukus* provide intense preparation to help him pass the high school and university entrance examinations he will soon be required to take. Taro spends hour after hour at these weekend *jukus* practicing taking entrance examinations and learning various test-taking strategies.

Because Taro is approaching these crucial entrance examinations, known more commonly to Japanese students as "examination hell," the whole life of his family revolves around facilitating his studies. These examinations are required not only for entrance into a university but before that for entrance into the distinguished high school Taro hopes to attend.

Taro ultimately hopes to work for either Mitsui or Sumitomo, Japan's two top companies. In Japan there is a very close correlation between the size of a corporation and the wages its employees receive, as well as career stability and social prestige. To ensure his chance of securing a job with one of these companies, Taro must attend Tokyo University, Japan's top ranked university. For it is from Tokyo University that Mitsui and Sumitomo recruit their new employees.

Because of Taro's high aspirations, Taro's parents are happy that they have provided him with all the educational advantages available in Gotemba. When Taro was three, he attended an infant training course. His parents felt that this training would increase the chances of Taro winning a place at a good kindergarten, which, in turn, would mean improved prospects of success in the top elementary school, top junior high school, top high school, and, finally, Tokyo University, the top university.

Taro hopes that the day will soon arrive when all the effort he is now expending will pay off—the day he passes the entrance examination into Tokyo University. He knows once he is accepted into Tokyo University, his future is sealed and a lifelong dream will come true—he will become an employee of either Mitsui or Sumitomo.

Yuki, an older brother of Taro's best friend, is now a freshman at Tokyo University. Yuki boasts of university life and how enjoyable his life has become. He has told Taro that he is now taking a four-year holiday in which he is clearing his brain of the huge volume of information soaked up over the previous fifteen years. Yuki claims that university life is a well-earned interlude between the stress of "examination hell" and working life. Yuki explains how it is quite normal for students to attend only a handful of lectures and seminars over their university career. The rest of their time is devoted to part-time jobs, parties, hiking, lying around watching television, and mastering the art of drinking in groups. After hearing Yuki's experiences with university life, Taro's motivation to succeed has been increased.

Taro is becoming more aware of the economic privations his parents have undergone to ensure that he has received every educational advantage. Taro has just recently learned that his parents are paying 950,000 yen (approximately $7,000) per year for his *juku* enrollments and that they are anticipating paying 1.5 million yen (approximately $10,000) per year when he attends Tokyo University. This is a sizable portion of his parents' income, but they are comforted by the knowledge that this long, hard period is coming to an end. Soon the education loans can be paid back, and after that Taro will be out in the world working for either Mitsui or Sumitomo, and then the tables will be turned. At last, Taro will be responsible for them.

LESSONS TO BE LEARNED: COMPARISONS MADE THROUGH WESTERN EYES

So what can Americans learn from the Japanese education system? Before lessons are transferred from one culture to another, a word of caution needs to be made. All the details shared here come from an American observer — thus, this is information on Japan as seen through Western eyes. Although countless comparisons exist, only four will be highlighted here.

Perhaps the very essence of Japanese education is carried by their emphasis on moral values in education and their specific delineation of what these values are. Japanese education strongly fosters "student responsibility," "group loyalty," and "endurance." They, in fact, have specific instruction time where these values are taught. It seems that these values are critical to the survival of a country that has the highest population density in the world. In contrast, the core of the American education system and the American culture, itself, is the development of "individualism." The creation of the United States has its roots in the desire to form a country allowing "individual freedoms" and "individual self-worth." So it seems that "to be Japanese" and "to be American" implies two totally different personal orientations.

The home life that Japanese and American children experience, along with the involvement of the home in the educational process, creates a second comparison. The Japanese students have their mothers who have devoted their entire life to ensuring the educational success of their children. Japanese mothers actively develop a strong support linkage between their home and their children's schools. A view of American home life provides almost the exact opposite picture. Current concerns for today's American educators include "latch-key children," single-parent families, and the general lack of parental involvement in their children's education.

The importance and impact that private education plays within the two societies provides a third contrast. *Jukus* are a very prevalent part of the Japanese education system. The majority of Japanese junior high and high school students attend *jukus* in addition to their public school classes. The Japanese private education sector, their *jukus*, focus their instruction on training their student body to pass entrance examinations. This is very unlike the private education sector within the American school system. Perhaps the most hotly discussed difference between American and Japanese students is their test scores. Could the differences in these scores be attributed to the differences in the ability to take tests rather than academic achievement?

The fourth contrast focuses on the status of the teaching profession within the two countries. *Sensei*, the Japanese word for teacher, itself highlights the status of the teaching profession within Japan. *Sensei* translates to mean the "most honored profession." Teachers in Japan earn salaries comparable to those of corporate employees and rarely leave their profession for "greener pastures." In comparison, the teaching profession within the United States is often linked with low salaries, low prestige, and even a commonly asked question — should a teacher be considered a "professional"?

In conclusion, the above four comparisons are not intended to be "lessons to be learned," where one contrasted concept is recommended to be transplanted from one culture to another. They are provided instead to present a summary picture of how different these two countries really are. An awareness of these differences will enable a deeper and more comprehensive learning process to evolve. Once differences are realized, understanding and appreciation of each culture will follow. Once understanding and appreciation are in place, both cultures will then be able to become aware of the influences each has on the other. Even though these two countries are on opposite sides of the world, they are truly interrelated and connected. And it is with this perspective that this cultural learning cycle will continue to grow.

REFERENCES

Asia Seminar on Educational Technology. (1985). *Computers in education: An outline of country experiences*. Tokyo.

Burstein, D. (1988). Japan is a super power. In W. Dudly (Ed.), *Japan: Opposing viewpoints*. San Diego, CA: Greenhaven Press.

George, P. S. (1989). *The Japanese junior high school: A view from the inside*. Columbus, OH: National Middle School Association.

Ikai, A. (1984). *Use of computer education in Japan*. Tokyo: National Institute for Educational Research in Japan.

Ravitch, D. (1986). Japan's smart schools. *The new republic*, January 6/13.

Reischauer, E. O. (1988). *The Japanese today: Changes and continuity*. Cambridge, MA: Harvard University Press.

Tasker, P. (1987). *Inside Japan: Wealth, work, and power in the new Japanese empire*. London: Sidgwick and Jackson.

Televised Distance Education
Overcoming "Expert"-Imposed Obstacles

Thomas L. Russell
Director of Instructional Telecommunications
North Carolina State University, Raleigh

In July 1989, the Association for Educational Communications and Technology (AECT) sponsored a professional development seminar entitled "The Role of Educational Technology in Distance Education," at Indiana University in Bloomington. This seminar was one of the professional high points of the year, and brought into focus the various applications of technology — primarily computer-based — that are in place or under development in distance education. Although there were some presentations on television-based distance education, the momentum seems to be taking us away from television toward the computer. If the television medium for distance education is about to fade away or have its role diminished, then it may well be that we have weighted it down with obstacles that could or should be lifted. We in the developed world may have the luxury of casting aside certain media as newer, more "glamorous," or perhaps interactive ones come along. In striving to assist those in the Third World, we may unintentionally be saddling them with unnecessary obstacles that signficantly reduce their chances for success.

To date, distance educators in most developing nations, and in developed nations, who have employed the medium of television and have achieved various degrees of success have found it to be an expensive and cumbersome experience. At least during the "honeymoon"/novelty stages, these systems do well as long as money is plentiful and large numbers of students are participating to justify the expense. Usually massive support from the developed world is necessary to establish and maintain such systems for Third World countries. One wonders about the ability of the Third World nations to continue these operations when outside support is withdrawn. What about others who have similar needs but do not have substantial resources? Can they even hope to utilize television to help meet their distance education needs? The answer is a resounding "Yes!"

To proceed it will be necessary to discuss certain obstacles that interfere with a rethinking process proven necessary if we are to achieve an affordable and manageable televised distance education system. These "expert"-imposed obstacles are the myths about the medium of television itself — more specifically, television in education and, of paramount importance, television in distance education. These obstacles are pervasive and must be exposed in light of the results of the Teacher Oriented Televised Education (TOTE) experience.

If one accepts the success of the TOTE program, then one needs to consider certain long-held beliefs about the medium of television in distance education as obstacles which, at best, apply part of the time or, at worst, are myths. A myth, according to *Webster's Seventh New Collegiate Dictionary*, is "an ill-founded belief held uncritically by an interested group." To elaborate, I'll add that a myth is: (1) a belief often repeated; (2) what people *want* to believe; and (3) a belief reinforced by others who want to believe it. These definitions would appear to describe the way the obstacles to television in distance education have been established.

OBSTACLES CONCERNING THE
MEDIUM OF TELEVISION

The basis for these obstacles is born of commercial television methods that have been accepted as *the* standard to emulate.

Obstacle 1. Television Is Expensive

The methods employed by commercial television are indeed expensive, having evolved out of the entertainment radio and motion picture industries where performance fees are usually so high that high production cost seems relatively insignificant. This industry has shown virtually no interest in seeking significant operational cost reductions, except in the areas employing robotic devices, which add sizable capital costs. While these commercial production costs are high, let me hasten to add that they might be justified by the potential for millions of viewers and the fact that sponsors are willing to pay premium rates for these large numbers. Blindly accepting this commercial model as the *only* way to employ the medium of television means acceptance of high costs. TOTE and similar projects have demonstrated that there is not only an *effective* alternative, but an *affordable* alternative.

Obstacles 2. Television Is a Visual Medium

Of course it is true that the visual element of television is pervasive; however, one need only compare the video and audio portions of most programming to realize that program messages are usually far more dependent on sound (narrative, dialogue, announcer) than on the picture. With most television programs (exceptions being primarily sporting events), one will benefit more by blanking out the picture and just listening than by turning off the sound and letting only the images tell the story. Try it.

Obstacle 3. A Picture Is Worth a Thousand Words

This cliché seems to have been accepted by all, regardless of the programming we experience. While it is true that vast amounts of information can be covered by images, it is also true that there are many words that would be worth many images. In most cases these images must be accompanied by words to adequately convey the messages. How many television programs have been produced without words, thousands of words? At the very least, words are practical. Imagine trying to produce an entire instructional program or series without words! Keep in mind that the academic world is verbally/printed-word oriented.

Obstacle 4. Television Producers Are
Creative and Know What Works

The professionals who design and produce programs for commercial television are lauded as the experts who know how to produce successfully. If that is so, then why do most new commercial programs presented annually fail to attract the intended audiences? Indeed, many other programs are never permitted the opportunity for broadcast. Again, if these professionals are so creative, why is it that so many programs look alike, even worldwide? If you were to travel around the world and just look at local newscasts, you would feel certain that the news program format developed in the United States in the 1950s was the only way it could be done anywhere.

Even experts who designed and continue to design television facilities lack imagination, which contributes to programming limitations. The television studio, which evolved from the radio studio of the 1930s, is essentially the same as it was back then — everywhere in the world!

OBSTACLES TO TELEVISION IN EDUCATION

As stated earlier, the medium of television was based on the specifications of the entertainment industry. The myths about television in education are derived from the almost universal acceptance of the commercial broadcasters' established standards. There is a paradox here, as the educator generally is one of the harshest critics of commercial television. Why then are educators so eager to embrace the "enemy's" techniques? Could it be that we are enamored of the entertainment aspect of the medium? Are we too timid to break tradition? Are we reluctant to recognize that *good* teaching can be as stimulating as *good* entertainment?

Obstacle 1. Television Is Expensive!

Television, when done according to the commercial standard, is expensive. This may be acceptable when commercials can be sold to provide revenue over and above cost, but no such opportunity exists for the educational television producer. All too often when one's educational television operation is looked at with the question, "Is it worth it?" the answer could easily be "No." The medium is said to be expensive because the conventional facilities, primarily studios, are designed to be expensive, not only to build but also to operate. Most of us are infatuated with the hardware and endeavor to build the "best quality studios we can buy." We will strive to get as close as possible to the sought-after "broadcast quality" whether we need it or not. Having built these studios, we will only then begin to worry about the huge operational/maintenance costs of this labor-intensive facility. Conventional television is expensive in both time and money. There are few producers who couldn't or wouldn't spend more money and/or time, if available, on any given program. Does anyone ever ask, "How much is it worth?" or, "Can't it be done cheaper?" or, "Do we really need opening music, titles, credits, and other reminders of the commercial world?"

Does anyone ever try to see how *little* they can spend on a program? Why is it admirable to keep costs down when we go shopping, but to do the opposite with instructional television? What about accountability, cost-effectiveness, profit? Television *can* be expensive; TOTE shows us that it *does not have to* be expensive.

Obstacle 2. Producing Programs Intimidates Teachers

Aside from the fact that teachers resist change (as most of us do), the standard television facility is designed and operated in such a way that it tends to intimidate the uninitiated, impose excessive changes in behavior, and, usually, elicit a poor performance. Quality television performance requires a talent that is no more prevalent among those of us in education than it is among the population in general. Because we can write does not necessarily mean we can write scripts. But the facility and methods can be changed so that faculty participation is encouraged and the best teaching performance is elicited. What we need are "teacher-friendly" (TOTE) studios.

Obstacle 3. Does the Teacher Resist Using Television?

Teacher resistance to utilizing television is significant, but it doesn't have to be. Teachers resist using television in their classrooms because it can be a bothersome, risky activity without appropriate administrative acknowledgement; occasional peer criticism is also a problem. Remove these stumbling blocks and teacher utilization will increase noticeably.

Obstacle 4. Television Improves Learning

While it seems acceptable to all that in many instances television and other media used correctly should improve learning, the vast body of often-contradictory research seems to say otherwise. When comparing learning in the classroom to learning by virtually any television system, no significant difference in learning has been shown. While this statement may seem to condemn the advocates of television, let me hasten to add that it also says that the classroom is no better than television.

Obstacle 5. Educational Television Is Better Suited to Technical Subject Matter

This statement might well be made by a teacher in the humanities. It is equally likely that a teacher of technical subjects would state with certainty that humanities subjects are far better suited for the televised medium. The truth is that there is no conclusive evidence that any particular subject cannot be successfully taught via television. It seems clear that any subject can be taught via television if the teacher believes it can.

Obstacle 6. Television Is Best as a Supplement to the Teacher

Insofar as the teacher is, at least some of the time, a presenter of information, then this function can certainly be taken over by television, thereby making the medium far more than a supplement. Those teachers who perceive of their role as that of a presenter will usually state that television is just a "tool" to be kept in its place. In fact, teachers have the power to keep technologies in their place as "tools" and "supplementers." Interestingly, we seem to go merrily along, with the public and professional education leaders perpetuating this myth while ignoring the significance of successful total teaching projects such as TOTE.

Obstacle 7. Educational Television Is
Best When Interactive

While it is true that at least some students benefit from immediate feedback, it seems equally true that many, especially those who are highly motivated, do just as well or better without it. Further, we often lose sight of the variance in learning styles that tell us that some students, especially the less outgoing, seem to thrive in a learning situation that does not include the stress of group interaction and exposure.

Obstacle 8. Noninteractive Television Is Passive

Of course, you cannot talk back to a television screen and be heard. But just as a good story on television is something that can elicit strong emotional reactions, so too can a good teaching performance bring about a kind of interaction that can involve the student and therefore facilitate learning and make learning more enjoyable. TOTE students tell of learning and knowing that they are learning. They mention that they feel as if they were with the teacher in the classroom and sometimes even feel compelled to speak aloud to the teacher. Naturally, interactivity is desirable for those who can benefit from it, but at what cost? Based on the TOTE experience, there is some question of interactivity being over-rated, especially in light of what is *not* being done because interaction is not practical.

Obstacle 9. Professional Television Programming Has Made
Academic Audiences Highly "Sophisticated" and Demanding

Again, the TOTE experience contradicts this statement. There is a strong indication that serious students, in fact, prefer the TOTE lecture format to what they had envisioned as less-than-totally comfortable instructors in a typical telelecture setting. Students usually find TOTE lectures to be a pleasant surprise. If they realized how much more cost would be involved in a conventional production and how it could impact their costs, I believe they would be even more supportive of the less sophisticated TOTE approach. The only ones who usually get defensive about the level of production sophistication are the instructional television producers. Are they unbiased?

Obstacle 10: The "Talking Head" Is to Be Avoided at All Costs

This point logically follows the previous myth, because teachers, when doing their own thing, are usually "talking heads." Talking heads are often spoken of in derisive terms. Talking heads on television are no more boring than they are in the classroom. Granted, some in the classroom are boring, but talking heads need not be boring. Good lecturers — knowledgeable, dynamic, competent — are good teachers, and television can effectively capture them and deliver them successfully.

Obstacle 11. Students' Attention Spans Are Shorter with Television

A boring lecturer is a boring lecturer. Attempts to improve a lecturer who is poor by adding "production" means we are destined to end up with a poorly presented, albeit slick, program. Often the producer's goals are really to add entertainment value. TOTE has proven that students participate in the program to learn, and they expect to be taught and taught well. For educators, good entertainment is far more difficult to attain than good instruction — so who needs it? Content and delivery of that content are far more valuable for students than production values, especially when high production values are accompanied by amateurish, stiff, uncomfortable presenters.

Obstacle 12. "Good" Television Programs Will be Properly Utilized by Teachers

No matter how you define "good instructional television," it will not likely be very successful if it is administered by unskillful, uncaring, or biased classroom instructors. Classroom instructors, when using instructional television programs — even excellent programs — in the classroom, can and have caused such experiences to be negative for the students. Interestingly, teachers with opposite attitudes have found ways to take mediocre programs and turn them into positive learning experiences.

Obstacle 13. When Teaching by Television, Teachers Must Make Significant Changes or They Will be Unsuccessful

This myth has contributed to the stereotyped uncomfortable teacher providing a stiff, albeit "slick," lesson. I have found that students, in general, respond more favorably to a comfortable teacher performing naturally than to an uncomfortable teacher performing for the camera. The cost of this improved performance is a complete change from the producer-oriented conventional instructional television method. The TOTE system is as successful as it is in part because teachers are not asked to make any significant changes in their normal mode of instruction. To achieve this, the facility and operational procedures had to be changed substantially, but the instructor changed little, if at all.

OBSTACLES TO TELEVISION IN DISTANCE EDUCATION

Obstacle 1. The British Open University (BOU) Is the Most Outstanding Example of Television Utilization in Distance Education

The BOU is indeed a splendid institution, but its utilization of television is insignificant and may be reduced even further. Its adamant position of adherence to the "highest" BBC production standards has practically forced it to abandon the medium. Certainly, as economic times have become difficult, their costly production methods have proven an unnecessary burden.

Obstacle 2. Distance Education Students Prefer Television to the Conventional Classroom

Distance education students, like most students everywhere, would prefer to go to school in the conventional classroom, provided: (1) the classroom is conveniently located; (2) the schedule fits their particular needs; and (3) small classes are taught by good instructors. When these conditions prove impractical, as they must with all distance education systems, television is a welcome second choice. It appears that TOTE students' acceptance is so high because TOTE delivers a quality classroom experience in an affordable, convenient, and timely manner.

This paper has presented nineteen obstacles concerning the medium of television that, in fact, may be more accurately described as part-time myths. All, at times, or perhaps most of the time, ring true. However, they are only part of the whole story. I believe we do not know about all of the other parts at this time. TOTE has provided strong evidence that there is more than one way to employ the components of the television medium. It has also shown us that good classroom teaching is not only effective, but desired, and is transferable to television intact and at low cost. Many other of the present practices of the medium need to be reexamined by impartial observers. It would be as ludicrous to proclaim TOTE as the best application of the television medium to education as it would be to proclaim that conventional methodology is best.

TOTE places the major burden of change onto those in the television production fields, not on the teacher. Therefore, as expected, the greatest resistance to TOTE methodology comes from the television production fraternity. The exceptions are found among those producers who perceive themselves more as educators and who are willing to embrace a new and promising alternative.

REFERENCES

Bates, Anthony. (1988). Television, learning and distance education. *ICDE Bulletin*, 29-38.

Beare, Paul L. (1989). The comparative effectiveness of videotape, audiotape, and tele-lecture in delivering continuing teacher education. *The American Journal of Distance Education, 3* (2).

Clark, Richard E. (1983). Reconsidering research on learning from media. *Review of Educational Research, 53* (4), 445-459.

Lipson, Joseph. (1977). *Technology and adult education: A report on the university of Mid-America experiment.*

Newby, Timothy J., & Ritchie, Helen. (1989). Classroom lecture/discussion vs. live televised instruction: A comparison of effects on student performance, attitude and interaction. *The American Journal of Distance Education, 3* (3), 36-45.

Peirpoint, Paul E. (1988). Faculty attitudes towards teaching in off-campus graduate programs. *International Journal of Innovative Higher Education, 5* (1, 2).

Russell, Thomas L. (1983). A classroom/media blend for small populations, *ICDE Bulletin, 3* (September), 24-28.

Russell, Thomas L. (1988). Media center administration: Al alternative for success. *The Australian Journal of Educational Technology, 4* (2), 146-159.

Russell, Thomas L. (1989). A study of foreign language instruction via TOTE. *Research in Distance Education* (July), 2-4.

Russell, Thomas L. (1989). Televised distance education at low cost. In *Research and Development in Higher Education*, Vol. II. Higher Education Research and Development Society of Australasia, 173-175.

Stone, Harvey. (1986). Non-tutored video instruction in graduate engineering education. *Monitor* (AMCEE Newsletter) (6), 2-4.

The Year in Review

Rockley L. Miller
and
John Sayers
Editors
The Videodisc Monitor

A full decade of progress in interactive video closed with a rash of long-awaited and long-overdue "discoveries": The computer world discovered "multimedia"; publishers discovered the videodisc; consumers discovered the combination player; and the interactive video industry discovered the need for standards. Perhaps most significantly, the markets may actually have discovered the need for interactive video.

THE TOP TEN STORIES OF 1989

• In January, the Society for Worldwide Interbank Financial Telecommunications (SWIFT) announces the sale of its award-winning interactive video programs to the Bank for Foreign Economic Affairs of the USSR. The capitalist programs prove so effective that they rapidly lead to the collapse of socialism throughout eastern Europe.

• In January, ABC News, in partnership with Optical Data Corporation, establishes the ABC News Interactive division to develop and distribute videodiscs for the education market — marking the first significant foray by a major news organization into multimedia publishing.

• In February, Sony Corporation of America introduces the VIW-5000 interactive work station that breaks the $5,000 barrier and incorporates IBM InfoWindow emulation. Further, the company unbundles its popular system and enters the board level market with its graphic overlay and videodisc control card.

• In March, Encyclopaedia Britannica and Pioneer sign an agreement to publish 100 Britannica K-12 titles on videodisc with bar-code access through accompanying workbooks. This creates an instant critical mass of product in the education market and establishes the low cost bar-code system as a force to be reckoned with.

• Also in March, the annual Microsoft CD-ROM conference found a major focus on multimedia and a confusing array of emerging business relationships. Philips, Sony, and Microsoft disclose specifications for the CD-ROM XA format. Intel and IBM agree to work together on DVI, while IBM and Microsoft announce joint development for an open industry standard for multimedia personal computing systems.

Reprinted from *The Videodisc Monitor*, January 1990.

- In May, Philips strengthens its potential CD-I position with the announcement of full motion video capabilities, to be incorporated in time for CD-I's consumer launch. Also, Sony and Matsushita join the effort to promote and market the format.
- In June, the Interactive Video Industry Association and International Developers Inc. announce plans to establish the Tech 2000 showcase and gallery at Techworld Plaza in Washington, DC—the first major interactive video demonstration site to be open to the public. At the November preview opening, the facility is supported by more than 85 vendors and developers of interactive systems and software.
- In August, Apple Computer Inc. highlights multimedia at MacWorld and weighs in with its Media Control Architecture and numerous second-party multimedia applications—all demonstrating the company's oft-stated commitment to leadership in the future of multimedia.
- In a busy October, Pioneer buys DiscoVision Associates, thus garnering key patents for both analog and digital optical disc technologies. In addition, Pioneer announces the development of a rewritable analog videodisc; and the firm takes a clear bead on the education market with its new LD-V2200 player.
- Finally, in November the US Army exercises its third option for Electronic Information Delivery Systems, bringing its total purchase to 14,000 units—surpassing General Motors as the single largest videodisc network to date.

1989: MONTH-BY-MONTH NEWS SUMMARIES

January

- In partnership with Optical Data Corporation, ABC News establishes the ABC News Interactive division to develop and distribute videodiscs for the education market. During the year, ABCNI releases several programs, including *The 88 Vote: Campaign for the White House*.
- The Dartmouth Medical School finishes *Choosing: Prostatectomy or Watchful Waiting*, an interactive videodisc *HyperCard* program to help patients decide for or against prostrate surgery.
- Domino's Pizza tests *Vincent Van Dough*, a disc-based literacy program developed under a US Department of Labor grant designed to teach employees the chemical processes of dough-making while simultaneously improving employee literacy.
- Hy-Test, a manufacturer of occupational safety footware, places ByVideo disc-based kiosks (Sears Occupational Footwear Centers) in Sears stores in Boston, Chicago, and Detroit.
- The Interactive Video Industry Association Compatibility Technical Working Group distributes its first draft report and survey for industry compatibility standards.
- SWIFT announces the sale of its interactive video programs to the Bank for Foreign Economic Affairs (USSR).
- About 55 firms attend the US Army EIDS Presolicitation Conference. As of January, US Army TRADOC has about 2,000 EIDS systems, with an additional 1,000 in May. Also in May, the National Guard receives 200 to 300 units of an anticipated 2,200 total units. The US Army Recruiting Command has 300 units and expects 3,000 units to be installed by September.

In other EIDS-related news, Matrox Electronic Systems Ltd. introduces Private Tutor II, an enhanced version of its EIDS-compatible system. The new system includes an AT-compatible computer, videodisc player, VGA/EGA graphics overlay, and audio subsystem.

In addition, Matrox offers an upgrade kit that makes the Zenith 248 computer an interactive videodisc-based work station compatible with the Army EIDS.

Also, Online Computer Systems unveils an integrated system which offers CD-ROM capability compatible with the US Army's EIDS.

• The first computer viruses are discovered in CD-ROM software. A strain of the nVIR virus is detected in *MegaROM* from Quantum Leap Technology. Almost half of the infected disks were shipped to members of the computer press for review.

• The US Information Agency awards the New England Technology Group a $545,900 contract to develop and produce interactive video-based exhibits for *Design USA*, a US-USSR cultural exchange exhibition.

February

• Apple Computer unveils *Macintosh Fundamentals and Beyond*, a videodisc/ *HyperCard* training series to augment the Macintosh Certification program for Apple employees and reseller personnel. The series will be delivered to 33 training centers (8-10 work stations each).

• Avesco Plc. acquires British interactive video firm VideoLogic Ltd.

• Digital Techniques has purchased all assets of Cramer Interactive for an unspecified amount of DTI stock.

• The International Communications Industries Association and the Association for Educational Communications and Technology jointly sponsor Infocomm in Dallas, Texas.

• Meridian Data markets a CD-ROM publishing system which combines its CD Publisher premastering unit with the *CD Answer* and *CD Author* publishing software from Dataware Technologies.

• The National Geographic Society opens the first phase of Geographica, its science center for geography, at its Explorers Hall in Washington, DC. Phase one includes four interactive exhibits created by Exhibit Technology.

• Nebraska Interactive Video finishes production for Combustion Engineering on its tenth surrogate travel videodisc in a series offered by CE to help nuclear power plants with training and job planning.

• The Nebraska Videodisc Design/Production Group and University of Nebraska-Lincoln Television develop *Japan: Toward the 21st Century*, a videodisc multimedia project designed to increase US awareness and understanding of the Japanese culture.

• PARS Travel Information Systems, owned by Northwest and TWA airlines, has begun offering to its 5,500 participating travel agencies the PARS Integrated Reservation Imaging System, which uses interactive videodisc and CD-ROM to provide agents with pictures, maps, and audio about the 18,000 properties represented on the PARS travel reservation system. Spectrum Interactive provides software engineering and videodisc production; the map CD-ROM is developed by ETAK Systems, owned by Rupert Murdoch.

• After a year-long test at FanClub locations, Reebok International announces a roll out of interactive video kiosks for in-store promotions.

• Sony unveils its VIW-5000 interactive work station which features IBM InfoWindow emulation, CGA/EGA/VGA graphics compatibility, small footprint, and compatibility with other Sony VGA-based systems for $4,995. Sony also demonstrates a Laser Videodisc Recording System comprised of the LVR-5000 recorder and LVS-5000 processor.

March

- More than 2,000 gather in Anaheim for Microsoft's fourth International Conference on CD-ROM. Philips, Sony, and Microsoft disclose professional specifications for the CD-ROM Extended Architecture (CD-ROM XA) format which incorporates audio and graphics technology from CD-I to serve as a bridge between CD-ROM and CD-I.

- Apple expands the interactive capabilities of its Apple IIe and IIgs with the introduction of the $549 Apple II Video Overlay Card. ISC Educational Systems introduces *Essential Teaching Skills* (designed for new and veteran school teachers), the first Level Three videodisc course to use the new card. Also, Whitney Educational Services announces its Video Overlay Synchronizer, a hardware interface which converts Apple Desktop Bus data into recordable audio cues.

- Encyclopaedia Britannica and Pioneer sign an agreement to publish 100 of EB's K-12 educational titles on videodisc during the summer. All the discs will be linear transfers in CAV mode, with chapter stops at headings and bar-code access provided in accompanying workbooks.

- Under the terms of a $17 million contract, Flight Safety Services installs 69 videodisc-based Aircrew Training Systems at six US Air Force sites across the country. The systems (developed by Rediffusion Simulation) are used to train pilots and flight engineers who operate the C-5A Galaxy aircraft.

- IBM and PDO announce *IW Assist*, a variation on the previously announced *CD Assist* package targeted for use with the IBM InfoWindow and *InfoWindow Presentation System (WPS)* authoring software.

- Intel and IBM agree to develop IBM Micro Channel Architecture boards that will bring Intel's DVI technology to the IBM PS/2 computer family. IBM will work with Intel to help define new DVI products, including boards, software, and integrated circuits ... Intel also introduces the Pro750 Application Development Platform for the development of DVI software and hardware products.

- Microsoft and IBM announce joint development for an open industry standard for multimedia personal computing systems. Bill Gates of Microsoft suggests three benchmarks for multimedia systems: *Level One* (available 1989): *MS-DOS* with *Microsoft Windows* and CD-ROM XA; *Level Two* (1990-1991), a superset of "Level One," adding memory, overlay; and *Level Three* (1991-1992): *OS/2 Presentation Manager* with CD-ROM XA drive and Intel DVI video compression.

- Due to the inability to find additional co-investors, JC Penney discontinues Telaction, the interactive video home shopping service being test-marketed in Chicago suburbs.

- Philips subsidiary Optical Disc Mastering introduces the LHH-8000 integrated manufacturing system for CD-ROM. The self-contained system requires no clean room; just a 50 × 50 square foot area, electricity, and three staffers.

- Pioneer announces its CDM-6 CD-ROM Changer, which can address six CD-ROM discs from one CPU.

- PDO announces a standards conversion service that allows conversion of NTSC master video tapes to PAL format and vice versa.

- Processor Sciences introduces the VGAVision I video overlay board which provides video/graphic overlay, color digitizing, and special effects for PC computers.

- At the March National Association of Retail Merchants convention, The Retail Network unveils its PICS Music Preview System, a disc-based, in-store sampling system that allows store customers to preview 30-second clips from 80 music videos.

- Rona-Botanix, a hardware and nursery supplies retailer, installs 22 Interactive Communication Systems produced by Techniform International. The systems give customers access to information on 1,000 different horticultural specimens in Canada and the eastern US.
- Script Systems introduces the *Script Title Encoding and Production System (STEPS)*, a complete CD-I development and testing environment.
- More than 1,500 participants pour into Orlando for the conferences on Interactive Instruction Delivery, Learning Technology in the Health Care Sciences, and Electronic Marketing and Consumer Information Delivery sponsored by the Society for Applied Learning Technology (SALT).
- Sony subsidiary Digital Audio Disc Corporation announces plans to press video-discs for the US consumer market under a five-year agreement with distributor Image Entertainment.
- Technidisc wins a videodisc pressing contract by Norton Air Force Base for approximately $133,000 (75 to 100 double-sided masters and about 3,500 replicas). The firm also wins a contract form the Joint Visual Information Activity ($277,800) which provides similar services for the Army and Navy.
- Universal Video Communications unveils its VP-2000 video compression technology that offers real-time compression and decompression of video images from any NTSC video source into standard PC data files. These files can be stored or transmitted via telephone or network lines.
- MetaMedia Systems completes the first "Level Four" disc for the US Army EIDS hardware platform. Developed under contract to Matrox Electronics Systems Ltd., the EIDS Electronic Operator Training Manual is the first disc to take advantage of the EIDS system standard capability for downloading digital data from the videodisc.
- Yamaha ships its Programmable Disc System, a write-once production recording system for compact discs of several formats (CD-A, CD-ROM, and CD-I). The system, developed in cooperation with Philips, uses a recordable disc pioneered by Fuji Film and becomes the engine in CD-ROM development systems from Meridian Data and Optical Media International.

April

- The Carnegie Museum of Natural History (Pittsburgh) unveils The Stratavator, an interactive videodisc system which simulates a descent three miles below the earth's surface.
- EmTech releases the first in a series of eight videodisc courses on Computer Assisted Software Engineering (CASE), which will comprise the software portion of the firm's EmTech Library turnkey learning system.
- Two disc-based visitor information systems welcome visitors to the new Archives building of the George Eastman House International Museum of Photography.
- Kodak implements an interactive employee training program that brings an IBM InfoWindow system to each of 140 district service and marketing offices. More than 15 programs provide training in marketing support and equipment repair.
- The Scottish Interactive Technology Centre is established on the campus of Moray House College in Edinburgh.
- Teac begins delivery of the LV-220P Auto-Turn player, a device that can play both sides of a Teac-specific 12" recordable videodisc without user intervention.
- The United Nations undertakes a project to convert 175,000 images from its photo collection to videodisc.

• Visage releases its V:Link 1910, a single-board videodisc overlay/controller for IBM AT-compatible computers; version 3.2 of its *V:Exec* system software, which includes an InfoWindow emulator; and the VXP Upgrade System, which provides components needed to upgrade an IBM PC/AT into an interactive work station.

May

• The BBC's interactive Television Unit develops *Gallery*, a training simulator for television directors. The two-screen system uses an Apple Macintosh computer, *HyperCard*, Philips videodisc player, and footage from the BBC series *Eastenders* to allow the user to mix video footage from four simulated camera angles.

• Encyclopaedia Britannica and Education Systems Corporation unveil *Compton's Multimedia Encyclopedia*, a networked, CD-ROM version of *Compton's Encyclopedia.*

• The Florida Department of Corrections implements a state-wide program that uses interactive videodisc to train corrections and probation officers.

• Fundacio Caixa de Pensions (Spain) sponsors INSYS 89 in Barcelona, which attracts 300 European delegates for two days of presentations and discussions on interactive media.

• Hertz installs 25 Amtech Interactive Video Transaction Consoles at 22 Hertz Business Center sites throughout the US.

• The J. Paul Getty Museum introduces its new interactive videodisc exhibit on illuminated manuscripts from the Middle Ages and Renaissance.

• Pioneer begins delivery of the top-of-the-line LD-V8000 industrial videodisc player (replacing the existing LD-V6000 series). The firm also announced a wireless, hand-held laser barcode scanner, an autochanger, and an innovative hardware leasing program for educators.

Also, Pioneer and its subsidiaries launch a campaign with film studios and hardware and software retailers to "establish laser videodisc as the new standard in home video entertainment."

Three new consumer players are introduced, and Pioneer promotes the technology through print ads, television spots, and a theater-style Dolby surround-sound display at malls in the New York and Los Angeles areas.

• Reed International (parent company of Online Computer Systems and MetaMedia Systems) buys the worldwide travel and electronic publishing businesses of Rupert Murdoch's News Corporation (known as the Travel Information Group). The purchase includes News Corporation subsidiary Comsell, a major interactive video producer.

• Selectra demonstrates "Digital Video Interactive Tape," which adds frame-grabbing and overlay technology to its Smart VCR to simulate interactive video on a tape machine.

• Sony and Matsushita plan to join Philips in promoting and marketing the CD-I format. Also, Philips announces that the format spec will be extended at some point to include full-screen, full-motion video capability.

June

• Some 2,500 people attend the Multimedia and Hypermedia Expo in San Francisco, sponsored by American Expositions.

• Analysis and Technology acquires training services firm Applied Science Associates.

• ByVideo installs its PACE Partner kiosk in 41 Denver PACE stores. The kiosk offers customers information on Goodrich tires and Delco batteries.

• Central Hardware announces plans to upgrade its 38 "Mr. Tinker" videodisc kiosks (produced by ByVideo) to make them fully transactional by Spring 1990.

• Comsell introduces *Financial Flashfax*, a series of nine videodisc programs which teach the basics of the financial industry, bank product knowledge, teller training, and bank security.

• IBM introduces several new utilities designed to enhance its position in interactive multimedia applications. Also, IBM's Advanced Education Systems division changes its name to the IBM Multimedia Solutions division.

• The Interactive Video Industry Association, in conjunction with Techworld developer International Developers inc., make plans to establish in Techworld Plaza (Washington, DC) the Tech 2000 showcase and gallery, the first major interactive information technology demonstration site open to the general public.

• Nearly 2,000 attendees gather for the 21st conference of the International Television Association in San Francisco.

• At the Summer Consumer Electronics Show (Chicago), more manufacturers jump onto the laser bandwagon: Pioneer shows five new consumer units; Sony introduces two new combination CD/videodisc units; and Yamaha weighs in with two consumer players. In the fall, Mitsubishi and Sharp US market combi players in the US.

• Scholastech releases *The Eye*, the first of 25 Level Two videodiscs in the firm's Anatomy Project disc series.

• Sony and Taiyo Yuden form the START Lab, a 50-50 venture to offer small-scale production of compact discs using Taiyo's CD write-once recorder technology. Sony will manufacture the recorder and Taiyo will produce the discs.

• Stewart Publishing and the Fuld Institute for Technology in Nursing Education (FITNE) co-sponsor Interactive Healthcare 89, attended by 200 delegates in Alexandria, Virginia.

• Nearly 300 delegates travel to Atlanta for the annual Electronic Retailing conference sponsored by Touche Ross.

July

• 3M Health Information Systems develops an interactive videodisc course to train hospital personnel on the use of its Pathlab III Laboratory Information System.

• Mergers and acquisitions ... American Business Mergers and Baker Productions merge, forming Baker Videoactive Corporation ... Andersen Consulting acquires Courseware Inc. ... And Crosfield Electronics (UK) is acquired by a joint venture of Du Pont and Fuji Film for price of £235 million.

• Ford Motor Credit upgrades its Level Two videodisc training network to a Level Three configuration with the addition of IBM PCs and InfoWindow units to its existing base of Sony LDP-1000A players. A total of 149 units have been upgraded at branch offices during the last year.

• General Motors ceases production on videodiscs for its extensive dealer network, and most of the video centers have been phased out. The network, installed in 1979 and including nearly 11,000 dealers, was the largest single installation of videodisc systems through 1990.

• Grolier Electronic Publishing ships an upgrade to its *Electronic Encyclopedia on CD-ROM* which can be read in either IBM PC or Macintosh environments.

- The Helene Fuld Trust awards grant monies totaling $1,355,000 to 33 schools for the purchase of interactive videodisc hardware.
- IBM Germany agrees to market VideoLogic's DVA-4000 technology as part of the IBM Learning Training System 90 work station, a turnkey system incorporating IBM PS/2, VGA monitor, and Sony LDP-1500P PAL or LDP-3600D dual standard disc player.
- Jan Bell Marketing plans to install interactive video jewelry kiosks in all 49 Pace Membership Warehouses.
- Jostens forms Jostens Learning Corporation, a wholly-owned subsidiary which combines disc veteran firms Education Systems Corporation and Prescription Learning Corporation.
- Learncom closes its Cambridge, Massachusetts, offices and moves its operations to parent company Sandy's headquarters in Troy, Michigan.
- Microsoft forms a new multimedia division to oversee development and marketing of multimedia systems software for consumer products.
- The Museum of International Folk Art (Santa Fe) installs a combination CD-ROM videodisc kiosk developed by Concentrics and Wilson Learning on the subject of Hispanic heritage ... And the New Mexico Museum of Natural History installs two disc-based exhibits (designed by Art and Technology) on geology.
- NASA contracts Bradford Communications to produce *Satellites and You*, the first D2 videotape transfer direct to videodisc (pressed by Pioneer). D2 is a new digital process for tape editing that eliminates generation loss.
- The National Board of Medical Examiners begins testing a new Computer-Based Examination (CBX) at 70 medical schools nationwide. The CBX includes a videodisc-based simulation that tests patient management skills.
- The National Interactive Video Centre (UK) awards Thorn EMI Business Communications a contract to provide 100 interactive videodisc work stations as part of NIVC's IVIFE (Interactive Video in Industry and Further Education) program.
- William R. Roach and Associates acquires a majority in the training and education business of Control Data Corporation, including CDC's PLATO Education Services. Roach was a former president of Advanced Systems and Applied Learning.
- After three years of often bitter dispute, a "Memorandum of Understanding" is reached among 15 Japanese and European hardware manufacturers, and music and recording associations to allow digital audio tape recorders to be sold in the US.

August

- Abbott Laboratories installs 20 InfoWindow systems to deliver *In Touch with Forklift Safety*, an interactive videodisc program to train some 2,000 internal drivers and pedestrians who work in warehouse facilities.
- The American Federation of Teachers and Apple announce plans for an interactive multimedia program to teach educators and policy makers about the complex issues of school restructuring. The prototype program integrates videodisc with *HyperCard* software, and is scheduled for roll out in 1990.
- At MacWorld Expo in Boston, Apple pushes the multimedia concept ... The firm plans to define by the end of the year a Media Control Architecture to provide a framework for all applications to access information from videodisc players, CD-audio players, videotape recorders, and other media devices.

Also several groups show product or prototype *HyperCard* videodisc or CD-ROM programs, including ABC News Interactive, BBC, JFK School of Government at Harvard, Newsweek, WGBH Television, and others.

- The Banco de Santiago and Bermac Communications develop Supermatico, the first completely interactive on-line banking system in Chile.
- The BBC makes plans to sell its Interactive Television Unit.
- Capitol Disc Interactive—a joint venture of Philips and Capitol Video Communications—begins taking orders for the Philips CD-I 180/181 professional CD-I system, for delivery "by 1 January 1990 or sooner."
- Caterpillar installs an interactive instructional support system at its York, Pennsylvania, facility to support a major shift from single-machine manufacturing to cell-based manufacturing.
- Compaq Computer releases *QuickFind*, a CD-ROM technical and product reference to help the firm's dealers provide improved customer service on its computer line.
- Comsell completes the first major installation of 250 videodisc-based travel reservation systems at 32 Utell International offices worldwide.
- Contact Interact completes a 30-store pilot test of its Health Check system, a stand-alone kiosk that combines a blood-pressure measuring machine with a disc system. A roll-out of 500 units is scheduled for January 1990.
- Image Entertainment establishes the Image Interactive label, which will offer consumers videodiscs of limited interactivity, including enhanced films and new productions.
- The Compatibility Committee of the Interactive Video Industry Association demonstrates that it is possible for an interactive videodisc application to run without modification on a number of different interactive video systems (IBM InfoWindow, Sony View, Matrox EIDS, Video Associates Labs, and Visage/Zenith).
- Kodak discontinues operations of its unsuccessful Discus Electronic Training subsidiary.
- The Library of Congress announces "The American Memory Project," which will use interactive technologies to disseminate to US libraries difficult-to-access or uncataloged portions of its collections—including manuscripts, photographs, films, and books.
- Rogers Cablesystems signs a $212,000 contract with Intercomm International for the development of a complete interactive videodisc customer service training program.
- The conferences on Interactive Videodisc in Education and Training, Development of Effective Interactive Instruction Materials, and Applications of Artificial Intelligence and CD-ROM in Education and Training (sponsored in Arlington, Virginia by the Society for Applied Learning Technology) draw more than 2,300 attendees.
- Video Associates Labs introduces the VALWIN hardware/software package that allows users of VAL's MicroKey Mark 10 EGA graphics overlay/videodisc control cards to run IBM InfoWindow applications.
- VideoLogic demonstrates an IBM PC/AT implementation of its Digital Video Architecture.

September

- 3M wins a $390,000 contract from Army Recruiting Command for mastering and replication services.
- Allstate Insurance installs 230 IBM InfoWindow systems at claim departments nationwide to provide training and sales support for the 60-110 employees at each office.
- Coats Viyella introduces in 12 British stores an interactive marketing and training kiosk which illustrates a line of bed linen, curtains, wallpapers, and accessories.
- The Los Angeles Zoo opens Adventure Island, a $7 million high-tech children's zoo that features several videodisc-based exhibits from Art and Technology.

- Metcalf and Eddy Services award Industrial Training Corporation a $500,000 contract to produce nine interactive video training programs for the Milwaukee Metropolitan Sewerage District.
- Consumer market introduction for the Philips CD-I format is bumped to the first quarter of 1991.
- British news service Reuters introduces *The Reuter File*, an encyclopedic interactive video program on every aspect of the organization, from its journalistic roots in Victorian times to its present role as an electronic publisher and global information giant.
- Shell Oil invests heavily in interactive training, with a 13-disc series on financial management for service station dealers (45 systems); and 60 InfoWindow systems at 12 oil refinery and chemical plants for on-site industrial training.

October

- Amigo Business Computers launches two interactive video kiosk systems based on the Commodore Amiga computer.
- At its annual Interactive conference in Brighton, England, the British Interactive Video Association (BIVA) changes its name to the British Interactive Media Association (BIMA) and presents its annual awards to 17 lucky winners.
- Chemical Bank (New York) develops its own self-service, transactional, point-of-information system. Fourteen terminals are installed in 10 locations in Manhattan, Brooklyn, Westchester, and Long Island, and a roll-out of 40 more systems is underway.
- Claims courts in the states of Colorado and Ohio separately install disc-based information systems.
- Digital Audio Disc Corporation presses a record 125,000 CD-ROM discs.
- Multimedia makes itself known at the CD-ROM Expo in Washington, DC, sponsored by IDG Conference Management Group and attended by 3,300.
- International Test Corporation installs 28 InfoWindow-based automobile driver testing systems in its US and Canadian testing centers. By April 1990, an additional 300 systems will be installed in Oregon and Canada.
- Microsoft releases *Microsoft Office*, a CD-ROM collection of four major Microsoft business packages for the Apple Macintosh.
- Nissan Motors' new Infiniti branch begins training all mechanics at its first 62 dealerships via interactive videodisc.
- Pioneer is busy this month ... The firm agrees to buy Discovision Associates from DVA joint venture partners IBM and MCA for $200 million ...

Pioneer and Kokusai Denshin Denwa announce a jointly-developed rewritable videodisc system capable of storing up to 30 minutes of motion video or up to 54,000 still frames in the analog Laserdisc format on a rewritable magneto-optic disc ...

Also, in the US the firm releases the LD-V2200, an industrial unit targeted at educators and priced between the LD-V2000 and LD-V4200 players ... In Britain, Pioneer introduces the model CLD-1450 combination videodisc CD player, which plays videodiscs pressed in both PAL and NTSC video formats ...

And Pioneer wins a $263,913 contract for videodisc mastering and replication from the Joint Visual Information Activity.

- Telerobotics International announces the Intercessor, a networkable, disc-based training station.
- Unisys installs 50 interactive video systems at 18 offices to provide sales training. An additional 60-system roll-out is planned for early 1990.

• The US Army exercises its third-year option to acquire 4,000 additional EIDS units from Matrox Electronic Systems Ltd. at a contract amount of $19,847,329.

• The US Coast Guard contracts Kinton to develop a series of videodisc simulations to train cutter crew on the COMDAC communications system. Approximately 20 systems will be used at the COMDAC training facility in Portsmouth, Virginia.

Also, The US Joint Tactical Fusion Training Development Project Office contracts Kinton to produce interactive operator training for a variety of hardware systems developed by JTFPO, a joint project that combines intelligence data collected by the Army and Air Force.

• Visage announces a $5,995 InfoWindow-compatible delivery system.

November

• During Corporate Video 89, the Association for Visual Communicators presents several of its annual Cindy Awards to interactive programs.

• IBM runs perilously low on InfoWindows, quoting delivery times of three and four months for the displays.

• Intel enhances the capabilities of its DVI technology to permit users to compress video footage in real time at 30 frames per second. The new capability, called RTV version 1.5 will be available in products starting in the first quarter of 1990.

• The Interactive Video Industry Association and Business Week sponsor the National Leadership Forum on Productivity and Learning in the Visual Information Age, featuring the Touch America Showcase of 60 Model Learning Programs from 33 states and a preview opening of Tech 2000.

• For the Interactive Video Science Consortium, Digital Techniques completes *Earth Over Time*, a videodisc-based geology exhibition.

• MPO Videotronics expands its network of videodisc-based food merchandising systems to 110 of the 130 Ralph's grocery stores and half of the 1,500 Safeway stores.

• The National Geographic Society and LucasFilm Ltd. launch GTV (Geography Television), an innovative computer/videodisc program for teaching American History.

• Pioneer allows rival makers of videodisc players to use its "LaserDisc" trademark free of charge.

• In its Castle's Great Hall, the Smithsonian Institution dedicates a new $2.7 million information center which includes 13 interactive visitor information systems.

• Sony unveils its HDL-2000 high-definition videodisc player that plays specially-pressed discs. The first US application is a public display at the St. Louis Zoo's Ecology Hall.

• The Society for Worldwide Interbank Financial Telecommunications initiates an effort to establish minimum courseware standards within its particular banking market.

• Touchtel formally launches the Discover Atlanta ad-based network of public information kiosks at 30 sites in Atlanta. A total of 200 units are expected by the end of 1990.

• The US Navy Memorial Foundation contracts Kodak to produce a videodisc of photographs to accompany new and existing text entries in the Navy Memorial Log, to be featured in the $15 million Navy Memorial and Visitors Center scheduled to open in Washington, DC next year.

• In Tokyo, Pioneer demonstrates a rewritable/WORM disk drive capable of handling both rewritable and write-once optical disk formats. Mass production is slated to begin in the spring.

December

• Apple and universities and schools in five states establish the Christopher Columbus Consortium—which will focus on the use of technology to improve education and classroom management.

• Colonial Mutual Group, a UK insurance firm, invests approximately £2.8 million in an interactive training initiative to serve 2,000 to 3,000 insurance representatives.

• Philips-owned Headstart Technologies releases the LX-CD and the III-CD, the first *MS-DOS* microcomputers to include a CD-ROM drive as standard equipment.

• LucasFilm Ltd. reintroduces the *EditDroid* videodisc-based video editing system— to be manufactured and marketed by Skywalker Sound South.

• Optical Data Corporation pushes hard for the use of technology in education as it submits its disc program *Window in Science* to the Texas Textbook Committee for adoption into the state's elementary science curriculum.

• Pioneer, United Artists Entertainment Corporation, and United International Holdings Inc. form Pioneer United MallVision Inc. to launch an ad-based, closed-circuit video network in shopping malls across the country.

• French car maker Renault and Philips International (France) announce the joint development of four compact disc-interactive (CD-I) programs (entitled *Ediris*) to train Renault mechanics and technicians in the automaker's worldwide dealer network. In the UK alone, Renault expects each of its 280 dealerships will install at least one CD-I system by the end of 1990.

• The Sears Discover Credit Card announces plans to invest $4-5 million to develop an automated interactive training network. Sixteen systems are installed to date, with three of seven disc-based programs from Applied Learning near completion.

• Southern California Edison Electric contracts River City Productions for 22 video-discs on electrotechnologies to be used in SCE's $15 million Customer Technology Applications Center in Irvine, California.

Part Three

Leadership Profiles in
Educational Media and Technology

Introduction

This year the editors continue the historical/biographical function of *EMTY* by providing biographical sketches of two significant leaders in educational technology. Both have been written by longtime associates of these leaders.

Harvey Raymond Frye
1917-1976

Harvey Raymond Frye
(1917-1976)

Don C. Smellie
Professor of Education
Utah State University, Logan

Harvey Frye was born on April 6, 1917, in Barrington, Illinois, to Raymond and Louise Agnes Hertrampf Frye. Harvey graduated from Barrington High School in 1936 and continued his education at DePauw University, where he received the Bachelor of Music and Art degree in 1940. His first job after completing his degree was as a teacher and part-time art and music supervisor for the Ansonia Public Schools, Ansonia, Ohio, during the 1940-1941 school year.

Harvey served in the United States Army during World War II (1941-1945). Following the war Harvey enrolled in a master's degree program at Indiana University and in 1947 was offered a position in the Audiovisual Center at the university as a part-time photographer. Harvey soon moved into a position as a production supervisor and in 1950 was appointed the first Supervisor of Graphic Arts in the AV Center. The year before, in 1949, he organized and taught one of the first courses of its kind, the Preparation of Inexpensive Instructional Materials. Students flocked to his classes to learn graphic teaching techniques but, even more important, they came to learn of his philosophy of teaching and of life itself. He somehow became friend and father surrogate to large numbers of his students. As a master storyteller, he was able to clarify many a difficult teaching or visualization principle with a yarn about his experiences as an infantry cook or about his early farm life.

Harvey Frye devoted the greatest portion of his energy to becoming a master teacher and in 1970 was named the Indiana University Teacher of the Year. Never content with the structure of his course or the way it was taught, he was forever experimenting and testing new methods and techniques. As a former art teacher, he was convinced teachers could be taught to successfully prepare and produce many of the projected and nonprojected instructional materials they needed in their classroom teaching.

At the same time, he also developed new processes for locally producing visual instructional materials and made famous the "Plan of Organization for Local Production." The plan included the areas of illustration, preservation, lettering, coloring, and photography. These five basic areas led to a sixth area, converting and duplication (see figure 1, page 208). Thousands of media professionals all over the world use this plan to organize local production programs. He developed a philosophy and rationale for local production which, when combined with his plan of organization, became the basic curriculum for courses in universities throughout the United States and in many foreign countries.

International students respected Harvey's knowledge and would seek him out for advice concerning methods and techniques to use media and technology in developing countries. As international and other alumni returned to the Indiana University campus, Harvey was one of the first individuals they would seek out for the purpose of being recharged intellectually and philosophically.

Figure 1.

Harvey discovered the "lifting" or what some individuals have termed the "picture transfer process," which is a method of converting pictures from magazines and other select sources to acetate so they can be projected. This process has improved the classroom instruction of thousands of teachers over the years since Harvey perfected the technique. Harvey was consulted by many large corporations requesting his input on the design of media equipment and ideas for developing graphic production materials. He did the field tests for many materials used today in graphic production, and some of the ideas based on his experiments that he fed to companies resulted in marketable products. Harvey received no personal financial gain for his ideas but always felt it was his responsibility as a professional to share ideas that could benefit humankind.

Fortunate indeed were the select individuals who had the opportunity to be one of Harvey's graduate assistants. Harvey would teach and work with his graduate students all day. But the "real education" started in the evenings and would typically go on into the night, many times not ending until one or two a.m., and only then with Harvey treating the financially impoverished students to a pizza supreme. It was common for students to visit with Harvey before making major career decisions because of their respect for him and his philosophy of life.

Harvey coauthored, with Ed Minor, a textbook entitled *Techniques for Producing Visual Instructional Media*, published by McGraw-Hill. At one time it became the most widely used text in graphics production, not only by teachers but also by industrial, military, and government producers. He also published several articles in leading journals, but his true enjoyment came from producing highly visualized handouts to support instruction in his courses. While most professors rely on their publications to influence others, Harvey Frye's effect on people was through his humane, sincere concern for the individual. He had the unique ability to cause individuals to stretch themselves far beyond what they thought possible.

His personal enjoyment of life, professional enthusiasm, outstanding speaking and presentation abilities, personal concern for people, and example will long remain in the thoughts of the many students and media professionals with whom he unselfishly shared his time, talents, and energy. Master teacher, craftsman, artist, Renaissance man, scholar, father, husband are but a few of the words that describe Harvey Raymond Frye. A strong proponent of creativity, he not only taught it, but also practiced it. When his children wanted something as simple as a toy or as complicated as a television set he would purchase the raw materials and components and they would be encouraged and taught how to build or produce it.

Harvey was an outstanding family man. He and his wife, Mary Jane Blanke, had four sons, Kent, Bruce, Perry, and Mark. His basement was a center of creativity for not only his sons but also for many graduate students who would use his workshop to develop experimental apparatus to support their research activities.

Harvey's philosophy was that he would never rust out from inactivity but preferred to wear out from activity and service to others. He was practicing that philosophy when he died unexpectedly on December 15, 1976.

The author is grateful for information from Robert Ostermeier in his memorial for Harvey Raymond Frye given at Arlington, Indiana, December 1976.

An Interview with Marie E. McMahan

Robert A. Honeywell
Director
Educational Resources Center
College of Education
Utah State University, Logan

Noting how much the field has progressed since I left it, I am inclined to say that my contribution wasn't very substantial. However, in defense of myself, I am compelled to say that I was in our field almost from the very beginning. Beginnings — foundations if you will — are important to buildings, to movements, to organizations; yes, even to educational fields.

Marie E. McMahan
October 1989

Marie E. McMahan retired from the field of educational technology in 1979, shortly after completing her term as president of the Association for Educational Communications and Technology (AECT). Her career of service and leadership began with a rural school teaching position in south central Michigan, and culminated over forty years later in northeastern Ohio, where she was director of the Instructional Resources Center and coordinator of undergraduate and graduate media programs in the College of Education at Kent State University.

Following her retirement from Kent State University, Marie McMahan moved to Hudsonville, Michigan. Recently, she responded to a series of questions about her professional preparation, career accomplishments, and perceptions concerning the future of educational technology.

Please describe your early teaching experience.

I came from a teaching family on both my father's [John] and mother's [Edith] sides. It was natural to assume that I would follow in the footsteps of my aunts and uncles. I had the bad fortune to graduate from high school five years after the beginning of the Great Depression [1929]. Due to financial restrictions, I accepted a contract to teach at a rural school after my first two years of preparation at Western State Teacher's College in Kalamazoo, Michigan [now Western Michigan University].

My first contract to teach seemed something of a miracle ... at that time at least. For teaching seven grades and kindergarten, for doing the janitorial work, and for being in charge of everything at the school, I received the magnificent sum of sixty dollars a month — five hundred forty dollars for my whole first year. Needless to say, teaching materials in that little rural school were limited. Numerous classes a day needed to be taught. What a challenge! It necessitated field trips into the rural countryside, encouraging students to develop simple projects, putting on an occasional program for parents, and other activities which broadened educational possibilities. It was certainly a good environment to stimulate a young beginning teacher to be innovative and to seek alternative methods of teaching. After two more years at that school, I decided it was time to return to Western to finish my B.S. degree and acquire a certificate to teach in a city system.

Being offered a job to teach second and third grade in the Battle Creek [Michigan] Public Schools was a happy development. The school system had a good reputation and I was fortunate to be accepted in that large a system with only my rural school experience. My first class consisted of thirty-seven children in a racially mixed school. I had a combined class, consisting of seven slow third graders and thirty fast second graders. A real challenge for a new teacher! (I could tell you interesting tales about moving from a one-room school to an advanced city system, working in an interracial situation after growing up in a completely one-color little town, having an unusually large two-grade class, and so forth.) Second and third graders were a delightful level with whom to work. I appreciated the fact that the Battle Creek system was very forward looking and that teachers were invited to teach in creative ways, use a variety of materials, and involve students in meaningful experiences. I think some of the activities in which I involved my students during those early Battle Creek years were a good basis for the audiovisual work I would do later.

I entered the audiovisual field during my sixth year in Battle Creek. I had no [previous] formal training in audiovisual techniques, only what was incidental to my teacher preparation. My experience in teaching had been with simple materials, such as charts, three-dimensional materials, dramatization, puppets, and other similar materials.

What caused you to get initially involved with the field of educational technology?

I completed my first five years in the Battle Creek school system about the time that World War II ended. Not too long before the war, educational motion pictures had come into being. During the war, considerable work was done with this teaching tool in attempting to elevate the educational levels of service men whose backgrounds were found to be deficient. Much success was achieved in this regard. Following the war, educators began to speculate as to whether such materials could be used in the schools. Quite rapidly after that, progressive educators began to set up audiovisual programs in their school systems and to locate persons to administer such programs. Dr. Virgil Rogers of the Battle Creek system was this kind of superintendent. He initiated a simple audiovisual services [department] in the Battle Creek system. I was given the title of Assistant in Audiovisual Aids and given the responsibility for administering the circulation and use of a library of silent films on American history.

I soon recognized my need for additional training and began to work on a master's degree with an emphasis in the audiovisual field. Even then, I felt that education should be more than book learning, that it should consist of techniques other than the question-answer routine so prominent at that time, that it should involve creativity on the part of teachers and varied experiences on the part of students. The research that had been done in the audiovisual field demonstrated not only the value of multisensory experiences in the retention of learning, but also the importance of student involvement in their own learning. The possibility of improving education through the creative use of multiple types of media began to challenge me.

What were the big issues concerning educational technology when you began your involvement in the field? Have these issues prevailed or changed through the years?

In attempting to identify the big issues, I note that a number of them are *still* basic questions. For although educational technology continues to change at a rapid pace, we are still attempting to resolve some of the same basic issues. Although our answers change from time to time, the questions themselves seem to remain the same:

A. What materials and/or experiences are encompassed by this field?

B. What is the most appropriate nomenclature for this field?

C. What persons are to be served by this field?

D. What services are to be provided?

E. What staff members are required to provide these services?

F. What are appropriate roles for each of these kinds of staff members?

G. What kinds of preparation and how extensive a preparation is required for each kind of staff member?

H. What skills in selection, production, and utilization of media do the *users* of technology tequire?

One major aspect of the growth of the educational technology field since those early days has been the development of the *instructional systems* concept. A basic question which must be asked in any given situation is: "What kind of instructional system are we developing? Is it a system which includes a teacher only? Is it a teacher plus media system? Is it a media-only system?"

Did you have difficulty gaining acceptance in a predominantly male field?

First of all, I should comment on why it was predominantly a male field. In the beginning, it was assumed that men would be more comfortable with sophisticated equipment. Now that the field has become associated with good education and good communication, it has become a more diversified field—one in which either sex can make an important contribution.

When I first entered the educational technology field, there were so few of us ... of either sex. At that time, we were each in our own small part of the world struggling with crowded space, inadequate materials, minimal amounts of equipment, and with insufficient time to do the job. Any person who had any kind of a program started was considered [to be] some kind of "expert"; anyone who had a few good ideas to share was invited to do so at teachers' institutes, state audiovisual meetings, in college extension classes, in Department of Audiovisual Education conventions, and so forth. I had many opportunities to do these kinds of things. People didn't care whether one was a man or a woman, and both were given opportunities and help in developing the field.

What developments in educational technology have you been a part of that will remain historically significant to future students in the field?

I was "on board" at a time when educational technology departments were first being developed in elementary and secondary schools. At first, these departments were being developed independently of previously existing print materials collections. After a few years, schools became aware of the fallacy of having two separate materials departments in the same school and began combining them into educational media departments, which incorporated both print and the newer technological materials.

Another important change that I was able to witness to a considerable degree was the development of state and national educational technology associations. These associations are instrumental in helping schools, universities, and a variety of other organizations use technology, to achieve their educational purposes more effectively through a wider range of instructional materials.

Initially, the theoretical basis for the use of the whole gamut of instructional materials was made of bits and pieces of research from a variety of educational fields. Within the past few years, however, another change of which I have been a part has been the use of the *systems concept* to bring together the many discrete components of the instructional milieu. This seems to be a functional way of dealing with the many elements in the instructional process and coping with the numerous interrelationships among them.

What feelings do you have about the directions that educational technology is taking?

As I peruse our journal, I am amazed at the rapid technological movement that has occurred in these past few years. I remember similar rapid technological advances while I was active in the field, and I would like to pose several questions:

A. In those instructional systems involving both men/women and media, are we conceptualizing them so that the human elements of the system are doing those things which only humans can do or which humans can do more effectively than machines?

B. If we are indeed to be members of instructional teams, do we relate to professionals in the area of curriculum and instruction in such ways that we are truly perceived as members of that team?

C. Are we making strong efforts to relate to those for whom we are preparing instructional systems so that they are psychologically and intellectually prepared to accept these systems and use them effectively?

D. What strategies are we employing to encourage an adequate degree of standardization of new equipment so that we can function efficiently in our departments?

E. Do we have adequate good research evidence dealing with optimum ways of using our many new technological devices? Have we researched them well enough so that we know which higher levels of learning (as suggested by Gagne) or which objectives (as suggested by Bloom) they can reach, or do we still tend to use these new technolgoical devices for only the simpler, less sophisticated kinds of learning tasks?

F. Have we adequately studied the characteristics of the new technologies, so that we can make appropriate plans regarding which ones to use for specific educational objectives and how to use them to achieve the desired objectives?

For what would you like to be especially remembered by your colleagues?

I would like to be remembered as one who was open to new ideas and situations, one who was creative in dealing with situations that required openness and change. I would like to be remembered, too, as one who—although fascinated by new developments in the world and by new technological devices—recognized that these are only tools which help us achieve our objectives. We are in charge of machines and not they of us. We need to be certain of the goals and values which we are seeking and we need to use the tools in ways that enable us to reach our goals and ensure that the sought-after values become an integral and permanent part of our lives. I would like to be remembered as one, who having been given the opportunity of working for a few short years in the field of education (specifically in the exciting new field of educational technology), has left the world a little bit better for having been here.

Marie McMahan's own period of career development coincided with the evolution of audiovisual hardware/software utilization into a comprehensive technology to improve teaching and learning. Local, state, and national education agencies played a vital collaborative role throughout this evolutionary process. Accordingly, Marie McMahan's writings and staff development efforts were directed toward accomplishing two objectives: (a) to strengthen working relationships between the emerging educational technologists and the existing elementary, secondary, and K-12 curriculum specialists; and (b) to further the development of a theoretical framework for the evaluation, selection, and utilization of educational media. She was nearly as involved with curriculum groups, such as the Association for the Supervision of Curriculum Development, as she was with the Michigan Audiovisual Association, the Michigan Education Association, the Ohio Educational Library-Media Association, the Department of Audiovisual Instruction (of the National Education Association), and the Association for Educational Communications and Technology.

Coupling her undergraduate and graduate studies with her in-the-field experience, Marie McMahan moved along a "continuum of educational emphases," from improving teaching/learning methodology, implementing programs, administering programs, evaluating programs, utilizing applied research, to synthesizing and articulating a theoretical framework for the emerging field of educational technology. At Western Michigan University, she received a bachelor of science degree with a major in science and a minor in English while earning an elementary-level teaching certificate. During her "Ann Arbor Years" at the University of Michigan, she focused on the administration and supervision of educational media as she completed a master of arts degree. In 1969, Marie McMahan received her Ed.D. degree from Michigan State University. Her dissertation, "A Study of the Feasibility of a System of Pre-Service Teacher Education in Media," utilized a systems approach to link educational theory and practice as a strategy for improving preservice teacher training competencies with media evaluation, selection, and utilization.

Throughout her career, Marie McMahan remained a steadfast advocate of both public education and the teaching profession. Because of her own extensive teaching background, she understood the challenges faced by elementary and secondary school teachers and consistently acknowledged their accomplishments. Likewise, she had high expectations of teachers. Marie McMahan expected teachers to be sensitive to the needs and learning styles of individual students, in addition to being knowledgeable about the content of either the grade level or subject area. She considered **creativity** to be a *required* competency in teachers because she considered it to be a required condition for learning. On at least one occasion Marie McMahan remarked, "I recognize that teachers may not be equally creative in all situations, but I believe that all teachers have some inherent creativity or they wouldn't want to teach." She was proud to be a school media consultant and whether at the district, state, or national level, she perceived as her mission to make good teachers *even better* teachers. During the later years of her career, Marie McMahan worked most directly with school media personnel and graduate students at the master's degree and doctoral degree levels who were committed to improving teaching and learning through the systems approach to instructional development. Even in the context of a university graduate studies program, she regarded her teaching role to be her major contribution and her students as her primary legacy. When asked what she considered to be the important accomplishments of her career, Marie McMahan remarked:

> *What a difficult question! Any accomplishments which last into the future and that make a difference will probably become evident as former students of mine work creatively in the field of educational technology, implementing some of the methods that we found to be useful and ascertaining that technological media are used in well-planned ways as integral parts of carefully constructed communications strategies.*

Marie E. McMahan will be remembered and revered both as a teacher of teachers and a teacher *for* teachers.

Part Four

Organizations and Associations in North America

Introduction

Brenda Branyan-Broadbent
Associate Professor
Department of Instructional Technology
Utah State University, Logan

Lois A. Ward
Staff Assistant II
Department of Instructional Technology
Utah State University, Logan

Part 4 of *EMTY* contains several hundred descriptions of media-related organizations and associations. They are organized into two general geographic areas: the United States and Canada.

The section on the United States includes a classified list with headings useful to professionals. This classification will be helpful in finding subject leads to the alphabetical list; such a classified list is not included for Canada. All organizations listed in part 4 were sent copies of the entry describing their organization that appeared in *EMTY 1989*. Respondents were invited to update and edit these entries. In most cases they responded; if they did not, the information included in *EMTY 1989* is repeated here so that the organization or association is represented in this directory.

The reader is reminded that changes in communications and media are frequent and extensive and information in this directory is as accurate as possible at the time of publication.

United States

This section of *EMTY 1990* includes annotated entries for several hundred associations and organizations headquartered in the United States whose interests are somehow significant to the fields of instructional technology/educational media, library and information science, communications, computer technology, training/management in business/industry, publishing, and many others.

Readers who know only the acronym for some association or organization of interest to them may refer to the index to obtain its full name.

CLASSIFIED LIST

Adult, Continuing, Distance Education
Audio (Records, Audiocassettes and Tapes,
    Telephone, Radio); Listening
Audiovisual (General)
Censorship
Children-, Youth-Related Organizations
Communication
Community Resources
Computers, Computer Software, Computer
    Hardware
Copyright
Databases; Networks
Education (General)
Education (Higher)
Equipment (Manufacturing, Maintenance,
    Testing, Operating)
ERIC-Related
Films—Educational/Instructional/ Documentary
Films—Theatrical (Film Study, Criticism,
    Production)
Films—Training
Futures

Games, Toys, Drama, Play, Simulation,
    Puppetry
Graphics
Information Science
InstructionalTechnology/Design/Development
International Education
Libraries—Academic, Research
Libaries—Public
Libraries—Special
Libraries and Media Centers—General, School
Microforms; Micrographics
Museums; Archives
Photography
Print—Books
Production (Media)
Publishing
Religious Education
Research
Selection, Collections, Processing (Materials)
Special Education
Training
Video (Cassette, Broadcast, Cable, Satellite,
    Videodisc, Videotex)

Adult, Continuing, Distance Education
(ALA) Reference and Adult Services Division (RASD)
Association for Continuing Higher Education (ACHE)
Association for Educational Communications and Technology (AECT)
ERIC Clearinghouse on Adult, Career, and Vocational Education (CE)
National University Continuing Education Association (NUCEA)
Network for Continuing Medical Education (NCME)
Society of Manufacturing Engineers (SME)
Superintendent of Documents

Audio (Records, Audiocassettes and Tapes Telephone, Radio); Listening
American Radio Relay League, Inc. (ARRL)
American Shortwave Listener's Club (ASWLC)
American Women in Radio and Television (AWRT)
Clearinghouse on Development Communication
Corporation for Public Broadcasting (CPB)
Federal Communications Commission (FCC)
International Tape/Disc Association (ITA)
National Association of Broadcasters (NAB)
National Association of Business and Educational Radio (NABER)
National Public Radio (NPR)
Oral History Association
Radio Free Europe/Radio Liberty (RFE-RL)
Recording for the Blind
Recording Industry Association of America, Inc.(RIAA)

Audiovisual (General)
Association for Educational Communications and Technology (AECT)
(AECT) Division of Educational Media Management (DEMM)
(AECT) Division of School Media Specialists (DSMS)
Association of Audio-Visual Technicians
HOPE Reports

Censorship
Freedom of Information Center (FOI)
Women's Institute for Freedom of the Press

Children-,Youth-Related Organizations
(ALA) Association for Library Service to Children (ALSC)
(ALA) Young Adult Services Division (YASD)
Association for Childhood Education International (ACEI)
Center for Children's Media (CCM)
Children's Television International, Inc.
Close Up Foundation
Council for Exceptional Children (CEC)

ERIC Clearinghouse on Elementary and Early Childhood Education (PS)
ERIC Clearinghouse on Handicapped and Gifted Children (EC)
National Association for Creative Children and Adults (NACCA)
National Association for the Education of Young Children (NAEYC)
National PTA
Technology and Media Division of CEC (TAM)

Communication
American Newspaper Publishers Association (ANPA) Foundation
American Radio Relay League, Inc. (AARL)
East-West Institute of Culture and Communication
ERIC Clearinghouse on Information Resources (IR)
ERIC Clearinghouse on Languages and Linguistics (FL)
ERIC Clearinghouse on Reading and Communication Skills (CS)
Freedom of Information Center (FoI)
International Association of Business Communicators (IABC)
International Communication Association
International Communications Industries Association (ICIA)
National Council of the Churches of Christ— Communication Commission
Speech Communication Association (SCA)
Women in Film (WIF)
World Pen Pals (WPP)

Community Resources
Teachers and Writers Collaborative (T&W)

Computers, Computer Software, Computer Hardware
(AECT) Division of Interactive Systems and Computers (DISC)
Association for Computer Educators (ACE)
Computer-Based Education Research Lab (CERL)
ISTE
Minnesota Educational Computing Corporation (MECC)
OCLC (Online Computer Library Center)
PLATO
Resources in Computer Education (RICE)
SOFTSWAP
Specialnet

Copyright
Copyright Clearance Center
International Copyright Information Center (INCINC)

Databases; Networks
ERIC (Educational Resources Information Center) (See separate entries for the various clearinghouses.)

ERIC Document Reproduction Service (EDRS)
ERIC Processing and Reference Facility
PLATO
RICE
SpecialNet

Education (General)

American Association of School Administrators
(AASA)
American Montessori Society (AMS)
American Society of Educators (ASE)
Association for Childhood Education International
(ACEI)
Association for Experiential Education (AEE)
(AECT) Minorities in Media (MIM)
Association of Teacher Educators (ATE)
Center for Instructional Research and Curriculum
Evaluation
Council for Basic Education
Education Development Center, Inc.
Environmental Quality Instructional Resources
Center
ERIC Clearinghouse on Counseling and Personnel
Services (CG)
ERIC Clearinghouse on Elementary and Early
Childhood Education (PS)
ERIC Clearinghouse on Handicapped and Gifted
Children (EC)
ERIC Clearinghouse on Rural Education and Small
Schools (RC)
ERIC Clearinghouse on Science, Mathematics, and
Environmental Education (SE)
ERIC Clearinghouse for Social Studies/Social
Science Education (ERIC/ChESS)
ERIC Clearinghouse on Teacher Education (SP)
ERIC Clearinghouse on Urban Education (UD)
International Reading Association (IRA)
National Art Education Association (NAEA)
National Association for the Exchange of Industrial
Resources (NAEIR)
National Association of Secondary School
Principals (NASSP)
National Association of State Boards of Education
(NASBE)
National Association of State Educational Media
Professionals (NASTEMP)
National Association of State Textbook Administra-
tors (NASTA)
National Center for Appropriate Technology
National Clearinghouse for Bilingual Education
National Council for Accreditation of Teacher
Education (NCATE)
National Education Association (NEA)
National Endowment for the Arts (NEA)
National Endowment for the Humanities (NEH)
National Science Foundation (NSF)
National Science Teachers Association (NSTA)
Project in Distance Education
Project in Educational Technology
Social Science Education Consortium

Education (Higher)

American Association of Community and Junior
Colleges (AACJC)
American Association of State Colleges and
Universities
Association for Continuing Higher Education
(ACHE)
(AECT) Community College Association for
Instruction and technology
(AECT) Northwest College and University
Council for the Management of Educational
Technology
Association of American Colleges (AAC)
ERIC Clearinghouse on Higher Education (HE)
University and College Designers Association
(UCDA)
University Film and Video Association (UFVA)

Equipment (Manufacturing, Maintenance, Testing, Operating)

(ALA) Library and Information Technology
Association (LITA)
American National Standards Institute (ANSI)
Association of Audio-Visual Technicians (AAVT)
EPIE Institute
ERIC Clearinghouse on Tests, Measurement, and
Evaluation (TM)
International Communications Industries Associa-
tion (ICIA)
National School Supply and Equipment Association
(NSSEA)
Society of Motion Picture and Television Engineers
(SMPTE)

ERIC-Related

ERIC (Educational Resources Information Center)
ERIC Clearinghouse on Adult, Career, and
Vocational Education (CE)
ERIC Clearinghouse on Counseling and Personnel
Services (CG)
ERIC Clearinghouse on Elementary and Early
Childhood Education (PS)
ERIC Clearinghouse on Handicapped and Gifted
Children (EC)
ERIC Clearinghouse on Higher Education (HE)
ERIC Clearinghouse on Information Resources (IR)
ERIC Clearinghouse on Languages and Linguistics
(FL)
ERIC Clearinghouse on Reading and Communica-
tion Skills (CS)
ERIC Clearinghouse on Rural Education and Small
Schools (RC)
ERIC Clearinghouse on Science, Mathematics, and
Environmental Education (SE)
ERIC Clearinghouse on Teacher Education (SP)
ERIC Clearinghouse on Urban Education (UD)
ERIC Document Reproduction Service (EDRS)
ERIC Processing and Reference Facility

Films—Educational/Instructional/ Documentary
Anthropology Film Center (AFC)

Association of Independent Video and Filmmakers
and the Foundation for Independent Video and
Film
Children's Film and Television Center of America
(CFTCA)
CINE Information
Council on International Non-theatrical Events
Film/Video Arts Inc.
National Aeronautics and Space Administration
(NASA)
National Alliance of Media Arts Centers (NAMAC)
National Audiovisual Center (NAC)
National Film Board of Canada (NFBC)
National Information Center for Educational Media
(NICEM)
Pacific Film Archive (PFA)
PCR: Films and Video in the Behavioral Sciences
Women's Media Project (WMP)

**Films—Theatrical (Film Study, Criticism,
Production)**
Academy of Motion Picture Arts and Sciences
(AMPAS)
American Society of Cinematographers
Film Advisory Board (FAB)
Film Arts Foundation (FAF)
Hollywood Film Archive
International Film and TV Festival of New York
National Film Information Service (NFIS)

Films—Training
(AECT) Industrial Training and Education Division
(ITED)
American Film and Video Association (AFVA)
Association of Independent Video and Filmmakers
and the Foundation for Independent Video and
Film
Council on International Non-theatrical Events
Great Plains National ITV Library
National Audiovisual Center
National Film Board of Canada
Training Media Association

Futures
Institute for the Future
Office of Technology Assessment (OTA)
World Future Society (WFS)

**Games, Toys, Drama, Play, Simulation,
Puppetry**
North American Simulation and Gaming Associa-
tion (NASAGA)
Puppeteers of America
Society for Computer Simulation (SCS)

Graphics
International Graphic Arts Education Association
(IGAEA)
Newspaper Features Council (NFC)

Health-Related Organizations
American Medical Writers Association (AMWA)
American Society for Healthcare Education and
Training of the American Hospital Associa-
tion (ASHET)
Health Sciences Communications Association
(HeSCA)
Lister Hill National Center for Biomedical
Communications of the National Library of
Medicine
Medical Library Association (MLA)
National Association for Visually Handicapped
(NAVH)
National Library of Medicine
Network for Continuing Medical Education
(NCME)

Information Science
International Information Management Congress
(IMC)

**Instructional Technology/Design/
Development**
Agency for Instructional Technology (AIT)
Association for Educational Communications and
Technology (AECT)
(AECT) Community College Association for
Instruction and Technology (CCAIT)
(AECT) Division of Educational Media Manage-
ment (DEMM)
(AECT) Division of Instructional Development
(DID)
National Society for Performance and Instruction
(NSPI)
Office of Technology Assessment (OTA)
Professors of Instructional Design and Technology
(PIDT)
Society for Applied Learning Technology (SALT)

International Education
(AECT) International Division (ITNL)
(AECT) International Visual Literacy Association,
Inc. (IVLA)
Council on International Educational Exchange
(CIEE)
East-West Institute of Culture and Communication
Institute of International Education
International Friendship League (IFL)
Office for International Networks in Education and
Development (INET)
United Nations Department of Public Information
U.S. Advisory Commission on Public Diplomacy
World Pen Pals (WPP)

Libraries—Academic, Research
American Library Association (ALA)
(ALA) Association of College and Research
Libraries (ACRL)

Libraries—Public
American Library Association (ALA)
(ALA) Audiovisual Committee (of the Public
Library Association)
(ALA) Library Administration and Management
Association (LAMA)
(ALA) Library and Information Technology
Association (LITA)
(ALA) Public Library Association (PLA)
(ALA) Reference and Adult Services Division
(RASD)
(ALA) Resources and Technical Services Division
(ALA) Young Adult Services Division (YASD)

Libraries—Special
American Library Association (ALA)
(ALA) Association for Library Service to Children
(ALSC)
(ALA) Association of Specialized and Cooperative
Library Agencies (ASCLA)
(ALA) Technology in Public Libraries Committee
Special Libraries Association (SLA)
Theater Library Association (TLA)

Libraries and Media Centers—General, School
American Library Association (ALA)
(ALA) American Association of School Librarians
(ALA) American Library Trustee Association
(ALTA)
Association for Educational Communications and
Technology (AECT)
(AECT) Division of School Media Specialists
(DSMS)
(AECT) National Association of Regional Media
Centers (NARMC)
(AECT) Northwest College and University
Association for Library and Information Science
Education
Catholic Library Association
Consortium of College and University Media
Centers
Continuing Library Education Network and
Exchange
Council for the Management of Educational
Technology
Council of National Library and Information
Associations
International Association of School Librarianship
(IASL)
Library of Congress
National Alliance of Media Arts Centers (NAMAC)
National Association of State Educational Media
Professionals (NASTEMP)
National Commission on Libraries and Information
Science (NCLIS)
National Council of Teachers of English (NCTE)
Commission on Media
On-Line Audiovisual Catalogers (OLAC)

Microforms; Micrographics
See ERIC-Related entries

Museums; Archives
American Federation of Arts (AFA)
(AECT) Archives
Association of Systematics Collections
Computer Museum
Hollywood Film Archive
International Museum of Photography at George
Eastman House
Lawrence Hall of Science
Museum Computer Network, Inc.
Museum of Broadcasting (MB)
Museum of Holography
Museum of Modern Art
National Gallery of Art (NGA)
Smithsonian Institution

Photography
International Center of Photography (ICP)
International Museum of Photography at George
Eastman House
Museum of Holography
National Press Photographers Association, Inc.
(NPPA)
Photographic Society of America (PSA)
Society for Photographic Education (SPE)
Society of Photo Technologists (SPT)
SPSE: The Society for Imaging Science and
Technology

Print—Books
American Booksellers Association (ABA)

Production (Media)
American Society of Cinematographers Association
for Educational Communications and
Technology (AECT)
(AECT) Media Design and Production Division
(MDPD)
Association of Independent Video and Filmmakers
and the Foundation for Independent Video and
Film
Film Arts Foundation (FAF)
Women in Film (WIF)
Women's Media Project (WMP)

Publishing
American Booksellers Association (ABA)
Association of American Publishers (AAP)
Authors' League of America
Government Printing Office (US GPO)
Magazine Publishers of America (MPA)
National Association of State Textbook Administra-
tors (NASTA)

Religious Education
Catholic Library Association
National Religious Broadcasters (NRB)

Research
American Educational Research Association
(AERA)

(AECT) Research and Theory Division (RTD)
(AECT) ECT Foundation
Center for Advanced Visual Studies
Center for Instructional Research and Curriculum
    Evaluation
Center for Interactive Programs
Clearinghouse on Development Communication
Council for Educational Development and Research
    (CEDaR)
Education Development Center, Inc.
ERIC clearinghouses. See ERIC-Related entries.
Far West Laboratory for Educational Research and
    Development (FWL)
HOPE Reports
Institute for Development of Educational Activities
    (IDEA)
Institute for Research on Teaching
National Technical Information Service (NTIS)
National Technology Center
NETWORK
Northwest Regional Educational Laboratory
    (NWREL)

Selection, Collections, Processing (Materials)
National Information Center for Educational Media
    (NICEM)

Special Education
Council for Exceptional Children
ERIC Clearinghouse on Handicapped and Gifted
    Children (EC)
National Association for Visually Handicapped
    (NAVH)

Training
American Management Association (AMA)
(AMA) Human Resources Division
American Society for Training and Development
    (ASTD)
Association for Educational Communications and
    Technology (AECT)
(AECT) Federal Educational Technology
    Association (FETA)
(AECT) Industrial Training and Education Division
    (ITED)
Bergwall

ERIC Clearinghouse on Adult, Career, and
    Vocational Education (CE)
Training Modules for Trainers (TMT)

**Video (Cassette, Broadcast, Cable, Satellite,
    Videodisc, Videotex)**
Agency for Instructional Technology (AIT)
American Women in Radio and Television
Association for Educational Communications and
    Technology (AECT)
(AECT) Division of Telecommunications (DOT)
Association of Independent Video and Filmmakers
    and the Foundation for Independent Video and
    Film
Central Educational Network (CEN)
Children's Television International, Inc.
Close Up Foundation
Corporation for Public Broadcasting (CPB)
Federal Communications Commission (FCC)
Great Plains National ITV Library (GPN)
International Tape/Disc Association (ITA)
International Telecommunications Satellite
    Organization (INTELSAT)
International Teleconferencing Association (ITCA)
International Television Association (ITVA)
National Association for Better Broadcasting
    (NABB)
National Association of Broadcasters (NAB)
National Cable Television Institute (NCTI)
National Federation of Community Broadcasters
    (NFCB)
National Telemedia Council (NTC)
Nebraska Videodisc Design/Production Group (VD-
    PG)
PBS ENCORE
PBS VIDEO
Public Broadcasting Service (PBS)
Public Service Satellite Consortium (PSSC)
Society of Cable Television Engineers (SCTE)
Society of Motion Picture and Television Engineers
    (SMPTE)
Telecommunications Research and Action Center
    (TRAC)
Television Licensing Center (TLC)
Women in Film (WIF)

ALPHABETICAL LIST

Academy of Motion Picture Arts and Sciences (AMPAS). 8949 Wilshire Blvd., Beverly Hills CA 90211. (213) 278-8990. An honorary organization composed of outstanding individuals in all phases of motion pictures. Seeks to advance the arts and sciences of motion picture technology and artistry. Presents annual film awards; offers artist-in-residence programs; operates reference library and National Film Information Service. *Publications: Annual Index to Motion Picture Credits*; and *Academy Players Directory*.

Agency for Instructional Technology (AIT). Box A, Bloomington, IN 47402. (812) 339-2203; (800) 457-4509. Edwin G. Cohen, Exec. Dir. Established to strengthen education through technology. In cooperation with state and provincial agencies, AIT develops instructional materials using video, computers, and other emerging technologies. AIT also acquires and distributes a wide variety of video, computer, and related print materials for use as major learning resources. From April 1973 to July 1984, AIT was known as the Agency for Instructional Television. Its predecessor organization, National Instructional Television, was founded in 1962. *Publications: AIT Newsletter;* and *AIT Catalog*.

American Association of Community and Junior Colleges (AACJC). One Dupont Circle NW, Suite 410, Washington, DC 20036-1176. (202) 293-7050. Dale Parnell, Pres. AACJC serves the nation's 1,211 community, technical, and junior colleges through advocacy, professional development, publications, and national networking. The annual convention draws more than 4,000 mid- and top-level administrators of two-year colleges. Staff and presidents offer expertise in all areas of education. Sixteen councils and six commissions address all areas of education. *Membership:* 1,110 inst., 150 int'l, 4 fdn., 75 corp., 103 educ. assn. *Dues:* Vary for institutions, corporations, foundations, and individuals. *Publications: Community, Technical and Junior College Journal*, bi-mo.; *AACJC Letter*, mo.; *College Times;* Community College Press (books, monographs, etc.); and publications program (directories, books, monographs, policy statements, etc.).

American Association of School Administrators (AASA). 1801 N. Moore St., Arlington, VA 22209. (703) 528-0700. Richard D. Miller, Exec. Dir. Represents professional administrators and managers in education in the United States and overseas, provides an extensive program of professional development through the National Academy for School Executives (NASE), and carries out Leadership for Learning projects such as that of the National Center for the Improvement of Learning. Also produces publications and audiovisual programs to increase knowledge and skills of administrators. *Membership:* 19,000. *Dues:* $175.00. *Publications: The School Administrator; Leadership News*; and numerous books and video programs.

American Association of State Colleges and Universities. One Dupont Circle NW, Suite 700, Washington, DC 20036-1192. (202) 293-7070. Allan W. Ostar, Pres. Membership is open to any regionally accredited institution of higher education, and those in the process of securing accreditation, which offer programs leading to the degree of bachelor, master, or doctor, and which are wholly or partially state-supported and state-controlled. Organized and operated exclusively for educational, scientific, and literary purposes, its particular purposes shall be to improve higher education within its member institutions through cooperative planning, studies, and research on common educational problems, and the development of a more unified program of action among its members; and to provide other needed and worthwhile educational services to the colleges and universities it may represent. *Membership:* 372 inst. *Dues:* Based on current student enrollment at institution. *Publications: MEMO: To the President; In Pursuit of Degrees with Integrity: A Value Added Approach to Undergraduate Assessment; Strategies for Effective Enrollment Management;* and *Early Planning for Now: A Guide for Families*.

American Booksellers Association (ABA). 137 W. 25th St., New York, NY 10001. (212) 463-8450; outside NY (800) 637-0037. Bernard Rath, Exec. Dir. A trade organization of large and small firms engaged in retail book sales. *Total Membership as of July 31, 1989:* 7,340 members, 4,981 stores and branches. *Dues*: $125.00 initially, sliding scale renewal on sales volume. *Publications: ABA Book Buyers Handbook; ABA Basic Book List; A Manual on Bookselling; American Bookseller; ABA Newswire*; and *ABA Sidelines Directory*.

American Educational Research Association (AERA). 1230-17th St. NW, Washington, DC 20036. (202) 223-9485. William J. Russell, Exec. Dir. A national professional organization of educators and behavioral scientists active and/or interested in educational research and its application to educational problems. Sponsors annual meetings featuring presentations of original research findings. *Membership*: 15,800. *Dues*: $45.00. *Publications: Educational Researcher; American Educational Research Journal; Journal of Educational Statistics; Educational Evaluation and Policy Analysis; Review of Research in Education*; and *Review of Educational Research*.

The American Federation of Arts (AFA). Headquarters, 41 E. 65th St., New York, NY 10011. (212) 988-7700, FAX (212) 861-2487. Myrna Smoot, Dir. Museum Services Div., 74 New Montgomery, San Francisco, CA 94105 (415) 974-1230, FAX (415) 974-5121. National nonprofit museum service which organizes exhibitions and film programs and circulates them to museums, university art galleries, and art centers throughout the country and abroad. *Membership*: 600. *Newsletter:* ARI, published quarterly.

American Film and Video Association (AFVA). 920 Barnsdale Rd., Suite 152, La Grange Park, IL (708) 482-4000. Ron MacIntyre, Exec. Dir. Formerly the Educational Film Library Association, the AFVA is recognized as the authoritative organization in assembling data about the 16mm and video fields, in encouraging quality production and appreciation of film generally, and in guidance in the proper use of these media. Serves as a national clearinghouse of information about films, conducts workshops on a variety of media-related topics, and sponsors the annual American Film and Video Festival. *Membership:* 1,300. *Dues*: $45.00 indiv., $175.00 inst. *Publications: SightLines; AFVA Bulletin*; and *AFVA Evaluations*.

American Library Association (ALA). 5O E. Huron St., Chicago, IL 60611. (312) 944-6780. Linda F. Crismond, Exec. Dir. The ALA is the oldest and largest national library association. Its 47,000 members represent all types of libraries—state, public, school, and academic, as well as special libraries serving persons in government, commerce, the armed services, hospitals, prisons, and other institutions. Chief advocate of achievement and maintenance of high-quality library information services through protection of the right to read, educating librarians, improving services, and making information widely accessible. *Membership*: 47,000. *Dues:* Basic dues $38.00 first year, $75.00 renewing members. *Publications*: *American Libraries*.

(ALA) American Association of School Librarians (AASL). 50 E. Huron St., Chicago, IL 60611. (312) 944-6780. Ann Carlson Weeks, Exec. Dir. Seeks general improvement and extension of school library/media services as a means of strengthening education. Gives special attention to evaluation, selection, interpretation, and use of library media. Activities and projects of the association are divided among 55 committees and three sections. *Membership*: 6,500. *Dues:* membership in ALA plus $35.00, $105.00 renewing member, $34.00 student member. *Publications*: *School Library Media Quarterly*; and others.

(ALA) American Library Trustee Association (ALTA). 50 E. Huron St., Chicago, IL 60611. (312) 944-6780. Sharon L. Jordan, Exec. Dir. Interested in the development of effective library service for people in all types of communities and libraries. Members, as policymakers, are concerned with organizational patterns of service, the development of competent personnel, the provision of adequate financing, the passage of suitable legislation, and the encouragement of citizen support for libraries. *Membership:* 1,700. *Dues*: $35.00 plus membership in ALA. *Publications: ALTA Newsletter*.

(ALA) Association of College and Research Libraries (ACRL). 50 E. Huron St., Chicago, IL 60611-2795. (312) 944-6780. JoAn Segal, Exec. Dir. Represents librarians and promotes libraries of postsecondary, research, and specialized institutions. Has available library standards for colleges, universities, and two-year institutions. Publishes statistics on academic libraries. Committees include Academic Status, Audiovisual, Professional Education, Legislation, Publications, and Standards and Accreditation. Free list of materials available. *Membership:* 10,000. *Dues:* $35.00 (in addition to ALA membership). *Publications: College & Research Libraries; College & Research Libraries News; Rare Books and Manuscripts Librarianship,* 11-section newsletter; and *Choice.*

(ALA) Association for Library Collections & Technical Services (ALCTS). 50 E. Huron St., Chicago, IL 60611. (312) 944-6780. Karen Muller, Exec. Dir. Nancy R. John, Pres. Dedicated to acquisition, identification, cataloging, classification, and preservation of library materials, the development and coordination of the country's library resources, and aspects of selection and evaluation involved in acquiring and developing library materials and resources. Sections include Cataloging and Classification, Preservation of Library Materials, Reproduction of Library Materials, Resources, and Serials. *Membership:* 6,039. *Dues:* $35.00 plus membership in ALA. *Publications: Library Resources & Technical Services* (q.); *RTSD Newsletter* (6/yr.).

(ALA) Association for Library Service to Children (ALSC). 50 E. Huron St., Chicago, IL 60611. (312) 944-6780. Susan Roman, Exec. Dir. Interested in the improvement and extension of library services for children in all types of libraries, evaluation, and selection of book and nonbook library materials, and the improvement of techniques of library services for children from preschool through the eighth grade or junior high school age. Annual conference and midwinter meeting with the ALA. Committee membership open to ALSC members. *Membership:* 3,500. *Dues:* $35.00 plus membership in ALA. *Publications: Journal of Youth Services in Libraries;* and *ALSC Newsletter.*

(ALA) Association of Specialized and Cooperative Library Agencies (ASCLA). 50 E. Huron St., Chicago, IL 60611. (312) 944-6780. Andrew Hansen, ALA Staff Liaison. Represents state library agencies, multitype library cooperatives, and libraries serving special clientele to promote the development of coordinated library services with equal access to information and material for all persons. The activities and programs of the association are carried out by 21 committees, three sections, and various discussion groups. Write for free checklist of materials. *Membership:* 1,700. *Dues:* (in addition to ALA membership) $30.00 personal members, $50.00 organizations, $500.00 state library agencies. *Publications: Interface.*

(ALA) Audiovisual Committee (of the Public Library Association). 50 E. Huron St., Chicago, IL 60611. (312) 944-6780. Promotes use of audiovisual materials in public libraries.

(ALA) Library Administration and Management Association (LAMA). 50 E. Huron St., Chicago, IL 60611. (312) 944-6780. Karen Muller, Exec. Dir. Provides an organizational framework for encouraging the study of administrative theory, for improving the practice of administration in libraries, and for identifying and fostering administrative skills. Toward these ends, the association is responsible for all elements of general administration which are common to more than one type of library. These may include: organizational structure—Buildings and Equipment Section (BES); Fundraising & Financial Development Section (FRFDS); Library Organization & Management Section (LOMS); Personnel Administration Section (PAS); Public Relation Section (PRS); Systems & Services Section (SASS); Statistic Section (SS), financial administration, personnel management and training, buildings and equipment, public relations, and fundraising. *Membership:* 5,000. *Dues:* $25.00 (in addition to ALA membership). *Publications: Library Administration & Management.*

(ALA) Library and Information Technology Association (LITA). 50 E. Huron St., Chicago, IL 60611. (312) 944-6780. Linda J. Knutson, Exec. Dir. Concerned with library automation, the information sciences, and the design, development, and implementation of automated systems in those fields, including systems development, electronic data processing, mechanized information retrieval, operations research, standards development, telecommunications, video communications, networks and collaborative efforts, management techniques, information technology, optical technology, artificial intelligence and expert systems, and other related aspects of audiovisual activities and hardware applications. *Membership*: 5,000. Dues: $30.00/yr. plus membership in ALA. *Publications*: *Information Technology and Libraries*; and *LITA Newsletter*.

(ALA) Public Library Association (PLA). 50 E. Huron St., Chicago, IL 60611. (312) 944-6780. Eleanor Jo Rodger, Exec. Dir.; Sarah Long, Pres. Concerned with the development, effectiveness, and financial support of public libraries. Speaks for the profession and seeks to enrich the professional competence and opportunities of public libraries. Sections include Adult Lifelong Learning, Armed Forces Library, Community Information, Metropolitan Libraries, Public Library System, Small and Medium-sized Libraries, Marketing Public Library Services, and Technology in Public Libraries. *Membership*: 6,200. *Dues*: $35.00/yr., open to all ALA members. *Publications: Planning and Role Setting for Public Libraries: A Manual of Options and Procedures; Output Measures for Public Libraries: A Manual of Standardized Procedures*, 2nd Edition; *Public Library Data Service, Statistical Report '89*.

(ALA) Reference and Adult Services Division (RASD). 50 E. Huron St., Chicago, IL 60611. (312) 944-6780. Andrew M. Hansen, Exec. Dir. Responsible for stimulating and supporting in every type of library the delivery of reference information services to all groups and of general library services and materials to adults. *Membership*: 5,201. *Dues*: $25.00 plus membership in ALA. *Publications*: *RQ; RASD Update*; and others.

(ALA) Technology In Public Libraries Committee (of the Public Library Association). 50 E. Huron St., Chicago, IL 60611. (312) 944-6780. John Blegen, Chair. Collects and disseminates information on technology applications in public libraries.

(ALA) Young Adult Services Division (YASD). 50 E. Huron St., Chicago, IL 60611. (312) 944-6780. Susan B. Madden, Pres. Seeks to improve and extend library services to young people, assumes responsibility within the ALA to evaluate and select books and nonbook media and to interpret and make recommendations regarding their use with young adults. Committees include Audiovisual Producers and Distributors Liaison, Best Books for Young Adults, Recommended Books for the Reluctant Young Adult Reader, Media Selection and Usage, Publishers' Liaison, and Selected Films for Young Adults. *Membership*: 2,400. *Dues*: $25.00 (in addition to ALA membership). *Publications: Journal of Youth Services in Libraries* (formerly *Top of the News); Best Books*; many others.

American Management Association (AMA). 135 W. 50th St., New York, NY 10020. (212) 586-8100. Thomas R. Horton, Chairman and CEO. The AMA is an international educational organization, membership-based and not-for-profit, dedicated to broadening the management knowledge and skills of people and, by so doing, strengthening their organizations. AMA operates management centers and offices in the United States and, through AMA/International, in Brussels, Belgium; São Paulo, Brazil; Toronto, Canada; and Mexico City, Mexico. AMA offers public meetings through the Center for Management Development, Presidents Association, AMA/International, AMA Planning Services, AMA On-Site, and Operation Enterprise where interchange of management information, ideas, and experience in each field is provided through large-scale national conferences, seminars, briefings and workshops. Other services offered by AMA include the Extension Institute (a self-study program), Film UDED, AMA, COM Books, The Management Information Service, and the AMA Library. *Membership* approx. 75,000. *Publications: Management Review* (membership periodical); *The President; Personnel; Management Solutions; Supervisory Sense; Compensation and Benefits Review; CompFlash; Workshop and International Executive.*

   (AMA) Human Resources Division. 135 W. 50th St., New York, NY 10020. (212)903-8234. Phyllis White, Div. Mgr. Offers conferences, courses, and briefings in such areas as compensation, employee relations, human resources administration, management and supervisory training and development, career development, employee benefits, flexible benefits, and organization development. Members of this AMA division are typically vice presidents for personnel, industrial relations managers, safety directors, strategic planning directors, training directors, and employee benefit professionals. *Publications: Management Review; Personnel; Organizational Dynamics.*

American Medical Writers Association (AMWA). 9650 Rockville Pike, Bethesda, MD 20814. (301) 493-0003. Lillian Sablack, Exec. Dir. An international society whose members are engaged in all media of communication in medicine and allied professions. Founded in 1940, it is the largest association dedicated to the advancement of medical communication. Aims to offer guidance in the art and techniques of medical communication and to develop courses and workshops in the field. *Membership:* 3,200. *Dues:* $65.00. *Publications: AMWA Journal;* and *Freelance Directory.*

American Montessori Society (AMS.) 150-5th Ave., New York, NY 10011. (212) 924-3209. Bretta Weiss, Nat. Dir. Dedicated to promoting better education for all children through teaching strategies consistent with the Montessori system. Membership is composed of schools in the private and public sectors employing this method, as well as individuals. It serves as a resource center and clearinghouse for information and data on Montessori, affiliates teacher training programs in different parts of the country, conducts a consultation service and accreditation program for school members, and distributes Montessori materials and books. Sponsors four regional educational conferences per year. *Dues:* Yr.—teachers, $30.00; parents, $25.00; inst., $192.50-927.50. *Publications: AMS Constructive Triangle;* and *Annual Report.*

American National Standards Institute (ANSI). 1430 Broadway, New York, NY 10018. (212) 354-3300, FAX (212) 302-1286. Manuel Peralta, Pres.; James N. Pearse, Chairman of the Board. ANSI is the coordinator of the U.S. voluntary standards system, approves American National Standards, and represents the U.S. in the International Organization for Standardization (ISO) and the International Electrotechnical Commission (IEC). The Institute does not write standards or codes but coordinates those developed through an open consensus process by more than 240 organizations, 1,000 businesses, and 20 government agencies that comprise its membership. *Publications: Catalog of Standards,* yearly, lists more than 8,000 standards of all topic areas; *ANSI Reporter,* monthly newsletter of the national and international standards community; and *Standards Action,* biweekly listing status of revisions on standards in the U.S and abroad.

American Newspaper Publishers Association (ANPA) Foundation. Box 17407, Dulles Airport, Washington, DC 20041. (703) 648-1000. Judith D. Hines, Exec. V.P. Seeks to advance professionalism of the press, to foster public understanding of a free press, to cultivate increased numbers of future newspaper readers, and to enhance minority opportunities in newspapering. Administers a national Newspaper in Education Program, encouraging local newspapers and school systems to cooperate in using the newspaper for various fields of study. Also administers a Literacy Program, encouraging newspapers to work in their communities to combat illiteracy. Sponsors a Minority Opportunity Program to foster diversity in the newspaper business and supports numerous efforts encouraging freedom of the press. *Dues:* payable to association by newspapers. *Publications:* Training materials for students and professionals.

American Radio Relay League, Inc. (ARRL). 225 Main St., Newington, CT 06111. (203) 666-1541. David Sumner, Exec. V.P. A noncommercial association of radio amateurs interested in radio communication, experimentation, and the relaying of messages for the advancement of the radio art and public welfare. *Membership:* 160,000. *Dues:* $25.00. *Publications:* Send for list.

American Shortwave Listener's Club (ASWLC). 16182 Ballad Lane, Huntington Beach, CA 92649-2204. (714) 846-1685. Stewart H. MacKenzie, Pres.. A hobbyist organization founded to advance shortwave listening on a worldwide basis. Research and educational programs include studies of radio signals from earth satellites, relay stations, frequency interference, radio astronomy, propagation monitoring, sunspot studies, and computer communications worldwide. *Membership*: 1,000. *Dues*: $18.00 annually. Sample copy of *SWL*, $1.00. *Publications*: *SWL, Equipment Survey*, and *Proper Reporting Guide.*

American Society for Healthcare Education and Training of the American Hospital Association (ASHET). 840 N. Lake Shore Dr., Chicago. IL 60611. (312) 280-6113. Eileen M. Meehan, Dir. Members include directors of health education and training, health educators, patient education coordinators, education managers, human resource development coordinators, staff development coordinators, media specialists and organization development practitioners who conduct and manage education and training programs in all types of health care institutions, and wellness/health promotion coordinators. *Membership*: 1,600. *Dues*: $90.00. *Publications: Healthcare Education Dateline*; and *Journal of Healthcare Education and Training.*

American Society for Training and Development (ASTD). 1630 Duke St., Box 1443, Alexandria, VA 22313. (703) 683-8100. Curtis Plott, Exec. V.P. Leading professional organization for individuals engaged in employee training and education in business, industry, government, and related fields. Members include managers, program developers, instructors, consultants, counselors, suppliers, and academics. The purpose of its extensive professional publishing program is to build an essential body of knowledge for advancing the competence of training and development practitioners in the field. Many special interest subgroups relating to industries or job functions are included in the organization. *Membership*: 24,000. *Dues*: $120/yr. indiv. (group discounts available). *Publications: Training and Development Journal; Info-Line; ASTD Video Directories; A Checklist for Technical Skills and Other Training and Development; Competency Analysis for Trainers: A Personal Planning Guide; ASTD Directory of Academic Programs in T&D/HRD; Evaluating Training Programs; Training and Development Handbook; National Report;* and others.

American Society of Cinematographers. 1782 N. Orange Dr., Hollywood, CA 90078. (213) 876-5080. Leonard South, Pres. *Membership*: 271. *Publications: American Cinematographer Magazine.*

American Society of Educators (ASE). 1429 Walnut St., Philadelphia, PA 19102. (215) 563-3501. A multifaceted professional organization that serves the nation's teachers by providing information and evaluation of media resources and technologies for effective classroom use. *Membership*: 41,000. *Dues*: $29.00/yr. $38.00/yr. foreign. *Publications: Media and Methods.*

American Women in Radio and Television (AWRT). 1101 Connecticut Ave. NW, Suite 700, Washington, DC 20036. (202) 429-5102. Susan Kudla Finn, Exec.. Dir. Organization of professionals in the electronic media including owners, managers, administrators, and those in creative positions in broadcasting, satellite, cable, advertising, and public relations. The objectives are to work worldwide to improve the quality of radio and television; to promote the entry, development, and advancement of women in the electronic media and allied fields; to serve as a medium of communications and idea exchange; and to become involved in community concerns. Organized in 1951. Student memberships available. *Membership:* 52 chapters. *Dues:* $105.00/yr. *Publications: News and Views; Resource Directory; Careers in the Electronic Media.*

Anthropology Film Center (AFC). Box 493-87504, 1626 Canyon Rd., Santa Fe, NM 87501. (505) 983-4127. Joan and Carroll Williams, Co-Dirs. Offers Documentary Film Program, a 34-week, full-time course in 16mm film production and theory. Also provides consultation, research, 16mm film equipment sales and rental, facilities rental, joint M.A. degree with Temple University, occasional seminars and workshops, and a specialized library. *Publications: A Filmography for American*

Indian Education; An Ixil Calendrical Divination (a 16mm color film); and *First Impressions of Ixil Culture,*16mm color film).

Association for Childhood Education International (ACEI). 11141 Georgia Ave. #200, Wheaton, MD 20902. (301) 942-2443. Lucy Prete Martin, Ed. and Dir. of Publications. Concerned with children from infancy through early adolescence. ACEI publications reflect careful research, broadbased views, and consideration of a wide range of issues affecting children. Many are media-related in nature. The journal (*Childhood Education*) is essential for teachers, teachers-in-training, teacher educators, daycare workers, administrators, and parents. Articles focus on child development and emphasize practical application. Regular departments include book reviews (child and adult); reviews on films, pamphlets, and software; research; and classroom idea-sparkers. Articles address timely concerns; of the five issues published yearly, one is a theme issue devoted to critical concerns. *Membership:* 15,000. *Dues:* $38.00/yr. *Publications: Childhood Education* (official journal); *ACEI Exchange* (newsletter); and *Journal of Research in Childhood Education* (new).

Association for Computer Educators (ACE). College of Business, IDS, James Madison University, Harrisonburg, VA 22807. (703) 568-6189. Dr. Cynthia Johnson, Pres. Membership for those who teach or have an interest in computers and information systems. *Membership:* 1,000 plus libraries. *Dues:* $35.00/yr. *Publications: The Journal of Computer Information Systems.*

Association for Continuing Higher Education (ACHE) Center for Continuing Education, University of Evansville, 1800 Lincoln Ave., Evansville, IN 47722. (812) 479-2472. Roger H. Sublett, Exec. V.P. An association of institutions and individuals having a commitment to providing opportunities in higher education for adults in traditional and nontraditional programs. *Membership:* 1,564 indiv. representing 585 institutions. *Dues:* $35.00/yr. professional, $200.00/yr. institutional. *Publications: 5 Minutes with ACHE; The Journal of Continuing Higher Education;* and *Proceedings.*

Association for Educational Communications and Technology (AECT). 1126-16th St. NW, Washington, DC 20036. (202) 466-4780. Stanley Zenor, Exec. Dir; Lucy Ainsley, Pres. Concerned with learning and educational technology; established in 1923, AECT members include instructional technologists; media or library specialists; university professors and researchers; industrial/ business training specialists; religious educators; government media personnel; school, school district, and state department of education media program administrators and specialists; educational/ training media producers; and numerous others whose professional work requires improvement of media and technology in education and training. AECT members also work in the armed forces, in public libraries, in museums, and in other information agencies of many different kinds, including those related to the emerging fields of computer technology. AECT serves as a central clearinghouse and communications center for its members. The association maintains TechCentral, a national electronic mail network and bulletin board service. Through its various committees and task forces, it compiles data and prepares recommendations to form the basis of guidelines, standards, research and information summaries on numerous topics and problems of interest to the membership. AECT professional staff members report on government activities of concern to the membership and provide current data on laws and pending legislation relating to the educational media/technology field. AECT also maintains the ECT Foundation, through which it offers a limited number of financial grants to further the association's work. Archives (see entry) are also maintained at the University of Iowa. The AECT annual convention features the nation's largest instructional media exposition, InfoCOMM International Exposition, held jointly with the International Communications Industries Association (ICIA). The next convention will be held Feb. 13 -17, 1991, in Orlando, Florida. *Membership:* 5,000, plus 9,000 additional subscribers, 9 divisions, 12 national affiliates, 46 state affiliates, Puerto Rico, Guam, and more than 30 national committees and task forces. *Dues:* $50.00/yr. regular, $20.00/yr. student and retired. *Publications: TechTrends* (6/yr., with membership, $30.00/yr. nonmember); *Report to Members* (newsletter); *Educational Technology Research & Development* (4/yr., $30.00/yr. member, $20.00/yr. student and retired, $45.00/yr. nonmember); various division publications; and a number of books and videotapes, including the following recent titles: *Copyright and Instructional Technologies: A Guide to Fair Use and Permissions Procedures* (second edition) 1989; *Doctoral Research in Instructional/Design and Technology: A Directory of Dissertations 1989; Information Power: Guidelines for School Library Media Programs 1988; Information Power Discussion Guide 1988; Masters Curricula in Educational Communications and Technology: A Descriptive Directory* (third edition) 1989; *Mediatoons* 1989; *Safety in the Library Media Program: A Handbook* 1987; *Standards for College and University Learning Resources Programs: Technology in Instruction* (second edition) 1989; *The Information Power Video* (videotape) 1988; *Introduction to HyperCard* (videotape) 1989; *Interactive Learning with HyperCard—Apple Macintosh Computers* (videotape) 1989; and *Interactive Video Demonstration Tapes—Video Archive Volume No. 1, Video Archive Volume No. 2, Video Archive Volume No. 3.*

Because of similarity of interests, the following organizations have chosen to affiliate with the Association for Educational Communications and Technology. (As many as possible have been polled for inclusion in *EMTY*.)

- Association for Multi-Image (AMI)
- Association for Special Education Technology (ASET)
- Community College Association for Instruction and Technology (CCAIT)
- Consortium of University Film Centers (CUFC)
- Federal Educational Technology Association (FETA)
- Health Science Communications Association (HeSCA)
- International Visual Literacy Association (IVLA)
- Minorities in Media (MIM)
- National Association of Regional Media Centers (NARMC)
- New England Educational Media Association
- Northwest College and University Council for the Management of Educational Technology
- Southeastern Regional Media Leadership Council (SRMLC)
- State University of New York Educational Communications Center

Two additional organizations are also related to the Association for Educational Communications and Technology:

- AECT Archives
- AECT ECT Foundation

Association for Educational Communications and Technology (AECT) Divisions:

(AECT) Division of Educational Media Management (DEMM). 1126-16th St. NW, Washington, DC 20036. (202) 464-4780. Barbara Duffy, Pres. Seeks to develop an information exchange network and to share information about common problems, solutions, and program descriptions of educational media management. Develops programs that increase the effectiveness of media managers, initiates and implements a public relations program to educate the public and administrative bodies as to the use, value, and need for educational media management, and fosters programs that will help carry out media management responsibilities effectively. *Membership*: 1,024. *Dues*: one division membership included in the basic AECT membership; additional division memberships are $10.00/yr. *Publications: Media Management Journal.*

(AECT) Division of Interactive Systems and Computers (DISC) 1126-16th St. NW, Washington, DC 20036. (202) 466-4780. Janet Azbell, Pres. Concerned with the generation, access, organization, storage and delivery of all forms of information used in the processes of education and training. The Division promotes the networking of its members to facilitate sharing of expertise and interests. *Membership*: 512. *Dues*: one division membership included in the basic AECT membership; additional division memberships are $10.00/yr. *Publications: Newsletter.*

(AECT) Division of Instructional Development (DID). 1126-16th St. NW, Washington, DC 20036. (202) 466-4780. Brockenbrough Allen, Pres. DID is composed of individuals from business, government, and academic settings concerned with the systematic design of instruction and the development of solutions to performance problems. Members' interests include the study, evaluation, and refinement of design processes; the creation of new models of instructional development; the invention and improvement of techniques for managing the development of instruction; the development and application of professional ID competencies; the promotion of academic programs for preparation of ID professionals; and the dissemination of research and development work in ID. *Membership*: 765. *Dues*: one division membership included in the basic AECT membership; additional division memberships are $10.00/yr. *Publications: DID Newsletter* and Occasional Papers; and *Journal of Instructional Development* (published by AECT).

(AECT) Division of School Media Specialists (DSMS). 1126-16th St. NW, Washington, DC 20036. (202) 466-4780. Tom Peterson, Pres. DSMS promotes communication among school media personnel who share a common concern in the development, implementation, and evaluation of school media programs; and strives to increase learning and improve instruction in the school setting through the utilization of educational media and technology. *Membership*: 860. *Dues:* one division membership included in the basic AECT membership; additional division memberships are $10.00/yr. *Publications: Newsletter.*

(AECT) Division of Telecommunications (DOT). 1126-16th St. NW, Washington, DC 20036. (202) 466-4780. Bill Barnhart, Pres. Seeks to improve education through use of television and radio, video and audio recordings, and autotutorial devices and media. Aims to improve the design, production, evaluation, and use of telecommunications materials and equipment; to upgrade competencies of personnel engaged in the field; to investigate and report promising innovative practices and technological developments; to promote studies, experiments, and demonstrations; and to support research in telecommunications. Future plans call for working to establish a national entity representing instructional television. *Membership*: 695. *Dues:* one division membership included in the basic AECT membership; additional division memberships are $10.00/yr. *Publications: Newsletter.*

(AECT) Industrial Training and Education Division (ITED). 1126-16th St. NW, Washington, DC 20036. (202) 466-4780. Robin Taylor, Pres. Seeks to promote the sensitive and sensible use of media and techniques to improve the quality of education and training; to provide a professional program that demonstrates the state-of-the-art of educational technology as a part of the AECT convention; to improve communications to ensure the maximum use of educational techniques and media which can give demonstratable, objective evidence of effectiveness. *Membership:* 250. *Dues:* one division membership included in the basic AECT membership; additional division memberships are $10.00/yr. *Publications: Newsletter.*

(AECT) International Division (INTL) 1126-16th St. NW, Washington, DC 20036. (202) 466-4780. John Nelson, Pres. Seeks to improve international communications concerning existing methods of design; to pretest, use, produce, evaluate, and establish an approach through which these methods may be improved and/or adapted for maximum use and effectiveness; to develop a roster of qualified international leaders with experience and competence in the varied geographic and technical areas; and to encourage research in the application of communication processes to support present and future international social and economic development. *Membership:* 200. *Dues:* one division membership included in the basic AECT membership; additional division memberships are $10.00/yr. *Publications: Newsletter.*

(AECT) Media Design and Production Division (MDPD). 1126-16th St. NW, Washington, DC 20036. (202) 466-4780. James King, Pres. Seeks to provide formal organized procedures for promoting and facilitating interaction between commercial and noncommercial, nontheatrical filmmakers, and to provide a communications link for filmmakers with people of similar interests. Also seeks to provide a connecting link between creative and technical professionals of the audiovisual industry. Advances the informational film producer's profession by providing scholarships and apprenticeships to experimenters and students and by providing a forum for discussion of local, national, and universal issues. Recognizes and presents awards for outstanding films produced and for contributions to the state-of-the-art. *Membership:* 300. *Dues:* one division membership included in the basic AECT membership; additional division memberships are $10.00 yr. *Publications: Newsletter.*

(AECT) Research and Theory Division (RTD). 1126-16th St. NW, Washington, DC 20036. (202) 466-4780. Marina McIsaac, Pres. Seeks to improve the design, execution, utilization, and evaluation of audiovisual communications research; to improve the qualifications and effectiveness of personnel engaged in communications research; to advise the educational practitioner as to use of the results of research; to improve research design, techniques, evaluation, and dissemination; and to promote both applied and theoretical research on the systematic use of all forms of media in the improvement of instruction. *Membership:* 337. *Dues:* one division membership included in the basic AECT membership; additional division memberships are $10.00/yr. *Publications: Newsletter.*

Association for Educational Communications and Technology (AECT)
Affiliate Organizations:

(AECT) Community College Association for Instruction and Technology (CCAIT). College of Dupage LRC, 22nd St. and Lambert Rd., Glen Ellyn, IL 60137. (312) 858-2800. Bernard Fradkin, Pres. A national association of community and junior college educators interested in the discovery and dissemination of information about problems and processes of media and technology in community and junior colleges. Facilitates member exchange of data, reports, proceedings, personnel, and other resources; sponsors AECT convention sessions and social activities. *Membership:* 200. *Dues:* $15.00. *Publications:* Monthly newsletter; and semiannual journal.

(AECT) Federal Educational Technology Association (FETA). James T. Cannon, Pres. 6210 Edsall Rd. #402, Alexandria, VA 22312. (202) 632-5444. Martha Brooke, Pres. Seeks to create an awareness of the concept of instructional technology; to provide a forum for the exchange of information and ideas related to the latest developments and programs within the field; to standardize approaches to the employment of instructional technology and to furnish guidelines for the continued pursuit of excellence in the production of educational media programs, all within the armed forces and U.S. government. Membership open to media and instructional technologists from government agencies and organizations supplying them, and to other interested persons.

(AECT) International Visual Literacy Association, Inc. (IVLA). Virginia Tech, Education Technologies Div., Learning Resources Center, Blacksburg, VA 24061. (703) 961-5879. Roberts Braden, Pres.. Provides a multi-disciplinary forum for the exploration of modes of visual communication and their application through the concept of visual literacy; promotes development of visual literacy and serves as a bond between the diverse organizations and groups working in that field. *Dues:* $25.00, regular; $35.00 comprehensive (includes *Journal*). *Publications:* newsletter; and *Journal of Visual/Verbal Languaging.*

(AECT) Minorities In Media (MIM). TV/Media Resources Ctr., 1819 Nickerson Blvd., Hampton City Schools, Hampton, VA 23663. (804) 851-8411. Barbara Noble, Pres. Seeks to encourage the effective use of educational media in the teaching/learning process; provide leadership opportunities in advancing the use of technology as an integral part of the learning process; provide a vehicle through which minorities might influence the use of media in institutions; develop an information exchange network to share information common to minorities in media; study, evaluate, and refine the educational technology process as it relates to the education of minorites; and encourage and improve the production of materials for the education of minorites. *Membership*: 100. *Dues*: $10.00. *Publications*: Annual newsletter.

(AECT) National Association of Regional Media Centers (NARMC). P.O. Box 5026, Lancaster, PA 17601. (717) 569-8561. Mark Richie, Pres. Seeks to foster the exchange of ideas and information among educational communications specialists responsible for the administration of regional media centers, through workshops, seminars, and national meetings. Studies the feasibility of developing joint programs that could increase the effectiveness and efficiency of regional media services. Disseminates information on successful practices and research studies conducted by regional media centers. *Membership*: 268 regional centers, 70 corporations. *Dues*: $35.00. *Publications: étin* (q. newsletter); *Annual Report.*

(AECT) Northwest College and University Council for the Management of Educational Technology. Instructional Media Center, Eastern Washington University, Cheney, WA 99004. Jerry Donen, Dir. The first regional group representing institutions of higher education in Alberta, Alaska, British Columbia, Idaho, Montana, Oregon, and Washington to receive affilate status in AECT. Membership is restricted to media managers with campuswide responsibilities for educational technical services, in the membership region. Corresponding membership is available to those who work outside the membership region. An annual conference and business meeting is held the last weekend of October each year, rotating throughout the region. Current issues under consideration include managing the emerging telecommunication technologies, copyright, accreditation, and certification. Organizational goals include identifying the unique status problems of media managers in higher education, and improving the quality of the major publication. *Membership*: approx. 85. *Dues*: $35.00. *Publications*: *NW/MET Bulletin.*

Other AECT-Related Organizations:

(AECT) Archives. University of Iowa, c/o Calvin E. Mether, N 159 Lindquist Center, Iowa City, IA 52240. (319) 335-5623. A collection of media, projection and reproduction equipment, photographic devices, manuscripts, and related materials representing important developments in visual and audiovisual education and in instructional/educational technology. Maintained by the University of Iowa in cooperation with AECT. It is not open to the public.

(AECT) ECT Foundation. 1126-16th St. NW, Washington, DC 20036. Robert E. de Kieffer, Chair. The ECT Foundation is a nonprofit organization whose purposes are charitable and educational in nature. Its operation is based on the conviction that improvement of instruction can be accomplished, in part, by the continued investigation and application of new systems for learning, and by periodic assessment of current techniques for the communication of information. In addition to awarding scholarships, internships, and fellowships, the foundation develops and conducts leadership training programs for emerging professional leaders.

Association for Experiential Education (AEE). CU Box 249, Boulder, CO 80309. (303) 492-1547. Daniel Garvey, Exec. Dir. AEE believes that the learner and the teacher should use the most powerful and effective means to interact with each other, and their environments, and to deal with the tasks at hand. Experience-based education emphasizes direct experience to increase the quality of learning. AEE helps to advance, expand, conceptualize, and formalize this learning process. *Membership*: 1,200. *Dues*: $35.00-$50.00 indiv., $125.00 inst. *Publications: Jobs Clearinghouse*; and *The Journal of Experiential Education*.

Association for Library and Information Science Education. c/o Ilse Moon, 5623 Palm Aire Drive, Sarasota, FL 34243. (813) 355-1795. Seeks to advance education for library and information science and produces annual Library and Information Science Education Statistical Report. Open to professional schools offering graduate programs in library and information science; personal memberships open to educators employed in such institutions, other memberships available to interested individuals. *Membership*: 600 indiv., 85 inst. *Dues*: inst., $250.00 full, $150.00 assoc., $75.00 international; personal, $40.00 full-time, $20.00 part-time, student, retired. *Publications: Journal of Education for Library and Information Science*; directory; *Library and Information Science Education Statistics*.

Association of American Colleges (AAC). 1818 R St. NW, Washington, DC 20009. (202) 387-3760. John W. Chandler, Pres. AAC, founded in 1915, is the national voice for liberal learning. Through programs, grants, publications, and workshops, AAC strives to enhance liberal education and secure its integration with professional programs and courses of study. Programs include the Project on the Status and Education of Women. *Membership*: 615. *Dues*: based on FTE and Eng. *Publications: Liberal Education*; and *On Campus with Women,* and monographs.

Association of American Publishers (AAP). 220 E. 23rd St., New York, NY 10010. (212) 689-8920 Ambassador Nicholas A. Veliotes, Pres. A group of 300 companies whose members produce the majority of printed materials sold to U.S. schools, colleges, libraries, bookstores, and homes. Range of member interests is reflected in textbooks, religious, scientific and media books, instructional systems, software, audio and videotapes, records, cassettes, slides, transparencies, and tests. Provides its members with information concerning trade conditions, markets, copyrights, manufacturing processes, taxes, duties, postage, freight, censorship movements, government programs, and other matters of importance. *Membership*: 300 companies. *Dues*: vary. *Publications: AAP Monthly Report.*

Association of Audio-Visual Technicians (AAVT). 2378 S. Broadway, Denver, CO 80210. (303) 698-1820. Elsa C. Kaiser, Exec. Dir. Proposes to increase communication and to assist audiovisual technicians in their work; holds seminars in conjunction with most of the major audiovisual shows. Maintains a lending library of programs on audiovisual equipment or production. Also has a lending library of old manuals for rent by AAVT members. *Membership:* 1,200. *Dues*: $35.00 indiv., $65.00 inst. *Publications: Fast Forword.*

Association of Independent Video and Filmmakers and the Foundation for Independent Video and Film. 625 Broadway, 9th floor, New York, NY 10012. (212) 473-3400. Lawrence Sapadin, Exec. Dir. The national trade association for independent video and filmmakers, representing their needs and goals to industry, government, and the public. Programs include domestic and foreign festival liaison for independents, screenings and seminars, insurance for members and groups, and information and referral services. Recent activities include monitoring status of independent work on public television, advocacy for cable access, and lobbying for modifications in copyright law. *Dues*: $45.00 indiv., $85.00 inst., $60.00 libs., $25.00 students. *Publications: The Independent.*

Association of Systematics Collections. 730-11th St. NW, 2nd floor, Washington, DC 20001. (202) 347-2850. K. Elaine Hoagland, Exec. Dir. Promotes the care, management, and improvement of biological collections, provides information on biological collections and biologists who offer taxonomic services, and publishes current information on endangered species and government permit regulations regarding the scientific use of plants and animals. *Membership:* 80 inst., 20 scientific societies. *Dues:* After election to membership. *Publications: Biogeography of the Tropical Pacific; Amphibian Species of the World; Collections of Frozen Tissues, Controlled Wildlife I, II, III;*

Sources of Federal Funding in the Biological Sciences; Guidelines to the Acquisition and Management of Biological Specimens; ASC Newsletter; The Systematic Community; A Guide to Museum Pest Control; Systematics: Relevance, Resources, Services, and *Management (a bibliography); Foundations for a National Biological Survey; and Crocodilian, Toatara,* and *Turtle Species of the World.*

Association of Teacher Educators (ATE). 1900 Association Dr., Suite ATE, Reston, VA 22091. (703) 620-3110. Robert J. Stevenson, Exec. Dir. Annual conference, usually held in February, and annual summer workshops. *Membership*: 4,000. *Dues*: $50.00. *Publications*: *Action in Teacher Education; ATE Newsletter*; and other miscellaneous publications.

Authors' League of America, Inc. 234 W. 44th St., New York, NY 10036. (212) 391-9198. Garson Kanin, Pres. A professional organization of authors of books, magazine materials, and plays. *Membership*: 14,500. *Publications: Dramatics Guild Quarterly;* and *Authors Guild Bulletin.*

Bergwall. 106 Charles Lindbergh Blvd., Uniondale NY 11553-3695. (516) 222-1111; (800) 645-3565. Charles Bergwall, Pres. The nation's largest producer of media for technical/vocational education. Catalog available.

Catholic Library Association. 461 W. Lancaster Ave., Haverford, PA 19041. (215) 649-5250. Natalie A. Logan, Exec. Dir. Seeks to improve libraries in general, and religion-oriented libraries in particular; promotes discriminating taste in literature and other communication media. Encourages compilation, publication, and use of religious reference tools, seeks to attract persons into librarianship through scholarships, fosters research and developments in librarianship and communication, and encourages cooperation with associations interested in the field. Produces continuing education programs on videotape. *Membership*: 3,000. *Dues*: $45.00-$500.00. *Publication: CLA Handbook and Membership Directory* (annual); *Catholic Library World* (6/yr.); and *Catholic Periodical and Literature Index* (6/yr.).

Center for Advanced Visual Studies. MIT Building W11, 40 Massachusetts Ave., Cambridge, MA 02139. (617) 253-4415. Otto Piene, Dir. Founded by Gyorgy Kepes in 1968, offers a unique situation in which artists explore and realize art work in collaboration with scientists and engineers. Has done significant work on lasers, holography, video, kinetics, environmental art, and sky art.

Center for Children's Media (CCM). 451 W. Broadway (#4N), New York, NY 10012-3156. Maureen Gaffney, Exec. Dir. Formerly the Media Center for Children, this is a resource for professionals who make or use media with children. All information is based on ongoing evaluation of short nontheatrical 16mm films and videotapes for children. Institutional services include workshops and courses for teachers, librarians, art and museum educators, hospital programmers, and film- or videomakers. Programming consultation available for libraries, museums, schools, hospitals, and community organizations. Production consultation available to individuals and institutions. *Publications: What to Do When the Lights Go On; Using Media to Make Kids Feel Good; 100 Best Films and Videos for Children; Basics of Film Programming; Using Folktale Films; Half-Inch Video; and Using Film and Video as Art with Grades 5-8* (in preparation).

Center for Instructional Research and Curriculum Evaluation. 1310 S. 6th St., Champaign, IL 61820. (217) 333-3770. Robert E. Stake, Exec. Dir. A unit within the College of Education, University of Illinois, the Center is primarily active in conducting education-related research and development projects in the U.S.A., but is of considerable interest to program evaluation specialists in foreign countries.

Central Educational Network (CEN). 1400 E. Touhy, Des Plaines, IL 60018. (312) 390-8700. James A. Fellows, Pres. Provides general audience, postsecondary programming, and ITV services. *Membership*: PTV stations and educational agencies.

Chidren's Film and Television Center of America (CFTCA). School of Cinema-TV, University of Southern California, 850 W. 34th St., Los Angeles, CA 90089. (213) 743-8632. Shanta Herzog, Exec. Dir.; Ann Knapp, Program Dir. CFTCA is a national organization of parents, children, teachers, librarians, entertainers, film producers, and distributors whose purpose is to encourage and support the production, distribution, and exhibition of excellent films for children. CFTCA represents the United States in the International Center of Films for Children and Young People in Paris. Activities include the International Children's Film Festival held in Los Angeles, the Ruby Slipper Awards for outstanding films, and sponsorship of film workshops for teachers and librarians in Los Angeles County. *Dues*: $25.00 indiv., $40.00 family. *Publications: Children's Film International, A Review Journal of the International Children's Film Festival*; quarterly newsletter.

Children's Television International, Inc. 8000 Forbes Pl., Suite 201, Springfield, VA 22151. (703) 321-8455. Ray Gladfelter, Pres.; Karen Shipman, Dir. of Customer Services. An educational organization that develops, produces, and distributes a wide variety of color television programming and television-related materials as a resource to aid children's social, cultural, and intellectual development. Program areas cover language arts, science, social studies, art, and business communications for home, school, and college viewing. *Publications: Teacher's Guides* which accompany instructional TV series.

CINE Information. 215 W. 90th St., New York, NY 10024. (212) 877-3999. Barbara Margolis. Exec. Dir. CINE Information is a nonprofit educational organization established to develop sound methods and tools for the more effective use of film by community groups and educational programmers. It produces and distributes materials about film and videotape use, and produces films on topics of social and cultural importance. Newest release is the American Film Festival Red Ribbon winner *Are We Winning Mommy? America and the Cold War* (feature documentary). Also featured at the Berlin, Toronto, Chicago, Denver, and Park City, Utah film festivals. *Publications*: *Adam Clayton Powell, Jr.*, an hour-long documentary, will premier in fall 1989 on "The American Experience" over PBS; *In Focus: A Guide to Using Films* by Linda Blackaby, Dan Georgakas, and Barbara Margolis, a complete step-by-step handbook for film and videotape users, with detailed discussions of how to use film and tape in educational, cultural, and fundraising activities.

Clearinghouse on Development Communication. 1815 N. Fort Meyer Dr., 6th floor, Arlington, VA 22209. (703) 527-5546. Michael Laflin, Dir. A center for materials and information on applications of communication technology to development problems. Operated by the Institute for International Research and funded by the Bureau for Science and Technology of the U.S. Agency for International Development. Visitors and written requests for information are welcome. *Dues:* subscription, $10.00. *Publications: Development Communication Report* (q.).

Close Up Foundation. 1235 Jefferson Davis Hwy., Arlington, VA 22202. (703) 892-5400, (800) 336-5479. Stephen A. Janger, Pres. An organization dealing with the involvement of citizens in government. Brings participants to Washington for a series of week-long, in-depth looks into the federal government. Produces several series of television programs telecast on the C-SPAN cable network for secondary school and home audiences. *Membership*: 24,000 participants annually. *Publications: Perspectives; Current Issues; Economic Choices; International Relations*; and videotapes on current domestic and foreign policy issues.

Computer-Based Education Research Laboratory (CERL). University of Illinois, 252 Engineering Research Laboratory, 103 South Mathews Avenue, Urbana, IL 61801. (217) 333-6210. Dr. Donald L. Bitzer, Director. CERL is a research laboratory dedicated to the development of hardware, software, and courseware for the delivery of cost-effective, interactive computer-based education. Delivery has been via a large-scale system (PLATO) linking more than 1,800 terminals to a central computer. CERL has also developed a Cluster System and stand-alone terminals. A new low-cost mainframe delivery system, NovaNET, is now in operation. It is capable of serving several thousand users via a network of satellite, cable television, or phone lines. PLATO originated at the

University of Illinois in 1960, NovaNET in 1986. *Publications:* Department and professional journal. Publications available upon request.

The Computer Museum. 300 Congress St., Boston, MA 02210. (617) 426-2800. Dr. Oliver Strimpel, Acting Exec. Dir. The world's only computer museum occupies 55,000 square feet in a renovated historic building on Boston's waterfront. The museum presents the history of the information revolution, from mammoth vacuum tube computers to state-of-the-art technology, through 60 hands-on exhibits, displays, films and animation, recreations of vintage computer installations, and the most extensive collection of computers and robots ever assembled. *Membership*: 2,000. *Dues*: $30.00 indiv., $45.00 family. *Publications*: *The Computer Museum Annual* (annual journal); *The Computer Museum News* (bimonthly newsletter); *Educational Group Tour Planner; Educational Activities Kit.*

Consortium of College and University Media Centers (formerly Consortium of University Film Centers). c/o Audio Visual Services, Kent State, 330 Library, Kent, OH 44242. (216) 672-3456. John P. Kerstetter, Exec. Dir. A professional group of higher education media personnel whose purpose is to improve education and training through the effective use of educational media. Assists educational and training users in business in making films, video, and educational media more accessible. Fosters cooperative planning among university media centers. Gathers and disseminates information on improved procedures and new developments in educational media and media center management. *Membership*: 200. *Dues*: $125/yr. constituents; $25 active; $125 sustaining (commercial); $15 students, $20 assoc. *Publications*: *The Educational Film/Video Locator; The Leader* (newsletter to members); and *16mm Film Maintenance Manual.*

Continuing Library Education Network and Exchange. Round Table of the American Library Association. 50 E. Huron, Chicago, IL 60611. (312) 944-6780. Elaine Wingate, ALA staff liaison; Gail McGovern, Pres.; Vee Friesner Carrington, V.P. Seeks to provide access to quality continuing education opportunities for librarians and information scientists and to create an awareness of the need for such education in helping individuals in the field to respond to societal and technological changes. *Membership:* 349. *Dues:* Open to all ALA members; indiv. members $15.00; $50.00 for organizations. *Publications*: *CLENExchange* (q.), available to nonmembers by subscription—$20.00/yr. U.S. zip, $25.00 non-U.S. zip.

Copyright Clearance Center (CCC). 27 Congress St., Salem, MA 01970. (500) 744-3350. Eamon T. Fennessy, Pres. An organization through which corporations, academic and research libraries, information brokers, government agencies, and other users of copyrighted information may obtain authorizations and pay royalties for photocopying these materials in excess of exemptions contained in the U.S. Copyright Act of 1976. In addition to offering a Transactional Reporting Service, CCC also operates an Annual Authorization Service, which is an annual-license program serving photocopy permissions needs of large U.S. corporations. *Membership*: 2,500 users, 6,400 publishers, 915,000 publications. *Publications*: *Publishers Photocopy Fee Catalog*; *CCC Report* (newsletter, q.); and *Handbook for Libraries and Other Organization Users,* irreg.

Corporation for Public Broadcasting (CPB) 1111-16th St. NW, Washington, DC 20036. (202) 955-5100. Donald E. Ledwig, Pres. and CEO. A private, nonprofit corporation authorized by the Public Broadcasting Act of 1967 to develop noncommercial television and radio services for the American people, while insulating public broadcasting from political pressure or influence. CPB supports station operations and funds radio and television programs for national distribution. CPB sets national policy that will most effectively make noncommercial radio and television and other telecommunications services available to all citizens. *Publications*: *CPB Report* (bi-wk., 3 yr. for $25.00); *Annual Report*; and *CPB Public Broadcasting Directory* ($10.00).

Council for Basic Education. 725-15th St. NW, Washington, DC 20005. (202) 347-4171. A. Graham Down, Exec. Dir. A vocal force advocating a broadly defined curriculum in the liberal arts for all students in elementary and secondary schools. *Membership*: 4,000. *Dues*: $40.00 members;

$25/yr. subscribers. *Publications: Basic Education; Perspective* (q., 2 yr. for $75.00 members or $45.00 subscribers); and various reports and books.

Council for Educational Development and Research (CEDaR). 1201-16th St. NW, Suite 305, Washington, DC 20036. (202) 223-1593. Dena G. Stoner, Exec. Dir. Members are educational research and development institutions. Aims to advance the level of programmatic, institutionally based educational research and development and to demonstrate the importance of research and development in improving education. Provides a forum for professional personnel in member institutions. Coordinates national dissemination program. Other activities include research, development, evaluation, dissemination, and technical assistance on educational issues. *Membership*: 14. *Publications: R & D Preview; Newsletter*; and *Directory*.

Council for Exceptional Children (CEC). 1920 Association Dr., Reston, VA 22091. (703) 620-3660. Jeptha Greer, Exec. Dir. A membership organization providing information to teachers, administrators, and others concerned with the education of handicapped and gifted children. Maintains a library and database on literature on special education; prepares books, monographs, digests, films, filmstrips, cassettes, and journals; sponsors annual convention and conferences on special education, provides information and assistance to lawmakers on the education of the handicapped and gifted; coordinates Political Action Network on the rights of exceptional persons. *Membership*: 54,000. *Dues*: Professionals, $55.00-$63.00, depending on state of residence; students, $24.00-$24.50, depending on state of residence. *Publications: Exceptional Children; Teaching Exceptional Children; Exceptional Child Educational Resources*; and numerous other professional publications dealing with the education of handicapped and gifted children.

Council of National Library and Information Associations. St. John's University, Library Room 322-Grand Central & Utopia Parkways, Jamaica, NY 11439. (718) 990-6735. Thomas Jay Kemp, Chair. The council is a forum for discussion of many issues of concern to library and information associations. Current committees at work are the Joint Committee on Association Cooperation and the Ad Hoc Committee on Copyright Implementation. *Membership*: 21 associations. *Dues*: Inquire.

Council on International Educational Exchange (CIEE) 205 E. 42nd St., New York, NY 10017. (212) 661-1414. Jack Egle, Exec. Dir. CIEE has been a pioneer in developing and encouraging educational exchange programs involving work and study and student travel since 1947. CIEE also has offices in Paris, Tokyo, London, Madrid, Rome, Kyoto, Hong Kong, Bonn, and in 25 U.S. cities. *Membership*: 200 colleges and universities. *Publications: Student Travel Catalog*, featuring information on programs involving work, study, and travel throughout the world, available free of charge.

Council on International Non-theatrical Events. 1001 Connecticut Ave. NW, Suite 1916, Washington, DC 20036. (202) 785-1136. FAX (202) 785-4114. Richard Calkins, Exec. Dir. Coordinates the selection and placement of U.S. documentary, television, short subject, and didactic films in more than 200 overseas film festivals annually. A Golden Eagle Certificate is awarded to each professional film considered most suitable to represent the United States in international competition. A CINE Eagle Certificate is awarded to winning adult amateur, youth, and university student-made films. Prizes and certificates won at overseas festivals are presented by embassy representatives at an annual awards luncheon. Deadlines for receipt of entry forms are 1 February and 1 August. *Publications: CINE Yearbook; Annual International U.S. Film Festival Directory*.

East-West Institute of Culture and Communication. East-West Center, 1777 East-West Rd., Honolulu, HI 96848. (808) 944-7666. Robert B. Hewett, Interim Dir. Dedicated to implementing the East-West Center's mission of fostering better understanding and relations among people of the East and West through programs and research activities related to culture and communication. Its three program groups study the creative expression of culture; cultural construction and national identity; and modernization, communication and change. Conducts international cooperative research, arranges international conferences and workshops; offers opportunities for participation;

and publishes books, papers, and materials on topics related to culture and communication in the Asian, Pacific, and United States regions.

Education Development Center, Inc. 55 Chapel St., Newton, MA 02160. (617) 969-7100. Janet Whitla, Pres. Seeks to improve education at all levels, in the United States and abroad, through curriculum development, institutional development, and services to school and the community. Produces filmstrips and videocassettes, primarily in connection with curriculum development and teacher training. *Publications: Annual Report*; and occasional papers.

Environmental Quality Instructional Resources Center. OSU, 1200 Chambers Rd., Room 310, Columbus, OH 43212. (614) 292-6717. Robert W. Howe, Dir. Emphasizes water quality education and training. Maintains IRIS (Instructional Resources Information System), an audiovisual library, and makes publications and audiovisual aids available. Publication lists and audiovisual lists are available. *Publications: EQ-IRC Bulletin; IRIS supplements*; and various monographs.

EPIE Institute (Educational Products Information Exchange). Box 839, Water Mill, NY 11976. (516) 283-4922. P. Kenneth Komoski, Exec. Dir. Involved primarily in assessing educational materials. Together with Consumers Union, provides evaluations of educational microcomputer software. EPIE's microcomputer product evaluations are accessible electronically via CompuServe. EPIE also provides inservice training and consultation, and microcomputer seminars on software evaluations. All of EPIE's services, including its Curriculum Alignment Services for Educators, are available to schools and state agencies, as well as individuals. *Membership*: 2,500. *Publications: EPIEgram* materials; *Equipment; MICROgram; Parents Guide to Educational Software*; and *The Educational Software Selector (T.E.S.S.)*

ERIC (Educational Resources Information Center). 555 New Jersey Ave. NW, Washington, DC 20208. (202) 357-6289. Robert Stonehill, Head. Coordinates the ERIC system of 16 clearinghouses (see following entries). ERIC's database contains citations to more than 250,000 unpublished or hard-to-find documents on various phases, levels, and subject areas of education, all of which are intended to assist professionals in locating data pertaining to classroom, administrative, and planning problems. The ERIC Clearinghouses have responsibility within the network for acquiring the significant educational literature within their particular areas, selecting the highest quality and most relevant material, processing (i.e., cataloging, indexing, abstracting) the selected items for input to the database, and also for providing information-analysis products and various user services based on the database. ERIC also catalogs and announces journal articles dealing with education from over 750 educational journals. Offers microfiche of uncopyrighted materials in over 760 collections throughout the world. The exact number of Clearinghouses has fluctuated over time in response to the shifting needs of the educational community. There are currently 16 Clearinghouses. These are listed below, together with full addresses, telephone numbers, and brief scope notes describing the areas they cover. *Dues:* None. *Publications: Resources in Education;* and *Current Index to Journals in Education.*

ERIC Clearinghouse on Adult, Career, and Vocational Education (CE). Ohio State University, Center on Education and Training for Employment, 1900 Kenny Rd.. Columbus, OH 43210-1090. (614) 292-4353; (800) 848-4815. All levels and settings of adult and continuing, career, and vocational/technical education. Adult education, from basic literacy training through professional skill upgrading. Career education, including career awareness, career decisionmaking, career development, career change, and experience-based education. Vocational and technical education, including new subprofessional fields, industrial arts, corrections education, employment and training programs, youth employment, work experience programs, education/business partnerships, entrepreneurship, adult retraining, and vocational rehabilitation for the handicapped.

ERIC Clearinghouse on Counseling and Personnel Services (CG). University of Michigan, School of Education, Room 2108, 610 East University St., Ann Arbor, MI 48109-1259. (313) 764-9492. Preparation, practice, and supervision of counselors at all educational levels and in all settings;

theoretical development of counseling and guidance; personnel procedures such as testing and interviewing and the analysis and dissemination of the resultant information; group work and case work; nature of pupil, student, and adult characteristics; personnel workers and their relation to career planning, family consultations, and student orientation activities.

ERIC Clearinghouse on Educational Management (EA). University of Oregon, 1787 Agate St., Eugene, OR 97403-5207. (503) 686-5043. The leadership, management, and structure of public and private educational organizations; practice and theory of administration; pre-service and inservice preparation of administrators; tasks and processes of administration; methods and varieties of organization and organizational change; and the social context of educational organizations. Sites, buildings, and equipment for education; planning, financing, constructing, renovating, equipping, maintaining, operating, insuring, utilizing, and evaluating educational facilities.

ERIC Clearinghouse on Elementary and Early Childhood Education (PS). University of Illinois, College of Education, 805 W. Pennsylvania Ave., Urbana, IL 61801-4897. (217) 333-1386. The physical, cognitive, social, educational, and cultural development of children from birth through early adolescence; prenatal factors; parental behavior factors; learning theory research and practice related to the development of young children, including the preparation of teachers for this educational level; educational programs and community services for children; and theoretical and philosophical issues pertaining to children's development and education.

ERIC Clearinghouse on Handicapped and Gifted Children (EC). Council for Exceptional Children, 1920 Association Dr., Reston, VA 22091-1589. (703) 620-3660. All aspects of the education and development of the handicapped and gifted, including prevention, identification and assessment, intervention, and enrichment, both in special and in integrated settings .

ERIC Clearinghouse on Higher Education (HE). George Washington University, One Dupont Circle, NW, Suite 630, Washington, DC 20036-1183. (202) 296-2597. Topics relating to college and university conditions, problems, programs, and students. Curricular and instructional programs, and institutional research at the college or university level. Federal programs, professional education (medicine, law, etc.), professional continuing education, collegiate computer-assisted learning and management, graduate education, university extension programs, teaching-learning, legal issues and legislation, planning, governance, finance, evaluation, inter-institutional arrangements, management of institutions of higher education, and business or industry educational programs leading to a degree.

ERIC Clearinghouse on Information Resources (IR). Syracuse University, Huntington Hall, Room 030, 150 Marshall St., Syracuse, NY 13244-2340. (315) 443-3640. Educational technology and library and information science at all levels. Instructional design, development, and evaluation are the emphases within educational technology, along with the media of educational communication: computers and microcomputers, telecommunications (cable, broadcast, satellite), audio and video recordings, film and other audiovisual materials, as they pertain to teaching and learning. Within library and information science, the focus is on the operation and management of information services for education-related organizations. All aspects of information technology related to education are considered within the scope.

ERIC Clearinghouse for Junior Colleges (JC). University of California at Los Angeles (UCLA), Mathematical Sciences Building, Room 8118, 405 Hilgard Ave., Los Angeles, CA 90024-1564. (213) 825-3931. Development, administration, and evaluation of two-year public and private community and junior colleges, technical institutes, and two-year branch university campuses. Two-year college students, faculty, staff, curricula, programs, support services, libraries, and community services. Linkages between two-year colleges and business/industrial organizations. Articulation of two-year colleges with secondary and four-year postsecondary institutions.

ERIC Clearinghouse on Languages and Linguistics (FL). Center for Applied Linguistics, 1118-22nd St., NW, Washington, DC 20037-0037. (202) 429-9551. Languages and language sciences; theoretical and applied linguistics; all areas of foreign language, second language, and linguistics instruction, pedagogy, or methodology; psycholinguistics and the psychology of language learning; cultural and intercultural context of languages; application of linguistics in language teaching; bilingualism and bilingual education; sociolinguistics; study abroad and international exchanges; teacher training and qualifications specific to the teaching of foreign languages and second languages; commonly and uncommonly taught languages, including English as a second language; related curriculum developments and problems.

ERIC Clearinghouse on Reading and Communication Skills (CS). Indiana University, Smith Research Center, 2805 East 10th St., Suite 150, Bloomington, IN 47405-2373. (812) 855-5847. Reading, English, and communication skills (verbal and nonverbal), pre-school through college; educational research and instruction development in reading, writing, speaking, and listening; identification, diagnosis, and remediation of reading problems; speech communication (including forensics), mass communication, interpersonal and small group interaction, interpretation, rhetorical and communication theory, speech sciences, and theater. Preparation of instructional staff and related personnel in these areas. All aspects of reading behavior with emphasis on physiology, psychology, sociology, and teaching; instructional materials, curricula, tests/measurement, and methodology at all levels of reading; the role of libraries and other agencies in fostering and guiding reading; diagnostics and remedial reading services in schools and clinical settings. Preparation of reading teachers and specialists. For list of most recent publications, write to ERIC/RCS at address above.

ERIC Clearinghouse on Rural Education and Small Schools (RC). Appalachia Educational Laboratory, 1031 Quarrier St., P.O. Box 1348, Charleston, WV 25325-1348. (800) 624-9120. Economic, cultural, social, or other factors related to educational programs and practices for rural residents; American Indians/Alaska Natives, Mexican Americans, and migrants; educational practices and programs in all small schools; outdoor education.

ERIC Clearinghouse for Science, Mathematics, and Environmental Education (SE). Ohio State University, 1200 Chambers Rd., Room 310, Columbus, OH 43212-1792. (614) 292-6717. Science, mathematics, and environmental education at all levels, and within these three broad subject areas, the following topics: development of curriculum and instructional materials; teachers and teacher education; learning theory/outcomes (including the impact of parameters such as interest level, intelligence, values, and concept development upon learning in these fields); educational programs; research and evaluative studies; media applications; computer applications.

ERIC Clearinghouse for Social Studies/Social Science Education (ERIC/ChESS). Indiana University, Social Studies Development Center, Suite 120, 2805 East Tenth St., Bloomington, IN 47405-2373. (812) 855-3838. All levels of social studies/social science education; contents and contributions of the social science disciplines (anthropology, economics, geography, civics, sociology, social psychology, political science) and selected humanities disciplines (history, art, music); education as a social science; comparative education (K-12); content and curriculum materials on social topics such as law-related education, ethnic studies, bias and discrimination, aging, adoption, women's equity, and sex education.

ERIC Clearinghouse on Teacher Education (SP). American Association of Colleges for Teacher Education, One Dupont Circle, NW, Suite 610, Washington, DC 20036-2412. (202) 293-2450. School personnel at all levels; teacher selection and training, preservice and inservice preparation, and retirement; the theory, philosophy, and practice of teaching; curricula and general education not specifically covered by other clearinghouses; all aspects of physical education, health education, and recreation education.

ERIC Clearinghouse on Tests, Measurement, and Evaluation (TM). American Institutes for Research (AIR), Washington Research Center, 3333 K St., NW, Washington, DC 20007-3893. (202) 342-5060. Tests and other measurement devices; methodology of measurement and evaluation; application of tests, measurement, or evaluation in educational projects or programs; research design and methodology in the area of testing and measurement/evaluation; learning theory in general.

ERIC Clearinghouse on Urban Education (UD). Teachers College, Columbia University, Institute for Urban and Minority Education, Main Hall, Room 300, Box 40, 525 W. 120th St., New York, NY 10027-9998. (212) 678-3433. Programs and practices in public, parochial, and private schools in urban areas and the education of particular racial/ethnic minority children and youth in various settings—local, national, and international; the theory and practice of educational equity; urban and minority experiences; and urban and minority social institutions and services.

ERIC Document Reproduction Service (EDRS). Computer Microfilm Corporation, 3900 Wheeler Ave., Alexandria, VA 22304-6409. (800) 227-ERIC (3742). Operates the document delivery arm of the ERIC system. Furnishes microfiche and/or paper copies of most ERIC documents. Address purchase orders to the above address. FAX order and delivery service available. FAX Number 1-703-823-0505.

ERIC Processing and Reference Facility. ARC Professional Services Group, Information Systems Division, 2440 Research Blvd., Suite 550, Rockville, MD 20850-3238. (301) 590-1420. Ted Brandhorst, Dir. A centralized information processing facility serving all components of the ERIC network, under policy direction of central ERIC. Services provided include editing, receiving and dispatch, document control and analysis, Lexicography, computer processing, file maintenance, database management, and others. Receives and edits abstracts from 16 ERIC clearinghouses for publication in *Resources in Education (RIE)*, and acquisitions update in the *ERIC Thesaurus*. *Publications: Resources in Education; ERIC Thesaurus; Source Directory; Report Number Index; Clearinghouse Number/ED Number Cross Reference Listing; Title Index; ERIC Processing Manual;* and numerous other listings and indexes.

Far West Laboratory for Educational Research and Development (FWL). 1855 Folsom St., San Francisco, CA 94103. (415) 565-3000. Dr. Dean Nafziger, Dir. Contributes to the improvement of the quality of learning experiences that support the values and functions of a humanistic society. FWL carries out its mission by producing new knowledge through research, by conducting programmatic development leading to new, high-quality products or processes that will serve the needs of all learners; by providing technical assistance in support of quality education for those who seek it; and by confronting and assessing educational issues in an impartial environment. FWL has established a strong development and technical assistance capability in instructional technology and media. FWL maintains a reference library with a complete ERIC microfiche collection and conducts information searches. *Publications.* Books; newsletters; handbooks; guides; research syntheses; reports; and training materials. *See also* Council for Educational Development and Research.

Federal Communications Commission (FCC). 1919 M St. NW, Washington, DC 20554. (202) 632-7000. Patti Grace Smith, Chief, Consumer Assistance and Small Business Div. An agency that regulates radio, television, telephone, and telegraph operations within the United States. Allocates frequencies and channels for different types of communications activities, issues amateur and commercial operators' licenses, and regulates rates of interstate communication services of many different kinds. *Publications:* Bulletins pertaining to educational broadcasting.

Film Advisory Board (FAB). 1727-1/2 Sycamore, Hollywood, CA 90028. (213) 874-3644. Elayne Blythe, Pres. Previews and evaluates films and film-type presentations in all formats, makes recommendations for improved family entertainment fare, and presents awards of excellence to outstanding motion pictures and TV programs and for innovations in these industries. Technical awards are also presented, and awards for outstanding contributions to the entertainment industry and for the most promising newcomers. Awards of excellence are presented for videocassettes; the FAB Winner Seal is featured worldwide on many of the family and child videocassettes for Prisms, Vestron's Children's Video Library, and others. Supplies film list to many national organizations encouraging them to support FAB award-winning products. *Membership*: 450. Dues: $35.00/yr. *Publications:* Monthly film list distributed to studios, libraries, churches, PR firms, youth groups, PTAs, clubs, and colleges. Now rating home videos with Film Advisory Board (FAB) rating system.

Film Arts Foundation (FAF). 346-9th St., 2nd floor, San Francisco, CA 94103. (415) 552-8760. Gail Silva, Dir. Service organization designed to support and promote independent film and video production. Services include low-cost 16mm editing facility, skills file, festivals file, resource library, group legal plan, seminars, workshops, work-in-progress screenings, proposal consultation, nonprofit sponsorship of selected film and video projects, and advocacy for independent film and video. *Membership*: 1,600. *Dues*: $35.00. *Publications: Release Print*.

Film/Video Arts, Inc. 817 Broadway, New York, NY 10003. (212) 673-9361. Encourages media production as an educational, vocational, and artistic experience. Provides an equipment resource center that includes equipment loans, a video synthesis studio, film-to-tape transfer service, and postproduction facilities; film and video training workshops including a scholarship program for minorities and women; and a film bureau which provides film rental and speaker subsidies to New York State nonprofit community organizations. *Dues*: $35.00 indiv., $50.00/nonprofit organ. (Oct. I-Sept. 30).

Freedom of Information Center (FoI). Box 858, University of Missouri, Columbia, MO 65205. (314) 882-4856. Kathleen Edwards, Center Mgr. Collects and indexes material on action by government, media, and society affecting the flow of information at international, national, state, and local levels. The center answers questions on the federal FoI Act, censorship issues, access to government at all levels, privacy, ethics, bar-press guidelines, and First Amendment issues. *Publications*: Back issues of FoI publications available for purchase.

Government Printing Office (US GPO). N. Capitol and H Sts. NW, Washington, DC 20401. (202) 275-2052, publications and order information (202) 783-3238. The GPO provides printing and binding services to Congress and the agencics of the federal government and distributes government publications through its Superintendent of Documents sales and depository library programs. Prints and binds materials from Congress and federal departments and agencies, and distributes and sells government publications (through the Superintendent of Documents).

Great Plains National ITV Library (GPN). Box 80669, Lincoln, NE 68501. (402) 472-2007; (800) 228-4630. Lee Rockwell, Dir. Dedicated to the use and sharing of instructional television courses produced by organizations across the country. Offers more than 100 videotaped (videocassette) courses and related teacher utilization materials. Users may lease or purchase. Also distributes instructional videodiscs. *Publications*: Quarterly newsletter; annual catalog; and occasional flyers and brochures.

Health Sciences Communications Association (HeSCA). 6105 Lindell Blvd., St. Louis, MO 63112. (314) 725-4722. Lionelle Elsesser, Exec. Dir. Draws together people with a wide variety of knowledge, professions, and experience in work toward the common goal of improved instructional design in all areas of health sciences communications. Recognizes excellence in biocommunications through its media festivals and awards programs. *Membership:* 700. *Dues*: $100 indiv.; $145 inst. (1st yr.); $750 sustaining; $35 students (without journal); $40 retired members. For additional categories, contact association office. *Publications*: *Patient Education Sourcebook; Feedback* (newsletter); *Journal of Biocommunications*; and directory of accredited institutions with programs in biomedical communications.

Hollywood Film Archive. 8344 Melrose Ave., Hollywood, CA 90069. (213) 933-3345. D. Richard Baer, Dir. Archival organization for information about feature films produced worldwide, from the early silents to the present. Offers comprehensive movie reference works for sale, including *Variety Film Reviews* (1907-1986), as well as copyright records. *Publications:* Reference books.

HOPE Reports. 1600 Lyell Ave., Rochester, NY 14606. (716) 458-4250. Thomas W. Hope, Pres. and Chair. Provides reports for the audiovisual/video communication field covering statistical and financial status, sales, salaries, trends, and predictions. Also provides calendar scheduling service of national/international events. Makes private surveys and has consulting service.

Institute for Development of Educational Activities, Inc. (IDEA). 259 Regency Ridge, Dayton, OH 45459. (513) 434-6969. FAX (513) 434-5203. Action-oriented research and development organization, originating from the Charles F. Kettering foundation, established to assist the educational community in bridging the gap that separates research and innovation from actual practice in the schools. Goal is to design and test new responses to problems in education and to create arrangements for their extensive application. Main activities include: developing new and improved processes, systems, and materials; providing information and services that facilitate use of improved methods and materials. Sponsors seminars.

Institute for Research on Teaching. College of Education, MSU, East Lansing, MI 48824. (517) 353-6413. Penelope Peterson and Jere Brophy, Co-Dirs. Funded primarily by the U.S. Department of Education and Michigan State University; conducts research on the continuing problems of practice encountered by teaching professionals, the teaching of subject matter disciplines in elementary schools (through the Center for the Learning and Teaching of Elementary Subjects), and publishes numerous materials detailing this research. *Publications*: *Research Series*; Occasional Papers; newsletter; Elementary Subjects Center research series; and annual catalog.

Institute for the Future (IFTF). 2740 Sand Hill Rd., Menlo Park, CA 94025. (415) 854-6322. Roy Amara, Pres. Works with organizations to plan their long-term futures. Helps them to evaluate the external environment and take advantage of the opportunities offered by new technologies. Founded in 1968, IFTF has emerged as a leader in action-oriented research for business, industry, and governments, having worked with more than 300 organizations. Typical projects include environmental scanning, strategic planning assistance, policy analyses, and market outlooks for new products and next-generation technologies. The success of the organization is based on several unique strengths including a pragmatic futures orientation, studies of emerging technologies, networking of ideas and people, use of scenarios to identify and analyze issues and options, and tailoring projects to meet client needs. *Publications*: List available from the institute free of charge.

Institute of International Education. 809 United Nations Plaza, New York, NY 10017. (212) 883-8200. Richard Krasno, Pres. A private, nonprofit organization administering public and private grants to enable U.S. students to study abroad and foreign students to study at universities in this country. *Membership*: 650 U.S. universities. *Publications: Academic Year Abroad; Vacation Study Abroad; Open Doors: Report on International Educational Exchange; English Language and Orientation Programs in the United States;* and numerous publications and directories for foreign nationals interested in study in the United States and for U.S. nationals interested in studying abroad.

International Association of Business Communicators (IABC). One Hallidie Plaza, Suite 600, San Francisco, CA 94102. (415) 433-3400. Norman G. Leaper, Pres. IABC is the worldwide association for the communication and public relations profession. It is founded on the principle that the better an organization communicates with all its audiences, the more successful and effective it will be in meeting its objectives. IABC is dedicated to fostering communication excellence, contributing more effectively to organizations' goals worldwide, and being a model of communication effectiveness. *Membership:* Over 11,000. *Dues*: $170.00 in addition to local and regional dues. *Publication: IABC Communication World.*

International Association of School Librarianship (IASL). Box 1486, Kalamazoo, MI 49005. (616) 343-5728. Jean E. Lowrie, Exec. Secy. Seeks to encourage development of school libraries and library programs throughout the world, to promote professional preparation of school librarians and continuing education programs, to achieve collaboration among school libraries of the world, and to facilitate loans and exchanges in the field. *Membership:* over 900. *Dues:* $20.00 personal and institution; based on membership for Associations. *Publications: IASL Newsletter; Annual Proceedings; Persons to Contact; Indicators of Quality for School Library Media Programs;* and occasional papers.

International Center of Photography (ICP). 1130-5th Ave., New York, NY 10128. (212) 860-1777. Cornell Capa, Dir. A comprehensive photographic institution whose exhibitions, publications, collections, and educational programs embrace all aspects of photography from aesthetics to technique; from the eighteenth century to the present; from master photographers to newly emerging talents; from photojournalism to the avant-garde. Changing exhibitions, lectures, seminars and workshops, a museum shop, and screening-room make ICP a complete photographic resource. *Membership:* 6,000. *Dues:* $35.00-$45.00 general memberships, supporting, photography circle. $500.00 silver card, $1,000.00 gold card; corporate memberships available. *Publications: Library of Photography;* and *Encyclopedia of Photography—Master Photographs from PFA Collection.*

International Communication Association. Box 9589, Austin, TX 78766. (512) 454-8299. Robert L. Cox, Exec. Dir. Established to study human communication and to seek better understanding of the process of communication. Engages in systematic studies of communication theories, processes, and skills, and disseminates information. *Membership:* 2,200. *Dues:* $40.00-$1,450.00. *Publications: Human Communication Research; A Guide to Publishing in Scholarly Communication Journals; Communication Theory* (q.); *and Communication Yearbook.*

International Communications Industries Association (ICIA). 3150 Spring St., Fairfax, VA 22031. (703) 273-7200. Kenton Pattie, Exec. V.P. An international association of media hardware and software producers and manufacturers, dealers, representatives, and others involved with educational, communications and information activities and services and products. Maintains close liaison with Congress in matters pertaining to media legislation. Annual convention and exhibit held each winter. Co-sponsors of the INFOCOMM International ™ Exposition, which houses over 90,000 square feet of communications media products annually. *Publications: Equipment Directory of Audio-Visual, Computer and Video Products; Communications Industries Report;* and various market research studies in the video industry.

International Copyright Information Center (INCINC). c/o Association of American Publishers, 1718 Connecticut Ave. NW, 7th Floor, Washington, DC 20009. (202) 232-3335. Carol A. Risher, Dir. Assists developing nations in their efforts to translate and/or reprint copyrighted works published in the United States.

International Film and TV Festival of New York. 5 W. 37th St., New York, NY 10018. (914) 238-4481. Gerald M. Goldberg, Pres. An annual competitive festival for industrial and educational film and video productions, filmstrips and slide programs, multi-image and multi-media presentations, and TV programs. Entry fees begin at $85.00. First entry deadline is June 30.

International Friendship League (IFL). 55 Mt. Vernon St., Boston, MA 02108. (617) 523-4273. F. W. Hatch, Pres. Organized in 1948 in 129 countries, the IFL aims to promote a better understanding of the world among young people through regular exchanges of personal letters. The largest percentage of mail matched is with secondary school students, although students of college age as well as adults participate. Send envelope for complete details or name, address, age, and interests with membership fee and self-addressed stamped envelope for faster service. *Membership:* 1,256,390. *Dues:* $3.00 (to 13 yrs.), $5.00 (14-18 yrs.), $8.00 (19-29 yrs.), $10.00 (30 yrs. and older—regular contributors).

International Graphic Arts Education Association (IGAEA). 4615 Forbes Ave., Pittsburgh, PA 15213. (412) 682-5170. Virgil Pufahl, Pres. The president's address is Department of Communication, University of Wisconsin, Platteville, WI 53818. An organization of professionals in graphic arts education and industry, dedicated to promoting effective research and disseminating information concerning graphic arts, graphic communications, and related fields of printing. *Dues:* $15.00 regular; outside North America, add $2.00. *Publications: Visual Communications Journal; Research and Resource Reports.*

International Information Management Congress (IMC). 345 Woodcliff Dr., Fairport, NY 14450. (716) 383-8330. George D. Hoffman, Exec. Dir. An educational association supporting education in the information management field, exchange of information, and publications. Organizes yearly conferences and exhibits in different parts of the world. *Membership:* 30 associations, 100 sustaining company members. *Dues:* $90 affiliates; $100 assoc.; varies for sustaining members. *Publications: IMC Journal* (bi-mo.).

International Museum of Photography at George Eastman House. 900 East Ave., Rochester, NY 14607. (716) 271-3361. James L. Enyeart, Dir. World-renowned museum of photographic history established to preserve, collect, and exhibit photographic materials and to present a variety of services and programs to promote a better understanding and appreciation of photographic art and science. Services include archives, traveling exhibtions, regional center for the conservation of photographic materials, and photographic print service. Educational programs, symposia, and internship stipends offered. *Dues:* $30 libraries; $45-$74 families; $35-$44 indiv.; $25-$34 student or senior citizen, $75-$124 Contributor; $125-$249 Sustainer; $250-$499 Patron; $500-$999 Benefactor. *Publications: IMAGE; Microfiche Index to Collections;* and *Newsletter.*

International Reading Association (IRA). 800 Barksdale Rd., Box 8139, Newark, DE 19714-8139. (302) 731-1600. Ronald W. Mitchell, Exec. Dir. Seeks to improve the quality of reading instruction at all levels, to develop awareness of the impact of reading, to sponsor conferences and meetings planned to implement the association's purposes, and to promote the development of reading proficiency commensurate with each individual's unique capacity. *Membership*: 90,000. Dues: $18.00 and up. *Publications: Reading Research Quarterly; Journal of Reading; The Reading Teacher;* and *Lectura y Vida.*

International Tape/Disc Association (ITA). 5005-8th Ave., New York, NY 10018. (212) 643-0620. Henry Brief, Exec. V.P. World's largest international audio/video/data trade association. Acts as a clearinghouse for information about the industry and holds seminars in audio, video, and data technology, marketing, merchandising, distribution, and programming. *Membership:* Over 450 companies. *Dues:* Based upon annual gross dollar volume in the audio/video/data area. *Publications: ITA Membership Newsletter; Seminar Proceedings;* and *ITA Source Directory.*

International Telecommunications Satellite Organization (INTELSAT). 3400 International Dr. NW, Washington, DC 20008. (202) 944-6800. Public Relations 944-7500. Dean Burch, Dir. Gen. Dedicated to the design, development, construction, establishment, operation, and maintenance of the global, international telecommunications satellite system which currently provides two-thirds of the world's international overseas telecommunications links and virtually all live international television services. *Membership*: 117 countries.

International Teleconferencing Association (ITCA). 1299 Woodside Dr., Suite 101. McLean, VA 22102. (703) 556-6115 J. Robert Brouse, Exec. Dir. Seeks to provide a clearinghouse for the exchange of information between users, researchers, and providers in the field of teleconferencing. *Membership*: 800. *Dues*: $500.00 organizational; $100 individual; $250 small business; $1,000 sustaining; $2,000 Gold Sustaining; $30, student. *Publications: ITCA Insider Newsletter* (m.).

International Television Association (ITVA). 6311 N. O'Connor Rd., Suite 230, LB 51, Irving, TX 75039. (214) 869-1112. Fred M. Wehrli, Exec. Dir. ITVA is the only organization dedicated to serving the needs of the professional video communicator in nonbroadcast settings. It has more than 95 chapters in North America and there are 3,000 international affiliate members in fourteen countries around the world. *Membership*: 9,000. *Dues*: $95.00/yr. indiv. *Publications: International Television News (ITN); Corporate Television* .

ISTE (formerly International Council for Computers in Education, ICCE). University of Oregon, 1787 Agate St., Eugene, OR 97403-9905 (503) 686-4414. David Moursand, Chief Exec. Officer. *Membership:* 13,000. *Dues:* $28.50 U.S., $31.00 outside U.S. *Publications:* Publishes guides to the instructional use of computers in instruction and in teacher training at pre-college level. These guides include *The Computing Teacher: 1989-1990 Educational Software Preview Guide; The Computer Coordinator; Guide for Microcomputer-Based Instructional Packages; Introduction to Computers in Education for Elementary/Middle School Teachers;* and *AppleWorks for Educators, a Beginning and Intermediate Workbook.*

Lawrence Hall of Science. University of California, Berkeley, CA 94720.(415) 642-3167. Linda Lipner, Dir. A center for research and public education. Its Math Education Project introduces visitors and teachers to computers through classes, workshops, exhibits, and the publication of software packages. *Publications:Teaching Basic Bit by Bit; Creative Play; What's in Your Lunch?;* and *Micros for Micros: Estimation, Numbers, Words, Music.*

Library of Congress. James Madison Bldg., 101 Independence Ave. SE, Washington, DC 20540. As the research arm of Congress and the national library, the library provides materials on interlibrary loan and prepares traveling exhibits of photographs. Cataloging data are available in card, book, and machine-readable formats. The American Folklife Center provides for the preservation and dissemination of folklife through research, performances, exhibits, publications, and recordings. The Copyright Office catalogs copyright entries. Many other divisions are of interest to media specialists. *Publications:* Listed in *Library of Congress Publications in Print.*

Lister Hill National Center for Biomedical Communications of the National Library of Medicine. Bldg. 38A, 8600 Rockville Pike, Bethesda, MD 20894. (301) 496-4441. Daniel R. Masys, M.D., Dir. The Center conducts research and development programs in three major categories: computer and information science as applied to the problems of medical libraries, of biomedical research, and health care delivery; biomedical image engineering, and including image acquisition, processing, storage retrieval, and communications; and use of new technologies for health professions education. It carries on research in the use of computer-assisted videodisc technology and has a Learning Center for Interactive Technology which demonstrates new applications to health sciences education.

Magazine Publishers of America (MPA). 575 Lexington Ave., Suite 540, New York, NY 10022. (212) 752-0055. Donald D. Kummerfeld, Pres. MPA is the trade association of the consumer magazine industry. MPA promotes the greater and more effective use of magazine advertising, with ad campaigns in the trade press and in MPA member magazines, presentations to advertisers and their ad agencies, and magazine days in cities around the United States. MPA runs educational seminars, conducts surveys of its members on a variety of topics, represents the magazine industry in Washington, DC, maintains an extensive library on magazine publishing, and carries on other activities. *Membership:* 230 publishers representing over 1,200 magazines. *Publications: Newsletter of Research; Newsletter of International Publishing; Magazine.*

Medical Library Association (MLA). 6 N. Michigan Ave., Suite 300, Chicago, IL 60602. (312) 419-9094. Frances Groen, Pres; Raymond A. Palmer, Exec. Dir. A group of professionals in the health sciences library field dedicated to fostering medical and allied scientific libraries, promoting educational and professional growth of health sciences librarians, and exchanging medical literature among members. *Membership:* 5,000. *Dues:* $95.00 indiv., $315.00 sustaining. *Publications: MLA News;* and *Bulletin of the Medical Library Association;* also monographs.

Minnesota Educational Computing Corporation (MECC). 3490 Lexington Ave. North, St. Paul, MN 55126-8097. (612) 481-3500. Dale LaFrenz, Pres. Since its inception in 1973, MECC has remained committed to serving education by listening and responding to the diverse and changing needs of students and educators. MECC promotes effective learning by developing high-quality, curriculum-based software in all major subject areas and by making them affordable through a variety of purchase plans. Approximately one-third of the nation's school districts have joined MECC through Direct License memberships, permitting them to duplicate MECC software product on site. MECC products are also available through authorized dealers nationwide or can be ordered directly from the MECC catalog. In addition to software products, MECC offers instructional management, emerging technology products, teacher training and development, and conferences. An academic research partnership, the MECC/University of Minneosta Center for the Study of Educational Technology, conducts a variety of studies on the impact of technology on education. MECC respects the challenges faced by modern educators and pledges to remain on the cutting edge of technology. *Membership:* Available; institutional memberships, MECC Club. *Publications: MECC Network Newsletter.*

Museum Computer Network, Inc. School of Information Studies, Syracuse University, Syracuse, NY 13244. (315) 443-5612. Deirdre C. Stam, Exec. Dir. A nonprofit service organization which works to improve museum collection documentation and facilitates the sharing of collection-related data among museums through effective use of modern data management technology. Explores and explains other computer applications appropriate to museums. Activities include annual conferences, regional workshops, technical advisory services, and publication of a quarterly newsletter. *Publications: Spectra* (newsletter).

Museum of Broadcasting (MB). 1 E. 53rd St., New York, NY 10022. Office (212) 752-4690. Information Tape (212) 752-7684. William S. Paley, Founder; Dr. Robert M. Batscha, Pres. A unique nonprofit institution with two equally important responsibilities: to collect and preserve radio and television programs; and to explore and interpret our broadcasting heritage through public exhibitions of the collection. Today the Museum houses 40,000 radio and television programs that reflect more than sixty years of broadcasting history. The informative card catalog is used for selecting programs for individual listening and viewing on two floors of easy-to-use consoles. The Museum also presents major exhibitions and seminars that highlight various aspects of radio and television. Exhibitions focus on topics of social, historical, popular, or artistic interest; and seminars feature in-person discussions with writers, producers, directors, actors, and others who have created landmark programming. In the fall of 1990, the Museum will move to a much larger, newly constructed facility located at 23 West 52nd St. in New York City. The Museum is supported by daily contributions, membership fees, and grants by individuals, corporations, foundations, and government agencies. *Publications: MB News;* exhibition catalogs; screening schedules; seminar monographs; and flyers.

Museum of Holography. 11 Mercer St., New York, NY 10013. (212) 925-0526. Maltha Tomko, Dir. Housed in a landmark cast-iron building, the museum boasts the world's largest collection of holograms, three-dimensional images. Through its extensive exhibition and education programs, the museum shows the work of artists working in the medium, and explains how holograms are made, how they work, and how they have become useful tools in art, science, and technology. The museum also maintains a library, a collection of slides and photographs, and an artist-in-residence program. *Publications: Holosphere, The International Directory of Holography.*

Museum of Modern Art, Circulating Film Library. 11 W. 53rd St., New York, NY 10019. (212) 708-9530. William Sloan, Libr. Sponsors film study programs and provides film rentals and sales. *Publications: Circulating Film Catalog.*

National Aeronautics and Space Administration (NASA). Washington, DC 20546. (202) 755-2320. NASA's primary responsibility is to implement congressional policy with regard to the peaceful purposes of space exploration and research. It has overall charge of the total U.S. space program. A portion of NASA's activities includes the development of training and demonstration programs, a wide-ranging information dissemination program for elementary and secondary schools. There are seven NASA educational office service centers located in various parts of the United States.

National Alliance of Media Arts Centers (NAMAC). 135 St. Pauls Ave., Staten Island, NY 10301. (718) 727-5593. Robert Haller, Secy./Treas. A nonprofit organization dedicated to increasing public understanding of and support for the field of media arts in the United States. Members include media arts centers and media artists, as well as other individuals and organizations providing services for production, education, exhibition, preservation and distribution of video, film, audio, and intermedia. NAMAC's information services are available to the general public, arts and nonarts organizations, businesses, corporations, foundations, government agencies, schools and universities. *Membership*: 150 organ., 150 indiv. *Dues*: Inst., ranges from $50.00.-$250.00/yr. depending on annual budget; $20.00/yr.. indiv. *Publications: Media Arts.*

National Art Education Association (NAEA). 1916 Association Dr., Reston, VA 22091. (703) 860-8000. Thomas A. Hatfield, Exec. Dir. A professional association of art educators in elementary school through university and continuing education. Purpose is to improve and expand visual art education at all levels of instruction. *Membership*: 13,200. *Dues*: contact the association. *Publications: Art Education; Studies in Art Education*; and *NAEA News.*

National Association for Better Broadcasting (NABB). 7918 Naylor Ave., Los Angeles CA 90045. (213) 641-4903. Frank Orme, Pres. Promotes the public interest in broadcasting through the development of greater awareness of the public's rights and responsibilities in broadcasting. *Publications: Better Radio and Television;* and *You Own More Than Your Set!*

National Association for Creative Children and Adults (NACCA). 8080 Springvalley Dr., Cincinnati, OH 45236. (513) 631-1777. Drs. Cheryl Wright and Scott Wright, Pres.; Ann Fabe Isaacs, Chief Exec. Off. Seeks to encourage the development of creativity in the general public and especially among gifted persons. Sponsors workshops, field terms, inservice training, and a yearly national conference. *Publications: It's Happening* (newsletter free with membership); *Creative Child and Adult Quarterly* (included with membership); *Common Sense Creativity;* additional publications including *NACCA Creativity Projects.*

National Association for the Education of Young Children (NAEYC). 1834 Connecticut Ave. NW, Washington, DC 20009. (202) 232-8777; (800) 424-2460. Offers professional development opportunities to early childhood educators designed to improve the quality of services to children from birth through age eight, the critical years of development. *Membership*: 70,000 in 390 local and state affiliate groups. *Dues*: $25.00 regular; $50.00 comprehensive. *Publications: Young Children* (journal); over 60 books, posters, videos, and brochures.

National Association for the Exchange of Industrial Resources (NAEIR). 560 McClure St., Box 8076, Galesburg, IL 61402. (309) 343-0704. Gary Smith, Pres. The organization operates as a clearinghouse for excess materials gathered from industrial sources and donated to participating school and nonprofit members. The materials must be new. Membership is restricted to schools and charitable service organizations within the United States that qualify as nonprofit entities exempt from federal income tax under Section 501(C)(3) of the Internal Revenue Code of 1954. *Membership*: 8,000 schools and nonprofit organizations in 50 states. *Dues*: $545.00. *Publications: NAEIR News*; and *The NAEIR Bulletin* .

National Association for Visually Handicapped (NAVH). 22 W. 21st St., New York, NY 10010. (212) 889-3141. Lorraine H. Marchi, Pres. Publishes and distributes newsletters at irregular intervals (*Seeing Clearly* for adults and *In Focus* for youth). Informational literature, most of which is in large print, is available to visually impaired individuals, their families, the professionals and paraprofessionals who work with them. Maintains a loan library (free) of large-print books, and offers counsel and guidance to visually impaired adults and their families, and to the parents of visually impaired children. *Membership*: 9,574. *Publications: Catalog of Large Print Materials; Selected List of LPM for Adults;* and *Loan Library List.*

National Association of Broadcasters (NAB). 1771 N St. NW, Washington, DC 20036-2891. (202) 429-5300. Edward 0. Fritts, Pres. and Chief Exec. Officer. A trade association that represents commercial broadcasters. Encourages development of broadcasting arts, and seeks to protect its members and to strengthen and maintain the industry so that it may best serve the public. *Membership*: More than 5,100 radio stations, 970 television stations, and all the major networks. *Dues*: Based on station revenue for radio and on market size for television. *Publications: Telemedia.* Also, weekly newsletters: *TV Today* and *Radio Week.*

National Association of Business and Educational Radio (NABER). 1501 Duke St., Alexandria, VA 22314. (703) 739-0300; (800) 759-0300. John Sherlock, Dir., Membership/Communications. Represents individuals whose business and professional needs interest them in the uses of TV-shared UHF, and 800 Mhz channels for communication purposes. *Membership*: 5,000. *Publications: Business Radio; ShopTalk; TechTalk; SMR Letter;* and *Private Carrier Pages.*

National Association of Secondary School Principals (NASSP). 1904 Association Dr., Reston, VA 22091. (703) 860-0200. Thomas F. Koerner, Ed. and Dir. Provides a national voice for secondary education, supports promising and successful educational practices, conducts research, examines issues, and represents secondary education at the federal level. *Membership*: 40,000. *Publications: NASSP Bulletin; NASSP NewsLeader; Curriculum Report; Legal Memorandum; Schools in the Middle; TIPS for Principals; AP Special; Practitioner;* and *Leadership Magazine.*

National Association of State Boards of Education (NASBE). 1012 Cameron St., Alexandria, VA 22314. (703) 684-4000. Gene Wilhoit, Exec. Dir. Studies problems and improves communication among members, exchanges information, provides educational programs and activities, and serves as a liaison with other educators' groups. *Membership*: 562. *Publications: The State Board Connection.*

National Association of State Educational Media Professionals (NASTEMP). Mary Jane Vinella, Library Media Consultant, New Mexico Department of Education, Education Building, Santa Fe, NM 87501-2786. (505) 827-6562. The overall purpose of this association is to strengthen and to improve education through the effective utilization of educational media. Membership: open to U.S. Department of Education and state and district agencies. *Membership:* 110. *Dues:* $10.00. *Publications: Aids to Media Selection for Students* and *Teachers; Quarterly Newsletter.*

National Association of State Textbook Administrators (NASTA). Division of Instructional Materials, Room 104 B, Ford Education Bldg., Little Rock, AR 72201. (501) 682-4337. Sam Bundy, Pres. Its purposes are (1) to foster a spirit of mutual helpfulness in adoption, purchase, and distribution of textbooks; (2) to arrange for study and review of textbook specifications; (3) to authorize special surveys/tests/studies; and (4) to initiate action leading to better quality textbooks. NASTA is unaffiliated with any parent organization. It works with the Association of American Publishers and the Book Manufacturers Institute. Services provided include a working knowledge of text construction, monitoring lowest prices, sharing adoption information, identifying trouble spots, and discussions in the industry. *Membership*: Approx. 22.

National Audiovisual Center (NAC). National Archives and Records Administration, 8700 Edgeworth Dr., Capitol Heights, MD 20743. (301) 763-1896. R. Kevin Flood, Dir. Central information and distribution source for more than 8,000 audiovisual programs produced by or for the U.S. government. Materials are made available for sale or rent on a self-sustaining basis at the lowest price possible. *Publications: Media Resource Catalog* (1986), listing 2,700 of the latest and most popular programs, is available free. Also available free are specific subject listings such as science, history, medicine, and safety and health.

National Cable Television Institute (NCTI). P.O. Box 27277, Denver, CO 80227. (303) 761-8554. Byron Leech, Pres. Provides technical educational materials and services for the upgrading of professional and technical competencies of cable television personnel. *Publications: Cable Technology.*

National Center for Appropriate Technology. P.O. Box 3838, Butte, MT 59702. (406) 494-4572. George Turman, Pres. A private, nonprofit organization whose mission is to promote energy conservation, renewable energy, and sustainable agriculture technologies, and whose do-it-yourself publications/projects may be of special interest as learning activities in science classes. *Publications:* Consumer and technical publications.

National Clearinghouse for Bilingual Education. 8737 Colesville Rd., Suite 900, Silver Spring, MD 20910. (301) 588-6898; (800) 647-0123. Harpreet Sandhu, Dir. National information center for the education of language minority students in grades K-12 and a producer of various publications related to the field of bilingual education. *Dues:* None. *Publications: FORUM* (bi-mo. newsletter).

National Commission on Libraries and Information Science (NCLIS). 1111-18th St. NW, Suite 310, Washington, DC 20036. (202) 254-3100. Dr. Susan K. Martin, Exec. Dir. An agency in the Executive Branch of the U.S. government charged with advising Congress and the President in the entire field of library and information services. The commission has four major roles: to serve as a resident expert for both the Executive and Legislative branches, to be an honest broker bringing together agencies in both branches to focus on problems of common interest, to serve as a forum for the entire library/information community, and to be a catalyst in getting programs implemented.

National Council for Accreditation of Teacher Education (NCATE). 2029 K St. NW, Suite 500, Washington, DC 20006. (202) 466-7496. Richard C. Kunkel, Exec. Dir. A consortium of professional organizations that establishes standards of quality and accredits professional education units in colleges and universities. Interested in the self-regulation and improvement of standards in the field of teacher education. *Membership:* 18 colleges and univ., 24 educational organ. *Publications: Standards, Procedures and Policies for the Accreditation of Professional Education Units;* and *Annual List* of accredited programs/units.

National Council of Teachers of English (NCTE) Commission on Media. 1111 Kenyon Rd., Urbana, IL 61801. (217) 328-3870. John C. Maxwell, Exec. Dir. An advisory body which identifies key issues in teaching of media. Reviews current projects and recommends new directions and personnel to undertake them, monitors NCTE publications on media, and suggests program ideas for the annual convention. *Publications: English Journal; College English; Language Arts; English Education Research in the Teaching of English; Teaching English in the Two-Year College.*

National Council of the Churches of Christ—Communication Commission. 475 Riverside Dr., New York, NY 10115. (212) 870-2567. Rev. Dr. J. Martin Bailey, Acting Assoc. General Secy. for Communications. Ecumenical agency for cooperative work of 19 Protestant and Orthodox denominations and agencies in broadcasting, film, cable, and print media. Offers advocacy to government and industry structures on media services. Services provided include liaison to network television and radio programming; film sales and rentals; distribution of information about syndicated religious programming; syndication of some programming; news and information to broadcast news media regarding work of the National Council of Churches, related denominations, and agencies; and cable television and emerging technologies information services. *Membership:* 32 denominations.

National Education Association (NEA). 1201-16th St. NW, Washington, DC 20036. (202) 833-4000. Mary Hatwood Futrell, Pres. The world's largest advocacy organization of teachers, other school employees, and college faculty. Seeks to improve American public education, conducts research on school problems and professional teacher welfare, maintains lobby relationships with the federal government, and provides information to inform the public about education and educational needs. *Membership:* 1.9 million. *Dues:* $75.00 active membership.

National Endowment for the Arts (NEA). 1100 Pennsylvania Ave. NW, Washington, DC 20506. The Arts in Education Program offers Special Project Grants which are available to a wide range of nonprofit arts and education organizations for projects of regional or national significance which advance progress toward the arts becoming a basic part of education, K-12. Funds are also used for Arts Endowment leadership initiatives to help improve arts education. For further information, contact the Arts in Education Program at (202) 682-5426 or the Office of Public Information (202) 682-5400. *Publications: Guideline Booklet.*

National Endowment for the Humanities (NEH). 1100 Pennsylvania Ave. NW, Room 426, Washington, DC 20506. (202) 786-0278. James Dougherty, Asst. Dir. for Media. Offers limited support for the planning, scripting, and production of radio and television projects pertaining to the humanities. Grants are available for children's, as well as adult, programming. The program has two deadlines each year, in March and in September. For further information, contact Media Program, Division of General Program, NEH. *Publications: Guidelines for Applications.*

National Federation of Community Broadcasters (NFCB). 1314-14th St. NW, Washington, DC 20005. (202) 797-8911. Lynn Chadwick, Pres. NFCB represents its members in public policy development at the national level, provides a wide range of practical services, and distributes programs to all noncommercial stations. *Membership*: 70 stations, 100 (assoc.) stations and production groups. *Dues*: Based on income, from $75.00 to $500.00 for assn.; $300.00 to $2,000.00 for participants. *Publications: Legal Handbook; Audio Craft*, 1989 edition; and *Community Radio Monthly.*

National Film Board of Canada (NFBC). 1251 Ave. of the Americas, New York, NY 10020. (212) 586-5131. John Sirabella, Nontheatrical Rep. Established in 1939, the NFBC's main objective is to produce and distribute high-quality audiovisual materials for educational, cultural, and social purposes. *Publications: U.S. Film Resource Guide.*

National Film Information Service (NFIS). 8949 Wilshire Blvd. Beverly Hills, CA 90211. (213) 278-8990. Provides an information service on films, lists library, and archives films. All inquiries must be accompanied by SASE.

National Gallery of Art (NGA). Department of Extension Programs, Washington, DC 20565. (202) 842-6273. Ruth R. Perlin, Head. This department of NGA is responsible for the production and distribution of an educational audiovisual program. Materials available (all loaned free to schools, community organizations, and individuals) include films, videocassettes, and color slide programs. A free catalog of programs is available upon request. A videodisc on the gallery and its collection is available for loan. *Publications: Catalogue of Programs.*

National Information Center for Educational Media (NICEM). P.O. Box 40130, Albuquerque, NM 87196. (505) 265-3591. Marjorie M. K. Hlava, Pres. NICEM, in conjunction with the Library of Congress, is a centralized facility that collects, catalogs, and disseminates information about nonbook materials of many different kinds. Its mission is to build and expand the database to provide current and archival information about nonbook educational materials; to apply modern techniques of information dissemination that meets user needs; and to provide a comprehensive, centralized nonbook database used for catalogs, indexes, multimedia publications, special search services, machine-readable tapes, online access, and statistical analysis. *Publications*: indexes to AV educational materials.

National Library of Medicine. 8600 Rockville Pike, Bethesda, MD 20894. (301) 496-6308. Donald A. B. Lindberg, M.D., Dir. Collects, organizes, and distributes literature on biomedicine; seeks to apply modern technology to the flow of biomedical information to health professionals; and supports development of improved medical library resources for the country. Responsible for MEDLINE, SDILINE, CATLINE, SERLINE, CANCERLIT, AVLINE, and TOXLINE. Maintains a collection of 17,000 health science audiovisual materials and supervises the Lister Hill Center for Biomedical Communications, and the National Center for Biotechnology Information. Maintains seven regional medical libraries. *Publications: National Library of Medicine Audiovisuals Catalog.*

National Press Photographers Association, Inc. (NPPA). 3200 Croasdaile Dr., Suite 306, Durham, NC 27705. (919) 383-7246. Charles Cooper, Exec. Dir. An organization of professional news photographers who participate in and promote photojournalism in publications, and through television and film. Sponsors workshops and contests, and maintains a tape library and collections of slides in the field. *Membership:* 10,000. *Dues:* $55.00, professional, $30.00 student. *Publications*: *News Photographer*; membership directory; and *Best of Photojournalism books.*

National PTA. 700 N. Rush St., Chicago, IL 60611. (312) 787-0977. Ann Lynch, Pres. A child advocacy association dedicated to improving the lives of our country's children through the school, home, community, and place of worship. Strengthens laws for the care and protection of children and youth. A drug and alcohol project seeks to strengthen parent-child communication in order to prevent use and/or abuse. *Membership:* 6.6 million. *Dues:* Vary, established by local units. *Publications: Children and Television; What Parents Can Do; PTA Today; Kids with Keys, Parents with Jobs: Who's in Charge? (English and Spanish); Home Helps for Learning: A Guide to Pre-School Development; How to Talk to Your Child About Sex; Drug Abuse and Your Teens:What Parents Should Know; Young Children and Drugs; What Parents Can Do;* and *What's Happening in Washington.*

National Public Radio (NPR). 2025 M Street NW, Washington, DC 20036. (202) 822-2300. Douglas J. Bennet, Pres. Through member stations in 48 states, Puerto Rico, and the District of Columbia, National Public Radio reaches a broad segment of the population. Its award-winning programs, "All Things Considered," "Morning Edition," and "Performance Today," have helped build an audience base of more than 11 million weekly listeners. With programs such as "Horizons," NPR's Department of Special Programs acknowledges the diversity in American society and provides programs which focus on minorities, the elderly, and the disabled. In addition to programming, NPR provides more than 370 member stations with distribution and representation support services.

National Religious Broadcasters (NRB). P.O. Box 1926, Morristown, NJ 07962-1926. (201) 428-5400. Ben Armstrong, Exec. Dir. Sponsors an annual Summer Institute of Communications and holds an annual national convention and seven regional conventions. *Membership:* 1,450 stations, indiv., and agencies. *Dues:* Based on income. *Publications: Religious Broadcasting Magazine; Annual Directory of Religious Broadcasting; Sourcebook for Religious Broadcasting;* and *Religious Broadcasting Cassette Catalog.*

National School Supply and Equipment Association (NSSEA). 2020 N. 14th St., Suite 400, Arlington, VA 22201. (703) 524-8819. Tim Holt, Exec. V.P. A service organization of 800 manufacturers, distributors, retailers, and independent manufacturers' representatives of school supplies, equipment, and instructional materials. Seeks to maintain open communications between manufacturers and dealers in the school market, to find solutions to problems affecting schools, and to encourage the development of new ideas and products for educational progress. *Publications: Tidings.*

National Science Foundation (NSF). Washington, DC 20550. (202) 357-9498. Primary purposes are to increase the nation's base of scientific knowledge; encourage research in areas that can lead to improvements in economic growth, productivity, and environmental quality; promote international cooperation through science; and develop and help implement science education programs to aid the nation in meeting the challenges of contemporary life. Grants go chiefly to colleges and other research organizations. Applicants should refer to the *NSF Guide to Programs.* Scientific material and media reviews are available to help the public learn about NSF-supported programs.

National Science Teachers Association (NSTA). 1742 Connecticut Ave. NW, Washington, DC 20009. (202) 328-5800. Bill Aldridge, Exec. Dir. International nonprofit association of science teachers ranging from kindergarten through university level. *Membership*: 44,000. *Dues:* $35.00/

yr. indiv. (includes one journal), $43.00/yr. inst. (includes one journal). *Publications: Science and Children; The Science Teacher; Journal of College Science Teaching*; and *Science Scope.*

National Society for Performance and Instruction (NSPI). 1126-16th St. NW, Suite 102, Washington, DC 20036. (202) 861-0777. Paul Tremper, Exec. Dir. NSPI is the leading association dedicated to increasing productivity in the workplace through the application of performance and instructional technologies. Founded in 1962, its 4,000 members are located throughout the United States, Canada, and 28 other countries. The society offers an awards program recognizing excellence in the field. The Annual Conference and Expo is held in the spring. *Membership*: 4,000. *Dues*: $95.00. *Publications: Performance Instruction Journal:* member directory; *Introduction to Performance Technology* Volume 1; *Performance Improvement Quarterly.*

The National Technical Information Service (NTIS). A self-supporting agency of the U.S. Department of Commerce that actively collects, organizes, and distributes technical information generated by United States and foreign governments in all areas of science and technology. There are two million titles in the NTIS permanent archives, some of which date as far back as 1945, and last year NTIS added 63,000 new titles to its collection. The entire collection is available at any time—whether a report dates from 20 years ago or last month. In addition, NTIS provides government-generated computer software and computerized data files on both tape and diskette through its Federal Computer Products Center. To keep pace with technology transfer activities, the NTIS Center for the Utilization of Federal Technology licenses federal inventions and makes them available to private industry and prepares and issues a number of publications, catalogs, and directories announcing federal technologies and resources. In the area of foreign technology, NTIS has recently increased its holdings—up to a third of the reports entering the collection are now from foreign sources. To get a free 32-page catalog describing NTIS products and services, contact the NTIS Order Desk, Springfield, VA 22161, (703) 487-4650, and ask for PR827/NCB.

National Technology Center. American Foundation for the Blind, 15 W. 16th St., New York, NY 10011. (212) 620-2080. Eliot M. Schreier, Dir. The Center has three components: National Technology Information System, Evaluations Laboratory, and Research and Development Laboratory. Provides a resource for blind and visually impaired persons and professionals in education, rehabilitation, and employment. Evaluations Laboratory: (212) 620-2051. John C. DeWitt, Eval. Coord. Collects and disseminates data regarding radio reading and information services for print-handicapped persons. Works with Congress, federal agencies, and private organizations on legislative and regulatory matters affecting print-handicapped persons. Provides consultation to existing and potential radio reading and information services and to individuals and organizations developing computer technology for print-handicapped persons.

National Telemedia Council (NTC). 120 E. Wilson St., Madison, WI 53703. (608) 257-7712. Dr. Marti Tomas, Pres.; Marieli Rowe, Exec. Dir. An organization to improve the quality of radio and television programming by educational means, through the development of media literacy, working with teachers in the classroom and with parents and others concerned with youth. Acts as a sponsoring organization for KIDS-4, the Sun Prairie, WI Children's Channel, a dedicated cable channel of television by and for children. NTC activities include conferences, Project Look-Listen, a newsletter, *Telemedium*, annual sponsor recognition awards, and special projects. *Dues:* $20.00 and up. *Publications: Telemedium;* and *Annual Look-Listen Opinion Report.*

National University Continuing Education Association (NUCEA). One Dupont Circle NW, Suite 615, Washington, DC 20036. (202) 659-3130. Daniel Shannon, Pres.; Kay J. Kohi, Exec. Dir. An association of public and private institutions concerned with making continuing education available to all population segments and to promoting excellence in the continuing higher education community. Many institutional members offer university and college film rental library services. *Membership*: 2,000. *Dues*: Dependent on membership category. *Publications:* Monthly newsletter; quarterly occasional papers; scholarly journal; *Independent Study Catalog*; *Conferences and Facilities Directory;* and several incidental publications.

Nebraska Videodisc Design/Production Group (VD-PG). KUON-TV, University of Nebraska, Box 83111, Lincoln, NE 68501. (402) 472-3611. Ron Nugent, Group Dir. A group of designers and producers concerned with the development and production of programs that exploit the unique capabilities of the videodisc. Hold annual symposium and workshops.

The NETWORK. 290 S. Main St., Andover, MA 01810. (617) 470-1080. D. Max McConkey, contact person. A research and service organization providing consultation, training, assistance, and materials to schools, other educational institutions, and private sector firms with educational interests. *Publications: Administering Writing Programs: A Training Package for the Coordination of Writing Programs; The Cumulative Writing Folder; Nutrition Education Curriculum; Sex Equity Curriculum; The Effective Writing Teacher; Eighteen Strategies; An Action Guide to School Improvement; People, Policies and Practices; Examining the Chain of School Improvement,* Vols. I-X. *See also* Council for Educational Development and Research.

Network for Continuing Medical Education (NCME). One Harmon Plaza, Secaucus, NJ 07094. (201) 867-3550; (800) 223-0272; in NJ (800) 624-2102. Jim Disque, Exec. Dir. Produces and distributes videocassettes to hospitals for physicians' continuing education. *Membership:* By subscription. *Dues:* Subscription Fees: VHS-$1,820; 3/4" $2,020.

Newspaper Features Council (NFC). Ward Castle, Comly Ave., Rye Brook, NY 10573. (914) 939-3919. John P. McNeel, Pres. Formerly the Newspaper Comics Council, Inc., NFC is a professional organization whose membership consists of newspapers, syndicates, editors, columnists, writers, syndicated cartoonists, and editorial cartoonists. Its purpose is to provide a forum for membership to exchange views, discuss common problems and mutual opportunities, and improve the content of newspapers for the betterment of the general public and the industry. A small uncataloged library is available to professional researchers. *Membership*: 150. *Dues*: newspaper syndicates $1,250/yr.; newspapers $160/yr.; creators (syndicated columnists and syndicated cartoonists) $75/yr. *Publications: Career for You in the Comics* ($2.00); *Cavalcade of American Comics* ($1.50); *Comics in the Classroom* ($1.00); and *Grapevine* (newsletter to members only). Tape order form also available, "How to Become Syndicated". The order form is free and lists prices of tapes.

North American Simulation and Gaming Association (NASAGA). c/o Community Systems Foundation, 1130 Hill St., Ann Arbor, MI 48104. (313) 761-1368. Fred Goodman, Exec. Dir. Provides a forum for the exchange of ideas, information, and resources among persons interested in simulation and games. Assists members in designing, testing, using, and evaluating simulations and/or games, and in using these as research tools. A computerized mailing list and cross-referencing service are available through national headquarters and UNC-Asheville. Sponsors various conferences. *Membership*: 800. *Dues*: $35.00 regular, $10.00 students. *Publications: Simulation and Games.*

Northwest Regional Educational Laboratory (NWREL). 101 SW Main St., Suite 500, Portland, OR 97204. (503) 275-9500. Robert R. Rath, Exec. Dir. Assists education, government, community agencies, and business and labor in bringing about improvement in educational programs and processes by developing and disseminating effective educational products and procedures, including applications of technology. Provides technical assistance and training in educational problem solving. Evaluates effectiveness of educational programs and processes. Sponsors and maintains Resources in Computer Education (RICE), a database developed by the MicroSIFT project of the Computer Technology Program at NWREL. RICE provides descriptive and evaluative information about microcomputer applications for elementary and secondary education. It also includes brief descriptive information about producers of educational software. Citations include references to educational software packages and their producers, featuring detailed software and hardware requirements, product descriptions and evaluations, information on intended end-user/audience, and further instructional information. *Membership*: 817. *Dues*: None. *Publications: Northwest Report* (newsletter).

OCLC (Online Computer Library Center). 6565 Frantz Rd., Dublin, OH 43017. (614) 764-6000. A nonprofit membership organization which engages in computer library service and research and makes available computer-based processes, products, and services for libraries and other educational organizations, and library users. From its facility in Dublin, Ohio, OCLC operates an international computer network that libraries use to acquire and catalog books, order custom-printed catalog cards and machine-readable records for local catalogs, arrange interlibrary loans, and maintain location information on library materials. OCLC also provides local decentralized computer systems and stand-alone microcomputer-based systems for individual libraries or clusters of libraries, and online and offline products and services for the electronic delivery of information. More than 10,000 libraries contribute to and/or use information in the OCLC Online Union Catalog. *Publications: OCLC Newsletter* (6/yr.); *Annual Report*; *Research Libraries OCLC: A Quarterly*.

Office for International Networks in Education and Development (INET). College of Education, MSU, 238 Erikson, East Lansing, MI 48824-1034. (517) 355-5522. Anne Schneller, Mgr. The INET office makes a number of publications available to development planners and practitioners working on behalf of persons in Africa, Asia, Latin America, and the Middle East. Such materials are distributed for sale or on an exchange basis; that is, the office sends publications in hopes that recipients will give the office further materials, especially those of a "fugitive" nature. Such materials may be in the form of books, working papers, surveys, occasional papers, annual reports, journals, or newsletters which are relevant to education and development. The INET office strongly encourages participants to continue this exchange of publications which has proved to be so important to low-cost dissemination of information throughout the Third World. INET is interested particularly in matters and materials related to formal and nonformal education for development. *Membership:* Free. *Dues:* None. *Publications: The INET Update*; annotated bibliographies; and occasional papers.

Office of Technology Assessment (OTA). U.S. Congress, Washington, DC 20510-8025. (202) 224-9241. John Gibbons, Dir. Established by Congress to study, report on, and assess the significance and probable impact of new technological developments upon U.S. society and to advise Congress on public policy implications and options. Recent assessments focusing on technology and education issues include *Information Technology R&D: Critical Trends and Issues (1985); Intellectual Property Rights in an Age of Electronics and Information (1986); Technology and Structural Unemployment: Retraining Adult Displaced Workers (1986);* and *Automation of America's Offices (1986)*. In addition, the assessment *Power On! New Tools for Teaching & Learning (1988)* includes an interim staff paper on "Trends and Status of Computers in Schools: Use in Chapter 1 Programs and Use with Limited English Proficient Students" (March 1987). OTA recently prepared a Special Report on Technologies for Learning at a Distance (released late fall of 1989). *Publications:* For a list, contact publishing office (202) 224-8996.

On-line Audiovisual Catalogers (OLAC). 3604 Suffolk, Durham, NC 27707. (919) 684-5896. Catherine Leonardi, Treas. Formed as an outgrowth of the ALA conference, OLAC seeks to permit members to exchange ideas and information and to interact with other agencies that influence audiovisual cataloging practices. *Membership:* 600. *Dues:* Available for single or multiple years, ranges from $7.00-$24.00 indiv., $13.00-$42.00 inst. *Publications: OLAC Newsletter.*

Oral History Association. 1093 Broxton Ave. #720, Los Angeles, CA 90024. (213) 925-0597. Richard Candida Smith, Exec. Sec. Seeks to develop the use of oral history as primary source material and to disseminate oral history materials among scholars. *Membership:* 1,400. *Publications: Oral History Newsletter; Oral History Review; Evaluation Guidelines; Annual Report and Membership Directory; Oral History and the Law;* and *Oral History in Secondary Education.*

Pacific Film Archive (PFA). University Art Museum, 2625 Durant Ave., Berkeley, CA 94720. (415) 642-1437. Sponsors the exhibition, study, and preservation of classic, international, documentary, animated, and avant-garde films. Provides media research and a service to locate film sources, books, and addresses.

PBS ENCORE. 1320 Braddock Pl., Alexandria, VA 22314. (703) 739-5225. Michael Patterson, Assoc. Dir. Distributes PBS programs with extant broadcast rights to public television stations. *Publications: PBS Encore Catalog, Monthly News & Update Memo.*

PBS VIDEO. 1320 Braddock Place, Alexandria, VA 22314. Outside Virginia (800) 424-7963; in Virginia (703) 739-5380. Jon Cecil, Dir. Markets and distributes PBS television programs for sale on videocassette to colleges, public libraries, schools, government, and other organizations and institutions. Top-selling programs include "Moyers: The Power of the Word," "Middle Ages School Kit," "Thinking Your Way to Better SAT Scores," "American Exerience II," "The Mind," "Eyes on the Prize II," and "France TV Magazine." *Publications: PBS VIDEO Program Catalog;* and *PBS Video News.*

PCR: Films and Video in the Behavioral Sciences. Special Services Bldg., Pennsylvania State University, University Park, PA 16802. (814) 863-3102; purchasing info. (800) 826-0132. Thomas McKenna, Mng. Ed. Collects and makes available to professionals 16mm films and video in the behavioral sciences judged to be useful for university teaching and research. A free catalog of the films in PCR is available. The PCR catalog now contains some 1,000 films in the behavioral sciences (psychology, psychiatry, anthropology, animal behavior, sociology, teaching and learning, and folklife). Some 7,000 professionals now use PCR services. Films and tapes are available on loan for a rental charge. Many films may also be purchased. Films may be submitted for international distribution. Contact the managing editor through PCR.

Photographic Society of America (PSA). 3000 United Founders Blvd., Suite 103, Oklahoma City, OK 73112 (405) 843-1437. Terry S. Stull, Operations Manager. A nonprofit organization for the development of the arts and sciences of photography and for the furtherance of public appreciation of photographic skills. Its members, largely amateurs, consist of individuals, camera clubs, and other photographic organizations. Divisions include color slide, motion picture, nature, photo-journalism, travel, pictorial print, stereo, and techniques. Sponsors national, regional, and local meetings, clinics, and contests. Request dues information from above address. *Publications: PSA Journal.*

PLATO/NovaNET Computer-based Education Research Laboratory (CERL). University of Illinois, 252 Engineering Research Laboratory, 103 S. Mathews Ave., Urbana, IL 61801. (217) 333-6210. Dr. Donald Bitzer, Dir. CERL is a research laboratory dedicated to the development of hardware, software, and courseware for the delivery of cost-effective, interactive, computer-based education. Delivery has been via a large-scale system (PLATO) linking more than 1,400 terminals to a central computer, a cluster system, and stand-alone terminals. A new, low-cost, PLATO-like delivery system, NovaNET, is now in operation. It is capable of serving several thousand users via a network of satellite, cable television, or phone lines. PLATO originated at the University of Illinois in 1960. *Publications:* Department and professional journal publications available on request.

Professors of Instructional Design and Technology (PIDT). School of Education, Indiana University, Bloomington, IN 47405. (812) 855-2854. Dr. Tom Schwen, contact person. An organization designed to encourage and facilitate the exchange of information among members of the instructional design and technology academic community. It also serves to promote excellence in the academic programs in instructional design and technology and to encourage research and inquiry that will benefit the field while providing leadership in the public and private sectors in its application and practice. Membership consists of faculty employed in higher education institutions whose primary responsibilities are teaching and research in this area, and of other persons interested in the goals and activities of the PIDT.

Project in Distance Education. Department of Educational Affairs, OAS, 1889 F St. NW, Washington DC 20036. (202) 458-3309. Arturo Garzon, contact person. Promotes development of distance education in Latin America and Caribbean countries through planning, human resource and institution building, and research. Main projects in Venezuela, Colombia, Argentina, Brazil,

Bahamas, Costa Rica, and Honduras and Panama. Mostly at post-secondary and teacher training level.

Project in Educational Technology. Department of Educational Affairs, OAS, 1889 F St. NW, Washington, DC 20036. (202) 458-3337. Contact Arturo Garzon. Maintains support, information, and personnel exchanges among educational technology centers in Brazil, Argentina, Chile, Ecuador, Colombia, and Mexico, with tie-ins to other Latin American countries. Emphasizes development of human resources through a variety of programs, seminars, short courses, on-site training, and technical assistance. Also disseminates information through its journal. *Publications: Revista de Tecnología Educativa.*

Public Broadcasting Service (PBS). 1320 Braddock Pl., Alexandria, VA 22314. (703) 739-5000. Bruce Christensen. Pres. Serves as a distributor of national public television programming, obtaining all programs from the stations or independent producers; PBS is not a production facility. Owned and operated by the licensees through annual membership fees. Funding for technical distribution facilities in part by the Corporation for Public Broadcasting. PBS services include national promotion, program acquisition and scheduling, legal services, development and fundraising support, engineering and technical studies, and research. Of special interest are the Adult Learning Service, which offers telecourses through college, public television station partnerships, and PBS VIDEO, which offers PBS programs for rent/sale to educational institutions. PBS is governed by a board of directors elected by licensees for 3-year terms. *Membership:* 173 licensees; 336 stations.

Public Service Satellite Consortium (PSSC). 600 Maryland Ave. SW, Suite 220, Washington, DC 20024. (202) 863-0890. Louis A. Bransford, Pres. Represents the telecommunication interests of nonprofit organizations; provides members with information, consultation, educational briefings, and representation to federal agencies and other organizations; assists members in contracting for operational functions such as systems engineering and networking; conducts workshops on new technologies and telecommunications issues. *Membership:* 100. *Dues:* $500.00/yr. nonprofit, $1,000.00/yr. corporate. *Publications: Report to Members Newsletter;* and *Teleguide: A Handbook on Video-Teleconferencing.*

Puppeteers of America. 5 Cricklewood Path, Pasadena, CA 91107. (818) 797-5748. Gayle Schulter, Membership Chair. Founded in 1937 to promote and develop the art of puppetry. It has a large collection of films and videotapes for rent in its audiovisual library and offers books, plays, and related items from the Puppetry Store. Puppeteers is a national resource center which offers regional festivals, workshops, exhibits, and a puppetry exchange. *Dues:* Various classes of membership which range from $15.00-$40.00. *Publications: Puppeteering Journal* (annual directory).

Radio Free Europe/Radio Liberty (RFE-RL, Inc.). 1201 Connecticut Ave. NW, Washington DC 20036. (202) 457-6900. An independent radio broadcast service funded by federal grants, which broadcasts to the Soviet Union; Bulgaria, Czechoslovakia, Hungary, Poland, and Romania; the Baltic States; and Afghanistan.

Recording for the Blind. 20 Roszel Rd., Princeton, NJ 08540. (609) 452-0606. Supported by volunteers and contributions from individuals, corporations, and foundations. Supplies free recordings of educational books for visually, percentually, and physically disabled students and professionals.

Recording Industry Association of America, Inc. (RIAA). 1020-19th St. NW, Suite 200, Washington, DC 20036. (202) 775-0101. Jason S. Berman, Pres. Compiles and disseminates U.S. industry shipment statistics by units and wholesale/retail dollar equivalents; establishes industry technical standards; conducts audits for certification of gold and platinum records and video awards; acts as the public information arm on behalf of the U.S. recording industry, provides antipiracy intelligence to law enforcement agencies; presents an RIAA cultural award for contributions to cultural activities in the United States and acts as a resource center for recording industry research projects. *Membership*: 50 sound recording manufacturers. *Publications: Statistical Report; Industry Sourcebook*; newsletter; and press releases.

RICE (Resources in Computer Education). MicroSIFT Project, Northwest Regional Educational Laboratory. 101 SW Main St., Suite 500, Portland, OR 97204. (503) 275-9625. Don Holznagel, Dir. of Technical Prog. RICE is a microcomputer database developed under the U.S. Department of Education-funded MicroSIFT Project. It contains information about software products appropriate for use in K-12 education. RICE is designed to produce custom search reports based on the subject, type, grade range, and hardware specified by the requestor. In addition to these initial parameters, the search report provides the titled, producer contact information, producer marketing policies, references to published reviews and a brief abstract for each product which matches the search parameters. To request a search, or for more information, contact the Technology Program at the address above.

Smithsonian Institution. c/o Margaret Langrall, Office of Public Affairs, Washington, DC 20560. (202) 357-1300. Robert McCormick Adams, Secy. An independent trust establishment which conducts scientific and scholarly research, administers the national collections, and performs other educational public service functions, all supported by Congress, trusts, gifts, and grants. Includes the National Museum of Natural History/National Museum of Man, National Museum of American History, National Air and Space Museum, Freer Gallery of Art, National Museum of American Art, National Portrait Gallery, National Museum of African Art, Cooper-Hewitt Museum of Design and Decorative Arts, Renwick Gallery, Hirshhorn Museum, and Sculpture Garden, Arthur M. Sackler Gallery, Anacostia Museum, and others. Museum is free and open daily except Christmas. (Exception: Cooper-Hewitt in New York City has entrance fees.) *Membership*: Smithsonian assoc., resident and national. *Dues*: Vary. *Publications: Smithsonian* .

Social Science Education Consortium (SSEC). 855 Broadway, Boulder, CO 80302. (303) 492-8154. James R. Giesc, Exec. Dir. The major goal of SSEC is to improve social studies instruction at all levels—elementary, secondary, and college. The consortium disseminates information about social studies materials, instructional methods, and trends. It assists educators in identifying, selecting, and using new ideas and methods in social studies and provides a forum for social scientists and educators to exchange ideas and views. A free catalog of publications and services is available on request. *Membership*: 140.

Society for Applied Learning Technology (SALT). 50 Culpeper St., Warrenton, VA 22186. (703) 347-0055. Raymond G. Fox, Pres. Seeks to advance the development of highest standards and practices in the application of technology to learning, to foster wide dissemination of understanding and knowledge in actual and potential uses of technology in learning, to foster wide dissemination of understanding and knowledge in actual and potential uses of technology in learning, and to provide an effective educational channel among scientists, managers, and users of training and learning technology. *Membership*: 700. *Dues:* $30.00. *Publications: Journal of Educational Technology Systems; Journal of Interactive Instructional Development*; send for list of books.

Society for Computer Simulation (SCS) . P.O. Box 17900, San Diego, CA 92117-7900. (619) 277-3888. Chip G. Stockton, Exec. Dir. A technical society devoted to the art and science of modeling and simulation. Its purpose is to advance the understanding, appreciation, and use of all types of computer models for studying the behavior of actual or hypothesized systems of all kinds. Sponsors local, regional, and national technical meetings and conferences such as Eastern & Western Simulation Multiconferences, Summer Computer Simulation Conference, National Educational Computing Conference, and others. *Membership*: 1,900. *Dues:* $50.00. *Publications: Simulation;* Simulation series; and *Transactions of SCS*. Additional office in Ghent, Belgium.

Society for Photographic Education (SPE). Campus Box 318, University of Colorado, Boulder, CO 80309. (303) 492-0588. Judith Thorpe, Exec. Dir. An association of college and university teachers of photography, museum photographic curators, writers, and publishers. It promotes higher standards of photographic education. *Membership*: 1,700. *Dues:* $50.00. *Publications: Exposure*; and newsletter.

Society of Cable Television Engineers (SCTE). 669 Exton Commons, Exton, PA 19341. (215) 363-6888. William W. Riker, Exec. V.P. SCTE is dedicated to the technical training and further education of members. A nonprofit membership organization for persons engaged in engineering, construction, installation, technical direction, management, or administration of cable television and broadband communication technologies. Also eligible for membership are students in communications, educators, government and regulatory agency employees, and affiliated trade associations. *Membership:* 5,800. *Dues:* $40.00/yr. *Publications: The Interval in Communications Technology.*

Society of Manufacturing Engineers (SME). 1 SME Dr., Box 930, Dearborn , MI 48121. (313) 271-1500. Steven R. Bollinger, Video Admin. A technical society which, among many other services, distribute videotapes for rent or purchase. Covers a wide range of manufacturing technology, including robots, lasers, manufacturing productivity, material processing, finishing, and product design. *Publication*: Free catalog.

Society of Motion Picture and Television Engineers (SMPTE). 595 W. Hartsdale Ave., White Plains, NY 10607-1824 (914) 761-1100. Lynette Robinson, Exec. Dir. Fosters the advancement of engineering and technical aspects of motion pictures, television, and allied arts and sciences; disseminates scientific information in these areas; and sponsors lectures, exhibitions, classes, and conferences. Open to those with clearly defined interest in the field. *Membership*: 9,500. *Dues*: $50.00. *Publications:* Booklets and reports related to nonbook media, such as *SMPTE Journal*; *Special Effects in Motion Pictures;* and test films.

Society of Photo Technologists (SPT). 6535 S. Dayton, Suite 2000, Englewood, CO 80111. (303) 799-0667. Karen A. Hone, contact person. An organization of photographic equipment repair technicians, which improves and maintains communications between manufacturers and independent repair technicians. *Membership*: 1,000. *Dues:* $105.00-$250.00. *Publications: SPT Journal; SPT Parts and Services Directory;* and *SPT Newsletter*.

SOFTSWAP. P.O. Box 271704, Concord, CA 94527-1704. (415) 685-7289. Hal Gibson, contact person. SOFTSWAP is an inexpensive, yet high-quality library of many teacher-developed and commercial educational programs for use in the Apple, IBM, and MAC computers. These copyrighted programs are organized onto disks which are sold for a nominal charge, with permission to copy. *Publications: Catalog; Newsletter*.

Special Libraries Association (SLA). 1700-18th St. NW, Washington, DC 20009. (202) 234-4700. David R. Bender, Exec. Dir. Members are librarians and information managers serving industry, business, research, educational and technical institutions, government, libraries, newspapers, museums, and other public and private organizations requiring or providing specialized information. SLA is an international professional association of individuals and organizations with educational, scientific, and technical interests in information management and technology. The association encourages its members to increase professional competencies and performance. Continuing education seminars keep members informed of new developments in the information field. *Membership:* 12,000. *Publications: Special Libraries; SpeciaList*; and a number of books.

SpecialNet. 2021 K St. NW, Suite 215, Washington, DC 20006. (202) 835-7300; (800) 468-8550. Mike Norman, contact person. A computerized fee-charging information database emphasizing special education resources.

Speech Communication Association (SCA). 5105 Backlick Rd., Bldg. E, Annandale, VA 22003. (703) 750-0533. James L. Gaudino, Exec. Dir. A voluntary society organized to promote study, criticism, research, teaching, and application of principles of communication, particularly of speech communication. *Membership*: 6,000. *Dues*: $50.00. *Publications: Spectra Newsletter* (mo.); *Quarterly Journal of Speech; Communication Monographs; Communication Education; Critical Studies in Mass Communication; Speech Communication Teacher; Index to Journals in Communication Studies through 1985; Speech Communication Directory of SCA and the Regional Speech Communication Organizations (CSSA, ECA, SSCA, WSCA).* For additional publications request brochure.

SPSE: The Society for Imaging Science and Technology, Exec. Dir. Seeks to advance the science and engineering of imaging materials and equipment and to develop means for applying and using imaging techniques in all branches of engineering and science. *Membership:* 3,000, 17 chapters. *Publications: Journal of Imaging Science;* and *Journal of Imaging Technology.*

Superintendent of Documents. U.S. Government Printing Office, Washington, DC 20402. (202) 783-3238. Functions as the principal sales agency for U.S. government publications. Has over 20,000 titles in its active sales inventory. For information on the scope of its publications, write for the free Subject Bibliography index listing of over 240 subject bibliographies on specific topics. Of particular interest is 258, *Grants and Awards, SB 114, Directories and Lists of Persons and Organizations,* and *SB 73, Motion Pictures, Films and Audiovisual Information.*

Teachers and Writers Collaborative (T&W). 5 Union Square West, New York, NY 10003. (212) 691-6590. Nancy Larson Shapiro, Dir. Sends writers and other artists into New York public schools to conduct long-term projects with classroom teachers and publishes materials on how to teach creative writing based on these materials. *Dues*: $35.00/yr., basic membership. *Publications: Teachers and Writers* magazine; *Journal of a Living Experiment: The First 10 Years of Teachers & Writers; The Whole Word Catologue, Vols. 1 & 2; Personal Fiction Writing; The Writing Workshop, Vols. 1 & 2; The Teachers & Writers Handbook of Poetic Forms; The Art of Science Writing; Like it Was: A Complete Guide to Writing Oral History; Moving Windows: Evaluating the Poetry Children Write; Poetic Forms: 10 Audio Programs.*

Technology and Media Division (TAM). Council for Exceptional Children, 1920 Association Dr., Reston, VA 22091. (703) 620-3660. The Technology and Media Division (TAM) of the Council for Exceptional Children (CEC) encourages the development of new applications, technologies, and medias for use as daily living tools by special populations. This information is disseminated through professional meetings, training programs, and publications. TAM members receive four issues annually of the *Journal of Special Education Technology* containing articles on specific technology programs and applications, and three issues of the TAM newsletter, providing news of current research, developments and products, conferences and special programs information. *Membership*: 1,500. *Dues*: $10.00 in addition to CEC membership.

Telecommunications Research and Action Center (TRAC). Box 12038, Washington, DC 20005. (202) 462-2520. Samuel Simon, counsel. Seeks to educate telecommunications consumers, to improve broadcasting, and to support local and national media reform groups and movements. *Dues*: $25.00/yr. *Publications: After Divestiture What the AT&T Settlement Means for Business and Residential Telephone Service; Citizens' Media Directory; A Citizens' Primer on the Fairness Doctrine; Phonewriting: A Consumer's Guide to the New World of Electronic Information Services.*

Television Licensing Center (TLC). 5547 N. Ravenswood Ave., Chicago, IL 60640. (312) 878-2600; (800) 323-4222. Offers licensing services for duplicating television programs from PBS, CBS, NBC, and others. *Publications: TLC Guide.*

Theater Library Association (TLA). 111 Amsterdam Ave., Room 513, New York, NY 10023. (212) 870-1670. Richard M. Buck, Secy. Treas. Seeks to further the interests of collecting, preserving, and using theater, cinema, and performing arts materials in libraries, museums, and private collections. *Membership:* 500. *Dues*: $20.00 indiv., $25.00 inst. *Publications: Broadside* (q.); and *Performing Arts Resources* (membership annual).

Training Media Association. 198 Thomas Johnson Dr., Suite 206, Frederick, MD 21701. (301) 662-4268. Robert A. Gehrke, Exec. Dir. An organization dedicated to the protection of film and videotape copyright and copyright education. *Membership:* 75. *Dues:* Based on number of employees. *Publications: The Monthly.*

Training Modules for Trainers (TMT). School of Education, University of Michigan, Ann Arbor, MI 48109. (313) 763-4668. Dr. Carl F. Berger, Director. Funded by the Michigan Department of Education, the TMT Project was conceived to provide materials for use by trainers in addressing the computing needs of the educational community. The materials consist of a set of modules, each containing an overview, goals, training leader prerequisites, competency list, issues narrative, references, activities, blackline masters, and a feedback form. In addition, there is a videotape and set of slides available to supplement certain modules. Module topics include training methods, district planning, instructional methods, applications concepts, software evaluation, hardware configuration, basic technical skills, instructional management, software design, computers in the curriculum, computer-mediated communication, administrative uses, future images, and computers and media services, emerging technology, artificial intelligence, CD-ROM, distance education, and videodiscs. *Publications: Training Modules for Trainers: A Resource for Training Leaders in The Educational Use of Computers* (set of 19).

United Nations Department of Public Information. United Nations Secretariat Bldg., New York, NY 10017. (212) 963-6934. Produces and distributes films, radio and television programs, still pictures, charts, posters, various publications, and audio materials about the United Nations. Distribution is worldwide and is accomplished in part through a network of approximately 60 United Nations information centers, as well as via distributors and direct from New York. Items are provided in a number of different languages, including English, French, Spanish, and Arabic.

U.S. Advisory Commission on Public Diplomacy. 301-4th St. SW, Room 600, Washington, DC 20547. (202) 485-2457. Dr. Edwin J. Feulner, Jr., Chair. Established by Congress in 1978 to advise the president, Congress, the secretary of state, and the director of the U.S. Information Agency on the formulation of U.S. Information Agency policies and programs concerning international educational and cultural activities and on the effectiveness with which those programs are conducted. Issues periodic reports. *Membership*: 6. *Publications: 1989 Annual Report.*

University and College Designers Association (UCDA). 2811 Mishawaka Ave., South Bend, IN 46615. (219) 288-UCDA. Barbara Esmark, Pres. Composed of individuals and institutions interested in better visual design to improve higher education communication through graphics, photography, signage, films, and other related media. *Membership*: 1,000. *Dues*: Regular $75.00, inst. $325.00, assn. $110.00, student $30.00. *Publications: Designer* (q.).

University Film and Video Association (UFVA). c/o Stanford University, Dept. of Comm., McClatchy Hall, Stanford, CA 94305. (415) 723-2300. Ben Levin, Pres.. Members are people involved in the arts and sciences of film and video. Promotes film and video production in educational institutions, fosters study of world cinema and video in scholarly resource centers, and serves as central source of information on film/video instruction, festivals, grants, jobs, production, and research. *Membership:* Approx. 800. *Dues*: Indiv. $35.00, students $15.00, inst. $75.00, commercial firms $150.00. *Publications: Journal of Film and Video; UFVA Digest*; and a membership directory .

Women in Film (WIF). 6464 Sunset, Suite 660, Hollywood, CA 90028. (213) 463-6040. Linda Valentino, Exec. Dir. For women in film, television, cable, etc., a communications network, an educational resource and a lobby to support women and women filmmakers. The purpose of Women in Film is to serve as a support group and act as a clearinghouse and source of information on qualified professional women in the entertainment industry. WIF conducts ongoing workshops, a series of lectures and open discussions by leaders in the industry who share their expertise with small groups of members. Subjects include directing, producing, contract negotiation, writing, production development, acting, and technical crafts. The Crystal Awards Luncheon is an annual event honoring outstanding women and men for their contributions toward improving the image and increasing participation of women in the industry. Women in Film Foundation has been instituted to offer grants, scholarships, and film finishing funds to qualified recipients. *Dues:* $100.00./yr. *Publications: Newsletter*, $25.00/yr. subscription.

Women's Institute for Freedom of the Press. 3306 Ross Pl. NW, Washington, DC 20008. (202) 966-7783. Dr. Donna Allen, Pres., Dr. Martha Leslie Allen, Dir. Conducts research and publishes reports on communications media and women. Annual conference held on restructuring the communications system and expanding communications for women nationally and internationally. Annual directory of women's media (1975-1989). *Membership*: Non-member assoc. structure. *Publications: The 1989 Directory of Women's Media* and *Syllabus Sourcebook on Media and Women.*

Women's Media Project (WMP) (formerly Media Project). 1333 H St. NW, 11th floor, Washington, DC 20005. (202) 682-0940. Alisa Shapiro, Dir. A project of the NOW Legal Defense and Education Fund. Feminist activists united to eliminate sex role stereotyping of women and men in the media and to increase the participation of women and minorities in broadcasting. Purposes are to: conduct public education campaigns with up-to-date information on issues that affect women; guide individuals and groups in developing effective dialogues with local broadcasters and publishers through community action campaigns; monitor compliance with equal employment legislation in the communications industry; encourage development and distribution of quality television and radio programming that offers realistic and contemporary images of women. Identifies programming promoting equality between women and men. Conducts research in broadcast employment. *Publications: Women's Media Campaign Workbook* (annual); research reports.

World Future Society (WFS). 4916 St. Elmo Ave., Bethesda, MD 20814-5089. (301) 656-8274. Edward Cornish, Pres. Organization of individuals interested in the study of future trends and possibilities. *Membership:* 30,000. *Dues:* For information, please write to address above. *Publications: The Futurist: A Journal of Forecasts, Trends and Ideas about the Future; Futures Research Quarterly;* and *Future Survey.* The society's bookstore offers audio and video tapes, books, films, and other items.

World Pen Pals (WPP). 1694 Como Ave., St. Paul, MN 55108. (612) 647-0191. Loni Fazendin, Secy. Cultivates appreciation of other cultures and customs through encouraging personal letter writing activities. The service charge is $3.00 indiv., $2.50 for groups (minimum of six names). Include a self-addressed stamped envelope.

Canada

This section on Canada includes information on Canadian organizations whose principal interests lie in the general fields of education, educational media, instructional technology, and library and information science. Organizations listed in the 1989 *EMTY* were contacted for updated information and changes have been made accordingly.

ACCESS NETWORK. Alberta Educational Communications Corporation, 16930-114 Ave., Edmonton AB T5M 3S2, Canada. (403) 451-7272. Established in 1973 to serve the educational needs of Albertans. Responsible for producing television and radio programs, multimedia kits, microcomputer-based programs, and learning support materials for educational use.

Association for Media and Technology in Education in Canada (AMTEC). Vancouver Community College, Instructional Media Services, Box 24700, Station C, Vancouver, BC, V5T 4N4, Canada. (604) 875-8293. Bruce MacLean, Pres. Promotes applications of educational technology in improving education and the public welfare. Fosters cooperation and interaction; seeks to improve professional qualifications of media practitioners; organizes and conducts media and technology meetings, seminars, and annual conferences; stimulates and publishes research in media and technology. *Membership:* 550. *Publications: Canadian Journal of Educational Communication; Media News;* Membership Directory (with membership).

Canadian Association of Broadcasters/Association canadienne des radiodiffuseurs (CAB/ACR). Box 627 Station B, Ottawa, ON K1P 5S2, Canada. (613) 233-4035. A nonprofit trade association representing privately owned Canadian AM and FM radio stations and television stations as well as various associated organizations and networks.

Canadian Book Publishers' Council (CBPC). 45 Charles St. E., 7th floor, Toronto, ON M4Y 1S2, Canada. (416) 964-7231. Jacqueline Hushion, Exec. Dir. CBPC members publish and distribute an extensive list of Canadian and imported materials to schools, universities, bookstores, and libraries. CBPC provides exhibits throughout the year and works through a number of subcommittees and groups within the organization to promote effective book publishing. *Membership:* 40 companies, educational institutions, or government agencies who publish books as an important facet of their work.

Canadian Broadcasting Corporation (CBC). 1500 Bronson Ave., Box 8478, Ottawa, ON K1G 3J5, Canada. (613) 724-1200. The CBC is a publicly owned corporation established in 1936 by an act of the Canadian Parliament to provide a national broadcasting service in Canada in the two official languages. The CBC is financed mainly by public funds voted annually by Parliament.

Canadian Education Association/Association canadienne d'éducation (CEA/ACE). 252 Bloor St. W., Suite 8-200, Toronto, ON M5S 1V5, Canada. (416) 924-7721. Robert E. Blair, Exec. Dir. The Canadian equivalent of the U.S. National Education Association. *Publications: CEA Handbook; Education Canada; CEA Newsletter; The Craft of Student Evaluation; Stress and Teachers; Marketing the School System; School Board Leave Policies; Dollars and Sense: How School Boards Save Money; Evaluation for Excellence: The Price of Quality; The Public Finance of Elementary and Secondary Education in Canada; Student Transportation in Canada: Facts and Figures; Federal Involvement in Public Education; Canada and Citizenship Education.*

Canadian Film Institute (CFI). 150 Rideau St., Ottawa, ON K1N 5X6, Canada. (613) 232-6727. FAX (613) 232-6315. Frank Taylor, Exec. Dir. Established in 1935, the institute promotes the study of film and television as cultural educational forces in Canada. It distributes over 7,000 films on the sciences and the visual and performing arts through the Canadian Film Institute Film Library, LM Media Marketing Services Ltd., 115 Torbay Rd., Unit 9, Markham, ON L3R 2M9. (416) 475-3750. FAX (416) 475-3756. *Publications: The Guide to Film Television and Communications Studies in Canada 1989; Canadian Film* series (monographs); *Northern Lights: A Programmer's Guide to the Festival of Festivals Retrospective.*

Canadian Library Association. 200 Elgin St., Suite 602, Ottawa, ON K1P 5E3, Canada. Beth Barlow, Pres.; Ernest Ingles, Pres.-elect (officers change July 1990); Sharon Henry, Exec. Dir.

Canadian Museums Association/Association des Musées Canadiens (CMA/AMC). 280 Metcalf St., Suite 400, Ottawa, ON K2P 1R7, Canada. (613) 233-5653. John G. McAvity, Exec. Dir. Seeks to advance public museum service in Canada. *Membership:* 2,000. *Publications: Museogramme* (mo. newsletter); *Muse* (q. journal); *Directory of Canadian Museums* (listing all museums in Canada plus information on government departments, agencies, and provincial and regional museum associations); and *CMA Bibliography* (an extensive listing of published material on the subjects of museology, museography, and museum and art gallery administration). CMA offers a correspondence course that serves as an introduction to museum operations and philosophy through selected readings.

National Film Board of Canada (NFBC). 1251 Ave. of the Americas, New York, NY 10020. (212) 586-5131. John Sirabella, Nontheatrical Rep. Established in 1939, the NFBC's main objective is to produce and distribute high-quality audiovisual materials for educational, cultural, and social purposes. *Publication: U.S. Film Resource Guide*

Ontario Film Association, Inc. 3-1750 The Queensway, Suite 1341, Etobicoke, ON M9C 5H5, Canada. A nonprofit organization whose primary objective is to promote the sharing of ideas and information about film and video through seminars, workshops, screenings, and publications. Sponsors the annual Grierson Documentary Seminar on film and video subjects, bringing together users, makers, and students interested in production and use. *Publication: Visual Media/Visuels Niedias.*

Part Five

Graduate Programs

Doctoral Programs in
Instructional Technology

Brenda Branyan-Broadbent
Associate Professor
Department of Instructional Technology
Utah State University, Logan

Lois A. Ward
Staff Assistant II
Department of Instructional Technology
Utah State University, Logan

This directory presents data on sixty-four doctoral programs (Ph.D. and Ed.D.) in instructional technology, educational communications/technology, media services, and closely allied programs currently being offered throughout the United States and the District of Columbia. Information in this section was obtained from, and updated by, the institutional deans, chairpersons, or their representatives, in response to an inquiry/questionnaire mailed to them during the summer of 1989. The survey conducted for *EMTY 1990* revealed that no new doctoral-level programs had been created. Unfortunately, the Cooperative Doctoral Program at San Jose State University has been dropped; and the program at the University of Massachusetts has been placed "on hold." Severe budget problems have impacted both programs.

Doctoral programs have experienced some changes in their administrative leadership. International student enrollments continue to increase; and as would be expected, most graduates seek positions as teachers in colleges or as instructional designers/developers in business and industry. Emerging interest in seeking employment in health-related fields, or in high-technology industries, or working with distance education technologies, can also be observed in data provided by the respondents. Coursework to support programs in educational computing appears to be maintaining its strength.

Entries provide the following data: (1) name and address of the institution; (2) chairperson or other individual in charge of the doctoral program; (3) types of degrees offered and specializations, including information regarding positions for which candidates are prepared; (4) special features of the degree program; (5) admission requirements, including minimal grade point average; (6) information on faculty; (7) number of full-time and part-time students participating in the program; (8) details of available financial assistance; (9) doctoral program trends; and (10) the number of foreign nationals, total number of men (m), and total number of women (w) who graduated with doctorates during the one-year period between 1 July 1988 and 30 June 1989.

Directors of advanced professional programs for instructional technology/media specialists should find the information furnished in this directory useful as a means of comparing their own offerings and requirements with those of institutions offering comparable programs. Then, too, those individuals seeking a school at which to pursue advanced graduate studies should be assisted by this listing to locate institutions that best suit their interests and requirements.

Additional information concerning programs listed, including instructions on applying for admission, may be obtained by contacting individual program coordinators. General or graduate catalogs usually will be furnished for a minimal charge, while specific program information normally will be sent at no charge.

In endeavoring to provide complete listings, we are greatly indebted to those individuals who responded to our requests for information. While considerable effort has been expended to ensure completeness of the listings, there may be institutions within the United States or its territories that now have programs and have been omitted. In those instances where repeated appeals for updated information were not responded to, the entry which appeared in *EMTY 1989* is included in order to have the program represented. Readers are encouraged to furnish new information to the publisher who, in turn, will follow up for the next edition of *EMTY*.

Institutions in this section are listed alphabetically by state.

ALABAMA

University of Alabama. Graduate School of Library Service, Tuscaloosa, AL 35487. J. Gordon Coleman, Jr., Coord., Doctoral Program, Graduate School of Library Service. *Specializations:* Ph.D. in Library and Information Science with specializations in school library media, youth services, library management, information studies, and historical studies. *Features*: Program is designed to fit the needs of the student using the resources of the entire university. Students may prepare for careers in teaching and research in colleges and universities or for innovative practice in the profession. *Admission Requirements*: Master's in library science, instructional technology or equivalent, Miller Analogy score of 55, Graduate Record Exam score of 1,100, 3.5 graduate QPA, three letters of recommendation, writing sample, curriculum vitae, and statement of purpose. *Faculty:* 12 full-time; 4 part-time. *Students:* 7 full-time; 3 part-time. *Assistance*: Six 20-hour assistantships paying $622/month with all tuition waived (in-state and out-of-state); some scholarships. *Doctoral Program Trends*: Doctoral program initiated in August 1988. *Doctorates Awarded 1988-89:* 0 (relatively new program).

ARIZONA

Arizona State University. College of Education, Tempe, AZ 85287-0611. Howard Sullivan, Prof., Div. of Psychology in Education, College of Education. *Specializations*: School offers programs of study leading to both the Ph.D. and the Ed.D. degrees in educational technology. Primary content focus of both programs is on instructional design and development. Ph.D. program also has strong research emphasis. Students may complement this focus with concentrated work in such areas as instructional media, computer-based education, training, development, etc. Preparation is for work as university faculty and instructional designers and trainers in business, industry, the military, and higher education. *Features:* Instructional development internships in public and higher education, or in business, industry, and the military. *Admission requirements:* Two months prior to enrollment: all university application forms, two transcripts from each institution in which previous academic work has been completed, three letters of reference, a score report for either the Miller Analogies Test (65 or higher) or the GRE (1,200 or higher verbal plus quantitative), statement of professional goals, and undergraduate GPA of 3.0 or better. *Faculty*: 3 full-time. *Students:* 9 full-time; 11 part-time. *Assistance*: Graduate assistantships $2,362-$18,330 per academic year; summer teaching opportunities; fellowships; scholarships; loans administered through the university financial aid office. *Doctoral Program Trends:* More than half of program graduates obtain faculty positions in universities; number of placements in high technology firms is increasing. *Doctorates Awarded 1988-89*: 1m, 4w.

CALIFORNIA

United States International University. School of Education, San Diego, CA 92131. Colin F. MacKinnon, Assoc. Prof. and Computer Program Coordinator, School of Education. *Specializations*: The Ed.D. Program is designed to attract students interested in a variety of emphases: computer literacy, teaching with or about computers, computer program coordination, instructional systems development, distance education, and microcomputer management. Prepares individuals to serve in a variety of positions: school district coordinators for instructional computing, specialists in designing learning strategies and training programs, university directors of learning resources, and change agents in industry and the military having teaching or training as a primary concern. *Features*: Program involves required core courses in human behavior and futuristics, concentration courses in leadership, cognitive theory, global education, statistics, and elective specialization courses including computer literacy, problem solving, microcomputer programming, microcomputer applications, issues in computer education, curriculum theory and design, and instructional systems development. The development of independent microcomputer use skills is emphasized. *Admission Requirements:* Admission to graduate program recommended by committee of faculty to the Dean of the School of Education. Evaluation of GRE or MAT test score, candidate's vita, three letters of recommendation, statement of purpose for study, and final committee interview. *Faculty*: 15 full-time; 5 part-time. *Students:* 40 full-time; 10 part-time. *Assistance:* A limited number of graduate assistantships offered in conjunction with research and development work undertaken at the University. *Doctoral Program Trends:* Increasing enrollment of international students from Taiwan interested in infusing computer technology into Taiwanese public schools. *Doctorates Awarded 1987-88:* 4m, 4w, including 4 foreign nationals.

University of California at Berkeley. School of Library and Information Studies, Berkeley, CA 94720. Michael K. Buckland, Prof., Coord., School of Library and Information Studies. *Specializations*: School offers two doctoral programs, Ph.D. and D.L.I.S. degrees in library and information studies. *Features*: Ph.D. requires original piece of research revealing high critical ability and powers of imagination and synthesis; the D.L.I.S. specifies candidate's command of a comprehensive knowledge and technical skills needed for initiating, organizing, and carrying out the investigation of significant problems in the field of library science. Both programs stress the need for familiarity with information processing technology, educational technology, database management systems, etc. *Admission Requirements:* Contingent upon admission to graduate standing including graduation from an accredited master's degree program with at least a B average. *Faculty*: 14 full-time; 5 part-time. *Students*: Data not available. *Assistance*: Scholarships, fellowships, assistantships (research and teaching), and readerships. *Doctoral Program Trends*: Cognitive science now a Ph.D. subfield. *Doctorates Awarded 1988-89*: 3w, 4m.

University of California at Los Angeles. Department of Education, Los Angeles, CA 90024-1521. Aimee Dorr, Prof. of Education, Dir. of Educational Technology, Learning and Instruction Specialization, Div. of Educational Psychology, Dept. of Education. *Specializations*: Offers Ph.D. and Ed.D. programs. Ph.D. program prepares graduates for research, teaching educational technology, and consultancies in the development of instructional materials. Ed.D. program prepares graduates for leadership roles in the development of instructional materials and educational technologies. *Features*: The program addresses the design and utilization principles and processes underlying all effective applications of instructional technologies and their products. Television and microcomputer-based systems are encouraged. *Admission Requirements*: Superior academic record, combined GRE score of 1,000 or better, and master's degree in a relevant area. For the Ed.D. program, two or more years of relevant field experience is desirable. *Faculty*: 8 faculty participate in learning and instruction, of whom 2 teach full-time in instructional technology and the remaining 6 (all with full-time academic appointments) teach part-time in instructional technology and part-time in other areas in the department. *Students:* 9 full-time; 2 part-time. *Assistance*: Includes fellowships, tuition remission, and some paid research and teaching assistantships. *Doctoral Program Trends*: Doctoral applications from high-quality students have increased in recent years, and more students are interested in the instructional uses of computers in education. *Doctorates Awarded 1988-89:* 1m, 2w.

University of Southern California. School of Education, Los Angeles, CA 90007. (213) 743-2383. Robert L. Baker, Prof., Chair., Dept. of Educational Psychology and Technology, School of Education. *Specializations:* M.A., Ph.D., Ed.D. to prepare individuals to teach instructional technology; manage educational media/training programs in business or industry, research and development organizations, and higher educational institutions; perform research in instructional technology and media; and deal with computer-driven interactive technology. *Features*: Special emphasis upon instructional design, systems analysis, and interactive video instruction. *Admission Requirements:* A bachelor's degree and satisfactory performance (combined score of 1,100) on the GRE aptitude test. *Faculty*: 11 full-time; 5 part-time. *Students:* 20 full-time; 75 part-time. *Assis-

tance: Part-time work available (instructional technology related) in the Los Angeles area and on the university campus. *Doctoral Program Trends:* Increasing enrollments of students seeking position placements in business/industry, instructional design/development, media production, and computer education. *Doctorates Awarded 1987-88:* 7m, 5w, including 4 foreign nationals. The University of Southern California also has a cooperative Ed.D. with San Jose State University with a major in instructional technology and emphasis placed on industrial applications. The first cycle of students includes 5 men and 5 women.

COLORADO

University of Colorado at Denver. School of Education, Denver, CO 80204. David H. Jonassen, Prof., Chair. of Instructional Technology Program, School of Education. *Specializations:* Ph.D. in instructional technology, in instructional development, and/or instructional computing for use in business/industry and higher education. *Features*: Courses in management and consulting, emphasizing instructional development, interactive video technologies, evaluation, and internship opportunities in a variety of agencies. *Admission Requirements:* Satisfactory GPA, GRE, writing/publication background, letters of recommendation, transcripts, and application form. *Faculty:* 5-1/2 full-time; 4 part-time. *Students*: 10 part-time; 2 full-time. *Assistance:* Corporate internships may be available. *Doctoral Program Trends:* Preparation of students seeking position placements in business/industry, government agencies, computer-related fields, higher education, and/or university teaching. *Doctorates Awarded 1987-88:* 0 (relatively new program).

University of Northern Colorado. College of Education, Greeley, CO 80639. David H. Roat, Prof., Dir., Div. of Research, Evaluation and Development, College of Education. *Specializations:* Ed.D. program in interdisciplinary studies including educational technology/instructional development. *Features:* Program tracks on "process" issues of analysis, design, and evaluation of learning systems. Issues are supported by a foundation based upon learning theory, measurement, evaluation, and instructional delivery, including instructional computing and distance education methodologies. Graduates are prepared for careers as curriculum specialists, course designers, trainers, instructional developers, media specialists, and human resource managers. *Admission Requirements:* GPA of 3.0 for master's program applicants, three letters of recommendation, congruency between applicant's statement of career goals and program goals, and GRE combined test score of 1,050. *Faculty:* 5 full-time; 2 part-time. *Students:* 18 doctoral; 52 M.A., 31 graduate certification. *Assistance:* A limited number of Colorado Fellowships are available for full-time incoming students; graduate and research assistantships are available for full-time students. *Doctoral Program Trends:* Information not available. *Doctorates Awarded 1988-89:* 1m, 2w.

CONNECTICUT

University of Connecticut. Storrs, CT 06269-2001. Phillip Sleeman, Dir., University Center for Instructional Media and Technology, and Prof. of Education. *Specializations*: Ph.D., sixth year, and master's degree programs involving advanced instructional media and technology to prepare individuals in instructional technology position of major responsibility in universities, colleges, community colleges, large school systems, state departments of education, government and industry, and other educational and media organizations of national scope. *Features*: The program seeks an optimum mix of competencies involved in solving instructional media and technology problems, with competencies in several fields of professional education (psychological foundations, social foundations, research and evaluation, business administration, curriculum and supervision, instructional media and technology, computers, videodiscs, teleconferencing, computer graphics, and data processing). *Admission Requirements:* Admission to graduate school; undergraduate GPA above 3.0; filing of Miller Analogies Test; evidence of scholarly attainments, interests, and potential for growth; the strength of validity of career motive, previous significant experience in the instructional media field; and at least five years of highly successful teaching experience (of which one or more years of administrative or supervisory experience would be desirable). *Faculty*: 2 full-time; 4 part-time. *Students*: Data not available. *Assistance*: A number of graduate assistantships, predoctoral fellowships, research fellowships, and federal and minority fellowships available competitively. *Doctoral Program Trends*: Interactive video, advanced learning theory, computer graphics, videodisc, and research. *Doctorates Awarded 1988-89:* 3m, 1w.

FLORIDA

Florida State University. College of Education, Tallahassee, FL 32306. Walter Wager, Prof. and Program Leader, Instructional Systems Program, Department of Educational Research, College of Education. *Specialization:* Ph.D. degree in instructional systems with specializations for persons planning to work in academia, business or industry, government, or military. *Features:* Core courses include systems and materials development, analysis of media, project management, psychological foundations, current trends in instructional design, and research and statistics. Internships are also required. *Admission Requirements:* Total score of 1,000 on the verbal and quantitative sections of the GRE, or a GPA of 3.0 for the last two years of undergraduate study, 3.3 GPA graduate. International students must provide TOEFL scores. *Faculty:* 10. *Assistance*: University and college fellowships; grant and contract-funded assistantships. *Doctoral Program Trends:* Increased enrollments of students interested in position placements in business and industry. *Doctorates Awarded 1988-89:* 5m, 5w, including 1 foreign national.

Nova University. Fort Lauderdale, FL 33314. John Scigliano, Dean and Dir., Center for Computer Based Learning. *Specializations:* Ed.D./CED, DAIS, D.A.T.L. and D.A.M.I.S. degrees designed for professionals concerned with educational use of microcomputers, networks, information management, and telecommunications. *Features*: Program enables individuals to advance in their professions through information handling, computer utilization, telecommunications, and learning theory. Emphases are placed on individual computer-based learning online (during evenings and weekends); interactive computer learning; teleconferences; seminars and field projects through a core curriculum of leadership; advanced programming; systems analysis; learning theory; educational research; and learning futures. *Admission Requirements:* Master's degree from an accredited university, appropriate work experience and related credentials, demonstrated computer literacy, and an aptitude for programming. *Faculty:* 7 full-time. *Students*: Full-time in each of the following programs: D.A. not reported; Computer Education, 110. *Assistance*: Guaranteed student loan program; some teaching assistantships. *Doctoral Program Trends:* Student attendance/participation at selected computing institutes; successful student participation in three practicums related to microcomputers and new technology. This new program is expanding rapidly and presently includes six foreign nationals as students. *Doctorates Awarded 1987-88*: 38.

University of Florida. College of Education, Gainesville, FL 32611. Lee Mullally, Assoc. Prof., Chair. Educational Media and Instructional Design Program, College of Education. *Specializations:* Ph.D. and Ed.D. programs that stress theory, research, training, teaching, evaluation, and instructional development. *Admission Requirements:* A composite score of at least 1,100 on the GRE, an undergraduate GPA of 3.0 minimum and a graduate GPA of 3.5 minimum, and three letters of recommendation. *Faculty:* 2 full-time; 1 part-time. *Students:* 8 full-time; 6 part-time. *Assistance:* 2 graduate assistantships. *Doctoral Program Trends:* Increasing enrollments of students interested in position placements in business/industry, instructional design/development, and computer education. *Doctorates Awarded 1988-89:* 1.

GEORGIA

Georgia State University. University Plaza, Atlanta, GA 30303. Rosalind Miller, Prof. of Library Media. *Specialization:* Ph.D. in instructional technology, instructional development, media management in schools, special libraries, or business. *Admission Requirements:* Three letters of recommendation, handwritten and autobiographical sketch, admission tests, and acceptance by department. *Faculty:* 3.5 full-time equivalent. *Students:* 18 full- and part-time. *Assistance:* Graduate research assistantships. *Doctoral Program Trends:* Budget has remained about the same; facilities including space, hardware, and software have been upgraded while faculty and staff have decreased slightly. *Doctorates Awarded 1988-89:* 0

University of Georgia. College of Education, Athens, GA 30602. Kent L. Gustafson, Chair, Dept. of Instructional Technology, College of Education. *Specializations:* M. Ed., Ed.S., and Ed.D. for leadership positions as specialists in instructional design and development. The program offers advanced study for individuals with previous preparation in instructional media and technology, as well as a preparation for personnel in other professional fields requiring a specialty in instructional systems/instructional technology. Representative career fields for graduates include designing/developing/evaluating new courses, tutorial programs, and instructional materials in a number of different settings; military/industrial training; medical/dental/nursing professional schools; allied health agencies; teacher education/staff development centers; state/local school systems; higher education/teaching/research; and publishers/producers of instructional products (textbooks, workbooks, films, etc.) *Features:* Minor areas of study available in a variety of other departments. Personalized programs are planned around a common core of courses; practica, internships, and/or clinical experiences. Research activities include special assignments, applied projects, and task forces, as well as thesis and dissertation studies. *Admission Requirements:* Application to graduate school, satisfactory GRE score, other criteria as outlined in *Graduate School Bulletin. Faculty:* 11 full-time. *Students:* 21 full-time. *Assistance:* Graduate assistantships available. *Doctoral Program Trends:* Increasing enrollments of students interested in position placements in business/industry, instructional design/development, and computer education. *Doctorates Awarded 1988-89:* 3m, 1w.

ILLINOIS

Northern Illinois University. College of Education, DeKalb, IL 60115. Dr. Gary L. McConeghy, Chair, Instructional Technology, College of Education—LEPS. *Specialization:* Ed.D., in instructional technology emphasizing instructional design and development, computer education, media administration, production, and preparation for careers in business, industry, and higher education. *Features:* Considerable flexibility in course selection, including advanced seminars, internships, individual study, and research. Program is highly individualized. A total of 60 courses offered by several departments, including Library Science, Radio/Television/Film, Art, Journalism, Educational Psychology, and Research and Evaluation. *Admission Requirements:* 2.75 undergraduate GPA, 3.5 M.S. GPA; combined score of 1,000 on GRE; a writing sample; and three references. *Faculty:* 5 full-time, with courses in other departments taught by several members of the graduate faculty; 3 part-time. *Students:* 55 part-time. *Assistance:* 9 assistantships available involving laboratory supervision, instruction, and instructional development activities on and off campus. Some additional fellowships and grants possible especially for minority students. *Doctoral Program Trends:* Increasing enrollments of students interested in positions in business/industry, health, instructional design/development, and computer education. *Doctorates Awarded 1988-89:* 2m, both foreign nationals.

Southern Illinois University. College of Education, Carbondale, IL 62901. Billy G. Dixon, Prof., Chair., Dept. of Curriculum and Instruction, College of Education. *Specializations:* Ph.D., and M.S. in education with specialty areas in instructional technology, instructional development, computer-based education, and school library media. *Features:* All specializations are oriented to multiple education settings. *Admission Requirements:* M.S., 2.7 GPA or better; Ph.D., 3.25 GPA or better; MAT or GRE score; letters of recommendation; and writing sample. *Faculty:* 5 full-time; 5 part-time. *Students:* Approximately 140 current graduate students in these specialty areas. *Assistance:* Six graduate scholarships available plus university fellowship program. *Doctoral Program Trends:* Graduate student enrollment has continued to increase. *Doctorates Awarded 1988-89:* 3m, 8w.

Southern Illinois University. School of Education, Edwardsville, IL 62026. Gene D. Allsup, Prof., Chair., Dept. of Educational Leadership. School of Education. *Specialization:* Ed.D. (all-school degree) in instructional processes emphasizing theory and research, teaching, evaluation, and instructional systems design and development. *Admission Requirements:* GRE, undergraduate GPA of B+. *Faculty:* 6 full-time; 1 part-time. *Students*: 4 full-time; 10 part-time. *Assistance:* 4 graduate assistantships, 2 fellowships. *Doctoral Program Trends*: Increasing enrollments of students interested in position placements in business/industry, health, government, instructional design/ development, and computer education. *Doctorates Awarded 1988-89:* 5m, including 1 foreign national.

University of Illinois at Urbana-Champaign. College of Education, Champaign, IL 61820. J. Richard Dennis, Assoc. Prof., Dept. of Curriculum & Instruction. College of Education. *Specializations:* Ph.D., Ed.D. programs (including advanced certificate program) with emphasis in the following areas: preparation of university research faculty, materials/training designers, computer resources managers, and continuing professional teacher training. *Features:* Programs designed to accommodate individuals with diverse background preparations. *Admission Requirements*: Master's degree, 4.0 out of 5.0 GPA, GRE submitted, a sample of scholarly writing in English, TOEFL scores for non-English-speaking students. *Faculty:* 8 full-time. *Students:* 65 full-time and part-time including 20 foreign nationals. *Assistance:* Limited fellowships available; some assistantships; tuition waiver support available for highly qualified applicants. *Doctoral Program Trends:* Increasing emphasis on application of artificial intelligence and the design of intelligence tutoring systems. *Doctorates Awarded 1988-89:* 3m, 2w, including 2 foreign nationals.

University of Illinois at Urbana-Champaign. Department of Educational Psychology. Champaign, IL 61820. Charles K. West, Prof., Div. of Learning and Instruction, Dept. of Educational Psychology. *Specialization*: Ph.D. in educational psychology with emphasis in educational computing. *Features:* Individually tailored program. Strongly research-oriented with emphasis on applications of cognitive science to instruction. *Admission Requirements:* Flexible: good academic record, high GRE scores, and strong letters of recommendation. *Faculty:* 17. *Students:* 1989-90, 25 enrolled. *Assistance:* Scholarships, research assistantships, and teaching assistantships available. *Doctoral Program Trends*: Data not available. *Doctorates Awarded 1988-89:* 5.

INDIANA

Indiana University. School of Education, Bloomington, IN 47405. Michael Molenda, Assoc. Prof., Chair., Dept. of Instructional Systems Technology, School of Education. *Features*: Three major emphasis areas—instructional design and development, message design and production, and organizational change. Students draw on all areas when planning their academic programs. Virtually all students are full-time residents. Many opportunities for students to combine practice with study by working in the AV center and other appropriate agencies on and off campus. *Admission Requirements:* Satisfactory GPA, verbal, quantitative, and analytical sections of the GRE. *Faculty*: 10 full-time, equivalent. *Students:* 83 Master's students. *Assistance:* Graduate assistantships, associate instructorships, fellowships, scholarships, and fee remissions. *Doctoral Program Trends*: Increasing enrollments of students interested in position placements in business/ industry, instructional design/development, and computer education. *Doctorates Awarded 1988-89:* 5m, 3w, including 3 foreign nationals.

Purdue University. School of Education, West Lafayette, IN 47907. James D. Russell, Prof. of Education, Dept. of Curriculum & Instruction. *Specialization:* Ph.D. programs to prepare individuals to direct instructional development in school districts, health, business, government and industry. *Admission Requirements:* GPA of 3.0 or better, three recommendations, scores of at least 1,000 on the GRE, statement by the applicant concerning his or her proposed goals and time schedule, and acceptance by the Department of Curriculum & Instruction. *Faculty:* 6 full-time. *Students*: 16 full-time. *Assistance:* Graduate teaching assistantships and graduate laboratory assistantships. *Doctoral Program Trends:* Increasing enrollments of students interested in position placements in business/industry, health, instructional design/development, and computer education. *Doctorates Awarded 1988-89:* 4m, 4w.

IOWA

Iowa State University. College of Education, Ames, IA 50011. Michael Simonson, Prof., Secondary Education, College of Education. *Specializations:* Master's or Ph.D. in education with an emphasis on media, computers, curriculum and instruction for public school and private corporate training, college and university supervision of media use, operation of an instructional materials center, and instructional development; higher education research and teaching, and teacher education programs; and positions in business, industry, or public and private agencies concerned with communications and teaching processes. *Features:* Practicum experiences related to professional objectives, supervised study and research projects tied to long-term studies within the program, development and implementation of new techniques, teaching strategies, and operational procedures in instructional resources centers and four computer labs. *Admission Requirements:* Admission to graduate school, master's degree in a field appropriate to the specialization, top half of undergraduate class, and successful professional and/or related experience relevant to the program, such as work or instructional activities. *Faculty:* 5 full-time. *Students:* 20 full-time; 20 part-time. *Assistance:* Graduate assistantships. *Doctoral Program Trends:* Increasing enrollments of students interested in position placements in business/industry and computer education. *Doctorates Awarded 1987-88:* 2m, 2w.

University of Iowa. College of Education, Iowa City, IA 52242. Leonard S. Feldt, Prof., Psychological and Quantitative Foundations, College of Education. *Specializations:* Computer applications, instructional development, training and human resource development. *Features:* Flexibility in planning to fit individual needs, backgrounds, and career goals. The program is interdisciplinary involving courses within divisions of the College of Education, as well as in the schools of Business, Library Science, Radio and Television, Linguistics, and Psychology. *Admission Requirements:* A composite score of at least 1,000 on GRE (verbal and quantitative) and a 3.2 GPA on all previous graduate work for regular admission. (Conditional admission may be granted.) Teaching or relevant experience may be helpful. *Faculty:* 4 full-time; 4 part-time. *Students:* 40 full-time and part-time. *Assistance:* Special assistantships (in the College of Education) for which students in any College of Education program may compete. Application deadlines for the special assistantships is 1 February. *Doctoral Program Trends:* Increasing enrollments of students interested in position placements in business/industry, instructional design/development, and computer education. *Doctorates Awarded 1988-89:* 4w.

KANSAS

Kansas State University. College of Education, Manhattan, KS 66506-5301. Jackson Byars, Prof., Dept. of Educational Media and Technology, College of Education. *Specializations:* Ph.D. and Ed.D. program. This program is offered on a semester basis and requires 90 credit hours including 60 in media and technology, one year of residency, and a dissertation. *Students:* 26. Faculty: 4, 0, 6. *Program Trends:* Increasing enrollments of students interested in position placements in business/industry, health, college teaching, instructional design/development, and computer education. *Doctorates Awarded 1987-88:* 4m, 4w.

University of Kansas. Instructional Technology Center, Lawrence, KS 66045. Ronald Aust, Asst. Prof., Curriculum and Instruction, Dir., Instructional Technology Center. *Specializations:* Ph.D., Ed.D. and Ed.S., and M.S. to prepare instructional technologists to serve in leadership roles in a variety of educational settings. Emphasis is on the use of research-based data to guide decision making in the various roles required of instructional technologists. Special attention is given to the principles and procedures for designing instruction with computers, video, interactive video and for distance learning applications. *Features:* The Instructional Technology Center provides a laboratory setting to assist in research projects and in the acquisition of production, instructional development, and media management skills. The department's microcomputer laboratories provide access to current equipment and software. Students are encouraged to work with faculty on appropriate projects. In addition to a common core, flexibility is built into the program so students may pursue their own interest. *Admission Requirements:* Regular admission, 3.5 GPA and 900 GRE; Provisional, 3.25 GPA and 900 GRE or 3.5 GPA with less than 900 GRE. *Faculty*: 3. *Students:* 5 full-time; 12 part-time. *Assistance:* 4 graduate teaching assistantships (apply by 1 March). *Doctoral Program Trends:* Increasing enrollment of students interested in position placements in college teaching, in business and industry training, and computer education. *Doctorates Awarded 1988-89:* 2m, 1w.

KENTUCKY

University of Kentucky. College of Education, Lexington, KY 40506. Gary Anglin, Assoc. Prof., Dept. of Curriculum and Instruction, College of Education. *Specialization:* Ed.D. program emphasizing instructional design/instructional technology, research, and teaching. *Features:* Data not available. *Admission Requirements*: A minimum composite score (verbal and quantitative) of 1,000 on the GRE, minimum undergraduate GPA of 2.5, minimum graduate GPA of 3.4. Concurrent applications to the Graduate School and Department are required, including letters of recommendation. *Faculty:* 2 full-time. *Students*: 12. *Assistance*: A limited number of teaching associateships and research assistantships are awarded on a competitive basis. Applicants for available minority fellowships are encouraged. Financial assistance package includes tuition remission. *Doctoral Program Trends:* Increasing enrollments of students interested in positions in business/industry, college teaching, instructional design/development, and computer education. *Doctorates Awarded 1988-89:* 0.

MARYLAND

The Johns Hopkins University. School of Continuing Studies, Baltimore, MD 21218. Marion Panyan. Prof., Div. of Education, School of Continuing Studies. *Specializations:* Ed.D. in human communications and its disorders—a dual-major degree in technology and one of the following areas: mild-moderate handicapped and severely/profoundly handicapped. The program requires 99 semester hours beyond the baccalaureate including 12 hours of dissertation research and 27 hours in computers and related rehabilitation educational technology. (A master's level program is also offered.) *Features:* Computer courses including but not limited to BASIC, authoring programs, and systems, LOGO, interactive video disc, hardware and adaptive devices, software selection/evaluation, expert systems, robotics, networking, and computerized information and data management in special education. Internships and practicum opportunities in special education and rehabilitation settings. *Admission Requirements:* Master's or doctorate from an accredited institution. *Faculty*: 3 full-time; 12 part-time. *Students*: 30 full-time and part-time. *Assistance*: Information available through Marion Panyan, Center for Technology and Human Disabilities, 2301 Argonne Street, Baltimore, MD 21218. *Doctoral Program Trends:* Emphasis on applications of microcomputers and related technology. *Doctorates Awarded 1988-89:* 1.

University of Maryland. College of Library and Information Services, College Park, MD 20742. Claude E. Walston, Prof. and Dean, College of Library and Information Services. *Specialization:* Ph.D. in Library Science and Educational Technology/Instructional Communication. *Features*: Program is broadly conceived and interdisciplinary in nature, using the resources of the entire campus. The student and the advisor design a program of study and research to fit the student's background, interests, and professional objectives. Students prepare for careers in teaching and research in information science and librarianship and elect concentrations including educational technology/instructional communication. *Admission Requirements:* Baccalaureate degree (the majority enter with master's degrees in library science, educational technology, or other relevant disciplines), GRE general tests, three letters of recommendation, and a statement of purpose. Interviews required when feasible. *Faculty:* 15-1/2 with doctorates and 16 part-time. *Students:* 22 full-time. *Assistance*: Some fellowships starting at $8,800, with remission of tuition; some assistantships also available. *Doctorates Awarded 1988-89:* 3.

MASSACHUSETTS

Boston University. School of Education, Boston, MA 02215. Gaylen B. Kelley, Prof., Chair., Program in Educational Media and Technology, School of Education. *Specializations*: Ed.D. for developing and teaching academic programs in instructional technology in community colleges and universities; or specialization in such application areas as business and industrial training, biomedical communication, or international development projects. Program specializations in instructional development, media production and design, and instructional facilities design for media and technology. Students participate in mandatory research sequence and may elect courses in other university schools and colleges. *Features:* Doctoral students have a great deal of flexibility in program planning and are encouraged to plan programs that build on prior education and experience that lead to specific career goals; there is strong faculty participation in this process. *Admission Requirements:* Three letters of recommendation, Miller Analogies Test score, copies of undergraduate and graduate transcripts, complete application form with statement of goals, and a personal interview with the department chair (may be waived). Minimum GPA is 2.7 with Miller Analogy Score of 50. Faculty: 3 full-time; 13 part-time. *Students:* 10 full-time; 57 part-time. *Assistance:* A number of assistantships and part-time instructor positions. *Doctoral Program Trends*: Increasing enrollments of students interested in position placements in business/industry, health, government, program administration, instructional design/development, media production, and computer education. *Doctorates Awarded 1988-89:* 4m, 5w, including 2 foreign nationals.

MICHIGAN

Michigan State University. College of Education, East Lansing, Ml 48824. Leighton A. Price, Prof., Coord. of the Educational Systems Development program in the Department of Counseling, Educational Psychology and Special Education. *Program Basis:* Quarter. *Specializations:* Ph.D. and Ed.D. to prepare individuals to improve the quality and effectiveness of instructional delivery systems, to improve learning at all educational and training levels, and to serve as instructional developers and highly qualified training personnel. Emphasis is given to systems design and analysis, to selection and evaluation of instructional computing and other educational technologies, to design and validation of instructional materials, and to research on attributes of teaching strategies and supporting technologies. *Features:* Individually designed doctoral programs, guided field experience in instructional design projects, and cognitive work in areas such as communication, higher education, or instructional resource management. *Admission Requirements:* Master's degree with an acceptable academic record, transcripts, teaching credentials (preferred), three letters of recommendation, acceptable verbal and quantitative GRE scores, statement describing professional goals and ways that the doctoral program may contribute to their achievement, and a personal interview. *Faculty:* 9 full-time, 1 part-time. *Students:* 15 Ph.D. candidates. *Assistance:* Some fellowship and graduate assistantship opportunities in instructional development and technology are available for qualified applicants. *Trends:* The program is responding to rapid developments in the field of educational technology. *Doctorates Awarded 1987-88:* 2m, 1w, including 1 foreign national.

University of Michigan. Department of Curriculum, Teaching and Psychological Studies. Ann Arbor, MI 48109-1259. Patricia Baggett, Assoc. Prof., Chair., Computers and Education. *Programs:* M.A., Ed.D. and joint M.A. and Ph.D. with the Computer Science Department. *Minimum Degree Requirements:* 30 credit hours for master's, 60 for doctorate. *Faculty:* 2 full-time, several partial appointments. *Graduate students:* approximately 10.

Wayne State University. College of Education, Detroit, MI 48202. Rita C. Richey, Coordinator, Instructional Technology Programs, Div. of Administrative and Organizational Studies, College of Education. *Specializations*: Ed.D. and Ph.D. programs to prepare individuals for leadership in business, industry, health care, and the K-12 school setting as instructional development specialists; media or learning resources managers or consultants; specialists in instructional video, and computer-assisted or computer-managed instruction; teachers in higher education; or research specialists. *Features:* Guided field experience and on-the-job training and participation in teaching and instructional development activities within the university and in business and industry. *Admission Requirements:* Master's, GPA of 3.5, strong professional recommendations, and an interview. *Faculty:* 4 full-time; 5 part-time. *Students:* 104 full-time and part-time. *Assistance:* contract industrial internships. *Doctoral Program Trends:* Increased enrollments of students seeking position placements in college teaching, instructional design/development, and computer education. *Doctorates Awarded 1988-89:* 1m, 5w.

MINNESOTA

University of Minnesota. College of Education, Minneapolis, MN 55455. Richard Kimpston, Prof., Chair., Curriculum and Instructional Systems, College of Education. *Specializations:* M.A., M.Ed., and Ph.D. in education are offered through the graduate school. Areas of study include instructional design and technology, computer-based instruction, and curriculum systems and instruction research. *Features:* Internships and special field experiences. *Admission Requirements:* General requirements for admission. *Faculty:* 6 full-time; 6 associate. *Students:* 200 full- and part-time. *Assistance:* Teaching fellowships, research, project assistantships, and internships are available. *Doctoral Program Trends:* Increasing enrollments of students interested in position placements in business/industry, college teaching, program administration, instructional design/development, and computer education. *Doctorates Awarded 1988-89:* 2m, 1w.

MISSOURI

University of Missouri—Columbia. College of Education, Columbia, MO 65211. John F. Wedman, Asst. Prof., Educational Technology Program, Curriculum and Instruction Dept., College of Education. *Specializations:* Ph.D. and Ed.D. programs to prepare individuals for positions in higher education and instructional development positions in both industry and the military. *Features:* Program deals with educational computing, instructional design, and media development. Support areas, such as adult education, communications, and management, are integrated with educational technology courses to form a degree plan that is both focused and broadbased. An internship experience, in a setting consistent with the career goals of the student, is also included. *Admission Requirements:* Graduate GPA above 3.5 and a combined score of 1,350 or better on the GRE or a graduate GPA of 3.2 and a combined score of 1,500 or better on the GRE. Minimum of two years of appropriate professional experience, letters of recommendation, and statement of purpose. A TOEFL score of 550 or better is required for students whose native language is not English. *Faculty:* 2 full-time; 3 part-time, plus selected faculty in interdisciplinary fields. *Students:* 12 students are currently active in the doctoral program. *Assistance:* Scholarships and fellowships, ranging from $200 to $8,000, available from several sources. Teaching and research assistantships available to qualifed individuals. Special financial support available for minority and foreign national students. *Doctoral Program Trends:* Research and development activities related to distance learning technologies used in various educational settings. *Doctorates Awarded 1988-89:* 2m (foreign nationals).

NEBRASKA

University of Nebraska. Teachers College, Lincoln, NE 68588-0515. Gordon F. Culver, Prof., Teachers College. *Specializations and Features:* Ph.D. and Ed.D. programs are in administration, curriculum, and instruction with an emphasis in instructional technology. Students in these programs demonstrate competencies for professions in instructional design, research in IT, and training by developing appropriate portfolios. Within the context of a balanced graduate experience in IT, extensive experiences in the use of videodisc technologies are possible. *Admission Requirements:* Admission standards are set by the graduate college. *Faculty:* 3 full-time faculty teach in the IT program; 5 are involved in videodisc design and production. *Assistance:* Scholarship and externally based funding support available. *Doctoral Program Trends:* Program emphasizes "design and theory" in the area of instructional technology. *Doctorates Awarded 1988-89:* None.

NEW JERSEY

Rutgers—The State University of New Jersey. The Graduate School, New Brunswick, NJ 08903. Brent D. Ruben, Prof., and Dir., Ph.D. Program, School of Communication, Information and Library Studies, The Graduate School. *Specializations:* Ph.D. programs in communication; information and communication in management and organizational processes; information systems, structures and users; information and communication policy and technology; and library and information services. *Features:* Program provides doctoral-level coursework for students seeking theoretical and research skills for scholarly and professional leadership in the information and communication fields. *Admission Requirements:* Typically, students should have completed a master's degree in information studies, communication, library science, or related field. The undergraduate GPA should be 3.0 or better. The GRE is required; TOEFL is also required for foreign applicants whose native language is not English. *Faculty:* 36 full-time. *Students:* 82 full-time and part-time. *Assistance:* Approximately 16 teaching assistantships and one Title II-B Fellowship available per year for full-time students. Research assistantships and other work opportunities are also available. *Doctoral Program Trends:* Increasing emphasis on relationship between communication and information, and the impact of both on human behavior. *Doctorates Awarded 1988-89:* 3m, 5w.

NEW YORK

Columbia University, Teachers College. New York, NY 10027. John B. Black, Prof. and Chair. *Specialization:* Ed.D. for individuals seeking careers in instructional technology; programs in instructional technology (in a department that also includes communication and computing in education). *Features:* Part-time employment is available and encouraged as part of the coursework of 90 semester hours (in addition to the dissertation). Programs are individually planned, interdisciplinary, and based on prior and present interests and anticipated future developments in instructional technology. Up to 45 credits of relevant coursework may be transferred. *Admission Requirements:* A record of outstanding capability, potential for leadership and creativity as indicated from academic records, recommendations, score on the GRE, statement of expressed interest and future plans. *Faculty:* 5 full-time; 2 part-time. *Students:* 12 full-time; 32 part-time. *Assistance:* Limited scholarships (applications must be received before 1 January for the following September semester) and work-study financial aid for qualified applicants. *Doctoral Program Trends:* Increasing enrollments of students interested in position placements in business/industry, instructional design/development, and computer education. *Doctorates Awarded 1987-88:* 3W.

New York University. New York, NY 10003. Donald T. Payne, Assoc. Prof., Dir., Educational Communication and Technology Program. *Specializations:* Preparation of individuals to perform as instructional media designers, developers, and producers in education, business and industry, health and medicine, community services, government, and other fields; to coordinate media communications programs in educational television centers, museums, schools, and corporate; health and medicine, and community organizations; to serve as directors and supervisors in audiovisual programs in all settings listed; and to teach in educational communications and instructional technology programs in higher education. *Features:* Emphasizes theoretical foundations, in particular a cognitive perspective of learning and instruction and their implications for designing media based learning environments; participation in special research and production projects in multi-image, television, microcomputers, and computer-based interactive multi-media systems. *Admission Requirements:* Combined score of 1,000 minimum on GRE, interview related to academic and/or professional preparation and career goals. *Faculty:* 2 full-time; 7 part-time. *Students:* 31. *Assistance:* Some financial aid and work-study programs. *Doctoral Program Trends:* Increasing enrollments of students interested in position placements in business, industry, health, instructional design/development, media production, and computer education. *Doctorates Awarded 1988-89:* 1m, 1w.

State University of New York at Buffalo. Graduate School of Education, Buffalo, NY 14214. T. A. Razik, Prof. of Education, Dept. of Educational Organization, Administration and Policy. *Specializations:* Ph.D., Ed.D., and Ed.M. to educate graduate students in the theories, resources, and dynamics of instructional design and management. Emphasis is on the systems approach, communication, computer-assisted instruction and model building, with a specific focus on the efficient implementation of media in instruction. *Features:* The program is geared to instructional development, systems analysis, systems design and management in educational and non-educational organizations; research is oriented to the analysis of communication and information theory. Laboratories are available to facilitate student and faculty research projects in educational and/or training settings. Specifically, the knowledges and skills are categorized as follows: planning and designing; delivery systems and managing; and evaluating. *Admission Requirements:* Satisfactory scores on the Miller Analogies Test and/or GRE, master's degree or equivalent in field of specialization, and minimum 3.0 GPA. *Faculty:* 3 full-time; 3 part-time. *Students:* 25 full-time; 35 part-time. *Assistance:* 3 graduate assistantships (apply by 10 March). *Doctoral Program Trends:* Increasing enrollments of students interested in position placements in business/industry, health, university teaching, instruction design/development, and computer application. *Doctorates Awarded 1987-88:* 4m, 3w, including 1 foreign national.

Syracuse University. School of Education, Syracuse, NY 13244-2340. Donald Ely, Prof., Chair., Instructional Design, Development, and Evaluation Program, School of Education. *Specializations:* Ph.D., Ed.D., and M.S. degree programs for instructional design of programs and materials, educational evaluation, human issues in instructional development, media production including computers and videodisc, and educational research and theory (learning theory, application of theory, and educational and media research). Graduates are prepared to serve as curriculum developers, instructional developers, program and product evaluators, researchers, resource center administrators, communications coordinators, trainers in human resource development, and instructors in education in higher education. *Features:* Field work and internships, special topics and special issues seminar, student and faculty initiated minicourses, seminars and guest lecturers, faculty-student formulation of department policies, and multiple international perspectives. *Admission Requirements:* A bachelor's degree from an accredited institution. *Faculty:* 7 full-time; 4 part-time. *Students:* 55 full-time; 45 part-time. *Assistance:* Some fellowships (competitive); and graduate assistantships entailing either research or administrative duties in instructional technology. *Doctoral Program Trends:* Increasing enrollments of students interested in position placements in business/industry, program administration, instructional design/development, and computer education. *Doctorates Awarded 1988-89:* 3m, 1w, including 2 foreign nationals.

OHIO

Kent State University. Instructional Technology Program, White Hall 405, KSU, Kent, OH 44242. (216) 672-2294. Dr. Drew Tiene, Program Coordinator. *Program Basis:* semester. *Tuition per credit:* $117 in-state, $209 out-of-state. *Summer:* Two 5-week sessions. *Specializations:* Ph.D. in Educational Psychology with courses in research methods, new technologies, instructional design, production and evaluation of media programming, change strategies, etc. *Features:* Program encourages students to take elective courses in relevant departments in the College of Education and across the university, for example in communications, psychology, technology, etc. *Admission Requirements:* Obtain a doctoral program application packet from the Graduate School of Education, White Hall 306. Send two completed copies of the application, a $10 application fee, transcripts, 5 letters of recommendation (at least 2 from previous instructors), score on one of the following: Miller Analogies Test, Terman Concept Mastery Test, or Graduate Record Exam. *Assistance:* Graduate assistantships and teaching assistantships available. *Faculty:* 4 Graduates: a few each year.

Ohio State University. College of Education, Columbus, OH 43210. Marjorie Cambre, Assoc. Prof., Contact Person, Instructional Design and Technology Program, College of Education. *Specialization:* Ph.D. in instructional design and technology for preparation of individuals to perform research and to teach in higher education, administer comprehensive media services, or engage in research, production and development leadership functions in higher education and related educational agencies. *Features*: Interdisciplinary work in other departments (photography, journalism, communications, radio and television, computer and information science); individual design of doctoral programs according to candidate's background, experience, and goals; and internships provided on campus in business and industries and in schools; integrated school media laboratory, microcomputer, and videodisc laboratory. *Admission Requirements:* Admission to graduate school and specific program area in the College of Education, GRE general test, minimum 2.7 GPA, and satisfactory academic and professional recommendations. *Faculty*: Regular faculty— 8 full-time in education. *Students:* 21 full-time; 14 part-time *Assistance:* Graduate fellowships and scholarships are often available, as well as departmental teaching and research assistantships and assistantship opportunities in media facilities on campus. *Doctoral Program Trends:* Increasing enrollments of students interested in position placements in business/industry, instructional design/ development, and computer education. *Doctorates Awarded 1987-88:* 6m, 1w, including 1 foreign national.

Ohio University. College of Education, Athens, OH 45701-2979. Seldon D. Strother, Assoc. Prof., Dir. of Educational Media, School of Curriculum & Instruction, College of Education. *Specializations:* Ph.D. programs in either Instructional Technology in School Settings or Instructional Technology in Higher Education, Business & Industry and the Health Sciences. *Features:* Each program requires a minimum of 30 quarter hours of instructional technology embracing courses such as interpersonal communication, telecommunications, computer science, and psychology. Aspects of program include a high degree of self-direction, scholarship, coursework, seminars, independent study, writing, and research. Curriculum and instruction practicums and research apprenticeships are also available. *Admission Requirements*: Acceptance by Office of Graduate Studies of the College of Education. A master's degree, or its equivalent, is also required. *Faculty:* 4 full-time; 2 part-time, plus selected personnel from the Curriculum and Instruction faculty, as appropriate. *Students:* New Program. *Doctoral Program Trends:* Anticipated enrollment of individuals whose interests are in position placements in the schools, higher education, business and industry, and the health sciences. *Doctorates Awarded 1987-88:* 0 (relatively new program).

University of Toledo. College of Education and Allied Professions, Toledo, OH 43606. Amos C. Patterson, Prof., Chair., Dept. of Curriculum and Educational Technology, College of Education and Allied Professions. *Features:* Research and theory in the areas of instructional design, development, evaluation, computers, video, and training and human resources. Emphasis is in the empirical study of systematic processes and procedures in instructional technology, 135 quarter hours beyond the baccalaureate degree or 90 quarter hours beyond the master's degree, including tool skill courses and dissertation credit. Residency requirement of one year or three full-time summer quarters depending on Ph.D. or Ed.D. option. Option of one or two minor areas of study to be included in total program hours. *Admission Requirements:* Miller Analogies Test at or above 50th percentile, three letters of recommendation, official transcripts of undergraduate and graduate work, and autobiographic sketch. *Tuition and Fees:* $62.30 per quarter hour. *Faculty:* 6, 5, 1. *Assistance:* Graduate assistantships require 20 hours of work per week. Basic stipend for assistantships of $4,800 with full tuition remission. *Doctoral Program Trends:* Increasing enrollments of students seeking position placements in business/industry, health, government, college teaching, program administration, instructional design/development, media production, and computer education. *Doctorates Awarded 1987-88:* 3m, 1w, including 3 foreign nationals.

OKLAHOMA

Oklahoma State University. College of Education, Stillwater, OK 74078. Douglas B. Aichele, Head, Dept. of Curriculum and Instruction, College of Education. *Specializations:* M.S. and Ed.D. programs in educational technology (microcomputers), media management/administration, materials production, utilization/application, theory and research, selection, college teaching, evaluation, instructional systems design, instructional development, curriculum foundations, and learning theory. *Admission Requirements:* Minimum of 3.0 GPA on undergraduate work (master's), Miller Analogies Test, and minimum of one year teaching experience (doctorate). *Faculty:* 3 full-time; 2 part-time. *Students:* 14 full-time; 18 part-time M.S. candidates; 8 full-time; 12 part-time Ed.D. candidates. *Assistance:* 9 graduate assistantships. *Doctoral Program Trends:* Increasing enroll- ments of students interested in position placements in business/industry, college teaching, program administration, and instructional design/development. *Doctorates Awarded 1988-89:* 2m.

University of Oklahoma. College of Education, Norman, OK 73069. Tillman J. Ragan, Prof., Head, Dept. of Educational Psychology, Educational Technology Program Area, College of Education. *Specializations:* Ph.D. and Ed.D. leading to specializations for research, teaching, management, and consulting in instructional technology (including preparation in instructional design and development, computer, video, computer-assisted video instruction—and preparation in management of instructional systems and programs). *Features:* Programs are designed through the vehicle of an advisory conference in which the student's background and goals are translated into a program of study and research proficiencies; a practicum is included to provide experiences resembling those related to the individual's career objectives. Computer emphasis area now available. *Admission Requirements:* Evidence of potential for contribution to the field, satisfactory performance on the GRE aptitude test, satisfactory performance on advisory conference in second semester of post-master's work. *Faculty:* 3 full-time; 3 part-time. *Assistance:* Graduate Assis- tantships involving teaching and service or research are available. *Doctoral Program Trends:* In- creasing enrollments of students interested in position placements in college teaching and computer education. *Doctorates Awarded 1988-89:* 1m, 1w.

OREGON

University of Oregon. Division of Teacher Education, Eugene, OR 97401. Judith Grosenick, Assoc. Dean, Division of Teacher Education. *Specializations:* Ph.D. or Ed.D. in Curriculum and Instruction leading to public school, junior college, college, and university supervision of media use and instructional development; higher education research and teaching; and positions in business, industry, and public and private agencies concerned with instructional development, computers- in-education, product development, and training. *Features:* A flexible program designed to meet a specific student's needs. *Admission Requirements:* Master's degree. *Faculty:* 2 full-time; 4 part- time. *Assistance:* Graduate assistantships available—8. *Doctoral Program Trends:* Increasing enrollments of students interested in computer-in-education, and in locating positions in non- traditional learning environments such as business and industry. *Doctorates Awarded 1988-89:* 4m, 2w.

Western Oregon State University. Department of Education, Monmouth, OR 97361. Richard Forcier, Prof. and Dir., Instructional Technology. *Program Basis:* Quarter. *Minimum Degree Re- quirements:* 45 credit hours including 36 in media; thesis optional. *Specialization:* Computer education; instructional systems. *Features:* Offers advanced courses in media management, media production, instructional systems, instructional development, and computer technology. Some specialization in "distance delivery" of instruction and computer-interactive video instruction. *Admission Requirements:* Bachelor's degree, minimum 2.75 GPA in undergraduate program, interview, satisfactory performance on GRE or Miller Analogies Test. *Faculty:* 6, 5, 1. *Graduates:* 6m, 10w, including 2 foreign nationals.

PENNSYLVANIA

Pennsylvania State University. Division of Curriculum and Instruction, University Park, PA 16802. Paul W. Welliver, Div. of Curriculum and Instruction. *Specializations:* Ph.D. and Ed.D. for individuals seeking professional pursuits in instructional systems design, development, manage- ment, evaluation and research in instructional endeavors within buiness, industrial, medical, health, religious, higher education, and public school settings. Present research emphases are on instruc- tional development, dissemination, implementation, and management; interactive video; computer-based education; and visual learning. *Features*: A common thread throughout all programs is that candidates have basic competencies in the understanding of human learning; curriculum; instructional design, development, evaluation; and research procedures. Practical experience is available in mediated independent learning, research, instructional development, computer-based education, and dissemination projects. *Admission Requirements:* GRE or MAT and acceptance as a prospective candidate by a graduate faculty member. *Faculty*: 5 full-time. *Students:* 32 full-time; 38 part-time. *Assistance:* Graduate assistantships in managing mediated independent study courses, operating media facilities, assisting in research projects, and participating in university instructional development projects. *Doctoral Program Trends*: Increasing enrollments of students interested in position placements in business/industry, program administration, instructional design/development, interactive video, and computer education. *Doctorates Awarded 1988-89:* 3m, 2w.

Temple University. College of Educational Media Program, College of Education, Dept. of Curriculum, Instruction & Technology, Philadelphia, PA 19122. Elton Robertson, Prof., Dept. of Educational Media. *Specialization:* Ed.D. in Curriculum, Instruction and Technology with emphasis in educational media for proficiency in employing instructional technology to enhance learning and teaching at elementary, secondary, and university levels, as well as in industrial training situations. *Features:* The program is designed to take into account the candidate's personal and professional goals. Practical experience is provided for those wishing to (1) teach media-related courses (2) apply the newer interactive technology to enhance the instructional development process, and (3) function in various administrative roles in support of learning resource and instructional resource centers. *Admission Requirements*: Bachelor's degree, master's degree or 24 credits in educational media, admission to the graduate school, media experience, and a satisfactory interview with the faculty. *Faculty:* 2 full-time. *Students*: 3 full-time, 27 part-time. *Assistance:* 4 departmental assistantships, fellowships. *Doctoral Program Trends*: Increasing enrollments of students interested in position placements in business/industry, government, instructional design/development, media production, and computer education. *Doctorates Awarded 1988-89:* 2m, 2w.

University of Pittsburgh. School of Education, Pittsburgh, PA 15260. Barbara Seels, Assoc. Prof., Prog. Coord., Program in Instructional Design and Technology, Dept. of Instruction and Learning, School of Education. *Specializations:* Ed.D. and M.Ed. programs for the preparation of generalists with skills in production, selection, use, instructional design, and CBI; certification programs for instructional technologists. Program prepares people for positions in which they can effect educational change through instructional technology. Program includes three competency areas: instructional design, technological delivery systems, and communications research. *Admissions Requirements:* Submission of written statement of applicant's professional goals, three letters of recommendation, demonstration of English proficiency, satisfactory GPA, sample of professional writing, GRE, and personal interviews. *Faculty:* 4 full-time; 2 part-time. *Students:* 20 full- time; 80 part-time, of which approximately 16 are foreign nationals. *Assistance:* Tuition scholarships and assistantships may be available. *Doctoral Program Trends:* Increasing enrollments of students interested in instructional design. *Doctorates Awarded 1988-89:* 5m, 4w, including 2 foreign students.

TENNESSEE

Memphis State University. College of Education, Memphis, TN 38152. Thomas Rakes, Prof., Interim Chair, Dept. of Curriculum and Instruction, College of Education. *Specializations:* Ed.D. offered in instructional design and technology with career emphasis in schools, health care, and business & industry. *Features:* Internship, special projects, and research opportunities. *Admission Requirement*: Master's degree or equivalent and acceptable GRE. *Faculty:* 3 full-time; 2 part-time. *Students:* Data not available. *Assistance:* Assistantships. *Doctoral Program Trends:* Applied instructional design research and applied CBI research. *Doctorates Awarded 1987-88:* 1m, 2w.

University of Tennessee. College of Education, Knoxville, TN 37996-3400. Alfred D. Grant, Coord., Instructional Media and Technology, College of Education. *Specializations:* Ed.D., Ed.S., and Ph.D. programs in curriculum and instruction with emphasis in instructional media and technology; coursework in media management, materials production, utilization/application, theory and research, selection, training, teaching, evaluation, and instructional development. *Admission Requirements:* 3 years full-time teaching experience (Ed.D.), minimum undergraduate GPA of 2.5 (M.A.), and graduate GPA of 3.25 (Ed.D.). *Faculty:* 1.5 full-time. *Students:* 1.5 full-time Ed.D. candidate. *Assistance:* None reported. *Doctoral Program Trends:* Increasing enrollments of students seeking position placements in the health and industrial fields. *Doctorates Awarded 1987-88:* 0.

TEXAS

East Texas State University. Dept. of Secondary and Higher Education, Commerce, TX 75428. Robert G. Munday, Prof. and Head, Dept. of Secondary and Higher Education. *Specializations:* Ed.D. is offered for individuals interested in specializing in educational technology within the broad area of supervision, curriculum, and instruction; master's degree with majors in educational technology or library science is offered. Programs are designed to prepare professionals in various aspects of instructional technology, including management, instructional design, production of instructional materials, use, theory and research, and teaching in public schools and higher education. *Features:* Programs are tailored to fit professional goals of individuals. Opportunities are provided for practical applications through internships, practicums, and assistantships. *Admission Requirements:* Satisfactory GPA and GRE score, evidence of literary and expository skills and aptitudes, and recommendations. *Faculty:* 5 full-time; 6 part-time. *Students:* 19 full-time; 68 part-time. *Assistance:* Graduate assistantships, which include stipends and waivers of out-of-state tuition. *Doctoral Program Trends:* Increasing enrollments of students interested in position placements in business/industry, college teaching, and computer education. *Doctorates Awarded 1987-88:* 3m, 2w.

Texas A&M University. College of Education, College Station, TX 77843. Ronald D. Zellner, Assoc. Prof., Coord., Educational Technology Program, College of Education. *Specializations:* Ph.D. and Ed.D. programs to prepare individuals to teach college and university courses in educational technology, manage learning resource centers, and apply educational technology skills and knowledges in various settings related to communication and instructional processes in higher education, public education, business and industry, and public and private agencies. *Features:* The doctoral programs are flexible and interdisciplinary; degrees are established and granted in conjunction with other departments in the College of Education; specialization areas include computer applications (CAI, CMI, interactive video), media, and video production; program provides laboratories, equipment, and a PBS television station. *Admission Requirements:* A bachelor's degree, admission to graduate college which includes satisfactory performance on the GRE; some requirements may vary with respect to the particular program in which the degree is housed. *Faculty:* 6 full-time; 2 part-time. *Students:* 4 full-time; 10 part-time. *Assistance:* Several graduate assistantships (teaching and project) and a limited number of fellowships; part-time employment on campus, in local school districts, and in surrounding communities. *Doctoral Program Trends:* Increasing emphasis on placement in government, industry, and computer education settings. *Doctorates Awarded 1988-89:* 1m, 1w.

University of Texas. College of Education, Austin, TX 78712. DeLayne Hudspeth, Assoc. Prof., Coord., Instructional Technology, Dept. of Curriculum and Instruction, College of Education. *Specialization:* Ph.D. program emphasizes research, design, and development of instructional systems and communications technology. *Features:* The program is interdisciplinary in nature, although certain competencies are required of all students. Programs of study and dissertation research are based on individual needs and career goals. Learning resources include a model LRC, computer labs and classrooms, a color television studio, and access to a photo and graphics lab. *Admission Requirements:* Minimum 3.0 GPA and a score of at least 1,100 on the GRE. *Faculty:* 4 full-time. Many courses are offered cooperativey by other departments, including Radio-TV Film, Computer Science, and Educational Psychology. *Students:* 20 full-time; 16 part-time. *Assistance:*

Assistantships are available in planning and developing instructional materials and in teaching undergraduate media courses; there are also some paid internships. *Doctoral Program Trends*: Increasing enrollments of students seeking positions in business/industry, health, program administration, instructional design/development, and computer education. *Doctorates Awarded 1988-89:* 2m, 3w, including 1 foreign national.

UTAH

Brigham Young University. Department of Instructional Science, Provo, UT 84602. Paul F. Merrill, Prof., Chair. *Specializations:* M.S. and Ph.D. degrees are offered in instructional science and technology. In the M.S. program, students may specialize in instructional design and production, computers in education, or research and evaluation. In the Ph.D. program students may specialize in instructional design, instructional psychology, or research and evaluation. *Features:* Course offerings include principles of learning, instructional design, assessing learning outcomes, evaluation in education, empirical inquiry in education, project and instructional resource management, quantitative reasoning, microcomputer materials production, naturalistic inquiry, and more. Students are required to participate in internships and projects related to development, evaluation, measurement, and research. *Admission Requirements*: For further information, write to Dr. Paul F. Merrill at the above address. *Faculty:* 11 full-time. *Students:* 20 M.S., 40 Ph.D. *Doctoral Program Trends:* Increasing enrollments of students interested in position placements in business/industry, health, college teaching, instructional design/development, and computer education. *Doctorates Awarded 1988-89:* 6.

Utah State University. College of Education, Logan, UT 84322-2830. Don C. Smellie, Prof., Chair., Dept. of Instructional Technology, College of Education. *Specialization:* Ed.D. in educational technology. Offered for individuals seeking to become professionally involved in instructional development and administration of media programs in public schools, community colleges, and universities. Teaching and research in higher education is another career avenue for graduates of the program. *Features:* A relatively small program allowing individual attention. The doctoral program is built on a strong master's and specialist's program in instructional technology. All doctoral students complete a core with the remainder of the course selection individualized, based upon career goals. *Admission Requirements*: 3.0 GPA, successful teaching experience or its equivalent, satisfactory performance on the GRE, written recommendations, and a personal interview. *Faculty*: 8 full-time; 7 part-time. *Students:* 130 M.S./M.Ed. candidates; 4 Ed.S. candidates; 21 Ed.D. candidates. *Assistance*: Approximately 18 to 26 assistantships (apply by 1 June). *Doctoral Program Trends:* Increasing enrollments of students seeking position placements in business/industry, college teaching, instructional design/development, and computer education. *Doctorates Awarded 1988-89:* 3w.

VIRGINIA

University of Virginia. Curry School of Education, Charlottesville, VA 22903. John B. Bunch, Assoc. Prof. of Education, Dept. of Educational Studies, School of Education. *Specializations:* Ed.D. or Ph.D. program for well-qualified students seeking professional training in the design, production, and evaluation of instructional programs and materials in school or nonschool settings. Students may also work with faculty to conduct research on the effective uses of technology for instruction or information exchange. Graduates are placed as instructional developers or media specialists in education, as training developers in business, industry, or government agencies, or as university faculty. *Features:* A relatively small program that enables the department to tailor programs to the needs and goals of individual students (including options of minor area concentrations in other professional schools). Specializations are available in interactive technologies (a multi-media approach employing computer, compact disc, and videodisc-based materials), or media production (including video and photography). *Admission Requirements:* Satisfactory performance on GRE, written recommendations, and a personal interview. *Faculty:* 3 full-time. *Students:*15 full-time; 25 part-time. *Assistance:* A number of graduate assistantships are avilable as well as a limited number of fellowships (application must be made prior to 1 April). *Doctoral Program Trends:* Increasing enrollments of students seeking positions in business/industry, health, college teaching, instructional design/development, media production, and computer education. *Doctorates Awarded 1988-89:* 0

Virginia Polytechnic Institute and State University. College of Education, Blacksburg, VA 24061. John K. Burton, Assoc. Prof., Program Area Leader, Instructional Systems Development, Curriculum & Instruction. *Specializations:* M.A., M.S., and Ed.D. programs in instructional technology. Preparation for education, business, and industry. *Features:* Areas of emphasis are instructional design, educational computing, evaluation, and media management. Psychology is the disciplinary theory/research perspective. The Instructional Systems Development Program houses the Self-Instructional Curriculum Lab (SICL) and the Education Microcomputer Lab (EML) which contains some 70 microcomputers (Apple, IBM, and Macintosh) including interactive video and speech synthesis capabilities. The program is also affiliated with the university's Learning Resources Center (LRC) which houses production services for graphics and video as well as satellite communications. Doctoral students are expected to intern either on campus (e.g., LRC) or off campus (e.g., Arthur Anderson Associates, AT&T, etc.) or both. *Admission Requirements:* 3.3 GPA for master's degree, three letters of recommendation, all transcripts. Experience in education recommended but not required. *Faculty:* 9 full-time; 2 split; 4 adjunct. *Students:* 10 full-time; 12 part-time. *Assistance:* Seven graduate assistantships; three tuition waivers; two to four additional graduate assistantships usually available due to contracts and grants. *Doctoral Program Trends:* Increasing use of computers for most production. Increasing liaison with private sector although most doctorates still take academic positions. Continued emphasis on graduate student research and publication presentation. *Doctorates Awarded 1988-89:* 3m, 2w.

WASHINGTON

University of Washington. College of Education, Seattle, WA 98195. William D. Winn, Prof. of Education, College of Education. *Specializations:* Ph.D. and Ed.D. for individuals in business, industry, higher education, public schools, and organizations concerned with education or communication (broadly defined). *Features:* Emphasis on instructional design as a process of making decisions about the shape of instruction; additional focus on research and development in such areas as message design (especially graphics and diagrams); electronic information systems; interactive instruction via videodisc, videotex, and computers. *Admission Requirements:* GRE scores, letters of reference, transcripts, personal statement master's degree or equivalent in field appropriate to the specialization, 3.5 GPA in master's program, two years of successful professional experience and/or experience related to program goals. *Faculty:* 2 full-time; 3 part-time. *Students:* 12 full-time; 32 part-time. *Assistance:* Assistantships awarded competitively and on basis of program needs; other assistantships available depending on grant activity in any given year. *Doctoral Program Trends:* Students increasingly interested in applying ID principles to interactive instructional environments. *Doctorates Awarded 1988-89:* 4.

WEST VIRGINIA

West Virginia University. College of Human Resources and Education, Morgantown, WV 26506. David McCrory Prof., Chair., Technology Education, Communication and Information Systems Sequence of Study, College of Human Resources and Education. *Specialization:* M.A. and Ed.D. degree programs in history of technical development, research, college teaching, instructional systems design, instructional development, and communication and information systems. *Admission Requirements:* GRE and Miller Analogies Test, minimum GPA 3.0. *Faculty:* 4 full-time; 2 part-time. *Students:* 10 full-time; 6 part-time. *Assistance:* Two teaching assistantships, three research assistantships. *Doctoral Program Trends:* Increasing enrollments of students seeking position placements in business/industry, government, program management, educational delivery systems, and computer education. *Doctorates Awarded 1988-89:* 2m.

WISCONSIN

University of Wisconsin. School of Education, Madison, WI 53706. Ann De Vaney, Prof., Dept. of Curriculum and Instruction, School of Education. *Specializations:* Ph.D. programs to prepare college and university faculty and staff, and instructional developers. *Features:* The program is coordinated with media operations of the university. Traditional instructional technology courses are processed through a social, cultural, and historical frame of reference. Current curriculum emphasizes communication, perception, and cognitive theories, critical cultural studies, and theories of textual analysis and instructional development. Strength in small format video production and computers. *Admission Requirements:* Previous experience in instructional technology preferred, previous teaching experience, minimum 2.75 GPA on all undergraduate work completed, acceptable scores on either the Miller Analogies Test or the GRE test, and a minimum 3.0 GPA on all graduate work. (Note: Exceptions may be made on some of these requirements if all others are acceptable.) *Faculty:* 5 full-time; 2 part-time. *Students:* 25 Ph.D.; 35 M.S. *Assistance:* A few stipends of approximately $1,000 a month for 20 hours of work per week; and other media jobs are also available. *Doctoral Program Trends:* Preparation of academics with strengths in social/cultural aspects of educational technology and the role of media in education. *Doctorates Awarded 1988-89:* 5m, 4w.

WYOMING

University of Wyoming. Department of Educational Foundations and Instructional Technology, Laramie, WY 82071. Barbara Hakes, Assoc. Prof., Head, Dept. of Educational Foundations and Instructional Technology. *Specializations:* The College of Education offers both the Ed.D. and the Ph.D. programs. Instructional technology is not currently offered as a separate degree. The Ed.D. or Ph.D. may be earned with an emphasis in instructional technology through programs in curriculum instruction, educational administration, adult education, or educational foundations. *Faculty:* 5 full-time; 4 part-time. *Students:* 5m, 12w. *Doctorates Awarded 1988-89:* 3m, 2w. For additional information, contact Dr. Barbara Hakes and see the university's master's degree programs.

Master's Degree and Six-Year Programs in Instructional Technology

Brenda Branyan-Broadbent
Associate Professor
Department of Instructional Technology
Utah State University, Logan

Lois A. Ward
Staff Assistant II
Department of Instructional Technology
Utah State University, Logan

Program data for this yearbook were updated by program chairpersons or their representatives in response to an inquiry/questionnaire submitted to them during the summer of 1989.

Six-year specialist/certificate programs in instructional technology and related media are included in this directory as was the case in 1989. Each of these specialist/certificate programs is identified by an asterisk and is placed immediately after an individual institution's master's degree program listing.

Institutions of learning that offer master's and/or six-year specialist certificate programs have remained fairly constant in terms of enrollment, program offerings, and graduates. Regrettably, four programs have been deleted from this year's directory at the request of the respondents. Computer proficiency requirements for graduation are evident in several programs, e.g., University of Arizona. There is also evidence of distance education delivery of instruction, e.g., Boise State University and Utah State University.

As of 1989, foreign nationals continue to represent a small but significant part of the enrollment. Slightly more than three out of every twenty instructional technology program graduates are foreign nationals. Presently, a small number of foreign nationals are coming from Europe, the Middle East, Africa, and South America. Most foreign nationals, however, are coming from the Pacific Rim nations (Taiwan, Southeast Asia, Korea, the Philippines, and China).

Each entry in the directory contains the following information: (1) name and mailing address of the institution; (2) name, academic rank, and title of program head; (3) name of the administrative unit offering the program; (4) the basis on which the program is offered, i.e., semester, quarter, or trimester; (5) minimum degree requirements; (6) faculty information; (7) the number of men (m) and the total number of women (w) who graduated with master's degrees from the program during the one-year period between 1 July 1988 and 30 June 1989; and (8) identification of those institutions offering six-year specialist degree programs in instructional technology. Several institutions have been listed twice since their computer technology programs are offered apart from their educational/ instructional technology programs.

In endeavoring to update and provide completeness in the listings which follow, we are greatly indebted to the staff members of the Association of Educational Communications and Technology (AECT) and the American Library Association (ALA); the state departments of education throughout the nation; and especially the instructional technology, educational communications, and media representatives of the participating colleges and universities in the United States. A special word of thanks is also due to those college/university secretaries who rendered special assistance.

To ensure completeness of this directory, considerable effort has been expended. However, readers who may know of either new programs or omissions are encouraged to provide information to the publisher who, in turn, will follow up on them for the next edition of *EMTY*. In those instances where repeated appeals for updated information were not responded to, the entry which appeared in *EMTY 1989* is included in order to have the program represented. Individuals who are interested in any of these graduate programs are encouraged to make direct contact with the head of the program to ensure that the most recent information available is acquired.

Institutions in this section are arranged alphabetically by state.

ALABAMA

Alabama State University. Library Education Media, School of Education, Montgomery, AL 36195. Katie R. Bell, Prof., Coord., Library Education Media, School of Education. *Program Basis:* Semester. *Minimum Degree Requirements:* 36 credit hours including 18 in media; thesis optional. *Faculty:* 2, 1, 0. *Graduates*: 3m, 31w.

*School also offers a six-year specialist degree program in instructional technology and library media. This 36-42 semester program includes 18 semester hours in an instructional support area, 12 hours in education including statistics on human development and behavior, and 3 hours in a research project. *Graduates*: Data not available.

Auburn University. Educational Foundations, Leadership, and Technology, Auburn, AL 36849. Jeffrey Garrell, Prof., Dept. Head, Educational Foundations, Leadership and Technology. *Program Basis:* Quarter. *Minimum Degree Requirements*: 52 credit hours including 36 in media. *Faculty:* 18, 9, 9. *Graduates:* 1m, 3w.

*School also offers a six-year specialist degree program in instructional technology. Program is offered as either a degree or a non-degree option. The program serves either to improve the certification of school media specialists or to provide higher level study in instructional design and/or the application of computers in the learning environment.

Jacksonville State University. Instructional Media Division, Jacksonville, AL 36265. Roland Thornburg. Acting Dept. Head, Dept. of Educational Resources Instructional Media Division. *Program Basis:* Semester. *Minimum Degree Requirements*: 33 credit hours including 18 in media; thesis optional. *Faculty:* 2. *Graduates:* 10w.

*School also offers a six-year specialist degree program in instructional media with emphasis in library media. Program entails minimum of 33 credit hours including 18 in media. *Graduates:* 2w.

University of Alabama. Graduate School of Library Services, Tuscaloosa, AL 35487-0252. Philip M. Turner, Prof., Dean of Graduate School of Library Service. *Program Basis:* Semester. *Minimum Degree Requirements:* 36 credits including 21 in media. *Faculty:* 13, 6, 0. *Graduates:* 3m, 36w, including 2 foreign nationals.

*School also offers a six-year specialist degree program in instructional technology which is highly flexible and tailored to the students' educational needs. The program, leading to an Ed.S. degree, consists of 30 semester hours of coursework, does not require a thesis, and requires 12 of the 30 hours be taken in library media. *Graduates*: 1m, 1w.

University of South Alabama. College of Education, Mobile, AL 36688. John G. Baylor, Assoc. Prof., Dept. of Behavioral Studies and Educational Technology, College of Education. *Program Basis:* Quarter. *Minimum Degree Requirements:* 48 credit hours including 38 in media; thesis optional. M.Ed. program in educational media is for state school library media certification; M.S. program in instructional design is for employment in business, industry, the military, etc.; the Ed.S. in educational media leads to higher certification in library media. *Faculty:* 8, 1, 0. *Graduates*: 2m, 4w.

*School also offers a six-year specialist degree program in instructional technology for the improvement of teaching. The specific course offerings relating to the specialty field of educational media add to and complement the common core of the program and provide additional information and skills the media specialist needs to support the classroom teacher's efforts. *Admission to Candidacy:* Refer to the College of Education general section of the school's *Bulletin* for specific requirements for admission. *Ed.S. Graduates:*1w.

ARIZONA

Arizona State University. College of Education, Tempe, AZ 85287-0611. Vernon S. Gerlach, Prof., Coord., Learning and Instructional Technology, Division of Psychology in Education, College of Education. *Program Basis:* Semester. *Minimum Degree Requirements:* 30 credit hours; thesis optional. *Faculty:* 4.5, 0. *Graduates:* M.A. Degree: 6m, 4w; M.Ed. Degree: 5m, 11w.

University of Arizona. Graduate Library School, 1515 East First Street, Tucson, AZ 85719. C. D. Hurt, Assoc. Prof. and Dir., Graduate Library School. *Program Basis:* Semester. *Minimum Degree Requirements:* 38 graduate credit hours including 12 hours of core courses and a computer proficiency requirement; comprehensive required. *Faculty:* 10, 0, 0. *Graduates:* 25m, 71w, including 6 foreign nationals (1988 calendar year).

ARKANSAS

Arkansas Tech University. Department of Instructional Technology, Russellville, AR 72801. Ray Mann, Asst. Prof., Head, Instructional Technology Program, School of Education. *Program Basis:* Semester. *Minimum Degree Requirements:* 36 credit hours including 24 in media and related courses; thesis optional. *Faculty:* 1, 1, 1. *Graduates:* 2m, 2w.

University of Arkansas. College of Education, Fayetteville, AR 72701. Donald Bumpass, Assoc. Prof., Prog. Coord. for Instructional Resources, College of Education. *Program Basis:* Semester. *Minimum Degree Requirements:* 33 credit hours including 18 in media. *Faculty:* 2, 2, 1. *Graduates:* 3m, 16w, including 2 foreign nationals.

University of Central Arkansas. Library Science Department, Conway, AR 73032. Selvin W. Royal, Prof., Chair., Educational Media/Library Science Dept. *Program Basis:* Semester. *Minimum Degree Requirements:* 36 credit hours. Faculty: 5, 3, 2. *Graduates:* 5m, 27w.

CALIFORNIA

California State University—Chico. College of Communications, Chico, CA 95929-0504. John Ittelson, Prof., Advisor, Instructional Technology Program and Communication Design, College of Communication. *Program Basis:* Semester. *Minimum Degree Requirements:* 30 credit hours; thesis or project required. *Faculty:* 6, 0, 0. *Graduates:* 2m, 5w, including 1 foreign national.

California State University—Dominguez Hills. Center for Quality Education, Carson, CA 90747. Peter Desberg, Prof., Coord., Computer-Based Education, Graduate Studies Department. *Program Basis:* Semester. *Minimum Degree Requirements:* 30 credit hours including 9 hours of educational common core units and 21 units of educational technology/computers; thesis optional. *Faculty:* 6, 1, 1. *Graduates:* 30m, 38w, including 7 foreign nationals.

California State University—Long Beach. Instructional Media, Long Beach, CA 90840. Richard J. Johnson, Prof., Chair., Dept. of Instructional Systems Technology. *Program Basis:* Semester. *Minimum Degree Requirements:* 30 credit hours including 21 in media; thesis optional. Faculty: 5, 1, 2.25 time. *Graduates:* 11m, 17w, including 3 foreign nationals.

California State University—Los Angeles. School of Education, Los Angeles, CA 90032. James H. Wiebe, Prof., Assoc. Chair., Div. of Educational Foundations, School of Education. *Program Basis:* Quarter. *Minimum Degree Requirements:* 45 credit hours including 33 in media, including 2 options in the M.A. degree program: (1) computer education, and (2) instructional media and design. *Faculty:* 6, 1, 13. *Graduates:* 12m, 13w, including 2 foreign nationals.

California State University—Northridge. School of Communication and Professional Studies, Northridge, CA 91330. Judith Marlane, Prof., Chair., Dept. of Radio-TV-Film. Master's program is in mass communication, offered jointly with Dept. of Journalism, R-TV-F Prog. Coord., Ants A. Leps, Prof. Emphasis on instructional media available within the Mass Communication program. *Program Basis:* Semester. *Minimum Degree Requirements*: 30 credit hours, plus needed prerequisites for students lacking needed undergraduate preparation. Seven 3-unit instructional media-oriented course offerings available to students. *Faculty:* 10, 4, 2. *Graduates*: 1m, 2w.

California State University—San Bernardino. Television Center, San Bernardino, CA 92407. R. A. Senour, Prof., Dir., Audiovisual and Instructional Television Center. *Program Basis*: Quarter. *Minimum Degree Requirements*: 45 credit hours including 15 in media; program in media required. *Faculty*: 1, 2, 3. *Graduates*: 2.

    *School also offers technical certificate programs in computer education and educational technology. *Graduates*: Data not available.

National University. School of Education, Vista, CA 92083. Aaron F. Ruble, Dir., Dept. of Instructional Technology, School of Education. *Program Basis*: Monthly. *Minimum Degree Requirements*: The equivalent of 60 quarter hours with media courses tailored to meet student needs; project required. *Faculty*: 7, 0, 2. *Graduates*: 26m, 11w.

Pepperdine University. Graduate School of Education and Psychology, Culver City, CA 90230. Terence R. Cannings, Prof. and Prog. Dir., Graduate School of Education and Psychology. *Program Basis*: Trimester. *Minimum Degree Requirements*: 30 unit hours in Educational Computing. *Faculty*: 5, 0, 0. *Graduates*: 14m, 27w, including 2 foreign nationals.

San Diego State University. Educational Technology, San Diego, CA 92182. Patrick Harrison, Prof., Chair., Dept. of Educational Technology. *Program Basis*: Semester. *Minimum Degree Requirements*: 30 credit hours including 27 in educational technology, instructional design, and training. *Faculty:* 9, 0, 0. *Graduates*: 20m, 30w, including 5 foreign nationals.

San Francisco State University. Center for Educational Technology, San Francisco, CA 94132. Eugene Michaels, Coordinator & Professor. *Program Basis*: Semester. *Minimum Degree Requirements*: 30 credit hours, specializations in Instructional Systems, Instructional Computing, and Instructional Video. Field study thesis or project required. *Faculty*: 4.5, 3. *Graduates*: 10m, 12w.

    *School also offers 18 unit Graduate Certificate in Training Systems Development which can be incorporated into the Master's program.

San Jose State University. Instructional Technology Program, School of Education, San Jose, CA 95192-0076. Leonard Espinosa, Prof., Dir., Instructional Technology Program, Eucational Leadership and Development Div., School of Education. *Program Basis*: Semester. *Minimum Degree Requirements:* 30 credit hours including 20 in media; thesis program. *Faculty*: 9, 2, 0. *Graduates:* 7m, 26w, including 7 foreign nationals.

United States International University. School of Education, San Diego, CA 92131. Colin F. MacKinnon, Assoc. Prof. and Comp., Prog. Coord., School of Education. *Program Basis*: Quarter. *Minimum Degree Requirements*: 45 quarter hours and nine-course M.A. in Computer Education tailored to meet computer literacy, problem-solving, software applications, curriculum development, and integrating microcomputers into instructional needs of classroom teachers, curriculum coordinators, and district-level specialists from the United States and a number of international countries. (International Summer 3-3-3 Master's Program available for candidates who wish to study abroad for one or two summers with a one-course per quarter load during the academic year.) *Faculty*: 4, 2, 2. *Graduates*: 10m, 24w, including 5 foreign nationals.

University of California-Berkeley. School of Library and Information Studies, Berkeley, CA 94720. Charlotte Nolan, Assoc. Dean, Library and Information Studies, School of Library and Information Studies. *Program Basis*: Semester. *Minimum Degree Requirements:* 28 credit hours in library science, computer science, and related. *Faculty:* 12, 6, 2. *Graduates*: 31m, 60w, including 8 foreign nationals.

*School also offers six-year specialist degree certificate program, 20 semester credit hours are required for each of the following four certificate programs: library and information studies; bibliography; library automation and information science; and library management. Students are expected to carry out an independent research or design project. There are no language requirements, qualifying examinations, or final comprehensive examinations to be met or passed in any of the programs. Each program of studies is drawn up by individual students in consultation with a faculty counselor. *Graduates:* 1m, 1w.

University of California—Los Angeles. Graduate School of Education, Los Angeles, CA 90024-1521. Aimee Dorr, Prof., Learning and Instruction Specialization, Div. of Educational Psychology, Graduate School of Education. *Program Basis:* Quarter. *Minimum Degree Requirements:* 36 credit hours with emphasis on all media of communication and instruction. *Faculty:* 2, 0, 6. *Graduates:* 4m, 6w, including 1 foreign national.

University of California—Santa Barbara. Department of Education, Santa Barbara, CA 93106. Willis D. Copeland, Prof., Program Leader, Instruction, Dept. of Education. *Program Basis:* Quarter. *Minimum Degree Requirements:* 40 credit hours including 28 required and 12 elective; thesis required. *Faculty:* 2, 4, 0. *Graduates:* 8m, 8w, including 3 foreign nationals.

University of Southern California. School of Education, Los Angeles, CA 90007-0031. Robert L. Baker, Prof., Chair., Dept. of Educational Psychology and Technology, School of Education. *Program Basis:* Semester. *Minimum Degree Requirements:* 31 credit hours including 12 hours in media; thesis optional. *Faculty:* 5, 11, 2. *Graduates:* 11m, 13w, including 8 foreign nationals.

COLORADO

University of Colorado—Denver. Instructional Technology Program, School of Education, Denver, CO 80204. David H. Jonassen, Prof. and Chair., Instructional Technology Program, School of Education. *Program Basis:* Semester. *Minimum Degree Requirements:* For several tracks—instructional computing; corporate training and development, library/media and instructional technology, 36 credit hours including comprehensive; project or internship required. *Faculty:* 5, 2, 0. Graduates: 3m, 10w.

University of Northern Colorado. College of Education, Greeley, CO 80639. David H. Roat, Prof., Dir., Div. of Research, Evaluation and Development, College of Education. *Program Basis:* Semester. *Minimum Degree Requirements:* For M.A. degrees in educational media, instructional development, and educational computing, 30 credit hours with media credit varying with M.A. emphasis; comprehensive required; thesis optional. *Faculty:* 5, 3 adj. *Graduates:* 10m, 22w.

CONNECTICUT

Central Connecticut State University. Department of Educational Technology and Media, New Britain, CT 06050. Mary Ann Pellerin, Assoc Prof., Chair., Dept. of Educational Technology and Media. *Program Basis:* Semester. *Minimum Degree Requirements:* 30 credit hours of which the number taken in media varies. *Faculty:* 3, 6. *Graduates:* 7m, 6w, M.S. 13; 7 Certified Library Media Specialists-2 females with library media certification.
　　*School offers 5th- and 6th-year planned programs in educational media.

Southern Connecticut State University. School of Library Science and Instructional Technology, New Haven, CT 06515. Emanuel T. Prostano, Dean and Prof., School of Library Science and Instructional Technology. *Program Basis:* Semester. *Minimum Degree Requirements:* For instructional technology only, 30 credit hours including 21 in media with comprehensive examination; 36 hours without examination. *Faculty:* 1, 2, 1. *Graduates:* 2m, 3w.

University of Connecticut. Center for Instructional Media, Storrs, CT 06268. Phillip J. Sleeman, Prof., Dir., Univ. Center for Instructional Media and Technology. *Program Basis*: Semester. *Minimum Degree Requirements*: 24 credit hours including 15 in media; thesis optional. *Faculty*: 2, 1, 4. *Graduates*: 5m, 7w, including 2 foreign nationals. Program for school certification is being discontinued.

DELAWARE

University of Delaware. College of Education, Newark, DE 19716. Richard Venezky, Prof., Coord., Dept. of Educational Studies, College of Education. *Program Basis*: Semester. *Minimum Degree Requirements*: 33 credit hours including 15 in computing; thesis required. *Faculty*: 10, 7, 7. *Graduates:* 5m, 7w.

DISTRICT OF COLUMBIA

Galludet University. School of Education, Washington, DC 20002. Ronald Nomeland, Prof., Chair., Dept. of Educational Technology, School of Education and Human Services. *Program Basis*: Semester. *Minimum Degree Requirements*: 32 credit hours including 26 in educational media and a related practicum. *Faculty*: 4, 0, 2. Graduates: 5w.

Howard University. School of Education, Washington, DC 20059. John W. Greene, Prof., Chair., Dept. of Educational Leadership and Community Services, School of Education, and Coord., Educational Technology Prog. *Program Basis*: Semester. *Minimum Degree Requirements*: 36 credit hours for M.Ed., including introduction to educational technology; computer-assisted instruction; individualized instruction; and instructional systems development; thesis required for M.A. degree. *Faculty*: 3, 3, 5. *Graduates:* 6m, 7w, including 1 foreign national.

*School also offers a certificate of advanced graduate study usually totalling 30 credit hours of which 12-20 hours are in educational technology. Foundation courses in philosophy, sociology, and human learning are also required. *Graduates:* Data not available.

University of the District of Columbia (UDC). College of Education and Human Ecology. 4200 Connecticut Ave., N.W., Washington, DC 20008. Leo Pickett, Assoc. Prof. and Chair., Dept. of Media/Library and Instructional Systems, College of Education and Human Ecology. *Program Basis*: Semester. *Minimum Degree Requirements*: For M.S. Degree in Instructional Systems, 30 hours of required courses and six hours of electives; for M.S. Degree in Library and Information Science, 30 hours of required courses and six hours of electives. *Faculty*: 6, 0, 2. *Graduates*: 11m, 10w, including 6 foreign nationals.

FLORIDA

Barry University. School of Computer Science, Miami Shores, FL 33161. Robert L. Burke, Dean, School of Computer Science and Joel S. Levine, Prof., and Dir. of Computer Education Programs. *Program Basis*: Four nine-week cycles plus two intensive three-week and one two-week summer cycle. *Minimum Degree Requirements*: 36 semester credit hours including 6 credits in one of the following: practicum, internship, or thesis. *Faculty:* 6, 0, 0. *Graduates*: 7m, 12w, including 4 foreign nationals.

*School also offers 36 credit hours above the master's degree leading to a specialist degree in computer education. This program, while adhering to the master's program description, emphasizes in-depth studies in the area of specialized technology and related applications. *Graduates*: 3m, 2w.

Florida Atlantic University. College of Education, Boca Raton, FL 33431. Dan Kauffman, Prof., Cognitive Science and Artificial Intelligence, College of Education. *Program Basis*: Semester. *Minimum Degree Requirements*: 33 credit hours with emphasis on cognitive science and educational technology; thesis optional, but recommended. Graduates must demonstrate competence in learning theory, research methodology, future technologies, hypertext/hypermedia, computer applications, chaos theory, and three computer languages. *Faculty*: 3, 0, 0. *Graduates*: 8w.

Florida State University. College of Education, Tallahassee, FL 32306. Walter Wager, Prof. and Prog. Leader, Instructional Systems Prog., Dept. of Educational Research, College of Education. *Program Basis*: Semester. *Minimum Degree Requirements*: 36 hours; no thesis required. *Faculty*: 10, 0, 0. Graduates: 6m, 5w, including 2 foreign nationals.

Jacksonville University. Division of Education, Jacksonville, FL 32211. Daryle C. May, Prof. and Dir. in Teaching Prog. in Computer Education, Div. of Education. *Program Basis*: Semester. *Minimum Degree Requirements:* 36 credit hours including 18 in computer-related major. *Faculty*: 4, 3, 0. *Graduates*: 6m, 7w.

Nova University. Center for Advancement of Education, Fort Lauderdale, FL 33314. Donald Stanier, Prog. Prof., M.S. and Ed.S. in Learning Resources, Center for Advancement of Education. *Program Basis*: Modules. *Minimum Degree Requirements*: 36 credit hours including 24 in media; practicum required instead of thesis. *Faculty*: 5, 2, 2. *Graduates*: 3m, 22w, including 15 foreign nationals. (Please refer to Nova's Doctoral Program.)

University of Central Florida. College of Education, Orlando, FL 32816. Donna Baumbach, Assoc. Prof., Dept. of Educational Services, Educational Media/Instructional Technology Programs, College of Education. *Program Basis*: Semester. *Minimum Degree Requirements*: 39-45 semester hours including 30 in technology/media; thesis, project, or research options required. *Faculty*: 4, 4, 5. *Graduates*: 10m, 18w.

University of Florida. Educational Media and Instructional Design, Gainesville, FL 32611. Lee J. Mullally, Assoc. Prof., Educational Media and Instructional Design, Prog. Leader. *Program Basis*: Semester. *Minimum Degree Requirements*: 36 credit hours including 24 in educational media and instructional design; thesis optional. *Faculty*: 2, 0, 1. *Graduates*: 1m, 5w.
    *The Education Specialist Program is an advanced degree program and has the same requirements for admission as the Ph.D. and Ed.D. Programs. A special research and/or development project is required for the Ed.S. It also requires 72 semester hours beyond the B.E.

University of Miami. School of Education and Allied Professions, Coral Gables, FL 33124. Charles E. Hannemann, Assoc. Prof., Area Coord. for Educational Technology, Dept. of Teaching & Learning, School of Education. *Program Basis*: Semester. *Minimum Degree Requirements*: 33 credit hours including 12 hours in media for M.S. Ed. in organizational training; 36 credit hours including 15 hours in media for M.S. Ed. in instructional design; no thesis required but comprehensive written exam required. *Faculty*: 7, 4, 3. *Graduates*: 6m, 5w.

University of South Florida. School of Library and Information Science, Tampa, FL 33620. Robert J. Grover, Prof., Dir., School of Library and Information Science. *Program Basis*: Semester. *Minimum Degree Requirements*: 36 hours, thesis optional. *Faculty*: 7, 3, 0. *Graduates*: 12m, 67w, including 2 foreign nationals.
    *The sixth-year specialist program allows students to specialize in areas such as services for special clientele and library management. Students pursue work in the School of Library and Information Science and in other departments depending on the student's particular needs and interests, i.e., communications, aging studies, guidance, and public administration. The 36 hours include 9 hours for a thesis or project. Application procedures are similar to those for the master's program. Admission requirements are (1) an undergraduate grade point average of 3.0, a minimum grade of B on the last half of the baccalaureate degree, or minimum GRE aptitude score of 1,000 (quantitative and verbal); (2) three letters of recommendation; and (3) a master's degree from an ALA-accredited library school. *Graduates*: Data not available.

GEORGIA

Georgia Southern College. School of Education, Statesboro, GA 30460. Jack A. Bennett, Assoc. Prof., Dept. of Educational Leadership, Technology, and Research. *Program Basis*: Quarter.

Minimum Degree Requirements: 60 quarter-credit hours including a varying number of hours of media for individual students. *Faculty:* 2, 0, 0. *Graduates:* M.Ed., 6w.

*School also offers a six-year specialist degree program. The six-year specialist program is designed to extend the leadership preparation of school media specialists through a combination of courses in administration, supervision, and advanced media processes. *Graduates:* 2m, 3w.

Georgia State University. School of Education, Atlanta, GA 30303. Rosalind Miller, Prof., Coord., Library, Media and Technology, Dept. of Curriculum and Instruction, School of Education. *Program Basis*: Quarter. *Minimum Degree Requirements*: 60 credit hours including 45 hours in media; thesis optional. *Faculty*: 3, 3, 0. *Graduates:* 14w.

*School also offers a 50-hour six-year specialist degree program in educational media. Program is designed for practicing media specialists who have a master's degree. Research, education, content courses, and a research paper are required. *Graduates:* 5m, 7w.

University of Georgia. College of Education, Athens, GA 30602. Kent L. Gustafson, Prof., Chair., Dept. of Instructional Technology, College of Education. *Program Basis*: Quarter. *Minimum Degree Requirements*: 60 credit hours including 25 in media; thesis optional. *Faculty*: 11, 0, 0., *Graduates*: 6m, 23w, including 6 foreign nationals.

*School also offers a 45-hour six-year specialist degree program in instructional technology. Program primarily designed to meet certification requirements. Coursework includes educational psychology, curriculum design, instructional design, production, media center management, and an applied project. *Graduates*: 2m, 9w, including 2 foreign nationals.

West Georgia College. Media Education Department, Education Center, Carrollton, GA 30118. Price Michael, Prof., Chair., Media Education Dept. *Program Basis*: Quarter. *Minimum Degree Requirements*: 60 credit hours. *Faculty*: 3 full-time. *Graduates*: 7w.

*School also offers a six-year specialist degree program. This program is designed to develop advanced competencies in such areas as curriculum design, information retrieval, development of instructional systems, design of media programs and facilities, skills in media research, and management. *Graduates:* New Program.

HAWAII

University of Hawaii-Manoa. Educational Technology Department, Honolulu, HI 96822. Geoffrey Z. Kucera, Prof., Chair., Educational Technology Dept. *Program Basis*: Semester. *Minimum Degree Requirements*: 39 credit hours, including 30 in educational technology; thesis and nonthesis available. *Faculty*: 4, 4, 0. *Graduates*: 3w.

IDAHO

Boise State University. College of Technology, Boise, ID 83725. Dean Spitzer, Assoc. Prof., Dir., Instructional/Performance Technology Program, College of Technology. *Program Basis*: Semester. *Minimum Degree Requirements:* 33 credit hours in instructional/performance technology and related coursework; project or thesis required (included in 33 credit hours). Program is also delivered through computer-mediated conferencing to students located anywhere in North America. *Faculty*: 2, 2, 0. *Graduates:* 8. Relatively new program.

ILLINOIS

Chicago State University. Department of Library Science and Communications Media, Chicago, IL 60628. Harry Liebler, Prof., Chair., Dept. of Library Science and Communications Media. *Program Basis*: Semester. *Minimum Degree Requirements:* 36 credit hours; thesis optional, but encouraged. *Faculty*: 4, 0, 0. *Graduates:* 8m, 40w, including 1 foreign national.

Eastern Illinois University. Secondary Education Department, Charleston, IL 61920. John T. North, Prof., Chair., Secondary Education and Foundations Dept. *Program Basis*: Semester.

Minimum Degree Requirements: 32 credit hours including 24 in library/media; thesis optional. *Faculty*: 2, 2, 1. *Graduates:* 2m, 6w, including 1 foreign national.

Governors State University. College of Arts and Sciences, University Park, IL 60466. Michael Stelnicki, Prof., Instructional and Training Technology, College of Arts and Sciences. *Program Basis*: Trimester. *Minimum Degree Requirements*: 36 credit hours, all in instructional and performance technology. *Faculty*: 2, 2, 0. *Graduates*: 5m, 5w.

Illinois State University. Department of Communication, Normal, IL 61761. Vincent Hazelton, Prof., Chair., Dept. of Communication. *Program Basis*: Semester. *Minimum Degree Requirements*: 32 credit hours including 18 in media; thesis optional. *Faculty*: 2, 0, 0. *Graduates*: 4m, 6w.

Northeastern Illlnois University. Instructional Media, Chicago, IL 60625. Christine Swarm, Prof., Coord. of Instructional Media. *Program Basis*: Trimester. *Minimum Degree Requirements*: 33 credit hours including 21 in media; thesis optional. *Faculty:* 2, 2, 0. *Graduates:* 11m, 24w, including 2 foreign nationals.

Northern Illinois University. College of Education, DeKalb, IL 60115. Dr. Gary L. McConeghy, Chair., Assoc. Prof., Instructional Technology, College of Education—LEPS. *Program Basis*: Semester. *Minimum Degee Requirements*: 39 credits including 24 in instructional technology; thesis optional. *Faculty*: 5, 3, 3. *Graduates*: 4m, 11w.

Rosary College. Graduate School of Library and Information Science, River Forest, IL 60305. Michael E. D. Koeing, Dean. *Program Basis*: Semester. *Minimum Degree Requirements*: 36 credit hours including media; nonthesis; required entrance examinations may include GRE and TOEFL. *Faculty*: 8, 15, 0. *Graduates*: 18m, 71w.
   *School also offers certificate programs in law librarianship, library administration, and technical services and several joint-degree programs.

Southern Illinois University—Carbondale. College of Education, Carbondale, IL 62901. Pierre Barrette, Assoc. Prof., Coord., Educational Technology Prog., Div. of Curriculum and Instruction, College of Education. *Program Basis*: Semester. *Minimum Degree Requirements*: 32 credit hours plus research paper; thesis optional. *Faculty*: 3, 1, 4. *Graduates*: 3m, 5w.

Southern Illnois University—Edwardsville. School of Education, Edwardsville, IL 62026. Gene D. Allsup, Prof., Chair., Dept. of Educational Administration and Instructional Technology, School of Education. *Program Basis*: Quarter. *Minimum Degree Requirements*: 52 degree credit hours including 36 in instructional technology; thesis optional. *Faculty*: 5, 5, 0. *Graduates*: 12m, 17w, including 2 foreign nationals.

University of Illinois at Urbana-Champaign. College of Education, Champaign, IL 61820. J. Richard Dennis, Assoc. Prof., Dept. of Curriculum & Instruction, College of Education. *Program Basis:* Semester. *Minimum Degree Requirements*: 32 credit hours with emphasis on theory and design of interactive instructional systems, educational psychology, and educational policy studies; 4.0 minimum GPA required; TOEFL scores for non-English-speaking students; and GRE submitted. *Faculty*: 9, 5, 0. *Graduates*: 7m, 19w, including 10 foreign nationals.
   *School also offers a six-year specialist degree program in instructional technology. Program requires two years of demonstrated professional service and admission requirements comparable to those required for the master's degree. This program also requires 32 credit hours beyond the master's, of which 16 are at the most advanced graduate level. *Graduates*: 1m.

University of Illinois at Urbana-Champaign. Department of Educational Psychology, Champaign, IL 61820. Thomas H. Anderson, Assoc. Prof., Div. of Learning and Instruction, Dept. of Educational Psychology. *Program Basis*: Semester. *Minimum Degree Requirements*: 8 units of credit, at least 3 of which must be in 400-level courses, 2 in the major field (gratuate courses are offered for 1 or 1/2 unit each); thesis required. *Faculty*: 1, 6, 5. *Graduates*: 2m, 3w.

Western Illinois University. Department of Learning Resources, Macomb, IL 61455. Don Crawford, Prof., Chair., Dept. of Learning Resources. (Offered in cooperation with Dept. of Educational Administration.) *Program Basis*: Semester. *Minimum Degree Requirements*: 32-36 credit hours including 18 in media; thesis optional. *Faculty*: 11, 5. Note: Faculty includes individuals also teaching undergraduate courses (our basic mission). We offer considerable graduate courses for support in other programs, but have few majors at the graduate level. *Graduates*: 2m, 4w.

INDIANA

Indiana State University. Media Technology, Terre Haute, IN 47809. James E. Thompson, Prof., Chair., Dept. of Educational Foundations and Media Technology. *Program Basis*: Semester. *Minimum Degree Requirements*: 32 credit hours including 18 in media; thesis optional. *Faculty*: 9, 8, 1. *Graduates*: 6m, 5w, including 4 foreign nationals.
    *School also offers a six-year specialist degree program in instructional technology.

Indiana University. School of Education, Bloomington, IN 47405. Michael Molenda, Assoc. Prof., Chair., Dept. of Instructional Systems Technology (IST), School of Education. *Program Basis*: Semester. *Minimum Degree Requirements*: 37 credit hours including 19 in IST; thesis optional. *Faculty*: 10, 2, 2. *Graduates*: 20m, 26w, including 16 foreign nationals.
    *School also offers a specialist degree program in instructional systems technology. The description of this program is the same as the school's doctoral program in instructional systems technology except for the *Students, Trends and Degrees Awarded* sections. *Graduates:* 3m, 3w, including 2 foreign nationals.

Purdue University. School of Education, West Lafayette, IN 47907. James Russell, Prof., Educational Computing and Instructional Development, Dept. of Curriculum & Instruction. *Program Basis*: Semester. *Minimum Degree Requirements*: 30 credit hours including 20 in instructional research and development; thesis optional. *Faculty*: 6, 0, 0. *Graduates*: 5m, 6w, including 2 foreign nationals.
    *School also offers a six-year specialist degree program in instructional technology and related fields with emphasis in instructional research and development. Admission to the program requires prior completion of a master's degree. In addition to 30 hours of coursework, each student conducts a research project. At least one unit of residence credit for this degree must be earned on campus. The degree is a terminal degree and is not an intermediate step between the master's and doctoral degrees. *Graduates*: 1m, 1w.

Purdue University—Calumet. Department of Education, Hammond, IN 46323. John R. Billard, Assoc. Prof., Coord., Educational Media Prog., Dept. of Education. *Program Basis*: Semester. *Minimum Degree Requirements*: 33 credit hours including 24 in media; thesis optional. *Faculty*: 2, 2, 2. *Graduates*: 3m, 5w.

IOWA

Clarke College. Computers in Education, Dubuque, IA 52001. Judith Decker, Prof., Coord. *Program Basis*: Semester. *Minimum Degree Requirements*: 20-22 credit hours in computers, 9 hours in education, and 2-4 of electives. *Faculty*: 2.25, 1, 3. *Graduates*: 2m, 4w.

Iowa State University. College of Education, Ames, IA 50011. Michael Simonson and Roger Volker, Profs. and Coords. of Professional Studies, Curriculum and Instructional Technology (including media and computers), College of Education. *Program Basis*: Semester. *Minimum Degree Requirements*: 30 credit hours including 15 in media; thesis optional. *Faculty*: 5, 6, 1. *Graduates*: 4m, 4w.

Marycrest College. Graduate and Adult Programs, 1607 W. 12th St., Davenport, IA 52804. Thomas Faguet, Dean, Graduate and Adult Programs. *Program Basis*: Semester. *Minimum Degree*

Requirements: For MA in Education: Computer Applications, 30 hours; For MS in Computer Science, 33 hours with thesis, 36 hours nonthesis. *Faculty*: 4, 0, 0. *Graduates*: 7m, 9w.

University of Iowa. College of Education, Iowa City, IA 52242. Leonard S. Feldt, Prof., Chair., Psychological and Quantitative Foundations, College of Education. *Program Basis*: Semester. *Minimum Degree Requirements*: 35 semester hours with or without thesis. *Faculty*: 4, 4, 0. *Graduates*: 9m, 12w, including 10 foreign nationals.

University of Northern Iowa. Department of Curriculum and Instruction, Cedar Falls, IA 50614. Robert R. Hardman, Prof. and Dir., Educational Media, Dept. of Curriculum and Instruction. *Program Basis*: Semester. *Minimum Degree Requirements*: For the educational media degree, 38 credit hours including 34 in media; thesis optional. For the communications and training technology degree, 38 credit hours including 32 in media; thesis optional. *Faculty*: 8, 4, 0. *Graduates*: 2m, 1w in educational media; and 5m, 8w in communications and training technology.

KANSAS

Emporia State University. School of Library and Information Management, Emporia, KS 66801. Martha L. Hale, Dean, School of Library and Information Management. *Program Basis*: Semester. *Minimum Degree Requirements*: Two programs—the ALA accredited MLS requires 42 credit hours; the School Library Media Certificate Program requires approximately 27 hours and a teaching certificate. Media technology is a component of both programs. *Faculty:* 10, 0, 0. *Graduates:* 13m, 70w, including 6 foreign nationals.
*School also offers a school library certification program which includes 27 hours of the MLS program plus technologies mainstreamed into other courses. Computer theory and use is integrated into practically every course. In addition, program offers three 2-hour computer courses and one 3-hour course which are combination theory and hands-on. *Graduates*: Data not available.

Kansas State University. College of Education, Manhattan, KS 66506. John A. Hortin, Prof., Dept. of Curriculum and Instruction, College of Education. *Program Basis*: Semester. *Minimum Degree Requirements*: 30 credit hours including 21 in media; thesis optional. *Faculty*: 4, 6, 0. *Graduates*: 7m, 24w.
*School also offers a supervisory certification program in instructional technology. *Graduates*: 2m, 12w.

University of Kansas. School of Education, Lawrence, KS 66045. Ronald Aust, Asst. Prof., Dir., Instructional Technology Center, School of Education. *Program Basis*: Semester. *Minimum Degree Requirements*: 30 credit hours including 10 in media; thesis optional. Faculty: 1, 1, 1. *Graduates*: 2m, 3w, including 1 foreign national.

KENTUCKY

University of Kentucky. College of Education, Lexington, KY 40506. Gary Anglin, Assoc. Prof., Instructional Design, Dept. of Curriculum and Instruction, College of Education. *Program Basis*: Semester. *Minimum Degree Requirements*: 36 credit hours including 24 in instructional design and technology; no thesis required. *Faculty*: 2, 2, 1. *Graduates:* 8m, 18w, including 1 foreign national.
*School also offers six-year specialist and doctoral degree programs in instructional technology. Admission requirements include a minimum grade level of 3.4 for all graduate work and 30 credit hours of work completed in education. Program requires a minimum of 30 hours beyond the master's degree including 15 hours of advanced graduate level courses. *Graduates*: Data not avaibble.

University of Louisville. School of Education, Louisville, KY 40292. Allan Dittmer, (M.Ed., Secondary) and Stanley I. Mour, (M.Ed., Elementary), Profs., Coords., Instructional Systems Technology Prog., School of Education. *Program Basis*: Semester. *Minimum M.Ed. Degree Requirements*: 30 credit hours including 12 in instructional systems development; thesis optional.

Faculty: 3, 1, 2. *Graduates:* 4m, 1w. Note: Greater effort is being expended to "mainstream" media utilization instruction within all education courses.

Western Kentucky University. Department of Teacher Education, Bowling Green, KY 42101. Robert C. Smith, Assoc. Prof., LME Coord., Dept. of Teacher Education. *Program Basis*: Semester. *Minimum Degree Requirements*: 33 credit hours including 21 in media; thesis optional. *Faculty*: 6, 3, 2. *Graduates*: 3m, 5w.

LOUISIANA

Louisiana State University. School of Library and Information Science, Baton Rouge, LA 70803. Kathleen M. Heim, Dean, Prof., School of Library and Information Science. *Program Basis*: Semester. *Minimum Degree Requirements*: 37 credit hours including comprehensive; residence student on full-time basis for semester or summer; and completion of degree program in five years. *Faculty*: 9, 0, 0. *Graduates*: 11m, 45w, including 2 foreign nationals.

McNeese State University. Department of Administration and Educational Technology, Lake Charles, LA 70609. Joe Savoie, Head., Dept. of Administration and Educational Technology. *Program Basis*: Semester. *Minimum Degree Requirements*: 30 credit hours including 15 in media; thesis not required. *Faculty*: 2, 1, 1. *Graduates*: 4m, 6w.

Southern University. College of Arts and Humanities, Baton Rouge, LA 70813. Henry Wiggins, Prof., Chair., Dept. of Mass Communications, College of Arts and Humanities. *Program Basis*: Semester. *Minimum Degree Requirements*: 30 credit hours including 21 in mass communications and instructional technology; thesis optional. *Faculty*: 4, 3, 4. *Graduates:* 19m, 13w, including 1 foreign national.

MARYLAND

The Johns Hopkins University. Division of Education, Baltimore, MD 21218. Dianne Tobin, Coord., Technology Training Program for Educators, Div. of Education. *Program Basis*: Semester. *Minimum Degree Requirements*: 33 credit hours, 8 required courses in computer-related technology and media with remaining courses being electives in several broad areas. *Faculty*: 4, 0, 1. *Graduates*: 19m, 17w, including 1 foreign national.

Towson State University. College of Education, Baltimore, MD 21204. Paul Jones, Assoc. Prof., Instructional Technology Program, General Education Department. *Program Basis*: Semester. *Minimum Degree Requirements:* 5, 4, 1. *Graduates*: 1m, 6w, including 1 foreign national. Concentrations available in Instructional Design and School Library Media.

University of Maryland. College of Library and Information Services, College Park, MD 20742. Claude E. Walston, Dean and Prof., College of Library and Information Services. *Program Basis*: Semester. *Minimum Degree Requirements*: 36 credit hours including majors in library media; no thesis required. *Faculty*: 15, 0, 0. *Graduates*: 2m, 22w.

University of Maryland (UMBC). Department of Education, Catonsville, MD 21228. David B. Young, Assoc. Prof., Coord., Instructional Systems Development Master's Degree Prog., Dept. of Education. *Program Basis*: Semester. *Minimum Degree Requirements:* 36 credit hours including 18 in systems development for each of three programs: (1) Training Systems, (2) English as a Second Language, and (3) School Instructional Systems and Post Baccalaureate Teacher Certification. *Faculty*: 4, 4, 5. *Graduates*: 1m, 6w.

Western Maryland College. Department of Education, Westminster, MD 21157. Margaret W. Denman-West, Assoc. Prof., Coord., Media/Library Science, Dept. of Education. *Program Basis*: Semester. *Minimum Degree Requirements*: 33 credit hours including 18 in media; thesis optional. *Faculty*: 2, 2, 2. *Graduates*: 2m, 8w.

MASSACHUSETTS

Boston College. Department of Education, Chestnut Hill, MA 02167. Walter M. Haney, Assoc. Prof., Dir., Educational Technology Prog., 523 McGuinn Hall, Dept. of Education, Graduate School of Arts and Sciences. *Program Basis*: Semester. *Minimum Degree Requirements*: 36 credit hours including 30 in media; practicum; thesis optional. *Faculty*: 4, 3, 1. *Graduates*: 4m, 5w.

   *School also offers a certificate of advanced education studies degree (30 credit hours) beyond M.Ed. and a special fifth-year M.Ed. program in instructional technology for Boston College undergraduates. *Graduates*: Data not available.

Boston University. School of Education, Boston, MA 02215. Gaylen B. Kelley, Prof., Prog. Dir. of Educational Media and Technology, Div. of Instructional Development, School of Education. *Program Basis*: Semester. *Minimum Degree Requirements*: 32 credit hours; thesis optional. *Faculty*: 3, 0, 13. *Graduates*: 1m, 12w, including 2 foreign nationals.

   *School also offers a six-year specialist degree program Certificate of Advanced Graduate Specialization (C.A.G.S.) in instructional technology and a corporate training program. This program is offered to those wishing to update their skills in instructional technology or those who wish to concentrate in a particular subdiscipline of the field. Concentrations are available in instructional television, facilities design for communications technology, instructional design, computer-based instruction, and library and information science. Program also provides a vehicle for those who wish to certify as Supervisors/Directors of Unified Media Programs for the Massachusetts Public Schools. Program requires 30 credit hours of course work for program completion. Students entering the program must have completed a master's degree. *Graduates*: 1m.

Bridgewater State College. Department of Media and Librarianship, Bridgewater, MA 02324. Alan Lander, Prof., Chair., Dept. of Media and Librarianship. *Program Basis*: Semester. *Minimum Degree Requirements*: 33 credit hours including 27 in media; thesis optional. *Faculty*: 4, 4, 0. *Graduates*: 2m, 3w.

   *School also offers a unified media specialist certification program which provides preparation and background in both print and nonprint resources and services. Enrollment is required in a master's degree program in instructional media, library science, or graduate school certification program to be eligible for this certification program. *Graduates*: Data not available.

Fitchburg State College. Communications/Media Department, Fitchburg, MA 01420. Lee DeNike, David Ryder, Profs., Communications/Media Dept. *Program Basis*: Semester *Minimum Degree Requirements*: 36 credit hours in communications/media management including a required thesis. *Faculty*: 5, 0, 0. *Graduates*: 2m, 1w.

Harvard University. Graduate School of Education, Cambridge, MA 02138. David N. Perkins, Senior Research Assoc., Coord., Interactive Technology in Education, Graduate School of Education. *Program Basis*: Semester. *Minimum Degree Requirements*: Semester courses including emphasis in technology and educational theory and practice. *Faculty*: 6, 0, 0. *Graduates*: 11m, 14w including 6 foreign nationals.

Lesley College. Division of Education and Special Education, Graduate School, Cambridge, MA 02138-2790. Nancy Roberts, Prof., Dir., Computers in Education Prog., Div. of Education and Special Education, Graduate School. *Program Basis*: Semester. *Minimum Degree Requirements*: 33 credit hours including 18 in computers. *Faculty*: 5, 3, 4. *Graduates*: 4m, 16w, including 2 foreign nationals.

Simmons College. Graduate School of Library and Information Science, Boston, MA 02115. Robert D. Stueart, Dean, Graduate School of Library and Information Science. *Program Basis*: Semester. *Minimum Degree Requirements*: 36 credit hours including 36 in library science and instructional technology. *Faculty*: 14, 0, 0. *Graduates*: 28m, 131w, including 18 foreign nationals.

MICHIGAN

Eastern Michigan University. Teacher Education Department, Ypsilanti, MI 48197. Thomas Bushey, Assoc. Prof., Coord., Educational Technology Concentration, Teacher Education Dept. *Program Basis*: Semester. *Minimum Degree Requirements*: 30 credit hours including 18 in educational technology. *Faculty*: 8, 2, 0. *Graduates*: 7m, 8w, including 8 foreign nationals.

Michigan State University. College of Education, East Lansing, MI 48824. Leighton A. Price, Prof., Coord., Educational Systems Development program in the department of Counseling, Educational Psychology and Special Education. *Program Basis:* Quarter. *Admission Requirements*: At least a 3.0 GPA during the last two years of undergraduate study. *Minimum Degree Requirements*: 45 credit hours with emphasis in instructional design or in educational technology and instructional computing applications; no thesis required. *Faculty*: 9, 0, 4. *Graduates*: 9m, 6w, including 1 foreign national.

*School also offers a six-year specialist degree program in instructional technology. The Educational Specialist Degree provides opportunities for advanced work in specialized aspects of Educational Systems Development (e.g., instructional design and development, computer-based education, instructional program administration) as well as opportunities to broaden foundations in education, communication, applied educational technologies, and other cognate fields. *Minimum Degree Requirements*: 45 credit hours beyond the master's, written comprehensive examination, demonstrated competence in statistics where appropriate, no dissertation required. *Graduates*: Data not available.

University of Michigan. Curriculum, Teaching and Psychological Studies, Ann Arbor, MI 48109. Robert B. Kozma, Assoc. Prof., Chair., Instructional Technology Committee, Dept of Curriculum, Teaching and Psychological Studies. *Program Basis*: Trimester. *Minimum Degree Requirements*: 30 credit hours including project. *Faculty*: 1, 0, 3. *Graduates*: 3m, 1w, including 3 foreign nationals.

Wayne State University. College of Education, Detroit, MI 48202. Rita C. Richey, Prof., Instructional Technology Prog. Coord., Div. of Administrative and Organizational Studies, College of Education. *Program Basis*: Semester. *Minimum Degree Requirements*: 36 credit hours including required project internship recommended. *Faculty*: 4, 0, 10. *Graduates*: 6m, 27w.

*School also offers a six-year specialist degree program in instructional technology. This 36-credit hour program includes required work in instructional design and evaluation with a core of additional work in the specialty area of concentration. Internships encouraged. *Graduates*: 1m, 5w.

MINNESOTA

Mankato State University. Library Media Education, Mankato, MN 56002. Frank Birmingham, Prof., Chair., Library Media Education. *Program Basis*: Quarter. *Minimum Degree Requirements:* 51 credit hours including 27 in media. *Faculty:* 4, 2, 0. *Graduates:* 20w.

*School also offers a six-year specialist degree program in the instructional technology/media field. The library media specialist degree prepares individuals as media administrators managing the human and material resources of the media program. An individual's program seeks an in-depth knowledge in a specific area, that is, administration, materials, production. Program may or may not lead to additional certification or licensure. The 45-quarter-credit-hour program includes a research course involving library automation; 21 hours in library media education, including library/media colloquium, or educational administration or curriculum and instruction; internship; 6 hours of elective coursework outside the College of Education; thesis/field study; 6 hours of elective courses in area of media specialization, and an oral examination, a comprehensive examination, and an oral thesis defense. *Graduates*: Data not available.

St. Cloud State University. College of Education, St. Cloud, MN 56301-4498. John Berling, Prof., Dir., Center for Information Media, College of Education. *Program Basis*: Quarter. *Minimum Degree Requirements*: 48 credit hours, thesis; 51 credit hours; research paper; 54 credit hours, portfolio. *Faculty*: 7, 0, 0. Graduates: 2m, 17w, including 1 foreign national.

*School also offers a 45-quarter-credit six-year specialist degree program in information media. This program is available to those who have completed a master's degree in media, another field, or comparable field. The program is designed to develop competencies for media supervisor licensure, and administrative positions in public, academic, or school district media programs. Most students are required to take the GRE. A minimum grade point average on all graduate work is 3.0. References also are required. *Graduates*: Data not available.

University of Minnesota. Curriculum and Instructional Systems, Minneapolis, MN 55455. Richard D. Kimpston, Prof., Chair., Curriculum and Instructional Systems. *Program Basis*: Quarter. *Minimum Degree Requirements*: 44 credit hours including 22 in instructional systems. *Faculty*: 6, 6 associates. *Graduates*: 8m, 7w, including 1 foreign national.

MISSISSIPPI

Jackson State University. School of Education, Jackson, MS 39217-0175. William Rush, Prof., Chair., Dept. of Educational Foundations and Leadership, School of Education. *Program Basis*: Semester. *Minimum Degree Requirements*: 36 credit hours including 24 in media; thesis and field practicum optional. *Faculty*: 3. *Graduates*: 1m, 1w, including 1 foreign national.

University of Southern Mississippi. School of Library Science, Hattiesburg, MS 39406-5146. Jeannine Laughlin, Assoc. Prof., Dir., School of Library Science. *Program Basis*: Semester. *Minimum Degree Requirements*: 41 credit hours, comprehensive required. *Faculty*: 9. *Graduates*: 12m, 29w, including 2 foreign nationals.

MISSOURI

Central Missouri State University. Department of Special Services and Instructional Technology. Warrensburg, MO 64093. Kenneth Brookens, Assoc. Prof., Coord., Instructional Technology. *Program Basis*: Semester. *Minimum Degree Requirements*: M.S.E., 32 credit hours in curriculum and instruction with emphasis on instructional technology. *Faculty*: 1, 1, 0. *Graduates*: 1m, 2w.

*School also offers a certification program in learning resources by arrangement. Inquiries about the status of this program should be directed to the Chair of the Department of Special Services.

Northwest Missouri State University. Department of Computer Science, Maryville, MO 64468. Phillip J. Heeler, Assoc. Prof., Dir., School Computer Studies Prog., Dept. of Computer Science. *Program Basis*: Semester. *Minimum Degree Requirements*: 32 credit hours for each of three master's degree programs: (1) M.S. in school computer studies includes 26 credit hours of core computer courses; (2) M.S.Ed. in educational uses of computers includes 14 credit hours of core computer courses and 12 hours of educational courses; and (3) M.S.Ed. in using computers in specific disciplines requires 7 hours of core computer courses, 12 hours of education courses, and 7 hours in technology-related areas. *Faculty*: 3, 1, 1. *Graduates*: 8m, 10w, including 6 foreign nationals.

University of Missouri—Columbia. College of Education, Columbia, MO 65211. John F. Wedman, Asst. Prof., Coord., Educational Technology Program, Curriculum and Instruction Dept., College of Education. *Program Basis*: Semester. *Minimum Degree Requirements*: 30 credit hours including 16 hours of upper level graduate work, educational technology core (12 hours including internship or equivalent), and one course in educational psychology or educational foundations. *Faculty*: 2, 0, 0. *Graduates*: 2m, 3w, including 1 foreign national.

*School also offers a six-year specialist degree program in instructional technology. Program consists of 30 semester hours beyond the master's degree level and includes 15 hours of upper level graduate work, a research course, a statistics course, and 12 hours of educational technology involving internship or equivalent (new program). *Graduates*: Data not available.

University of Missouri—St. Louis. School of Education, St. Louis, MO 63121. Donald R. Greer, Assoc. Prof., Coord. of Educational Technology, Dept. of Educational Studies, School of Education. *Program Basis*: Semester. *Minimum Degree Requirements*: 32 credit hours including 18 in media. *Faculty*: 1, 1, 2/3. *Graduates*: 3m, 2w, including 1 foreign national.

Webster University. Instructional Technology, St. Louis, MO 63119. Paul Steinmann, Assoc. Dean and Dir., Graduate Studies and Instructional Technology. *Program Basis*: Semester. *Minimum Degree Requirements*: 33 credit hours including 24 in media; internship required. *Faculty*: 3, 1, 0. *Graduates*: 3m, 9w, including 2 foreign nationals.

MONTANA

University of Montana. School of Education, Missoula, MT 59812. Geneva Van Horne, Prof. of Library/Media, School of Education. *Program Basis*: Quarter. *Minimum Degree Requirements*: 54 credit hours including 32 in media; thesis optional. *Faculty:* 2, 1, 0. *Graduates:* 4m, 11w.
   *School also has an endorsement program in addition to the master's program.

NEBRASKA

Kearney State College. Department of Educational Administration, Kearney, NE 68849. Daniel W. McPherson, Assoc. Prof., Supervisor of Educational Media, Dept. of Educational Administration. *Program Basis*: Semester. *Minimum Degee Requirements*: 36 credit hours including 15 in media; thesis optional. Since this is a cooperative program, Kansas State University provides the 15 hours required for media and computer course work, and the supporting faculty. *Graduates*: 4 (relatively new program).

University of Nebraska—Lincoln. Instructional Technology, Teachers College, Lincoln NE 68588. David W. Brooks, Prof., Coord., Instructional Technology Dept., Teachers College. *Program Basis*: Semester. *Minimum Degree Requirements*: 36 credit hours including 24 in media; thesis optional. *Faculty*: 1, 1.5, 0. *Graduates*: 1m, 2w.

University of Nebraska—Omaha. Omaha, NE 68182. Verne Haselwood, Prof., Educational Media Program in Teacher Education. *Program Basis*: Semester. *Minimum Degree Requirements*: 36 credit hours including 27 in media; thesis optional. *Faculty*: 2, 0, 3. *Graduates*: 3m, 14w.

NEVADA

University of Nevada—Reno. College of Education, Reno, NV 89557. George R. McMeen, Assoc. Prof., Dir. of the Learning and Resource Center, Curriculum and Instruction Dept., College of Education. *Program Basis*: Semester. *Minimum Degree Requirements*: 36 credit hours including 16 or more in (a) computer education—media or (b) library—media; thesis optional. *Faculty*: 22, 15, 7. Graduates: 0m, 2w.
   *School also offers a six-year specialist degree program in curriculum and instruction with an emphasis in (a) or (b) above. *Graduates*: Data not available.

NEW JERSEY

Glassboro State College. School and Public Librarianship, Glassboro, NJ 08028. Rinehart S. Potts, Graduate Advisor and Program Coord. for School and Public Librarianship. *Program Basis*: Semester. *Minimum Degree Requirements*: 39 credit hours including required thesis project. *Faculty*: 1, 4, 0. *Graduates*: 3m, 9w, including 1 foreign national.

Jersey City State College. Division of Administration, Curriculum and Instruction, Jersey City, NJ 07305. Mildred Goodwin, Prof., Chair., Div. of Administration, Curriculum and Instruction. *Program Basis*: Semester. *Minimum Degree Requirements*: 45 credit hours including 36 in media; thesis optional. *Faculty*: 7, 5, 2. *Graduates*: 4m, 4w, including 1 foreign national.

Montclair State College. Department of Reading and Educational Media, Upper Montclair, NJ 07043. Robert R. Ruezinsky, Dir. of Media and Technology. *Program Basis*: Semester. No degree program exists. Two certification programs, AMS and EMS, exist on the graduate level. *Faculty*: includes 5 administrators and 1 adj., teaching on an overload basis.

*School also offers Associate Media Specialist and Educational Media Certificate programs for state level certification: 18-21 credit hours of media and technology are required for the AMS program and 30-33 hours for the EMS program.

Rutgers—The State University of New Jersey. School of Communication, Information and Library Studies, New Brunswick, NJ 08903. Betty J. Turock, Acting Chairperson, Dept. of Library and Information Studies, School of Communication, Information and Library Studies. *Program Basis*: Semester. *Minimum Degree Requirements*: 36 credit hours in which the hours for media vary for individual students. *Faculty*: 17. *Graduates*: 23m, 112w, including 14 foreign nationals.

*School also offers a six-year specialist certificate program. This 24 credit-hour program must be completed within a three-year period. Some courses may be taken in the library/information, an advanced curriculum that includes one or more doctoral seminars and a project culminating in a thesis, survey, film, etc. Other courses may be taken in related fields. Admission criteria include a master's degree; at least a B average and distinction in proposed area of advanced study; a minimum of two years of successful demonstrated experience; a description of applicant's area of interest; a proposed independent study project; and two letters of recommendation. *Graduates*: Data not available.

Saint Peter's College. Computer Education, Jersey City, NJ 07306. Henry F. Harty, Dir., Graduate Prog. in Computer Education. *Program Basis*: Semester. *Minimum Degree Requirements*: 39 credit hours including 27 in computers. *Faculty*: 9, 0, 0. *Graduates:* 12m, 33w.

Seton Hall University. Division of Educational Media, College of Education and Human Services, South Orange, NJ 07079. Rosemary W. Skeele, Asst. Prof., Dir., Graduate Prog. in Educational Media, Div. of Educational Media, College of Education and Human Services. *Program Basis*: Semester. *Minimum Degree Requirements*: 36 credit hours including 24 in media; mediated project instead of thesis. *Faculty*: 3, 1, 0. *Graduates*: 11m, 6w.

*School also offers an educational specialist certificate—36 credits may lead to state certification as media specialist.

William Paterson College. School of Education, Wayne, NJ 07470. Amy Job, Librarian, Assoc. Prof., Coord., Prog. in Library/Media, Curriculum and Instruction Dept. *Program Basis*: Semester. *Minimum Degree Requirements*: 30 credit hours in media including research. *Faculty*: 1, 0, 0. *Graduates*: 4w.

NEW MEXICO

University of New Mexico. College of Education, Albuquerque, NM 87131. Dr. Frank Field, Chair or Guy A. Watson, Assoc. Prof., Technological and Occupational Education, College of Education. *Program Basis*: Semester. *Minimum Degree Requirements*: Master's: 36 credit hours in Learning Technologies; Ed.D., 72 hours minimum; Ph.D., 78 hours. *Faculty*: 11, 0, 3. *Graduates*: 18m, 22w.

NEW YORK

Fordham University. Communications Department, Bronx, NY 10458. James A. Capo, Assoc. Prof., Chair., Director of Graduate Studies, Communications Dept. *Program Basis*: Semester. *Minimum Degree Requirements*: 30 credit hours; internship or thesis required. *Faculty*: 9. *Graduates*: 4m, 5w, including 1 foreign national.

Ithaca College. School of Communications, Ithaca, NY 14850. Diane M. Gayeski, Assoc. Prof., Chair, Graduate Corporate Communications, School of Communications. *Program Basis*: Semester. *Minimum Degree Requirements*: 36 credit hours including 30 in communications; thesis optional. *Faculty*: 8, 0, 0. *Graduates*: 3m, 13w.

The New School for Social Research. Media Studies Program, New York, NY 10011. Peter L. Haratonik, Dir., Media Studies Program. *Program Basis*: Semester. *Minimum Degree Requirements*: 36 credit hours in media; thesis encouraged. *Faculty*: 6, 1, 2. *Graduates*: 44m, 63w, including 18 foreign nationals.

New York Institute of Technology. Graduate Communication Arts, Old Westbury, NY 11568 (also in NYC). Adrienne O'Brien, Dean, School of Media and Arts. *Program Basis*: Semester. *Minimum Degree Requirements*: 32/34 credit hours with one specialization in television, film, electronic journalism, advertising/public relations, computer graphics, studio arts or media generalist; thesis optional. *Faculty*: 18, 0, 21. *Graduates*: 41m, 48w, including 15 foreign nationals.

New York Institute of Technology. Graduate Programs in Training and Learning Technology, School of Media and Arts, Old Westbury, NY 11568 (also in NYC). Dr. Angus Reynolds, School of Media and Arts. *Program Basis*: Semester. *Minimum Degree Requirements*: 37 credits with a specialization in management of training, computer applications, or instructional media; required thesis project in an instructional system. *Faculty*: 4, 0, 2. *Graduates*: 8m, 8w, including 4 foreign nationals.

New York University. School of Education, Health, Nursing and Arts Professions. New York, NY 10003. Donald T. Payne, Assoc. Prof. and Dir., Program in Educational Communication and Technology, School of Education, Health, Nursing and Arts Professions. *Program Basis:* Semester. *Minimum Degree Requirements*: 36 credit hours including 24 in media; terminal experience required; thesis optional. *Faculty*: 2, 0, 6. *Graduates*: 3m, 7w, including 3 foreign nationals.

*School also offers an 18-credit-hour certificate and a 30-credit-hour, six-year specialist program in educational communication and technology. Specializations for the six-year program are located in the school's doctoral program description. Admissions requirements include a master's degree with a 3.0 cumulative average. Students work closely with master's and doctoral program students who are in the same courses. *Faculty*: 2, 0, 6. *Graduates*: 0.

New York University—Tisch School of the Arts. Interactive Telecommunications Program, 721 Broadway, New York, NY 10003. Red Burns, Prof., Chair., The Interactive Telecommunications Program/Institute of Film and Television. *Program Basis*: Semester. *Minimum Degree Requirements*: 60 credit hours (15 courses at 4 credit hours each; program is two years for full-time students) including 5 required courses and thesis. *Faculty*: 3, 1, 4. *Graduates*: 20m, 20w, including 2 foreign nationals.

Queens College. City University of New York, Flushing, NY 11367-0904. Ray Cafolla. Asst. Prof., Post-Master Certificate Program in Educational and Learning Technology. *Program Basis:* Semester (1-year program, beginning each Aug.). *Minimum Degree Requirements*: 18 hours in Educational and Learning Technology. *Faculty*: 2, 2, 0. *Graduates*: 2 (new program).

Rochester Institute of Technology. Information Technology, Rochester, NY 14623-0887. Clint Wallington, Prof., Dir. of the Dept. of Information Technology, College of Applied Science and Technology. *Program Basis:* Quarter. *Minimum Degree Requirements:* 48 credit hours including an instructional development project (noncredit). *Faculty*: 4, 3, 1. *Graduates:* 8m, 11w.

St. John's University. Library and Information Science, Jamaica, NY 11439. Emmett Corry, Assoc. Prof., Dir., Div. of Library and Information Science. *Program Basis*: Semester. *Minimum Degree Requirements:* 36 credit hours including 21 in media; no thesis required. *Faculty:* 7, 3, 3. *Graduates:* 4m, 21w, including 4 foreign nationals.

*School also offers a six-year specialist program, which is a 24-credit-hour, advanced certificate program that can be tailored to the student's individual needs. *Graduates:* Data not available.

State University College of Arts and Science. School of Professional Studies, Potsdam, NY 13676. Norman Licht, Prof., Coord. Instructional Technology and Media Management, Center for Mathematics, Science and Technology, School of Professional Studies. *Program Basis:* Semester. *Minimum Degree Requirements:* 33 credit hours including emphasis in instructional technology, media, and computer education; thesis optional. *Faculty:* 6, 6, 0. *Graduates:* 8m, 13w, including 6 foreign nationals.

State University of New York at Albany. Department of Program Development and Evaluation, Albany, NY 12222. Joseph Bosco, Prof., Acting Chair, Coord. of Instructional Design and Technology Program, Dept. of Program Development and Evaluation. *Program Basis:* Semester. *Minimum Degree Requirements:* 30 credit hours including 15 in instructional design and technology; thesis optional. *Faculty:* 2, 3, 0. *Graduates:* 6m, 3w, including 2 foreign nationals.

State University of New York at Buffalo. Graduate School of Education, Buffalo, NY 14260. Taher Razik, Prof., Instructional Design and Management, Dept. of Education, Organization, and Policy, Faculty of Educational Studies. *Program Basis:* Semester. *Minimum Degree Requirements:* 33 credit hours including 21 hours in instructional design and management; thesis or project required; comprehensive examination. *Faculty:* 3, 0, 3. *Graduates:* 1m, 2w, including 1 foreign national.
   *School also offers a certificate program in instructional technology.

State University of New York at Buffalo. School of Information and Library Studies, Buffalo, NY 14260. George S. Bobinski, Dean, School of Information and Library Studies. *Program Basis:* Semester. *Minimum Degree Requirements:* 36 credit hours including 15 in media; thesis optional. *Faculty:* 9, 6, 0. *Graduates:* 22m, 71w, including 6 foreign nationals.
   *School also offers a sixth-year 30-credit-hour certificate program in instructional technology. *Graduates:* Data not available.

State University of New York at Stony Brook. College of Engineering and Applied Sciences, Stony Brook, NY 11794-2250. Thomas T. Liao, Prof., Chair, Dept. of Technology and Society, College of Engineering and Applied Sciences. *Program Basis:* Semester. *Minimum Degree Requirements:* 30 credit hours with emphasis in technological systems, industrial, management, educational computing, and environmental and waste management. *Faculty:* 8, 0, 0. *Graduates:* 29m, 21w, including 10 foreign nationals.

Syracuse University. School of Education, Syracuse, NY 13244-2340. Donald P. Ely, Prof., Chair, Instructional Design, Development and Evaluation Prog., School of Education, *Program Basis:* Semester. *Minimum Degree Requirements:* 30 credit hours. *Faculty:* 6, 1, 1. *Graduates:* 6m, 7w, including 4 foreign nationals.

Teachers College, Columbia University. Program in Communication, New York, NY 10027. John B. Black, Prof., Chair, Dept. of Communication, Computing and Technology in Education. *Program Basis:* Semester. *Minimum Degree Requirements:* M.A., 32 credit hours including 18 in media, core courses in communication and computing, thesis optional; M.A. media specialist (certification), 36 credit hours, core in School of Library Service, internship, research paper. *Faculty:* 5, 2, 1. *Graduates:* 3m, 7w, including 3 foreign nationals.

NORTH CAROLINA

Appalachian State University. Department of Library Science and Educational Foundations. Boone, NC 28608. John H. Tashner, Prof., Coord., Department of Library Science and Educational Foundations, College of Education. *Program Basis:* Semester. *Minimum Degree Requirements:* 36 credit hours including 15 in computer education; thesis optional. *Faculty:* 2, 0, 0. *Graduates:* 1 (relatively new program).

Appalachian State University. College of Education, Boone, NC 28608. Ken McEwin, Prof., Coord., Dept. of Curriculum and Instruction, Library/Media Studies, College of Education. *Program Basis:* Semester. *Minimum Degree Requirements:* 42 credit hours including selected sources in media; thesis optional. *Faculty:* 6, 0, 0. *Graduates:* 8m, 17w.

East Carolina University. Department of Library and Information Studies, Greenville, NC 27858. Lawrence Auld, Assoc. Prof., Chair., Dept. of Library and Information Studies. *Program Basis*: Semester. *Minimum Degree Requirements*: 44 credit hours in library service and media. *Faculty*: 10, 7, 0. *Graduates*: 1m, 7w.

North Carolina Central University. Department of Education, Durham, NC 27707. Marvin E. Duncan, Prof., Dir., Learning Resources Center, School of Education. *Program Basis*: Semester. *Minimum Degree Requirements*: 33 credit hours including 21 in media; thesis or project required. *Faculty*: 4, 1, 0. *Graduates*: 6m, 8w, including 4 foreign nationals.

University of North Carolina. School of Education, Chapel Hill, NC 27514. Ralph E. Wileman, Prof., Chair., Educational Media and Instructional Design, School of Education. *Program Basis*: Semester. *Minimum Degree Requirements*: 36 credit hours including 21 in media and comprehensive examination. *Faculty*: 2.5, 0, 0. *Graduates*: 2m, 12w.

Western Carolina University. Department of Administration, Curriculum and Instruction, Cullowhee, NC 28723. John W. McFadden, Prof., Coord., Dept. of Administration, Curriculum and Instruction. *Program Basis:* Semester. *Minimum Degree Requirements*: 30 credit hours including 18 in media. *Faculty*: 5, 4, 0. *Graduates*: 1m, 5w, including 1 foreign national. (Program continues to remain on an inactive status.)

OHIO

Kent State University. Instructional Technology Program, White Hall 405, KSU, Kent, OH 44242. (216) 672-2294. Dr. Drew Tiene, Prog. Coodinator. *Program Basis*: Semester. Tuition per credit: $117 in-state, $209 out-of-state. Summer: Two 5-week sessions. *Minimum Degree Requirements*: 34 credit hours including 14-20 hours of instructional technology coursework, depending upon certification sought. *Faculty*: 4. *Graduates*: approx. 10-15 per year.

Miami University. School of Education and Allied Professions, Oxford, OH 45056. Joe Waggener, Assoc. Prof., Coord., Instructional Technology Program, School of Education and Allied Professions. *Program Basis:* Semester. *Minimum Degree Requirements*: 30 credit hours; thesis optional. *Faculty*: 5, 4, 1. *Graduates*: Data not available.

Ohio State University. College of Education, Columbus, OH 43210. Marjorie Cambre, Assoc. Prof., Prog. contact person, Instructional Design and Technology, College of Education. *Program Basis*: Quarter. *Minimum Degree Requirements*: M.A. degree 50 credit hours including an individualized number of hours in media; thesis optional. *Faculty*: 8, *Graduates*: 4m, 12w.
   *School media certification is available.

Ohio University. College of Education, Athens, OH 45701. Seldon D. Strother, Assoc. Prof., Dir. of Educational Media, College of Education. *Program Basis:* Quarter. *Minimum Degree Requirements*: 52 credit hours including 26 in media; thesis optional. *Faculty*: 4, 2, 0. *Graduates*: 1w.

University of Toledo. Department of Educational Technology, Toledo, OH 43606. Amos C. Patterson, Prof., Group Leader, Dept. of Educational Technology. *Program Basis*: Quarter. *Minimum Degree Requirements*: 48 credit hours including 36 in media; master's project. *Faculty*: 6, 5, 1. *Graduates*: 16m, 14w, including 6 foreign nationals.
   Master's Program: Library/Media, Human Resources Development, Educational Computing. Annette Lamb, Asst. Professor. *Faculty*: 6, 5, 1. *Doctoral Program*: Educational Technology:

Graduates: 3m, 2w. School also offers a six-year specialist degree program in educational technology. *Program Basis*: Quarter. *Minimum Degree Requirements*: 45 credit hours including 5-credit-hour supervised internship. *Faculty*: 6, 5, 1. *Graduates*: 1m, 4w.

Wright State University. 244 Millett Hall, Dayton, OH 45435. Bonnie Mathies, Assoc. Prof., Chair., Department of Educational Technology and Vocational Education, College of Education and Human Services. *Program Basis:* Quarter. *Minimum Degree Requirements*: 48 credit hours; thesis optional. *Faculty*: 4. *Graduates*: 2m, 13w.

Xavier University. Department of Education, Cincinnati, OH 45207. John Pohlman, Asst. Prof., Dir., Graduate Programs in Educational Media, Dept. of Education. *Program Basis*: Semester. *Minimum Degree Requirements*: 30 credit hours including 18 in media; nonthesis but field practicum required. *Faculty*: 2, 1, 0. *Graduates*: 1m, 15w.

OKLAHOMA

Central State University. College of Education, Edmond, OK 73034-0193. Frances Alsworth, Assoc. Prof., Library Media Education, Dept. of Curriculum and Instruction, College of Education. *Program Basis*: Semester. *Minimum Degree Requirements*: 32 credit hours including 17 in media. *Faculty:* 2, 0, 1. *Graduates*: 4w.

Oklahoma State University. Curriculum and Instruction Department, Stillwater, OK 74078. Douglas B. Aichele, Prof., Head, Curriculum and Instruction Dept. *Program Basis:* Semester. *Minimum Degree Requirements:* 30 credit hours including 18 in media; thesis optional. *Faculty*: 3, 3 Teaching Assistants. *Graduates*: 4m, 4w.

Southwestern State University. School of Education, Weatherford, OK 73096. Lessley Price, Asst. Prof., Coord. of Library/Media Prog., School of Education. *Program Basis*: Semester. *Minimum Degree Requirements*: 32 credit hours including 24 in media; thesis optional. *Faculty*: 2, 2, 0. *Graduates*: 18w.

University of Oklahoma. Educational Technology, Norman, OK 73019. Tillman J. Ragan Prof., Area Head, Educational Technology Prog. Area, Dept. of Educational Psychology. *Program Basis*: Semester. *Minimum Degree Requirements*: 32 credit hours including 21 in educational technology; no thesis required. *Faculty*: 3, 3, 4. *Graduates*: 1m, 7w.

OREGON

Portland State University. School of Education, P.O. Box 751, Portland, OR 97207. Joyce Petrie, Prof., Coord., Educational Media, School of Education. *Program Basis*: Quarter. *Minimum Degree Requirements:* 45 credit hours including 42 in media; thesis optional. *Faculty*: 6, 2, 4. *Graduates*: 14m, 23w.

University of Oregon. Division of Teacher Education, 1787 Agate St., Eugene, OR 97403. Gary W. Ferrington, Program Head. Master's Degree: Curriculum and Instruction with a specialization in Instructional Systems Technology. *Program Basis*: Quarter. *Minimum Degree Requirements*: 45-48 credit hours including 30 in instructional technology or computers-in-education; thesis, synthesis paper, or field study. *Faculty:* 1 full-time, 5 part-time. *Graduates:* 4m, 3w, including 2 foreign nationals.

Western Oregon State College. Department of Secondary Education, Monmouth, OR 97361. Richard C. Forcier, Prof., Dir., Div. of Information Technology, Dept. of Secondary Education. *Program Basis:* Quarter. *Minimum Degree Requirements*: 45 credit hours including 36 in media; thesis optional. *Faculty*: 4, 3, 1. *Graduates*: 4m, 9w, including 2 foreign nationals.

PENNSYLVANIA

Clarion University of Pennsylvania. Department of Communication, Clarion, PA 16214. William Lloyd, Asst. Prof., Chair., Dept. of Communication. *Program Basis*: Semester. *Minimum Degree Requirements*: 36 credit hours including 27 in media; nonthesis but interactive video, research design and research study required. *Faculty*: 11, 6, 0. *Graduates*: 16m, 14w, including 4 foreign nationals.

Drexel University. College of Information Studies, Philadelphia, PA 19104. Richard H. Lytle, Prof. and Dean, College of Information Studies. *Program Basis*: Quarter. *Minimum Degree Requirements:* M.S. degree program of 48 credit hours comprised primarily of five functional groupings: organization and retrieval information; information technology; resources and their use; information services; and management and evaluation; nonthesis. *Faculty*: 15, 5, 0. *Graduates*: 56w, including 2 foreign nationals.

Indiana University of Pennsylvania. Department of Communications, Indiana, PA 15701. Kurt P. Dudt, Assoc. Prof., Chair., Dept. of Communications Media. *Program Basis*: Semester. *Minimum Degree Requirements*: 36 credit hours including 21 in media; thesis optional. *Faculty:* 11, 2, 0. *Graduates*: 12m, 9w, including 10 foreign nationals.

Lehigh University. Lehigh University School of Education, Bethlehem, PA 18105. Leroy J. Tuscher, Prof., Dir., Educational Technology Center, Lehigh University School of Education. *Program Basis*: Semester. *Minimum Degree Requirements*: 30 credit hours including 15 in media; thesis optional. *Faculty*: 4, 2, 3. *Graduates*: 5m, 9w, including 3 foreign nationals.

Pennsylvania State University. Division of Curriculum and Instruction, University Park, PA 16802. Paul W. Welliver, Prof., contact person, Instructional Systems Prog., Div. of Curriculum and Instruction. *Program Basis:* Semester. *Minimum Degree Requirements*: 30 credit hours including either a thesis or project paper. *Faculty*: 5, 0, 0. *Graduates*: 4m, 4w, including 2 foreign nationals.

Shippensburg University. Department of Communications and Journalism, Shippensburg, PA 17257. Dr. Pat Wallermeyer, Assist. Prof., Dept. of Communications and Journalism, College of Arts and Sciences. *Program Basis*: Semester. *Minimum Degree Requirements*: 30 credit hours in media/communications studies; thesis optional. *Faculty*: 7, 0, 0. *Graduates*: 6m, 7w, including 2 foreign nationals. (Program stresses mass communications.)

Temple University. Educational Media Department, Philadelphia, PA 19122. Elton Robertson, Prof., Chair., Educational Media Program. *Program Basis*: Semester. *Minimum Degree Requirements*: 33 credit hours including 24 in media; thesis optional. *Faculty*: 2, 2, 5. *Graduates*: 9m, 7w, including 1 foreign national.

University of Pittsburgh. Instructional Design and Technology, School of Education, Pittsburgh, PA 15260. Barbara Seels, Assoc. Prof., Prog. Coord., Instructional Design and Technology, Dept. of Instruction and Learning, School of Education. *Program Basis:* Trimester. *Minimum Degree Requirements:* 36 credit hours including 18 in instructional technology, 9 in core courses, and 9 in electives; comprehensive examination. *Faculty*: 3, 0, 0. *Graduates*: 3m, 2w, including 9 foreign nationals.
*School also offers a six-year specialist certification program. This instructional design and technology program offers a sequence of courses leading to Pennsylvania state certification as an instructional technologist. This option provides for study of media design and production, design of in-service programs, application of instructional technology to the curriculum, curriculum development, group processes, leadership skills, selection and utilization of materials with consideration for a multicultural society, evaluation strategies, and administration of media programs. The certification program can be taken concurrently with a master's degree sequence. *Graduates*: Data not available.

West Chester University. School of Education, West Chester, PA 19380. Joseph Spiecker, Prof., Chair., Instructional Media Dept., School of Education. *Program Basis*: Semester. *Minimum Degree Requirements*: 34 credit hours including 28 in media; thesis optional. *Faculty*: 5, 1, 1. *Graduates*: 5m, 4w, including 1 foreign national.

RHODE ISLAND

Rhode Island College. Department of Leadership Foundations and Technology, Providence, RI 02908. James E. Davis, Assoc. Prof., Chair., Dept. of Leadership Foundations and Technology. *Program Basis*: Semester. *Minimum Degree Requirements*: 30 credit hours including 21 in media; thesis optional. *Faculty*: 3, 2, 0. *Graduates*: 6m, 3w.

The University of Rhode Island. Graduate School of Library and Information Studies, College of Arts and Sciences, Kingston, RI 02881-0815. Elizabeth Futas, Prof., Dir., Graduate School of Library and Information Studies. *Program Basis*: Semester. *Minimum Degree Requirements*: 36 credit hours including specializations in areas such as media programs (in academic, school, or special libraries), information science, cataloging and reference, and bibliography. *Faculty:* 8, 12, 3. *Graduates*: 7m, 41w.

SOUTH CAROLINA

University of South Carolina. Educational Psychology Department, Columbia, SC 29208. J. C. Rotter, Prof., Chair., Educational Psychology Dept. *Program Basis*: Semester. *Minimum Degree Requirements*: 33 credit hours including 3 each in administration, curriculum, and research, 9 in production, and 3 in instructional theory; no thesis required. *Faculty*: 3, 1, 2. *Graduates*: 1m, 3w, including 1 foreign national.

Winthrop College. School of Education, Rock Hill, SC 29733. George Robinson, Assoc. Prof., Educational Media Coord., School of Education. *Program Basis:* Semester. *Minimum Degree Requirements*: 36-42 credit hours including 15-33 in media depending on media courses a student has had prior to this program; nonthesis. *Faculty*: 2, 0, 2. *Graduates*: 2m, 15w.

TENNESEE

East Tennessee State University. College of Education, Johnson City, TN 37614-0002. Rudy Miller, Assoc. Prof. of Instructional Communication, College of Education. *Program Basis*: Semester. *Minimum Degree Requirements:* 36 credit hours including 18 in instructional technology; thesis optional. *Faculty*: 1, 1, 3. *Graduates*: 6w, including 1 foreign national.

Memphis State University. College of Education, Memphis, TN 38152. Thomas A. Rakes, Prof., Chair., Dept. of Curriculum and Instruction, College of Education. *Program Basis*: Semester. *Minimum Degree Requirements*: 33 credit hours including 15 in instructional design and technology; thesis optional. *Faculty*: 2, 1, 0. *Graduates*: 3m, 12w.

*School also offers a six-year specialist degree program in instructional technology. Program comprised of 66 credit hours including 36 in major, 3 hours in educational research, 21 hours of supportive collateral, and two years teaching experience or equivalent. *Graduates*: Data not available.

Middle Tennessee State University. Department of Youth Education and School Personnel Services, Murfreesboro, TN 37132. Ralph L. White, Prof. and Chair., Dept. of Youth Education and School Personnel Services. *Program Basis*: Semester. *Minimum Degree Requirements*: 33 credit hours including 15 in media; no thesis required. *Faculty*: 2, 1, 0. Graduates: 7m, 23w.

University of Tennessee. College of Education, Knoxville, TN 37906-3400. Alfred D. Grant, Assoc. Prof., Coord. of Academic Media and Technology Program, Dept. of Curriculum and

Instruction, College of Education. *Program Basis:* Semester. *Minimum Degree Requirements:* 33 credit hours including individualized number of media hours; thesis optional. *Faculty:* 2, 2, 2. *Graduates*: 2m, 2w, including 1 foreign national.

*School also offers a six-year specialist degree program under the School of Education's Dept. of Curriculum and Instruction. Major emphasis of program is in instructional technology. This new program consists of 26 credit hours of courses plus a seminar research paper or a non-research paper.

TEXAS

East Texas State University. Dept. of Secondary and Higher Education, Commerce, TX 75428. Robert S. Munday, Prof., Head, Dept. of Secondary and Higher Education. *Program Basis*: Semester. *Minimum Degree Requirements:* 30 credit hours with thesis; 36 nonthesis including 18 in media. *Faculty:* 7, 3, 1. *Graduates:* 8m, 19w, including 12 foreign nationals.

North Texas State University. College of Education, Denton, TX 76203-3857. J. L. Poirot, Prof., Prog. Coord., Computer Education and Cognitive Systems, College of Education. *Program Basis:* Semester. *Minimum Degree Requirements*: 36 hours including 27 hours in instructional technology and computer education; nonthesis. *Faculty*: 7, 1, 0. *Graduates*: 5m, 8w, including 10 foreign nationals.

Prairie View A&M University. Department of School Services, Prairie View, TX 77446. Marion Henry, Prof., Dir., Educational Media and Technology Program. *Program Basis*: Semester. *Minimum Degree Requirements:* 36 credit hours, 21 in media; no thesis required. *Faculty:* 6, 2, 0. *Graduates:* 6w.

Texas A&M University. College of Education, College Station, TX 77843. Ronald D. Zellner, Assoc. Prof., Coord., Educational Technology Prog., College of Education. *Program Basis*: Semester. *Minimum Degree Requirements*: 37 credit hours including 19 in educational technology; nonthesis. *Faculty*: 6, 5, 1. *Graduates*: 5m, 6w, including 4 foreign nationals.

Texas Tech University. College of Education, Box 4560, Lubbock, TX 79409. Robert Price, Assoc. Prof., Dir., Instructional Technology Program, College of Education. *Program Basis:* Semester. *Minimum Degree Requirements*: 39 credit hours; nonthesis. *Faculty*: 3, 3, 0. *Graduates*: 9m, 8w, including 2 foreign nationals.

University of Texas. College of Education, Austin, TX 78712. De Layne Hudspeth, Assoc. Prof., Coord., Area of Instructional Technology, Dept. of Curriculum and Instruction, College of Education. *Program Basis*: Semester. *Minimum Degree Requirements:* 36 credit hours including 18 in instructional technology plus research course; thesis optional. A six-hour minor is required outside the department. *Faculty:* 6, 0, 0. *Graduates:* 12w, including 4 foreign nationals.

The University of Texas Southwestern Medical Center at Dallas. Biomedical Communications Department, Dallas, TX 75235. Mike Sheridan, Chair., Instructional Development Progs., Biomedical Communications Dept. *Program Basis*: Semester. *Minimum Degree Requirements*: 36 credit hours including 24 in media; thesis required. *Faculty*: 7, 5, 1. *Graduates*: 9m, 18w, including 3 foreign nationals.

UTAH

Brigham Young University. Instructional Science Department, Provo, UT 84602. Paul F. Merrill, Prof., Chair. *Program Basis:* Semester. *Minimum Degree Requirements*: 36 credit hours including 13 in core; thesis required. *Faculty:* 11, 0, 0. *Graduates*: 2m, 3w.

Utah State University. Department of Instructional Technology, Logan, UT 84322-2830. Don C. Smellie, Prof., Head, Department of Instructional Technology. *Program Basis*: Quarter. *Minimum*

Degree Requirements: 60 credit hours including 45 in media; thesis or practicum encouraged. Programs in school library media administration and master resource teacher/educational technology are also delivered via an electronic distance education system. *Faculty:* 8, 7, 1. *Graduates*: 17m, 15w, including 1 foreign national.

*School also offers a six-year specialist degree program in instructional technology. Program prepares individuals in the design, development, and evaluation of learning programs and materials for use in education, industry, and government. Admission requires 3.2 GPA, 900 GRE, or 46 MAT, master's degree, three letters of recommendation, and individual's written statement of goals and philosophy. Program includes minimum of 45 quarter hours emphasizing research, core, electives plus either a developmental practicum project or practicum internship. Graduates: 1w.

VIRGINIA

James Madison University. Dept. of Educational Resources, Harrisonburg, VA 22807. Alvin Pettus, Head, Dept. of Educational Resources. *Program Basis*: Semester. *Minimum Degree Requirements*: 33 credit hours including 21 in media; thesis optional. *Faculty*: 2, 2, 1. *Graduates:* 4w.

Radford University. Educational Media, Radford, VA 24142. Gary Ellerman, Prof., Academic Advisor, Educational Media, Human Services. *Program Basis:* Semester. *Minimum Degree Requirements:* 30 credit hours including 26 in media; thesis optional. *Faculty*: 3, 1, 0. *Graduates*: 3m, 4w.

University of Virginia. Curry School of Education, Charlottesville, VA 22903. John Bunch, Assoc. Prof., Coord., Instructional Technology Prog., Dept. of Educational Studies, Curry School of Education. *Program Basis:* Semester. *Minimum Degree Requirements*: 35 credit hours including 18 in media and computers. *Faculty*: 3, 2, 1. *Graduates*: 3m, 2w.

*School also offers a post-master's certificate program in instructional technology. Applicants for the Ed.S. degree must hold a master's degree; have earned a grade point average of B or better; submit an application for admission and official transcripts of all undergraduate and graduate work; be recommended by two persons qualified to judge his or her potential; submit basic aptitude test scores for the GRE; and submit a statement of professional goals. To earn the degree, a minimum of 30 credit hours is required in the student's program area and a written comprehensive exam of 8-10 hours is also required. *Graduates:* Data not available.

Virginia Commonwealth University. Division of Teacher Education, Richmond, VA 23284. Edward Caffarella, Assoc. Prof., Core Coord. of Instructional Technology, Div. of Teacher Education. *Program Basis:* Semester. *Minimum Degree Requirements*: 36 semester hours including 24 in media plus externships; thesis optional. *Faculty*: 2, 0, 1/3. *Graduates*: 6w.

Virginia Polytechnic Institute and State University (Virginia Tech). College of Education, Blacksburg, VA 24061-0313. John K. Burton, Assoc. Prof., Program Area Leader, Instructional Systems Development, Curriculum and Instruction. *Program Basis*: Semester. *Minimum Degree Requirements*: 30 credit hours including 15 in instructional technology; thesis optional. *Faculty*: 9, 0, 0. *Graduates:* 4m.

Virginia State University. School of Education, Petersburg, VA 23803. Vykuntapathi Thota, Coord., Educational Media. *Program Basis*: Semester. *Minimum Degree Requirements*: 30 credit hours plus thesis for master of science; 33 semester hours plus project for the master of education.

WASHINGTON

Eastern Washington University. Schools of Mathematical Science, Cheney, WA 99004. Donald R. Horner, Prof., Computer Science, School of Mathematical Sciences and Technology. *Program Basis*: Quarter. *Minimum Degree Requirements*: 48 credit hours with emphasis in computer science. *Faculty*: 6, 0, 0. *Graduates*: 5m, 5w.

University of Washington. Department of Education, Seattle, WA 98195. William D. Winn, Prof., Prog. in Educational Communication and Technology, School of Education. *Program Basis:* Quarter. *Minimum Degree Requirements:* 45 credit hours including 24 in media; thesis optional. *Faculty:* 2, 3, 0. *Graduates:* 3w, including 1 foreign national.

Western Washington University. School of Education, Bellingham, WA 98225. Tony Jongejan, Assist. Prof., Div. of Educational Technology, Dept. of Educational Administration and Foundations. *Program Basis:* Quarter. *Minimum Degree Requirements:* 45 credit hours including 22 in media; thesis optional. *Faculty:* 3, 3, 8. *Graduates:* 5w.

WEST VIRGINIA

Marshall University. Department of Instructional Technology and Library Science, Huntington, WV 25701. Virginia D. Plumley, Prof., Chair., Dept. of Instructional Technology and Library Science. *Program Basis:* Semester. *Minimum Degree Requirements:* 36 credit hours including 30 in media; thesis optional. *Faculty:* 3, 5, 0. *Graduates:* 5m, 2w, including 2 foreign nationals.

West Virginia University. Morgantown, WV 26506. David McCrory, Prof., Chair., Technology Education Program, Communication and Information Systems, College of Human Resources and Education. *Program Basis:* Semester. *Minimum Degree Requirements:* 36 credit hours including 15 hours in communication technology; thesis optional. *Faculty:* 2, 5, 0. *Graduates:* 3m, 1w, including 1 foreign national.

WISCONSIN

University of Wisconsin—La Crosse. La Crosse, WI 54601. Clyde L. Greve, Dir., Educational Media Program, College of Education. *Program Basis:* Semester. *Minimum Degree Requirements:* 30 credit hours including 15 in media; nonthesis. *Faculty:* 3, 0, 0. *Graduates:* 3m, 9w.

University of Wisconsin—Madison. School of Education, Madison, WI 53706. Ann DeVaney, Prof., Coord., Educational Communications and Technology, Dept. of Curriculum and Instruction, School of Education. *Program Basis:* Semester. *Minimum Degree Requirements:* 30 credit hours including 22 hours in media; thesis or project required. *Faculty:* 5, 3, 2. *Graduates:* 42m, 33w, including 14 foreign nationals.

University of Wisconsin—Oshkosh. Oshkosh, WI 54901. Richard R. Hammes, Prof. Coord., Dept. of Human Services and Professional Leadership, College of Education and Human Services. *Program Basis:* Semester. *Minimum Degree Requirements:* 30 credit hours including 15-21 in library, media, and technology. *Faculty:* 2, 0, 4. Graduates: 6m, 2w.

University of Wisconsin—Stout. Menomonie, WI 54751. David L. Graf, Prof., Program Dir., Media Technology Dept. *Program Basis:* Semester. *Minimum Degree Requirements:* 32 credit hours including 15 in media; thesis optional. *Faculty:* 4, 2, 4. *Graduates:* 5m, 4w, including 5 foreign nationals.

WYOMING

University of Wyoming. College of Education, Laramie, WY 82071. Barbara Hakes, Prof., Head, Instructional Technology, College of Education. *Program Basis:* Semester. *Minimum Degree Requirements:* 36 credit hours including 32 in instructional technology and 4 in thesis option, or 36 hours of coursework including project option. Three tracks are available: (a) Instructional Design, (b) Library/Media Management, and (c) Computer-based Education. *Degree Title:* Master of Science in Instructional Technology. *Faculty:* 6, 0, 0. *Graduates:* 12m, 10w.

Graduate Programs in Educational Computing

Brenda Branyan-Broadbent
Associate Professor
Department of Instructional Technology
Utah State University, Logan

Lois A. Ward
Staff Assistant II
Department of Instructional Technology
Utah State University, Logan

When the directory of graduate programs in educational computing first appeared in the 1986 *EMTY*, there were only fifty programs. This year's listing consists of 82 such programs. The information in this section has been revised and updates the information assembled by Leticia Ekhaml from West Georgia College for *EMTY 1989*. Individuals who are considering graduate study in educational computing should contact the institution of their choice for current information.

Data in this section include institution, degree offered, year the program began, number of full- and part-time faculty, number of students currently enrolled, academic credit information, degree requirements, information on outside funding for the department, availability of summer sessions, tuition, and contact person with phone number.

Appalachian State University. Department of Library Science and Educational Foundations, Boone, NC 28608. Department offers M.A. in Educational Media (Instructional Technology-Computers). Master's started in 1986. In fall 1989, had 2 full-time and 1 part-time faculty. *Selective admissions. Semester credit basis. Minimum Degree Requirements*: 36 hours (usually complete 45+ semester hours); thesis optional; internship required. *Outside funding for the department*: No. *Summer sessions*: 2 five-week terms. *Tuition*: $480 full-time, residents (in-state, 9 hours or more). Dr. John H. Tashner, (704) 262-2243.

Arizona State University. Educational Media and Computers. FMC Payne 146, Tempe, AZ 85287-0111. Department offers M.A. and Ph.D. in Educational Media and Computers. Master's started in 1971 and doctorate started in 1976. In fall 1989, had 9.5 full-time faculty members on the master's and doctoral levels; 25 male and 29 female students on the master's level, and 7 male and 6 female students on the doctoral level. *Semester credit basis. Minimum Degree Requirements*: Master's—33 hours (21 hours in educational media and computers, 9 hours in education, 3 hours outside education); thesis not required; internship required; practicum required. Doctorate—93 hours (24 hours in educational media and computers, 57 hours in education, 12 hours outside education); thesis required; internship required; practicum required. *Outside funding for the department*: yes (various grants). *Summer session*: 10 weeks. *Tuition per credit*: $67 residents (summer and 6 hours or less, $681 for 7 hours or more); $67 nonresidents (summer and 6 hours or less, cost varies for 7-11 hours, $2,742 for 12 hours or more). Dr. Gary Bitter, Coordinator, Educational Media and Computers, (602) 965-7192.

Buffalo State College. 1300 Elmwood Ave., Buffalo, NY 14222-1095. School offers M.S. in Ed. in Educational Computing. Master's started in 1988. In fall 1989, had 0 full-time and 10 part-time faculty members; 22 male and 28 female students. *Semester credit basis. Minimum Degree Requirements*: 33 hours (18 hours in computers, 12-15 hours in education, no hours outside education);

thesis or project required; internship not required; practicum not required. *Outside funding for the department*: no. *Summer session*: three 3-week sessions, two 6-week sessions. *Tuition per credit*: $90 residents; $192 nonresidents. Dr. Thomas C. Kinsey, Coordinator of M.S. in Education in Educational Computing, (716) 878-4732.

Cardinal Stritch College. Department of Educational Computing, 6801 North Yates Road, Milwaukee, WI 53217. Department offers an M.E. in Educational Computing and M.S. in Computer Science Education. Master's program started in 1984. In fall 1989 had 3 full-time and 3 part-time faculty members in the master's program; 56 male and 48 female students. *Semester credit basis. Minimum degree requirements*: Master of Education—30-32 hours (15-21 hours in computer, 6-15 hours in education, no hours outside education); degrees may be completed via coursework option or one of the culminating experiences: thesis, field experience, or software project. Master of Science—30-32 hours (24-26 hours in computer, 3-6 in education, no hours outside education). *Outside funding for the department:* no. *Summer session*: 6 weeks generally; although there are courses which span 1 week, 4 weeks. *Tuition per credit:* $180 on-campus (residents and nonresidents); $150 off-campus (residents and nonresidents). Dr. Jim Kasum, Chair, Department of Educational Computing, (414) 352-5400.

Central Missouri State University. Lovinger 300, Warrensburg, MO 64093. School offers M.S.E. Curriculum and Instruction emphasis Educational Computing. Master's started in 1986. In fall 1989 had 15 full-time and 2 part-time faculty members; 3 male students and 4 female students. *Semester credit basis. Minimum degree requirements*: 32 hours (15 hours in computers, 10 hours in education, 7 hours outside education). *Outside funding for the department*: not specified. *Summer session*: 8-12 weeks. *Tuition per credit hour*: $75 residents; $136 nonresidents. Dr. Max McCulloch, Professor, (816) 429-4235.

Clarke College. Graduate Studies, 1550 Clarke Drive, Dubuque, IA 52001. Clarke offers an M.A. in Education: Computers in Education. Master's started in 1964, this program in 1980. Four regular Clarke faculty and occasional adjunct instructors teach the technology courses in the predominantly summer program. *Students, summer 1989:* 10 male, 15 female. *Minimum Degree Requirements:* 21 s.h. in computer courses, 9 in education, 6 hr. elective. Non-thesis program; internships or practica available but not required. *Outside funding for the program*: no. Summer courses vary in length, spreading over seven weeks. *Summer 1989 tuition:* $150 per semester hour. Dr. Marge Clark, BVM, Ed.D., Director, Graduate Studies, (319) 588-6331.

Concordia College. 7400 Augusta, River Forest, IL 60305-1499. School offers M.A. in Mathematics/Computer Science Education. Master's started in 1987. In fall 1989, had 8 full-time and 3 part-time faculty members. *Students*: 11 male and 19 female. *Minimum Degree Requirements:* 48 quarter hours; no thesis, internship, practicum required. *Outside funding for the department:* none. *Summer session*: 9 weeks. *Tuition per credit*: $148 for all students. Dr. Paul T. Kreiss, Assoc. Dean, Graduate School. (312) 771-8300, ext. 363.

Eastern Michigan University. College of Education, Boone Hall, Ypsilanti, MI 48197. College offers M.A. in Educational Psychology with an Educational Technology area of concentration. Master's started in 1983. In fall 1989 had 5 full-time and 12 part-time faculty members; 55 male and 137 female students. *Semester credit basis. Minumum Degree Requirements:* 30 hours (22 hours in computers, 8 hours in education); thesis not specified; internship not specified; practicum not required. *Outside funding for the department:* no. *Summer session:* 6 weeks. Dr. James T. Bushey, Professor, Department of Teacher Education (313) 487-3260.

Eastern Washington University. Department of Mathematics and Computer Science, Cheney, WA 99004. Department offers M.Ed. in Computer Education (elementary), M. Ed. in Computer Education (secondary), and M.S. in Computer Education (interdisciplinary). Master's started in 1983. In fall 1989 had 5 full-time and 0 part-time faculty; total number of students is about 50, most active in summers only. *Quarter credit basis. Minimum degree requirements:* Master of Science—

52 hours (30 hours in computers, 0 hours in education, 8 hours outside education—not specifically computer science; the hours do not total to 52 because of freedom to choose where Methods of Research is taken, where 12 credits of supporting courses are taken, and where additional electives are taken); thesis not required; (a research project with formal report is required although it need not be a thesis in format); internship not required; practicum not required. Master of Education—48 hours minimum (24 hours in computer science, 16 hours in education, 8 hours outside education). *Outside funding for the department:* no. *Summer session:* 8 weeks. *Tuition per credit:* $59 residents and nonresidents. Dr. Donald R. Horner, Professor of Computer Science, (509) 359-7092.

Edgewood College. Department of Education, 855 Woodrow Street, Madison, WI 53711. Department offers M.A. in Education with emphasis on computer-based education. Master's started in 1987. In fall 1989 had 1 full-time and 4 part-time faculty members; 8 male and 20 female students. *Semester credit basis. Minimum degree requirements:* 36 hours (18 hours in computers, 30 hours in education, 6 hours outside education); thesis not required; internship not required; practicum not required. *Outside funding for the department:* no. *Summer session:* yes (number of weeks not specified). *Tuition per credit:* $215 residents; $215 nonresidents. Dr. Joseph E. Schmiedicke, Chair, Department of Education (608) 257-4861, ext. 2293.

Fitchburg State College. Graduate Program in Educational Technology, 160 Pearl Street, Fitchburg, MA 01420. Program offers M.Ed. in Computers in Education. Master's started in 1983. In fall 1989 had 9 full-time faculty members, 5 part-time faculty (adjunct status); 85 students (about 50 on campus and 35 off campus). *Semester credit basis: Minimum Degree Requirements:* 39 hours (30 hours in educational computers, 9 hours outside education; [electives]); thesis not required; internship not required; practicum not required. *Outside funding for the department*: yes (students pay educational services fees—$15 per lab course—used for purchasing software). *Summer session*: 4 weeks. *Tuition per credit*: $90 credit MA resident; $110 credit non-resident. Lab has been upgraded—(networked) 2 MacPlus, 15 Apple IIg's, 5 Apple IIe's. Dr. Sandy Miller-Jacobs, Chair, Graduate Program, (508) 345-2151, ext. 3308.

Florida Institute of Technology. Computer Education Department, 150 West University Boulevard, Melbourne, FL 32901-6988. Department offers M.S. in Computer Education. Master's started in 1984. In fall 1989 had 5 full-time and 4 part-time faculty members; 10 male and 9 female students on the master's level. *Quarter credit basis. Minimum degree requirements*: 48 hours (18 in computer, 18 in education, 12 outside education); thesis and internship not required; practicum required. *Outside funding for the department*: no. *Summer session*: 8 weeks. *Tuition per credit:* $189 residents; $189 nonresidents. Dr. Robert Fronk, Head of Computer Education Department, (407) 768-8000, ext. 8126.

Fontbonne College. 6800 Wydown Blvd., St. Louis, MO 63105. School offers M.S. in Computer Education. Master's program started in 1986. Thus far 49 have graduated from program, levels K-junior college. Currently 74 students. *Semester credit basis. Minimum degree requirements:* 33 hours (33 hours in computers [some overlap with education, e.g., Educational Psychology and Computers]), 0 hours outside education; thesis not required; internship not required; practicum not required. *Outside funding for the department:* no. *Summer session*: 6 weeks. *Tuition per credit:* $200 per credit hour for residents with 15 percent discount for full-time employees of educational facility; same for nonresidents. Dr. Mary K. Abkemeier, Master of Science in Computer Education, (314) 862-3456, ext. 365.

George Mason University. Center for Interactive Educational Technology, 4400 University Drive, Fairfax, VA 22030. Center offers M.Ed. in Curriculum and Instruction, specialization in Instructional Applications and Microcomputers (I.A.M.), and D.A.Ed. specialization in Instructional Computing. Master's started in 1983 and doctorate in 1984. In fall 1989 had 2 full-time and 2 part-time faculty members on the master's level, and 3 full-time and 2 part-time faculty members on the doctoral level; 10 male and 36 female students on the master's level, and 2 male and 3 female students on the doctoral level. *Semester credit basis. Minimum degree requirements*: Master's school-based computer coordinator—30 hours (12 hours in computers, 18 hours in education, 0 hours outside education); thesis an option; internship an option; practicum an option. Master's computer science educator—30 hours (15 hours in computers [12 of 15 are the "outside education" hours], 15 in education, 12 outside education); thesis an option; internship an option; practicum an option. Doctorate—69 hours beyond Master's, (54 hours in education [12 of these are computer courses], 15 hours outside education); thesis required; internship required; practicum required. *Outside funding for the department*: yes (various grants and contracts, generally federal and state). *Summer session*: yes (three 5-week sessions, one 8-week session). *Tuition per credit*: $95.50 residents; $211.50 nonresidents. Dr. Charles S. White, Center Director and I.A.M. Coordinator, (703) 764-6099.

The George Washington University. 2101 G. Street, Washington, DC 20052. School offers M.A. in Educational Technology Leadership. Master's started in 1988. In fall 1989 had 5 full-time and 0 part-time faculty members; number of students not specified. *Semester credit basis. Minimum degree requirements:* 36 hours (15 hours in computers, 9 hours in education, 12 hours electives inside or outside education); thesis required; internship not required; practicum not required. *Outside funding for the department*: no. *Summer session*: varying length sessions—normally 6-8 weeks. *Tuition per credit:* $358 residents and nonresidents. Mary Louise Ortenzo, Coordinator of Admissions, (202) 994-6160.

Georgia State University. Educational Foundations Department, Atlanta, GA 30303. Department offers M.A. and Ph.D. in Educational Psychology (emphasis option in educational computers). Master's and doctorate started in 1984. In fall 1989 had 2 full-time and 4 part-time faculty members on the master's and doctoral levels; 5 male and 2 female students on the master's level, and 4 male and 7 female students on the doctoral level. *Quarter credit basis. Minimum degree requirements*: Master's—60 hours (25 hours in computers, 35 hours in education); thesis required; internship not required; practicum not required. Doctorate—90 hours (35 hours in computers, 40 hours in education, 15 hours outside education); thesis required; internship not required; practicum not required. *Outside funding for the department*: no. *Summer session*: 6 and 8 weeks. *Tuition per credit:* $22 residents; $74 nonresidents. Dr. Dave O'Neil, Associate Professor, (404) 651-2582

Governors State University. College of Education, University Park, IL 60466. College offers M.A. in Education (with computer education as specialization). Master's started in 1986. In fall 1989 had 3 full-time and 5 part-time faculty members; 25 male and 26 female students. *Semester credit basis. Minimum degree requirements:* 36-39 hours (15 hours in computer, 21-24 hours in education, 0 hours outside education); thesis/project required; internship not required; practicum required. *Outside funding for the department:* no. *Summer session*: 8 weeks. *Tuition per credit*: $70 residents; $210 nonresidents. Dr. David Blood, University Professor, (312) 534-5000, ext. 2354.

Grambling State University. College of Education, Grambling, LA 71245. College offers Ed.D. in Developmental Education with an Instructional Systems and Technology specialization. Doctoral program started in 1986. In fall 1989 had 6-8 full-time and 46 part-time faculty members; exact number of students not specified (40 admitted candidates, 120+ taking classes and applying for admission, mostly female, 40 percent white and 60 percent black). *Semester credit basis. Minimum degree requirements:* 90+ hours (6 hours CAI, 6 hours design, 6 hours educational psychology, 6 hours video, 6 hours theory, 36 hours minimum in education, 0 hours outside education [but encouraged as cognate]) dissertation required; internship required; practicum not required. *Outside funding for the department*: no. *Summer session*: yes (number of weeks 6-10). *Tuition per credit*: residents, 1-3 units, $303; 12 units $637; nonresidents, 1-3 units $303; 12 units, $1,312. Dr. JoAnne Dauzat, Professor/Director of Doctoral Program, (318) 274-2656, and Dr. Ben Lowery, Assistant Professor, (318) 274-2238.

Hampton University. School of Education, Hampton, VA 23668. School offers M.A. in Computer Education. Master's started in 1983. In fall 1989 had 0 full-time and 5 part-time faculty members; 4 male and 15 female students. *Semester credit basis. Minimum degree requirements*: 36 hours (21 hours in computers, 15 in education, 0 hours outside education); thesis not required; internship not required; practicum required. *Outside funding for the department:* no. *Summer session*: 8 weeks. *Tuition per credit*: $115 residents and nonresidents. Dr. Carlton E. Brown, Dean, School of Education, (804) 727-5793.

Harvard University. Graduate School of Education, 111 Longfellow Hall, Cambridge, MA 02138. School offers Ed.M. with a concentration in interactive technology. Master's started in 1983. In fall 1989 had 1 full-time and 4 part-time faculty members; number of students not specified (students do not have to declare a concentration until the beginning of their last semester). *Semester credit basis. Minimum degree requirements*: 32 hours (number of hours in computers, education, and outside education not specified); thesis not required; internship not required; practicum not required. *Outside funding for the department*: not specified. *Summer session*: no. *Tuition per credit*: $1,529/course (4 credit hours) residents and nonresidents. Ms. Carly Moreno, Director of Admissions, (617) 495-3414

Iona College. New Rochelle, NY 10801. College offers M.S. in Educational Computing. Master's started in 1982. In fall 1989 had 5 full-time and 0 part-time faculty members; 50 male and 50 female students. *Trimester credit basis. Minimum degree requirements*: 36 hours ("all hours listed in educational computing"); thesis not required; internship not required; practicum not required. *Outside funding for the department:* no. *Summer session*: two 5-week sessions and 2-week institute. *Tuition per credit:* $240 residents and nonresidents. Dr. Catherine Ricardo, Coordinator and Associate Professor, Computer and Information Sciences, (914) 633-2578.

Iowa State University. College of Education, Ames, IA 50011. College offers Master's and Ph.D. in Curriculum and Instructional Technology with an emphasis in instructional computing. Master's and doctorate started in 1967. In fall 1989 had 4 full-time and 5 part-time faculty members on the master's and doctoral levels; 10 male and 24 female students on the master's level, and 2 male students on the doctoral level. *Semester credit basis. Minimum degree requirements* Master's—30 hours (6 hours in computers, other hours not specified); thesis required; internship not required; practicum not required. Doctorate— 78 hours, thesis required; internship not required; practicum not required. *Summer session*: 4 or 8 weeks. *Tuition per credit*: not specified for residents and nonresidents. Dr. Michael R. Simonson, Associate Professor, (515) 294-5287.

Jacksonville University. Department of Education, 2800 University Boulevard North, Jacksonville, FL 32211. Department offers MAT in Computer Education. Master's program started in 1983. In fall 1989 had 5 full-time and 2 part-time faculty members; 6 male and 4 female students. *Semester credit basis. Minimum degree requirements:* 36 hours (21 hours in computer, 15 hours in education, 0 hours outside education); thesis not required; internship not required; practicum not required; comprehensive exam required. *Outside funding for the department*: no. *Summer session*: 6 weeks. *Tuition per credit:* $210/semester-hour, residents and nonresidents. Dr. Daryle C. May, Director, Teacher Education and MAT Program, (904) 744-3950.

Johns Hopkins University. Div. of Education, Rm. 101 Whitehead Hall, Baltimore, MD 21218. Division offers M.S. in Education, concentration Technology for Educators, and C.A.S.E. in Technology for Educators, and Ed.D. in Human Communication and Its Disorders—Technology and Special Education. Master's started in 1980 and doctorate in 1984. In fall 1989 had 3 full-time and 25 part-time faculty members on the master's and doctoral levels; number of students not specified. *Semester credit basis. Minimum degree requirements*: Master's—33 hours (24 hours in computers, 9 hours in education [computer courses are all education related)]; thesis not required; internship required; practicum required. Specialist's—30 hours (30 hours in computers and education [computer courses are all education related]); thesis not required; internship required; practicum required. Doctorate—99 hours (hours in computers and education vary); thesis required; internship required; practicum required. *Outside funding for the department:* yes (for doctoral program only, sources not specified). *Summer Session:* yes. (number of weeks varies). Special summers only master's degree offered. *Tuition per credit:* $165 residents and nonresidents. Dr. Dianne Tobin, Assistant Professor, (301) 338-8273.

Kansas State University. Educational Technology and Computer Ed., 253 Bluemont Hall, Manhattan, KS 66506. Department offers M.S. in Elementary or Secondary Education with specialization in computer-based education, Ed.D. in computer education, and Ph.D. in computer education. Master's started in 1982; doctorate in 1984. In fall 1989 had 4 full-time and 3 part-time faculty members on the master's level, and 4 full-time and 0 part-time faculty members on the doctoral level; 10 male and 10 female students on the master's level, and 6 male and 3 female students on the doctoral level. *Semester credit basis. Minimum degree requirements:* Master's—30 hours (minimum of 9 in computer education); thesis not required; internship not required; practicum not required (but these are possible). Doctorate—90 hours (minimum of 18 in computer education, 12 hours outside education); thesis required; internship and practicum not required but encouraged. *Outside funding for the department:* yes (WEEA Grant, others pending). *Summer session:* 8 weeks. *Tuition per credit:* fall and spring—residents, part-time $37-$45, full-time $550-$600; nonresidents, part-time $118-$126, full-time $1,765-$1,885. Dr. Jackson A. Byars, Chair, Educational Technology and Computer Education, (913) 532-5556.

Kearney State College. Kearney, NE 68849. School offers M.S. in Educational Technology. Master's started in 1984. In fall 1989 had 3 full-time and 5 part-time faculty members; 19 male and 7 female students. *Semester credit basis. Minimum degree requirements:* 36 hours (18 hours in computers, 18 hours in education); internship not required; practicum not required. *Outside funding for the department:* no. *Summer session:* 8 weeks. *Tuition per credit:* $38.50 residents; $54.00 nonresidents. Dr. Lynn Johnson, Chair, Professional Teacher Education, (308) 234-8513.

Kent State University. Educational Technology Program, 405 White Hall, KSU, Kent, OH 44242. *Program Basis:* semester. *Tuition per credit:* $117 in-state, $209 out-of-state. *Summer:* Two 5-week sessions. *Minimum degree requirements:* 34 credit hours, incl. 15-20 hrs. in computer studies, 12-17 in education. *Faculty:* 4. *Graduates:* approx. 10 per year. Dr. Drew Tiene, Program Coordinator. (216) 672-2294.

Lesley College. 29 Everett Street, Cambridge, MA 02238. College offers M.A. in Computers in Education and C.A.G.S. in Computers in Education. Master's started in 1980. In fall 1989 had 5 full-time and 12 part-time faculty members on the master's and specialist levels; 10 male and 30 female students on the master's level, and 2 male and 3 female students on the specialist level. *Semester credit basis. Minimum degree requirements:* Master's—33 hours in computers (number of hours in education and outside education not specified); thesis not required; internship not required; practicum not required. Specialist—36 hours (hours in computers, in education, and outside education not specified); thesis, internship, practicum not specified. *Outside funding for the department:* yes (NSF Grant). *Summer session:* two 3-week sessions. *Tuition per credit:* $244 residents and nonresidents. Dr. Nancy Roberts, Professor of Computer Education, (617) 868-9600.

Long Island University. C. W. Post, Brookville, NY 11548. School offers M.S. in Education, concentration in computers in education. Master's started in 1985. In fall 1989 had 3 full-time and 0 part-time faculty members; number of students not specified. *Semester credit basis. Minimum degree requirements:* 36 hours (27 hours in computers, 9 hours in education, 0 hours outside education); thesis required; internship not required; practicum not required. *Outside funding for the department:* no. *Summer session:* 3 sessions, 5 weeks each. *Tuition per credit:* $260 per credit, $25 computer lab fee, residents; for nonresidents not specified. Ms. Rayzel B. Sachs, Academic Advisor of Educational Technology, (516) 299-2147.

Mankato State University. Education Technology M.S. Program, Box 20, Mankato, MN 56002. Program offers M.S. in Educational Technology (integrated interdisciplinary degree). Master's started in 1986. In fall 1989 had 8 full-time and 0 part-time faculty members: 25 male and 13 female students. *Quarter credit basis. Minimum degree requirements:* 51 hours (6-15 hours in computers, 12-15 hours in education, 12-18 hours [optional] outside education); thesis not required; internship required; practicum not required. *Outside funding for the department:* no. *Summer session:* yes (number of weeks not specified). *Tuition per credit:* $47.90 residents; $66.95 nonresidents. Kenneth C. Pengelly, Professor and Coordinator of Educational Technology M.S. Program, (507) 389-1965.

Minot State University. 500 Urn Avenue West, Minot, ND 58702. School offers M.S. in Audiology, M.S. in Education of the Deaf, M.S. in Elementary Education, M.S. in Learning Disabilities, M.S. in Special Education, M.S. in Speech-Language Pathology, MAT in Mathematics, M.S. in Criminal Justice. Master's program started in 1963. In fall, had 22 full-time and 9 part-time faculty members; 8 male and 53 female students. *Quarter credit basis. Minimum degree requirements*: 45 hours (hours in computers, in education and outside education vary according to program). *Outside funding for the department*: yes (Federal Grants in Special Education and Speech-Language Pathology). *Summer session:* 8 weeks. *Tuition*: full-time students: $532 residents (Minnesota Reciprocity $572); $1,330 nonresidents (contiguous states/provinces $656). Dr. Carol Sue Butts, Dean, Graduate School, (701) 857-3822.

National College of Education. Department of Computer Education, 2840 Sheridan Road, Evanston, IL 60201. Department offers M.Ed., M.S., C.A.S. in Computer Education (certificate of advanced studies), and Ed.D. in Instructional Leadership with minor concentration in computer education. Master's started in 1983, specialist in 1983, and doctorate in 1984. In fall 1989 had 2 full-time faculty and 4 part-time faculty members on the master's, specialist, and doctoral levels; 15 male and female students in the master's program, 31 male and female students in the specialist program, and 5 female students in the doctoral program (had 92 graduates). *Semester credit basis. Minimum degree requirements:* Master's—34 hours (18 hours in computers, 10 hours in education, and 0 hours outside education); thesis optional; internship not required, practicum not required. Specialist's, C.A.S. (certificate of advanced studies)—30 hours (18 hours in computers, 4 hours in education, 0 hours outside education); thesis not required; internship not required; practicum not required. Doctorate—63 hours (14 hours in computers, 37 hours in education, 0 hours outside education); thesis required; internship required; practicum not required. *Outside funding for the department:* no. *Summer session*: 6 weeks. *Tuition per credit:* $215 per semester hour, residents; $215 per semester hour, nonresidents. Dr. Sandra V. Turner, Chair, Department of Computer Education, (312) 475-1100, ext. 2256.

North Carolina State University. Department of Curriculum and Instruction, P.O. Box 7801, Raleigh, NC 27695-7801. Department offers M.A. in Instructional Technology—Computers (program track within one master's in Curriculum and Instruction). Master's started in 1986. In fall 1989 had 3 full-time faculty members; 18 male and female students. *Semester credit basis. Minimum degree requirements*: 36 hours; thesis optional; internship not required; practicum required. *Outside funding for the department:* no. *Summer session*: yes (number of weeks not specified). *Tuition per credit*: not specified for residents and nonresidents. Dr. Ellen Vasu, Associate Professor, Department of Curriculum and Instruction, (919) 737-3221.

Northern Illinois University. College of Education, DeKalb, IL 60115. College offers M.S.Ed. in Instructional Technology with a concentration in Microcomputers in Education and Training. Master's started in 1985. In fall 1989 had 5 full-time and 0 part-time faculty members; number of students not specified. *Semester credit basis. Minimum degree requirements:* 36 hours (24 hours in computers, 9 hours in education, 0 hours outside education); thesis not required; internship not required; practicum not required. *Outside funding for the department:* no. *Summer session*: 8 weeks. *Tuition per credit:* not specified. Dr. Gary L. McConeghy, Chair, Instructional Technology, (815) 753-0465.

Nova University. Ed.D./CED Program, Ft. Lauderdale, FL 33314. Program offers M.S., Ed.D., and Ed.S. in Computer Education. Master's started in 1985; specialist in 1984; doctorate in 1984. In fall 1989 had 2 full-time and 0 part-time faculty members on the master's level, and 8 full-time and 0 part-time faculty members on the doctoral level (specialist program is phasing out); 35 male and 35 female students on the master's level, 2 male and 3 female students on the specialist's level, and 55 male and 44 female students on the doctoral level. *Semester credit basis. Minimum degree requirements*: Master's—36 hours (24 hours in computer, 12 hours in education, 0 hours outside education); no thesis required; no internship required; practicum required. Doctorate—66 hours (33 hours in computer, 21 hours in education, 12 hours outside education); thesis required; internship not required; practicum required. *Outside funding for the department*: no. *Summer session*: number of weeks not specified. *Tuition per credit*: Master's, $150 residents and nonresidents; doctorate, $205 residents and nonresidents. Dr. John Kingsbury, Director of Marketing, (305) 475-7047.

The Ohio State University. 225 Ramseyer Hall, 29 W. Woodruff Avenue, Columbus, OH 43210-1177. Since 1980, school offers M.A. and Ph.D. in Computers in Education in the Program area of Instructional Design and Technology. In fall 1989 had 8 full-time and 4 part-time graduate faculty members: 34 students in the master's program and 29 students in the doctoral program. *Quarter credit basis. Minimum degree requirements:* M.A. 50 credit hours—18 hrs. core, 6 hrs. foundations, 3 hrs. multicultural—minimum; Ph.D. 135 hrs. post-bachelor's, general examination (written and oral), dissertation. *Outside funding for the department:* no. *Summer session:* 3, 5, 8, and 10 weeks. *Tuition per credit:* 1 credit Ohio resident, $108, out-of-state, $144; 10 or more credits Ohio resident $867, out-of-state $2,230. Dr. Marjorie A. Cambre, Associate Professor, The Ohio State University, (614) 292-4872.

Pace University. Department of Educational Administration, White Plains, NY 10606. Department offers M.S. in Curriculum and Instruction with a concentration in computers. Master's started in 1986. In fall 1989 had 0 full-time and 15 part-time faculty members; 20 male and 33 female students. *Semester credit basis. Minimum degree requirements:* 33-34 hours (15 hours in computers, 15 hours in education); thesis not required; internship not required; practicum not required; comprehensive exam required. *Outside funding for the department:* no. *Summer session:* 4 weeks. *Tuition per credit:* $300 residents and nonresidents. Dr. Lawrence Roder, Chair, Department of Educational Administration, (914) 681-4198.

The Pennsylvania State University. University Park, PA 16802. School offers M.S. in Instructional Systems, M.Ed. in Instructional Systems, Ph.D. in Instructional Systems, and D.Ed. in Instructional Systems. Master's started in 1980. In fall 1989 had 5 full-time and 2 part-time faculty members on the master's and doctoral levels; 12 male and 13 female students on the master's level, and 12 male and 15 female students on the doctoral level. *Semester credit basis. Minimum degree requirements:* Master's—30 hours (15 hours in computers, 9 hours in education, 6 hours outside education); thesis not required; internship not required; practicum not required. Doctorate—90 hours (27 hours in computers, 33 hours in education, 15 hours outside education); thesis required; internship not required; practicum not required. *Outside funding for the department:* yes. *Summer session:* 3-, 6-, and 8-week sessions. *Tuition per credit:* $176 residents; $349 nonresidents. Paul W. Welliver, Professor of Education, (814) 865-1500.

Purdue University. School of Education, West Lafayette, IN 47907. Department of Curriculum and Instruction offers M.S., Ed.S., and Ph.D. in Educational Computing and Instructional Development. Master's started in 1984 and specialist's and doctorate in 1985. In fall 1989 had 6 full-time and 0 part-time faculty members at all levels; 11 students on the master's level, and 9 students on the doctoral level. *Semester credit basis. Minimum degree requirements:* Master's—36 hours (15 in computer, 9 in education, 12 unspecified); thesis optional. Specialist—60-65 hours (15-18 in computer, 30-35 in education); thesis required; internship required; practicum required. Doctorate—70-82 hours (15-18 in computer, 42-45 in education); thesis required; internship required; practicum/project/report required. *Outside funding:* no. *Summer session:* 8 weeks. *Tuition per credit:* $69 residents; $206 nonresidents. Dr. James Russell, Chair, Educational Computing and Instructional Development, (317) 494-5673.

Saint Peter's College. Graduate Programs in Education, 2641 Kennedy Boulevard, Jersey City, NJ 07306. School offers M.A. in Education-Computer Science/Data Processing. Master's started in 1979. In fall 1989 had 9 full-time and 8 part-time faculty members; 12 male and 47 female students. *Semester credit basis. Minimum degree requirements:* 39 hours (27 hours in computers, 12 hours in education, 0 hours outside education); thesis not required; internship not specified; practicum not specified. *Outside funding for the department:* no. *Summer session:* 5 weeks. *Tuition per credit:* $227 residents and nonresidents. Dr. Henry F. Harty, Director, Graduate Programs in Education, (201) 915-9254.

San Diego State University. Department of Educational Technology, San Diego, CA 92182-0311. Department offers M.A. in Education with specializations in Educational Technology, and Educational Computing. In fall 1988 had 8 full-time and 3 part-time faculty members; 45 male and 65 female students. *Semester credit basis. Minimum degree requirements:* 36 hours (9 hours in education, hours in computers and outside education not specified); thesis not required; internship not required; practicum required. *Outside funding for the department:* yes (local companies, gifts from Apple Computer, federal and state grants). *Summer session:* 12 weeks. *Tuition per credit:* $70/unit residents and nonresidents (differs in summer). Dr. Pat Harrison, Chair, Department of Educational Technology, (619) 594-6718.

Southern Illinois University—Carbondale. Department of Curriculum and Instruction, Carbondale, IL 62901. Department offers M.S. in Curriculum and Instruction with a specialization in computer-based education and Ph.D. in Curriculum and Instruction with a specialization in instructional technology. Master's started in 1983 and doctorate in 1983. In fall 1989 had 5 full-time and 5 part-time faculty members on the master's and doctoral levels; 11 male and 14 female students on the master's level, and 5 male and 6 female students on the doctoral level. *Semester credit basis. Minimum degree requirements:* Master's—32 hours (specialty in computer-based education: 21 hours in computers, 9 hours in education, 2-6 outside education); thesis optional; internship not required; practicum not required. Doctorate—64 hours (specialty in instructional technology: hours in computers vary, 17 hours in education, hours outside education vary); thesis required; internship not required; practicum not required. *Outside funding for the department:* $1,000,000+ in the areas of early childhood, science education, math education, and teacher education. *Summer session:* 8 weeks. *Tuition per credit:* $65 residents; $195 nonresidents. Dr. Pierre Barrette, Coordinator, Department of Curriculum and Instruction, (618) 536-2441.

Southwest Baptist University. School of Education, 1601 South Springfield, Bolivar, MO 65613. School offers M.S. in Education with specialization in Computer Education. Master's started in 1982. In fall 1989 had 2 full-time and 3 part-time faculty members; 9 male and 19 female students. *Semester credit basis. Minimum degree requirements:* 36 hours (18 hours in computers, 18 hours in education, 0 hours outside education); thesis not required; internship not required; practicum required. *Outside funding for the department:* no. *Summer session:* two 4-week terms. *Tuition per credit:* $80 residents and nonresidents. Dr. Fred A. Teague, Dean, School of Education, (417) 326-1710.

Spalding University. Education Technology Program, 851 South Fourth Avenue, Louisville, KY 40203. Program offers Ed.S. in Computers in Education and M.A. in Education Technology. Master's program started in 1983; specialist in 1983. In fall 1989 had 1 full-time and 1 part-time faculty members; 11 students in the master of arts and 8 on the specialist's levels; *Semester credit basis. Minimum degree requirements:* Master's—30-36 hours (21-27 in computers, 9 hours in education, 0 hours outside education); thesis not required; internship not required; practicum required (directed study and position paper). Specialist's—30-36 hours (21-27 hours in computers, 9 hours in education, 0 hours outside education); thesis not required; internship not required; practicum required (directed study and position paper). Students may obtain Kentucky certificate endorsements (K-12) as specialist in Computerized Instruction (36 graduate semester hours) and Indiana certificate endorsement (K-12) as Computer Educator (15 graduate semester hours). *Outside funding for the department:* no. *Summer session:* 2 sessions of 5 weeks each. *Tuition per credit:* $175 plus fees, residents and nonresidents. Dr. Eileen Boyle Young, Director, Education Technology Program, (502) 585-9911, ext. 237.

State University College of Arts and Science at Potsdam. 204 Satterlee Hall, Potsdam, NY 13676. School offers M.S. in Education, Instructional Technology, and Media Management with educational computing concentration. Master's started in 1981. In fall 1989 had 6 full-time and 4 part-time faculty members; 41 male, 73 female students, and 10 foreign students (Taiwan). *Semester credit basis. Minimum degree requirements:* 33 hours (18 hours in computers, 15 hours in education, 0 hours outside education); thesis required; internship or practicum required. *Outside funding for* *the department*: no. *Summer session*: 5 weeks (two sessions, early and regular). *Tuition per credit*: $90 residents; $156 nonresidents. Dr. Norman Licht, Professor of Education, (315) 267-2527.

State University of New York. Department of Technology and Society, Stonybrook, NY 11794. Department offers Master's in Technological Systems Management with a 15-credit concentration in educational computing. Master's started in 1979. In fall 1989 had 4 full-time and 3 part-time faculty members; 21 male and 18 female students. *Semester credit basis. Minimum degree requirements*: 30 hours (hours in computer, education, and outside education not specified); thesis required; internship not specified; practicum not specified. *Outside funding for the department*: yes (source not specified). *Summer session:* 6 weeks. *Tuition per credit:* $90 residents; $192 nonresidents. Dr. Thomas T. Liao, Professor and Chairperson, (516) 632-8767.

Texas A&M University. Department of Interdisciplinary Education, Educational Technology Program, College Station, TX 77843. Department offers M.Ed. in Educational Technology, emphasis in computer applications. Master's started in 1984. In fall 1989 had 6 full-time and 2 part-time faculty members; 10 male and 8 female students. *Semester credit basis. Minimum degree requirements*: 37 hours (12 hours in computers, 6 hours in education); thesis not required; internship or practicum required. *Outside funding for the department:* no. *Summer session:* two 6-week sessions. *Tuition per credit*: $16 residents; $120 nonresidents. Dr. Ronald Zellner, Coordinator, Educational Technology, (409) 845-7276.

Texas Christian University. P.O. Box 32925, Fort Worth, TX 76129. School offers Master of General Education with specialization in computers in education. Master's started in 1984. In fall 1989 had 1 full-time and 1 part-time faculty member; number of students not specified. *Semester credit basis. Minimum degree requirements:* 36 hours (18 hours in specialization, 6 hours in professional education, 6 hours thesis, 6 hours elective); thesis required; internship not required; practicum required. *Outside funding for the department*: no. *Summer session*: one 3-week session, two 5-week sessions. *Tuition per credit:* not specified (fianancial assistance is available). Dr. Sherrie Reynolds, Assistant Professor, (817) 921-7660.

Texas Tech University. College of Education, Box 4560, TTU, Lubbock, TX 79409. College offers M.Ed. in Instructional Technology (educational computing) and Ed.D. in Instructional Technology (educational computing). Master's started in 1981; doctorate in 1982. In fall 1989 had 3 full-time and 2 part-time faculty members on the master's and doctoral levels; 28 students on the master's level and 17 students on the doctoral level. *Semester credit basis. Minimum degree requirements*: Master's—39 hours (24 hours in computing, 15 hours in education or outside education); thesis not required; internship not required; practicum required. Doctorate—81 hours (33 hours in computers, 24 hours in education, 24 hours outside education); thesis not specified; internship not required; practicum required. *Outside funding for the department:* no. *Summer session*: two 6-week sessions. *Tuition per credit*: $16 residents; $120 nonresidents. Dr. Robert Price, Director, Instructional Technology, (806) 742-2362.

Texas Wesleyan University. School of Education, Fort Worth, TX 76105. School offers M.S. in Computers in Education. Master's started in 1982. In fall 1989 had 3 full-time and 1 part-time faculty members; 10 male and 19 female students. *Semester credit basis. Minimum degree requirements:* 36 hours (18 hours in computers, 18 hours in education, 0 hours outside education); thesis required; internship not required; practicum required. *Outside funding for the department:* no. *Summer session:* two 5-week sessions. *Tuition per credit*: $155/hr. residents and nonresidents. Dr. Allen Henderson, Dean, School of Education, (817) 531-4940.

Texas Woman's University. Denton TX 76204. School offers M.A. and M.Ed. major in elementary education. Master's program started in 1985. In fall 1989 had 3 full-time faculty members (all are partially involved); 4 female and 0 male students. *Semester credit basis. Minimum degree requirements:* 36 hours (6 hours in computer science, 30 hours in education, [6-9 hours in computers in education]); thesis not specified; internship not specified; practicum not specified. *Outside* *funding for the department*: not specified. *Summer session:* 12 weeks. Tuition per credit: varies for residents (minimum of $100 through 6 hours); $120 per hour for nonresidents. Vera T. Gershner, Professor, (817) 898-2256.

United States International University. School of Education, 10455 Pomerado Rd., San Diego, CA, 92131. School offers M.A. in Computer Education and Ed.D. with specialization in computer education. Master's and doctorate started in 1983. In fall 1989 had 4 full-time and 4 part-time faculty members on the master's and doctoral levels; 40 male and 60 female students on the master's level and 25 male and 25 female students on the doctoral level. *Quarter credit basis. Minimum degree requirements:* Master's—45 hours (30 hours in computers, 15 hours in education, 0 hours outside education); thesis not required; internship not required; practicum required. Doctorate—95 hours (60 hours in computers, 35 hours in education, 0 hours outside education); thesis required; internship required; practicum required. *Outside funding for the department*: no. *Summer session*: 6 weeks. *Tuition per credit:* $170 residents and nonresidents. Colin MacKinnon, Associate Professor and Coordinator of Computer Education Programs,(619) 693-4721.

University of Colorado—Colorado Springs. School of Education, P.O. Box 7150, Colorado Springs, CO, 80933-7150. School offers M.A. in Curriculum and Instruction with an emphasis in Educational Computing and Technology. Master's program started in 1983. In fall 1989 had 2 full-time and 4 part-time faculty members in the master's program; 12 male and 13 female students. *Semester credit basis. Minimum degree requirements:* 33 hours (27 hours required in educational technology; 6 hours in education; 0 hours outside education); no thesis required; no internship required; no practicum required. *Outside funding for the department:* no. *Summer session*: 4 weeks. *Tuition per credit*: $70 residents; $203 nonresidents. Dr. Doris Carey, Graduate Faculty, (719) 593-3299.
  *Students reflect K-12 track for educators or CBT instructional design track for corporate trainers.

University of Delaware. College of Education, Newark, DE 19716. College offers M.A. in Educational Studies with specialization in computer-based education. Master's started in 1980. Number of faculty members and students not specified. *Semester credit basis. Minimum degree requirements*: 30 hours (12 hours in computers, 12 hours in education); research project required; 6 hours internship; practicum not required. *Outside funding for the department:* yes (NIE, NIMH, NSF). *Summer session:* 5 weeks. *Tuition per credit:* $143 residents; $350 nonresidents. Dr. Richard Venezky, Professor, Department of Educational Studies, (302) 451-8126.

University of Denver. School of Education, Denver, CO 80208. School offers M.A. in Curriculum and Instruction or in Educational Psychology. Master's started in 1984. In fall 1989 had 3 full-time and 3 part-time faculty members; 2 male and 2 female students. *Quarter credit basis. Minimum degree requirements*: 45 hours (20 hours in computers, 35 hours in education, 0-10 hours outside education); thesis not required; internship not required; practicum not required. *Outside funding for the department*: no. *Summer session:* yes (number of weeks not specified). Tuition per credit: $300 residents and nonresidents. Dr. Raymond Kluever, Coordinator, Graduate Study in Education, (303) 871-2508.

University of Florida. College of Education, G-518 Norman Hall, Gainesville, FL 32611. College offers Ed.S. and Ph.D. in Computers in Education. Specialist's started in 1984 and doctorate in 1984. In fall 1989 had 2 full-time and 1 part-time faculty members on the specialist and doctoral levels; 2 male and 1 female students on the specialist level, and 3 male and 2 female students on the doctoral level. *Semester credit basis. Minimum degree requirements:* Specialist's—hours vary (dependent on student's background); a minor in computer science (not computers in education) is required; thesis not required; internship not required; practicum required. Doctorate—hours vary (dependent on student's background); a minor in computer science is required; thesis required; internship not required; practicum not required. *Outside funding for the department:* no. *Summer session*: two 6-week terms. *Tuition per credit:* not specified. Dr. Roy Bolduc, Professor, (904) 392-5049.

University of Georgia. College of Education, Athens, GA 30602. College offers M.Ed. in Computer-Based Education. Master's started in 1985. In fall 1989 had 2 full-time and 6 part-time faculty members; 12 students. *Quarter credit basis. Minimum degree requirements*: 60 hours (25 hours in computers, 10 hours in education, 25 hours not specified [55 hours with applied project]); thesis not required; internship and practicum optional. *Outside funding for the department*: no. *Summer session*: variable (2-8 weeks). *Tuition per credit*: $44 residents; $132 nonresidents. Dr. C. Hugh Gardner, Associate Professor of Instructional Technology, (404) 542-3810.

University of Hartford. Math Education and Educational Computing, 200 Bloomfield Avenue, West Hartford, CT 06117. School offers M.S. in Educational Computing. Master's started in 1985. In fall 1989 had 2 full-time and 2 part-time faculty members; 3 male and 28 female students. *Semester credit basis. Minimum degree requirements:* 30 hours (21 hours in computers, 9 hours in education); thesis not specified; internship not specified; practicum not specified. *Outside funding for the department:* yes (NSF Grant). *Summer session:* 7 courses/1 week per course. *Tuition per credit:* $170 residents and nonresidents. Dr. Marilyn Schaffer, Associate Professor of Educational Computing, (203) 243-4277.

University of Hawaii. Department of Educational Technology, 1776 University Avenue, W 105, Honolulu, HI 96822. Department offers M.Ed. in Educational Technology. Master's started in 1983. In fall 1989 had 4 full-time and 1 part-time faculty members; 3 male and 9 female students. *Semester credit basis. Minimum degree requirements*: 39 minimum (21 hours in computers, 12 hours in education, 12 hours outside education); thesis available; internship required; practicum required. *Outside funding for the department:* no. *Summer session:* 12 weeks. *Tuition per credit:* $61 residents; $183 nonresidents. Dr. Geoffrey Z. Kucera, Department Chairman, (808) 948-7671.

University of Houston. University Park, College of Education, Houston, TX 77204-5872. College offers M.Ed. and Ed. D. in curriculum and instruction with emphasis in instructional technology, specialization in computer education. Master's started in 1981; doctorate in 1981. In fall 1989 had 3 full-time and 5 part-time faculty members on the master's and doctoral levels; about 50 students on the master's level, and about 12 students on the doctoral level. *Semester credit basis. Minimum degree requirements*: Master's—36 hours without thesis; internship not required; practicum not required. Doctorate—60 dissertation hours beyond Master's. *Outside funding for the department*: yes (NSF, U.S. Dept. of Ed., Texas Educational Agency, Institutional Grants). *Summer session*: 12 weeks. *Tuition per credit*: $18 residents; $122 nonresidents. Dr. George W. Bright, Director, Microcomputer Center, College of Education, (713) 749-1685.

University of Kentucky. Department of Special Education, Lexington, KY 40506-0001. Department offers Ed.S. degree in Special Education Microcomputer Specialist Program. Specialist's started in 1984. In fall 1989 had 0 full-time and 5 part-time faculty members; 3 male and 10 female students. *Semester credit basis. Minimum degree requirements*: 35 hours (35 hours in education [all courses offered in Special Education Department and focus on computer applications], 0 hours outside education); thesis required; internship not required; practicum required. *Outside funding for the department:* yes (Office of Special Education Programs, U.S. Department of Education). *Summer session:* 8 weeks. *Tuition per credit:* not specified. Dr. A. Edward Blackhurst, Professor, (606) 257-4713.

University of Lowell. College of Education, One University Avenue, Lowell, MA 01854. College offers M.Ed. in Curriculum and Instruction, C.A.G.S. in Curriculum and Instruction, Ed.D. in Leadership in Schooling. (Note: An option, called *Technology and Learning Environments*, is offered within broader program streams at M.Ed., C.A.G.S., and Ed.D. levels.) Master's, specialist's, doctorates started in 1984. In fall 1989 had 1 full-time (plus courses taught by other faculty) and 2 part-time (including lecturers) on the master's, specialist's, and doctoral levels; number of students not specified. *Semester credit basis. Minimum degree requirements:* Master's—33 hours (hours in computers, education, and outside education not specified); thesis not required; internship not required; practicum required. Doctorate—60 hours beyond master's plus dissertation (hours in computers, education, and outside education not specified); thesis required; internship not required; comprehensive exams required. *Outside funding for the department:* no. *Summer session:* yes (individual courses, schedule varies). *Tuition per credit:* residents, $61.50 plus fees; nonresidents, $195.95 plus fees. Dr. John LeBaron, Associate Professor, College of Education, (508) 934-4621.

University of Maryland. College of Education, College Park, MD 20742-1175. College offers M.A., M.Ed., and Ph.D. in Curriculum and Instruction with emphasis in computer education. Master's started in 1984 and doctorate in 1984. In fall 1989 had 2 full-time and 1 part-time faculty members on the master's and doctoral levels; 6 female and 1 male students on the master's level, and 4 male and 2 female students on the doctoral level. *Semester credit basis. Minimum degree requirements:* Master's—30 hours (12 hours in computers, 3 hours in education, 0 hours outside education); thesis optional; internship required; practicum not required. Doctorate—90 hours (15 hours in computers, 12 hours in education, no hours outside education); thesis required; internship not required; practicum not required. *Outside funding for the department*: no. *Summer session*: 12 weeks. *Tuition per credit:* $100 residents; not specified for nonresidents. Dr. Joseph Krajcik, Assistant Professor, (301) 454-7346.

University of Minnesota. Department of Curriculum and Instructional Systems, 104 Burton Hall, 178 Pillsbury Drive S.E., Minneapolis, MN 55455. Department offers M.Ed., M.A., Ph.D. in Computers in Education. Master's and doctorate started in 1972. In fall 1989 had 5 full-time and 4 part-time faculty members on the master's and doctoral levels; 150 students in the master's program, and 50 students in the doctoral program. *Quarter credit basis. Minimum degree requirements*: Master's—45 hours (18 hours in computers, 45 hours in education, 0 hours outside education); thesis (4 credits) required; internship not required; practicum not required. Doctorate—136 hours (136 hours in education, 0 hours outside education); thesis (36 credits) required; internship not required; practicum not required. *Outside funding for the department*: yes (assistantships with business). *Summer session*: two 5-week sessions. *Tuition per credit:* $59.23 residents (M.Ed.); $148.08 nonresidents (M.Ed.); varies for M.A. and Ph.D. (residents: one credit=$247.52, six credits=$631.24, 7-15 credits=$891.16; nonresidents: one credit=$495.04, six credits=$1,262.48, 7-15 credits=$1,782.32). Dr. Greg Sales or Richard Kimpston, Curriculum and Instructional Systems, (612) 624-2034 or (612) 625-8355.

University of Missouri—Kansas City. School of Education, 5100 Rockhill Road, Kansas City, MO 64110. School offers M.A. in Curriculum and Instruction/Computer Education. Master's started in 1987. In fall 1989 had 1 full-time and 2 part-time faculty members; 15 male and 10 female students. *Semester credit basis. Minimum degree requirements:* 30 hours (15 hours in computers, 15 hours in education); thesis not required; internship not required; practicum not required. *Outside funding for the department:* no. *Summer session:* 8 weeks. *Tuition per credit:* $83 residents; $212.20 nonresidents. Dr. Gary Nahrstedt, Chairman, Division of Curriculum and Instruction, (816) 276-2457.

University of Nevada—Reno. College of Education, Reno, NV 89557. College offers M.Ed. in Curriculum/Instruction. Master's started in 1986. In fall 1989 had 2 full-time and 2 part-time faculty members; 15 male and 20 female students. *Semester credit basis. Minimum degree requirements:* 36 hours (12 hours in computers, 24 in education); thesis not required; internship not required; practicum not required. *Outside funding for the department:* no. *Summer session:* two 5-week sessions. *Tuition per credit:* $40 residents; $1,100 nonresidents for 7 or more credits + $40 per credit. Dr. LaMont Johnson, Professor, Department of Curriculum and Instruction, (702) 784-4961.

University of North Carolina—Charlotte. College of Education, Charlotte, NC 28223. College offers M.A. in Media and Technology-Computer Education. Master's started in 1987. In fall 1989 had 0 full-time faculty and 6 part-time faculty members (full-time faculty devoting part of time to computer education program); 3 male and 12 female students. *Semester credit basis. Minimum degree requirements:* 36 hours (12 hours in computers, 15 hours in education, 9 hours outside education); thesis not required; internship required; practicum not required. *Outside funding for the* *department:* no. *Summer session:* two 5-week sessions. *Tuition per credit:* residents, $144 per 3-semester-hour course; nonresidents, $1,104 per 3-semester-hour course. Dr. Clarence Smith, Professor of Education, (704) 547-4542.

University of North Carolina—Greensboro. School of Education, 1000 Spring Garden Street, Greensboro, NC 27412. School offers M.Ed. in Computers in Education. Master's started in 1987. In fall 1989 had 1 full-time and 2 part-time faculty members; 5 male and 8 female students. *Semester credit basis. Minimum degree requirements:* 36 hours (12-18 in computers, 18 in education, 6 outside education); thesis not required; internship not required; practicum required. *Outside funding for the department:* no. *Summer session:* no. *Tuition per credit:* $63 residents; $557 nonresidents. Dr. Kieth C. Wright, Professor, (919) 334-5100, ext. 82.

University of North Texas. Department of Computer Education and Cognitive Systems, Box 5155, Denton, TX 76203. Department offers M.S. in Computer Education and Cognitive Systems. Master's started in 1987. In fall 1989 had 7 full-time and 3 part-time faculty members; 30 male and 50 female students. *Semester credit basis. Minimum degree requirements:* 36 hours (30 in computers, 6 in education); thesis not specified; internship not specified; practicum not specified. *Outside funding for the department:* yes (computer grant for equipment). *Summer session:* two 5-week terms. *Tuition per credit:* $16 residents; $120 nonresidents. Dr. J. L. Poirot, Chair, (817) 565-3790.

The University of Oklahoma. Educational Technology Graduate Program, Norman, OK 73019. Program offers M.Ed. in Education and Technology-Computer emphasis option. Master's started in 1982. In fall 1989 had 3 full-time and 2 part-time faculty members; 12 male and 17 female students. *Semester credit basis. Minimum degree requirements:* 33 hours (12 hours in computers, 21 hours in education [including above 12]); thesis not required; internship required; practicum not required. *Outside funding for the department:* yes (Special Educational Technology Grant—Office of Education). *Summer session:* 8 weeks. *Tuition per credit:* residents $61.50 as of 11/88; nonresidents, $190.40 as of 11/88. Dr. Tillman J. Ragan, Professor and Area Head, (405) 325-1521.

University of Oregon. ISTE, Eugene, OR 97403. College offers M.S., M.A., M.Ed. and D.Ed/Ph.D. in Curriculum and Instruction with specialization in computers in education. Master's started in 1970 and doctorate in 1971. Number of faculty members not specified; 38 students on the master's level, and 36 students on the doctoral level. *Quarter credit basis. Minimum degree requirements:* Master's—45-48 hours; thesis optional. Doctoral programs are individualized, but include a residency requirement. *Outside funding for the department:* not specified. *Summer session:* 8 weeks. *Tuition:* academic year: 9-16 hours (resident) $854; 9-16 hours (nonresident) $1,388. Dr. David Moursund, Professor, ISTE, (503) 686-4414.

University of Texas. College of Education, Austin, TX 78712. College offers M.S. and M.A. in Computers in Education. Master's programs started in 1984. In fall 1989, had 4 full-time and 1 part-time on the master's levels; about 25 students. *Semester quarter basis. Minimum degree requirements:* 12-18 hours in computers, 18-24 hours in education, 6 hours outside education; thesis and internship optional. *Outside funding for the department:* yes (source not specified). *Summer session:* two 6-week sessions. *Tuition per credit:* not specified for residents and nonresidents. Dr. DeLayne Hudspeth, Associate Professor, (512) 471-5211.

University of Virgin Islands. St. Thomas, VI 00802. School offers M.A. with emphasis in Computers and Technology in Education. Master's started in 1989 (January). In fall 1989 had 1 full-time and 0 part-time faculty member. Anticipated enrollment of 60 students. *Semester credit basis. Minimum degree requirements:* 36 credits (21 credits in computers, 15 credits in education, 0 credits outside education); thesis optional; internship not required; practicum required. *Outside funding for the department:* U. S. Dept. of Educ. *Summer session:* 6 weeks. *Tuition per credit:* $82 residents; $164 nonresidents. Dr. Dennis O. Harper, Associate Professor of Computer Ed., (809) 776-9200.

Virginia Polytechnic Institute and State University. Education Micro Computer Lab, Blacksburg, VA 24061-0313. School offers M.S. in Computers in Education and Ed.D. in Computers in Education. Master's started in 1982 and doctorate in 1982. In fall 1989 had 7 full-time and 0 part-time faculty members on the master's level, and 7 full-time and 3 part-time faculty members on the doctoral level; 2 male and 6 female students on the master's level, and 4 male and 1 female on the doctoral level. *Semester credit basis. Minimum degree requirements:* Master's—30 hours (12 hours in computers, 18 hours in education, 6 hours outside education); thesis required; internship required; practicum not specified. Doctorate—90 hours (18 hours in computers, 52 hours in education, 9 hours outside education); thesis required; internship required; practicum not required. *Outside funding for the department:* yes (State Department of Virginia; State Department of West Virginia). *Summer session:* two 5-week sessions, one 8-week session. *Tuition per credit:* $148 residents; $163 non-residents. Dr. John K. Burton, Program Leader and Associate Professor, Instructional Systems Development, (703) 231-5587.

Western Carolina University. Cullowhee, NC 28723. Department offers M.A.Ed. in Supervision, with concentration in Educational Technology-Computers. Master's started in 1987. In fall 1989 had 25+ full-time and 0 part-time faculty members; 6 male and 7 female students. *Semester credit basis. Minimum degree requirements:* 41 hours (18 hours in computers, 20 hours in education, 3 hours outside education); thesis not required; internship required; practicum not required. *Outside funding for the department:* no. *Summer session:* two 5-week sessions. *Tuition per credit:* residents, $71.05 per semester hour; nonresidents, $551.05 per semester hour. Dr. Don Chalker, Head, Department of Administration, Curriculum and Instruction, (704) 227-7415.

Western Washington University. School of Education, Bellingham, WA 98225. School offers M.Ed., in Computers in Education. Master's started in 1981. In fall 1989 had 2 full-time and 7 part-time faculty members; 10 male and 15 female students. *Quarter credit basis. Minimum degree requirements:* 52 hours (15 hours in computers, 24 hours in education, 0 hours outside education); thesis required; internship and practicum possible. *Outside funding for the department:* no. *Summer session:* 9 weeks. *Tuition per credit:* $82 residents; $248 nonresidents (up to 10 credits). Prof. Tony Jongejan, Assistant Professor of Education, (206) 676-3381.

Widener University. Center for Education, Chester, PA 19013. School offers M.Ed. in Computer Science Education. Master's started in 1986. In fall 1989 had 1 full-time and 4 part-time faculty members; 40 male and 51 female students. *Semester credit basis. Minimum degree requirements:* 30 hours (18 hours in computers, 6-12 hours in education, up to 6 hours outside education); thesis not required; internship not required; practicum not required. *Outside funding for the department:* no. *Summer session:* three 10-week terms. *Tuition per credit:* $450 residents and nonresidents. Dr. James P. Randall, Assistant Professor of Instructional Technology, (215) 499-4497.

Wright State University. Department of Educational Technology and Vocational Education, 244 Millett Hall, Dayton, OH 45435. Department offers M.E. Computer Education, M.E. Computer Coordinator, M.A. Computer Education. Master's programs started in 1985. In fall 1989 had 2 full-time and 4 part-time faculty members; 5 male and 12 female students in master's program in computer education, and 3 male and 10 female students in master's program in computer coordination. *Quarter credit basis. Minimum degree requirements:* 48 hours (hours in computers, education, and outside education not specified); thesis required for M.A. degree only; internship required (for computer education); practicum required (for computer coordination). *Outside funding for the department:* no (not yet). *Summer session:* two 5-week sessions. *Tuition per credit:* residents, $84 per quarter hour to 10.5 hours, $890 for 11-18 hours; nonresidents, $151 per quarter hour to 10.5 hours, $1,598 for 11-18 hours. Dr. Bonnie K. Mathies, Chair, Department of Educational Technology and Vocational Education, (513) 873-2509.

Xavier University. Department of Mathematics and Computer Science, 3800 Victory Parkway, Cincinnati, OH 45207. Department offers M.Ed. with concentration in computer science. Master's started in 1981. In fall 1989 had 4 full-time faculty members in Computer Science and 24 part-time in Education; 11 male and female students. *Semester credit basis. Minimum degree requirements:* 30 hours (12 hours in computers, 12 hours in education, 6 hours either computers or education). *Outside funding for the department:* no. *Summer session:* 6 weeks. *Tuition per credit:* $150 residents and nonresidents. Dr. David D. Berry, Director, Computer Science, (513) 745-3462.

Scholarships, Fellowships, and Awards

Brenda Branyan-Broadbent
Associate Professor
Department of Instructional Technology
Utah State University, Logan

Lois A. Ward
Staff Assistant II
Department of Instructional Technology
Utah State University, Logan

In the instructional technology/media-related fields, various scholarships, fellowships, and awards have been established. Many of these are available to those who either are or will be pursuing advanced degrees at the master's, six-year specialist, and/or doctoral levels.

Since various colleges, universities, professional organizations, and/or governmental agencies offer scholarships, fellowships, and awards and may wish to have them included in this section, it would be greatly appreciated if those knowledgeable of such financial awards would contact either the editors or the publisher for inclusion of such entries in the next edition of *EMTY*.

We are greatly indebted to the staff members of the Association for Educational Communications and Technology (AECT) and to Dr. Donald Ely, the editor of *EMTY 1988*, for initiating this interest area.

Information is furnished in the following sequence:

- Overview of AECT and ECT Foundation Awards

- AECT Awards

- ECT Foundation Awards

AECT AND ECT
FOUNDATION AWARDS

The Association for Educational Communications and Technology recognizes and rewards the outstanding achievement of its members and associates through a program which provides for three major annual awards — Achievement, Special Service, and Distinguished Service — and through the ECT Foundation, which provides awards in the areas of leadership, scholarship, and research.

AECT encourages members and associates to apply for these awards and to disseminate information about the awards to professional colleagues. Specific information about each award is available from the AECT national office. The deadline for submitting award applications is 1 November, each year.

All ECT Foundation and AECT awards are presented during the AECT National Convention and INFOCOMM International Exposition. In 1991, the convention and exposition will be held in Orlando, Florida, February 13 through 16.

For additional information on all awards, please contact:

AECT Awards Program
1126 Sixteenth Street NW
Washington, DC 20036

(202) 466-4780

AECT Awards

The Association for Educational Communications and Technology (AECT) provides for three annual awards:

Special Service Award: Granted to a person who has shown notable service to AECT as a whole or to one of its programs or divisions (must have been a member of AECT for at least 10 years and must not be currently an AECT officer, board member or member of the Awards Committee).

Distinguished Service Award: Granted to a person who has shown outstanding leadership in advancing the theory and/or practice of educational communications and technology over a substantial period of time (nominee need not be an AECT member but must not have received this award previously).

Annual Achievement Award: Honors the individual who during the past year has made the most significant contribution to the advancement of educational communications and technology (nominee need not be a member of AECT and the award can be given to the same person more than once).

ECT Foundation Awards

The ECT Foundation, a non-profit organization which carries out the purposes of AECT that are charitable and educational in nature, coordinates the following awards:

AECT/SIRS Intellectual Freedom Award (in conjunction with the Social Issues Resources Services Inc.): Recognizes a media specialist at any level who has upheld the principles of intellectual freedom as set forth in AECT's publication, "Media, the Learner, and Intellectual Freedom," and provides $1,000 for the individual and $1,000 for the media center of the recipient's choice (recipient must be a personal member of AECT).

AECT Annual Conference and Earl F. Strobehn Internship Award: Provides complimentary registration and housing at the annual conference plus a cash award for four full-time graduate students (applicant must be a member of AECT and enrolled in a recognized program in educational communications and technology).

Richard B. Lewis Memorial Award: Presented to the outstanding school district media utilization program along with a cash award (awarded to either a public or private school having media utilization programs in place).

AECT Leadership Development Grants: Supports innovative leadership development activities undertaken by affiliates, divisions, or regions with cash grants (special consideration will be given to proposals that demonstrate a commitment to leadership development, that propose programs unique to the applicant's organization, and that include activities of potential benefit to other AECT programs).

AECT Memorial Scholarship Award: Donations given in memory of specific past leaders of the field provide a scholarship fund which gives annual cash grants to AECT members enrolled in educational technology graduate studies (three letters of recommendation are required).

Dean and Sybil McClusky Research Award: Recognizes the year's outstanding doctoral thesis proposal that has been approved by the student's university and offers a cash reward to defray the research expenses (the winner must agree to complete the proposed study).

Carl F. & Viola V. Mahnke Film Production Award: Honors excellence in message design for film and video products created by undergraduate students who are members of AECT (products must have been completed within a two-year period prior to the competition).

Robert M. Gagné Instructional Development Research Award: Recognizes the most significant contribution by a graduate student to the body of knowledge on which instructional development is based with a plaque and a cash prize (the research must have been done in past three years while the candidate was enrolled as a graduate student).

James W. Brown Publication Award: Recognizes the outstanding publication in the field of educational technology in any media format during the past year with a cash award (excluded from consideration are doctoral, master's, or other types of dissertations prepared in fulfillment of degree program requirements).

ECTJ Young Scholar Award: Recognizes fresh, creative approach to research and theory in educational technology by a young scholar (applicant must be an individual who does not hold a doctorate degree or who has received a doctorate degree within the past three years).

Young Researcher Award: Recognizes an outstanding unpublished report of research of an experimental, descriptive, or historical nature by a researcher who has not yet attained the doctorate or is less than three years beyond the degree (jointly published papers are not accepted).

Jerry R. Coltharp Award: Recognizes innovative media management practices which enhance the provision of instructional media services or advance media applications.

DOT-AECT Crystal Award: Recognizes the most innovative and outstanding instructional telecommunications project for 1990.

AECT Special Service Award

Qualifications

- Award is granted to a person who has shown notable service to AECT. This service may be to the organization as a whole, one of its programs, or one of its divisions.
- Nominee currently must be a member of AECT and have at least ten years of service to AECT.

Disqualifications

- Recipient may not now be serving as an elected officer of AECT nor as a member of the Board of Directors.
- Nominee must not be currently serving as a member of the AECT Awards Committee.

Nomination

Nominations are judged and selected on the basis of an outstanding contribution to a division, committee, commission, or program of AECT, but not an affiliate organization. Please provide as much information as you can.

- Write in one hundred words or less why you think nominee would receive this award. Include a description of his/her contribution.
- What year did nominee join AECT?

AECT Distinguished Service Award

Qualifications

- Award is granted to a person who has shown outstanding leadership in advancing the theory and/or practice of educational communications and technology over a substantial period of time.
- The nominee need not be a member of AECT.
- Award may be given posthumously.

Disqualifications

- Nominee must not have received this award previously.
- Nominee must not be currently serving as a member of the AECT Awards Committee.

Nomination

Nominations are judged primarily on the distinction or magnitude of the nominee's leadership in advancing the field rather than the association.

Categories

- The following categories suggest areas in which the nominee may have rendered distinguished service to the field. The nominee may not be represented in these areas. Use those that apply or add others.

    • Leadership   • Research/Theory   • Development/Production   • Writing
        • Major Contribution to Education Outside the U.S.

AECT Annual Achievement Award

Qualifications

- Recipient may be one person or a group.
- The AAA honors the individual who during the past year has made the most significant contribution to the advancement of educational communications and technology.
- The nominee need not be a member of AECT.
- The contribution being honored should be publicly visible—a specific thing or event.
- It must be timely—taking place within approximately the past year.
- Award can be given to the same person more than once.

Nomination

The nature of this award precludes the use of a single checklist or set of categories for nomination. The nomination and selection are inherently subjective. You are asked simply to present a succinct argument in favor of your nominee. Your statement ought to answer the following questions:

- What is the specific achievement being honored?
- What impact has this achievement had, or is likely to have, on the field?
- How is the nominee connected with the achievement?

ECT Foundation
1991 AECT/SIRS Intellectual Freedom Award

Purpose: To recognize, annually, a media professional at any level who has upheld the principles of intellectual freedom as set forth in *Media, the Learner, and Intellectual Freedom: A Handbook*, published by AECT.

The Award: The award shall consist of:

1. a plaque and $1000 for the winning media professional, to be presented at the AECT National Convention and INFO-COMM International Exposition;

2. a framed certificate plus $1000 for the media center designated by the recipient;

3. the opportunity for the recipient to present a session on intellectual freedom at the AECT National Convention and COMMTEX International Exposition.

Selection: The following criteria will be used in the selection process:

1. the recipient will be a media specialist at any level.

2. the recipient will be a member of AECT.

3. the recipient shall not have received another intellectual freedom award in the same year if that award was sponsored by SIRS, Inc.

4. the recipient will meet at least one of the following criteria:

   • has developed and implemented an exemplary selection policy/challenge procedure for educational nonprint material.

   • has developed an innovative information program on intellectual freedom for nonprint media.

   • has upheld intellectual freedom principles in the face of a challenge to educational nonprint media

   • has been active in the establishment and/or continuation of a coalition relating to intellectual freedom.

   • has been active in the development of a legal base for the continued enjoyment of intellectual freedom.

Selection
Committee: A subcommittee of the AECT Intellectual Freedom committee is responsible for the selection of the winner.

ECT Foundation
1991 AECT National Convention—
Earl F. Strobehn Internship Program

Awards:

Six students will be chosen as convention interns. The winners will receive complimentary convention registration, complimentary housing, and a $100 cash award. The interns will be expected to arrive at the convention on Thursday and to stay until Tuesday. (Applicants are encouraged to request financial support for transportation and on-site expenses from their institutions or state affiliate organizations.)

Program
Activities:

Each intern will be expected to participate fully in a coordinated program of activities. These activities include private seminars with selected association and professional leaders in the field; observation of the AECT governance and program committees; and behind-the-scenes views of the convention itself. Each intern will also be responsible for specific convention-related assignments, which will require approximately fifteen hours of time during the convention. A former intern, who is now a member of the AECT Leadership Development Committee, will serve as the program coordinator.

Eligibility:

To qualify for consideration, an applicant must be a full-time student throughout the current academic year in a recognized graduate program in educational communications and technology, and must be a member of AECT. (Applicant may join AECT when applying for the award.)

Application
Process:

To apply for the Internship Program, qualified graduate students must complete and return the enclosed application form, and must submit two (2) letters of recommendation.

ECT Foundation
1991 Richard B. Lewis Memorial Award

Award:
$500, provided by the Richard B. Lewis Memorial Fund for "Outstanding School District Media Utilization," is awarded to the winner.

Selection
Process:
The winner will be selected by a unified committee appointed from the divisions of Educational Media Management (DEMM) and School Media Specialists (DSMS) of the Association for Educational Communications and Technology, and the National Association of Regional Media Centers (NARMC).

Selection
Criteria:
• Evidence of strong media utilization as gathered from:

1. special utilization studies conducted by or for the school district;

2. specific instances of good utilization as described in writing by school district or other personnel.

• Evidence of having provided in the school district budget means of implementing good utilization programs in its schools, and the degree to which AECT/ALA media standards are met for services, equipment, and personnel.

• Assessment of applicant's statements as to how the $500 (if awarded) would be spent, such as for:

1. attending national, regional, or state conferences or workshops related to media utilization;

2. selecting media specialist(s) to attend advanced training programs;

3. buying software or hardware needed to improve media utilization programs;

4. other purposes (indicating especially creative approaches).

• Recognition by an AECT state, regional, or national affiliate organization or representative, or from a National Association of Regional Media Centers state or regional representative:

1. through prior recognition or awards;

2. through a recommendation

Eligibility:
All school districts, public and private, having media utilization programs in place, and conforming to the above criteria, are eligible.

Other:
The winning district will receive a plaque as part of this award.

ECT Foundation
1991 Leadership Development Grants

Grants: Grants of up to $250 are provided by the ECT Foundation and administered by the AECT Leadership Development Committee. The grants are awarded to assist AECT affiliates, AECT divisions, and AECT regional organizations to undertake leadership development activities that will improve participants' skills as leaders in the professional organization or in educational technology.

Selection: Grant awards will be recommended by the Leadership Committee's subcommittee on Leadership Development Grants.

Criteria
for
Selection: All AECT state affiliates, divisions, and regional organizations are eligible for these competitive grants. An application from a previous grant recipient will not be considered unless a summary report has been submitted to the Leadership Development Committee and the AECT national office. Organizations that have not received a grant in the past are particularly invited to apply. Funds must be intended for some unique aspect or function not previously undertaken. Proposals that demonstrate a commitment to leadership development, that propose programs that are unique to the applicant's organization, and that include activities or products of potential benefit to other AECT programs will be given special consideration.

Awards: The awards will be presented during the AECT National Convention and INFOCOMM International Exposition.

ECT Foundation
1991 AECT Memorial Scholarships

Awards:

One scholarship of $750 and one scholarship of $500 are awarded to graduate students in educational communications/technology to carry out a research project in the field. The scholarships may be used to assist the recipients to further their education in a summer session or academic year of graduate study at any accredited college or university in the United States or Canada. Programs of study may be at the master's or doctoral level.

Eligibility:

All recipients must be members of AECT, and accepted in or enrolled in a graduate-level degree program as outlined above.

Selection
Criteria:

Selections will be based on the following:

1. scholarship;

2. experience related to the field of educational media, communications, or technology, such as employment, field experience, course work, assistantships, publications, etc.;

3. service to the field through AECT activities and membership in other related professional organizations;

4. three letters of recommendation from persons familiar with the candidate's professional qualifications and leadership potential;

5. the candidate's own knowledge of key issues and opportunities facing the educational communications/technology field today, with respect to their own goals.

ECT Foundation
1991 Dean and Sybil McClusky
Research Award

Award: $500 will be awarded for the best submitted doctoral research proposal
                        in educational technology, as selected by a jury of researchers from
                        AECT's Research and Theory Division.

Guidelines
for Preparing
and Submitting
Papers: Submitted proposals may follow acceptable formats of individual
                        schools but must include at least:

                        1. The definition of the problem including a statement of
                            significance.

                        2. A review of pertinent literature.

                        3. Research hypothesis to be examined.

                        4. Research design and procedures including statistical
                            techniques.

                        Applicants are encouraged to review pages 157-161 of Isaac, Stephen,
                        and Michaels, William B., *Handbook in Research and Evaluation*,
                        Robert R. Knapp, San Diego, CA, 1971.

Eligibility: Applicants must be presently enrolled in a doctoral program in educa-
                        tional technology and have obtained committee acceptance of their
                        proposal. The winner will be expected to sign a statement to the effect
                        that he/she will complete the proposed doctoral study in accordance
                        with the sponsoring University's graduate school policies (including any
                        time limitations) or be required to return the funds received.

ECT Foundation
1991 Carl F. and Viola V. Mahnke
Film Production Award

Award:
$500 will be awarded to honor a film or video product that demonstrates excellence in message design and production for educational purposes. In addition, Certificates of Merit will be awarded to entries with outstanding qualities worthy of recognition. In the event that no entry demonstrates excellence, in the opinion of the judges, no award will be given.

Eligibility:
Eligibility is limited to film and video products that are educational in nature and produced by undergraduate or graduate students. The winners must be members of AECT. Only entries completed within a two-year period prior to the competition will qualify.

Formats:
All entries must be either on film or videotape. Film entries are limited to 16mm. Video entries can either be ½-inch VHS or ¾-inch U-matic.

Judging:
All entries will be judged during the AECT National Convention by a panel of judges from the AECT Media Design and Production Division.

Entry Fee:
Entrants must include an entry fee of $10 per program, made payable to MDPD-AECT. For programs consisting of more than one film or videocassette, each must be submitted separately. An entry form must be completed for each entry. The entry form may be duplicated if necessary.

ECT Foundation
1991 Robert M. Gagné Award for Graduate Student
Research in Instructional Technology

Purpose:	To provide recognition and financial assistance for outstanding research done by a graduate student in the field of Instructional Development.
Description:	The Robert M. Gagné Award Fund is coordinated by the ECT Foundation, a nonprofit organization sponsored and controlled by the Association for Educational Communications and Technology (AECT). The Division of Instructional Development will solicit nominations for the Gagné Award and will select the winner. The ECT Foundation is responsible for the administration of the award fund and will issue the cash award to the recipient.
Award:	$500 is awarded for the most significant contribution to the body of knowledge upon which instructional development is based. The Gagné Award competition is sponsored by the Association for Educational Communications and Technology (AECT) and its Division of Instructional Development. A jury of scholars will select the winning contribution. The award will be presented to the recipient during the AECT National Convention. The winner will receive the cash award and a plaque.
Eligibility:	The work must have been completed after December 31, 1987, while the award candidate was enrolled as a graduate student.
Nomination Procedure:	You may nominate any individual (including yourself) for the Gagné Award.

ECT Foundation
1991 James W. Brown Publication Award

Award:　　　　　$200 will be given to the author or authors of an outstanding publication in the field of Educational Technology. The award will be presented during the 1991 AECT National Convention and INFOCOMM International Exposition in Orlando, Florida, February 13 through 16.

Eligibility:　　　Nominated items are not restricted to books or print; they may be in any media format (film, video, broadcast program, book, etc.). Any nonperiodic publication in the field of Educational Technology is eligible if it bears a publication date of 1988 or 1989.

Guidelines
for
Nominations:　　Nominations are solicited from all possible sources: AECT members; media-related publishers and producers; authors themselves; the AECT nonperiodic publications committee; and others.

Criteria:　　　　Nominated publications shall be judged on the basis of:

1. Significance of the item's content for the field of media/instructional technology, as defined in the *Definition of Educational Technology*, published by AECT in 1977, or in any subset of the publication.

2. Professional quality of the item.

3. Potential impact of the item's content on the field of media/instructional technology, as defined in the *Definition of Educational Technology*.

4. Technical quality of the item.

ECT Foundation
1991 ECTJ Young Scholar Award

Award:
$250 plus a certificate suitable for framing will be presented to the winner. Additionally, the winning paper will be published in *ECTJ*, the refereed scholarly research journal published by the Association for Educational Communications and Technology (AECT).

For:
The best paper discussing a theoretical construct that could guide research in educational technology, considered worthy by a panel of judges.

Eligibility:
An individual who does not hold a doctorate degree, or who received a doctorate not more than three (3) years ago as of September 1, 1990.

Guidelines
for Preparing
and Submitting
Papers:

1. Papers must deal with research and theory in educational technology and must include:

   • A problem area stated within a well-explicated theoretical construct;

   • Supporting citations and analyses of related research;

   • A concluding discussion centering on what directions future research might take, with specific regard to variables, subjects, settings, etc., and, if appropriate, suggestions concerning other theoretical constructs that should be taken into consideration;

2. The paper should not be a report of a specific study;

3. A fresh, imaginative approach—which may go beyond the data—is encouraged;

4. The paper must be an original unpublished work;

5. The paper should be about 35 (or less) double-spaced typewritten pages long;

6. The paper must be submitted in publishable journal format and must conform to the *American Psychological Association Style Manual*, 3rd edition.

Selection
of
Winner:
The selection of the winning paper will be the responsibility of the editor and editorial board of *ECTJ*. Only the best paper judged worthy of the award will win. (There may not be a recipient of this award every year.)

ECT Foundation
1991 Young Researcher Award

Award:
$500 for the best report of an experimental, descriptive, or historical study in Educational Technology. The Young Researcher Award competition is sponsored by the Research and Theory Division of the Association for Educational Communications and Technology (AECT). A jury of scholars will select the best contribution for presentation at the AECT National Convention and INFOCOMM International Exposition. The winner will receive the cash award plus a certificate suitable for framing.

Eligibility:
Anyone who is not more than three (3) years beyond a doctorate, as of December 31, 1990. A doctorate is *not* required. Jointly published papers are not acceptable.

Guidelines
for Preparing
and Submitting
Papers:
Papers must report an original, unpublished research effort of experimental, descriptive, or historical nature and must include the following:

1. problem area stated within a well-explicated theoretical construct(s);

2. supporting citations and analyses of related research;

3. exemplary reporting of research design or procedures and full description of statistical procedures where applicable;

4. concluding discussion that centers on directions for future research and implications for future directions in the field.

Other:
Manuscripts may be a maximum of 35 double-spaced typewritten pages. The manuscript must be submitted in publishable journal format and must conform to the *American Psychological Association Style Manual*, 3rd edition. The author's name should be included *only* on the cover sheet. All manuscripts will be coded and reviewed "blind."

ECT Foundation
1991 Jerry R. Coltharp Memorial
Innovative Media Management Award

Award:
This award is funded and coordinated by DEMM. One $400 award is presented annually, in recognition of innovative media management practices which enhance the provision of instructional media services or advance media applications.

Eligibility:
Media service programs in schools, school districts, colleges and universities, regional media centers, government/military, allied health, and business and industry are eligible for the award.

Submission:
Projects which demonstrate exemplary management practices and a potential for enhancing associated media services are to be described in an article format not to exceed ten double-spaced typed pages. Supporting photographs and/or graphic materials are encouraged. Article organization may be determined by the author but must include a definition of the specific need to be addressed, a review of the management approach applied, and an evaluation of the effectiveness of the project. Project categories are unrestricted and may encompass such areas as staff development, client training, public relations, service assessment, facilities design, etc.

Selection:
Submissions are reviewed and the recipient is determined by a selection committee appointed by the president of the AECT Division of Educational Media Management.

Criteria:
Criteria for evaluating submissions are as follows:

> *Originality*: Did the project demonstrate a unique approach to addressing specific needs?

> *Need*: Did the need to be addressed relate to the enhancement of media services or the advancement of media utilization?

> *Design*: Was the structure of the project appropriate to the need?

> *Impact*: Was the project successful in meeting the defined needs?

Reporting:
Articles detailing project parameters shall be considered for publication in an AECT publication. Publication rights will be assumed by AECT.

Other:
Manuscripts may be a maximum of 35 double-spaced typewritten pages. The manuscript must be submitted in publishable journal format and must conform to the *American Psychological Association Style Manual*, 3rd edition. The author's name should be included *only* on the cover sheet. All manuscripts will be coded and reviewed "blind."

1991 DOT-AECT Crystal Award

Purpose:	To recognize the most innovative and outstanding instructional tele-communications project for 1990.
Sponsor:	The Division of Telecommunications of the Association for Educational Communications and Technology (AECT).
Eligibility:	Limited to telecommunications projects that include a video component, that are instructional in nature and are designed for any age level, and that have been completed since September 30, 1989. Awards will be presented to the producing agency.
Entry Fee:	A $25.00 fee must accompany each entry. Make checks payable to DOT-AECT.
Judging:	Entries will be judged by a "blue ribbon" panel chosen by the President of DOT.
Criteria:	Entries will be judged using the following criteria:

- Instructional value and relevance
- Quality of production
- Evidence of successful utilization and implementation
- Evidence of achievement of goals and objectives

Entry
Information: The following information must be provided for each entry. Please provide the essential information only. This information may not exceed 4 pages.

1. Contact person's name, title, address and telephone number
2. Official name of submitting agency
3. Name of individual to accept award for producing agency, if selected as winner
4. Intended audience(s)
5. Goals and objectives of project
6. Design and production process, including names of principal project staff
7. Time line for project
8. Budget and sources of funding
9. Evidence of successful utilization and implementation
10. Samples of all project components
11. Return address for all items sent.

Part Six

Mediagraphy
Print and Nonprint Resources

Introduction

Warren E. Babcock
Reference Librarian
Merrill Library
Utah State University, Logan

This current resource section of *EMTY 90* represents journal articles and other recent publications in areas of potential interest to professionals in the field and other individuals interested in educational technology. It is planned that the comprehensive list of professional publications such as that which appeared in *EMTY 88* will be revised on a three-year schedule. In the interim editions of *EMTY*, a mediagraphy of current resources will appear.

Data for entries in this section were collected by using Books in Print Plus (CD-ROM), ERIC ONDISC, and through database searches online. Generally, to be included in this mediagraphy, all publications had to have been published in 1989. A few entries with earlier publication dates have been included because it was felt they would be of general interest and because they did not appear in the last edition of *EMTY*. It is anticipated that the method of organization of the citations will prove to be helpful to the reader.

ORDERING INFORMATION

The names of publishers or producers that are identical to the titles of the periodicals in the mediagraphy have not been repeated. Users are reminded that name and address data are provided in the "Directory of Producers, Distributors, and Publishers" appearing at the end of this section. It is suggested that users refer directly to the index in cases where names of individuals or organizations are known but specific titles are not.

OBTAINING ERIC DOCUMENTS

All entries in this section carrying "EDRS" identifying numbers (ED ...) are publications available from the Educational Resources Information Center (ERIC). Copies of most of these publications can be obtained from the ERIC Documents Reproduction Service (EDRS), 3900 Wheeler Ave., Alexandria, VA 22304-5110. (Phone toll free: 1-800-227-3742.)

Most publications can be obtained in both paper and microfiche. Up-to-date information about costs and ordering procedures is available in the publication entitled *Resources in Education* (*RIE*), which is available in most large libraries. Also many large libraries maintain an ERIC microfiche collection where these publications can be located and used generally without charge.

ARRANGEMENT

The citations are classified according to major subject emphases and are listed under a main entry. Journals, newsletters, and other periodically published items are listed alphabetically in the "Journal Articles" section.

The following is a list of major subject headings used in this bibliography:

- Adult Education

- Artificial Intelligence and Robotics

- CD-ROM

- Communication Systems

- Computers and Instructional Uses of Computers

- Databases, Online Searching, Networking, Telecommunications

- Distance Education

- Educational Research

- Educational Technology

- Electronic Publishing

- Information Science

- Instructional Design, Training

- Instructional Media

- Libraries, Media Centers, Technical Applications

- Microforms and Micrographics

- Videodisc Technology

Mediagraphy

ADULT EDUCATION

Reference Tools/ERIC Documents

Basic Principles for Adult Education. Office of Vocational and Adult Education, Washington, D.C. Division of Adult Education. March 1989. (ED 305 492. EDRS, 1989.) 9p. A basic set of principles for adult education reflects what should be found in each state and local program.

Communications Technologists in Adult, Career, and Vocational Education. ERIC Digest No. 81. Kerka, Sandra. 1989. (ED 305 494. EDRS, 1989.) 3p. The rapidly developing communications technologies (CT) have the potential to deliver education to more learners in more satisfactory ways.

A Computer-Based Curricular Provision for Rural Communities (RP110). Further Education Unit, London (England). 1989. (ED 306 048. EDRS, 1989.) 50p. Discussion of a project at East Devon College of Further Education which sought to identify learning needs in scattered rural communities, particularly among the unemployed, and to meet those needs with distance education technology.

Computer Conferencing: A Technology for Adult Education. Technical Report No. 1. Florini, Barbara M. February 1989. (ED 305 463. EDRS, 1989.) 23p. Computer conferencing is a promising technology for use in adult education because it eliminates time and geography as barriers to learning.

Books

Adult Education as Theory, Practice & Research: The Captive Triangle. Usher, Robin, and Bryant, Ian. (Routledge, Chapman & Hall, 1989.) 224p., $35.00. Examines the reasons for the diverse education of adults and offers more productive ways of considering the relationships between theory, research, and practice.

Adult Learning, 3d ed. Rogers, Jenny. (Taylor & Francis, 1989.) 256p., $18.00.

Adult Learning Methods. Galbraith, Michael W., editor. (Krieger, 1989.) $29.50. This is a "how-to" book that provides an overview of the major aspects of understanding and facilitating adult learning and an array of methods and techniques that can be employed.

Effective Strategies of Teaching Adults. Seaman, Don F., and Fellenz, Robert A. (Merrill, 1989.) 208p., $29.95.

The Handbook of Adult & Continuing Education. Merriam, Sharan B., and Cunningham, Phyllis M., editors. (Jossey-Bass, 1989.) 670p., $49.95. Identifies and analyzes the major issues and problems facing today's adult and continuing education professionals. Contains a chapter on new educational technologies for the future.

Improving Higher Education Environments for Adults: Responsive Programs & Services from Entry to Departure. Schlossberg, Nancy K., Lynch, Ann Q., and Chickering, Arthur W. (Jossey-Bass, 1989.) 208p., $22.95. Details the programs and services colleges and universities must implement to effectively meet the needs of the growing number of adult learners.

The Meaning of Adult Education. Lindeman, Eduard, and Long, Huey B. (University of Oklahoma, Oklahoma Center for Continuing Professional & Higher Education, 1989.) 150p., $14.95.

Journal Articles

Askov, Eunice N. "Using Computers for Teaching Basic Skills to Adults." **Lifelong Learning, 12** (6), 28-31, April 1989. (EJ 388 171.) Explains how using computers allows adults to learn basic skills in new ways and to avoid reliving experiences with frustration, failure, and humiliation that they may have endured as children in school.

Morrison, Ian, and Rubenson, Kjell. "Adult Training in an Information Economy." **Learning** (Canada), **5** (2), 4-9, 1989. (EJ 384 938.) Discusses how human resource investments are increasingly viewed as critical to the process of human development.

Putman, Anthony O. "Computer-Based Coaching: The Trainer's Missing Piece." **Training and Development Journal, 43** (3), 34-37, March 1989. (EJ 384 942.) The author discusses using computer-based coaching to help employees apply their training on the job.

Woodall, Robbie, and Pulliam, Quenton. "Accounting Telecourse Offers Needed Flexibility." **Business Education Forum, 43** (6), 14-16, March 1989. The authors describe the telecourse at Nashville State Technical Institute.

ARTIFICIAL INTELLIGENCE AND ROBOTICS

Reference Tools

Artificial Intelligence Abstracts Annual 1989. (Bowker A&I, 1990.) 470p., $395. Provides a timely review of developments in the field of artificial intelligence.

Artificial Intelligence and Instruction: A Selected Bibliography. Milheim, William D. (Educational Technology, 1989.) 55p., $14.95. A bibliography that covers the field of AI. Contains over 500 references.

Artificial Intelligence Handbook, 2 vols. Nisenfeld, A. E. Vol. 1, Concepts & Theory. Vol. 2, Applications. (Instrument Society of America, 1989.) Focuses on AI as one tool in a set of tools which can be used in problem solving.

The Facts on File Dictionary of Artificial Intelligence. Smith, Raoul. (Facts on File, 1989.) 330p., $29.95. It defines all of the field's generally accepted terms and describes all of its major expert systems.

Books

Expert Systems in Education and Training. McFarland, Thomas D., and Parker, Reese. (Educational Technology, 1989.) 200p., $34.95. Provides knowledge and information in the evaluation of the field of AI and its contribution to the work of educators.

Future Mind: Artificial Intelligence: The Merging of the Mystical & the Technological in the 21st Century. Glenn, Jerome C. (Acropolis Books, 1989.) 320p., $19.95.

Hypertext: Theory into Practice. McAleese, Ray, editor. (Ablex, 1989.) 192p., $32.50. This is an introduction to hypertext practice and represents an interesting cross-section of researchers and topics on hypertext.

IEEE International Conference on Robotics & Automation, 6th, 1989: Proceedings. (IEEE Computer Society Press, 1989.) 1,868p., $198.00. Contains the papers presented at the 1989 conference.

Knowledge-Based Control with Applications to Robots. De Silva, C. W., and MacFarlane, A. G. (Springer-Verlag New York, 1989.) 196p., $32.00.

Knowledge Representation & Organization in Machine Learning. Morik, K., editor. (Springer-Verlag New York, 1989.) 319p., $26.90.

The Philosophy of Artificial Intelligence. Boden, Margaret A. (Oxford University Press, 1989.) 288p., $49.95.

Progress in Robotics and Intelligent Systems. Volume 1. Ho, C. Y., and Zobrist, George W. (Ablex, 1989.) 352p., $49.50. Focuses on state-of-the-art developments in robotics and intelligent systems. Also provides insight, guidance, and specific techniques vital to those concerned with the design and implementation of robotics and intelligent system applications.

Journal Articles

Bitter, Gary G. "Artificial Intelligence: The Expert Way." **Media and Methods, 25** (5), 22-23, 25, May-June 1989. (EJ 394 004.) This discussion of artificial intelligence (AI) and expert systems focuses on their use in education.

"Fourth and Fifth Generation Programming Languages. Resources in Technology." **Technology Teacher, 48** (6), 15-22, March 1989. (EJ 384 917.) Discusses the history of programming languages, emphasizing the newer fourth- and fifth-generation languages that are increasingly human-like in their intelligence.

Mandell, Alan, and Lucking, Robert. "Investigating AI with BASIC and LOGO: Helping the Computer to Make Decisions." **Journal of Computers in Mathematics and Science Teaching, 8** (2), 94-99, Winter 1989. Compares a program written both in BASIC and LOGO on its inferential and decision-making ability. The author explains the steps in each program and how deductions and decisions are made.

Masuch, Michael, and LaPotin, Perry. "Beyond Garbage Cans: An AI Model of Organizational Choice." **Administrative Science Quarterly, 34** (1), 38-67, March 1989.

CD-ROM

Reference Tools

Microsoft CD-ROM Yearbook, 1989-1990. Forward by Gates, Bill. Introduction by Yee, Min S. (Microsoft, 1989.) 935p., $79.95. Contains current facts, statistics, and forecasts of the CD-ROM industry.

Books

Online & CD-ROM Databases in School Libraries: Readings. Lathrop, Ann. (Libraries Unlimited, 1989.) 250p., $29.50. School library media specialists describe their own experiences in integrating online databases into the established curriculum.

Using CD-ROM: A Collection of Product Appraisals by Users. Brown, Jane E., and Helgerson, Linda W., editors. (Langley Books, 1989.) 435p., $27.95.

Using CD-ROM as a Public Access Catalogue. Akeroyd, John, and others. (British Library Research & Development Department and distributed in the U.S. by the American Library Association, 1988.) Reviews the CD-ROM Public Access Catalogue Systems in use. Cost, ease of use and interface, hardware, and stage of development are discussed for each system examined.

Journal Articles

Gery, Gloria J. "CD-ROM: The Medium Has a Message." **Training, 26** (1), 45-51, January 1989. Discusses if and how compact disc technology can make trainers more effective in improving human performance within organizations.

Harwood, Jim. "Enter Erasable CDS: Hard Time for Hardisks." **Educational Technology, 29** (7), 53-54. July 1989. The rewritable optical media are finally here.

Saffady, William. "Read-Only Optical Disks: A State of the Art Survey." **Micrographics and Optical Storage Equipment Review**, 13, 3-72, 1988. Emphasizes the CD-ROM format, but also deals with videodiscs and other types of compact disks.

COMMUNICATION SYSTEMS

Reference Tools/ERIC Documents

Satellite Communications and High School Education: Perceptions of Students, Teachers, and Administrators. Simonson, Michael R., and others. (ED 308 841. EDRS, 1989.) 32p. Paper presented at the Annual Meeting of the Association for Educational Communications and Technology (Dallas, February 1-5, 1989). Contains a report series of research studies completed during 1988.

Books

Communication & Networking, 3d ed. Jordan, Larry. (Prentice Hall, 1989.) 108p., $24.95.

Data Communications Networking Devices. 2d ed. Held, Gilbert. (John Wiley & Sons, 1989.) 400p., $49.95. Provides a comprehensive coverage of the numerous devices employed in the design, modification, or optimization of data communications networks.

EMail in Libraries. Dewey, Patrick. (Meckler, 1989.) 150p., $35.00. Explores and explains how EMail is used in libraries, the effect of it on library function, and its advantages over paper mail.

Everybody's Networking Book: A Common-Sense Guide to Sharing Computer Information. O'Dell, Peter. (Ventana, 1989.) 310p., $24.95.

1989 National Directory of Bulletin Board Systems (annual). (Meckler, 1989.) 108p., $39.95. Lists thousands of bulletin boards by state and area code.

Journal Articles

Fuwen, Gao, and others. "A PC-Based Audio/Graphics/Video Image Satellite Communication Education System and Its Application." **Educational & Training Technology International, 26** (3), 248-53, August 1989. The paper offers some concrete suggestions for teleteaching and teleconferencing development.

George, Penny. "Interactive Television: A New Technology for Teaching and Learning." **CALICO Journal, 6** (3), 43-46, March 1989. Describes an interactive television program in which one Spanish teacher reached 3,959 elementary school students at nine different sites through the use of studio and classroom cameras and television.

Jordahl, Gregory. "Communications Satellites: A Rural Response to the Tyranny of Distance." **Educational Technology, 29** (2), 34-38, February 1989. Provides an overview of several current satellite-based instructional systems and assesses their potential role in rural education.

Lake, Dan. "Two Projects That Worked: Using Telecommunications as a Resource in the Classroom." **Computing Teacher, 16** (4), 17-19, December-January 1989. Describes projects developed through the Long Distance Learning Network (LDLN) which experimented with using telecommunications in classrooms in the United States and Canada.

Langenberg, Donald N. "Supporting the Global Scholar." **Academic Computing, 3** (5), 12-16, January 1989. (EJ 389 288.) Explores the impact of information technologies on the institutional and organizational arrangements through which scholarly research is supported.

McCarty, Robert. "The Advantages of Using a Network." **Electronic Learning, 9** (1), 32-38, September 1989. Discusses how networks offer educators numerous benefits in instruction and management.

Naisbitt, John. "Ten New Megatrends as We Approach the Year 2000." **Educational Facility Planner, 27** (1), 4-7, January-February 1989. (EJ 387 093.) Special issue featuring the programs presented at the Annual Conference of the Council for Educational Facility Planners, International (Milwaukee, October 9-12, 1988.)

Ornstein, Allan C. "Emerging Curriculum Trends: An Agenda for the Future." **NASSP Bulletin, 73** (514), 37-48, February 1989. (EJ 385 222.) Summarizes new trends and emerging issues, such as telecommunications, computer literacy, and futuristic study.

Phillips, Gerald M., and Santoro, Gerald M. "Teaching Group Discussion via Computer-Mediated Communication." **Communication Education, 38** (2), 151-61, April 1989. (EJ 388 655.) Examines a traditional group discussion course redesigned to operate via computer-mediated communication.

COMPUTERS AND INSTRUCTIONAL USES OF COMPUTERS

Reference Tools/ERIC Documents

The Annual Guide to Highest-Rated Educational Software, 1990 Edition. Pre-School-Grade 12. (R. R. Bowker, 1989.) 130p., $26.95. Identifies over 375 programs, from among 8,000 programs evaluated, that have received high grades in the past 12 months from 32 respected evaluation services.

Computers to Enhance Science Education: An Inservice Designed to Foster Classroom Implementation. Roseman, Jo Ellen, and Brearton, Mary Ann. (ED 307 153. EDRS, 1989.) 32p. A paper presented at the Annual Meeting of the National Association for Research in Science Teaching (San Francisco, March 30-April 1, 1989.) Describes an inservice project designed to help teachers acquire the skills necessary to effectively integrate computer technology into science instruction.

The Complete Directory of Public Domain & Shareware for Apple Macintosh Computer, rev. ed. Queen, John E., and Apel, Alan A. (Budgetbytes, 1989.) 160p.

Encyclopedia of Microcomputers. Volumes 3-4. Kent, Allen, and Williams, James G., editors. (Marcel Dekker, 1989.) $160.00. The articles in this work are exhaustive and self-contained, yet concise and readable.

Integrating Instructional Technology in Educational Institutions: The Proper Role for Teachers. Aust, Ronald, and others. (ED 308 808. EDRS, 1989.) 16p. A paper presented at the Annual Meeting of the Association for Educational Communications and Technology. (Dallas, February 1-5, 1989.) Examines teacher attitudes toward the integration of instructional technology into instructional programs.

Using Technology to Improve the Curriculum of Small Rural Schools. ERIC Digest. Monk, David. (ED 308 056. EDRS, 1989.) 3p. Reviews the promise and drawbacks of computerized learning programs and telecommunication technologies for small rural schools.

Books

Computer Assisted Learning. Kibby, M. R., and Mayes, J. T. (Pergamon, 1989.) 263p., $60.00.

Computers and Reading: Lessons from the Past and the Technologies of the Future. Balajthy, Ernest. (Prentice Hall, 1989.) 256p. Designed to meet the needs of teachers who want to increase sophistication in the use of computers in reading and language arts.

Computers in Elementary Mathematics Education. Clements, Douglas H. (Prentice Hall, 1989.) 256p., $31.00.

Evaluating Educational Software: A Guide for Teachers. Sloane, Howard, and others. (Prentice Hall, 1989.) 144p., $15.00. Offers practical guidelines for assessing student needs, evaluating instructional software for use in the school system, and evaluating the adequacy of a program.

School District Instructional Computer-Use Evaluation Manual. Morton, Chris, and Beverly, Don. (Educational Technology, 1989.) 50p., $19.95. Provides guidance in assessing the use of technology in the schools.

Teachers, Computers, and Curriculum: Microcomputers in the Classroom. Geisert, Paul G., and Furtrell, Mynga K. (Allyn & Bacon, 1990.) 384p., $33.00. Focuses on decision-making which will help teachers effectively integrate computers into their classrooms. A complete chapter on acquiring and evaluating courseware is included.

Understanding Hypercard. 2d ed. Harvey, Greg. (Sybex, 1989.) 654p., $24.95.

Journal Articles

Brown, Christopher R. "Taking Some of the 'Hype' out of HyperCard." **The Computing Teacher**, 17 (4), 50-52, December-January 1989-90. Discusses some of the misconceptions concerning HyperCard and the importance of good programming skills.

Raker, Elizabeth. "Hypermedia: New Technology Tools for Educators." **The Computer Teacher**, 17 (1), 18-19, August-September 1989. An example of a hyper-resource for teachers.

DATABASES, ONLINE SEARCHING, NETWORKING, TELECOMMUNICATIONS

Reference Tools

Online Database Selection. A User's Guide to the Directory of Online Database. (Elsevier Science, 1989.) 80p., $19.50. Devised to help users locate relevant databases more quickly, effectively, and accurately.

Books

Democratizing Information: Online Databases and the Rise of End-User Searching. Pfaffenberger, Bryan. (G. K. Hall, 1989.) 175p., $32.50. Discusses the role of the search intermediary and the emerging pattern of the end-user. Demonstrates the rewards of end-user searching.

Issues in Online Database Searching. Tenopir, Carol. (Libraries Unlimited, 1989.) 175p., $26.50. Contains over 50 selected articles from the author's column in *Library Journal*, some of which have been rewritten to reflect the latest developments or products.

Online Searching. Lee, Joann H. (Libraries Unlimited, 1989.) 230p., $30.00. Presents a clear picture of how to set up, operate, implement, and administer an online reference program. Also includes a chapter on the CD-ROM.

Telecommunications in the Classroom. Clark, Chris. (International Society for Technology in Education, 1989.)

Journal Articles

Carr, Carol. "Aids for Teaching Online Searching of the Chemical Literature." **Journal of Chemical Education, 66** (1), 21-24, January 1989. (EJ 387 848.) Describes some support programs and materials that facilitate preparation of an effective and inexpensive classroom program on online searching of the chemical literature.

Hancock, Joelie. "Learning with Databases." **Journal of Reading, 32** (7), 582-89, April 1989. (EJ 388 487.) Discusses a variety of ways that teachers at all levels are using databases in their classrooms and how databases can be integrated into the curriculum.

Hawkins, Brian L. "Campus-Wide Networking at Brown University." **Academic Computing, 3** (5), 32-33, 36-39, 44, 46-49, January 1989. (EJ 389 293.) Describes the development and current status of a campus-wide computer network at Brown University.

Oley, Elizabeth. "Information Retrieval in the Classroom." **Journal of Reading, 32** (7), 590-97, April 1989. (EJ 388 488.) Explores aspects of information retrieval skills such as end-user training, and Boolean logic.

DISTANCE EDUCATION

Reference Tools/ERIC Documents

Research in Distance Education: Methods and Results. McIsaac, Marina Stock, and others. (ED 308 827. EDRS, 1989.) 8p. Paper presented at the Annual Meeting of the Association for Educational Communications and Technology (Dallas, February 1-5, 1989). The purpose of the study was to examine the variety of research emerging on distance education and to suggest a method for synthesizing the results.

Books

Evaluating Open and Distance Learning. Thorpe, Mary. (Nichols, 1989.) 210p., $21.50. Outlines a specific approach to evaluation and provides practical examples. Emphasis on a team approach and the effective use of evaluation findings.

Mindweave: Communication, Computers & Distance Education. Mason, Robin D., and Kaye, Anthony, editors. (Pergamon, 1989.) 280p., $34.95.

Readings in Distance Learning & Instruction. Moore, Michael G., and Clark, G. Christopher, editors. (American Center for the Study of Distance Education, 1989.) 160p., $12.00. The second in a series on distance education.

Readings in Principles of Distance Education. Moore, Michael G., and Clark, G. Christopher, editors. (American Center for the Study of Distance Education, 1989.) 110p., $10.00. The first in a series on distance education.

Theory and Practice of Distance Education. Holmberg, Borje. (Routledge, Chapman & Hall, 1989.) 240p., $47.50. Discusses the arguments for and against different lines of thought and different influential models.

Journal Articles

Barker, Bruce O., and others. "Broadening the Definition of Distance Education in Light of the New Telecommunications Technologies." **American Journal of Distance Education, 3** (3), 20-29, 1989. (EJ 392 471.) Presents a categorization of distance education methodologies in the form of a taxonomy that compares correspondence study-based distance education approaches with telecommunications-based approaches.

Barron, Daniel D. "The School Library Media Specialist and Distance Education." **School Library Media Activities Monthly, 5** (6), 47-50, February 1989. (EJ 387 474.) Provides a brief history and overview of current projects in distance education and describes the potential roles of the library media specialist.

Clark, Thomas A., and Verduin, John R., Jr. "Distance Education: Its Effectiveness and Potential Use in Lifelong Learning." **Life Learning, 12** (4), 24-27, January 1989. (EJ 383 359.) Looks at what distance education is, and what its applications are in adult education.

Murgatroyd, Stephen, and Woudstra, Andrew. "Issues in the Management of Distance Education." **American Journal of Distance Education, 3** (1), 4-19, 1989. Examines key issues facing administrators at Athabasca University and discusses their implications for distance education organizations.

Saba, Farhad, and Twitchell, David. "Integrated Services Digital Networks: How It Can Be Used for Distance Education." **Journal of Educational Technology Systems, 17** (1), 15-25, 1989. (EJ 380 456.) Describes Integrated Services Digital Networks (ISDN) which when combined with desktop workstations will provide access to voice, text, and video telecommunications.

Tait, Alan. "The Politics of Open Learning." **Adult Education Quarterly, 61** (4), 308-13, March 1989. (EJ 388 179.) Examines the background and purposes of open learning in Great Britain. Political motives are emphasized.

Taylor, Dianne J., and others. "Communications Technology for Literacy Work with Isolated Learners." **Journal of Reading, 32** (7), 634-39, April 1989. (EJ 388 494.) Describes satellite-delivered education for isolated learners wherein students interact with both teacher and fellow students using voice, video, and data.

Woodall, Robbie, and Pulliam, Quenton. "Accounting Telecourse Offers Needed Flexibility." **Business Education Forum, 43** (6), 14-16, March 1989. (EJ 384 886.) The telecourse program at Nashville State Technical Institute is described.

EDUCATIONAL RESEARCH

Reference Tools/ERIC Documents

Educational Research and Theory Perspectives on Intelligent Computer-Assisted Instruction. Tennyson, Robert D., and Christensen, Dean L. (ED 308 847. EDRS, 1989.) 15p. Defines the next generation of intelligent computer-assisted instructional systems (ICAI) by depicting the elaborations and extensions offered by educational research and theory perspectives to enhance the ICAI environment.

The Educator's Desk Reference: A Sourcebook of Educational Information & Research (EDR). Freed, Melvyn N., and others. (Macmillan, 1989.) 512p., $49.95. Provides easy access to a wide range of information sources needed by professionals in all areas and at all levels of education.

Facts on File Dictionary of Education. Shafritz, Jay M., and others. (Facts on File, 1989.) 503p., $40.00. Comprising more than 5,000 alphabetical entries, the book covers all aspects of educational administration in primary, middle, and high schools.

Problems and Perspectives on the Evaluation of Regional and National Computer-Related Educational Activity. Collis, Betty. (ED 307 284. EDRS, 1989.) 15p. Paper presented at the Annual Meeting of the American Educational Research Association (San Francisco, March 27-31, 1989.)

Books

Controlling the "Out of Control" Costs of Education: The Critical Changes. Stewart, Don. (SLAT E. Services, 1989.) 432p., $17.45.

Disciplined Inquiry: Understanding & Doing Educational Research. Eichelberger, R. Tony. (Longman, 1989.) 320p., $20.80.

Educational Research, 5th ed. Borg, Walter R., and Gall, Meredith D. (Longman, 1989.) 944p., $29.56. Covers the entire field of educational research process, from identifying the problem to writing the thesis. Also introduces the individual to every research technique in common use.

The Nature of Social & Educational Inquiry: Empiricism vs. Interpretation. Smith, John K. (Ablex, 1989.) 192p., $32.50. Describes in a clear, concise fashion the underlying issues involved in the current discussion over different approaches (empiricist vs. interpretive, quantitative vs. qualitative, scientific vs. naturist) to social and educational inquiry.

Research & the Teacher: A Qualitative Introduction to School Based Research. Hitchcock, Graham, and Hughes, David. (Routledge, Chapman & Hall, 1989.) 304p., $55.00. Explains the methodologies, language, and relevance of research, and the ways teachers can apply qualitative research techniques in school-based investigation.

Research in Education: A Conceptual Introduction, 2d ed. McMillan, James H., and Schumacher, Sally. (Scott, Foresman, 1989.) 608p., $31.95.

Journal Articles

Abraham, Michael R. "Research & Teaching: Research on Instructional Strategies." **Journal of College Science Teaching, 18** (3), 185-87, 200, December-January 1989. (EJ 387 817.) Examines two instructional strategies, the traditional and learning cycle approaches, and compares them with regard to the variables of sequence, format, and necessity.

Brophy, Jere. "Research: Safe Harbor from Political Winds." **School Administrator, 46** (1), 26-27, January 1989. (EJ 383 838.) Presents the idea that new research suggests that teaching for conceptual understanding and higher-order application requires sustained focus on fewer topics but in greater depth.

Chesley, Robert. "Finding and Using Education Research." **Thrust for Educational Research, 18** (5), 22-25, February-March 1989. (EJ 387 002.) Describes several databases relevant to the education field.

Cziko, Gary A. "Unpredictability and Indeterminism in Human Behavior: Arguments and Implications for Educational Research." **Educational Researcher, 18** (3), 17-25, April 1989. (EJ 390 024.) Argues that the complex human behavior studied by educational researchers is by its nature unpredictable if not indeterminate.

EDUCATIONAL TECHNOLOGY

Reference Tools/ERIC Documents

Educational Technology: Integrations? Christensen, Dean L., and Tennyson, Robert D. (ED 308 811. EDRS, 1989.) 10p. A paper presented at the Annual Meeting of the Association for Educational Communications and Technology (Dallas, February 1-5, 1989.) Contains perspectives on the current state of technology-assisted instruction integrating computer language, artificial intelligence (AI), and cognitive science applied to instruction.

Dictionary of Library and Educational Technology. 3d ed. Rosenberg, Kenyon C., and Elsbree, John J. (Libraries Unlimited, 1989.) 196p., $32.50. Defines over 1,000 terms relating to audiovisual equipment, reprography, computer software and hardware, telecommunications, micrographies, photography, and mass storage (e.g., CD-ROM and videodiscs).

Hypertext: A New Medium for Reading and Writing. Davis, Ken. (ED 307 625. EDRS, 1989.) 11p. Paper presented at the Annual Meeting of the Conference on College Composition and Communication (Seattie, March 16-18, 1989.)

Hypertext, Behind the Hype. ERIC Digest. Bevilacqua, Ann F. (ED 308 882. EDRS, 1989.) 4p. Defines the concept of hypertext and describes the two types of hypertext — static and dynamic.

The International Encyclopedia of Education Technology. Eraut, Michael, editor. (Pergamon, 1989.) 700p., $105.00. A collection of state-of-the-art reports concerning the entire field of educational technology. One-volume format with contributions thematically arranged in five sections.

International Yearbook of Educational and Training Technology, 1989. Osborne, Chris. (Nichols, 1989.) 600p., $69.50. A world-wide directory of organizations and institutions in over 90 countries that are actively involved in the development of educational and training technology.

Trends in Educational Technology: 1989. ERIC Digest. Ely, Donald P. (ED 308 858. EDRS, 1989.) 4p. Provides a state-of-the-art analysis of the field of educational technology based on the results of a content analysis of its literature.

Books

Aspects of Educational Technology XXII. Bell, Chris, and others. (Nichols, 1989.) Proceedings of the 1988 Conference of the Association for Educational and Training Technology.

The Electronic Text: Learning to Write, Read and Reason with Computers. Costanzo, William V. (Educational Technology, 1989.) 300p., $32.95. Provides an overview of the entire range of software that affects the way individuals learn about, and use, the written word.

The Evolution of American Educational Technology. Saettler, Paul. (Libraries Unlimited, 1990.) 500p., $38.00. A scholarly work which focuses on the historical foundations of the theoretical and methodical approaches to educational technology.

Hypertext-Hypermedia. Jonassen, David H. (Educational Technology, 1989.) 100p., $24.95. Identifies characteristics, rationales, and applications of hypertext systems while exploring some of the problems in using and authoring hypertext.

Technology in Education: Looking toward 2020. Nickerson, Raymond, and Zophiastes, Philip, editors. (Lawrence Erlbaum Associates, 1989.) 352p., $19.95. The contributors describe their visions of the future for education and prescribe the steps necessary to achieve them.

Journal Articles

Bork, Alfred. "The introduction of Computers in Norwegian Schools: An International Report." **Technological Horizons in Education**, 16 (6), 83-86, December-January 1989. (EJ 386 143.) Discusses Norway's effort to determine what steps should be taken following its National Program for Computers in Education.

Bruder, Isabelle. "Future Teachers: Are They Prepared?" **Electronic Learning**, 8 (4), 32-39, January-February 1989. (EJ 387 513.) Article discusses whether or not teachers are prepared for computer use in the classroom and focuses on preservice teacher training.

Feuer, Michael J. "Investing in School Technology. Weigh Today's Expense against Tomorrow's Gain." **American School Board Journal**, 176 (3), 37-39, March 1989. (EJ 385 329.) Discusses some studies of school technology to demonstrate that cost-effective analysis allows similar programs to be compared.

McCarthy, Robert. "Educational Technology Time Line: 1980-1989." **Electronic Learning**, 9 (3), 30-35, November-December 1989. Takes a look back at educational technology and other events of the period.

Mehan, Hugh. "Microcomputers in Classroom: Educational Technology or Social Practice?" **Anthropology and Educational Quarterly**, 20 (1), 4-22, March 1989. (EJ 386 583.) Studies the use of microcomputers in four elementary school classrooms and their effect on classroom organization, teacher-student relations, and curriculum.

Moonen, Jef. "Involvement and Information. Fifteen Challenges for Computers in Education." **Educational Technology**, 29 (12), 7-11, December 1989. Discusses the need to adopt policies relative to the introduction of information technology into the educational system.

Reigeluth, Charles M. "Educational Technology at the Crossroads: New Mindsets and New Directions." **Educational Technology and Research and Development**, 37 (1), 67-80, 1989. (EJ 389 281.) Discusses changes needed in the field of educational technology and recommends future directions.

ELECTRONIC PUBLISHING

Books

Electronic Publishing: Evaluation, Procurement & Management. Gater, David W., and Ferguson, Bill. (TAB Books, 1989.) 304p., $29.95.

The Macintosh Press: Desktop Publishing for Libraries. Johnson, Richard D., and Johnson, Harriett H. (Meckler, 1989.) 185p., $34.50. Gives practical advice on how the Mac and available software can be used for library publishing.

Structured Documents. André, Jacques, and Quint, Vincent. (Cambridge University, 1989.) 232p., $49.50. Explores the structured representation of documents in computer document preparation systems. Using this approach to documents allows their logical structure to be represented both descriptively and analytically.

Journal Articles

Bowman, Joel P., and Renshaw, Debbie A. "Desktop Publishing: Things Gutenberg Never Taught You." **Journal of Business Communication, 26** (1), 57-77, Winter 1989. (EJ 386 893.) Provides a desktop publishing (DTP) overview including such topics as the advantages and disadvantages; hardware and software requirements; and future development.

DeLoughry, Thomas J. "Scholarly Journals in Electronic Form Seen as Means to Speed Pace of Publication and Promote Dialogue." **Chronicle of Higher Education, 35** (28), A11, 16, March 22, 1989. (EJ 387 395.) The technology to replace printed journals with electronic counterparts is now available. It is also likely to have greater impact on traditional means of disseminating scholarship than will desktop publishing and offers the potential for improved peer review.

Huprich, Violet M. "Desktop Publishing: The New Wave in Business Education." **Business Education Forum, 43** (7), 17-19, April 1989. (EJ 386 668.) Discusses the challenges of teaching desktop publishing.

Kember, David, and Kemp, Neal. "Computer-Aided Publishing and Open Learning Materials." **British Journal of Educational Technology, 20** (1), 11-26, January 1989. (EJ 389 297.) Discusses computer-aided publishing hardware and software, emphasizing their impact on the production of printed learning materials.

Parker, Roger C. "Ten Common Desktop Design Pitfalls." **Currents, 15** (1), 24-26, January 1989. (EJ 384 197.) Users of desktop publishing may be distracted from clear communication by the advanced features of the technology.

Turner, Judith Axler. "'Electrocopies' Seen Surpassing Photocopies as Threat to Copyright." **Chronicle of Higher Education, 35** (25), A1, 16, March 1, 1989. (EJ 385 693.) The unauthorized reproduction of printed material in electronic form, particularly using optical scanning, is rising and is becoming nearly impossible to monitor.

Wilson, Phil. "More Than Just Desktop Design." **Currents, 15** (1), 18-23, January 1989. (EJ 384 195.) Cornell University's Office of Publications' experiences in the process of computerization are discussed, including rationale, choice of equipment, and decisions concerning the services to be offered, and the lessons learned.

INFORMATION SCIENCE

Reference Tools

French Dictionary of Information Technology. Pyper, Terry. (Routledge, Chapman & Hall, 1989.) 592p., $92.50. Approximately 30,000 entries in French and English that cover not only terminology used in telecommunications, electronics, and computer science, but also developments in related disciplines.

Books

Coming Information Age: An Overview of Technology, Economics & Politics, 3d ed. Dizard, Wilson P. (Longman, 1989.) 224p., $14.95.

Effective Access to Information: Today's Challenge, Tomorrow's Opportunity. Trezza, Alphonse F. (G. K. Hall, 1989.) 176p., $22.50. Contains the complete papers of a conference held at Florida State University in 1988 entitled "Effective Access to Information."

Hypertext Hands On!: An Introduction to a New Way of Organizing & Accessing Information. Shneiderman, Ben, and Kearsley, Greg. (Addison-Wesley, 1989.) $26.95.

Information Literacies for the 21st Century. Blake, Virgil L., and Tjoumas, Renee. (G. H. Hall, 1990.) 350p., $29.95. Contains over 40 papers that were delivered at "Information Literacies for the Twenty-first Century," a national conference held in 1988 at Queens College, New York.

Information Literacy: Revolution in the Library. Breivik, Patricia S., and Gee, E. Gordon. (Macmillan, 1989.) 256p., $24.95. A university president and a library director take a close, critical look at new roles for academic libraries as resources for information literacy.

Information Technology and Global Independence. Jussawalla, Meheroo, and others. (Greenwood, 1989.) 344p., $39.95. The book is based on a series of recent conferences and contains a discussion of potential repercussions arising from the worldwide dissemination of IT.

Journal Articles

Caissy, Gail A. "Curriculum for the Information Age." **Educational Horizons, 68** (1), Fall 1989. Discusses new basic skills needed for the information age and how to integrate them into the curriculum.

Gayeski, Dianne M. "Why Information Technologies Fail." **Educational Technology, 29** (2), 9-17, February 1989. (EJ 389 333.) Discusses successes and failures in the field of instructional technology and suggests methods to design more appropriate systems that would present fewer barriers to adoption.

INSTRUCTIONAL DESIGN, TRAINING

Reference Tools/ERIC Documents

Cognitive Science and Instructional Technology: Improvements in Higher Order Thinking Strategies. Tennyson, Robert D. (ED 308 846. EDRS, 1989.) 23p. Paper presented at the Annual Meeting of the Association of Educational Communications and Technology (Dallas, February 1-5, 1989.) Examines the cognitive processes associated with higher-order thinking strategies.

Educational Administration (Curriculum and Instructional Design): An Annotated Bibliography. Pautler, Albert J. (ED 303 894. EDRS, 1989.) 23p. A collection of over 140 references which concerns educational administration research in the area of curriculum and instructional design.

EPIE Institute's Report on Computer-Based Integrated Instructional Systems. (EPIE Institute, 1989.) $250.00. Provides independently researched evaluative and descriptive data on all major Integrated Instructional Systems (IIS) being marketed to schools.

Books

How to Develop and Present Staff Training Courses. Sheal, Peter R. (Nichols, 1989.) 176p., $32.50. Covers setting up and monitoring the training program right down to assessing results.

Instruction: A Model Approach. Gunter, Mary Alice, and others. (Allyn & Bacon, 1990.) 352p., $33.00. Step-by-step approach that encourages self-learning by students. New models of teaching-cooperative learning resolution of conflict are included.

Instructional Design: New Alternative for Effective Education and Training. Johnson, Kerry A., and Foa, Lin J. (Macmillan, 1989.) 236p. $29.95. Presents both a comprehensive history of instructional design and new concepts to help create effective programs based on an analysis of learners, content, and the learning environment.

A Nonprogrammer's Guide to Designing Instruction for Microcomputers. Tessmer, Martin, and others. (Libraries Unlimited, 1989.) 228p. $26.50. Guides the teacher, whether novice or expert, through the courseware development process.

Programming Instructional Software: Applesoft Basic Edition. Ragan, Tillman, and Smith, Patricia. (Educational Technology, 1989.) 460p., $29.95 (includes a computer diskette). A guide meant for teachers and trainers who want to learn how to design and program their own instructional software in BASIC.

The Well-Trained Computer: Designing Systematic Instructional Material for the Classroom Microcomputer. Futrell, Mygna K., and Geisert, Paul. (Educational Technology, 1989.) 290p., $32.95. Provides guidance on design factors.

Journal Articles

Bruder, Isabelle. "Teacher Education: New Ideas for Professional Development." **Electronic Learning,** 9 (3), 22-28, November-December 1989. A report on EL's second annual technology leadership conference.

Fuchs, Lynn S., and others. "Effects of Curriculum-Based Measurement on Teachers' Instructional Planning." **Journal of Learning Disabilities,** 22 (1), 51-59, January 1989. (EJ 385 387.) The study assesses effects of computer-assisted or noncomputer-assisted curriculum-based measurement (CBM) on the instructional planning of 30 special education teachers.

Galagan, Patricia A. "IBM Gets Its Arms around Education." **Training and Development Journal,** 43 (1), 34-41, January 1989. (EJ 381 472.) Education at IBM has jumped to the top of company priorities, joining key business functions such as manufacturing and finance that report directly to top management. It is also moving out of the classroom into a world of advanced technology.

McCleary, Iva Dene, and Egan, M. Winston. "Program Design and Evaluation: Two-Way Interactive Television." **American Journal of Distance Education,** 3 (1), 50-60, 1989. Describes a study that examined the effects of using two-way interactive television in a three-course sequence of teacher education courses.

Merrill, M. David, and Li, Zhongmin. "An Instructional Design Expert System." **Journal of Computer-Based Instruction, 16** (3), 95-101, Summer 1989. The paper describes a prototype instructional design expert system which supports the instructional design phase of Instructional System Development.

Reigeluth, Charles, and Schwartz, Ellen. "An Instructional Theory for the Design of Computer-Based Simulations." **Journal of Computer-Based Instruction, 16** (1), 1-10, Winter 1989. A simulation is described in terms of its three major design aspects: the scenario, the underlying model, and the instructional overlay. The major focus is on the instructional overlay.

Tyre, Terian. "Technology Update: CMI Seen as Possible Solution to Quality of Education Issue." **Technological Horizons in Education, 16** (5), 17, 20, 25, December-January 1989. (EJ 386 140.) Discusses the current state of computer-managed instruction (CMI) and the advantages it affords both teachers and students.

INSTRUCTIONAL MEDIA

Reference Tools/ERIC Documents

Audio Video Market Place, 1989 (AVMP). (R. R. Bowker, 1989.) 802p., $75.00. A comprehensive directory of audiovisual equipment and services for business, education, government, and the library world. Updated annually.

Equipment Directory of Audio-Visual, Computer and Video Products, 1989-1990. (International Communications Industries Association. Distributed by Libraries Unlimited, 1989.) Features over 200 different categories of equipment, with more than 2,500 products, 400 manufacturers, and over 800 dealers represented.

Only the Best. The Annual Guide to Highest-Rated Educational Software. 1990 Edition. Neill, Shirley Boes, and Neill, George W. (R. R. Bowker, 1989.) 136p., $26.95. Identifies over 375 programs, from among 8,000 programs evaluated, that have received high grades in the past 12 months from 32 respected evaluation services.

Software for Schools 1987-1988. (R. R. Bowker, 1987.) 1,158p., $49.95. A comprehensive guide to educational microcomputer software that is suitable for use in formal educational settings from preschool through 12th grade.

The Video Register and Teleconferencing Resources Directory, 1988, 10th ed. (Knowledge Industry Publications.) 348p., $74.50. Provides the name, addresses, and phone numbers of over 6,000 video and teleconferencing companies and professionals.

What Do Teachers Need to Know about Instructional Media in the Computer Age? Savenye, Wilhelmina C. (ED 308 839. EDRS, 1989.) 10p. Paper presented at the Annual Meeting of the Association for Educational Communications and Technology (Dallas, February 1-5, 1989). Explores teacher training needs related to effective use of technology in the classroom.

Books

Cooperative Learning & Educational Media: Collaborating with Technology and Each Other. Adams, Dennis, and others. (Educational Technology, 1989.) 196p., $32.95. Designed to guide the reader through the ideas, issues, trends, and possibilities for linking cooperative learning to educational technology.

Planning for Video: A Guide to Making Effective Training Videos. Taylor, Margaret H. (Nichols, 1989.) 250p., $34.50. Relates video techniques directly to training theory and practices, and presents a systematic approach to the strategies required to design, produce, and evaluate training programs.

Secrets of Video Training. The Training with Video Casebook. Cartwright, Steve R. (Knowledge Industry Publishing, 1989.) 150p., $39.95. Contains a collection of over 30 case studies of companies which have used home video for training.

The Society of Text: Hypertext, Hypermedia and the Social Construction of Information. Barrett, Edward, editor. (MIT, 1989.) 350p., $37.50. A collection of essays that continues Barrett's investigations into implementing networked online systems. Focuses on specific hypermedia systems.

Journal Articles

Chen, Milton, and Marsh, William. "Belying the Myths about Instructional Television." **Education Week, 8**, 32-35, May 24, 1989. Discusses how instructional television can booster progress toward the twenty-first century.

D'Ignazio, Fred. "Through the Looking Glass: The Multiple Layers of Multimedia." **The Computer Teacher, 17** (4), 25-31, December-January 1989-90. The article discusses various ways to use a multimedia computer and provides definitions of words and terms.

Litchfield, Brenda C., and Mattson, Susan A. "The Interactive Media Science Project: An Inquiry-Based Multimedia Science Curriculum." **Journal of Computers in Mathematics and Science Teaching, 9** (1), 37-43, Fall 1989. This paper focuses on the philosophy and development of an inquiry-based, level three interactive videodisc project (nine discs) funded by the National Science Foundation and Houghton Mifflin Company and designed specifically to promote critical thinking.

Thompson, James G., and Jorgensen, Sally. "How Interactive Is Instructional Technology?" **Educational Technology, 29** (2), 24-26, February 1989. (EJ 389 335.) Examines the relationship between instructional technology and cognition and discusses interactions between the learner and instructional media.

LIBRARIES, MEDIA CENTERS, TECHNICAL APPLICATIONS

Reference Tools/ERIC Documents

ALA Yearbook of Library and Information Services 1989: A Review of Library Events 1988. Parent, Roger. (American Library Association, 1989.) 350p., $85.00. Contains over 130 review essays on library events and activities.

School Library Media Annual, 1990. Smith, Jane Bandy, editor. (Libraries Unlimited, 1990.) xxii, 384p., $29.50. Contains sections on the best books and software, state and national awards, research findings and projects in progress, and trends in automation.

Trends in Library and Information Science: 1989. ERIC Digest. Eisenberg, Michael B. ERIC Clearinghouse on Information Resources, Syracuse, N.Y., September 1989. (ED 308 884. EDRS, December 1989.) 4p. Trends are drawn from content analysis of professional journals, conference proceedings, ERIC documents, annuals, and dissertations in library and information science.

Books

Collection Management: Background Principles. Wortman, William A. (American Library Association, 1989.) 172p., $25.00. Discusses the essential principles and best practices of collection management, and closely examines every aspect of this complex area of library administration.

Descriptive Statistical Techniques for Librarians. Hafner, Arthur W. (American Library Association, 1989.) 266p., $20.00. A self-teaching manual that introduces simple statistical methods to evaluate and plan library services. Contains more than 75 charts and graphs based on pertinent library examples.

HyperCard, Hypertext, and Hypermedia for Libraries and Media Centers. Gluck, Myke. (Libraries Unlimited, 1989.) 274p., $28.50 (includes a disk). Gives an overview of Hypertext, Hypermedia products and a detailed explanation of the myriad uses for the Mac's HyperCard 1-2. An accompanying disk provides exercises to help the librarian gain hands-on experience.

Library Media Center Series (videotapes). Orange County Department of Education. (Orange County Department of Education, 1989.) 5 video tapes, $375.00. Contains the following titles: A Principal's Analysis of the Library Media Center; Mending: A Practical Guide to Book Repair; Weeding: Cultivating Your Library; The Effective Library Media Center Program: A General Analysis; and Library Inventory.

The Library of the Future. Alternative Scenarios for the Information Profession. Shuman, Bruce A. (Libraries Unlimited, 1989.) 140p., $24.50. Examines such issues as the growth of information and how the future public library will meet its users' needs.

Library Services in Theory and Context. 2d ed. Buckland, Michael K. (Pergamon, 1988.) 268p., $36.00. Provides a coherent synthesis of the cognitive, economic, political, and technical aspects of librarianship and relates them to social values and cultural contexts.

Managing Media Services: Theory and Practice. Vlcek, Charles W., and Wiman, Raymond V. (Libraries Unlimited, 1989.) 426p., $38.00. Covers every aspect of the administration of media services.

101 Microcomputer Projects to Do in Your Library: Putting Your Micro to Work. Dewey, Patrick. (American Library Association, 1989.) 176p., $22.50. Describes creative, ingenious microcomputer applications now being used in all types of libraries across the U.S. and Canada.

Technology for the Nineties. Nelson, Nancy Melin, editor. (Meckler, 1990.) $35.00. Seven experts formulate and forecast how technology will affect librarians during the final decade of this century.

Journal Articles

Boone, Barbara, and others. "The Impact of High Technology: A Survey of Rural, Urban, and Suburban Library Media Centers." **Educational Technology, 29** (1), 38-42, January 1989. (EJ 389 242.) Reports on the results of a survey that assessed the extent of use of computer and video technology in library media centers (LMCs) located in rural, suburban, and urban elementary schools in Texas.

Edwards, Karlene K. "Principals' Perceptions of Librarians: A Survey." **School Library Journal, 35** (5), 28-31, January 1989. (EJ 387 499.) A survey of Arizona principals covered topics related to school media specialists, their roles, and responsibilities.

Holloway, Mary A. "Automating the Media Center." **Technological Horizons in Education, 16** (2), 95-99, September 1988. (EJ 384 542.) Discusses the need to develop more efficient information retrieval skills by using new technology.

Patrick, Retta B. "Information Power: The Planning Process." **School Library Media Quarterly, 17** (2), 88a-88j, Winter 1989. (EJ 389 226.) Discusses the planning process described in "Information Power," recently published guidelines for school library media programs.

White, Herbert S. "The Value-Added Process of Librarianship." **Library Journal, 114** (1), 62-63, January 1989. (EJ 387 512.) Discusses the importance of the role of librarians in the educational process.

MICROFORMS AND MICROGRAPHICS

Reference Tools

Guide to Microforms in Print: 1989 Supplement. (Meckler, 1989.) 670p., $95.00. A cumulative annual listing of microform titles, comprising books, journals, newspapers, government documents, archival material, collections, etc., that are currently available from micropublishing organizations throughout the world.

Journal Articles

Andrew, Harry C. "Technological Advances and the Future of Electronic Imaging." **IMC Journal, 25** (5), 6-10, September-October 1989. Discusses the right questions to ask in information management.

Crowley, Mary Jo. "Optical Digital Disk Storage: An Application for News Libraries." **Special Libraries, 79** (1), 34-42, Winter 1988. (EJ 365 092). Describes the technology, equipment, and procedures necessary for converting a historical newspaper clipping collection to optical disk storage.

Jones, Virginia A. "Advances Continue in Micrographics Techniques." **Office, 110** (3), 80-81, September 1989. Discusses the price of the new systems and the legal acceptance of digitized facsimile signatures.

McDonald, Peter. "Color Microforms: New Possibilities." **Microform Review, 17** (3), 146-49, August 1988. (EJ 380 529.) Explores the advantages and disadvantages of using color microforms.

Torok, Andrew G., and Torok, Stephen. "Library Education and Micrographics Enter a New Phase." **Inform, 3** (3), 24-27, March 1989. Discusses the need to train micrographics professionals and the role of library schools.

Turner, Jeffrey H. "The Suitability of Diazo Films for Long Term Storage." **Microform Review, 17** (3), 142-45. August 1988. (EJ 380 528.) Outlines the suitability of diazo film for the use of micrographics in libraries.

VIDEODISC TECHNOLOGY

Reference Tools/ERIC Documents

Interactive Video and Cognitive Structures: A Technique for Enhancing the Effectiveness of Interactive Simulations and Games. Alexander, J., and others. (ED 308 852. EDRS, 1989.) 29p. Paper presented at the Annual Meeting of the Association for Educational Communications and Technology (Dallas, February 1-5, 1989.)

Books

The Computing Technology Videodisc (videodisc). (Sunbelt Technologies, 1989.) This disc is an organized collection of approximately 1,000 still visuals and 18 brief video motion segments on the topic of computers and related technologies. The CAV format disc is designed for instruction in computer literacy, computer science, data processing, educational computing, and other aspects of computer education. A detailed printed index allows users to access any frame or chapter at random through use of the player's controller.

Interactive Video. (Educational Technology, 1989.) $24.95. A compilation of articles that have appeared in the journal *Educational Technology* in the recent past.

Opening Minds: The Evolution of Videodiscs and Interactive Learning. Haynes, George R. (Kendall/Hunt, 1989.) $29.95. Contains a history of videodiscs in education.

Using Video: Interactive and Linear Designs. Arwady, Joseph W., and Gayeski, Diane M. (Educational Technology, 1989.) 180p., $34.95. A practice guide about video production and specific design tools.

Journal Articles

Atkins, Madeleine, and Blissett, Gill. "Learning Activities and Interactive Videodisc: An Exploratory Study." **British Journal of Educational Technology, 20** (1), 47-56, January 1989. (EJ 389 300.) Reports findings of a small-scale study on middle school students' use of interactive videodisc.

Geber, Beverly. "Whither Interactive Videodisc?" **Training, 26** (3), 47-49, March 1989. (EJ 384 851.) Probably with the next 10 years, current videodisc technology will be surpassed by something even more useful to corporate trainers.

Hall, Wendy, and others. "Using HyperCard and Interactive Video in Education: An Application in Cell Biology." **Educational & Training Technology International, 26** (3), 207-13, August 1989. This paper suggests an alternative model for the development of interactive video material for education by using existing videodiscs and Apple's HyperCard.

Hofmeister, Alan M., and others. "Teaching with Videodiscs and Teaching Fractions with Videodiscs and Mainstreaming Students with Learning Disabilities for Videodisc Math Instruction." **Teaching Exceptional Children, 21** (3), 52-60, Spring 1989. (EJ 387 229.) Presented is an introduction to laser videodisc technology, covering both hardware and courseware considerations and technological applications to special education.

Hughes, Helena. "Conversion for a Teacher-Delivered Course into an Interactive Videodisc-Delivered Program." **Foreign Language Annals, 22** (3), 283-94, May 1989. (EJ 389 024.) Discusses a Spanish language course using interactive videodisc.

Underwood, John. "Hypercard and Interactive Video." **CALICO Journal, 6** (3), 7-20, March 1989. (EJ 387 283.) Describes the use of HyperCard to author an interactive Spanish videodisc using a videodisc version of "Zarabanda," a Spanish-instruction soap opera.

Directory of Producers, Distributors, and Publishers

This directory provides, in one alphabetical listing, the names and addresses of producers, distributors, and publishers whose media-related products are mentioned in the Mediagraphy.

This arrangement saves space that would otherwise be required for duplications of addresses. At the same time, a useful directory is provided for quick reference by those requiring address information.

The directory itself is arranged alphabetically, by principal name. Foreign and U.S. entries are interfiled.

Users of this list are reminded that addresses of this type change often. Accuracy of addresses was carefully checked, however, and is believed to be correct as of 1 January 1990.

Ablex Publishing Corporation
355 Chestnut Street
Norwood, NJ 07648

Acropolis Books, Ltd.
A Subsidiary of Colortone Press, Inc.
Colortone Building
2400 17th Street, N.W.
Washington, DC 20009-0064

Addison-Wesley Publishing Co., Inc.
1 Jacob Way
Reading, MA 01867

Allyn & Bacon, Inc.
A Division of Simon & Schuster
160 Gould Street
Needham Heights, MA 02194-2310

**American Center for the Study of
   Distance Education**
Pennsylvania State University
University Park, PA 16803

American Library Association
50 East Huron Street
Chicago, IL 60611-2729

R. R. Bowker
A Division of Reed Publishing USA
245 West 17th Street
New York, NY 10011

Budgetbytes, Inc.
P. O. Box 2248
Topeka, KS 66609

Cambridge University Press
40 West 20th Street
New York, NY 10011

Marcel Dekker, Inc.
270 Madison Avenue
New York, NY 10016

Educational Technology Publications, Inc.
720 Palisade Avenue
Englewood Cliffs, NJ 07632

Elsevier Science Publishing Co., Inc.
A Subsidiary of Elsevier NDU NV
655 Avenue of the Americas
New York, NY 10010

EPIE Institute
P.O. Box 839
Water Mill, NY 11976

Facts on File
Subsidiary of Commerce Clearing House
460 Park Avenue, South
New York, NY 10016

Greenwood Press, Inc.
P.O. Box 5007
88 Post Road West
Westport, CT 06881

G. K. Hall
A Division of Macmillan
70 Lincoln Street
Boston, MA 02111

IEEE Computer Society Press
A Subsidiary of IEEE Computer Society
1730 Massachusetts Avenue, N.W.
Washington, DC 20036-1903

Instrument Society of America
P.O. Box 12277
67 Alexander Drive
Research Triangle Park, NC 27709

**International Society for Technology
   in Education**
1787 Agate Street
Eugene, OR 97403-9905

John Wiley & Sons, Inc.
605 Third Avenue
New York, NY 10158

Jossey-Bass, Inc., Publishers
Subsidiary of Maxwell Communications
   Corp.
350 Sansome Street
San Francisco, CA 94104-9825

Kendall/Hunt
Subsidiary of Wm. C. Brown Co.,
   Publishers
2460 Kerper Boulevard
Dubuque, IA 52001

Knowledge Industry Publications
Subsidiary of Knowledge Sciences, Inc.
701 Westchester Avenue
White Plains, NY 10604

Langley Books, Inc.
6609 Rosecroft Plain
Falls Church, VA 22043-1828

Lawrence Erlbaum Associates, Inc.
365 Broadway
Hillsdale, NJ 07642

Libraries Unlimited, Inc.
P.O. Box 3988
Englewood, CO 80155-3988

Longman, Inc.
A Division of Addison-Wesley Publishing
Co.
Longman Building
95 Church Street
White Plains, NY 10601

Macmillan Publishing Co., Inc.
866 Third Avenue
New York, NY 10022

Meckler Corporation
11 Ferry Lane West
Westport, CT 06880

Merrill Publishing Company
A Division of Bell & Howell Co.
1300 Alum Creek Drive
Columbus, OH 43216

Microsoft Press
A Division of Microsoft Corp.
P.O. Box 97017
16011 NE 36th Way
Redmond, WA 98073-9717

MIT Press
55 Hayward Street
Cambridge, MA 02142

Nichols Publishers Co.
P.O. Box 96
New York, NY 10024

Orange County
Department of Education
200 Kalmus Drive
Costa Mesa, CA 92626

Oxford University Press, Inc.
200 Madison Avenue
New York, NY 10016

Pergamon Press, Inc.
Subsidiary of Maxwell Communications
Corp.
Maxwell House
Fairview Park
Elmsford, NY 10523

Prentice Hall
A Division of Simon & Schuster
Route 9 West
Englewood Cliffs, NJ 07632

Routledge, Chapman & Hall, Inc.
Subsidiary of International Thomson
Organization (ITO)
29 East 35th Street
New York, NY 10001-2291

Scott, Foresman
Subsidiary of Times, Inc.
1900 East Lake Avenue
Glenview, IL 60025

Springer-Verlag New York, Inc.
A Subsidiary of Springer-Verlag Gmbh
& Co. KG
175 Fifth Avenue, 19th floor
New York, NY 10010

Sunbelt
P.O. Box 4447
Texas Tech University
Lubbock, TX 79409

SYBEX, Inc.
2021 Challenger Drive
Alameda, CA 94601

Taylor & Francis
79 Madison Avenue
New York, NY 10016

University of Oklahoma
Oklahoma Center for Continuing Profes-
sional and Higher Education
Norman, OK 73019

Ventana
P.O. Box 2468
Chapel Hill, NC 27515

Index

This index gives page locations of names of associations and organizations, authors, titles, and subjects. Subject entries are in boldface type. In addition, acronyms for all organizations and associations are cross-referenced to the full name. Please note that a classified list of U.S. organizations and associations appears on pages 221 to 226.